the
inclusive
new
testament

the inclusive new testament

PRIESTS FOR EQUALITY
Brentwood, Maryland

PRIESTS FOR EQUALITY
P.O. Box 5243
W. Hyattsville, MD 20782-0243

Printed in the United States of America
99 98 97   5 4 3rd printing

Cover illustration by Melissa Cooper
Book designed by Craig R. Smith
Typeset in Book Antiqua and American Uncial

Library of Congress Catalog Card Number: 94-73346
ISBN 0-9644279-0-7

table of
contents

acknowledgments

*t*he title of c.s. lewis' book <u>surprised by joy</u> has always struck me as something of an oxymoron. It seems oddly appropriate, however, in considering the who's and how's of *The Inclusive New Testament*—and in some cases even the why's.

The first joyful surprise came from **Dignity, San Francisco**, who gave Priests for Equality complete permission to use and revise their inclusive lectionary set. It's not a surprise that this book would not exist but for their generosity early on.

The most significant "joyful surprise" throughout this decade-long project came, and continues to come, from our constituency—priests, religious women and men, and lay women and men: the refusal to relent in our quest for inclusivity. Women of faith must be singled out because they have been a storm of energy with their suggestions, comments, critiques, candor and financial support. In a world where no one is indispensable, they have been the exception that proves the rule. Their joy in hope—a willingness to love a church that oppresses—is awesome. It foretells that we will, indeed, overcome.

A number of members of our Technical Committee deserve special recognition.

Mark Buckley (Systematic Theology), who participated in the project from the beginning, played a pivotal role in the early planning and implementation of *The Inclusive New Testament*. His departure from the project in the Spring of 1994, just prior to the final push, was sorely felt.

Angela Williams (Feminism) did editing work on the three-year Sunday inclusive language lectionary texts. Angela, who was also an artist, a poet and an auto mechanic, proved to be full of surprises—all of them joyful—with her resourcefulness.

Melissa Cooper (Feminist Theology) edited, designed and coordinated the publication of the two-volume daily lectionary texts. Melissa, a former seminarian who is now a professional graphic designer, also designed the cover for this volume. Her calm demeanor reflects a depth that makes her a joy to work with. Her strong feminism contributed an invaluable wealth of insights in developing, in their formative stages, the inclusive texts from which *The Inclusive New Testament* sprang.

A very successful fundraising campaign in the Spring of 1994 assured a staff for the final push. **Jennifer Bacon** (Systematic Theology), a seminarian at the Virginia Theological Seminary, did editing on the final version of *The Inclusive New Testament*. **Elizabeth Burke** (Feminist Theology), fifth-year undergraduate in French at the University of Maryland, also did editing. Their joyful insights and solid work ethic kept joy alive during the summer months. **Kate Barfield and Ken Jozwiak** (Feminist Theology) provided important proofing of the final drafts. Their wisdom and extraordinary attention to detail eliminated an unnecessary embarrassment or two.

Finality is a difficult challenge in an inclusive work—one is always searching for a better way to express oneself. However, our choice of the final editor of *The Inclusive New Testament*—a difficult decision in any world—was our final joyful surprise, for the decision didn't even merit discussion: it was meant to be. The choice fell to **Craig R. Smith**, our Scripture member of the Technical Committee since the publication of the daily lectionaries, which he also edited. Craig's work is exceptional. Generously open to suggestions, scrupulously careful with the original Greek texts, and relentless in any discussion, Craig has helped us refine, like silver, seven times over. He is a wonderful writer, an excellent scholar, and a fine and sensitive editor. Craig also designed the superb layout for *The Inclusive New Testament* and did the desktop publishing, and helped coordinate the book's publication as well.

In the midst of all this joy comes a reality check—a sad, though not entirely surprising one. Not all who worked with us on this project are acknowledged above. For while they made exceptional contributions, they could not be recognized out of fear for their ministry, career or job.

This project would be doomed to failure in a certain kind of world, but this one succeeded because it was graced from the start. It is, we believe, a righteous endeavor that we think will fill you with God's life, as it has us in the very act of working (and tinkering) with these sacred texts. We offer them to you joyfully. And we hope that you, too, will be surprised by joy.

Rev. Joseph A. Dearborn
National Secretary

acknowledgments

introduction

Priests for equality is a movement of women and men—lay, religious and clergy—that works for the full participation of women and men in the church and society.

One of Priests for Equality's founding goals, in the words of its seventeen-point charter, is to "eliminate sexist language." A prime focus of our Inclusive Language Project has been to make scripture accessible to those who have been excluded from it for so long.

The project began in 1988 when PFE received permission to use inclusive language texts developed by Dignity, San Francisco. We distributed them to our constituency; their feedback spurred us to revise the texts significantly—revisions that reflected their actual use at the grassroots, in the very settings in which they were being used: college campuses, parishes, chapels, houses of formation, convents, religious communities and living rooms.

In a formal follow-up survey, with close to 300 responses, our users reported back—emphatically, and with near-unanimity—that their top priority in lectionary revision was "God-language." About this time, the National Conference of Catholic Bishops—who were undertaking to revise the Catholic lectionary—explicitly voted not to change the masculine God-language. This was particularly ironic, since the bishops had already named sexism as a sin in their draft of a pastoral letter on women's concerns.

Our audience reacted swiftly and vocally. It quickly became clear that we—the rank-and-file of the church, feminists, feminist-oriented priests, and Priests for Equality—must now assume the responsibility for the creation of an inclusive lectionary. The bishops' decision confirmed what most of the Inclusive Language Project participants had suspected all along: if change were to come, it had to be at the grassroots. A new readiness to implement inclusive language at the local level took hold, and there was a new energy at all levels to make inclusive language the issue of the '90s.

Priests for Equality went on to create a two-volume set of daily lectionary readings, and again revised its three-year Sunday lectionaries, to much acclaim. But the demand for an inclusive-language version of the complete New Testament began to grow, and we happily undertook the project. In all, *The Inclusive New Testament* took seven years (and the work of many dedicated individuals) to complete. In truth, however, we feel the project was far bigger than all of us: we believe it has come about in answer to much earnest prayer, and we in turn pray that it will satisfy the longing of many hearts.

☙   ☙   ☙

While *The Inclusive New Testament* is certainly an inclusive language translation of the New Testament, it is much more: it is a re-imaging of the holy scriptures and our relationship to them.

The Inclusive New Testament is a fresh, dynamic translation into modern English, carefully crafted to let the power and poetry of the language shine forth, particularly when read aloud, while giving it an immediacy and intimacy that is rarely found in translations of the Bible. While striving to be faithful to the original Greek, we sought new and non-sexist ways to express the same ancient truths.

One of the biggest misconceptions about inclusive language is that it involves a mere "spot cleaning" for male pronouns. The intent of inclusive language is to make the Bible accessible to everyone, particularly to those who have felt that sexist language creates an uncomfortable (and, at times, insurmountable) barrier to their devotional life. Yet many people equate that intent with tossing in a few "sisters" wherever brothers are mentioned, or taking out all the "he's" and "him's." Were that the case, a good word processor might have, with a few global search-and-replaces, wrapped it up in a day or so. Instant inclusivity.

Another misconception, perhaps related to the first, is that it is in fact possible to entirely "eliminate sexist language." In our work on *The Inclusive New Testament*, there were places, particularly in some of the epistles, where either the linguistic idiom or the point of the passage itself was so encrusted that to remove the sexist language would necessitate removing the text itself. It was at those moments, when the text lay there in all its naked and unabashed bias, that its underlying and oppressive patriarchy became plain. It became increasingly clear why some Christian feminists have abandoned the Bible: simply because they must.

The truth is, "editing" cannot erase all of scripture's language problems. Efforts such as ours to remove sexist, classist or other inequitable terminologies—as if they were simply thick patinas over an otherwise fair and just portrait—are overly hopeful endeavors. Sometimes there is no clear picture underneath. Or worse: the picture is almost too clear, in its narrow, patriarchal view, so that many people can no longer see it as divinely inspired. Strip away the layers—the Jerusalem, the American Standard, the Revised Standard, the King James, the Vulgate—and go back to the original *koiné* Greek where Paul writes "in his own hand," and there he is, still talking about subjugating women. What do we do with that? Despise Paul? Leave the church? Rewrite the Bible?

Our approach has been to engage in the sort of critical discourse that Elisabeth Schüssler Fiorenza describes—letting the language inspire the questions to which our faith will supply the answers.

As Fiorenza says in her groundbreaking book *In Memory of Her: A Feminist Theological Reconstruction of Christian Origins*, a truly theological understanding of scripture recognizes that "inspiration—the life-giving breath and power of Sophia-Spirit—does not reside in texts: it dwells among people. She did not cease once the process of canonization ended. She is still at work today." Such scriptural authority rests not in wielding the Bible like a rule book or a recipe for right living, but in personal and collective discernment in the presence of the Spirit. Fiorenza again: "The main task of feminist theological hermeneutics is not to defend biblical authority. Rather it is to engender critical discourses which can claim theological authority of the 'others' to engage in a deliberative process of biblical interpretation."

So the task becomes more a matter of overhauling theologies rather than tinkering with texts. True, our project did involve great attention to "he's" and "him's,' and to explicitly including "sisters" each time "brothers" was mentioned. But the root of our attention is founded in the heartfelt belief that Jesus, as the incarnate Word, came for all people; and that the mercy, power and grace of God works through—and even in spite of—our fallen human languages and our attempts to articulate that message over several thousand years. The "act of theological interpretation," writes Fiorenza in *Bread Not Stone: The Challenge of Feminist Biblical Interpretation*, is "a moment in the global praxis of liberation." We undertook this project and present this finished version as a testament to the abiding, equalizing power of the Spirit to take that praxis of liberation and make it truly universal.

ᘓ   ᘓ   ᘓ

Our inclusive scripture work—and *The Inclusive New Testament* is a case in point—is essentially a four-step process.

The first step involves the creation of a working document. We begin with raw text, then edit it according to a carefully-crafted style sheet we have developed, meticulously reworking sexist, classist and racist language.

Our Technical Committee, which serves as an editorial board, represents four disciplines: Scripture, Feminism and Feminist Theology, Systematic Theology, and Pastoral Theology. In this crucial second step, the Technical Committee works through the text line by line. The committee is small by design—three to five persons at any given time—with a number of different individuals representing the four disciplines over time, and with, on occasion, one individual representing more than one discipline. Throughout the process, the Technical Committee remains a constant critical entity. This arrangement also allows us to use various consultants during the process, while assuring continuity throughout.

We owe a particular debt of gratitude to a handful of feminist theologians and scripture scholars whose writings have influenced our work tremendously: Rosemary Radford Reuther; Elisabeth Schüssler Fiorenza; Phyllis Trible; Elizabeth Johnson, CSJ; Anne Carr, BVM; Dianne Bergant, CSA; Mary Jo Weaver; Pheme Perkins; Anne E. Patrick, SNJM; and Sandra Schneiders, IHM, to name a few.

In step three, the text is reviewed by an independent scriptural scholar who is responsible for editing the texts based on a careful review—and often a completely new translation—of the original Greek. The texts are then returned to the Technical Committee for final review and acceptance. Any specific words or phrases requiring more research, review or dialogue are handled separately by the Technical Committee and the scripture scholar.

Outside consultants handle the desktop publishing, copy editing and proofreading. The important last step is a fresh and independent reading of the final draft by each member of the Technical Committee, after which the Committee meets and, in consultation with the scriptural scholar, comes to consensus on the final version, which then goes on to publication.

Our work was guided by the following criteria:

❖ *To create a "critical feminist biblical interpretation" of the New Testament in an inclusive language translation.*

From the project's inception, our efforts have involved grassroots feedback, the guidance of feminist theology and scripture, and an editing process that included women and men skilled in both the theological and social aspects of feminist, pastoral and scriptural critique.

❖ *To present the text in a layout that enhances the flow of the biblical narratives, while retaining the traditional chapters and verses.*

The modern divisions of the books of the Bible into chapters most likely happened in the 13th century; separating the text into numbered verses occurred in the 16th century. Unfortunately these divisions don't always make for very good reading—the sense of the passage is often seriously disrupted by the chapter and verse divisions—which in turn may have a deleterious impact on the doctrine, story, parable or instruction. Our solution was to create three levels of section breaks, designed to reflect the natural divisions of the text rather than artificial chapter-and-verse divisions:

- large breaks (indicated by the use of uncials in the text, and a citation showing the chapters and verses covered in that section), reflecting a major shift in theme or time, rather like chapter divisions in modern books;
- medium-sized breaks (indicated by three fleurons), reflecting a shift in scene or topic; and
- small breaks (indicated by a simple space in the text), reflecting minor groupings such as parables, sayings and pericopes.

This format gives greater attention to the story line of each book, while de-emphasizing its "bibleness." At the same time, however, we retain the traditional chapter and verse numbering, and include book and chapter indications at the bottom of each page; not only does this make for quick reference when looking up a favorite passage, it also allows *The Inclusive New Testament* to be read from the pulpit, and encourages systematic Bible study.

❖ *To make a clear distinction between linguistic convention and overt bias in passages that appear sexist.*

A case in point is Revelation 17:1—19:10. The offending phrases— "Whore of Babylon" and "Great Prostitute"—are both sexist and genderist. In the standard translations, the word "whore" automatically recalls a feminine image, even though male prostitution is as old as female prostitution. In this passage, she is portrayed as a remorseless tempter, inveigling and incriminating the otherwise pure hearts of men. We didn't wish to promulgate such misogyny, but more than that, we realized that the key to the passage lay not in its feminine or adulterous implications, but in its idolatrous motives: these titles have more to do with cultic practices and economic excesses—and their debauched consequences. Our translation therefore, as in Revelation 17:5, is closer to the underlying meaning of the text: "This cryptic name is written on its forehead: 'Babylon the Great, Source of All Idolatry and of the Abominations of the Earth.' "

A different approach was taken in 1 Corinthians 11:1-16, based in part on Fiorenza's commentary on the passage. We took Paul's objectionable insistence that while men are to pray and prophesy bare-headed, women must do so with their heads covered, and turned it into a relatively fair-minded reply to the Corinthians' own inquiry on the subject—as well as a discussion of the prophetic authority that women were to have in the church.

At the other extreme is 1 Timothy 2:9-15. One commentator likens our translation work to the removing of the centuries-old grime and dirt from the ceiling of the Sistine Chapel. But what does one do when the text lies there in its naked and unabashed sexism? We let Paul say, without defense, that "women are to be quiet and completely submissive during religious instruction. I don't permit a woman to teach or have authority over a man. She must remain silent."

We have managed, thankfully, to keep such offensive verses to an absolute minimum. One of the problems we faced, however, was that in our desire to present a non-sexist message of redemption, we ran into the danger of covering over the history of oppression from which we need to be redeemed. In the scriptures, we are confronted not only by God's redeeming Word, but also by the sinful response to that Word, both in the texts and in our lives. The history of exclusion must never be covered over by making the reading comfortably inclusive. We struggled with this aspect of the scriptures in trying to present an inclusive text, and have attempted to retain that history while refusing to consecrate the sexism that we found in the texts and in our own lives.

❖ *To distinguish between those passages which simply exclude women, and those which actively vilify women.*

That the Bible is the history of salvation throughout the Judeo-Christian dispensation is ample justification for the genealogies of the New Testament to be inclusive. We do this where we can. In the story of Lazarus and the wealthy person, for example, Lazarus goes to rest in the bosom of Sarah and Abraham, not just Abraham. In the letter to the Hebrews, we include her in the discussion about faith and the establishment of the Covenant. And we always include Rebecca when Isaac is mentioned, and Leah and Rachel when Jacob is discussed.

We also emphasize those areas in which scripture employs feminine imagery for the divine or for spiritual things. *Ruach*, the Hebrew word for "spirit," is always feminine, as is God's *shekinah*, or presence. Accordingly, in our translation the Holy Spirit is always referred to in the feminine.

Normally we render the parables gender-neutral, except when specifying gender adds directly to the passage—as in the story of the widow of Nain. The parable of the prodigal son, however, is the exception that proves the rule. The length of the parable, together with the numbers of male pronouns used in the original, made an inclusive translation too awkward.

❖ *To humanize and equalize those relegated to society's margins.*

In the pre-Civil Rights days it was common practice in the South to call male African Americans "boy." Such a constant practice generated an immensely oppressive power over its victim. Our goal throughout has been to humanize and equalize the Christian story of Our God in the world so that people come to see and live it more fully. To that end we strive to acknowledge the dignity of each individual by the simple expedient of how we address them. We do not identify people *as* their afflictions, impoverishments or infirmities. We do not refer to "the poor," but rather, "poorer people" or "people in need"—to show that poverty is not an absolute, easily-delineated category of people, but a relative condition that touches everyone. "A cripple" becomes "someone who couldn't walk"; "a leper" becomes "a person with leprosy."

❖ *To restore the role and status of women in the New Testament.*

Our revisions go well beyond word choice. Entire passages have been considered, reconsidered and revised according to a more theologically sound center. One mechanism for restoring the role and status of women is to stress the mutuality of human relationships. For example, in Luke 1:7, Elizabeth is no longer described as "barren"; instead "they (Elizabeth and Zechariah) were unable to conceive." We wanted to stress that parents are partners: in the genealogy in Matthew, for instance, where traditional lists read, "Isaac was the father of Jacob," we have "Rebecca and Isaac begot Jacob." In Luke 1:25, Elizabeth thanks God not for removing "her disgrace," but for relieving "*our* disappointment at not being able to conceive."

❖ *To stress the mutuality and equality of human relationships.*

Just as we emphasize that parents are partners, we stress that spouses are partners as well. And we deliberately and frequently use the term "partner" in marriage terminology to acknowledge and value non-traditional relationships.

❖ *To use terminology that acknowledges the many forms in which God appears in our lives.*

Our research—through many surveys and countless written responses to our queries—indicates that the biggest hurdle, both qualitatively and quantitatively, was God-language. Among women, the most offensive word is the term "Lord," and it has posed an especially difficult challenge because of its confessional implications. To call Jesus Lord is to acknowledge God's presence in the person of Jesus, and to make a personal commitment to Christ. To confess that Jesus is Lord is to confess that Caesar is *not* Lord. The word has taken on the status of an icon. We therefore look to the underlying import of the word, and find other terms that convey a similar impact. Hence we say that Jesus is *Sovereign*, or *Savior*, or talk about Jesus' reign or rulership. Such a decision, however, involves a paradigm shift in the manner in which scripture is represented to—and for—the entire community of faith.

While the sacred Name (YHVH or YHWH, or, in its common spelling, Yahweh) does not occur in the New Testament, the Greek word for "Lord," the traditional circumlocution for the divine Name, is frequently used in its place. In those cases we use *Our God*, both to stress the relational aspects of God in covenant with humankind, and to respect Jewish sensitivity to pronouncing the Name. In those places where "Lord" was meant to indicate sovereignty, we use *Most High*, *Almighty* and *Sovereign*—terms free of oppressive connotations, but rich with the idea of God's absolute reign.

In John's gospel, Jesus frequently refers to God as "the Father." We wanted to retain the idea of intimacy of relationship while de-emphasizing the idea of fatherhood, so we substitute the term *Abba God*—hearkening back to Jesus' own appeal to God as *Abba* in the garden of Gethsemane.

Our terms for Jesus also stress relationship rather than hierarchy. We use *Only Begotten*, *Firstborn*, and *God's Own* in place of "Son" to express Jesus' relationship to the Godhead. Occasionally Jesus is addressed as "Lord" out of simple respect; here we substitute *Teacher* or *Rabbi*.

"Son of Man" is more of a challenge because the phrase has several different shades of meaning. The term's roots in the Hebrew scriptures are similarly varied: it designates one who was chosen for a particular task, as in an anointing for service; it refers to the Messiah as the representative of God in the apocalyptic prophecies of the end of the age; and it is often simply a euphemism for "human being." We know, however, that the phrase as it appears in the Gospels was used by Jesus as one that best described his own self-understanding. Our translation strives to capture both the prophetic and the apocalyptic connotations of the phrase. We use *Chosen One* when it seems to refer to Jesus' self-understanding of his prophetic, earthly mission, and *Promised One* when Jesus appears to be describing the apocalyptic figure.

Beyond removing male pronouns and patriarchal metaphors from the text, our intent in representing Jesus Christ was to emphasize humanity over maleness. The significance of the Incarnation, for us, is not that God became a man, but that God—all-powerful, all-knowing and seeing, absolute Divinity—became flesh, took on human life and suffering and weakness. To that end, we have kept (though de-emphasized) male pronouns in passages describing Jesus' earthly ministry, but have removed them following the Resurrection.

In the belief that the Spirit encourages truly communal, egalitarian *koinonia* among Christian believers, we have modified terms of community. We replace the sexist "kingdom," which defines a group of people by its (male) ruler, with the more communal (albeit coined) term *kindom*, which defines a group by the ties that unite it. This new word had a somewhat mysterious beginning (and we still can't get a clear history): the story goes that it sprang, fully formed, from a community of women religious in formation; the term moved from person to person, convent to convent, community to community, until it arrived at our doorstep. Accordingly, we use the terms *kindom of God* and *kindom of heaven* as the heart of Jesus' proclamation, or occasionally *reign of God* when the emphasis is more on the action of God rather than the community.

The prolific number of king/servant references throughout the New Testament have been replaced. "King" is always *ruler*; "servant" is *attendant*, *aide* or *worker*, except where the text is referring to service to God—and even then we tend to emphasize the individual's faithfulness, devotion or ministry.

Anyone who has visited the Holocaust Museum in Washington, D.C. comes away seared with the visual scars of the Nazis' manifest hatred of the Jews. No wonder the very sound of the word "Jew" rings negatively when it is hurled as an epithet. For this reason, where the texts use the word "Jew" indiscriminately—and especially in places where the early church's polemic against non-messianic Jews was especially virulent—we particularize the text by substituting *Temple authorities* or *Jewish people*. We do use the term, however, when it compares to or contrasts with another people, e.g., "neither Jew nor Greek." We have taken a similar approach in deference to our African American sisters and brothers, who are two and three generations removed from slavery. We modify the term "slave" in most cases; when the context emphasizes the idea of domination, however, we talk openly about subjugation and oppression. The term "slave" is reserved solely for Paul's metaphor of being a "slave to sin."

CR   CR   CR

The Inclusive New Testament focuses on those whom society has marginalized: women, ethnic and racial minorities, lesbians and gay people, and those typecast in terms of their afflictions. It is our perception that there is a critical mass, especially among these faithful, who are yearning for the opportunity to experience the Word of God in a more meaningful way than the traditional proclamation of the lectionary readings.

All their lives women struggle with sexist customs, language and stereotyping. And it is not just a Catholic problem: while much has been accomplished in several Protestant denominations, most scriptures read in worship services are still grossly sexist. The continued self-destructiveness of an all-male clergy is creating a void that cries out to be filled; there is an abdication of duty, a lack of prophetic leadership. But women and men of faith the world over are stepping forward to fulfill that sense of calling, and it is to them that our work is dedicated. *The Inclusive New Testament* is for lay people and clergy alike who thirst for reform in establishment Christianity, and for those who, having despaired of change, are striking out on their own, both individually and through intentional communities. The texts are also directed to those who use the scriptures for spiritual reading and meditation on a regular basis.

And we direct the translation especially to those who will be initially exploring scripture while searching for broader goals in their spiritual life. One does not need a course on pain in order to understand it. Nor does every sin need to be experienced in order to teach morality. By the same token, neither young people nor inquirers into the faith need to experience the sin of sexist language such at an early stage in their spiritual lives. There is ample time to learn the more painful lessons of the hierarchical church once they are firmly established in the faith community.

Spiritual reading and meditation is another case. The purpose of spiritual exercises is to spend time in another place, as it were. Just as runners experience the rush of adrenaline and the pleasant release of endorphins as they push their bodies to the limit, so too with our spiritual lives. Spiritual exercises are routine activities in which we deliberately and consciously "work out," in order to put ourselves in another place, another state of awareness—and acquire not an adrenaline rush, but a state of calm and confident centeredness. This state is a participation in Other. And while the tools for this exercise are manifold, one of the most essential tools is scripture. With *The Inclusive New Testament* we choose to present a text without "rocks" or "potholes" in the path to union. A circumlocution here and there helps keep one focused.

Inclusive language is not an act of denial but rather an effort to put old wine into new wineskins. What we have created, essentially, is a *midrash* of the original texts. The word *midrash* (which is found in the Hebrew scriptures but came into its own in the rabbinical literature) refers generally to the study of sacred texts, but more particularly to the practice of creating a commentary on the text or giving a homiletic explanation. John L. McKenzie, S.J., in his *Dictionary of the Bible*, says that *midrash* "looked for the maximum of edifying lessons: it is a meditation on the sacred text or an imaginative reconstruction of the scene and episode narrated. Its goal is always the practical application to the present; thus a precept may be restated or an episode retold not in the terms of its own historical context, but in such a way that it gives light and direction to the generation that writes the *midrash*."

Our commitment to the original Greek text of the New Testament is unwavering: we have taken great pains to be faithful to the underlying message of the words. There are passages, however, where no amount of finagling and fiddling with the text will suffice. Because the writers of the New Testament were creatures of their own time and culture, not everything—even in this translation—is going to be politically correct or pleasing by contemporary standards.

While the patriarchy and sexism of the first century clearly oppressed women, it was just as clearly part of the mores of the time, and for that reason it may be considered amoral rather than immoral. But when, in the course of time, such oppression comes to be seen as sinful—and yet continues to exist in the church, with the approval of its leaders—it becomes our license to introduce *midrash* into the text and begin to right a two-thousand-year-old wrong.

℘   ℘   ℘

We come to the Liturgy of the Word to hear the message of liberation, but what we hear in non-inclusive texts are words of oppression. Scripture is the Word of God in human language, but we often forget how much our language represents our own limitations and sinfulness. Like a virus, sexism infects our celebrations of God's grace and sabotages our reception of the Liberating Word. Half of the community of grace has been systematically excluded from full participation in that community by the very words we claim to have come from God.

Such an outcome was not unforeseeable. Sexism is as much a part of our worldview as it was part of the worldview of those who wrote the scriptures. Our language and our culture are ingrained with such biases. Sacred scripture itself has a power to capture our imaginations, to form and inform the ways in which we look at the world. It has the power to challenge—or confirm—our worst cultural biases.

This being the case, we need to distinguish the canonicity of the sacred text from the the social and cultural worldview in which the texts were written—as well as from the worldview in which the texts are heard. The Word became flesh as a particular individual, born at a time and in a culture far distant from our own. The Word continues to become flesh in the retelling, in different times and in different cultures. Yet Jesus was a challenge to the status quo of his own time, rejecting the sexism and classism in first century Palestine. In contemporary retelling of the story of Jesus, however, we often don't allow the Word to be as challenging to our own biases and cultural conventions as Jesus was to his. The danger of equating our own worldview with the Word of God is that we allow this worldview, and the biases implicit within it, to become the measure of our understanding of scripture. We often allow the canons of our language to overrule the Word of God.

The Word became flesh within a culture where sexist structures and institutions were considered the norm. The texts went through varieties of translations into other languages and cultures, and each time the people of those times and places had to find ways of expressing the Word in their own limited way. So too are our translations of scripture layered with cultural baggage—and sexism, being very much a part of that cultural baggage, continues to permeate our reading of scripture.

At the same time, we also know that the Word of God is not bound by such cultural restraints. The Word of God is countercultural, challenging our most sacred cows. When we say that scripture is inspired, one of the things we mean is that scripture makes present the liberating activity of God in the experience of the believing community. Our increasing awareness of structural sexism helps us recover this liberating message, allowing it to burst forth and challenge sexism in our church and our society. To continue equating the Word with historical forms of institutional structures and concepts can only undermine the power of the Word to challenge us.

Hence the need for an inclusive language New Testament. The awareness of this need is not new. At the 1987 Women in the Church Conference, Bishop Francis Murphy said, "In preaching, I believe the priest has a wonderful opportunity to use feminine images of God. As celebrant of liturgy, he must make sure that the readings of scripture and the Eucharistic Prayers reflect inclusive language."

What we are presenting, then, is a complete re-imaging of the holy scriptures and our relationship with them. One of the truths this project has reinforced is that the Bible is not itself the Word of God, for that would be idolatry. Rather, the Bible *contains* the Word of God—or better yet, the Bible is the unique document of human beings' encounters with the Living God over the span of several thousand years. For the Word of God is always and everywhere a trinity: it is the message itself; the proclamation of that message; and the becoming, the incarnating, of that proclaimed message in our person. That Word, that truth, is thankfully one that no alphabet can fully capture—and therefore one that no scribe or scholar can corrupt in written text.

Any translation of scripture is a task to be undertaken with the utmost discretion and humility. Beyond that recognition, our only defense for errors and arbitrary decisions on our part, whether detectable or hidden, is that the text to which our labors are addressed speaks of mysteries beyond the reach of any translator. Our hope is that we are respectful of that mystery, which will outlast any attempt to capture it in words.

Advent 1994

the gospel according to
matthew

*t*his is the family record of jesus christ, descendant of Bathsheba and David, descendant of Sarah and Abraham:

²Sarah and Abraham begot Isaac; Rebecca and Isaac begot Jacob; Leah and Jacob begot Judah and his sisters and brothers; ³Tamar and Judah begot Perez and Zerah; Perez begot Hezron; Hezron begot Ram; ⁴Ram begot Amminadab; Amminadab begot Nahshon; Nahshon begot Salmon; ⁵Rahab and Salmon begot Boaz; Ruth and Boaz begot Obed; Obed begot Jesse; ⁶and Jesse begot David, the ruler.

Bathsheba—who had been the wife of Uriah—and David begot Solomon; ⁷Solomon begot Rehoboam; Rehoboam begot Abijah; Abijah begot Asa; ⁸Asa begot Jehoshaphat; Jehoshaphat begot Joram; Joram begot Uzziah; ⁹Uzziah begot Jotham; Jotham begot Ahaz; Ahaz begot Hezekiah; ¹⁰Hezekiah begot Manasseh; Manasseh begot Amon; Amon begot Josiah; ¹¹Josiah begot Jeconiah and his sisters and brothers at the time of the Babylonian captivity.

¹²After the Babylonian captivity, Jeconiah begot Shealtiel; Shealtiel begot Zerubbabel; ¹³Zerubbabel begot Abiud; Abiud begot Eliakim; Eliakim begot Azor; ¹⁴Azor begot Zadok; Zadok begot Achim; Achim begot Eliud;

¹⁵Eliud begot Eleazar; Eleazar begot Matthan; Matthan begot Jacob; ¹⁶Jacob begot Joseph, the husband of Mary. And from her Jesus was born.

¹⁷Thus there were fourteen generations from Sarah and Abraham to Bathsheba and David, fourteen generations from Bathsheba and David to the Babylonian captivity, and fourteen generations from the Babylonian captivity to the Messiah.

℞   ℞   ℞

¹⁸This is how the birth of Jesus came about.

When Jesus' mother, Mary, was engaged to Joseph, but before they lived together, she was found to be pregnant through the Holy Spirit. ¹⁹Joseph, her husband, an upright person unwilling to disgrace her, decided to divorce her quietly.

²⁰This was Joseph's intention when suddenly the angel of God appeared in a dream and said, "Joseph, heir to the House of David, don't be afraid to wed Mary; it is by the Holy Spirit that she has conceived this child. ²¹She is to have a son, and you are to name him Jesus—'Salvation'—because he will save the people from their sins." ²²All this happened to fulfill what God has said through the prophet:

²³"The virgin will be with child
      and give birth,
   and the child will be named
      Immanuel"

—a name which means "God is with us."

²⁴When Joseph awoke, he did as the angel of God had directed, and they went ahead with the marriage. ²⁵He did not have intercourse with her until she had given birth; she had a son, and they named him Jesus.

℞   ℞   ℞

2·¹After Jesus' birth—which happened in Bethlehem of Judea, during the reign of Herod—astrologers from the East arrived in Jerusalem ²and asked, "Where is the newborn ruler of the Jews? We observed his star at its rising, and have come to pay homage." ³At this news Herod became greatly disturbed, as did all of Jerusalem. ⁴Summoning all the chief priests and religious scholars of the people, he asked them where the Messiah was to be born.

⁵"In Bethlehem of Judea," they informed him. "Here is what the prophet has written:

⁶'And you, Bethlehem, land of Judah,
    are by no means least among the leaders of Judah,
  since from you will come a ruler
    who is to shepherd my people Israel.' "

⁷ Herod called the astrologers aside and found out from them the exact time of the star's appearance. ⁸ Then he sent them to Bethlehem, after having instructed them, "Go and get detailed information about the child. When you have found him, report back to me—so that I may go and offer homage, too."

⁹ After their audience with the ruler, they set out. The star which they had observed at its rising went ahead of them until it came to a standstill over the place where the child lay. ¹⁰ They were overjoyed at seeing the star and, ¹¹ upon entering the house, found the child with Mary, his mother. They prostrated themselves and paid homage. Then they opened their coffers and presented the child with gifts of gold, frankincense and myrrh.

¹² They were warned in a dream not to return to Herod, so they went back to their own country by another route.

¹³ After the astrologers had left, the angel of God suddenly appeared in a dream to Joseph with the command, "Get up, take the child and his mother and flee to Egypt. Stay there until I tell you otherwise. Herod is searching for the child to destroy him." ¹⁴ Joseph got up, awakened Jesus and Mary, and they left that night for Egypt. ¹⁵ They stayed there until the death of Herod, to fulfill what God had said through the prophet: "Out of Egypt I have called my Own."

¹⁶ Herod became furious when he realized that the astrologers had outwitted him. He gave orders to kill all male children that were two years old and younger living in and around Bethlehem. The age of the children was based on the date Herod had learned from the astrologers. ¹⁷ Then what was spoken through the prophet Jeremiah was fulfilled:
    ¹⁸ "A voice was heard in Ramah
      sobbing and lamenting loudly:
   it was Rachel weeping for her children;
      she refused to be consoled,
      for they were no more."

¹⁹ After Herod's death, the angel of God appeared in a dream to Joseph in Egypt ²⁰ with the command, "Get up, take the child and his mother, and set out for the land of Israel. Those who had designs on the life of the child are dead."

²¹ Joseph got up, awakened Jesus and Mary, and they returned to the land of Israel. ²² Joseph heard, however, that Archelaus had succeeded Herod as

ruler of Judea, and Joseph was afraid to go back there. Instead, because of a warning received by Joseph in a dream, the family went to the region of Galilee. ²³ There they settled in a town called Nazareth. In this way, what was said through the prophets was fulfilled: "He will be called a Nazarene."

3:1–7:29

𝒶𝓉 this time John the Baptizer appeared in the desert of Judea, proclaiming, ² "Change your hearts and minds, for the reign of heaven is about to break in upon you!"

³ It was John that the prophet Isaiah described when he said,

> "A herald's voice cries in the desert:
> 'Prepare the way of Our God,
> make straight the paths of God!' "

⁴ John was clothed in a garment of camel's hair and wore a leather belt around his waist. Grasshoppers and wild honey were his food. ⁵ At that time, Jerusalem, all Judea and the whole region around the Jordan were going out to him. ⁶ John baptized them in the Jordan River as they confessed their sins.

⁷ When he saw that many of the Pharisees and Sadducees were coming to be baptized, John said to them, "You pack of snakes! Who told you to flee from the coming wrath? ⁸ Give some evidence that you mean to reform! ⁹ And don't pride yourselves on the claim, 'Sarah and Abraham are our parents.' I tell you, God can raise children for Sarah and Abraham from these very stones!

¹⁰ "Even now the ax is laid to the root of the tree. Every tree that is not fruitful will be cut down and thrown into the fire. ¹¹ I will baptize you in water if you have a change of heart, but the One who will follow me is more powerful than I. I'm not fit even to untie the sandals of the Coming One! That One will baptize you in the Holy Spirit and fire, ¹² whose winnowing-fan will clear the threshing floor. The grain will be gathered into the barn, but the chaff will be burned in unquenchable fire."

¹³ Then Jesus came from Galilee to the Jordan to be baptized by John. ¹⁴ John tried to dissuade Jesus, saying, "I should be baptized by you, and yet you come to me!"

¹⁵ But Jesus replied, "Leave it this way for now. We must do this to completely fulfill God's justice." So John reluctantly agreed.

¹⁶ Immediately after Jesus had been baptized and was coming up out of

the water, the sky suddenly opened up and Jesus saw the Spirit of God descending as a dove and hovering over him. ¹⁷With that, a voice from the heavens said, "This is my Own, my Beloved, on whom my favor rests."

ଔ   ଔ   ଔ

⁴¹Then Jesus was led into the desert by the Spirit, to be tempted by the Devil. ²After fasting for forty days and forty nights, Jesus was hungry. ³Then the tempter approached and said, "If you are the Only Begotten, command these stones to turn into bread."

⁴Jesus replied, "Scripture has it,

'We live not on bread alone
but on every utterance that comes
from the mouth of God.' "

⁵Next the Devil took Jesus to the Holy City, set him on the parapet of the Temple ⁶and said, "If you are the Only Begotten, throw yourself down. Scripture has it,

'God will tell the angels to take care of you;
with their hands they will support you
that you may never stumble on a stone.' "

⁷Jesus answered, "Scripture also says, 'Do not put God to the test.' "

⁸The Devil then took Jesus up a very high mountain and displayed all the dominions of the world in their magnificence, ⁹promising, "All these I will give you if you fall down and worship me."

¹⁰At this, Jesus said to the Devil, "Away with you, Satan! Scripture says, 'You will worship the Most High God; God alone will you adore.' "

¹¹At that the Devil left, and angels came and attended Jesus.

ଔ   ଔ   ଔ

¹²When Jesus heard that John had been arrested, he went back to Galilee. ¹³He left Nazareth and settled in Capernaum, a lakeside town near the territory of Zebulun and Naphtali. ¹⁴In this way the prophecy of Isaiah was fulfilled:

¹⁵"Land of Zebulun, land of Naphtali,
the way to the sea on the far side of the Jordan,
Galilee of the Gentiles:
¹⁶the people who lived in darkness
have seen a great light;
on those living in the land of the shadow of death
a light has dawned."

¹⁷From that time on, Jesus began proclaiming the message, "Change your hearts and minds, for the kindom of heaven is at hand!"

 ᛅ ᛅ ᛅ

¹⁸ As Jesus was walking along the Sea of Galilee, he watched two brothers—Simon, who was called Peter, and Andrew—casting a net into the sea. They fished by trade. ¹⁹ Jesus said to them, "Come follow me, and I will make you fishers of humankind." ²⁰ They immediately abandoned their nets and began to follow Jesus.

²¹ Jesus walked along further and caught sight of a second pair of brothers—James and John, begot of Zebedee. They too were in their boat, mending their nets with their father. Jesus called them, ²² and immediately they abandoned both boat and father to follow him.

²³ Jesus traveled throughout Galilee, teaching in the synagogues, proclaiming the Good News of the kindom of heaven and healing all kinds of diseases and sicknesses among the people. ²⁴ His fame spread throughout Syria, and people suffering from illnesses and painful ailments of all kinds—those who were demon-possessed, those who were epileptic, those who were paralyzed—were brought to Jesus, and he healed them. ²⁵ Large crowds followed Jesus, coming from Galilee, the Decapolis, Jerusalem, Judea and Transjordania.

ᛅ ᛅ ᛅ

5:1 When Jesus saw the crowds, he went up on the mountainside, and after he sat down and the disciples had gathered around, ² Jesus began to teach them:

³ "Blessed are those who are poor in spirit:
    the kindom of heaven is theirs.
⁴ Blessed are those who are mourning:
    they will be consoled.
⁵ Blessed are those who are gentle:
    they will inherit the land.
⁶ Blessed are those who hunger and thirst for justice:
    they will have their fill.
⁷ Blessed are those who show mercy to others:
    they will be shown mercy.
⁸ Blessed are those whose hearts are clean:
    they will see God.
⁹ Blessed are those who work for peace:
    they will be called children of God.

¹⁰ Blessed are those who are persecuted
because of their struggle for justice:
the kindom of heaven is theirs.

¹¹ "You are fortunate when others insult you and persecute you, and utter every kind of slander against you because of me. ¹² Be glad and rejoice, for your reward in heaven is great; they persecuted the prophets before you in the very same way.

¹³ "You are the salt of the earth. But what if salt were to lose its flavor? How could you restore it? It would be fit for nothing but to be thrown out and trampled underfoot.

¹⁴ "You are the light of the world. You don't build a city on a hill, then try to hide it, do you? ¹⁵ You don't light a lamp, then put it under a bushel basket, do you? No, you set it on a stand where it gives light to all in the house. ¹⁶ In the same way, your light must shine before others so that they may see your good acts and give praise to your Abba God in heaven.

¹⁷ "Don't think I've come to abolish the Law and the Prophets. I have come not to abolish them, but to fulfill them. ¹⁸ The truth is, until heaven and earth pass away, not the smallest letter of the Law, not even the smallest part of a letter, will be done away with until it is all fulfilled. ¹⁹ That's why whoever breaks the least significant of these commands and teaches others to do the same will be called the least in the kindom of heaven. Whoever fulfills and teaches these commands will be called great in the kindom of heaven.

²⁰ "I tell you, unless your sense of justice surpasses that of the religious scholars and the Pharisees, you will not enter the kindom of heaven.

²¹ "You've heard that our ancestors were told, 'No killing' and, 'Every murderer will be subject to judgment.' ²² But I tell you that everyone who is angry with sister or brother is subject to judgment; anyone who says to sister or brother, 'I spit in your face!' will be subject to the Sanhedrin; and anyone who vilifies them with name-calling will be subject to the fires of Gehenna.

²³ "If you bring your gift to the altar and there remember that your sister or brother has a grudge against you, ²⁴ leave your gift there at the altar. Go to be reconciled to them, and then come and offer your gift.

²⁵ "Lose no time in settling with your opponents—do so while still on the way to the courthouse with them. Otherwise your opponents may hand you over to the judge, and the judge hand you over to the bailiff, who will

throw you into prison. ²⁶I warn you, you won't get out until you have paid the last penny.

²⁷ "You've heard the commandment, 'No committing adultery.' ²⁸But I tell you that those who look lustfully at others have already committed adultery with them in their hearts. ²⁹If your right eye causes you to sin, pluck it out and throw it away. It's better to lose part of your body than to have it all cast into Gehenna. ³⁰And if your right hand causes you to sin, cut it off and throw it away! It's better to lose part of your body than to have it all cast into Gehenna.

³¹ "It was also said, 'Whenever a couple divorces, each partner must get a decree of divorce.' ³²But I tell you that everyone who divorces—except because of adultery—forces the spouse to commit adultery. Those who marry the divorced also commit adultery.

³³ "Again, you have heard that our ancestors were told, 'Don't break your vow; fulfill all oaths made to Our God.' ³⁴But I tell you not to swear oaths at all. Don't swear by heaven, for it is God's throne; ³⁵don't swear by the earth, for it is God's footstool. Don't swear by Jerusalem, for it is the city of the great Ruler. ³⁶And don't swear by your own head, for you can't make a single hair white or black. ³⁷Say 'Yes' when you mean 'Yes' and 'No' when you mean 'No.' Anything beyond that is from the Evil One.

³⁸ "You've heard the commandment, 'An eye for an eye and a tooth for a tooth.' ³⁹But I tell you, don't resist an evil person. When someone strikes you on the right cheek, turn and offer the other. ⁴⁰If anyone wants to sue you for your shirt, hand over your coat as well. ⁴¹Should anyone press you into service for one mile, go two miles. ⁴²Give to those who beg from you. And don't turn your back on those who want to borrow from you.

⁴³ "You have heard it said, 'Love your neighbor—but hate your enemy.' ⁴⁴But I tell you, love your enemies and pray for your persecutors. ⁴⁵This will prove that you are children of God. For God makes the sun rise on bad and good alike; God's rain falls on the just and the unjust. ⁴⁶If you love those who love you, what merit is there in that? Don't tax collectors do as much? ⁴⁷And if you greet only your sisters and brothers, what is so praiseworthy about that? Don't Gentiles do as much? ⁴⁸Therefore be perfect, as Abba God in heaven is perfect.

6:1 "Beware of practicing your piety before others to attract their attention; if you do this, you will have no reward from your Abba God in heaven.

² "When you do acts of charity, for example, don't have it trumpeted before you; that is what hypocrites do in the synagogues and the streets, that they may be praised by others. The truth is, they've already received their reward in full. ³ But when you do acts of charity, don't let your left hand know what your right hand is doing; ⁴ your good deeds must be done in secret, and your Abba God—who sees all that is done in secret—will repay you.

⁵ "And when you pray, don't behave like the hypocrites; they love to pray standing up in the synagogues and on street corners for people to see them. The truth is, they have received their reward in full. ⁶ But when you pray, go to your room, shut the door, and pray to God who is in that secret place, and your Abba God—who sees all that is done in secret—will reward you.

⁷ "And when you pray, don't babble like the Gentiles. They think God will hear them if they use a lot of words. ⁸ Don't imitate them. Your God knows what you need before you ask it. ⁹ This is how you are to pray:

'Abba God in heaven,
    hallowed be your name!
¹⁰ May your reign come,
    may your will be done on earth as it is in heaven:
        ¹¹ give us today the bread of Tomorrow.
¹² And forgive us our debts,
    as we hereby forgive those who are indebted to us.
¹³ Don't put us to the test,
    but free us from evil.'

¹⁴ "If you forgive the faults of others, Abba God will forgive you yours. ¹⁵ If you don't forgive others, neither will Abba God forgive you.

¹⁶ "And when you fast, don't look depressed like the hypocrites. They deliberately neglect their appearance to let everyone know that they are fasting. The truth is, they have already received their reward. ¹⁷ But when you fast, brush your hair and wash your face. ¹⁸ Don't let anyone know you're fasting except your Abba God, who sees all that is done in secret. And Abba God—who sees everything that is done in secret—will reward you.

¹⁹ "Don't store up earthly treasures for yourselves, which moths and rust destroy and thieves can break in and steal. ²⁰ But store up treasures for yourselves in heaven, where neither moth nor rust can destroy them and thieves cannot break in and steal them. ²¹ For where your treasure is, there will your heart be as well.

²² "The lamp of the body is the eye. If your eye is sound, your whole body will be filled with light; ²³ but if your eye is diseased, your whole body will

be in darkness. And if the light inside you is darkness, how great that darkness will be!

24 "No one can serve two superiors. You will either hate one and love the other, or be attentive to one and despise the other. You cannot give yourself to God and Money. 25 That's why I tell you not to worry about your livelihood, what you are to eat or drink or use for clothing. Isn't life more than just food? Isn't the body more than just clothes?

26 "Look at the birds in the sky. They don't sow or reap, they gather nothing into barns, yet Our God in heaven feeds them. Aren't you more important than they? 27 Which of you by worrying can add a moment to your lifespan? 28 And why be anxious about clothing? Learn a lesson from the way the wildflowers grow. They don't work; they don't spin. 29 Yet I tell you, not even Solomon in full splendor was arrayed like one of these. 30 If God can clothe in such splendor the grasses of the field, which bloom today and are thrown on the fire tomorrow, won't God do so much more for you—you who have so little faith?

31 "Stop worrying, then, over questions such as, 'What are we to eat,' or 'what are we to drink,' or 'what are we to wear?' 32 Those without faith are always running after these things. God knows everything you need. 33 Seek first God's reign, and God's justice, and all these things will be given to you besides. 34 Enough of worrying about tomorrow! Let tomorrow take care of itself. Today has troubles enough of its own.

7:1 "Don't judge, or you yourself will be judged. 2 Your judgment on others will be the judgment you receive. The measure you use will be used to measure you. 3 Why do you look at the splinter in your neighbor's eye and never see the board in your own eye? 4 How can you say to your neighbor, 'Let me remove the splinter in your eye,' when the whole time there's a two-by-four in your own? 5 Hypocrite! Remove the board from your own eye first; then you'll be able to see clearly to remove the splinter from your neighbor's eye.

6 "Don't give dogs what is sacred; don't throw your pearls to pigs. If you do, they'll just trample them underfoot—then turn and tear you to pieces.

7 "Ask and keep asking, and you will receive. Seek and keep seeking, and you will find. Knock and keep knocking, and the door will be opened to you. 8 For the one who keeps asking, receives. The one who keeps seeking, finds. And the one who keeps knocking, enters.

9 "Is there any among you who would hand your daughter a stone when she asked for bread? 10 Would one of you hand your son a snake when he

asked for a fish? ¹¹ If you, with all your faults, know how to give your children what is good, how much more will your Abba God in heaven give good things to those who ask!

¹² "Therefore treat others as you would have them treat you. This is the whole meaning of the Law and the prophets.

¹³ "Enter by the narrow gate. The wide gate puts you on the spacious road to damnation, and many take it. ¹⁴ But it's a small gate, a narrow road that leads to Life, and only a few find it.

¹⁵ "Be on your guard against false prophets who come to you disguised as sheep, but underneath are ravenous wolves. ¹⁶ You will be able to tell them by their fruit. Can people pick grapes from thorns, or figs from thistles? ¹⁷ In the same way, a sound tree produces good fruit and a rotten tree produces bad fruit. ¹⁸ A sound tree cannot produce rotten fruit, and a rotten tree cannot produce good fruit. ¹⁹ Any tree that does not produce good fruit is cut down and thrown in the fire. ²⁰ I repeat, you'll be able to tell them by their fruit.

²¹ "It isn't those who cry out, 'My Savior! My Savior!' who will enter the kindom of heaven; rather, it is those who do the will of Abba God in heaven. ²² When that day comes, many will plead with me, 'Savior! Savior! Have we not prophesied in your name? Have we not exorcised demons in your name? Didn't we do many miracles in your name as well?' ²³ Then I will declare to them, 'I never knew you. Out of my sight, you evildoers!'

²⁴ "Anyone who hears my words and puts them into practice is like the sage who built a house on rock. ²⁵ When the rainy season set in, the torrents came and the winds blew and buffeted the house. It didn't collapse because it had been set solidly on rock. ²⁶ Anyone who hears my words but does not put them into practice is like the fool who built a house on sandy ground. ²⁷ The rains fell, the torrents came, the winds blew and lashed against the house. And it collapsed and was completely ruined."

²⁸ Jesus finished speaking and left the crowds spellbound at his teaching, ²⁹ because he taught with an authority that was unlike their religious scholars.

*W*hen Jesus came down from the mountain, large crowds followed. ² Suddenly a person with leprosy came forward, knelt down and said, "Rabbi, if you are willing, you can make me clean."

³Jesus reached out and touched the person. "I am willing. Be clean!" Immediately the leprosy disappeared. ⁴Jesus then said, "See to it that you tell no one. Go and show yourself to the priest and offer the gift Moses commanded. That should be the proof they need."

⁵As Jesus entered Capernaum, a centurion approached him and said, ⁶"Rabbi, my young attendant is at home in bed paralyzed, suffering in great pain."

⁷Jesus said, "I will come and heal your attendant."

⁸The centurion replied, "Teacher, I am not worthy to have you under my roof, but just say the word and my boy will be cured. ⁹I, too, am a person subject to authority and have soldiers subject to me. I say to some, 'Go!' and off they go; to others, 'Come here!' and they come; to my attendants, 'Do this!' and they do it."

¹⁰When Jesus heard this, he was amazed and said to those nearby, "The truth is, I've found no one in Israel with such great faith. ¹¹I tell you, many will come from the East and the West and will take their places at the feast with Sarah and Abraham, Rebecca and Isaac, and Leah and Rachel and Jacob in the kindom of heaven, ¹²while the natural heirs of the kindom will be thrown outside, into the darkness, where there will be weeping and gnashing of teeth." ¹³Then Jesus said to the centurion, "Go home, it will be done just as you believed it would." And the attendant was healed that very hour.

¹⁴Entering Peter's house, Jesus found Peter's mother-in-law in bed with a fever. ¹⁵Jesus touched her hand and the fever left, and she got up and went about her work.

¹⁶As evening drew near, they brought many to Jesus who were possessed. He expelled the spirits with a word and healed all who were ill, ¹⁷thereby fulfilling what had been said through Isaiah the prophet: "You took on our infirmities and endured our sufferings."

¹⁸Jesus, seeing a crowd gathering, gave orders to cross the lake to the other shore.

¹⁹Then a religious scholar approached and said, "Rabbi, I will follow you wherever you go."

²⁰Jesus replied, "The foxes have holes, the birds in the sky have their nests, but the Chosen One has nowhere to lie down."

²¹Another, a disciple, said to him, "Teacher, let me go and bury my mother first."

²²Jesus said, "Follow me, and let the dead bury their own dead."

²³ Then Jesus got into a boat and the disciples followed. ²⁴ Without warning, a violent storm broke over the lake, and the boat began to take on water. But Jesus was sleeping, ²⁵ so they shook him awake, exclaiming, "Save us! We are lost!"

²⁶ Jesus replied, "Why are you afraid? You have so little faith!" Then Jesus stood up and rebuked the winds and the sea, and there was a great calm. ²⁷ The others, dumbfounded, said, "Who is this, whom even the winds and the sea obey?"

²⁸ When Jesus landed at the Gadarene boundary, he encountered two demon-possessed people coming out of the tombs. They were so violent that no one could pass by there. ²⁹ "What do you want from us, Only Begotten of God," they shouted. "Have you come to torture us before the appointed time?" ³⁰ Some distance away a large herd of pigs was feeding. ³¹ The demons pleaded with Jesus and said, "If you expel us, send us into the herd of pigs."

³² Jesus answered, "Out with you!" With that they came forth and entered the pigs. The whole herd charged down the cliff into the lake and drowned in the water.

³³ The swineherds fled and, upon arriving in the town, told everything that had happened, including the story of the pair possessed by demons. ³⁴ Then the entire town came out to meet Jesus and implored him to leave the neighborhood.

9:1 Jesus got back into the boat, crossed the lake and returned to his own town. ² Then some people appeared, bringing a person who was paralyzed, stretched out on a pallet. Seeing their faith, Jesus said to the paralyzed person, "Courage, my child, your sins are forgiven."

³ At that, some of the religious scholars said to themselves, "This is blasphemy!"

⁴ Jesus was aware of their thoughts and said, "Why do you harbor evil thoughts? ⁵ Which is easier to say, 'Your sins are forgiven,' or 'stand up and walk'? ⁶ But to prove to you that the Chosen One has authority on earth to forgive sins—" Jesus then turned to the paralyzed person—"Stand up! Take up your mat, and go home." ⁷ With that, the afflicted one got up and went home. ⁸ The crowd was filled with awe when they saw this, and they praised God for giving such authority to mortals.

⁹ As Jesus walked on, he saw Matthew, a tax collector, at his post. Jesus approached and said, "Follow me," and Matthew got up and followed.

¹⁰ Now it happened that, while Jesus was at table in Matthew's house, many tax collectors and notorious "sinners" came to join Jesus and the disciples at dinner. ¹¹ The Pharisees saw this and complained to the disciples, saying, "What reason can the Teacher have for eating with tax collectors and sinners?"

¹² Overhearing the remark, Jesus said, "People who are in good health don't need a doctor; sick people do. ¹³ Go and learn the meaning of the words, 'I desire compassion, not sacrifices.' I have come to call not the righteous but sinners."

¹⁴ The disciples of John the Baptizer came to Jesus and said, "Why is it that while we and the Pharisees fast, your disciples don't?" ¹⁵ Jesus replied, "How can the guests at a wedding feast mourn while they are still all together? The time will come when the guests will be left alone; then they will fast.

¹⁶ "No one sews a piece of unshrunken cloth onto an old cloak, because the patch will pull away from the cloak and the tear will get worse. ¹⁷ Nor do people put new wine into old wineskins—if they do, the skins will burst, the wine will run out, and the skins will be ruined. No, they put new wine into new wineskins, and both are preserved."

℞   ℞   ℞

¹⁸ As Jesus was speaking, a synagogue official came up, knelt down and said, "My daughter has just died. But if you come and lay hands on her, she will live." ¹⁹ Jesus got up and went with the official, and so did the disciples.

²⁰ As they were going along, a woman who had suffered from hemorrhages for twelve years came up behind him and touched the hem of his cloak; ²¹ she was saying to herself, "If only I can touch his cloak, I will be healed."

²² Jesus turned around and saw her. "Courage, daughter," he said, "your faith has healed you." That very moment the woman was healed.

²³ When Jesus arrived at the house of the synagogue official, a noisy crowd had gathered, and the flute players who served as mourners had already arrived. ²⁴ When he saw them he said, "Get out! The child is not dead—only asleep." They all laughed at him.

²⁵ After the crowd had been put out, he entered and took the girl by the hand, and she got up. ²⁶ And the news spread throughout the countryside.

²⁷ As Jesus moved on from Capernaum, two blind people followed and cried out, "Heir to the House of David, have pity on us!"

²⁸ When Jesus reached his lodgings, they caught up with him. Jesus said to them, "Do you believe I can do this?"

They said, "Yes, Rabbi."

²⁹ Then he touched their eyes and said, "Because of your faith, it will be done to you." ³⁰ And their sight returned.

Then Jesus sternly warned them, "See that no one learns of this." ³¹ But they went off and talked about him all over the countryside.

³² As they were leaving, some people brought Jesus a person who was possessed by a demon and unable to speak. ³³ Once the demon was expelled, the individual began to speak—to the great surprise of the crowd. "Nothing like this has ever been seen in Israel!" they said.

³⁴ But the Pharisees said, "He casts out demons through the power of demons."

³⁵ Jesus continued touring all the towns and villages, teaching in their synagogues, proclaiming the Good News of God's reign and curing all kinds of diseases and sicknesses.

³⁶ At the sight of the crowds, Jesus' heart was moved with pity because they were distressed and dejected, like sheep without a shepherd. ³⁷ Jesus said to the disciples, "The harvest is bountiful but the laborers are few. ³⁸ Beg the overseer of the harvest to send laborers out to bring in the crops."

℞   ℞   ℞

10∶¹ Jesus summoned the Twelve, and gave them authority to expel unclean spirits and heal sickness and diseases of all kinds.

² These are the names of the twelve apostles: the first were Simon, nicknamed Peter—that is, "Rock"—and his brother Andrew; then James, begot of Zebedee, and his brother John; ³ Philip and Bartholomew; Thomas; Matthew, the tax collector; James, begot of Alphaeus; Thaddaeus; ⁴ Simon the Zealot; and Judas Iscariot, who betrayed Jesus.

⁵ These twelve Jesus sent out after giving them the following instructions:

"Don't visit Gentile regions, and don't enter a Samaritan town. ⁶ Go instead to the lost sheep of the house of Israel. ⁷ As you go, make this proclamation: 'The reign of heaven has drawn near.'

⁸ "Heal those who are sick, raise the dead, cure leprosy, expel demons. You received freely—now freely give.

⁹ "Take neither gold nor silver nor copper for your money belts— ¹⁰ no traveling bag, no change of clothes, no sandals, no walking staff—for workers deserve their keep.

¹¹"Look for worthy people in whatever town or village you come to, and stay with them until you leave. ¹²As you enter a house, bless it. ¹³If the home is deserving, your peace will descend on it. If it isn't, your peace will return to you.

¹⁴"If anyone does not receive you or listen to what you have to say, leave that house or town and, once outside it, shake its dust from your feet. ¹⁵The truth is, on Judgment Day it will go easier for the towns of Sodom and Gomorrah than it will for that town.

¹⁶"I am sending you out like sheep among wolves. So you must be as clever as snakes, but as innocent as doves. ¹⁷Be on your guard. People will haul you into court, they will flog you in the synagogues. ¹⁸For my sake you will be dragged before rulers and governors as witnesses to them and to the Gentiles.

¹⁹"When they hand you over, don't worry about how to speak or what to say. You'll be given what you should say when the time comes, ²⁰because it is not you speaking but the Spirit of your Abba God speaking through you.

²¹"Sibling will betray sibling to death, and parents their children; children will rise up against their parents and have them executed. ²²Everyone will hate you because of me. But whoever stands firm until the end will be saved. ²³When you are persecuted in one place, flee to another. The truth is, you will not have visited all the towns of Israel before the Chosen One comes.

²⁴"A student is not superior to the teacher; the follower is not above the leader. ²⁵The student should be glad simply to become like the teacher, the follower like the leader.

"If the head of the house has been called Beelzebul, how much more the members of the household!

²⁶"Don't let people intimidate you. Nothing is concealed that will not be revealed, and nothing is hidden that will not be made known. ²⁷What I tell you in darkness, speak in the light. What you hear in private, proclaim from the housetops.

²⁸"Don't fear those who can deprive the body of life but can't destroy the soul. Rather, fear the one who can destroy both body and soul in Gehenna.

²⁹"Are not the sparrows sold for pennies? Yet not a single sparrow falls to the ground without your Abba God's knowledge. ³⁰As for you, every hair of your head has been counted. ³¹So don't be afraid of anything—you are worth more than an entire flock of sparrows.

³²"Whoever acknowledges me before others, I will acknowledge before Abba God in heaven. ³³Whoever disowns me before others, I will disown before Abba God in heaven.

³⁴"Don't suppose that I came to bring peace on earth. I came not to bring peace, but a sword. ³⁵I have come to turn

'A son against his father,
    a daughter against her mother,
    in-law against in-law.
³⁶One's enemies will be
    the members of one's own household.'

³⁷"Those who love mother or father, daughter or son more than me are not worthy of me. ³⁸Those who will not carry with them the instrument of their own death—following in my footsteps—are not worthy of me.

³⁹"You who have found your life will lose it, and you who lose your life for my sake will find it.

⁴⁰"Those who welcome you also welcome me, and those who welcome me welcome the One who sent me.

⁴¹"Those who welcome prophets just because they are prophets will receive the reward reserved for the prophets themselves; those who welcome holy people just because they are holy will receive the reward of the holy ones.

⁴²"The truth is, whoever gives a cup of cold water to one of these lowly ones just for being a disciple will not lack a reward."

11:1 When Jesus had finished instructing the Twelve, he left the area to teach and preach in the outlying towns of the region.

11:2–13:58

While John was in prison, he heard about the works the Messiah was performing, and sent a message by way of his disciples ³to ask Jesus, "Are you 'The One who is to come' or do we look for another?"

⁴In reply, Jesus said to them, "Go back and report to John what you hear and see:

⁵'Those who are blind recover their sight;
    those who cannot walk are able to walk;

those with leprosy are cured;
    those who are deaf hear;
the dead are raised to life;
    and the *anawim*—the "have-nots"—
have the Good News preached to them.'

6 "Blessed is the one who finds no stumbling block in me."

7 As the messengers set off, Jesus began to speak to the crowds about John: "What did you go out to the wasteland to see—a reed swaying in the wind? 8 Tell me, what did you go out to see—someone luxuriously dressed? No, those who dress luxuriously are to be found in royal palaces. 9 So what did you go out to see—a prophet? Yes, a prophet—and more than a prophet! 10 It is about John that scripture says,

'I send my messenger ahead of you
    to prepare your way before you.'

11 "The truth is, history has not known a person born of woman who is greater than John the Baptizer. Yet the least born into the kindom of heaven is greater than he.

12 "From the time of John the Baptizer until now, the kindom of heaven has been advancing with power, and powerful people take hold of it. 13 The Law and the Prophets prophesied until John came. 14 And he, if you will believe me, is the Elijah who was to return. 15 Let those who have ears to hear, hear this!

16 "What comparison can I make with this generation? They are like children shouting to others as they sit in the marketplace, 17 'We piped you a tune, but you wouldn't dance. We sang you a dirge, but you wouldn't mourn.' 18 For John came neither eating nor drinking, and they say, 'He is possessed.' 19 The Chosen One comes, eating and drinking, and they say, 'This one is a glutton and a drunkard, a friend of tax collectors and sinners.' Wisdom will be vindicated by her own actions."

20 Then Jesus began to denounce the cities where most of the miracles had been performed, because they did not repent. 21 "Woe to you, Chorazin! Woe to you, Bethsaida! For if the miracles worked in you had been worked in Tyre and Sidon, they would have repented long ago in sackcloth and ashes! 22 But The truth is, it will go easier for Tyre and Sidon than for you on the Judgment Day.

23 "As for you, Capernaum, do you intend to ascend to the heavens? No, you will go down to the underworld! If the miracles worked for you had taken place in Sodom, it would be standing today. 24 But the truth is, it will go easier for Sodom than for you on the Judgment Day."

²⁵ Then Jesus prayed, "Abba God, Creator of heaven and earth, to you I offer praise; for what you have hidden from the learned and the clever, you have revealed to the youngest children. ²⁶ Yes, Abba, everything is as you want it to be."

²⁷ Jesus continued,

> "Everything has been handed over to me
>   by Abba God.
> No one knows the Only Begotten
>   except Abba God,
> and no one knows Abba God
>   except the Only Begotten—
> and those to whom the Only Begotten
>   wants to give that revelation.
> ²⁸ Come to me,
> all you who labor and carry heavy burdens,
>   and I will give you rest.
> ²⁹ Take my yoke upon your shoulders
>   and learn from me,
>   for I am gentle and humble of heart.
> Here you will find rest for your souls,
>   ³⁰ for my yoke is easy
>   and my burden is light."

ↁ   ↁ   ↁ

12:1 One Sabbath, Jesus walked through the standing grain. The disciples were hungry and began to pick some heads of grain and eat them. ² When the Pharisees saw this, they said to Jesus, "Look! Your disciples are doing something that is forbidden on the Sabbath."

³ Jesus replied, "Have you not read what David did when he and his followers were hungry, ⁴ how he entered God's house and ate the holy bread—something forbidden to him and his followers or anyone other than the priests? ⁵ Have you not read in the Law how priests, when they are serving in the Temple, can break the Sabbath rest without incurring guilt? ⁶ I tell you, something greater than the Temple is here. ⁷ If you understood the meaning of the text, 'I desire compassion, not sacrifices,' you wouldn't have condemned the innocent. ⁸ For the Chosen One is ruler of the Sabbath."

⁹ He left there and went into their synagogue. ¹⁰ A person with a withered hand was also in the synagogue. The Pharisees tried to trap Jesus with a trick question: "Is it lawful to heal on the Sabbath?"

¹¹ But Jesus replied, "Which one of you, if your sheep were to fall in a ditch

on the Sabbath, would not grab it and lift it out? ¹²Certainly a person is more valuable than a sheep! So then, yes, it is lawful to do good on the Sabbath."

¹³Then he said to the person with the withered hand, "Stretch it out." And immediately it was healed and as sound as the other hand.

¹⁴At this, the Pharisees went outside and began to plot against Jesus to find a way to destroy him. ¹⁵Jesus knew this and withdrew from the district.

ରେ   ରେ   ରେ

Many followed Jesus and he healed them all, ¹⁶but he warned them not to make public what he had done. ¹⁷This silence was to fulfill what the prophet Isaiah said:

¹⁸"You are my Faithful One, whom I have chosen;
 my Beloved, the One in whom I delight:
on you I will put my Spirit,
 and you will proclaim justice to the nations.
¹⁹You will not quarrel or cry out,
 and your voice will not be heard in the streets;
²⁰you will not break the bruised reed
 or snuff out the smoldering wick
 until justice is led to victory.
²¹In your name the nations will find their hope."

²²Then they brought someone to Jesus who was demon-possessed, blind and mute; Jesus healed the person and restored both sight and speech. ²³All the people were astonished, and said, "Could this be the promised Heir to the House of David?"

²⁴When the Pharisees heard this, they muttered, "The only way he drives out demons is by Beelzebul, the ruler of demons."

²⁵But Jesus knew what they were thinking and said to them, "Any realm divided against itself will be ruined, and any town or household divided against itself cannot stand. ²⁶If Satan drives out Satan, the Devil's domain is divided against itself. How then can it stand?

²⁷"And if I drive out demons by Beelzebul, by whom do your authorities drive them out? Your own people will stand in judgment of you! ²⁸But if I drive out demons through the Spirit of God, then the reign of God has come upon you!

²⁹"Again, how can burglars break into a house and carry off its property unless they first tie up the people inside? Only then can they ransack the house.

³⁰ "Those who are not with me are against me. Those who don't gather with me scatter. ³¹ Therefore, I tell you, every sin and blasphemy will be forgiven, except for blasphemy against the Holy Spirit. ³² Anyone who says a word against the Promised One will be forgiven, but anyone who speaks against the Holy Spirit will not be forgiven, either in this age or in the next.

³³ "Make the tree healthy and its fruit will be healthy; neglect the tree and its fruit will be rotten. A tree is known by its fruit.

³⁴ "You brood of vipers! How can what you say be good when you are full of evil? Our words flow from the fullness of our heart: ³⁵ a good person brings good things out of a good storehouse; a bad person brings bad things out of a bad storehouse.

³⁶ "I tell you, on Judgment Day all will give an account of every careless word they ever spoke. ³⁷ Your own words will either acquit you or condemn you."

³⁸ Then some of the religious scholars and Pharisees spoke up: "Teacher, we want to see a miraculous sign from you."

³⁹ Jesus answered, "It is an evil and unfaithful generation that asks for a sign! The only sign to be given is the sign of Jonah the prophet. ⁴⁰ For as Jonah was in the whale's belly for three days and three nights, so will the Chosen One be three days and three nights in the bowels of the earth.

⁴¹ "On Judgment Day the citizens of Nineveh will stand up against this generation and condemn it, because they repented when Jonah preached— but now one greater than Jonah is here. ⁴² On Judgment Day the Queen of Sheba will rise up against this generation and condemn it, because she came from the ends of the earth to hear Solomon—but now one greater than Solomon is here.

⁴³ "When an unclean spirit goes out of a person it wanders through arid places searching for rest. When it finds none, ⁴⁴ it says, 'I will return to the home I left.' And upon returning, it finds its old house empty and swept clean. ⁴⁵ Then it goes and brings back seven other spirits more evil than itself, and they enter and set up housekeeping; the person ends up far worse than before. And that is how it will be with this evil generation!"

⁴⁶ While Jesus was still speaking to the crowd, his family stood outside, wanting to speak to him. ⁴⁷ Someone said to Jesus, "Your mother and kin are standing outside, and they are anxious to speak with you." ⁴⁸ Jesus replied, "Who is my mother? Who are my kin?" ⁴⁹ Pointing to the disciples,

Jesus said, "This is my family. ⁵⁰Whoever does the will of Abba God in heaven is my sister and brother and mother."

ભ   ભ   ભ

13:₁ Later that day, Jesus left the house and sat down by the lake shore. ²Such great crowds gathered that he went and took a seat in a boat, while the crowd stood along the shore. ³He addressed them at length in parables:

"One day, a farmer went out sowing seed. ⁴Some of the seed landed on a footpath, where birds came and ate it up. ⁵Some of the seed fell on rocky ground, where there was little soil. This seed sprouted at once since the soil had no depth, ⁶but when the sun rose and scorched it, it withered away for lack of roots. ⁷Again, some of the seed fell among thorns, and the thorns grew up and choked it. ⁸And some of it landed on good soil, and yielded a crop thirty, sixty, even a hundred times what was sown. ⁹Let those who have ears to hear, hear this!"

¹⁰When the disciples came to Jesus, they asked, "Why do you speak to the people in parables?" ¹¹Jesus answered, "The secrets of the kindom of heaven are for you to know, but not for them. ¹²To those who have, more will be given until they have an abundance; those who have not will lose what little they have.

¹³"I use parables when I speak to the people because they look but don't see, they listen but don't hear or understand. ¹⁴Isaiah's prophecy is being fulfilled in them, which says,

> 'You will be ever listening, but never understanding;
> you will be ever looking, but never perceiving.
> ¹⁵For this people's heart
> has become calloused;
> they hardly hear with their ears,
> and they have closed their eyes.
> Otherwise they might see with their eyes,
> and hear with their ears,
> and understand with their hearts
> and turn back to me,
> and I would heal them.'

¹⁶"But blessed are your eyes because they see, and your ears because they hear. ¹⁷The truth is, many prophets and holy people longed to see what you see but never saw it, to hear what you hear but never heard it.

¹⁸"Now listen to the parable of the sower. ¹⁹When people hear the message about the kindom of God without understanding it, the Evil One comes along and snatches away what was sown in their hearts. This is the

seed sown along the path. ²⁰ Those who received the seed that fell on rocky ground are the ones who hear the word and at first welcome it with joy. ²¹ But they have no roots, so they last only for a while. When some setback or persecution comes because of the message, they quickly fall away. ²² Those who receive the message that fell among the thorns are the ones who hear the word, but then worldly anxieties and the lure of wealth choke it off, and the message produces no fruit. ²³ But those who receive the seed that fell on rich soil are those who hear the message and understand it. They produce a crop that yields a hundred, or sixty or thirty times what was sown."

²⁴ Jesus presented another parable to those gathered: "The kindom of heaven is like a farmer who sowed good seed in a field. ²⁵ While everyone was asleep, an enemy came and sowed weeds among the wheat and then made off. ²⁶ When the crop began to mature and yield grain, the weeds became evident as well.

²⁷ "The farmer's workers came and asked, 'Did you not sow good seed in your field? Where are the weeds coming from?'

²⁸ "The farmer replied, 'I see an enemy's hand in this.'

"They in turn asked, 'Do you want us to go out and pull them up?'

²⁹ " 'No,' replied the farmer, 'if you pull up the weeds, you might take the wheat along with them. ³⁰ Let them grow together until the harvest, then at harvest time I will order the harvesters first to collect the weeds and bundle them up to burn, then to gather the wheat into my barn.' "

³¹ Jesus presented another parable to the crowds: "The kindom of heaven is like the mustard seed which a farmer sowed in a field. ³² It is the smallest of all seeds, but when it has grown it is the biggest shrub of all—it becomes a tree so that the birds of the air come to perch in its branches."

³³ Jesus offered them still another parable: "The kindom of heaven is like the yeast a baker took and mixed in with three measures of flour until it was leavened all through."

³⁴ Jesus spoke all these things to the crowd in parables. He spoke to them in parables only, ³⁵ to fulfill what had been said through the prophet:

"I will open my mouth in parables,
I will announce things hidden
    since the creation of the world."

³⁶ Then Jesus left the crowd and went into the house. The disciples also came in and said, "Explain the parable about the weeds in the field."

³⁷ Jesus answered, "The farmer sowing the good seed is the Chosen One,

[38] the field is the world, and the good seed, the citizens of the kindom. The weeds are the followers of the Evil One, [39] and the enemy who sowed them is the Devil. The harvest is the end of the world, while the harvesters are the angels. [40] Just as weeds are collected and burned, so it will be at the end of the age. [41] The Chosen One will send the angels who will weed out the kindom of everything that causes sin and all who act lawlessly. [42] The angels will throw them into the fiery furnace, where there will be weeping and gnashing of teeth. [43] But those who are just will shine like the sun in the kindom of their Abba God. Let those who have ears to hear, hear this!

[44] "The kindom of heaven is like a buried treasure found in a field. The ones who discovered it hid it again, and, rejoicing at the discovery, went and sold all their possessions and bought that field.

[45] "Or again, the kindom of heaven is like a merchant's search for fine pearls. [46] When one pearl of great value was found, the merchant went back and sold everything else and bought it.

[47] "Or again, the kindom of heaven is like a net thrown into the sea, which collected all kinds of fish. [48] When it was full, the fishers hauled it ashore. Then, sitting down, they collected the good ones in a basket and threw away those that were of no use. [49] This is how it will be at the end of time. The angels will come and separate the wicked from the just [50] and throw the wicked into the blazing furnace, where there will be weeping and the gnashing of teeth.

[51] "Have you understood all this?"

"Yes," they answered.

[52] To this Jesus replied, "Every religious scholar who has become a student of the kindom of heaven is like the head of a household who can bring from the storeroom both the new and the old."

[53] When Jesus had finished these parables, he left the area [54] and came to his home town and began teaching the people in the synagogue, and the people were amazed. They said to one another, "Where did he get this wisdom and these miraculous powers? [55] Isn't this the carpenter's child? Isn't his mother's name Mary, and his brothers James and Joseph and Simon and Judah? [56] His sisters, too, aren't they all here with us? But where did such gifts come from?" [57] And they found him altogether too much for them.

Jesus said to them, "Prophets are only despised in their own home town and in their own households." [58] And Jesus did not work many miracles there because of their lack of faith.

At this time, Herod the tetrarch heard about the reputation of Jesus, ² and he said to his attendants, "This is John the Baptizer, who has risen from the dead. That is why miraculous powers are at work in him."

³ For Herod had arrested John, bound him and thrown him in prison because of Herodias, his brother Philip's wife. ⁴ For John had told Herod, "It is against the Law for you to have her." ⁵ He had wanted to kill John but was afraid of the people, who regarded John as a prophet.

⁶ Then, during the celebration of Herod's birthday, the daughter of Herodias danced for them and pleased Herod ⁷ so much that he promised on oath to give her whatever she asked. ⁸ Prompted by her mother, she said, "Give me the head of John the Baptizer on a platter."

⁹ Herod was distressed, but because his dinner guests had heard the oath, he ordered that her request be granted ¹⁰ and had John beheaded in the prison. ¹¹ The head was brought in on a platter and given to the young woman, who carried it to her mother. ¹² John's disciples came and took the body and buried it, then went and told Jesus.

ℭ ℭ ℭ

¹³ When Jesus heard about the beheading, he left Nazareth by boat and went to a deserted place to be alone. The crowds heard of this and followed him from their towns on foot. ¹⁴ When Jesus disembarked and saw the vast throng, his heart was moved with pity, and he healed their sick.

¹⁵ As evening drew on, the disciples approached Jesus and said, "This is a deserted place and it is already late. Dismiss the crowds so they can go to the villages and buy some food for themselves."

¹⁶ Jesus said to them: "There is no need for them to disperse. Give them something to eat yourselves."

¹⁷ "We have nothing here," they replied, "but five loaves and a couple of fish."

¹⁸ "Bring them here," Jesus said. ¹⁹ Then he ordered the crowds to sit on the grass. Taking the five loaves and two fish, Jesus looked up to heaven, blessed the food, broke it, and gave it to the disciples, who in turn gave it to the people. ²⁰ All those present ate their fill. The fragments remaining, when gathered up, filled twelve baskets. ²¹ About five thousand families were fed.

²² Jesus insisted that the disciples get into the boat and precede him to the other side. ²³ Having sent the crowds away, he went up on the mountain by

himself to pray, remaining there alone as night fell. ²⁴ Meanwhile the boat, already a thousand yards from shore, was being tossed about in the waves which had been raised by the fierce winds.

²⁵ At about three in the morning, Jesus came walking toward them on the lake. ²⁶ When the disciples saw Jesus walking on the water, they were terrified. "It is a ghost!" they said, and in their fear they began to cry out.

²⁷ Jesus hastened to reassure them: "Don't worry, it's me! Don't be afraid!"

²⁸ Peter spoke up and said, "If it is really you, tell me to come to you across the water."

²⁹ "Come!" Jesus said.

So Peter got out of the boat and began to walk on the water toward Jesus. ³⁰ But when he saw how strong the wind was, he became frightened. He began to sink, and cried out, "Save me!"

³¹ Jesus immediately stretched out his hand and caught Peter. "You have so little faith!" Jesus said to him. "Why did you doubt?"

³² Once they had climbed into the boat, the wind died down. ³³ Those who were in the boat showed great reverence, declaring to Jesus, "You are indeed God's Own!"

³⁴ After making the crossing, they landed at Gennesaret. ³⁵ When the people of that place recognized Jesus, they sent word to all the surrounding villages. They brought to Jesus all those who were sick, ³⁶ who begged him to let them just touch the hem of his cloak, and all who touched it were healed.

ᴄᴙ   ᴄᴙ   ᴄᴙ

15:1 Some Pharisees and teachers of the Law from Jerusalem then came to Jesus and said, ²"Why do your disciples violate the tradition of the elders? They don't perform a ritual hand-washing before they eat."

³ Jesus replied, "And why do you violate the commandments of God for the sake of your tradition? ⁴ For God said, 'Honor your mother and your father,' and 'Those who curse their mother or father must be put to death.' ⁵ But you say, 'Whoever says to their parents, "Any support you might have had from me is dedicated to God," is no longer obligated to support them.' ⁶ You therefore nullify the word of God for the sake of your tradition! ⁷ You hypocrites! Isaiah prophesied well when he said of you:

⁸ 'These people honor me with their lips,
    while their hearts are far from me.
⁹ Their worship of me is worthless,
    and their doctrines are mere human rules.' "

[10] Jesus called the crowd together and said to them, "Hear this and understand: [11] it's not what enters your mouth that defiles you—it's what comes out of your mouth that defiles you."

[12] Then the disciples approached him and said, "Do you realize that the Pharisees were offended by what you said?"

[13] Jesus replied, "Every plant that my Abba God in heaven has not planted will be pulled up by the roots. [14] Ignore them—they are blind people leading other blind people. And when the blind lead the blind, they all will fall into a ditch."

[15] Then Peter said to him, "Explain this parable to us."

[16] Jesus replied, "Do you still not understand? [17] Don't you realize that everything that goes into the mouth passes into the stomach and eventually finds its way into the sewer and is gone? [18] But what comes out of the mouth comes from the heart. This is what makes a person 'unclean.' [19] For from the heart come all sorts of evil intentions—murder, sexual infidelity, promiscuity, stealing, lying, even foul language. [20] These things make a person unclean—not eating with unwashed hands!"

[21] Jesus left there and departed for the district of Tyre and Sidon. [22] It happened that a Canaanite woman living in that area came and cried out to Jesus, "Heir to the House of David, have pity on me! My daughter is horribly demon-possessed."

[23] Jesus gave her no word of response. The disciples came up and repeatedly said to him, "Please get rid of her! She keeps calling after us."

[24] Finally Jesus turned to the woman and said, "My mission is only to the lost sheep of the House of Israel."

[25] She then prostrated herself before him with the plea, "Help me, Rabbi!"

[26] He answered, "But it isn't right to take the children's food and throw it to the dogs."

[27] "True, Rabbi," she replied, "but even the dogs get to eat the scraps that fall from the table."

[28] Jesus then said in reply, "Woman, you have great faith! Your wish will come to pass." At that very moment her daughter was healed.

℞   ℞   ℞

[29] Going on from there, Jesus came to the shore of the Sea of Galilee, then went up into the hills. He sat there, [30] and large crowds gathered, bringing with them people who had physical deformities, or couldn't walk, or were blind or deaf, and many others; these they put down at Jesus' feet, and he healed them. [31] The crowds were astonished as they saw people who had

been mute speaking, people who had been deformed whole again, people who had been lame walking about, and people who had been blind seeing. And they gave glory to the God of Israel.

³²Jesus called together the disciples and said, "My heart goes out to all the people. By now they have been with us three days and have nothing to eat. I don't want to send them away hungry—they might collapse on the way home."

³³The disciples said to Jesus, "Where could we get enough food in this deserted place to feed such a crowd?"

³⁴Jesus asked, "How many loaves of bread do you have?"

"Seven," they replied, "and a few small fish."

³⁵Then he directed the crowd to sit down on the ground. ³⁶He took the seven loaves and the fish and gave thanks, then broke them and gave them to the disciples, who gave them to the crowds. ³⁷All ate until they were full. When they gathered up the leftover fragments, they filled seven baskets. ³⁸Four thousand families were fed.

³⁹After Jesus had dismissed the crowd, he got into the boat and sailed to the region of Magadan.

16:1The Pharisees and the Sadducees came and asked Jesus for a sign from heaven in order to test him.

²He replied, "In the evening you say, 'Tomorrow will be fair, for the sky is red.' ³In the morning you say, 'It will storm today because the sky is red and overcast.' How is it that you can read the signs in the sky, but don't know how to read the signs of the times?

⁴"It is an evil and unfaithful generation that asks for a sign, and you will get no sign from me—except the sign of Jonah." Then he left them and went away.

⁵Once they had crossed to the far shore of the lake, the disciples realized that they had forgotten to bring bread. ⁶Jesus said to them, "Be alert; stay on your guard against the yeast of the Pharisees and the Sadducees."

⁷They discussed this among themselves and concluded, "It is because we didn't bring bread."

⁸Jesus was aware of their discussion and said, "You have so little faith! Why do you talk among yourselves about having no bread? ⁹Don't you understand yet? Don't you remember the five loaves for the five thousand, and how many baskets of leftovers you collected? ¹⁰Or the seven loaves for the four thousand, and how many baskets you collected? ¹¹How could you fail to comprehend that I wasn't talking about bread? I said to be on your

guard against the yeast of the Pharisees and Sadducees." ¹²Then they realized that he was warning them about the teaching of the Pharisees and Sadducees, not the yeast in bread.

ᛜ   ᛜ   ᛜ

¹³When Jesus came to the neighborhood of Caesarea Philippi, he asked the disciples this question: "What do people say about who the Chosen One is?" ¹⁴They replied, "Some say John the Baptizer, others say Elijah, still others Jeremiah or one of the prophets."

¹⁵"And you," he said, "who do you say that I am?"

¹⁶"You are the Messiah," Simon Peter answered, "the Firstborn of the Living God!"

¹⁷Jesus replied, "Blessed are you, Simon begot of Jonah! No mere mortal has revealed this to you, but my Abba God in heaven. ¹⁸I also tell you this: your name now is 'Rock,' and on bedrock like this I will build my community, and the jaws of death will not prevail against it.

¹⁹"Here—I'll give you the keys to the reign of heaven:
> whatever you declare bound on earth
>> will be bound in heaven,
> and whatever you declare loosed on earth
>> will be loosed in heaven."

²⁰Then Jesus strictly ordered the disciples not to tell anyone that he was the Messiah.

ᛜ   ᛜ   ᛜ

²¹From that time on, Jesus began to explain to the disciples that he must go to Jerusalem, to suffer many things at the hands of the elders, chief priests and religious scholars, and that he must be killed, and on the third day raised to life.

²²Peter took him aside and began to rebuke him. "Never, Rabbi!" he said. "This will never happen to you!"

²³Jesus turned to Peter and said, "Get yourself behind me, you Satan! You are trying to make me stumble and fall. You're setting your mind not on the things of God, but of mortals."

²⁴Then Jesus said to the disciples, "If you wish to come after me, you must deny your very selves, take up the instrument of your own death and begin to follow in my footsteps.

²⁵"If you would save your life, you will lose it; but if you would lose your

life for my sake, you will find it. ²⁶ What profit would you show if you gained the whole world but lost yourself? What can you offer in exchange for your very self?

²⁷ "The Promised One will come in the glory of Abba God accompanied by the angels, and will repay all according to their conduct. ²⁸ The truth is, some of you standing here will not taste death before you see the coming of the Promised One's reign."

17:1 Six days later, Jesus took Peter, James and John up on a high mountain to be alone with them.

² And before their eyes, Jesus was transfigured—his face becoming as dazzling as the sun and his clothes as radiant as light.

³ Suddenly Moses and Elijah appeared to them, conversing with Jesus. ⁴ Then Peter said, "Rabbi, how good that we are here! With your permission I will erect three shelters here—one for you, one for Moses and one for Elijah!"

⁵ Peter was still speaking when suddenly a bright cloud overshadowed them. Out of the cloud came a voice which said, "This is my Own, my Beloved, on whom my favor rests. Listen to him!"

⁶ When they heard this, the disciples fell forward on the ground, overcome with fear. ⁷ Jesus came toward them and touched them, saying, "Get up! Don't be afraid." ⁸ When they looked up, they did not see anyone but Jesus.

⁹ As they were coming down the mountainside, Jesus commanded them, "Don't tell anyone about this until the Chosen One has risen from the dead."

¹⁰ The disciples asked, "Why do the religious scholars claim that Elijah must come first?"

¹¹ Jesus replied, "Elijah is indeed coming and will restore all things. ¹² But the truth is, Elijah has already come; they didn't recognize him, but treated him as they pleased. The Chosen One will suffer at their hands in the same way." ¹³ Then the disciples realized that Jesus had been speaking to them about John the Baptizer.

¹⁴ One of the crowd came up to Jesus, knelt before him and said, ¹⁵ "Teacher, have pity on my child, who has seizures and is very ill. The child will often fall into the fire or the water. ¹⁶ Even your disciples have failed to effect a cure."

¹⁷ In reply Jesus said, "What an unbelieving and perverse generation you are! How long must I endure you? Bring the child to me." ¹⁸ Then Jesus

rebuked the demon and it came out, and the child was healed from that moment.

[19] The disciples then came to Jesus and asked, "Why couldn't we expel the demon?"

[20] Jesus answered, "Because you have so little faith. The truth is, if you have even as much faith as the tiny mustard seed, you can be able to say to this mountain, 'Move from here to there,' and it will move. Nothing will be impossible for you."*

[22] When Jesus and the disciples gathered again in Galilee, he said to them, "The Chosen One is going to be put into the hands of others [23] and be killed, but will be raised again on the third day." And the disciples were filled with grief.

ભ   ભ   ભ

[24] When they entered Capernaum, the collectors of the Temple tax approached Peter and asked, "Doesn't your Teacher pay the Temple tax?"

[25] Peter responded, "Of course he does."

When Peter came into the house, Jesus spoke to him first: "Simon, what is your opinion? Do the rulers of the world collect taxes or levies from their own children, or from foreigners?"

[26] Simon replied, "From foreigners."

Jesus observed, "Then their children are exempt. [27] But so we don't offend these people, go to the lake and cast a line, and catch the first fish that bites. Open its mouth and you will find a coin worth twice the Temple tax. Take it and give it to them for both you and me."

ભ   ભ   ભ

18[1] The disciples came up to Jesus with the question, "Who is the greatest in the kindom of heaven?"

[2] Jesus called for a little child to come and stand among them. [3] Then Jesus said, "The truth is, unless you change and become like little children, you will not enter the kindom of heaven. [4] Those who make themselves as humble as this child are the greatest in the kindom of heaven.

[5] "Whoever welcomes a little child like this in my name welcomes me. [6] But those who would cause any of these little ones who believe in me to

---

* Verse 21 is a later addition: *"But this kind of demon doesn't leave except by prayer and fasting."*

stumble would be better off thrown into the sea with millstones around their necks.

⁷"Woe to the world because of its stumbling blocks! Stumbling blocks are inevitable, but woe to those through whom they come!

⁸"If your hand or foot causes you to sin, cut it off and throw it away. It is better to enter Life without your limbs than to have two hands or two feet and be hurled into the eternal fire. ⁹And if your eye causes you to sin, pluck it out and throw it away. It is better to enter Life without sight, than to have two eyes and be hurled into the eternal fire.

¹⁰"See to it that you never despise one of these little ones, for I swear that their angels in heaven are continually in the presence of my Abba God.*

¹²"What do you think? Suppose a shepherd has a hundred sheep and one of them strays away—won't the shepherd leave the ninety-nine on the hillside and go in search of the stray? ¹³If the shepherd finds it, the truth is, there is more joy over the one found than over the ninety-nine that didn't stray. ¹⁴In the same way, it is never the will of your Abba God in heaven that one of these little ones should be lost.

¹⁵"If your sister or brother should commit some wrong against you, go and point out the error, but keep it between the two of you. If she or he listens to you, you have won a loved one back; ¹⁶if not, try again, but take one or two others with you, so that every case may stand on the word of two or three witnesses. ¹⁷If your sister or brother refuses to listen to them, refer the matter to the church. If she or he ignores even the church, then treat that sister or brother as you would a Gentile or a tax collector.

¹⁸"The truth is, whatever you declare bound on earth will be bound in heaven, and whatever you declare loosed on earth will be loosed in heaven.

¹⁹"Again I tell you, if two of you on earth join in agreement to pray for anything whatsoever, it will be granted you by my Abba God in heaven. ²⁰Where two or three are gathered in my name, I am there in their midst."

²¹Peter came up and asked Jesus, "When a sister or brother wrongs me, how many times must I forgive? Seven times?"

²²"No," Jesus replied, "not seven times; I tell you seventy times seven. ²³And here's why.

"The kindom of heaven is like a ruler who decided to settle accounts with the royal officials. ²⁴When the audit was begun, one was brought in who owed tens of millions of dollars. ²⁵As the debtor had no way of paying, the

---

* Some manuscripts add verse 11: *"The Promised One has come to save what was lost."*

ruler ordered this official to be sold, along with family and property, in payment of the debt.

²⁶ "At this, the official bowed down in homage and said, 'I beg you, your highness, be patient with me and I will pay you back in full!' ²⁷ Moved with pity, the ruler let the official go and wrote off the debt.

²⁸ "Then that same official went out and met a colleague who owed the official twenty dollars. The official seized and throttled this debtor with the demand, 'Pay back what you owe me!'

²⁹ "The debtor dropped to the ground and began to plead, 'Just give me time and I will pay you back in full!' ³⁰ But the official would hear none of it, and instead had the colleague put in debtor's prison until the money was paid.

³¹ "When the other officials saw what had happened, they were deeply grieved and went to the ruler, reporting the entire incident. ³² The ruler sent for the official and said, 'You worthless wretch! I cancelled your entire debt when you pleaded with me. ³³ Should you not have dealt mercifully with your colleague, as I dealt with you?' ³⁴ Then in anger, the ruler handed the official over to be tortured until the debt had been paid in full.

³⁵ "My Abba in heaven will treat you exactly the same way unless you truly forgive your sisters and brothers from your hearts."

19:1 When Jesus finished teaching there, he left Galilee and moved on to the area of Judea across the Jordan River. ² Large crowds followed him, and Jesus healed them there.

19:3 – 25:46

Some Pharisees approached Jesus to test him. They said, "May we get divorced for any reason whatsoever?"

⁴ Jesus replied, "Haven't you read that in the beginning, the Creator 'made them male and female' ⁵ and declared, 'This is why one person leaves home and cleaves to another, and the two become one flesh'? ⁶ Consequently they are no longer two, but one flesh—and what God has joined together, let no one separate."

⁷ The Pharisees said to Jesus, "Then why did Moses command that a formal decree be written when we divorce?"

⁸ "Because of your stubbornness, Moses let you divorce," he replied, "but at the beginning it was not that way. ⁹ I say to you now that whoever di-

vorces and marries another — except when the other partner has committed adultery — commits adultery themselves."

¹⁰The disciples said to Jesus, "If that's the case between husband and wife, it's better not to marry!"

¹¹Jesus replied, "Not everyone can accept this teaching — only those to whom it is given to do so. ¹²Some people are incapable of sexual activity from birth. Some have been made this way by human beings. And there are some who have renounced sexual relations for the sake of the kindom of heaven. Let anyone who can accept this teaching do so."

¹³Then small children were brought to Jesus so he could lay hands on them and pray for them. The disciples began to scold the parents, ¹⁴but Jesus said, "Let the children alone — let them come to me. The kindom of heaven belongs to such as these." ¹⁵And after laying his hands on them, Jesus left that town.

¹⁶Someone came up to Jesus and asked, "Teacher, what good must I do to possess eternal life?"

¹⁷Jesus replied, "Why do you ask me about what is good? There is only One who is good. But if you wish to enter into Life, keep the commandments."

¹⁸"Which ones?" the youth asked.

Jesus replied, "No killing. No committing adultery. No stealing. No bearing false witness. ¹⁹Honor your parents. Love your neighbor as yourself."

²⁰The youth said to Jesus, "I have kept all these. What more do I need to do?"

²¹Jesus said, "If you want to be perfect, go and sell what you own and give the money to poor people, and you will have treasure in heaven. Then come and follow me." ²²Upon hearing this the youth, whose possessions were many, went away sadly.

²³Jesus said to the disciples, "The truth is, it is difficult for a rich person to enter the kindom of heaven. ²⁴I'll say it again — it is easier for a camel to pass through the Needle's Eye gate than for the wealthy to enter the kindom of heaven."

²⁵When the disciples heard this, they were astonished. "Then who can be saved?" they said.

²⁶Jesus looked at them and said, "For mortals it is impossible, but for God everything is possible."

²⁷Then Peter spoke: "We have left everything and followed you. What then will there be for us?"

28 Jesus said, "The truth is, when all is made new and the Promised One sits on the throne of glory, you who have followed me will sit on twelve thrones, judging the twelve tribes of Israel. 29 And everyone who has left home, sisters, brothers, mother, father, children or land for my sake will be repaid a hundredfold, and will also inherit eternal life.

30 "Many who are first will be last and the last will be first.

20:1 "The kindom of heaven is like the owner of an estate who went out at dawn to hire workers for the vineyard. 2 After reaching an agreement with them for the usual daily wage, the owner sent them out to the vineyard.

3 "About mid-morning, the owner came out and saw others standing around the marketplace without work, 4 and said to them, 'You go along to my vineyard and I will pay you whatever is fair.' 5 At that they left.

"Around noon and again in the mid-afternoon, the owner came out and did the same. 6 Finally, going out late in the afternoon, the owner found still others standing around and said to them, 'Why have you been standing here idle all day?'

7 " 'No one has hired us,' they replied.

"The owner said, 'You go to my vineyard, too.'

8 "When evening came, the owner said to the overseer, 'Call the workers and give them their pay, but begin with the last group and end with the first.' 9 When those hired late in the afternoon came up, they received a full day's pay, 10 and when the first group appeared they assumed they would get more. Yet they all received the same daily wage.

11 "Thereupon they complained to the owner, 12 'This last group did only an hour's work, but you've put them on the same basis as those who worked a full day in the scorching heat.'

13 " 'My friends,' said the owner to those who voiced this complaint, 'I do you no injustice. You agreed on the usual wage, didn't you? 14 Take your pay and go home. I intend to give this worker who was hired last the same pay as you. 15 I'm free to do as I please with my money, aren't I? Or are you envious because I am generous?'

16 "Thus the last will be first and the first will be last."

℞   ℞   ℞

17 Jesus was on his way to Jerusalem when he took the Twelve aside and said to them, 18 "We're going up to Jerusalem now. There the Chosen One will be handed over to the chief priests and religious scholars, and will be condemned to death. 19 They will turn the Chosen One over to the Gentiles

to be mocked, scourged and crucified. But on the third day, the Chosen One will rise again."

20 Then the mother of Zebedee's children brought James and John to Jesus, and knelt down beg to a favor of him.

21 "What do you want?" Jesus asked.

She answered, "Promise me that in your kindom these children of mine will sit, one at your right hand and the other at your left."

22 Jesus replied, "Do you know what you are asking? Can you drink the cup that I am going to drink?"

"We can," they said.

23 "Very well," said Jesus, "you will drink my cup. But as for seats at my right hand and my left, these are not mine to give. They belong to those for whom they've been prepared by my Abba God."

24 The other ten, on hearing this, were indignant with the two brothers. 25 But Jesus said to them, "You know how the leaders of the Gentiles push their people around. 26 This is not to happen among you. Anyone among you who aspires to greatness must serve the rest. 27 And anyone among you who wishes to be first must serve the needs of all, as if enslaved— 28 just as the Chosen One came not to be served but to serve, and to die in ransom for many."

ભ   ભ   ભ

29 Jesus and the disciples left Jericho with a large crowd trailing behind. 30 Two blind people sat by the roadside and when they heard that it was Jesus passing by, they began to shout, "Jesus, Heir to the House of David, take pity on us!"

31 The crowd shushed them, but they cried out all the louder, "Rabbi, Heir to the House of David, take pity on us!"

32 Jesus stopped and called them over and said, "What do you want me to do for you?"

33 They answered, "Rabbi, we want our eyes to be opened."

34 Jesus, moved with pity, touched their eyes. Their sight returned immediately, and they followed him.

21:1 As they approached Jerusalem, entering Beth-Phage at the Mount of Olives, Jesus sent off two disciples 2 with the instructions, "Go into the village straight ahead of you, and immediately you will find a tethered donkey with her colt standing beside her. Untie them and lead them back to me. ³ If anyone questions you, say, 'The Rabbi needs them.' Then they will let them go at once."

⁴ This came about to fulfill what was said through the prophet:

⁵ "Tell the daughter of Zion,
    'Your Sovereign comes to you without display,
riding on a donkey, on a colt—
    the foal of a beast of burden.' "

⁶ So the disciples went off and did what Jesus had ordered. ⁷ They brought the donkey and her colt, and after they laid their cloaks on the animals, Jesus mounted and rode toward the city.

⁸ Great crowds of people spread their cloaks on the road, while some began to cut branches from the trees and lay them along the path. ⁹ The crowds—those who went in front of Jesus and those who followed—were all shouting,

"Hosanna to the Heir to the House of David!
    Blessed is the One who comes
in the name of the Most High!
    Hosanna in the highest!"

¹⁰ As Jesus entered Jerusalem, the whole city was stirred to its depths, demanding, "Who is this?"

¹¹ And the crowd kept answering, "This is the prophet Jesus, from Nazareth in Galilee!"

¹² When Jesus entered the Temple, he drove out all those who were selling and buying there. He overturned the tables of the money-changers and the seats of those selling doves. ¹³ He said to them, "Scripture says, 'My house is called a house of prayer,' but you make it a den of thieves!"

¹⁴ Those who were blind or couldn't walk came to him in the Temple, and he healed them. ¹⁵ When the chief priests and teachers of the Law saw the wonderful things Jesus did, and heard the children shouting "Hosanna to the Heir to the House of David!" throughout the Temple area, they became indignant.

¹⁶ "Do you hear what the children are shouting?" they asked him.

"Yes," Jesus replied. "Have you never read, 'From the mouths of children and nursing babies, you have brought forth praise'?" ¹⁷ After leaving them, he went out to Bethany to spend the night.

¹⁸ When he returned to the city early in the morning, Jesus grew hungry. ¹⁹ Seeing a fig tree by the road, he walked over to it but found only leaves.

So he said to it, "You will never bear fruit again." And immediately the tree withered.

²⁰ The disciples were amazed when they saw this. "How was it," they asked, "that the tree withered on the spot like that?"

²¹ Jesus answered, "The truth is, if you have faith and don't doubt, not only can you do what I did to the fig tree, but you can even say to this mountain, 'Get up and throw yourself into the sea!' and it will happen. ²² Everything you pray for in faith, you will receive."

ର   ର   ର

²³ Jesus entered the Temple precincts and began teaching. The chief priests and the elders of the people came to him and said, "By what authority are you doing what you do? Who gave you this authority?"

²⁴ "And I," replied Jesus, "will ask you a single question; if you give me the answer, I will tell you my authority for these actions. ²⁵ What was the origin of John's right to baptize? Was it divine or was it human?"

They discussed it among themselves and said, "If we say, 'divine,' he will respond, 'Then why did you refuse to believe him?' ²⁶ But if we say 'human,' we have the people to fear, for they regard John as a prophet." ²⁷ So they replied to Jesus, "We don't know."

Jesus said in reply, "Neither will I tell you by what authority I am doing these things."

²⁸ Jesus continued, "What do you think? There was a landowner who had two children. The landowner approached the elder and said, 'My child, go out and work in the vineyard today.' ²⁹ This first child replied, 'No, I won't,' but afterwards regretted it and went. ³⁰ The landowner then came to the second child and said the same thing. The second child said in reply, 'I'm on my way,' but never went. ³¹ Which of the two did what was wanted?"

They said, "The first."

Jesus said to them, "The truth is, tax collectors and prostitutes are entering the kindom of God before you. ³² When John came walking on the road of justice, you didn't believe him, but the tax collectors and the prostitutes did. Yet even when you saw that, you didn't repent and believe.

³³ "Listen to another parable. There was a property owner who planted a vineyard, put a hedge around it, installed a winepress and erected a tower. Then the owner leased it out to tenant farmers and went on a journey.

³⁴ "When vintage time arrived, the owner sent aides to the tenants to divide the shares of the grapes. ³⁵ The tenants responded by seizing the aides.

They beat one, killed another and stoned a third. ³⁶ A second time the owner sent even more aides than before, but they treated them the same way. ³⁷ Finally, the owner sent the family heir to them, thinking, 'They will respect my heir.'

³⁸ "When the vine-growers saw the heir, they said to one another, 'Here's the one who stands in the way of our having everything. With a single act of murder we could seize the inheritance.' ³⁹ With that, they grabbed and killed the heir outside the vineyard. ⁴⁰ What do you suppose the owner of the vineyard will do to those tenants?"

⁴¹ They replied, "The owner will bring that wicked crowd to a horrible death and lease the vineyard out to others, who will see to it that there are grapes for the proprietor at vintage time."

⁴² Jesus said to them, "Did you ever read in the scriptures,

'The stone which the builders rejected
has become the chief cornerstone;
it was Our God's doing
and we find it marvelous to behold'?

⁴³ "That's why I tell you that the kindom of God will be taken from you and given to people who will bear its fruit.

⁴⁴ "Those who fall on this stone will be dashed to pieces, and those on whom it falls will be smashed."

⁴⁵ When the chief priests and the Pharisees heard these parables, they realized that Jesus was speaking about them. ⁴⁶ Although they sought to arrest him, they feared the crowds, who regarded Jesus as a prophet.

22·1 Then Jesus spoke to them again in parables. He said, ² "The kindom of heaven is like this: there was a ruler who prepared a feast for the wedding of the family's heir; ³ but when the ruler sent out workers to summon the invited guests, they wouldn't come. ⁴ The ruler sent other workers, telling them to say to the guests, 'I have prepared this feast for you. My oxen and fattened cattle have been slaughtered, and everything is ready; come to the wedding.' ⁵ But they took no notice; one went off to his farm, another to her business, ⁶ and the rest seized the workers, attacked them brutally and killed them. ⁷ The ruler was furious, and dispatched troops who destroyed those murderers and burned their town.

⁸ "Then the ruler said to the workers, 'The wedding feast is ready, but the guests I invited don't deserve the honor. ⁹ Go out to the crossroads in the town and invite everyone you can find.' ¹⁰ The workers went out into the streets and collected everyone they met, good and bad alike, until the hall was filled with guests.

¹¹ "The ruler, however, came in to see the company at table, and noticed

one guest who was not dressed for a wedding. ¹²'My friend,' said the ruler, 'why are you here without a wedding garment?' But the guest was silent. ¹³Then the ruler said to the attendants, 'Bind this guest hand and foot, and throw the individual out into the darkness, where there will be weeping and gnashing of teeth.'

¹⁴"Many are called, but few are chosen."

⁓ ⁓ ⁓

¹⁵Then the Pharisees went off and began to plot how they might trap Jesus by his speech. ¹⁶They sent their disciples to Jesus, accompanied by sympathizers of Herod, who said, "Teacher, we know you're honest and teach God's way sincerely. You court no one's favor and don't act out of respect for important people. ¹⁷Give us your opinion, then, in this case. Is it lawful to pay tax to the Roman emperor, or not?"

¹⁸Jesus recognized their bad faith and said to them, "Why are you trying to trick me, you hypocrites? ¹⁹Show me the coin which is used to pay the tax." When they handed Jesus a small Roman coin, ²⁰Jesus asked them, "Whose head is this, and whose inscription?"

²¹"Caesar's," they replied.

At that, Jesus said to them, "Then give to Caesar what is Caesar's, but give to God what is God's."

²²When they heard this, they were astonished and went away.

²³Later that day, some Sadducees—who teach that there is no resurrection—came to Jesus and questioned him: ²⁴"Teacher, Moses said that if a man dies without producing children, his brother must marry his widow and raise up children so that the family name will continue. ²⁵Now, let's say there were seven brothers: the first marries and dies childless, so his brother marries his widow; ²⁶then the second brother dies childless, then the third, and so forth down to the seventh. ²⁷Last of all, the woman dies. ²⁸In this 'resurrection,' whose wife will she be? They had all been married to her!"

²⁹Jesus replied, "The reason you are mistaken is because you understand neither the scriptures nor the power of God. ³⁰In the resurrection, people don't marry at all—they are like God's angels. ³¹But on the subject of the resurrection, haven't you read what God told you? ³²'I am the God of Abraham and Sarah, the God of Isaac and Rebecca, the God of Jacob and Rachel and Leah!' God is not the God of the dead, but of the living."

³³When the crowds heard this, they were astonished at Jesus' teaching.

³⁴ When the Pharisees heard that Jesus had left the Sadducees speechless, they gathered together, ³⁵ and one of them, an expert on the Law, attempted to trick Jesus with this question: ³⁶ "Teacher, which commandment of the Law is the greatest?"

³⁷ Jesus answered:

> " 'You must love the Most High God
>> with all your heart,
>> with all your soul and
>> with all your mind.'

³⁸ "That is the greatest and first commandment. ³⁹ The second is like it: 'You must love your neighbor as yourself.' ⁴⁰ On these two commandments the whole Law is based—and the Prophets as well."

⁴¹ While the Pharisees were gathered around him, Jesus asked them this question: ⁴² "What do you think about the Messiah? Whose descendant is the Messiah?"

They said, "David's."

⁴³ Then Jesus asked, "Then how is it that David, inspired by the Spirit, calls the Messiah 'Sovereign'? For he says,

> ⁴⁴ 'The Most High said to my Sovereign,
>> "Sit at my right hand
>> until I place your enemies under your foot." '

⁴⁵ "If David calls the Messiah 'Sovereign,' how can the Messiah be a descendant of David?"

⁴⁶ No one could reply, and from that day on no one dared ask him any more questions.

ભ   ભ   ભ

23¹ Jesus told the crowds and the disciples, ² "The religious scholars and the Pharisees have succeeded Moses as teachers; ³ therefore, perform every observance they tell you to. But don't follow their example; even they don't do what they say. ⁴ They tie up heavy loads and lay them on others' shoulders, while they themselves will not lift a finger to help alleviate the burden.

⁵ "All their works are performed to be seen. They widen their phylacteries and wear huge tassels. ⁶ They are fond of places of honor at banquets and the front seats in synagogues. ⁷ They love respectful greetings in public and being called 'Rabbi.'

⁸ "But as for you, avoid the title 'Rabbi.' For you have only one Teacher,

and you are all sisters and brothers. ⁹ And don't call anyone on earth your 'Mother' or 'Father.' You have only one Parent—our loving God in heaven. ¹⁰ Avoid being called leaders. You have only one leader—the Messiah.

¹¹ "The greatest among you will be the one who serves the rest. ¹² Those who exalt themselves will be humbled, but those who humble themselves will be exalted.

¹³ "Woe to you religious scholars and Pharisees, you frauds! You shut the doors of heaven's kindom in people's faces, neither entering yourselves, nor allowing others to enter who want to.

¹⁴ "Woe to you religious scholars and Pharisees, you frauds! You go on and on with prayer for show, all the while devouring the only security that widows have—their houses; you, therefore, will be given the greater punishment.

¹⁵ "Woe to you religious scholars and Pharisees, you frauds! You travel over land and over sea to make a single convert, and once that person is converted, you create a proselyte twice as wicked as yourselves.

¹⁶ "Woe to you, blind guides! You say, 'If anyone swears by the Temple, it means nothing. But if anyone swears by the gold of the Temple, that person is bound by the oath.' ¹⁷ You blind fools! For which is of greater worth—the gold, or the Temple that makes the gold sacred? ¹⁸ You also say, 'If anyone swears by the altar, it means nothing; but those who swear by the gift on the altar are bound by their oath.' ¹⁹ Hypocrites! Which is greater—the offering, or the altar which makes the offering sacred? ²⁰ Those who swear by the altar are swearing by it and by everything on it. ²¹ Those who swear by the Temple are swearing by it and by the One who dwells there. ²² Those who swear by heaven are swearing by God's throne and by the One who is seated on it.

²³ "Woe to you religious scholars and you Pharisees, you frauds! You pay your tithes on mint, dill and cumin while neglecting the weightier matters of the Law—justice, mercy and faithfulness! These you should have practiced, without neglecting the others. ²⁴ You blind guides! You strain out gnats, but swallow camels in the process!

²⁵ "Woe to you religious scholars and Pharisees, you frauds! You clean the outside of the cup and the dish, leaving the inside filled with plunder and lust. ²⁶ Blind Pharisees! First clean the inside of the cup so that the outside may become clean as well.

²⁷ "Woe to you religious scholars and Pharisees, you frauds! You are like whitewashed tombs, beautiful to look at on the outside, but on the inside full of filth and the bones of the dead. ²⁸ In the same way you present a holy exterior to others, but on the inside you are full of hypocrisy and wickedness.

²⁹ "Woe to you religious scholars and Pharisees, you frauds! You build tombs for the prophets and decorate monuments of holy people, ³⁰ saying, 'We never would have joined in shedding the blood of the prophets, had we lived in our ancestors' days.' ³¹ Ha! Your own evidence testifies against you! You are the descendants of those who murdered the prophets! ³² Now it's your turn: finish what your ancestors started.

³³ "You snakes! You brood of vipers! How can you escape eternal damnation? ³⁴ Look, then: I'm sending you prophets, sages and religious scholars—some of whom you'll murder and crucify, some you'll whip in your synagogues, some you'll hunt down from town to town. ³⁵ And thus you will call down upon yourselves the guilt of all the righteous blood shed on earth, beginning with the blood of Abel the righteous, up to the blood of Zechariah begot of Berekiah—the one you murdered between the Temple and the altar. ³⁶ The truth is, all of this will happen to this generation.

³⁷ "Oh Jerusalem, Jerusalem—you murder the prophets, and you stone those sent to you! Oh, how often have I yearned to gather you together, like a hen gathering her chicks under her wings! But you would have none of it. ³⁸ Therefore your house is being left to you—abandoned.

³⁹ "I tell you, you will not see me again until you say, 'Blessed is the one who comes in the name of Our God!' "

ை   ை   ை

24 ¹ Jesus left the Temple. As he was leaving, the disciples approached and called his attention to the Temple buildings.

² He replied to them, "Do you see all these buildings? The truth is, not a single stone will be left upon another. All of it will be destroyed."

³ As Jesus sat on the Mount of Olives, the disciples approached him privately and asked, "Tell us, when will this happen? What will be the sign of your Coming and the end of the age?"

⁴ Jesus replied to them, "Make sure that no one deceives you. ⁵ For many will come in my name, saying, 'I am the Messiah,' and they will deceive many. ⁶ You will hear of wars, and rumors of more wars. Don't be alarmed, for these things must happen; but that does not mean it's the end. ⁷ For nation will war against nation, and empire against empire; there will be famines and earthquakes all over the world, ⁸ yet all these are only the beginning of the labor pains.

⁹ "Then they will hand you over to be tortured and executed. And you will be despised by all nations because of my name. ¹⁰ At that time many will lose their faith, and they will betray and hate one another.

[11] Many false prophets will rise up to deceive you. [12] Lawlessness will increase, and people's love will grow cold. [13] But those who persevere to the end will be saved.

[14] "The Good News of the kindom will be proclaimed to the whole world as a witness to all the nations. Then the end will come.

[15] "So when you see 'the abomination that causes desolation' that Daniel the prophet speaks of, standing in the holy place"—let the reader understand—[16] "then those in Judea must flee to the mountains. [17] People on a housetop must not go downstairs to collect their belongings. [18] Those in the field must not go back to fetch their cloaks. [19] How terrible it will be at that time for pregnant women and nursing mothers! [20] Pray that your escape will not happen in winter or on the Sabbath. [21] At that time there will be terrible turmoil, unmatched from the beginning of time until now, never to be matched again. [22] And if those days were not been shortened, no one would survive. That time will be shortened for the sake of the chosen.

[23] "If anyone says to you, 'Look, here's the Messiah!' or, 'There's the Messiah!' don't believe it. [24] False messiahs and false prophets will arise, performing impressive signs and wonders in order to deceive, if it were possible, even the chosen. [25] Look: I have told you everything ahead of time.

[26] "So if anyone says to you, 'The Messiah is in the desert,' don't go. If they say, 'The Messiah is in hiding,' don't believe them. [27] For just as the lightning flashes in the East and is visible in the West, so it will be at the coming of the Promised One. [28] It will be as obvious as vultures circling a corpse.

[29] "Immediately after the distress of those days,

'The sun will grow dark,
the moon will lose its light,
the stars will fall from the sky
and the powers of heaven will be shaken.'

[30] "Then the sign of the Promised One will appear in the sky, and all the tribes of the earth will mourn; they will see the Promised One coming on the clouds of heaven with great power and glory. [31] The Promised One will send forth the angels with a loud trumpet blast to gather the chosen from the four winds, and from one end of heaven to the other.

[32] "Take a lesson from the fig tree. When its branches are tender and its leaves sprout, you know that summer is near. [33] In the same manner, when you see all these things, know that the Promised One is near, at the very door.

[34] "The truth is, this generation will not pass away until all these things

have taken place. ³⁵ Heaven and earth will pass away, but my words never will.

³⁶ "No one knows that day and that hour—not the angels of heaven, nor even the Only Begotten—only Abba God.

³⁷ "The coming of the Promised One will be just like Noah's time. ³⁸ In the days before the flood, people were eating and drinking, having relationships and getting married, right up to the day Noah entered the ark. ³⁹ They were totally unconcerned until the flood came and destroyed them. So it will be at the coming of the Promised One. ⁴⁰ Two people will be out in the field; one will be taken and one will be left. ⁴¹ Two people will be grinding meal; one will be taken and one will be left. ⁴² Therefore be vigilant! For you don't know the day your Savior is coming.

⁴³ "Be sure of this: if the owner of the house had known when the thief was coming, the owner would have kept a watchful eye and not allowed the house to be broken into. ⁴⁴ You must be prepared in the same way. The Promised One is coming at the time you least expect.

⁴⁵ "Who is the faithful, farsighted worker whom the owner of the house puts in charge of the household to provide for their needs at the appropriate times? ⁴⁶ Happy are the workers whom the owners find at their work upon their return. ⁴⁷ The truth is, they will be given more responsibility. ⁴⁸ But if the worker is worthless and thinks, 'The owners will be away a long time,' ⁴⁹ and browbeats the other workers, eating and drinking to excess, ⁵⁰ the owners will return on a day when least expected, at the unknown hour. ⁵¹ They will scourge the lout, assigning the hypocrite to that place where there is wailing and the grinding of teeth.

25:1 "Then again, the kindom of heaven could be likened to ten attendants who took their lamps and went to meet the bridal party. ² Five of them were wise, five were foolish. ³ When the foolish ones took their lamps, they didn't take any oil with them, ⁴ but the wise ones took enough oil to keep their lamps burning. ⁵ The bridal party was delayed, so they all fell asleep.

⁶ "At midnight there was a cry: 'Here comes the bridal party! Let's go out to meet them!' ⁷ Then all the attendants rose and trimmed their lamps. ⁸ The foolish ones said to the wise, 'Give us some of your oil, for our lamps are going out.' ⁹ But the wise replied, 'Perhaps there won't be enough for us; run to the dealers and get some more for yourselves.'

¹⁰ "While the foolish ones went to buy more oil, the bridal party arrived; and those who were ready went to the marriage feast with them, and the door was shut. ¹¹ When the foolish attendants returned, they pleaded to be let in. ¹² The doorkeeper replied, 'The truth is, I don't know you.'

¹³ "So stay awake, for you don't know the day or the hour.

¹⁴ "Again, it's like a wealthy landowner who was going on a journey and called in three workers, entrusting some funds to them. ¹⁵ The first was given five thousand dollars, the second two thousand, and the third one thousand, according to each one's ability. Then the landowner went away. ¹⁶ Immediately the worker who received the five thousand went and invested it and made another five. ¹⁷ In the same way, the worker who received the two thousand doubled that figure. ¹⁸ But the worker who received the one thousand instead went off and dug a hole in the ground and buried the money.

¹⁹ "After a long absence, the traveler returned home and settled accounts with them. ²⁰ The one who had received the five thousand came forward bringing the additional five, saying, 'You entrusted me with five thousand; here are five thousand more.'

²¹ "The landowner said, 'Well done! You are a good and faithful worker. Since you were dependable in a small matter, I will put you in charge of larger affairs. Come, share my joy!'

²² "The one who had received the two thousand then stepped forward with the additional two, saying, 'You entrusted me with two thousand; here are two thousand more.'

²³ "The landowner said to this one, 'Cleverly done! You too are a good and faithful worker. Since you were dependable in a small matter, I will put you in charge of larger affairs. Come, share my joy!'

²⁴ "Finally the one who had received the one thousand stepped forward and said to the landowner, 'Knowing your ruthlessness—you who reap where you did not sow and gather where you did not scatter—²⁵ and fearing your wrath, I went off and buried your thousand dollars in the ground. Here is your money back.'

²⁶ "The landowner exclaimed, 'You worthless, lazy lout! So you know that I reap where I don't sow and gather where I don't scatter, do you? ²⁷ All the more reason to deposit my money with the bankers, so that on my return I could have had it back with interest! ²⁸ You, there! Take the thousand away from this bum and give it to the one with the ten thousand.

²⁹ " 'Those who have will get more until they grow rich, while those who have not will lose even the little they have. ³⁰ Throw this worthless one outside into the darkness, where there is wailing and grinding of teeth.'

³¹ "At the appointed time the Promised One will come in glory, escorted by all the angels of heaven, and will sit upon the royal throne, ³² with all the nations assembled below. Then the Promised One will separate them from

one another, as a shepherd divides the sheep from the goats. ³³The sheep will be placed on the right hand, the goats on the left.

³⁴"The ruler will say to those on the right, 'Come, you blessed of my Abba God! Inherit the kindom prepared for you from the creation of the world! ³⁵For I was hungry and you fed me; I was thirsty and you gave me drink. I was a stranger and you welcomed me; ³⁶naked and you clothed me. I was ill and you comforted me; in prison and you came to visit me.' ³⁷Then these just will ask, 'When did we see you hungry and feed you, or see you thirsty and give you drink? ³⁸When did we see you as a stranger and invite you in, or clothe you in your nakedness? ³⁹When did we see you ill or in prison and come to visit you?' ⁴⁰The ruler will answer them, 'The truth is, every time you did this for the least of my sisters or brothers, you did it for me.'

⁴¹"Then the ruler will say to those on the left, 'Out of my sight, you accursed ones! Into that everlasting fire prepared for the Devil and the fallen angels! ⁴²I was hungry and you gave me no food; I was thirsty and you gave me nothing to drink. ⁴³I was a stranger and you gave me no welcome; naked and you gave me no clothing. I was ill and in prison and you did not come to visit me.' ⁴⁴Then they in turn will ask, 'When did we see you hungry or thirsty, or homeless or naked, or ill or in prison, and not take care of you?' ⁴⁵The answer will come, 'The truth is, as often as you neglected to do this to one of the least of these, you neglected to do it to me.' ⁴⁶They will go off to eternal punishment, and the just will go off to eternal life."

26:1–28:20

Jesus now finished all he had to say, and he told the disciples, ²"Passover starts in two days, and the Chosen One will be handed over to be crucified."

³Then the chief priests and the elders of the people gathered in the palace of the high priest, Caiaphas. ⁴They planned to arrest Jesus under some pretext and execute him—⁵"But not during the Festival," they agreed, "or we might have a riot on our hands."

⁶Now when Jesus was in Bethany, at the house of Simon, who had leprosy, ⁷a woman approached Jesus with an alabaster jar of very expensive ointment. She poured it on his head while he reclined at the table. ⁸The disciples, witnessing this, were indignant. "What a waste!" they said. ⁹"This could have been sold at a high price, and the money given to needier people."

¹⁰ Jesus, aware of their concern, said, "Why do you upset the woman? She has done me a good deed. ¹¹ You'll always have poor people with you, but you won't always have me. ¹² When she poured the oil on my body, she was preparing me for burial. ¹³ The truth is, wherever the Good News is proclaimed in the world, she will be remembered for what she has done for me."

¹⁴ One of the Twelve, the one named Judas Iscariot, went off to the chief priests ¹⁵ and said, "What are you willing to give me if I hand Jesus over to you?"

They paid him thirty pieces of silver. ¹⁶ And from that moment he looked for an opportunity to betray Jesus.

ల   ల   ల

¹⁷ On the first day of the Feast of Unleavened Bread, the disciples came up to Jesus and said, "Where do you want us to prepare the Passover for you?"

¹⁸ Jesus told them to go to a certain person in the city and say, "The Teacher says, 'My appointed time draws near. I am to celebrate the Passover in your house.' " ¹⁹ The disciples did as Jesus ordered and prepared the Passover supper.

²⁰ When it grew dark, he reclined at table with the Twelve. ²¹ And while they were eating he said, "The truth is, one of you is about to betray me."

²² They were greatly distressed and started asking him in turn, "Surely, it is not I, Teacher?"

²³ Jesus replied, "The one who has dipped his hand into the dish with me is the one who will hand me over. ²⁴ The Chosen One will go as the scriptures foretold—but woe to the one by whom the Chosen One is betrayed! It would be better for that one never to have been born at all."

²⁵ Then Judas, who was betraying Jesus, said, "Surely it is not I, Rabbi?"

Jesus answered, "You have said it yourself."

²⁶ During the meal Jesus took bread, blessed it, broke it and gave it to the disciples. "Take this and eat it," Jesus said. "This is my body." ²⁷ Then he took a cup, gave thanks, and gave it to them. "Drink from it, all of you," he said. ²⁸ "This is my blood, the blood of the Covenant, which will be poured out on behalf of many for the forgiveness of sins. ²⁹ The truth is, I will not drink this fruit of the vine again until the day when I drink it anew with you in my Abba's kindom."

³⁰ Then, after singing the Hallel, they walked out to the Mount of Olives.

ନ୍ଦ   ନ୍ଦ   ନ୍ଦ

³¹ Jesus then said to them, "Tonight you will all fall away because of me, for scripture says, 'I will strike the shepherd, and the sheep will be scattered.' ³² But after I have been raised, I will go to Galilee ahead of you."

³³ Peter responded, "Though all may fall away because of you, I never will!"

³⁴ Jesus replied, "The truth is, before the cock crows tonight, you will deny me three times."

³⁵ Peter said, "Even if I must die with you, I will never disown you." And all the other disciples said the same.

³⁶ Then Jesus went with them to a place called Gethsemani and said to the disciples, "Stay here while I go over there and pray." ³⁷ Jesus took along Peter, James and John and started to feel grief and anguish. ³⁸ Then he said to them, "My soul is deeply grieved, to the point of death. Please, stay here, and stay awake with me."

³⁹ Jesus went on a little further and fell prostrate in prayer: "Abba, if it is possible, let this cup pass me by. But not what I want—what you want."

⁴⁰ When Jesus returned to the disciples, he found them asleep. He said to Peter, "Couldn't you stay awake with me for even an hour? ⁴¹ Be on guard, and pray that you may not undergo trial. The spirit is willing, but the body is weak."

⁴² Withdrawing a second time, Jesus prayed, "Abba, if this cup cannot pass me by without my drinking it, your will be done!"

⁴³ Once more Jesus returned and found the disciples asleep; they could not keep their eyes open. ⁴⁴ Jesus left them again, withdrew somewhat and prayed for a third time, saying the same words as before. ⁴⁵ Finally Jesus returned to the disciples and said to them, "Are you still sleeping? Still taking your rest? The hour is upon us—the Chosen One is being betrayed into the hands of sinners. ⁴⁶ Get up! Let us be on our way! Look, my betrayer is here."

⁴⁷ While Jesus was still speaking, Judas, one of the Twelve, arrived—accompanied by a great crowd with swords and clubs. They had been sent by the chief priests and elders of the people. ⁴⁸ Judas had arranged to give them a signal. "Whomever I embrace is the one," he had said; "take hold of him." ⁴⁹ He immediately went over to Jesus and said, "Shalom, Rabbi!" and embraced him.

[50] Jesus said to Judas, "Friend, just do what you're here to do!" At that moment, the crowd surrounded them, laid hands on Jesus and arrested him.

[51] Suddenly, one of those who accompanied Jesus drew a sword and slashed at the high priest's attendant, cutting off an ear. [52] Jesus said, "Put your sword back where it belongs. Those who live by the sword die by the sword. [53] Don't you think I can call on my Abba God to provide over twelve legions of angels at a moment's notice? [54] But then how would the scriptures be fulfilled, which say it must happen this way?"

[55] Then Jesus said to the crowd, "Am I a robber, that you have come armed with swords and clubs to arrest me? Every day I sat teaching in the Temple precincts, yet you never arrested me." [56] All this happened in fulfillment of the writings of the prophets. Then all the disciples deserted Jesus and fled.

Ș Ș Ș

[57] Those who had seized Jesus led him off to Caiaphas, the high priest, where the religious scholars and elders had convened. [58] Peter followed at a distance as far as the high priest's residence. Going inside, Peter sat down with the guards to await the outcome. [59] The chief priests, with the whole Sanhedrin, were busy trying to obtain false testimony against Jesus, so that they might put him to death. [60] They discovered none, despite the many false witnesses who took the stand.

Finally two came forward [61] who stated, "This man has declared, 'I can destroy God's sanctuary and rebuild it in three days."

[62] The high priest rose and addressed Jesus, "Have you no answer? What about this testimony leveled against you?" [63] But Jesus remained silent. The high priest then said to him, "I order you to tell us under oath, before the living God, whether or not you are the Messiah, the Firstborn of God?"

[64] "You have said it yourself," Jesus replied. "But I tell you: soon you will see the Chosen One seated at the right hand of the Power, and coming on the clouds of heaven."

[65] At this, the high priest tore his robes and said, "Blasphemy! What further need do we have of witnesses? You yourselves have heard the blasphemy. [66] What is your verdict?"

They responded, "He deserves death!" [67] Then they spat at his face and struck him with their fists. Others slapped Jesus, [68] saying, "Play the prophet for us, Messiah! Who struck you?"

[69] While this was happening, Peter was sitting in the courtyard. One of

the attendants came over and said, "You were with Jesus the Galilean too, weren't you?"

⁷⁰ But Peter denied it in front of everyone. He said, "I don't know what you're talking about!"

⁷¹ When Peter went out to the gate, another attendant saw him and said to those nearby, "This one was with Jesus of Nazareth."

⁷² Again he cursed and denied it: "I don't know him!"

⁷³ A little while later, some bystanders came over to Peter and said, "You certainly are one of them! Even your accent gives you away!"

⁷⁴ At that, Peter began cursing and swore, "I don't know the man!"

Just then a rooster began to crow, ⁷⁵ and Peter remembered the prediction Jesus had made: "Before the rooster crows, you will disown me three times." Peter went out and cried bitterly.

27:1 At daybreak, all the chief priests and the elders of the people took formal action against Jesus to put him to death. ² They bound him and led him away to be handed over to Pilate, the governor.

༒   ༒   ༒

³ When he saw that Jesus had been condemned, Judas, who had betrayed Jesus, felt remorse. He took the thirty pieces of silver back to the chief priests and elders, ⁴ and said, "I have sinned! I have betrayed innocent blood!"

"What's that to us?" they answered. "That's your affair!" ⁵ So Judas flung the money into the sanctuary and left. Then he went off and hanged himself.

⁶ The chief priests picked up the silver, observing, "It's against the Law to deposit this in the Temple treasury, since it is blood money." ⁷ After some discussion, they used the money to buy Potter's Field as a cemetery for foreigners. ⁸ That is why that field, even today, is called Blood Field. ⁹ On that occasion, what was said through Jeremiah the prophet was fulfilled:

> "They took thirty pieces of silver,
>   the price for the One
> whose price was set
>   by the children of Israel,
> ¹⁰ and they paid it out for Potter's Field
>   just as Our God commanded me."

¹¹ Then Jesus was arraigned before Pontius Pilate, the governor, who questioned him. "Are you the King of the Jews?"

Jesus replied, "You say that I am."

¹² Yet when Jesus was accused by the chief priests and elders, he made no reply. ¹³ Pilate said to Jesus, "Surely you hear how many charges they bring against you?" ¹⁴ But Jesus did not answer Pilate on a single count, much to the governor's surprise.

¹⁵ Now, on the occasion of a festival, the governor was accustomed to release one prisoner, whomever the crowd would designate. ¹⁶ At the time they were holding a notorious prisoner named Barabbas. ¹⁷ So when the crowd gathered, Pilate asked them, "Which one do you wish me to release for you? Barabbas? Or Jesus, the so-called Messiah?" ¹⁸ Pilate knew, of course, that it was out of jealousy that they had handed Jesus over.

¹⁹ While Pilate was still presiding on the bench, his wife sent him a message: "Have nothing to do with that innocent man. I had a dream about him last night which has been troubling me all day long."

²⁰ But the chief priests and elders convinced the crowds that they should ask for Barabbas, and have Jesus put to death. ²¹ So when the governor asked them, "Which one do you wish me to release for you?" they all cried, "Barabbas!"

²² Pilate said to them, "Then what am I to do with Jesus, the so-called Messiah?"

"Crucify him!" they all said.

²³ "Why? What crime has he committed?" Pilate asked.

But they only shouted louder, "Crucify him!"

²⁴ Pilate finally realized that he was getting nowhere with this—in fact, a riot was breaking out. Pilate called for water and washed his hands in front of the crowd, declaring as he did so, "I am innocent of this man's blood. The responsibility is yours." ²⁵ The whole crowd said in reply, "Let his blood be on us and on our children." ²⁶ At that, Pilate released Barabbas to them. But he had Jesus whipped with a cat-o'-nine-tails, then handed him over to be crucified.

²⁷ The governor's soldiers took Jesus inside the Praetorium and assembled the whole cohort around him. ²⁸ They stripped off his clothes and wrapped him in a scarlet military cloak. ²⁹ Weaving a crown out of thorns, they pressed it onto his head, and stuck a reed in his right hand. Then they be-

gan to mock Jesus by dropping to their knees, saying, "All hail, King of the Jews!" ³⁰ They also spat at him. Afterward they took hold of the reed and struck Jesus on the head. ³¹ Finally, when they had finished mocking him, they stripped him of the cloak, dressed him in his own clothes and led him off to crucifixion.

³² On their way out, they met a Cyrenian named Simon, whom they pressed into service to carry the cross. ³³ Upon arriving at a site called Golgotha—which means Skull Place—³⁴ they gave Jesus a drink of wine mixed with a narcotic herb, which Jesus tasted but refused to drink.

³⁵ Once they had nailed Jesus to the cross, they divided his clothes among them by rolling dice; ³⁶ then they sat down and kept watch over him. ³⁷ Above his head, they put the charge against him in writing: "This is Jesus, King of the Jews." ³⁸ Two robbers were crucified along with Jesus, one at his right and one at his left.

³⁹ People going by insulted Jesus, shaking their heads ⁴⁰ and saying, "So you are the one who was going to destroy the Temple and rebuild it in three days! Save yourself, why don't you? Come down off that cross if you are God's Own!"

⁴¹ The chief priests, the religious scholars and the elders also joined in the jeering: ⁴² "He saved others but he cannot save himself! So he's the King of Israel! Let's see him come down from that cross, and then we will believe in him. ⁴³ He trusts in God; let God rescue him now, if God is happy with him! After all, he claimed to be God's Own!" ⁴⁴ The robbers who had been crucified with Jesus jeered at him in the same way.

⁴⁵ At noon, a darkness fell over the whole land until about three in the afternoon. ⁴⁶ At that hour Jesus cried out with a loud voice, " 'Eli, Eli, lama sabachthani?' " which means, "My God, My God, why have you forsaken me?" ⁴⁷ This made some of the bystanders who heard it remark, "He is calling for Elijah!" ⁴⁸ One of them hurried off and got a sponge. He soaked the sponge in cheap wine and, sticking it on a reed, tried to make Jesus drink. ⁴⁹ The others said, "Leave him alone. Let's see whether Elijah comes to his rescue."

⁵⁰ Once again, Jesus cried out in a loud voice, then he gave up his spirit. ⁵¹ Suddenly, the curtain in front of the Holy of Holies was ripped in half from top to bottom. The earth quaked, boulders were split ⁵² and tombs were opened. Many bodies of holy ones who had fallen asleep were raised. ⁵³ After Jesus' resurrection, they came out of their tombs and entered the holy city, and appeared to many.

⁵⁴ The centurion and his cohort, who were standing guard over Jesus' body, were terror-stricken at seeing the earthquake and all that was happening, and said, "Clearly, this was God's Own!"

⁵⁵ A group of women were present, looking on from a distance. These were the same women who had followed Jesus from Galilee as ministers to him. ⁵⁶ Among them were Mary of Magdala; Mary, the mother of James and Joseph; and the mother of Zebedee's children.

⁵⁷ When evening fell, a wealthy man from Arimathea named Joseph, who had become a disciple of Jesus, ⁵⁸ came to request the body of Jesus; Pilate issued an order for its release. ⁵⁹ Taking the body, Joseph wrapped it in fresh linen ⁶⁰ and laid it in his own tomb, which had been hewn out of rock. Then Joseph rolled a huge stone across the entrance of the tomb and went away. ⁶¹ But Mary of Magdala and the other Mary remained sitting there, facing the tomb.

⁶² The next day—the one following the Day of Preparation—the chief priests and the Pharisees called at Pilate's residence ⁶³ and said, "We recall that, while he was still alive, the impostor made the claim, 'After three days I will rise again.' ⁶⁴ Therefore, please issue an order to keep the tomb under surveillance until the third day. Otherwise, Jesus' disciples might go and steal his body and tell the people, 'Jesus has been raised from the dead!' This final deception would be worse than the first."

⁶⁵ Pilate said to them, "You have a guard. Go and secure the tomb as best you can." ⁶⁶ So they went to seal the tomb and post a guard.

☙   ☙   ☙

28:1 After the Sabbath, as the first day of the week was dawning, Mary of Magdala came with Mary to inspect the tomb.

²Suddenly, there was a severe earthquake, and an angel of God descended from heaven, rolled back the stone, and sat on it. ³ The angel's appearance was like lightning, with garments white as snow. ⁴ The guards shook with fear and fell down as though they were dead.

⁵ Then the angel spoke, addressing the women: "Don't be afraid. I know you are looking for Jesus the crucified, ⁶ who is no longer here. Jesus has been raised, exactly as it was foretold. Come and see the burial place. ⁷ Then go quickly and tell the disciples that Jesus has risen from the dead and now goes ahead of you to Galilee. You will see Jesus there. That is the message I have for you."

⁸ The women hurried away from the tomb with awe and great joy and ran to carry the good news to the disciples.

⁹ Suddenly Jesus stood before them and said, "Shalom!" The women came up, embraced Jesus' feet and worshiped. ¹⁰ At this, Jesus said to them, "Don't be afraid! Go tell the disciples to go to Galilee, where they will see me."

¹¹ While the women were on their way, some of the guards went into the city and reported to the chief priests what had happened. ¹² The chief priests in turn held a meeting with the elders and, after working out their strategy, gave a considerable amount of money to the soldiers, ¹³ with these instructions: "You are to say, 'His disciples came during the night and stole him away while we were asleep.' ¹⁴ And if any word of this gets to the governor, we will straighten it out with him and keep you out of trouble." ¹⁵ The soldiers took the money and carried out their instructions. This is the story that circulates among Judeans to this very day.

¹⁶ The Eleven made their way to Galilee, to the mountain where Jesus had summoned them. ¹⁷ At the sight of the risen Christ they fell down in homage, though some doubted what they were seeing. ¹⁸ Jesus came forward and addressed them in these words:

> "All authority has been given me
>   both in heaven and on earth;
> ¹⁹ go, therefore, and make disciples of all the nations.
> Baptize them in the name
>   of Abba God,
>   and of the Only Begotten,
>   and of the Holy Spirit.
> ²⁰ Teach them to carry out
>   everything I have commanded you.
> And know that I am with you always,
>   even until the end of the world!"

the gospel according to
mark

*t*he gospel of jesus christ, god's own,
² begins as it was written in Isaiah the prophet:
> "I send my messenger before you
> to prepare your way,
> ³ a herald's voice in the desert, crying,
> 'Make ready the way of Our God,
> Clear a straight path.' "

⁴ And so John the Baptizer appeared in the desert, proclaiming a baptism of repentance for the forgiveness of sins. ⁵ The whole Judean countryside and all the people of Jerusalem went out to John and were baptized by him in the Jordan River as they confessed their sins. ⁶ John was clothed in camel's hair and wore a leather belt around his waist, and he ate nothing but grasshoppers and wild honey. ⁷ In the course of his preaching, John said, "One more powerful than I is to come after me. I am not fit to stoop and untie his sandal straps. ⁸ I have baptized you in water, but the One to come will baptize you in the Holy Spirit."

⁹ It was then that Jesus came from Nazareth in Galilee and was baptized in the Jordan River by John. ¹⁰ Immediately upon coming out of the water,

Jesus saw the heavens opening and the Spirit descending on him like a dove. ¹¹ Then a voice came from the heavens: "You are my Beloved, my Own. On you my favor rests."

¹² Immediately the Spirit drove Jesus out into the wilderness, ¹³ and he remained there for forty days, and was tempted by Satan. He was with the wild beasts, and the angels looked after him.

CB CB CB

¹⁴ After John's arrest, Jesus appeared in Galilee proclaiming the Good News of God:

¹⁵ "This is the time of fulfillment. The reign of God is at hand! Change your hearts and minds, and believe this Good News!"

CB CB CB

¹⁶ While walking by the Sea of Galilee, Jesus saw the brothers Simon and Andrew casting their nets into the sea, since they fished by trade. ¹⁷ Jesus said to them, "Follow me; I will make you fishers of humankind." ¹⁸ They immediately abandoned their nets and followed Jesus.

¹⁹ Proceeding a little further along, Jesus saw the brothers James and John, begot of Zebedee. They too were in their boat, putting their nets in order. ²⁰ Immediately Jesus called them, and they left their father Zebedee standing in the boat with the hired help, and went off in the company of Jesus.

CB CB CB

²¹ They came to Capernaum, and on the Sabbath Jesus entered the synagogue and began to teach. ²² The people were spellbound by the teaching, because Jesus taught with an authority that was unlike their religious scholars.

²³ Suddenly a person with an unclean spirit appeared in their synagogue. It shrieked, ²⁴ "What do you want from us, Jesus of Nazareth? Have you come to destroy us? I know who you are—the Holy One of God!"

²⁵ Jesus rebuked the spirit sharply: "Be quiet! Come out of that person!" ²⁶ At that the unclean spirit convulsed the possessed one violently, and with a loud shriek it came out.

²⁷ All who looked on were amazed. They began to ask one another, "What is this? A new teaching, and with such authority! This person even gives orders to unclean spirits and they obey!" ²⁸ Immediately news of Jesus spread throughout the surrounding region of Galilee.

²⁹ Upon leaving the synagogue, Jesus entered Simon's and Andrew's house with James and John. ³⁰ Simon's mother-in-law lay ill with a fever, and immediately they told Jesus about her.

³¹ Jesus went over to her, took her by the hand and helped her up, and the fever left her. Then she went about her work.

³² After sunset, as evening drew on, they brought to Jesus all who were ill and possessed by demons. ³³ Everyone in the town crowded around the door. ³⁴ Jesus healed many who were sick with different diseases, and cast out many demons. But Jesus would not permit the demons to speak, because they knew who he was.

³⁵ Rising early the next morning, Jesus went off to a lonely place in the desert and prayed there. ³⁶ Simon and some companions managed to find Jesus ³⁷ and said to him, "Everybody is looking for you!"

³⁸ Jesus said to them, "Let us move on to the neighboring villages so that I may proclaim the Good News there also. That is what I have come to do." ³⁹ So Jesus went into their synagogues proclaiming the Good News and expelling demons throughout the whole of Galilee.

⁴⁰ A person with leprosy approached Jesus, knelt down and begged, "If you are willing, you can heal me."

⁴¹ Moved with pity, Jesus stretched out a hand, touched the person with leprosy and said, "I am willing. Be cleansed."

⁴² Immediately the leprosy disappeared, and the person with the disease was cured. ⁴³ Jesus gave a stern warning and sent the person off. ⁴⁴ "Not a word to anyone," Jesus said. "Go off and present yourself to the priest and make an offering for your healing as Moses commanded, as a testimony to the religious authorities."

⁴⁵ But the person who had been healed went off and began to proclaim the whole matter freely, making the story public. As a result it was no longer possible for Jesus to enter a town openly, and Jesus stayed in lonely places. Even so, people kept coming to him from all directions.

2:1 Jesus came back to Capernaum after several days, and word spread that he was home. ² People began to gather in such great numbers that there was no longer any room for them, even around the door.

While Jesus was delivering God's word to them, ³ some people arrived bringing a paralyzed person. The four who carried the invalid ⁴ were unable to reach Jesus because of the crowd, so they began to open up the roof directly above Jesus. When they had made a hole, they lowered the mat on which the paralyzed one was lying. ⁵When Jesus saw their faith, he said to the sufferer, "My child, your sins are forgiven."

⁶Now some of the religious scholars were sitting there asking themselves, ⁷"Why does Jesus talk in that way? He commits blasphemy! Who can forgive sins but God alone?"

⁸Jesus immediately perceived in his spirit that they reasoned this way among themselves and said to them, "Why do you harbor such thoughts? ⁹Which is easier, to say to this paralyzed person, 'Your sins are forgiven,' or to say, 'Stand up, pick up your mat and walk'? ¹⁰But so you all may know that the Promised One has authority on earth to forgive sins—" Jesus then turned to the paralyzed person—¹¹"I tell you, stand up! Pick up your mat and go home."

¹²The paralyzed person stood up, picked up the mat and walked outside in the sight of everyone. They were awestruck, and they all gave praise to God and said, "We have never seen anything like this!"

℞   ℞   ℞

¹³Jesus went out again and walked along the lake shore, but people kept coming to him in crowds to listen to his teachings. ¹⁴As he passed by, Jesus saw Levi, begot of Alphaeus, sitting in the tax office. Jesus said, "Follow me," and Levi got up and followed him.

¹⁵While Jesus was reclining to eat in Levi's house, many other tax collectors and notorious "sinners" joined him and the disciples at dinner. There were many people following Jesus. ¹⁶When the religious scholars who belonged to the Pharisee sect saw that he was eating with tax collectors and sinners, they complained to the disciples, "Why does the Teacher eat with these people?"

¹⁷Overhearing the remark, Jesus said to them, "People who are healthy don't need a doctor; sick ones do. I have come to call sinners, not the righteous."

¹⁸Now John's disciples and the Pharisees fasted regularly. Some people came to Jesus with the objection, "Why do John's disciples and those of the Pharisees fast, while yours don't?"

¹⁹Jesus replied, "How can wedding guests fast while the bridegroom is still among them? So long as the bridegroom stays with them, they cannot fast. ²⁰The day will come, however, when the bridegroom will be taken away; on that day they will fast.

²¹"No one sews a patch of unshrunken cloth on an old cloak. Otherwise, the patch pulls away from it—the new from the old—and the tear gets

worse. ²²Similarly, no one pours new wine into old wineskins. If one does, the wine will burst the skins, and both wine and skins will be lost. No, new wine is poured into new wineskins."

²³One Sabbath day Jesus took a walk through the grain fields, and the disciples began to pick ears of grain as they went along. ²⁴The Pharisees said to Jesus, "Look, why are they doing something on the Sabbath day that is forbidden?"

²⁵And Jesus replied, "Did you never read what David did in his time of need when he and his followers were hungry— ²⁶how David went into the house of God when Abiathar was high priest and ate the loaves of offering, which only the priests are allowed to eat, and how he also gave some to those with him?"

²⁷Then Jesus said to them, "The Sabbath was made for people, not people for the Sabbath. ²⁸That is why the Chosen One is ruler even of the Sabbath."

3:1 Returning to the synagogue, Jesus met someone who had a withered hand. ²Now the religious authorities were watching to see if Jesus would heal the individual on the Sabbath day, as they were hoping for some evidence to use against Jesus. ³He said to the afflicted one, "Stand and come up front!"

⁴Then he turned to them and said, "Is it permitted to do a good deed on the Sabbath—or an evil one? To preserve life or to destroy it?"

At this they remained silent. ⁵Jesus looked around at them with anger, for he was deeply grieved that they had closed their hearts so. Then Jesus said to the person, "Stretch out your hand." The other did so, and the hand was perfectly restored.

⁶The Pharisees went out and at once began to plot with the Herodians, discussing how to destroy Jesus.

J
3:7–6:6

esus withdrew with the disciples to the lakeside. A great crowd followed him from Galilee, ⁸and an equally great multitude came from Judea, Jerusalem, Idumea, Transjordan and the neighborhood of Tyre and Sidon, because they had heard what he had done.

⁹In view of their numbers, Jesus told the disciples to have a fishing boat ready so that he could avoid the pushing of the crowd. ¹⁰Because he had healed many, all who had afflictions kept pressing forward to touch him.

¹¹ Unclean spirits would catch sight of him, fling themselves down at his feet and shout, "You are God's Own," ¹²while he kept ordering them sternly not to reveal who he was.

ᴒᴙ   ᴒᴙ   ᴒᴙ

¹³Jesus went up the mountain and summoned those followers he wanted, who came and joined him. ¹⁴He named twelve as his companions whom he would send to preach ¹⁵and to have authority to expel the demons.

¹⁶He appointed the twelve as follows: Simon, to whom he gave the name Peter; ¹⁷James, begot of Zebedee, and John, his brother, to whom he gave the name Boanerges, or "children of thunder"; ¹⁸Andrew; Philip; Bartholomew; Matthew; Thomas; James begot of Alphaeus; Thaddaeus; Simon, the Zealot; ¹⁹and Judas Iscariot, who betrayed Jesus.

ᴒᴙ   ᴒᴙ   ᴒᴙ

²⁰Then Jesus went home, and again such a crowd gathered that he and the disciples were unable even to eat a meal. ²¹When Jesus' relatives heard of this, they went out to take charge of him, thinking that he had lost his mind.

²²The religious scholars who had come down from Jerusalem said of Jesus, "He is possessed by Beelzebul," and, "He casts out demons through the ruler of demons."

²³Summoning them, Jesus spoke in parables: "How can Satan cast out Satan? ²⁴If a realm is torn by civil strife, it cannot last. ²⁵If a household is divided according to loyalties, it will not survive. ²⁶Similarly, if Satan has suffered mutiny in the ranks and is torn by dissension, the Devil is finished and cannot endure. ²⁷No attacker can enter a stronghold unless the defender is first put under restraint. Only then can the attacker plunder the stronghold.

²⁸"The truth is, every sin and all the blasphemy the people utter will be forgiven, ²⁹but those who blaspheme against the Holy Spirit will never have forgiveness. They are guilty of an eternal sin." ³⁰Jesus spoke all this because they said, "He is possessed by an unclean spirit."

³¹Jesus' mother and brothers arrived and sent in a message asking for him. ³²A crowd was sitting around Jesus, and they said to him, "Your mother and brothers are outside looking for you." ³³Jesus replied, "Who is my mother? Who is my family?" ³⁴And looking around at everyone there, Jesus said, "This is my family! ³⁵Anyone who does the will of God, that person is my sister, my brother, my mother."

4:1 Again Jesus began to preach beside the lake. But such a huge crowd gathered around that he got into a boat and sat there, while the crowd remained on the shore.

2 Jesus taught them many things in the form of parables and, in the course of his teaching, said, 3 "Listen carefully. Imagine a sower going out to sow, scattering the seed widely. 4 Some of the seed fell on the edge of the path, and the birds came and ate it. 5 Some seed fell on rocky ground where it found a little soil, and sprang up immediately because the soil had little depth—6 but then, when the sun came up and scorched it, it withered for lack of roots. 7 Some seed fell into thorns, and the thorns grew up and choked it, and it produced no crop. 8 And some seed fell into rich soil and grew tall and strong, producing a crop thirty, sixty, even a hundredfold." 9 Jesus ended by saying, "If you have ears to hear, then listen."

10 Now when Jesus was away from the crowd, the Twelve, and others who formed the community, asked what the parable meant. 11 Jesus said, "The secret of the kindom of God is given to you, but to those who are outside, it comes in parables, 12 so that 'they may look and look again, but not perceive; they may listen and listen again, but not understand.' Otherwise they might be converted and be forgiven."

13 Jesus continued, "Don't you understand this parable? Then how will you understand any of the parables? 14 The sower is sowing the message. 15 Those on the edge of the path where the message is sown are people who have no sooner heard it, than Satan comes and carries away the message that was sown in them. 16 Similarly, those who receive the seed on patches of rock are people who, when first they hear the message, immediately welcome it with joy. 17 But they have no root in themselves, they do not last; when trials or persecutions rise because of my message, they immediately fall away. 18 Then there are others who receive the seed in thorns. These have heard the message, 19 but the worries of this world, the lure of riches and all the other passions come in and choke the message, so it produces nothing. 20 And there are those who have received the seed in rich soil. They hear the message and accept it, and they bear fruit, thirty, sixty, and a hundredfold."

21 He also said to the crowd, "Would you bring in a lamp and put it under a bushel basket or hide it under the bed? Surely you'd put in on a lampstand! 22 Things are hidden only to be revealed at a later time. They are made secret only to be brought out into the open. 23 If you have ears to hear, then listen!"

²⁴ He continued, "Listen carefully to what you hear. The amount you measure out is the amount you will receive—and more besides. ²⁵ To those who have, more will be given; from those who have not, what little they have will be taken away."

²⁶ Jesus said further, "The reign of God is like this: a sower scatters seed on the ground, ²⁷ then goes to bed at night and gets up day after day. Through it all the seed sprouts and grows without the sower knowing how it happens. ²⁸ The soil produces a crop by itself—first the blade, then the ear, and finally the ripe wheat in the ear. ²⁹ When the crop is ready, the sower wields the sickle, for the time is ripe for harvest."

³⁰ Jesus went on to say, "What comparison can we use for the reign of God? What image will help to present it? ³¹ It is like a mustard seed which people plant in the soil: it is the smallest of all the earth's seeds, ³² yet once it is sown, it springs up to become the largest of shrubs, with branches big enough for the birds of the sky to build nests in its shade."

³³ Using many parables like these, Jesus spoke the message to them, as much as they could understand. ³⁴ Everything was spoken in parables, but Jesus explained everything to the disciples later when they were alone.

ᘓ   ᘓ   ᘓ

³⁵ With the coming of evening that same day, Jesus said to the disciples, "Let's cross over to the other shore." ³⁶ Leaving the crowd behind, they took Jesus in the boat in which he was sitting. There were other boats with them.

³⁷ Then a fierce gale arose, and the waves were breaking into the boat so much that it was almost swamped. ³⁸ But Jesus was in the stern through it all, sound asleep on a cushion. They woke him and said, "Teacher, doesn't it matter to you that we're going to drown?"

³⁹ Jesus awoke, rebuked the wind and said to the sea, "Quiet! Be calm!" And the wind dropped and everything was perfectly calm. ⁴⁰ Jesus then said to the disciples, "Why were you so frightened? Have you no faith?"

⁴¹ But they became filled with fear and said to one another, "Who is this, whom even the wind and sea obey?"

5:1 They came to the region near Gerasa, on the other side of the lake. ² And when he had disembarked, immediately a person with an unclean spirit met them. ³ The possessed one lived among the tombs and could no longer be restrained, even with a chain. ⁴ In fact, shackles and fetters had been used as restraints to no avail. No one had proved strong enough to subdue the demoniac.⁵ The sufferer would use stones to gash the flesh, howling day and night among the tombs and the mountain crags without interruption.

⁶Catching sight of Jesus, the bedeviled one ran up and bowed down to Jesus, ⁷but then started shrieking in a loud voice, "What do you want with me, Jesus, Firstborn of the Most High God? Swear by God that you won't torture me!" ⁸For Jesus had been saying, "Come out of this person, unclean spirit!"

⁹"What is your name?" Jesus asked.

"My name is Legion, for there are many of us," was the reply. ¹⁰And the possessed one begged Jesus not to send them all out of the area.

¹¹Now there was a large herd of pigs feeding on the mountainside, ¹²and the unclean spirits begged Jesus, "Send us to the pigs so we can enter them." ¹³Jesus gave them permission. And with that, the unclean spirits came out and entered the pigs, and the herd of about two thousand went rushing down the cliff into the lake, and there they were drowned.

¹⁴The swineherds ran off and reported this in the town and in the countryside, and the people came to see what really had happened. ¹⁵As they approached Jesus, they caught sight of the one who had been possessed sitting fully clothed and perfectly sane. And they were filled with fear. ¹⁶The spectators explained what had happened to the possessed person, and told the townspeople about the pigs. ¹⁷Then the crowd began to implore Jesus to leave their district.

¹⁸As Jesus was getting into the boat, the one who had been healed came up and begged to be allowed to go with him. ¹⁹Jesus answered, "Go home to your people and tell them what Our God has done for you." ²⁰So the former demoniac went off and proceeded to proclaim throughout the Ten Cities what Jesus had done. Everyone was amazed at what they heard.

²¹When Jesus had crossed again to the other shore in the boat, a large crowd gathered, and he stayed by the lakeside.

²²Then one of the synagogue officials—Jairus by name—came up and, seeing Jesus, fell down ²³and pleaded earnestly, saying, "My little daughter is desperately sick. Come and lay your hands on her to make her better and save her life." ²⁴Jesus went with him and a large crowd followed, pressing from all sides.

²⁵Now there was a woman who had suffered from hemorrhages for twelve years; ²⁶after long and painful treatment from various doctors, she had spent all she had without getting better—in fact, she was getting worse. ²⁷She had heard about Jesus, and she came up behind him in the crowd and touched his cloak. ²⁸"If I can touch even the hem," she had told her-

self, "I will be well again." ²⁹ Immediately the flow of blood dried up, and she felt in her body that she was healed of her affliction.

³⁰ Immediately aware that healing power had gone out from him, Jesus turned to the crowd and said, "Who touched my clothes?"

³¹ The disciples said, "You see how the crowd is pressing you and yet you say, 'Who touched me?' "

³² But Jesus continued to look around to see who had done it. ³³ Then the woman came forward, frightened and trembling because she knew what had happened to her, and she fell at Jesus' feet and told him the whole truth.

³⁴ "My daughter," Jesus said, "your faith has saved you; go in peace and be free of your affliction."

³⁵ While Jesus was still speaking, some people arrived from the house of the synagogue official to say, "Your daughter is dead. Why put the Teacher to any further trouble?"

³⁶ But Jesus overheard the remark and said to the official: "Don't be afraid. Just believe." ³⁷ Jesus allowed no one to follow him except Peter and James and James' brother John.

³⁸ They came to the official's house and Jesus noticed all the commotion, with people weeping and wailing unrestrainedly. ³⁹ Jesus went in and said to them, "Why all this commotion and crying? The child is not dead, but asleep." ⁴⁰ At this, they began to ridicule him, and he told everyone to leave.

Jesus took the child's mother and father and his own companions and entered the room where the child lay. ⁴¹ Taking her hand, he said to her, *"Talitha, koum!"* which means, "Little girl, get up!" ⁴² Immediately the girl, who was twelve years old, got up and began to walk about.

At this they were overcome with astonishment. ⁴³ Jesus gave the family strict orders not to let anyone know about it, and told them to give the little girl something to eat.

ര   ര   ര

6:1 After leaving there, Jesus came into his own town, followed by the disciples.

² When the Sabbath came, he began to teach in the synagogue, and the many listeners were astonished and said, "Where did he learn all this? What is this wisdom that has been granted, and these miracles that are performed by his hands? ³ Isn't this the carpenter, the son of Mary, the brother of James and Joses and Judah and Simon? Are not his sisters here with us?" They found these things to be stumbling blocks.

⁴Jesus said to them, "Prophets are not without honor, except in their home towns and among their own relatives and in their own households." ⁵And he could work no miracles there, apart from laying his hands upon a few sick people and healing them; ⁶their lack of faith astounded him. He made the rounds of the neighboring villages instead, and spent the time teaching.

6:7–8:30

Chen Jesus summoned the Twelve and began to send them out in pairs, giving them authority over unclean spirits. ⁸He instructed them that they should take nothing for their journey, except a mere staff—no bread, no bag, no money in their belts. ⁹They were to wear sandals but, he added, "Do not take a spare tunic."

¹⁰And Jesus said to them, "Whenever you enter a house, stay there until you leave town. ¹¹Any place that does not receive you or listen to you, as you leave it, shake off the dust from the soles of your feet as a testimony against them."

¹²And so they set off, proclaiming repentance as they went. ¹³They cast out many demons, and anointed many sick people with oil and healed them.

℞   ℞   ℞

¹⁴Meanwhile Herod, the ruler of Judea, had heard about Jesus, whose reputation had become widespread. Some people were saying, "John the Baptizer has been raised from the dead, and that is why such miraculous powers are at work in him." ¹⁵Others said, "He is Elijah"; still others, "He is a prophet, like one of the prophets of old." ¹⁶When Herod heard of Jesus, he exclaimed, "John, whom I beheaded, has risen from the dead!"

¹⁷Now it was Herod who had ordered John arrested, chained and imprisoned on account of Herodias, the wife of his brother Philip, whom Herod had married. ¹⁸For John had told Herod, "It is against the Law for you to have your brother's wife." ¹⁹As for Herodias, she was furious with John and wanted to kill him but was unable to do so. ²⁰Herod feared John, knowing him to be good and holy, and kept him in custody. When Herod heard John speak he was very much disturbed; yet he was moved by John's words.

²¹Herodias had her chance one day when Herod on his birthday held a dinner for the court circle, military officers and leaders of Galilee. ²²When

the daughter of Herodias came in and danced, this delighted Herod and the guests so much that he told the young woman, "Ask me anything you like and I will give it to you." ²³ And Herod swore an oath, "I will give you anything you ask, even half of my entire realm!"

²⁴ She went out and said to her mother, "What should I ask for?"

Herodias replied, "The head of John the Baptizer."

²⁵ The woman hurried back to Herod and made her request: "I want you to give me the head of John the Baptizer on a platter."

²⁶ Herod was deeply distressed by this request, but remembering the oath he swore before the guests, he was reluctant to break his oath to her. ²⁷ So Herod immediately sent one of the bodyguards with orders to bring John's head. The guard beheaded John in prison, ²⁸ then brought the head in on a platter and gave it to the young woman, who gave it to her mother.

²⁹ When John's disciples heard about this, they came and took the body away and laid it in a tomb.

ㅤㅤㅤㅤ℧ㅤㅤㅤ℧ㅤㅤㅤ℧

³⁰ The apostles came back to Jesus and reported all that they had done and taught. ³¹ Jesus said to them, "Come away by yourselves to someplace more remote, and rest awhile." For there were many people coming and going, and the apostles hadn't had time to eat. ³² So they went away in a boat to a deserted area.

³³ The people saw them leaving and many recognized them, so they ran together on foot from all the cities and got there ahead of the apostles. ³⁴ When Jesus went ashore, there was a large crowd waiting for him, and he felt compassion for them because they were like sheep without a shepherd. So he began to teach them many things.

³⁵ By now it was getting very late, and his disciples came up to him and said, "This is a deserted place and it's very late. ³⁶ Why not dismiss them so they can go to the nearby farms and villages and buy something to eat?"

³⁷ Jesus replied, "Give them something to eat yourselves."

They answered, "You want us to spend half a year's wages on bread for them to eat?"

³⁸ "How many loaves do you have?" Jesus asked. "Go look."

When they found out they reported back, "Five, and two fish."

³⁹ Jesus told them to have the people sit down on the grass ⁴⁰ in groups of hundreds and fifties. ⁴¹ Then Jesus took the five loaves and two fish, raised his eyes to heaven and said the blessing. Jesus broke the loaves and handed them to the disciples to distribute among the people. He also passed out the two fish among them.

⁴²They all ate until they had their fill. ⁴³The disciples gathered up the left-overs and filled twelve baskets of broken bread and fish. ⁴⁴In all, five thousand families ate that day.

⁴⁵Immediately Jesus made the disciples get in the boat and go on ahead to Bethsaida, while he dismissed the crowd. ⁴⁶After leaving them, he went up the hillside to pray.

⁴⁷When evening came, the boat was far out on the lake, and Jesus was alone on land. ⁴⁸He saw that the disciples were worn out with rowing, because the wind was against them. About three in the morning, Jesus went out to them, walking on the water. He was about to pass them by ⁴⁹when they saw him and—thinking it was a ghost—cried out. ⁵⁰For they had all seen him and were terrified.

Jesus hastened to reassure them: "Calm yourselves! It's me. Don't be afraid." ⁵¹Jesus got into the boat with them, and the wind died down. They were completely amazed by what had happened, ⁵²for they hadn't understood about the loaves. Their minds were closed.

⁵³After crossing the lake, Jesus and the disciples came ashore at Gennesaret and tied up their boat there. ⁵⁴No sooner had they stepped out of the boat than people recognized Jesus. ⁵⁵The crowds started hurrying about the countryside and brought the sick on stretchers wherever Jesus went. ⁵⁶Wherever he appeared—in villages, in towns or in the countryside—they laid down the sick in the open places, begging him to let them touch just the fringe of his cloak, and all who touched Jesus got well.

℞   ℞   ℞

7:1The Pharisees and some of the religious scholars who had come from Jerusalem gathered around Jesus. ²They had noticed that some of the disciples were eating with unclean hands—that is, without ritually washing them. ³For the Pharisees, and Jewish people in general, follow the tradition of their ancestors and never eat without washing their arms as far as the elbow. ⁴Moreover, they never eat anything from the market without first sprinkling it. There are many other traditions which have been handed down to them, such as the washing of cups and pots and dishes.

⁵So these Pharisees and religious scholars asked Jesus, "Why do your disciples not respect the tradition of our ancestors, but eat their food with unclean hands?"

⁶Jesus answered, "How accurately Isaiah prophesied about you hypocrites when he wrote,

'These people honor me with their lips,
  while their hearts are far from me.
⁷ The worship they offer me is worthless;
  the doctrines they teach are only human precepts.'
⁸ You disregard God's commandments and cling to human traditions."

⁹ Jesus went on to say, "How ingeniously you evade the commandment of God in order to preserve your own tradition! ¹⁰ For Moses said, 'Honor your mother and your father' and, 'Anyone who curses mother or father must be put to death.' ¹¹ But you say that if someone says to their mother or father, 'Any support you might have had from me is *korban'* "—that is, dedicated to God—¹² "then they're allowed to do nothing more for their parents. ¹³ In this way you nullify God's word in favor of the traditions you have handed down. And you do many other things like this."

¹⁴ Jesus summoned the crowd again and said to them, "Listen to me, all of you, and try to understand. ¹⁵ Nothing that enters us from the outside makes us impure; it is what comes out of us that makes us impure. ¹⁶ If you have ears to hear, then listen."

¹⁷ When Jesus got home, away from the crowd, the disciples questioned him about the parable. ¹⁸ He said to them, "Are you also incapable of understanding? Don't you see that whatever enters us from outside cannot make us impure? ¹⁹ It doesn't enter our heart, just our stomach—then passes out into the sewer." In this way, Jesus pronounced all food clean.

²⁰ He went on, "It is what comes out of us that makes us unclean. ²¹ For it is from within—from our hearts—that evil intentions emerge: promiscuity, theft, murder, adultery, ²² greed, malice, deceit, obscenity, envy, slander, pride, foolishness. ²³ All these evils come from within and make us impure."

છ   છ   છ

²⁴ Jesus left Gennesaret and went to the territory of Tyre and Sidon. There he went into a certain house and wanted no one to recognize him, but he could not pass unrecognized.

²⁵ A woman whose young daughter had an unclean spirit heard about him. She approached Jesus and fell at his feet. ²⁶ The woman, who was Greek, a Syro-Phoenician by birth, begged Jesus to expel the demon from her daughter.

²⁷ He told her, "Let the children of the household satisfy themselves at table first. It is not right to take the food of the children and throw it to the dogs."

²⁸ She replied, "Yes, Rabbi, but even the dogs under the table eat the family's scraps."

²⁹ Then Jesus said to her, "For saying this, you may go home happy; the demon has left your daughter." ³⁰ When she got home, she found her daughter in bed and the demon gone.

³¹ Jesus left the region of Tyre and returned by way of Sidon to the Sea of Galilee, into the district of the Ten Cities.

³² Some people brought an individual who was deaf and had a speech impediment, and begged Jesus to lay hands on that person. ³³ Jesus took the afflicted one aside, away from the crowd, put his fingers into the deaf ears and, spitting, touched the mute tongue with his saliva. ³⁴ Then Jesus looked up to heaven and, with a deep sigh, said, "*Ephphatha!*"—that is, "Be opened!" ³⁵ At once the deaf ears were opened and the impediment cured; the one who had been healed began to speak plainly.

³⁶ Then Jesus warned them not to tell anyone; but the more he ordered them not to, the more they proclaimed it. ³⁷ Their amazement went beyond all bounds: "He has done everything well! He even makes the deaf hear and the mute speak!"

CR   CR   CR

8:¹ Once again a large crowd assembled, and they had nothing to eat. Jesus called over the disciples and said, ²"My heart goes out to these people. By now they have been with us for three days and have nothing to eat. ³ If I send them away hungry, they will collapse on the way, for some have come a long distance."

⁴ The disciples replied, "How can anyone give these people enough bread in this desolate place?"

⁵ Jesus asked them, "How many loaves do you have?"

"Seven," they replied.

⁶ Then Jesus directed the crowd to sit down. Taking the seven loaves, he gave thanks, broke them and gave them to the disciples to distribute, and they handed them out to the crowd. ⁷ They also had a few small fish; asking a blessing on the fish, Jesus told them to distribute these also.

⁸ The people in the crowd ate until they were filled—yet they gathered seven wicker baskets of leftovers. ⁹ Those who had eaten numbered about four thousand.

Jesus dismissed them ¹⁰ and then got into the boat with the disciples to go to the region of Dalmanutha.

¹¹ The Pharisees came forward and began to argue with Jesus. They demanded a sign from heaven—as a test. ¹² With a sigh that came straight from his heart, Jesus said, "Why does this generation demand a sign? The truth is, no sign will be given to this generation." ¹³ And leaving them again and getting back into the boat, he went away to the opposite shore.

¹⁴ The disciples had forgotten to bring bread along, and they had only one loaf with them in the boat. ¹⁵ Then Jesus gave them this warning: "Keep your eyes open. Be on guard against the yeast of the Pharisees and the yeast of Herod."

¹⁶ And they said to one another, "It's because we forgot the bread."

¹⁷ Aware of this, Jesus reprimanded them: "Why are you talking about having no bread? Don't you see or understand yet? Are your minds closed? ¹⁸ Have you 'eyes that don't see, ears that don't hear'? Don't you remember ¹⁹ when I broke the five loaves for the five thousand? How many baskets of fragments did you collect?"

They answered, "Twelve."

²⁰ "And when I broke the seven loaves for the four thousand, how many baskets of scraps did you collect?"

"Seven," they replied.

²¹ Then he said to them, "And you still don't understand?"

ಇ   ಇ   ಇ

²² When they arrived at Bethsaida, some people brought a blind villager and begged Jesus for a healing. ²³ Jesus led the blind person by the hand to the outskirts of the village. When he had spat on the person's eyes and laid hands on them, Jesus asked, "Do you see anything?"

²⁴ The blind one answered, "I see people, but they look like trees walking around."

²⁵ Then Jesus laid hands on the eyes a second time, and the villager was restored to clear and distinct sight. ²⁶ Jesus sent the healed person home, warning, "Don't even go into the village."

ಇ   ಇ   ಇ

²⁷ Then he and the disciples set out for the villages around Caesarea Philippi. On the way, Jesus asked the disciples this question: "Who do people say that I am?"

²⁸ They replied, "Some say John the Baptizer; others, Elijah; still others, one of the prophets."

²⁹ "And you," he went on to ask, "who do you say that I am?"

Peter answered, "You are the Messiah!" ³⁰ But Jesus gave them strict orders not to tell anyone about him.

8:31–10:52

*t*hen Jesus began to teach them that the Promised One had to suffer much, be rejected by the elders, chief priests and religious scholars, be put to death and rise again three days later. ³² Jesus said these things quite openly.

Peter then took him aside and began to take issue with him. ³³ At this, Jesus turned around and, eyeing the disciples, reprimanded Peter: "Get out of my sight, you Satan! You are judging by human standards rather than by God's!"

³⁴ Jesus summoned the crowd and the disciples and said, "If you wish to come after me, you must deny your very self, take up your cross and follow in my footsteps. ³⁵ If you would save your life, you'll lose it, but if you lose your life for my sake, you'll save it. ³⁶ What would you gain if you were to win the whole world but lose your self in the process? ³⁷ What can you offer in exchange for your soul? ³⁸ Whoever in this faithless and corrupt generation is ashamed of me and my words will find, in turn, that the Promised One and the holy angels will be ashamed of that person, when all stand before Our God in glory."

9:1 Jesus also said to them, "The truth is, some of you standing here won't taste death before you see God's reign established in power."

² Six days after that, Jesus took Peter and James and John and led them up a high mountain where they could be alone.

And there Jesus was transfigured before their eyes; ³ the clothes Jesus wore became dazzlingly white—whiter than any earthly bleach could make them.

⁴ Elijah appeared to them, as did Moses, and the two were talking with Jesus. ⁵ Then Peter spoke to Jesus. "Rabbi," he said, "how wonderful it is for us to be here! Let us make three shelters—one for you, one for Moses and one for Elijah!" ⁶ Peter did not know what he was saying, so overcome were they all with awe.

⁷ Then a cloud formed, overshadowing them; and there came a voice from out of the cloud: "This is my Beloved, my Own; listen to this One." ⁸ Then

suddenly, when they looked around, they saw no one with them any-more—only Jesus.

⁹ As they were coming down from the mountain, Jesus gave them orders not to tell anyone what they had seen until after the Promised One had risen from the dead. ¹⁰ They agreed to this, though they discussed among themselves what "rising from the dead" could mean.

¹¹ And they put the question to Jesus, "Why do the religious scholars say that Elijah must come first?"

¹² He said, "Because Elijah does indeed come first, to restore all things. Yet why does it say in scripture that the Promised One must suffer much and be rejected? ¹³ But I tell you, Elijah has already come, and they have done to him everything they wished, just as it is written."

¹⁴ As they approached the other disciples, they saw a large crowd stand-ing around and some religious scholars arguing with them. ¹⁵ As soon as the crowd caught sight of Jesus, they were awestruck and ran up to greet him.

¹⁶ He asked them, "What are you all discussing?"

¹⁷ "Teacher," someone in the crowd replied, "I have brought to you my child, who is possessed by a mute spirit. ¹⁸ Whenever it comes, it seizes my child and throws the little one into convulsions. My child foams at the mouth and becomes rigid. Just now I asked your disciples to expel the spirit, but they were unable to do so."

¹⁹ Jesus said to the crowd, "What an unbelieving lot you are! How long must I remain with you? How long can I endure you? Bring the child to me."

²⁰ When they did, the spirit caught sight of Jesus and immediately threw the child into convulsions. The child fell to the ground, rolling around and foaming at the mouth.

²¹ Then Jesus questioned the parent, "How long has this been happen-ing?"

"From infancy," was the reply. ²² "Often it throws our little one into the fire and into the water. But if you can do anything, have pity on us and help us!"

²³ " 'If you can'?" replied Jesus. "Everything is possible to those who be-lieve!"

²⁴ The child's parent answered, "I do believe. Help my unbelief!"

²⁵ Jesus, on seeing the crowd rapidly gathering, reprimanded the unclean spirit and said, "Mute and deaf spirit, I command you: come out of this child and never again return!"

²⁶ It screamed and threw the child into convulsions, then it came out. The child became like a corpse, and many said, "The little one is dead." ²⁷ But with assistance from Jesus, the child stood up.

²⁸ When Jesus arrived at the house, the disciples asked him privately, "Why is it that we could not expel it?" ²⁹ Jesus replied, "This kind can't be driven out at all—except through prayer."

ଔ   ଔ   ଔ

³⁰ They left that district and began a journey through Galilee, but Jesus did not want anyone to know about it. ³¹ He was teaching the disciples along these lines: "The Promised One is going to be delivered into the hands of others and will be put to death, but three days later this One will rise again." ³² Though they failed to understand these words, they were afraid to question him.

³³ They returned home to Capernaum. Once they were inside the house, Jesus began to ask them, "What were you discussing on the way home?" ³⁴ At this they fell silent, for on the way they had been arguing about who among them was the most important. ³⁵ So Jesus sat down and called the Twelve over and said, "If any of you wants to be first, you must be the last one of all and at the service of all."

³⁶ Then Jesus brought a little child into their midst and, putting his arm around the child, said to them, ³⁷ "Whoever welcomes a child such as this for my sake welcomes me. And whoever welcomes me welcomes not me but the One who sent me."

³⁸ John said to Jesus, "Teacher, we saw someone using your name to expel demons, and we tried to stop it since this person was not part of our group."

³⁹ Jesus said in reply, "Don't try to stop it. No one who performs a miracle using my name can speak ill of me soon thereafter! ⁴⁰ Anyone who is not against us is with us. ⁴¹ The truth is, anyone who gives you a cup of water in my name because you belong to the Messiah will certainly not go without a reward.

⁴² "Rather than make one of these little ones who believe in me stumble, it would be better to be thrown into the sea with a large millstone hung around your neck.

⁴³ "If your hand causes you to sin, cut it off. It would be better to enter Life crippled than to have hands and go into Gehenna, where the fire never

goes out.* ⁴⁵ If your foot causes you to sin, cut it off. It is better to enter Life crippled than to have two feet and be thrown into Gehenna.* ⁴⁷ And if your eye causes you to sin, pluck it out. It would be better to enter the kindom of God with one eye than to have two eyes and be drawn into Gehenna, ⁴⁸ where 'the worm never dies and the fire never goes out.'

⁴⁹ "Everyone will be salted with fire.

⁵⁰ "Salt is good. But if salt loses its flavor, how can you make it salty again?

"Have salt in yourselves, and live in peace with one another."

10·1 Jesus left there and came to the districts of Judea and the other side of the Jordan. Once more the crowds gathered around and as usual Jesus began to teach them.

² Some Pharisees approached Jesus and, as a test, asked, "Is it permissible for husbands to divorce wives?"

³ In reply Jesus asked, "What command did Moses give?"

⁴ They answered, "Moses permitted a husband to write a decree of divorce and to put her away."

⁵ But Jesus told them, "Moses wrote the commandment because of your hardness of heart. ⁶ From the beginning of creation,

> 'God made them male and female.
> ⁷ This is why one person leaves home
>   and cleaves to another,
> ⁸ and the two become one flesh.'

They are no longer two, but one flesh. ⁹ What God has united, therefore, let no one divide."

¹⁰ Back in the house again, the disciples questioned Jesus once more about this. ¹¹ He told them, "If a man divorces his wife and marries another, he commits adultery against her; ¹² and if a woman divorces her husband and marries another, she commits adultery."

¹³ People were bringing their children to Jesus to have him touch them, but the disciples scolded them for this.

¹⁴ When Jesus saw this he was indignant and said to them, "Let the children come to me; do not stop them. It is to just such as these that the kindom of God belongs. ¹⁵ The truth is, whoever doesn't welcome the kindom of God as a little child won't enter it."

¹⁶ And Jesus took the children in his arms and blessed them, laying his hands on them.

---

* Most manuscripts omit verses 44 and 46, which are identical to verse 48.

17 As he was setting out on a journey, someone came running up and asked, "Good Teacher, what must I do to share in everlasting life?" 18 Jesus answered, "Why do you call me good? No one is good but God alone. 19 You know the commandments: No killing. No committing adultery. No stealing. No bearing false witness. No defrauding. Honor your mother and your father."

20 The other replied, "Teacher, I have kept all these since my childhood."

21 Then Jesus looked at the person with love and said, "There is one thing more that you must do. Go and sell what you have and give it to those in need; you will then have treasure in heaven. After that, come and follow me."

22 At these words, the inquirer, who owned much property, became crestfallen and went away sadly.

23 Jesus looked around and said to the disciples, "How hard it is for rich people to enter the kindom of God!"

24 The disciples could only marvel at these words. So Jesus repeated what he had said: "My children, how hard it is to enter the realm of God! 25 It is easier for a camel to pass through the Needle's Eye gate than for a rich person to enter the kindom of God!"

26 The disciples were amazed at this and said to one another, "Then who can be saved?"

27 Jesus looked at them and said, "For mortals it is impossible—but not for God. With God all things are possible."

28 Peter was moved to say to Jesus, "We have left everything to follow you!"

29 Jesus answered, "The truth is, there is no one who has left home, sisters or brothers, mother or father, children or fields for me and for the sake of the Gospel 30 who won't receive a hundred times as much in this present age—as many homes, brothers, sisters, mothers, fathers, children and property, though not without persecution—and, in the age to come, everlasting life.

31 "Many who are first will be last, and the last will be first."

ℭ   ℭ   ℭ

32 They were on their way up to Jerusalem, with Jesus leading the way. The disciples were baffled by this move, while the other followers were afraid. Taking the Twelve aside once more, Jesus began to tell them what was going to happen.

33 "We are on our way up to Jerusalem where the Promised One will be

handed over to the chief priests and the religious scholars. Then the Promised One will be condemned to death and handed over to the Gentiles ³⁴ to be mocked, spat upon, flogged and finally killed. Three days later the Promised One will rise."

³⁵ Zebedee's children James and John approached Jesus. "Teacher," they said, "we want you to grant our request."

³⁶ "What is it?" Jesus asked.

³⁷ They replied, "See to it that we sit next to you, one at your right and one at your left, when you come into your glory."

³⁸ Jesus told them, "You do not know what you are asking. Can you drink the cup I will drink or be baptized in the same baptism as I?"

³⁹ "We can," they replied. Jesus said in response, "From the cup I drink of, you will drink; the baptism I am immersed in, you will share. ⁴⁰ But as for sitting at my right or my left, that is not mine to give; it is for those to whom it has been reserved."

⁴¹ The other ten, on hearing this, became indignant at James and John.

⁴² Jesus called them together and said, "You know how among the Gentiles those who exercise authority are domineering and arrogant; those 'great ones' know how to make their own importance felt. ⁴³ But it can't be like that with you. Anyone among you who aspires to greatness must serve the rest; ⁴⁴ whoever wants to rank first among you must serve the needs of all. ⁴⁵ The Promised One has come not to be served, but to serve—to give one life in ransom for the many."

⁴⁶ They came to Jericho. As Jesus was leaving Jericho with the disciples and a large crowd, a blind beggar named Bartimaeus, begot of Timaeus, was sitting at the side of the road. ⁴⁷ When he heard that it was Jesus of Nazareth, he began to shout and to say, "Heir of David, Jesus, have pity on me!"

⁴⁸ Many people scolded him and told him to be quiet, but he shouted all the louder, "Heir of David, have pity on me!"

⁴⁹ Jesus stopped and said, "Call him here."

So they called the blind man. "Don't be afraid," they said. "Get up; Jesus is calling you." ⁵⁰ So throwing off his cloak, Bartimaeus jumped up and went to Jesus.

⁵¹ Then Jesus said, "What do you want me to do for you?"

"Rabbuni," the blind man said, "I want to see."

⁵² Jesus replied, "Go, your faith has saved you." And immediately Bartimaeus received the gift of sight and began to follow Jesus along the road.

 s they approached Jerusalem and came to Bethphage and Bethany at the Mount of Olives, Jesus sent off two of the disciples [2] with this instruction: "Go to the village straight ahead of you, and as soon as you enter it you will find tethered there a colt on which no one has ridden. Untie it and bring it back. [3] If anyone says to you, 'Why are you doing that?' say, 'The Rabbi needs it, but will send it back very soon.' "

[4] So they went off, and finding a colt tethered out on the street near a gate, they untied it. [5] Some of the bystanders said to them, "What do you mean by untying that colt?" [6] They answered as Jesus had told them to, and the people let them take it.

[7] They brought the colt to Jesus and threw their cloaks across its back, and he sat on it. [8] Many people spread their cloaks on the road, while others spread leafy branches which they had cut from the fields. [9] And everyone around Jesus, in front or in back of him, cried out,

> "Hosanna!
>> Blessed is the One who comes
>> in the name of Our God!
> [10] Blessed is the coming reign of our ancestor David!
>> Hosanna in the highest!"

[11] Jesus entered Jerusalem and went into the Temple precincts. He inspected everything there, but since it was already late in the afternoon, he went out to Bethany accompanied by the Twelve.

ભ   ભ   ભ

[12] The next day when they were leaving Bethany, Jesus felt hungry. [13] Observing a fig tree covered with foliage some distance off, he went over to see if the tree contained any fruit, but upon inspecting it found only leaves—it was not the season for figs. [14] Jesus addressed the fig tree and said, "No one will ever eat fruit from you again." And the disciples witnessed this.

[15] Then they went on to Jerusalem. Jesus entered the Temple and began driving out those engaged in selling and buying. He overturned the money-changers' tables and the stalls of those selling doves; [16] moreover, he would not permit anyone to carry goods through the Temple area.

[17] Then he began to teach them: "Doesn't scripture say, 'My house will be called a house of prayer for all the peoples'? But you have turned it into a den of thieves!"

¹⁸ The chief priests and the religious scholars heard about this and began looking for a way to destroy him. At the same time, they were fearful because the whole crowd was under the spell of his teaching.

¹⁹ When evening came, Jesus and the disciples went out of the city. ²⁰ Early the next morning, as they were walking along, they saw the fig tree withered to its roots. ²¹ Peter remembered and said, "Rabbi, look! The fig tree you cursed has withered up."

²² In reply Jesus said, "Put your trust in God. ²³ The truth is, if any of you say to this mountain, 'Get up and throw yourself into the sea,' and you don't doubt in your heart, but believe that what you say will happen, it will happen. ²⁴ That's why I tell you that whatever you ask for in prayer, believe that you have already received it, and it will be done for you.

²⁵ "And when you stand praying, forgive anyone against whom you have a grievance, so that your loving God in heaven may in turn forgive you your faults."*

℞   ℞   ℞

²⁷ They came to Jerusalem again, and as Jesus was walking through the Temple, the chief priests, the religious scholars and the elders asked, ²⁸ "On what authority are you doing these things? Who has given you the power to do them?"

²⁹ "I will ask you a question—only one," Jesus replied. "If you give me an answer, I will tell you on what authority I do the things I do. ³⁰ Tell me, was John's baptism of divine origin, or merely human?"

³¹ They thought to themselves, "If we say, 'divine,' he will ask, 'Then why did you not put faith in it?' ³² But can we say 'merely human'?"—for they had reason to fear the people, who regarded John as a true prophet. ³³ So their answer to Jesus was, "We do not know."

In turn, Jesus said to them, "Then neither will I tell you on what authority I do the things I do."

12¹ Once more Jesus began to address them in parables: "A farmer planted a vineyard, put a hedge around it, dug out a vat and erected a tower. Then the farmer leased it to tenants and went on a journey.

² "In due time the farmer sent a subordinate to the tenants to obtain from them the owner's share of the produce from the vineyard. ³ But they seized

---

* Verse 26 is a later addition: *"If you don't forgive, your loving God in heaven won't forgive your faults either."*

the subordinate, who, after a beating, was sent off empty-handed. ⁴ Then the owner sent them a second subordinate; this one they treated shamefully too; ⁵ and they killed a third subordinate. So too with many others: some they beat, others they killed.

⁶ "There was one more to send—the farmer's own beloved child. 'They will respect my heir,' thought the farmer. ⁷ But the tenants said to one another, 'Here is the one who will inherit everything. Come, let us kill the heir, and the inheritance will be ours.' ⁸ Then they seized and killed the heir and dragged the body outside the vineyard.

⁹ "What do you suppose will happen? The farmer will come and destroy those tenants and turn the vineyard over to others! ¹⁰ Are you not familiar with this passage of scripture:

'The stone rejected by the builders
    has become the cornerstone of the building.
¹¹ This is Our God's doing,
    and it is marvelous in our eyes.' "

¹² At these words they wanted to arrest Jesus, but they had reason to fear the crowd. They knew well enough that the parable was directed at them. Finally they went away.

¹³ Some Pharisees and Herodians were sent after Jesus to catch him in his speech. ¹⁴ The two groups approached Jesus and said, "Teacher, we know you are truthful and unconcerned about the opinion of others. It is evident you aren't swayed by another's rank, but teach God's way of life sincerely. So: is it lawful to pay tax to the emperor or not? ¹⁵ Are we to pay or not to pay?"

Knowing their hypocrisy, he said to them, "Why are you trying to trick me? Let me see a coin." ¹⁶ When they handed him one, he said to them, "Whose image and inscription do you see here?"

"Caesar's," they answered.

¹⁷ Then Jesus said, "Give to Caesar what is Caesar's, and give to God what is God's." This reply took them completely by surprise.

¹⁸ Then some Sadducees, who hold that there is no resurrection, came to Jesus with a question: ¹⁹ "Teacher, Moses wrote that if anyone dies leaving a wife but no child, his brother must marry the wife and produce offspring. ²⁰ So let's say there were seven brothers. The eldest married a woman and died leaving no children. ²¹ The second married her, and he too died childless. The same happened to the third; ²² in fact, none of the seven left any children behind. Last of all, the woman also died. ²³ At the resurrection,

when they all come back to life, whose wife will she be? All seven married her."

²⁴ Jesus said, "You just don't see, because you fail to understand the scriptures or the power of God. ²⁵ When people rise from the dead, they neither marry nor are given in marriage, but live like the angels of heaven. ²⁶ As to the raising of the dead, have you not read in the book of Moses, in the passage about the burning bush, how God told him, 'I am the God of Sarah and Abraham, the God of Rebecca and Isaac, the God of Leah and Rachel and Jacob'? ²⁷ God is the God of the living, not of the dead. You are very much mistaken."

²⁸ One of the religious scholars who had listened to them debating and had observed how well Jesus had answered them, now came up and put a question to him: "Which is the foremost of all the commandments?"

²⁹ Jesus replied, "This is the foremost: 'Hear, O Israel, God, our God, is one. ³⁰ You must love the Most High God with all your heart, with all your soul, with all your mind and with all your strength.' ³¹ The second is this: 'You must love your neighbor as yourself.' There is no commandment greater than these."

³² The scholar said to Jesus, "Well spoken, Teacher! What you have said is true: the Most High is one and there is no other. ³³ To love God with all your heart, with all your understanding and strength, and to love your neighbor as yourself—this is far more important than any burnt offering or sacrifice."

³⁴ Jesus, seeing how wisely this scholar had spoken, said, "You are not far from the kindom of God." And after that no one dared to question Jesus any more.

³⁵ Later, as Jesus was teaching in the Temple, he went on to say, "How can the religious scholars claim, 'The Messiah is David's heir'? ³⁶ David himself, inspired by the Holy Spirit, said,

> 'God said to my Sovereign:
>> "Sit at my right hand
>> until I place your enemies under your foot."'

³⁷ If David addresses this one as 'Sovereign,' how can the Sovereign be David's heir?" The large crowd listened to this with delight.

³⁸ In his teaching, Jesus said, "Beware of the religious scholars who like to walk about in long robes, be greeted obsequiously in the market squares, ³⁹ and take the front seats in the synagogues and the places of honor at banquets. ⁴⁰ These are the ones who swallow the property of widows and offer

lengthy prayers for the sake of appearance. They will be judged all the more severely."

⁴¹Jesus sat down opposite the collection box and watched the people putting money in it, and many of the rich put in a great deal. ⁴²A poor widow came and put in two small coins, the equivalent of a penny.

⁴³Then Jesus called out to the disciples and said to them, "The truth is, this woman has put in more than all who have contributed to the treasury; ⁴⁴for they have put in money from their surplus, but she has put in everything she possessed from the little she had—all she had to live on."

℧   ℧   ℧

13·¹As Jesus was leaving the Temple, one of the disciples commented in passing, "Look, Teacher! What huge stones these are! What wonderful buildings!"

²Jesus replied, "See these great buildings? Not a single stone will be left on another. Everything will be torn down."

³As Jesus was sitting on the Mount of Olives facing the Temple, Peter, James, John and Andrew asked him privately, ⁴"Tell us, when will all this happen? What will be the sign that all this is about to take place?"

⁵Jesus began by saying, "Be on your guard that no one deceives you. ⁶Many will come in my name saying, 'I am the One,' and they will deceive many. ⁷When you hear of wars and rumors of war, do not be alarmed. Things like this must happen, but the end is still to come. ⁸Nation will rise against nation and empire against empire; there will be earthquakes throughout the world and famines—yet this is only the beginning of the labor pains.

⁹"Be on your guard. They will hand you over to the courts, and they will flog you in the synagogues. You will stand before governors and rulers because of me, as a witness before them, ¹⁰for the Good News must first be proclaimed to all. ¹¹Whenever you are arrested and put on trial, do not fret about what you are going to say. Say whatever is given to you at the time, for it will not be you speaking, but the Holy Spirit.

¹²"Sisters and brothers will betray each other to the point of death, and parents will betray their children. Children will rebel against parents and have them put to death. ¹³You will be hated by all because of my name. Yet the one who perseveres to the end will be saved.

¹⁴"When you see 'the abomination that causes desolation' set up where it should not be"—let the reader understand—"then those in Judea must escape to the mountains. ¹⁵Those on the housetop must not come down

into the house to collect their belongings. ¹⁶ Those in the fields must not take time to pick up their cloaks. ¹⁷ Woe to the pregnant women and the nursing mothers in those days! ¹⁸ Pray that this doesn't happen in winter. ¹⁹ For the distress at that time will be unequalled from the beginning of time when God created the world, until now and for all time to come. ²⁰ If the Sovereign One were not to shorten those days, no one would be saved. Because of the chosen ones, God has cut short those days.

²¹ "And if anyone says to you at that time, 'Look, there is the Messiah!' or, 'Look, here is the Messiah!,' don't believe it. ²² For false Messiahs and false prophets will appear, and will work signs and wonders in order to deceive even the chosen, if that were possible. ²³ So be on your guard. I have told you everything beforehand.

²⁴ "But in those days, after that time of distress, the sun will be darkened, the moon will lose its brightness, ²⁵ the stars will fall from the sky and the powers in the heavens will be shaken. ²⁶ Then they will see the Promised One coming in the clouds with great power and glory; ²⁷ then the angels will be sent to gather the chosen from the four winds, from the ends of the earth to the ends of heaven.

²⁸ "Take the fig tree as a parable: as soon as its twigs grow supple and its leaves come out, you know that summer is near. ²⁹ In the same way, when you see these things happening, know that the Promised One is near, right at the door. ³⁰ The truth is, before this generation has passed away, all these things will have taken place. ³¹ Heaven and earth will pass away, but my words will not pass away.

³² "But as for that day or hour, nobody knows it—neither the angels of heaven, nor the Only Begotten—no one but Abba God. ³³ Be constantly on the watch! Stay awake! You do not know when the appointed time will come.

³⁴ "It is like people traveling abroad. They leave their home and put the workers in charge, each with a certain task, and those who watch at the front gate are ordered to stay on the alert. ³⁵ So stay alert! You do not know when the owner of the house is coming, whether at dusk, at midnight, when the cock crows or at early dawn. ³⁶ Do not let the owner come suddenly and catch you asleep. ³⁷ What I say to you, I say to all: stay alert!"

Passover and the Feast of Unleavened Bread were to be observed in two days' time. The chief priests and religious scholars were looking for

14:1–15:47

some excuse to arrest Jesus and kill him. ²But they said, "Not during the festival, or the people may riot."

³While Jesus was in Bethany reclining at table in the house of Simon, who was afflicted with leprosy, a woman entered carrying an alabaster jar of perfume made from expensive aromatic nard. After breaking the jar, she began to pour the perfume on his head.

⁴Some said to themselves indignantly, "What is the point of this extravagant waste of perfume? ⁵It could have been sold for over three hundred silver pieces, and the money given to those in need!" They were infuriated with her.

⁶But Jesus said, "Let her alone. Why do you criticize her? She has done me a kindness. ⁷You will always have poor people among you, and you can do them good whenever you want, but you will not always have me. ⁸She has done what she could. She has anointed my body and is preparing it for burial. ⁹The truth is, wherever the Good News is proclaimed throughout the world, what she has done will be told in her memory."

¹⁰Then Judas Iscariot, one of the Twelve, went off to the chief priests to hand Jesus over to them. ¹¹Hearing what he had to say, they were jubilant and promised to give him money. Then Judas started looking for an opportune moment to betray Jesus.

¹²On the first day of the Feast of Unleavened Bread, when it was customary to sacrifice the paschal lamb, the disciples said to Jesus, "Where do you want us to prepare the Passover supper for you?"

¹³He directed two of the disciples and said to them, "Go into the city, and you will come upon a man carrying a water jar. Follow him ¹⁴into a house he enters and say to the owner, 'The Teacher asks, "Where is my guest-room? I want to eat the Passover meal there with my disciples." ' ¹⁵Then you will be shown an upstairs room, spacious, furnished, with everything in order. That is the place you are to get ready for us."

¹⁶Then the disciples went off. When they reached the city, they found it just as Jesus had told them, and they prepared the Passover supper.

¹⁷As it grew dark, Jesus arrived with the Twelve. ¹⁸They reclined at table, and in the course of the meal Jesus said, "The truth is, one of you is about to betray me—one who is eating with me."

¹⁹They were very upset at these words, and one by one they said to him, "Surely it's not me!"

²⁰Jesus replied, "It is one of you Twelve—one who dips into the dish with me. ²¹The Chosen One is going the way the scriptures foretell. But woe to

the one by whom the Chosen One is betrayed! It were better had that person never been born."

²² During the meal Jesus took bread, blessed and broke it, and gave it to them saying, "Take this and eat. This is my body." ²³ He likewise took a cup, gave thanks and passed it to them, and they all drank from it. ²⁴ Jesus said to them, "This is my blood, the blood of the Covenant, which will be poured out on behalf of many. ²⁵ The truth is, I will never again drink of the fruit of the vine until the day I drink it anew in the kindom of God."

²⁶ After singing songs of praise, they walked out to the Mount of Olives.

As they were walking ²⁷ Jesus said to them, "You will all fall away, for scripture says, 'I will strike the shepherd and the sheep will be scattered.' ²⁸ But after I have been raised, I will go to Galilee ahead of you."

²⁹ Peter said to Jesus, "Even though everyone may fall away, I will not."

³⁰ Jesus said to him, "The truth is, this very night before the cock crows twice, you will deny me three times."

³¹ But Peter said vehemently, "Even if I have to die with you, I will not disown you!" All the other disciples said the same thing.

☙   ☙   ☙

³² Then they came to a place named Gethsemane. Jesus said to them, "Sit down here while I pray." ³³ Jesus took along with him Peter, James and John. Then he began to be very distressed and troubled, ³⁴ and said to them, "My heart is filled with sorrow to the point of death. Stay here and keep watch."

³⁵ Jesus went a little further off and fell to the ground, praying that if it were possible this hour might pass him by. ³⁶ He said, "Abba, you have the power to do all things. Take this cup away from me. But let it be not my will, but your will."

³⁷ When Jesus returned he found them asleep. He said to Peter, "Asleep, Simon? Could you not stay awake for even an hour? ³⁸ Be on guard and pray that you not be put to the test. The spirit is willing, but the flesh is weak."

³⁹ Going back again, Jesus began to pray in the same words. ⁴⁰ Upon returning Jesus found them asleep once again. They could not keep their eyes open, nor did they know what to say to him.

⁴¹ He returned a third time and said, "Still sleeping? Still taking your rest? It will have to do. The hour is upon us—the Chosen One is being handed into the clutches of evildoers. ⁴² Get up, let's go. Look! Here comes my betrayer."

⁴³ While Jesus was still speaking, Judas, one of the Twelve, came up accompanied by a crowd carrying swords and clubs; they had been sent by the chief priests, the religious scholars and the elders. ⁴⁴ The betrayer had arranged this signal for them:"Whomever I embrace is the one; arrest him and take him away under guard." ⁴⁵ Judas went directly to Jesus, embraced him and said, "Rabbi!" ⁴⁶ At this, they laid hands on Jesus and arrested him.

⁴⁷ One of the bystanders drew a sword and struck the high priest's attendant, cutting off an ear. ⁴⁸ Jesus then said, "Why have you come to arrest me with swords and clubs, as though I were a robber? ⁴⁹ I was within your reach daily, teaching in the Temple precincts, yet you never arrested me. But let the scriptures be fulfilled."

⁵⁰ With that, all the disciples deserted Jesus and fled. ⁵¹ Following Jesus was a youth wearing nothing but a linen cloth, whom they also tried to arrest ⁵² but who fled naked, leaving the cloth behind.

⁵³ Then they led Jesus off to the high priest, and all the chief priests, elders and religious scholars gathered together. ⁵⁴ Peter followed at a distance right into the high priest's courtyard, where he found a seat with the Temple guard and began to warm himself at the fire.

⁵⁵ The chief priests with the whole Sanhedrin were busy soliciting testimony against Jesus that might lead to his death, but they could not find any. ⁵⁶ Many gave false testimony against Jesus, but their stories did not agree. ⁵⁷ Some, for instance, on taking the stand, testified falsely by saying, ⁵⁸ "We heard him declare, 'I will destroy this Temple made by human hands, and in three days I will build another made without hands!' " ⁵⁹ But even in this, their testimony did not agree.

⁶⁰ The high priest stood up before the court and began to interrogate Jesus: "Have you no answer to what these people are testifying against you?" ⁶¹ But Jesus remained silent and made no reply. Once again the high priest interrogated him: "Are you the Messiah, the Only Begotten of the Blessed One?"

⁶² Jesus replied, "I am! And you will see the Chosen One seated at the right hand of the Power and coming with the clouds of heaven."

⁶³ At that, the high priest tore his robes and said, "What further need do we have of witnesses? ⁶⁴ You have heard the blasphemy. What is your verdict?" They all said Jesus was guilty and condemned him to death.

⁶⁵ Some of them began to spit on Jesus. They blindfolded and hit him, saying, "Prophesy!" The guards beat him too.

⁶⁶ While Peter was down in the courtyard, one of the attendants of the high priest came along. ⁶⁷ When she noticed Peter seated near the fire, she looked more closely at him and said, "You too were with Jesus of Naza-

reth." [68] Peter said, "I don't know what you're talking about! What do you mean?" Then Peter went out into the gateway. At that moment a rooster crowed.

[69] The woman, keeping an eye on him, started again to tell the bystanders, "He's one of them." [70] Once again Peter denied it. A little later the bystanders said to him once more, "You are certainly one of them! You're a Galilean, aren't you?" [71] Peter began to curse, and swore, "I don't even know who you're talking about!" [72] The cock crowed a second time. And Peter recalled the prediction Jesus had made: "Before the cock crows twice, you will deny me three times." He rushed away, weeping.

15:1 As soon as it was daybreak the chief priests, the elders and religious scholars and the whole Sanhedrin reached a decision. They bound Jesus and led him away, and handed him over to Pilate, [2] who interrogated him. "Are you the King of the Jews?" he asked.

Jesus responded, "You are the one who is saying it."

[3] The chief priests then brought many accusations against him. [4] Pilate interrogated Jesus again: "Surely you have some answer? See how many accusations they are leveling against you!" [5] But to Pilate's astonishment, Jesus made no further response.

[6] Now whenever there was a festival, Pilate would release for them one prisoner—anyone they asked for. [7] There was a prisoner named Barabbas who was jailed along with the rioters who had committed murder in the uprising. [8] When the crowd came to ask that Pilate honor the custom, [9] Pilate rejoined, "Do you want me to release for you the King of the Jews?" [10] Pilate was aware, of course, that it was out of jealousy that the chief priests had handed Jesus over. [11] But the chief priests incited the crowd to have him release Barabbas instead. [12] Pilate again asked them, "What am I to do with the one you call the King of the Jews?"

[13] The people shouted back, "Crucify him!"

[14] "Why?" Pilate asked. "What crime has he committed?"

But they shouted all the louder, "Crucify him!"

[15] So Pilate, wishing to satisfy the crowd, released Barabbas to them, and, after having Jesus scourged, handed him over to be crucified.

ഗ   ഗ   ഗ

[16] The soldiers led Jesus away into the hall known as the Praetorium; then they assembled the whole battalion. [17] They dressed Jesus in royal purple, then wove a crown of thorns and put it on him. [18] They began to salute him: "All hail! King of the Jews!" [19] They kept striking Jesus on the head with a

reed, spitting at him and kneeling in front of him pretending to pay homage. ²⁰ When they had finished mocking him, they stripped him of the purple and dressed him in his own clothes. Then they led him out to be crucified.

²¹ A passerby named Simon of Cyrene, the father of Alexander and Rufus, was coming in from the fields. The soldiers pressed him into service to carry Jesus' cross. ²² Then they brought Jesus to the site of Golgotha—which means "Skull Place."

²³ They tried to give him wine drugged with myrrh, but he would not take it. ²⁴ Then they nailed him to the cross and divided up his garments by rolling dice for them to see what each should take. ²⁵ It was about nine in the morning when they crucified him.

²⁶ The inscription listing the charge read, "The King of the Jews." ²⁷ With Jesus they crucified two robbers, one at his right and one at his left.*

²⁹ People going by insulted Jesus, shaking their heads and saying, "So you were going to destroy the Temple and rebuild it in three days! ³⁰ Save yourself now by coming down from that cross!" ³¹ The chief priests and the religious scholars also joined in and jeered, "He saved others, but he can't save himself! ³² Let 'the Messiah, the King of Israel' come down from that cross right now so that we can see it and believe in him!" Those who had been crucified with him hurled the same insult.

³³ When noon came, darkness fell on the whole countryside and lasted until about three in the afternoon. ³⁴ At three, Jesus cried out in a loud voice, " 'Eloi, eloi, lama sabachthani?' " which means, "My God, My God, why have you forsaken me?" ³⁵ A few of the bystanders who heard it remarked, "Listen! He is calling on Elijah!" ³⁶ Someone ran and soaked a sponge in sour wine and stuck it on a reed to try to make Jesus drink, saying, "Let's see if Elijah comes to take him down."

³⁷ Then Jesus uttered a loud cry and breathed his last. ³⁸ At that moment the curtain in the sanctuary was torn in two from top to bottom. ³⁹ The centurion who stood guard over Jesus, seeing how he died, declared, "Clearly, this was God's Own!"

⁴⁰ There were also some women present looking on from a distance. Among them were Mary of Magdala; Mary, the mother of James the younger and Joses; and Salome. ⁴¹ These women had followed Jesus when he was in Galilee and attended to his needs. There were also many others who had come up with him to Jerusalem.

⁴² As it grew dark—it was Preparation Day, that is, the eve of the Sab-

---

* Some manuscripts add: ²⁸ This fulfilled the scripture, "He let himself be counted among sinners."

bath—⁴³a distinguished member of the Sanhedrin, Joseph from Arimathea, arrived. He was waiting for the reign of God, and he gathered up courage and sought an audience with Pilate, and asked for the body of Jesus.

⁴⁴Pilate was surprised that Jesus should have died so soon. He summoned the centurion and inquired whether Jesus was already dead. ⁴⁵Upon learning that this was so, Pilate released the body to Joseph.

⁴⁶Then, having bought a linen shroud, Joseph took the body of Jesus down, wrapped him in the linen and laid him in a tomb which had been cut out of rock. Finally, he rolled a large stone across the entrance of the tomb. ⁴⁷Meanwhile, Mary of Magdala and Mary, the mother of Joses, were looking on and observed where Jesus had been laid.

16:1-8

When the Sabbath was over, Mary of Magdala, Mary the mother of James, and Salome bought perfumed oils so that they could anoint Jesus. ²Very early, just after sunrise on the first day of the week, they came to the tomb.

³They were saying to one another, "Who will roll back the stone for us from the entrance to the tomb?" ⁴When they looked, they found that the huge stone had been rolled back.

⁵On entering the tomb, they saw a young person sitting at the right, dressed in a white robe. They were very frightened, ⁶but the youth reassured them: "Do not be amazed! You are looking for Jesus of Nazareth, the One who was crucified. He has risen; he is not here. See the place where they laid him. ⁷Now go and tell the disciples and Peter, 'Jesus is going ahead of you to Galilee, where you will see him just as he told you.'"

⁸They made their way out and fled from the tomb bewildered and trembling; but they said nothing to anyone, because they were so afraid.

The gospel ends here. Two different endings were added by later writers.

the "shorter ending"

[9] And immediately they reported all these instructions to Peter and his companions. After this, through them, Jesus sent forth the holy and imperishable proclamation of eternal salvation.

the "longer ending"

[9] Jesus rose from the dead early on the first day of the week, appearing first to Mary of Magdala, out of whom the savior had cast seven devils. [10] She went and reported it to Jesus' companions, who were grieving and weeping. [11] But when they heard that Jesus was alive and had been seen by her, they refused to believe it.

[12] Later on, as two of them were walking along on their way to the country, Jesus appeared to them in a different form. [13] These two went back and told the others, who did not believe them either.

[14] Finally, the risen Christ appeared to the Eleven themselves while they were at table, and scolded them for their disbelief and their stubbornness, since they had put no faith in those who had seen Jesus after the resurrection.

[15] Then Jesus told them, "Go into the whole world and proclaim the Good News to all creation.

[16] "The one who believes it and is baptized will be saved; the one who refuses to believe it will be condemned. [17] Signs such as these will accompany those who have professed their faith: in my name they will expel demons; they will speak in new tongues; [18] they will be able to handle poisonous snakes; if they drink anything deadly, it will not harm them; and the sick upon whom they lay their hands will recover."

[19] Then, after speaking to them, the savior was taken up into heaven and was seated at God's right hand. [20] The disciples went forth and preached everywhere. Christ worked with them and confirmed their message through the signs which accompanied them.

the gospel according to
luke

Many others have undertaken to compile a narrative of the events which have been fulfilled among us, ²exactly as those happenings were passed on to us by the original eyewitnesses and ministers of the Word. ³I too have investigated everything carefully from the beginning and have decided to set it down in writing for you, noble Theophilus, ⁴so that you may see how reliable the instruction was that you received.

ଔ   ଔ   ଔ

⁵In the days of the ruler Herod, there was a priest named Zechariah, of the priestly class of Abijah. His wife Elizabeth was a descendant of Aaron. ⁶Both were worthy in the sight of God and scrupulously observed all the commandments and observances of Our God. ⁷They were childless—unable to conceive—and they were both advanced in years.

⁸Now it was the turn of Zechariah's priestly class to serve. And as he was fulfilling his priestly office before God, ⁹it fell to him by lot, according to priestly usage, to enter the sanctuary of Our God and offer incense.

¹⁰ While the full assembly of people was praying outside at the time of day when the incense was offered, ¹¹ an angel of Our God appeared to him, standing to the right of the altar of incense. ¹² Zechariah was deeply disturbed upon seeing the angel, and was overcome with fear.

¹³ The angel said to him, "Don't be frightened, Zechariah. Your prayer has been heard. Your wife Elizabeth will bear a son, whom you'll name John. ¹⁴ He will be your joy and delight and many will rejoice at his birth, ¹⁵ for he will be great in the sight of Our God. He must never drink wine or liquor, and he will be filled with the Holy Spirit from his mother's womb. ¹⁶ And he will bring many of the children of Israel back to their God Most High. ¹⁷ He will go before God as a forerunner, in the spirit and power of Elijah, to turn the hearts of parents to their children, and the rebellious to the wisdom of the just—to make ready a people prepared for Our God."

¹⁸ Zechariah said to the angel, "How can I be sure of this? I am an old man, and my wife too is advanced in age."

¹⁹ The angel replied, "I am Gabriel, who stands before God. I was sent to speak to you and bring you this good news. ²⁰ But because you have not trusted my words, you'll be mute—unable to speak—until the day these things take place. They'll all come true in due season."

²¹ Meanwhile, the people were waiting for Zechariah and wondered about his delay in the sanctuary. ²² When he finally came out he was unable to speak to them, and they realized that he had seen a vision inside. But he could only make signs to them and remained mute. ²³ Then, when his time of priestly service was over, he went home.

²⁴ Some time later, Elizabeth conceived. She went into seclusion for five months, ²⁵ saying, "Our God has done this for me. In these days, God has shown favor to us and taken away the disgrace of our having no children."

$$\text{ᘓ} \qquad \text{ᘓ} \qquad \text{ᘓ}$$

²⁶ Six months later, the angel Gabriel was sent from God to a town in Galilee called Nazareth, ²⁷ to a young woman named Mary; she was engaged to a man named Joseph, of the house of David. ²⁸ Upon arriving, the angel said to Mary, "Rejoice, highly favored one! God is with you! Blessed are you among women!"

²⁹ Mary was deeply troubled by these words and wondered what the angel's greeting meant. ³⁰ The angel went on to say to her, "Don't be afraid, Mary. You have found favor with God. ³¹ You'll conceive and bear a son, and give him the name Jesus—'Deliverance.' ³² His dignity will be great, and he will be called the Only Begotten of God. God will give Jesus the

judgment seat of David, his ancestor, ³³ to rule over the house of Jacob forever, and his reign will never end."

³⁴ Mary said to the angel, "How can this be, since I have never been with a man?"

³⁵ The angel answered her, "The Holy Spirit will come upon you, and the power of the Most High will overshadow you—hence the offspring to be born will be called the Holy One of God. ³⁶ Know too that Elizabeth, your kinswoman, has conceived a child in her old age; she who was thought to be infertile is now in her sixth month. ³⁷ Nothing is impossible with God."

³⁸ Mary said, "I am the servant of God. Let it be done to me as you say." With that, the angel left her.

೧೩   ೧೩   ೧೩

³⁹ Within a few days Mary set out and hurried to the hill country to a town of Judah, ⁴⁰ where she entered Zechariah's house and greeted Elizabeth.

⁴¹ As soon as Elizabeth heard Mary's greeting, the child leaped in her womb and Elizabeth was filled with the Holy Spirit. ⁴² In a loud voice she exclaimed, "Blessed are you among women, and blessed is the fruit of your womb! ⁴³ But why am I so favored, that the mother of the Messiah should come to me? ⁴⁴ The moment your greeting reached my ears, the child in my womb leaped for joy. ⁴⁵ Blessed is she who believed that what Our God said to her would be accomplished!"

⁴⁶ Mary said:

> "My soul proclaims your greatness, O God,
> ⁴⁷ and my spirit rejoices in you, my Savior.
> ⁴⁸ For you have looked with favor
> upon your lowly servant,
> and from this day forward
> all generations will call me blessed.
> ⁴⁹ For you, the Almighty, have done great things for me,
> and holy is your Name.
> ⁵⁰ Your mercy reaches from age to age
> for those who fear you.
> ⁵¹ You have shown strength with your arm,
> you have scattered the proud in their conceit,
> ⁵² you have deposed the mighty from their thrones
> and raised the lowly to high places.
> ⁵³ You have filled the hungry with good things,
> while you have sent the rich away empty.

⁵⁴ You have come to the aid of Israel your servant,
    mindful of your mercy—
⁵⁵ the promise you made to our ancestors—
    to Sarah and Abraham
    and their descendants forever."

⁵⁶ Mary stayed with Elizabeth about three months and then returned home.

   ❧   ❧   ❧

⁵⁷ When the time came for Elizabeth to deliver, she gave birth to a son. ⁵⁸ When her neighbors and relatives heard that God had been merciful to her, they shared her joy. ⁵⁹ When all had assembled for the circumcision on the eighth day, they intended to name the baby after his father Zechariah. ⁶⁰ But his mother spoke up, "No, he is to be called John."

⁶¹ They pointed out to her, "But no one in your family has this name." ⁶² Then they made signs to the father to find out what he wanted the child to be named. ⁶³ The father asked for a writing tablet and wrote, "His name is John." They were all astonished.

⁶⁴ Immediately Zechariah's mouth was opened and his tongue was loosed, and he began to speak in praise of God. ⁶⁵ Their neighbors were all filled with awe, and throughout the hill country of Judea, people were talking about these events. ⁶⁶ All who heard the news stored it in their hearts and said, "What will this child turn out to be?" For God's hand was with him.

⁶⁷ Zechariah, John's father, was filled with the Holy Spirit and prophesied:

⁶⁸ "Blessed are you, the Most High God of Israel—
    for you have visited and redeemed your people.
⁶⁹ You have raised up a mighty savior for us
    of the house of David,
⁷⁰ as you promised through the mouths of your holy ones,
    the prophets of ancient times:
⁷¹ salvation from our enemies
    and from the hands of all our foes.
⁷² You have shown mercy to our ancestors
    by remembering the holy Covenant
    you made with them,
⁷³ the oath you swore to Sarah and Abraham,
    ⁷⁴ granting that we,
delivered from the hands of our enemies,
    might serve you without fear,

⁷⁵ in holiness and justice,
in your presence all our days.

⁷⁶ And you, my child, will be called
the prophet of the Most High,
for you'll go before Our God
to prepare the way for the Promised One,
⁷⁷ giving the people the knowledge of salvation
through forgiveness of their sins.
⁷⁸ Such is the tender mercy of our God,
who from on high
will bring the Rising Sun to visit us,
⁷⁹ to give light to those who live
in darkness and the shadow of death
and to guide our feet
into the way of peace."

⁸⁰ In the meantime, the child grew up and became strong in spirit. He lived out in the desert until the day he appeared openly in Israel.

ര   ര   ര

2:¹ In those days, Caesar Augustus published a decree ordering a census of the whole Roman world. ² This first census took place while Quirinius was governor of Syria. ³ All the people were instructed to go back to the towns of their birth to register. ⁴ And so Joseph went from the town of Nazareth in Galilee to "the city of David"—Bethlehem, in Judea, because Joseph was of the house and lineage of David; ⁵ he went to register with Mary, his espoused wife, who was pregnant.

⁶ While they were there, the time came for her delivery. ⁷ She gave birth to her firstborn, a son; she put him in a simple cloth wrapped like a receiving blanket, and laid him in a feeding trough for cattle, because there was no room for them at the inn.

⁸ There were shepherds in the area living in the fields and keeping nightwatch by turns over their flock. ⁹ The angel of God appeared to them, and the glory of God shone around them; they were very much afraid.

¹⁰ The angel said to them, "You have nothing to fear! I come to proclaim good news to you—news of a great joy to be shared by the whole people. ¹¹ Today in David's city, a savior—the Messiah—has been born to you. ¹² Let this be a sign to you: you'll find an infant wrapped in a simple cloth, lying in a manger."

¹³Suddenly, there was a multitude of the heavenly host with the angel, praising God and saying,

¹⁴"Glory to God in high heaven!
And on earth, peace to those on whom God's favor rests."

¹⁵When the angels had returned to heaven, the shepherds said to one another, "Let's go straight to Bethlehem and see this event that God has made known to us." ¹⁶They hurried and found Mary and Joseph, and the baby lying in the manger; ¹⁷once they saw this, they reported what they had been told concerning the child. ¹⁸All who heard about it were astonished at the report given by the shepherds.

¹⁹Mary treasured all these things and reflected on them in her heart. ²⁰The shepherds went away glorifying and praising God for all they had heard and seen, just as they had been told.

℞   ℞   ℞

²¹When the eighth day arrived for the child's circumcision, he was named Jesus, the name the angel had given him before he was conceived.

²²When the day came for them to be purified, as laid down by the Law of Moses, the couple took Jesus up to Jerusalem and presented him to God. ²³For it's written in the Law of Our God, "Every firstborn heir is to be consecrated to God." ²⁴They likewise came to offer in sacrifice "a pair of turtledoves or two young pigeons," in accord with the dictate of the Law of Our God.

²⁵Now there lived in Jerusalem a man named Simeon. He was devout and just, anticipating the consolation of Israel, and he was filled with the Holy Spirit. ²⁶She had revealed to Simeon that he wouldn't see death until he had seen the Messiah of God. ²⁷Prompted by her, Simeon came to the Temple; and when the parents brought in the child to perform the customary rituals of the Law, ²⁸he took the child in his arms and praised God, saying,

²⁹"Now, O God, you can dismiss your servant in peace,
    just as you promised;
³⁰because my eyes have seen the salvation
    ³¹which you have prepared for all the peoples to see—
³²a light of revelation to the Gentiles
    and the glory of your people Israel."

³³As the child's mother and father stood there marveling at the things that were being said, ³⁴Simeon blessed them and said to Mary, the mother, "This child is destined to be the downfall and the rise of many in Israel,

and to be a sign that is rejected, ³⁵ so that the secret thoughts of many may be laid bare. And a sword will pierce your heart as well."

³⁶ There was a woman named Anna, the daughter of Phanuel, of the tribe of Asher, who was also a prophet. She had lived a long life, seven years with her husband, ³⁷ and then as a widow to the age of eighty-four. She never left the Temple, worshiping day and night, fasting and praying. ³⁸ Coming up at that moment, she gave thanks to God and talked about the child to all who anticipated the deliverance of Jerusalem.

³⁹ When the couple had fulfilled all the prescriptions of the Law of God, they returned to Galilee and their own town of Nazareth. ⁴⁰ The child grew in size and strength. He was filled with wisdom, and the grace of God was with him.

℞   ℞   ℞

⁴¹ The parents of Jesus used to go every year to Jerusalem for the feast of Passover, ⁴² and when Jesus was twelve, they went up for the celebration as was their custom. ⁴³ As they were returning at the end of the feast, the child Jesus remained behind in Jerusalem, unbeknownst to Mary and Joseph. ⁴⁴ Thinking Jesus was in their caravan, they continued their journey for the day, looking for him among their relatives and acquaintances.

⁴⁵ Not finding Jesus, they returned to Jerusalem in search of him. ⁴⁶ On the third day, they came upon Jesus in the Temple, sitting in the midst of the teachers, listening to them and asking them questions. ⁴⁷ All who heard Jesus were amazed at his understanding and his answers.

⁴⁸ When Mary and Joseph saw Jesus, they were astonished, and Mary said, "Son, why have you done this to us? You see that your father and I have been so worried, looking for you." ⁴⁹ Jesus said to them, "Why were you looking for me? Did you not know I had to be in my Abba's house?"

⁵⁰ But they didn't understand what he told them. ⁵¹ Then Jesus went down with them to Nazareth and was obedient to them. Mary stored these things in her heart, ⁵² and Jesus grew in wisdom, in years and in favor with God and people alike.

3:1–4:13

In the fifteenth year of Tiberius Caesar, Pontius Pilate was governor of Judea, Herod tetrarch of Galilee, Philip his brother tetrarch of the region of Ituraea and Trachonitis, and Lysanias tetrarch of Abilene. ² In those days, during the high-priesthood of Annas and Caiaphas, the Word of God came to John, begot of Zechariah, in the desert. ³John went through the entire region of the Jordan proclaiming a baptism of repentance for the forgiveness of sins, ⁴as is written in the words of Isaiah, the prophet:

> "A herald's voice in the desert, crying,
>> 'Make ready the way of Our God;
>> clear a straight path.
> ⁵Every valley will be filled,
>> and every mountain and hill will be leveled.
> The twisted paths will be made straight,
>> and the rough road smooth—
>>> ⁶and all humankind will see the salvation of God.' "

⁷John said to the crowds who came out to be baptized by him, "You pack of snakes! Who warned you to escape the wrath to come? ⁸Produce good fruit as a sign of your repentance. And don't presume to say to yourselves, 'We have Sarah and Abraham as our mother and father,' for I tell you that God can raise children for Sarah and Abraham from these very stones. ⁹The ax is already laid at the root of the tree; every tree that doesn't produce good fruit will be cut down and tossed into the fire."

¹⁰When the people asked him, "What should we do?" ¹¹John replied, "Let the one with two coats share with the one who has none. Let those who have food do the same."

¹²Tax collectors also came to be baptized, and they said to John, "Teacher, what are we to do?"

¹³John answered them, "Exact nothing over and above your fixed amount."

¹⁴Soldiers likewise asked, "What about us?" John told them, "Don't bully anyone. Don't accuse anyone falsely. Be content with your pay."

¹⁵The people were full of anticipation, wondering in their hearts whether John might be the Messiah. ¹⁶John answered them all by saying, "I am baptizing you in water, but someone is coming who is mightier than I, whose sandals I am not fit to untie! This One will baptize you in the Holy Spirit and in fire. ¹⁷A winnowing-fan is in his hand to clear the threshing floor and gather the wheat into the granary, but the chaff will be burnt in unquenchable fire." ¹⁸Using exhortations like this, John proclaimed the Good News to the people.

¹⁹But Herod the tetrarch—whom John rebuked for his wickedness, including his relationship with his sister-in-law, Herodias—²⁰committed another crime by throwing John into prison.

²¹When all the people were baptized, Jesus also came to be baptized. And while Jesus was praying, the skies opened ²²and the Holy Spirit descended

on the Anointed One in visible form, like a dove. A voice from heaven said, "You are my Own, my Beloved. On you my favor rests."

℞ ℞ ℞

23 When Jesus began to teach, he was about thirty years old. He was begot, as it was thought, of Joseph, who was begot of Heli, 24 begot of Matthat, begot of Levi, begot of Melchi, begot of Jannai, begot of Joseph, 25 begot of Mattathias, begot of Amos, begot of Nahum, begot of Esli, begot of Naggai, 26 begot of Maath, begot of Mattathias, begot of Semein, begot of Josech, begot of Joda, 27 begot of Joanan, begot of Rhesa, begot of Zerubbabel, begot of Shealtiel, begot of Neri, 28 begot of Melchi, begot of Addi, begot of Cosam, begot of Elmadam, begot of Er, 29 begot of Joshua, begot of Eliezer, begot of Jorim, begot of Matthat, begot of Levi, 30 begot of Simeon, begot of Judah, begot of Joseph, begot of Jonam, begot of Eliakim, 31 begot of Melea, begot of Menna, begot of Mattatha, begot of Nathan, begot of David, 32 begot of Jesse, begot of Obed, begot of Boaz, begot of Sala, begot of Nahshon, 33 begot of Amminadab, begot of Admin, begot of Arni, begot of Hezron, begot of Perez, begot of Judah, 34 begot of Jacob, begot of Issac, begot of Abraham, begot of Terah, begot of Nahor, 35 begot of Serug, begot of Reu, begot of Peleg, begot of Eber, begot of Shelah, 36 begot of Cainan, begot of Arphaxad, begot of Shem, begot of Noah, begot of Lamech, 37 begot of Methuselah, begot of Enoch, begot of Jared, begot of Mahalaleel, begot of Cainan, 38 begot of Enosh, begot of Seth, begot of Eve and Adam, begot of God.

℞ ℞ ℞

4:1 Jesus returned from the Jordan filled with the Holy Spirit, and she led him into the desert 2 for forty days, where he was tempted by the Devil. Jesus ate nothing during that time, at the end of which he was famished.

3 The Devil said to Jesus, "If you are God's Own, command this stone to turn into bread." 4 Jesus answered, "Scripture has it, 'We don't live on bread alone.'"

5 Then the Devil took Jesus up higher and showed him all the nations of the world in a single instant. 6 The Devil said, "I'll give you all the power and the glory of these nations; the power has been given to me and I can give it to whomever I wish. 7 Prostrate yourself in homage before me, and it will all be yours."

8 In reply, Jesus said, "Scripture has it:
　　　'You will worship the Most High God;

God alone will you adore.' "

⁹ Then the Devil led Jesus to Jerusalem, set him up on the parapet of the Temple and said, "If you are God's Own, throw yourself down from here, ¹⁰ for scripture has it,

> 'God will tell the angels to take care of you;
>> ¹¹ with their hands they'll support you,
>> that you may never stumble on a stone.' "

¹² Jesus said to the Devil in reply, "It also says, 'Do not put God to the test.' "

¹³ When the Devil had finished all this tempting, Jesus was left alone. The Devil awaited another opportunity.

4:14–9:50

*J*esus returned in the power of the Spirit to Galilee, and his reputation spread throughout the region. ¹⁵ He was teaching in the Galilean synagogues, and all were loud in their praise.

¹⁶ Jesus came to Nazareth, where he had been brought up. Entering the synagogue on the Sabbath, as was his habit, Jesus stood up to do the reading. ¹⁷ When the book of the prophet Isaiah was handed him, he unrolled the scroll and found the passage where it was written:

> ¹⁸ "The Spirit of Our God is upon me:
>> because the Most High has anointed me
>> to bring Good News to those who are poor.
> God has sent me to proclaim liberty to those held captive,
>> recovery of sight to those who are blind,
>> and release to those in prison—
> ¹⁹ to proclaim the year of Our God's favor."

²⁰ Rolling up the scroll, Jesus gave it back to the attendant and sat down. The eyes of all in the synagogue were fixed on him. ²¹ Then he said to them, "Today, in your hearing, this scripture passage is fulfilled."

²² All who were present spoke favorably of him; they marveled at the eloquence of the words on Jesus' lips. They said, "Surely this isn't Mary and Joseph's son!"

²³ Jesus said to them, "Undoubtedly you'll quote me the proverb, 'Physician, heal yourself,' and say, 'Do here in your own country the things we heard you did in Capernaum.' ²⁴ But the truth is, prophets never gain acceptance in their hometowns.

²⁵ "The truth is, there were many women who were widowed in Israel in

the days of Elijah, when the heavens remained closed for three and a half years and a great famine spread over the land. ²⁶ It was to none of these that Elijah was sent, but to a woman who had been widowed in Zarephath, near Sidon. ²⁷ Recall, too, that many had leprosy in Israel in the time of Elisha the prophet, yet not one was cured except Naaman the Syrian."

²⁸ At these words, the whole audience in the synagogue was filled with indignation. ²⁹ They rose up and dragged Jesus out of town, leading him to the brow of the hill on which the city was built, with the intention of hurling him over the edge. ³⁰ But he moved straight through the crowd and walked away.

CR　　CR　　CR

³¹ Jesus went down to Capernaum, a town in Galilee. He would teach there on the Sabbath. ³² And the teaching made a great impression on them, because he spoke with authority.

³³ In the synagogue one day, there was a person possessed by the spirit of an unclean demon, which shouted in a loud voice, ³⁴ "Leave us alone! What do you want with us, Jesus of Nazareth? Have you come to destroy us? I know who you are: the Holy One of God!"

³⁵ But Jesus said sharply, "Be quiet! Come out!" And the demon threw the person down in front of everyone, then went out without doing any harm.

³⁶ Everyone was struck with astonishment, and they said to one another, "What is this teaching? He commands the unclean spirits with authority and power, and they leave!" ³⁷ And reports of him spread throughout the surrounding countryside.

³⁸ On leaving the synagogue, Jesus entered the house of Simon and his family. Simon's mother-in-law was in the grip of a high fever, and they asked him to help her.

³⁹ Jesus stood over her and rebuked the fever, and it left. She got up immediately and went about her work.

⁴⁰ At sunset, all who had people sick with a variety of diseases brought them to Jesus, and he laid hands on each and cured them. ⁴¹ Demons departed from many, crying out as they did so, "You are the Firstborn of God!" Jesus rebuked them and forbade them to speak, for they knew who the Messiah was.

⁴² The next morning, Jesus left the house and went to a lonely place. The crowds followed and, when they found Jesus, they tried to keep him from

leaving them. ⁴³But Jesus said, "I must proclaim the Good News of God's reign to the other towns too, because that is what I was sent to do." ⁴⁴And he continued preaching in the synagogues of Judea.

଼ଆ   ଼ଆ   ଼ଆ

⁵:¹One day, Jesus was standing by Lake Gennesaret, and the crowd pressed in on him to hear the word of God. ²He saw two boats moored by the side of the lake; the fishers had disembarked and were washing their nets. ³Jesus stepped into one of the boats, the one belonging to Simon, and asked him to pull out a short distance from the shore; then, remaining seated, he continued to teach the crowds from the boat.

⁴When he had finished speaking, he said to Simon, "Pull out into deep water and lower your nets for a catch."

⁵Simon answered, "Rabbi, we've been working hard all night long and have caught nothing; but if you say so, I'll lower the nets."

⁶Upon doing so, they caught such a great number of fish that their nets were at the breaking point. ⁷They signaled to their mates in the other boat to come and help them, and together they filled the two boats until they both nearly sank.

⁸After Simon saw what happened, he was filled with awe and fell down before Jesus, saying, "Leave me, Rabbi, for I'm a sinner." ⁹For Simon and his shipmates were astonished at the size of the catch they had made, ¹⁰as were James and John, Zebedee's sons, who were Simon's partners.

Jesus said to Simon, "Don't be afraid; from now on you'll fish among humankind." ¹¹And when they brought their boats to shore, they left everything and followed him.

଼ଆ   ଼ଆ   ଼ଆ

¹²In one town Jesus was in, there was a person with leprosy. Seeing Jesus, the sufferer fell to the ground and implored him, "Teacher, if you are willing, you can heal me."

¹³Jesus stretched out his hand, touched the person and said, "I am willing: be cleansed." Immediately the leprosy disappeared.

¹⁴Jesus then gave this stern warning: "Tell no one, but go and show yourself to the priest and make the offering for your healing that Moses prescribed, as a testimony to them."

¹⁵The reputation of Jesus continued to grow. Large crowds gathered to hear him and to be healed of their sicknesses. ¹⁶But Jesus often withdrew to some place where he could be alone and pray.

¹⁷ One day, as Jesus was teaching, there were Pharisees and experts on the Law sitting there, who had come from every village of Galilee and from Judea and Jerusalem. And the power of God was present for Jesus to heal the sick.

¹⁸ Then some people appeared, carrying a paralyzed person on a mat; they tried to carry the individual into the house, to set in front of Jesus. ¹⁹ But the crowd made it impossible to get in, so they went up on the roof, made an opening in the tiles and lowered the paralyzed one into the middle of the gathering, in front of Jesus.

²⁰ Seeing their faith, Jesus said, "My friend, your sins are forgiven you."

²¹ The religious scholars and the Pharisees began to murmur among themselves, "Who is this person talking blasphemy? Who can forgive sins but God alone?"

²² But Jesus, aware of their thoughts, responded to them and said, "Why do you harbor such thoughts in your hearts? ²³ Is it easier to say, 'Your sins are forgiven you,' or to say, 'Get up and walk'? ²⁴ But to prove to you that the Chosen One has authority on earth to forgive sins—" then he turned to the paralyzed person—"I tell you, get up, take up your mat and go home."

²⁵ Immediately the individual stood up in front of them, picked up the mat and went home, praising God. ²⁶ They were all filled with awe and praised God, saying, "We have seen remarkable things today!"

²⁷ When Jesus went out after this, he saw a tax collector named Levi sitting at his tax booth. "Follow me," Jesus said, ²⁸ and Levi got up, left everything and followed him.

²⁹ Levi gave a big reception at his house for Jesus, and there was a large crowd of tax collectors and others at dinner with them. ³⁰ The Pharisees and the religious scholars complained to Jesus' disciples, "Why do you eat and drink with tax collectors and 'sinners'?"

³¹ Jesus answered them, "It's not the healthy who need a doctor, but the sick. ³² I have come to call not the virtuous, but sinners to repentance."

³³ Then they said to him, "John's disciples fast frequently and offer prayers; the disciples of the Pharisees do the same. Yours, on the contrary, go on eating and drinking."

³⁴ Jesus replied, "Can you make the wedding guests fast while the bridal party is still with them? ³⁵ The day will come when the bridal party will be taken from them; then they'll fast."

³⁶ Jesus then told them this parable: "People never tear a piece from a new

garment and sew it on an old one. If they do, not only will they have torn the new garment, but the piece taken from the new will not match the old. ³⁷ And people never put new wine in an old wineskin. If they do, the new wine will burst the skin; the wine will spill out and the skin will be ruined. ³⁸ No, new wine must be put into fresh wineskins.

³⁹ "People never want new wine after they've been drinking the old. They say, 'We like the old better.' "

6:1 One Sabbath, Jesus was walking through the grainfields. The disciples were picking heads of grain, rubbing them with their hands and eating them. ² Some of the Pharisees asked, "Why are you doing what is prohibited on the Sabbath?"

³ Jesus said, "Haven't you read what David did when he and the troops were hungry—⁴ how he entered the House of God and took the consecrated bread and ate it and gave the rest to the others, loaves which only the priests are allowed to eat?"

⁵ Then Jesus said to them, "The Chosen One is ruler over the Sabbath."

⁶ On a different Sabbath, Jesus came to teach in a synagogue where there was a person with a withered right hand. ⁷ The religious scholars and Pharisees were looking for a reason to accuse Jesus, so they watched him closely to see if he would heal on the Sabbath.

⁸ But Jesus knew their thoughts and said to the person with the withered hand, "Get up and stand here in front." So the afflicted one got up and stood in front of everyone. ⁹ Jesus said to the others, "I ask you, is it lawful on the Sabbath to do good—or evil? To preserve life—or destroy it?" ¹⁰ He looked around at them all, then said to the one with the infirmity, "Stretch out your hand." The other did so, and the hand was perfectly restored.

¹¹ At this they were furious and began to discuss with one another what they could do to Jesus.

ભ્ર   ભ્ર   ભ્ર

¹² It was about this time that Jesus went out to the mountains to pray, spending the night in communion with God. ¹³ At daybreak, he summoned the disciples and picked out twelve of them, whom he named as apostles: ¹⁴ Simon—to whom he gave the name Peter—and his brother Andrew; James and John; Philip and Bartholomew; ¹⁵ Matthew and Thomas; James, begot of Alphaeus, and Simon, who was called the Zealot; ¹⁶ Judas, begot of James, and Judas Iscariot, who became a traitor.

¹⁷ Coming down the mountain with them, Jesus stopped in a level area where there were a great number of disciples. A large crowd of people was with them from Jerusalem and all over Judea, to as far north as the coastal region of Tyre and Sidon—¹⁸ people who had come to hear Jesus and be healed of their diseases, and even to be freed from unclean spirits. ¹⁹Indeed, the whole crowd was trying to touch Jesus, because power was coming out of him and healing them all.

²⁰ Looking at the disciples, Jesus said:

"You who are poor are blessed,
    for the reign of God is yours.
²¹ You who hunger now are blessed,
    for you'll be filled.
You who weep now are blessed,
    for you'll laugh.
²² You are blessed when people hate you,
    when they scorn and insult you
and spurn your name as evil
    because of the Chosen One.
²³ On the day they do so,
    rejoice and be glad:
your reward will be great in heaven,
    for their ancestors treated the prophets the same way.
²⁴ But woe to you rich,
    for you are now receiving your comfort in full.
²⁵ Woe to you who are full,
    for you'll go hungry.
Woe to you who laugh now,
    for you'll weep in your grief.
²⁶ Woe to you when all speak well of you,
    for their ancestors treated the false prophets
    in the same way.

²⁷ "To you who hear me, I say: love your enemies. Do good to those who hate you, ²⁸ bless those who curse you, and pray for those who mistreat you. ²⁹ When they slap you on one cheek, turn and give them the other; when they take your coat, let them have your shirt as well. ³⁰ Give to all who beg from you. When someone takes what is yours, don't demand it back.

³¹ "Do to others what you would have them do to you. ³² If you love those who love you, what credit does that do you? Even 'sinners' love those who love them. ³³ If you do good only to those who do good to you, what credit does that do you? Even 'sinners' do as much. ³⁴ If you lend to those you expect to repay you, what credit does that do you? Even 'sinners' lend to

other 'sinners,' expecting to be repaid in full. ³⁵ Love your enemies and do good to them. Lend without expecting repayment, and your reward will be great. You'll rightly be called children of the Most High, since God is good even to the ungrateful and the wicked.

³⁶ "Be compassionate, as your loving God is compassionate. ³⁷ Don't judge, and you won't be judged. Don't condemn, and you won't be condemned. Pardon, and you'll be pardoned. ³⁸ Give, and it will be given to you: a full measure—packed down, shaken together and running over—will be poured into your lap. For the amount you measure out is the amount you'll be given back."

³⁹ He also told them a parable: "Can a blind person act as guide to another who is blind? Won't they both fall into a ditch?

⁴⁰ "The student is not above the teacher. But all students will, once they are fully trained, be on a par with their teacher.

⁴¹ "How can you look at the splinter in another's eye, yet miss the plank in your own? ⁴² How can you say to another, 'Let me remove the splinter from your eye,' but fail to see the board lodged in your own? Hypocrite, remove the board from your own eye first; then you'll see clearly enough to remove the splinter from the eye of another.

⁴³ "A good tree doesn't produce bad fruit any more than a bad tree produces good fruit. ⁴⁴ Each tree is known by its yield. Figs are not taken from thorn bushes, or grapes picked from briars. ⁴⁵ Good people produce goodness from the good they've stored up in their hearts; evil people produce evil from the evil stored up in their hearts. People speak from the fullness of their hearts.

⁴⁶ "Why do you call out, 'Rabbi, Rabbi,' but don't put into practice what I teach you? ⁴⁷ Those who come to me and hear my words and put them into practice—I'll show you who they're like: ⁴⁸ they are like the person who, in building a house, dug deeply and laid the foundation on a rock. When a flood arose, the torrent rushed against the house, but failed to shake it because of its solid foundation. ⁴⁹ On the other hand, anyone who has heard my words, but has not put them into practice, is like the person who built a house on sand, without any foundation. When the torrent rushed upon it, the house immediately collapsed and was completely destroyed."

ପ୍ର   ପ୍ର   ପ୍ର

7:1 After having finished this discourse in the hearing of the people, Jesus entered Capernaum. ² A centurion had a favorite attendant who was, at that moment, sick to the point of death. ³ Hearing about Jesus, the centurion sent some Jewish elders to ask him to come and save the attendant's life. ⁴ The elders approached Jesus and petitioned earnestly. "This centurion deserves this favor from you," they said; ⁵"he loves our nation and was the one who built our synagogue."

⁶Jesus set out with them. When he was only a short distance from the house, the centurion sent out friends to convey this message: "Rabbi, don't trouble yourself, for I am not worthy to have you enter my house. ⁷That's why I didn't presume to come to you myself. Just give the order and my attendant will be cured. ⁸I, too, know the meaning of an order, having soldiers under my command. I give orders, and they obey."

⁹On hearing this, Jesus was amazed, and turned to the crowd that was following and said, "I tell you, I've never found this much faith among the Israelites."

¹⁰When the messengers returned to the house, they found the attendant in perfect health.

¹¹Soon afterward, Jesus went to a town called Nain, and the disciples and a large crowd accompanied him. ¹²As Jesus approached the gate of the town, a dead body was being carried out—the only son of a widowed mother. A considerable crowd of townspeople were with her.

¹³Jesus was moved with pity upon seeing her and said, "Don't cry." ¹⁴Then Jesus stepped forward and touched the coffin; at this, the bearers halted. Jesus said, "Young man, get up."

¹⁵The dead youth sat up and began to speak, and Jesus gave him back to his mother.

¹⁶Fear seized them all, and they began to praise God. "A great prophet has risen among us," they said, and, "God has truly visited us." ¹⁷This was the report that spread about Jesus throughout Judea and the surrounding country.

¹⁸John's disciples reported these things to him. John summoned two of them ¹⁹and sent them to Jesus with the question, "Are you the One who is to come, or must we wait for someone else?"

²⁰When the couriers came to Jesus, they said, "John the Baptizer has sent us to you to ask, 'Are you the One who is to come, or must we wait for someone else?'"

²¹Immediately Jesus went and healed many people of diseases, sicknesses and evil spirits, and gave sight to many who were blind. ²²Then he gave the couriers this answer: "Go and report to John what you have seen and heard. Those who are blind recover their sight, those who are crippled walk, those with leprosy are cured, those who are deaf hear,

the dead are raised to life, and those who are poor have the Good News preached to them. ²³ Happy is the one who doesn't lose faith in me."

²⁴ When John's messengers had left, Jesus began to talk about John to the crowds: "What did you go out into the wilderness to see? A reed swaying in the breeze? ²⁵ What, really, did you go out to see? Someone dressed in fine clothes? No—those who dress in fine clothes and live luxuriously are to be found in mansions. ²⁶ But what did you go out to see? A prophet? Yes, I tell you, and much more than a prophet.

²⁷ "This is the one about whom scripture says, 'I send my messenger ahead of you, to prepare your way before you.' ²⁸ I tell you, there is no one born of woman who is greater than John. But the least in the kindom of God is greater than he is."

²⁹ All the people who heard him, even tax collectors, acknowledged God's goodness, because they had received baptism from John. ³⁰ The Pharisees and the experts on the Law, on the other hand, thwarted God's plan for themselves because they had refused John's baptism.

³¹ Jesus continued, "To what can I compare the people of this generation? What are they like? ³² They are like children sitting in the marketplace and calling out to one another, 'We piped you a tune but you wouldn't dance, we sang you a dirge but you wouldn't weep.' ³³ What I mean is that John the Baptizer came neither eating bread nor drinking wine, and you said, 'He is demon-possessed!' ³⁴ The Chosen One came and both ate and drank, and you say, 'Here is a glutton and a drunkard, a friend of tax collectors and sinners!' ³⁵ Wisdom, however, is vindicated by all her children."

℘   ℘   ℘

³⁶ One of the Pharisees invited Jesus to dinner. Jesus went to his house and reclined at table. ³⁷ A woman who had a low reputation in that town came to the house. She had learned that Jesus was dining with the Pharisee, so she brought with her an alabaster jar of perfumed oil. ³⁸ She stood behind Jesus, crying, and her tears fell on his feet. Then she dried his feet with her hair, kissed them, and anointed them with the oil.

³⁹ When the Pharisee saw this, he said to himself, "If this fellow were the Prophet, he'd know who this woman is that is touching him, and what a low reputation she has."

⁴⁰ In answer to the Pharisee's thoughts Jesus said, "Simon, I have something to tell you."

"Tell me, Teacher," he said.

⁴¹ "Two people owed money to a creditor. One owed the creditor the equivalent of two years' wages; the other, two months' wages. ⁴² Both were

unable to pay, so the creditor wrote off both debts. Which of them was more grateful to the money-lender?"

⁴³ Simon answered, "I suppose the one who owed more."

Jesus said, "You are right."

⁴⁴ Turning to the woman, he said to Simon, "See this woman? I came into your house and you gave me no water to wash my feet, but she has washed them with her tears and dried them with her hair. ⁴⁵ You gave me no kiss of greeting, but she covered my feet with kisses. ⁴⁶ You didn't anoint my head with oil, but she anointed my feet with oil. ⁴⁷ For this reason, I tell you, her sins, which are many, have been forgiven—see how much she loves! But the one who is forgiven little, loves little."

⁴⁸ Then Jesus said to the woman, "Your sins are forgiven."

⁴⁹ Those also sitting at the table began to ask among themselves, "Who is this who even forgives sins?"

⁵⁰ Meanwhile Jesus said to her, "Your faith has saved you. Go in peace."

℞   ℞   ℞

8:1 Now soon after this, Jesus journeyed through the towns and villages proclaiming the Good News of God's reign. With Jesus went the Twelve, ² as well as some women he had healed of evil spirits and sicknesses; Mary of Magdala, from whom he had cast out seven demons; ³ Joanna, the wife of Herod's steward Chuza; Suzanna; and many others who were contributing to the support of Jesus and the Twelve with their own funds.

⁴ With a large crowd gathering, and people from every town finding their way to him, Jesus used this parable: ⁵ "A farmer went out to sow some seed. In the sowing, some seed fell on the footpath where it was walked on, and the birds of the air ate it up. ⁶ Some fell on rocky ground, sprouted up, then withered through lack of moisture. ⁷ Some fell among thorns, and the thorns growing up with it stifled it. ⁸ But some seed fell on good ground, grew up and yielded grain a hundredfold."

Whenever Jesus would say something like this, he would exclaim, "Whoever has ears to hear, hear this!"

⁹ The disciples began asking Jesus what the meaning of this parable might be.

¹⁰ He replied, "To you the mysteries of the kindom of God have been confided, but the rest have only parables—so that 'they may look but never see, listen but never understand.'

¹¹ "This is the meaning of the parable. The seed is the word of God. ¹² Those on the footpath are people who hear, but the Devil comes and takes

the word out of their hearts, lest they believe and be saved. ¹³ Those on the rocky ground are the ones who, when they hear the word, receive it with joy. But they have no roots; they believe for a while, but fall away in time of testing. ¹⁴ The seed that fell among thorns are those who hear, but their progress is choked by the cares, riches and pleasures of life, so they don't mature and produce fruit. ¹⁵ The seed on good ground are those who hear the word in a spirit of openness, hold it close, and bear fruit through perseverance.

¹⁶ "People never light a lamp only to put it under a basket or under a bed; they put it on a lampstand so that whoever comes in may see the light. ¹⁷ There is nothing hidden that will not be exposed, nothing concealed that will not be known and brought to light. ¹⁸ Take care, therefore, how you listen: to those who have, more will be given; those without will lose even the little bit they thought they had."

℞   ℞   ℞

¹⁹ Now Jesus' mother and kin came to see him, but they couldn't get near him because of the crowd. ²⁰ Someone told Jesus, "Your mother and kin are outside, waiting to see you."

²¹ Jesus replied, "My mother and my kin are those who hear the word of God and put it into practice."

℞   ℞   ℞

²² One day Jesus boarded a boat with the disciples and said, "Let's cross to the other side of the lake." So they cast off. ²³ As they were sailing, Jesus took a nap.

Soon a squall came down on the lake, and they began to take on water to a dangerous degree. ²⁴ They woke him and said, "Rabbi, Rabbi! We're sinking!"

Jesus got up, and reprimanded the wind and the waves. Immediately the storm subsided and all was calm again. ²⁵ "Where is your faith?" he asked them.

But they were both afraid and amazed, and they said to one another, "Who is this, who gives orders to the wind and the waves, and they obey him?"

²⁶ They came to the region of the Gerasenes, which is opposite Galilee. ²⁷ Jesus was stepping from the boat when he was met by a person from the

town who was possessed by demons. The demoniac had not worn clothes for a long time, and was homeless, living among the tombs instead.

²⁸ Seeing Jesus, the individual cried out and fell at his feet, shouting loudly, "What do you want with me, Jesus, Only Begotten of the Most High God? I beg you, don't torture me!" ²⁹—for Jesus was ordering the unclean spirit to come out of the person. This spirit had seized the demoniac many times in the past, who then needed to be restrained with chains and shackles and kept under guard—yet every time, the possessed person would break the bonds and be driven by the demon into deserted places.

³⁰ "What is your name?" Jesus asked.

"Legion," it replied, because many demons had entered the person. ³¹ And they pleaded with Jesus not to order them to depart into the abyss.

³² A large herd of pigs was feeding nearby on the hillside. The demons pleaded with Jesus to allow them to enter the swine, and he gave them permission. ³³ The demons left the person and entered the pigs, and the herd rushed down the hillside into the lake and drowned.

³⁴ When the swineherds saw what had happened, they ran away to tell the story in town and throughout the countryside. ³⁵ The local residents came out to see what happened. And as they approached Jesus, they also saw the exorcised person sitting at Jesus' feet, clothed and of a right mind. And they were afraid. ³⁶ Those who had witnessed it told the others how the possessed one had been made whole. ³⁷ Panic overcame the whole population of the region of the Gerasenes, and they asked Jesus to leave them.

When Jesus had gotten into the boat to leave, ³⁸ the person who had been healed asked to go with him. But Jesus said, "No, ³⁹ go back home and tell everyone what God has done for you." So the one who had been made whole went off and proclaimed throughout the region what Jesus had accomplished.

⁴⁰ When Jesus returned, a crowd of people was waiting for him and welcomed him. ⁴¹ A man named Jairus, an official of the synagogue, stepped forward and fell at Jesus' feet. He begged Jesus to come to his house, ⁴² for his only daughter—who was twelve years old—was dying.

As Jesus moved along, the crowd almost crushed him. ⁴³ In the crowd was a woman who had suffered from hemorrhages for twelve years, and had found no one who could heal her. ⁴⁴ She came up behind Jesus and touched the fringe of his cloak, and immediately the bleeding stopped.

⁴⁵ "Who touched me?" Jesus asked.

When no one nearby responded, Peter said, "Rabbi, it's the crowd pressing around you."

⁴⁶ But Jesus said, "Someone touched me. I felt power leave me."

⁴⁷ When the woman realized that she had been noticed, she approached in fear and knelt before him. She explained in front of the crowd why she had touched him and how she had been instantly healed.

⁴⁸ Jesus said to her, "Daughter, your faith has healed you. Go in peace."

⁴⁹ While Jesus was still talking, someone from the house of Jairus, the synagogue official, arrived and said, "Your daughter died. Don't trouble the Teacher anymore."

⁵⁰ But when Jesus heard this, he said to the messenger, "Don't be afraid. Have faith, and she will be made well."

⁵¹ When he arrived at the house, Jesus ordered no one to enter with him except Peter, John, James and the girl's parents. ⁵² Everyone was weeping and wailing for the child, but Jesus said, "Stop crying. She is not dead, just sleeping." ⁵³ But they ridiculed him, for they knew she was dead.

⁵⁴ Jesus took her hand and said softly, "Get up, child." ⁵⁵ Her breath returned to her and she got up immediately. And he told them to give her something to eat. ⁵⁶ The parents were astonished, but he ordered them to tell no one what had happened.

ॐ   ॐ   ॐ

9:1 Jesus called the Twelve together and gave them power and authority to overcome all demons and to cure diseases. ² He sent them forth to proclaim the kindom of God and to heal the afflicted.

³ Jesus told them, "Take nothing for the journey, neither walking staff, nor travelling bag, nor bread, nor money. Don't even take a change of clothes. ⁴ Stay at whatever house you enter, and proceed from there. ⁵ As for those who don't receive you, leave that town and shake its dust from your feet as a testimony against them."

⁶ So they set out and went from village to village, spreading the Good News everywhere and healing people.

⁷ Now Herod the tetrarch heard of all that Jesus was doing, and was perplexed, for some were saying, "John has been raised from the dead"; ⁸ others, "Elijah has appeared"; and still others, "One of the prophets of old has risen."

⁹ But Herod said, "I myself had John beheaded. Who is this about whom I hear all these reports?" And Herod kept trying to see Jesus.

¹⁰ When the apostles returned, they reported to Jesus what they had done. Taking them with him, he retreated to the town of Bethsaida where they could be by themselves.

¹¹ But when the crowd found out, they followed him. Jesus welcomed the

crowd and spoke to them about the reign of God, and healed all who were in need of healing.

¹² As sunset approached, the Twelve came and said to Jesus, "Dismiss the crowd, so they can go into the surrounding villages and countryside and find lodging and food, for this is a remote and isolated area."

¹³ Jesus answered them, "Give them something to eat yourselves!" The disciples replied, "We have nothing but five loaves and two fish. Or do you want us to go and buy food for all these people?" ¹⁴ There were about five thousand gathered.

Jesus said to the disciples, "Have them sit down in groups of fifty or so." ¹⁵ They did so and got them seated. ¹⁶ Then, taking the five loaves and two fishes, Jesus raised his eyes to heaven, said a blessing over them, broke them and gave them to the disciples for distribution to the crowd.

¹⁷ They all ate until they were satisfied and, when the leftovers were collected, there were twelve baskets full.

೭   ೭   ೭

¹⁸ One day when Jesus was praying in seclusion and the disciples were with him, he put the question to them, "Who do the crowds say that I am?"

¹⁹ "John the Baptizer," they replied, "and some say Elijah, while others claim that one of the prophets of old has returned from the dead."

²⁰ "But you—who do you say that I am?" Jesus asked them.

Peter replied, "God's Messiah."

²¹ Jesus strictly forbade them to tell this to anyone.

²² "The Chosen One," Jesus said, "must suffer grievously, be rejected by the elders, the chief priests and the religious scholars, be put to death and then be raised up on the third day."

²³ Then Jesus said to all of them, "You who wish to be my followers must deny your very self, take up your cross—the instrument of your own death—every day, and follow in my steps. ²⁴ If you would save your life, you'll lose it, and if you would lose your life for my sake, you'll save it. ²⁵ What profit is there in gaining the whole world if you lose or forfeit yourselves in the process?

²⁶ "Those who are ashamed of me and of my words, of them will the Chosen One be ashamed in that coming, in the glory of Abba God and of the holy angels. ²⁷ The truth is, there are some standing here right now who will not taste death before they see the kindom of God."

²⁸ About eight days after saying this, Jesus took Peter, John and James and went up onto a mountain to pray. ²⁹ While Jesus was praying, his face changed in appearance and the clothes he wore became dazzlingly white. ³⁰ Suddenly two people were there talking with Jesus—Moses and Elijah. ³¹ They appeared in glory and spoke of the prophecy that Jesus was about to fulfill in Jerusalem.

³² Peter and the others had already fallen into a deep sleep, but awakening, they saw Jesus' glory—and the two people who were standing next to him. ³³ When the two were leaving, Peter said to Jesus, "Rabbi, how good it is for us to be here! Let's set up three tents, one for you, one for Moses and one for Elijah!" Peter didn't really know what he was saying.

³⁴ While Peter was speaking, a cloud came and overshadowed them, and the disciples grew fearful as the others entered it. ³⁵ Then from the cloud came a voice which said, "This is my Own, my Chosen One. Listen to him!"

³⁶ When the voice finished speaking, they saw no one but Jesus standing there. The disciples kept quiet, telling nothing of what they had seen at that time to anyone.

³⁷ The following day, when they came down the mountain, a large crowd awaited him. ³⁸ A man stepped out of the crowd and said, "Teacher, please come and look at my son, my only child. ³⁹ A demon seizes him and he screams, and it throws him into convulsions until he foams at the mouth. It releases the boy only with difficulty, and when it does, he is exhausted. ⁴⁰ I begged your disciples to cast it out, but they couldn't."

⁴¹ Jesus said in reply, "You unbelieving and perverse generation! How much longer must I be among you and put up with you? Bring the child to me." ⁴² As the boy approached, the demon dashed the child to the ground and threw him into a violent convulsion. But Jesus reprimanded the unclean spirit, healed the child and returned him to his father. ⁴³ All present were awestruck at the greatness of God.

In the midst of all the crowd's amazement at these things, Jesus said to the disciples, ⁴⁴ "Let these words sink in: the Chosen One must be delivered into the hands of others." ⁴⁵ But they failed to understand this statement; its meaning was so concealed from them that they didn't grasp it at all, and they were afraid to question Jesus about the matter.

℞   ℞   ℞

⁴⁶ A dispute arose among the disciples as to which of them was the greatest.

⁴⁷ Jesus, who knew their thoughts, took a little child and had it stand next

to him. ⁴⁸Then he said to them, "Whoever welcomes this child in my name welcomes me. And anyone who welcomes me, welcomes the One who sent me. For the lowliest among you is the greatest."

⁴⁹John said, "Rabbi, we saw someone casting out devils in your name, and—because the individual doesn't follow along with us—we tried to put a halt to it."

⁵⁰Jesus replied, "Don't stop it, for anyone who is not against you is for you."

9:51–19:27

as the time approached when he was to be taken from this world, Jesus firmly resolved to proceed toward Jerusalem ⁵²and sent messengers on ahead. They entered a Samaritan town to make preparations for him, ⁵³but the Samaritans wouldn't welcome Jesus because his destination was Jerusalem.

⁵⁴When the disciples James and John saw this, they said, "Rabbi, do you want us to call down fire from heaven and destroy them?" ⁵⁵But Jesus turned and reprimanded them.* ⁵⁶Then they set off for another town.

⁵⁷As they were making their way along, they met a fellow traveler who said to Jesus, "I'll follow you wherever you go."

⁵⁸Jesus replied, "Foxes have lairs, the birds of the sky have nests, but the Chosen One has nowhere to rest."

⁵⁹To another traveler Jesus said, "Follow me."

The traveler replied, "Let me bury my father first."

⁶⁰Jesus said in return, "Let the dead bury their dead; you go and proclaim the reign of God everywhere."

⁶¹Yet another traveler approached Jesus in this way: "I'll be your follower, Rabbi, but first let me say goodbye to my people at home."

⁶²Jesus answered, "Whoever puts a hand to the plow but keeps looking back is unfit for the reign of God."

 জ   জ   জ

10¹ After this, Jesus appointed seventy-two others, and sent them on

---

* Later manuscripts read: ...them: "You don't know what kind of spirit this is coming from. ⁵⁶ The Chosen One came not to destroy people's lives, but to save them." Then they...

ahead in pairs to every town and place he intended to visit. ²He said to them, "The harvest is rich, but the workers are few; therefore, ask the overseer to send workers to the harvest.

³"Be on your way, and remember: I am sending you as lambs in the midst of wolves. ⁴Don't carry a walking stick or knapsack; wear no sandals and greet no one along the way. ⁵And whatever house you enter, first say, 'Peace be upon this house!' ⁶If the people live peaceably there, your peace will rest on them; if not, it will come back to you. ⁷Stay in that house, eating and drinking what they give you, for the laborer is worth a wage. Don't keep moving from house to house.

⁸"And whatever city you enter, after they welcome you, eat what they set before you ⁹and heal those who are sick in that town. Say to them, 'The reign of God has drawn near to you.' ¹⁰If the people of any town you enter don't welcome you, go into its streets and say, ¹¹'We shake the dust of this town from our feet as testimony against you. But know that the reign of God has drawn near.' ¹²I tell you, on that day the fate of Sodom will be less severe than that of such a town.

¹³"Woe to you, Chorazin! And woe to you, Bethsaida! If the miracles worked in your midst had occurred in Tyre and Sidon, they would long ago have repented in sackcloth and ashes! ¹⁴It will go easier on the day of judgment for Tyre and Sidon than for you. ¹⁵And as for you, Capernaum, will you exalt yourself to the skies? No, you'll be hurled down to Hades!

¹⁶"Anyone who listens to you, listens to me. Anyone who rejects you, rejects me; and those who reject me, reject the One who sent me."

¹⁷The seventy-two disciples returned with joy, saying, "Rabbi, even the demons obey us in your name!"

¹⁸Jesus replied, "I watched Satan fall from the sky like lightning. ¹⁹Look: I've given you the power to tread on snakes and scorpions—even all the forces of the enemy—and nothing will ever injure you. ²⁰Nevertheless, don't rejoice in the fact that the spirits obey you so much as that your names are inscribed in heaven."

²¹At that moment Jesus rejoiced in the Holy Spirit and said, "I offer you praise, Abba, ruler of heaven and earth, because what you have hidden from the learned and the clever you have revealed to mere children. Yes, Abba, you have graciously willed it so. ²²Everything has been entrusted to me by you. No one knows me except through you, and no one knows you except through me—and those to whom I choose to reveal you."

²³Turning to the disciples, Jesus spoke to them privately: "Blessed are the eyes that see what you see. ²⁴For I tell you, many prophets and rulers

wanted to see what you see but never saw it, to hear what you hear but never heard it."

ભ   ભ   ભ

[25] An expert on the Law stood up to put Jesus to the test and said, "Teacher, what must I do to inherit everlasting life?"

[26] Jesus answered, "What is written in the law? How do you read it?"

[27] The expert on the Law replied:

> "You must love the Most High God
>> with all your heart,
>> with all your soul,
>> with all your strength
>> and with all your mind,
> and your neighbor as yourself."

[28] Jesus said, "You have answered correctly. Do this and you'll live."

[29] But the expert on the Law, seeking self-justification, pressed Jesus further: "And just who is my neighbor?"

[30] Jesus replied, "There was a traveler going down from Jerusalem to Jericho, who fell prey to robbers. The traveler was beaten, stripped naked, and left half-dead. [31] A priest happened to be going down the same road; the priest saw the traveler lying beside the road, but passed by on the other side. [32] Likewise there was a Levite who came the same way; this one, too, saw the afflicted traveler and passed by on the other side.

[33] "But a Samaritan, who was taking the same road, also came upon the traveler and, filled with compassion, [34] approached the traveler and dressed the wounds, pouring on oil and wine. Then the Samaritan put the wounded person on a donkey, went straight to an inn and there took care of the injured one. [35] The next day the Samaritan took out two silver pieces and gave them to the innkeeper with the request, 'Look after this person, and if there is any further expense, I'll repay you on the way back.'

[36] "Which of these three, in your opinion, was the neighbor to the traveler who fell in with the robbers?"

[37] The answer came, "The one who showed compassion."

Jesus replied, "Then go and do the same."

ભ   ભ   ભ

[38] As they traveled, Jesus entered a village where a woman named Martha welcomed him to her home. [39] She had a sister named Mary, who seated herself at Jesus' feet and listened to his words.

⁴⁰ Martha, who was busy with all the details of hospitality, came to Jesus and said, "Rabbi, don't you care that my sister has left me all alone to do the household tasks? Tell her to help me!"

⁴¹ Jesus replied, "Martha, Martha! You're anxious and upset about so many things, ⁴² but only a few things are necessary—really only one. Mary has chosen the better part, and she won't be deprived of it."

ભ   ભ   ભ

11:1 One day Jesus was praying, and when he had finished, one of the disciples asked, "Rabbi, teach us to pray, just as John taught his disciples."

² Jesus said to them, "When you pray, say,

'Abba God,
hallowed be your Name!
May your reign come.
³ Give us today
Tomorrow's bread.
⁴ Forgive us our sins,
for we too forgive everyone who sins against us;
and don't let us be subjected to the Test.' "

⁵ Jesus said to them, "Suppose one of you has a friend, a neighbor, and you go to your neighbor at midnight and say, 'Lend me three loaves of bread, ⁶ because friends of mine on a journey have come to me, and I have nothing to set before them.'

⁷ "Then your neighbor says, 'Leave me alone. The door is already locked and the children and I are in bed. I can't get up to look after your needs.' ⁸ I tell you, though your neighbor will not get up to give you the bread out of friendship, your persistence will make your neighbor get up and give you as much as you need.

⁹ "That's why I tell you, keep asking and you'll receive; keep looking and you'll find; keep knocking and the door will be opened to you. ¹⁰ For whoever asks, receives; whoever seeks, finds; whoever knocks, is admitted. ¹¹ What parents among you will give a snake to their child when the child asks for a fish, ¹² or a scorpion when the child asks for an egg? ¹³ If you, with all your sins, know how to give your children good things, how much more will our heavenly Abba give the Holy Spirit to those who ask?"

ભ   ભ   ભ

¹⁴ Jesus was casting out a demon that made its host unable to talk. When the demon left, the mute person spoke, to the crowd's amazement. ¹⁵ Some

said, "It's by Beelzebul, the prince of demons, that he casts out demons." ¹⁶Still others, to test Jesus, were demanding a sign from heaven.

¹⁷Jesus knew what they were really thinking and said to them, "Every nation divided against itself will be ruined, and a house divided against itself will fall. ¹⁸If the realm of Satan is divided against itself, how can it stand?—since you say it's by Beelzebul that I cast out demons. ¹⁹If I cast out demons by Beelzebul, by whom do your people cast them out? In that case, let them act as your judges. ²⁰But if it is by the finger of God that I cast out demons, then the reign of God has come upon you.

²¹"When strong, fully armed guards protect the courtyard, its possessions go undisturbed. ²²But when a stronger force comes and overpowers the guards, the victors carry off and divide the spoils.

²³"Those who are not with me are against me, and those who don't gather with me, scatter.

²⁴"When an unclean spirit has gone out of a person, it wanders through arid wastes, searching for a resting place; failing to find one, it says, 'I'll go back to where I came from.' ²⁵It then returns, to find the house swept and tidied. ²⁶Next it goes out and returns with seven other spirits far worse than itself, who enter in and dwell there—with the result that the person is then far worse off than at the outset."

²⁷While Jesus was speaking, a woman from the crowd called out, "Blessed is the womb that bore you and the breasts that nursed you!"

²⁸"Rather," Jesus replied, "blessed are those who hear the word of God and obey it!"

²⁹When the crowds pressed around Jesus, he began to speak to them in these words: "This is a wicked generation! It asks for a sign, but none will be given except the sign of Jonah. ³⁰For just as Jonah was a sign for the Ninevites, so will the Promised One be a sign for this generation. ³¹Sheba, the ruler of the South, will rise at the Judgment along with the members of this generation, and she will condemn them. For she came from the ends of the earth to listen to Solomon's wisdom, but now One greater than Solomon is here. ³²The people of Nineveh will stand up at the Judgment with this generation and condemn it. For they repented at the preaching of Jonah, and now One greater than Jonah is here.

³³"You don't light a lamp only to hide it in the cellar or to put it under a bucket. You put it on a stand where people see it when they come in.

³⁴"The lamp of your body is your eye. If your eye is sound, the whole body is filled with light. But if your eye is diseased, your body is filled with darkness. ³⁵See to it then that the light in you doesn't fade into darkness.

[36] If your whole body is full of light, however, with no darkness in it, it will be completely lit—the way it is when the light of a lantern shines on you."

℞   ℞   ℞

[37] After Jesus finished talking, a Pharisee invited him home to dine. Jesus entered and reclined at the table for the meal. [38] Seeing this, the Pharisee was surprised that Jesus had not performed the ritual washings prescribed before eating.

[39] Jesus said, "You Pharisees! You cleanse the outside of cup and dish, but within, you are filled with thievery and wickedness. [40] Fools! Didn't the One who made the outside make the inside too? [41] But if you give to those poorer than you, all things will be clean for you.

[42] "Woe to you Pharisees! You pay tithes on mint, rue and all the garden plants, while neglecting justice and the love of God. These are the things you should practice, without omitting the others.

[43] "Woe to you Pharisees! You love the front seats in synagogues and the marks of respect in public.

[44] "Woe to you! You are like hidden tombs over which people walk unaware."

[45] In reply, one of the experts in the Law said, "Teacher, in speaking this way you insult us too."

[46] Jesus replied, "Woe to you lawyers as well! You lay impossible burdens on the people, but won't lift a finger to lighten them.

[47] "Woe to you! You build monuments to the prophets, but it was your ancestors who murdered them. [48] You show that you stand behind the deeds of your ancestors: they did the murdering and you build the monuments! [49] That's why the wisdom of God has said, 'I'll send them prophets and apostles, some of whom they'll persecute and others they'll kill, [50] so that this generation will have to account for the blood of all the prophets shed since the foundation of the world.' [51] Their guilt stretches from the blood of Abel to the blood of Zechariah, who met his death between the altar and the sanctuary! Yes, I tell you, this generation will have to account for it.

[52] "Woe to you experts on the Law! You have taken away the key to knowledge. And not only haven't you gained access, you have stopped others who were trying to enter!"

[53] When Jesus was leaving this gathering, the religious scholars and Pharisees began to be extremely hostile to him and question him closely on a

multitude of subjects, ⁵⁴setting traps to catch Jesus with something he might say.

12¹Meanwhile thousands of people had gathered, a crowd so dense that they were trampling each other. Jesus spoke first to the disciples:

"Be on your guard against the yeast of the Pharisees, which is hypocrisy.

²"There is nothing concealed that will not be revealed, nothing hidden that will not be made known. ³Everything you have said in the dark will be heard in the daylight; what you have whispered in locked rooms will be proclaimed from the rooftops.

⁴"I tell you, my friends: don't be afraid of those who kill the body and then can do no more. ⁵I'll tell you whom you ought to fear: fear the one who has the power to kill you and then cast you into Gehenna. Yes, I tell you, this is the one to fear. ⁶Aren't five sparrows sold for a few pennies? Yet not one of them is neglected by God. ⁷In fact, even the hairs on your head are counted! Don't be afraid: you are worth more than a whole flock of sparrows.

⁸"I tell you, if you acknowledge me in front of other people, the Chosen One will acknowledge you before the angels of God. ⁹But those who disown me in the presence of mortals will be disowned in the presence of the angels of God.

¹⁰"Those who speak against the Chosen One will be forgiven, but those who blaspheme the Holy Spirit will never be forgiven.

¹¹"When they bring you before synagogues, rulers and authorities, don't worry about how to defend yourselves or what to say. ¹²The Holy Spirit will teach you at that moment all that should be said."

¹³Someone in the crowd said to Jesus, "Teacher, tell my brother to give me my share of our inheritance."

¹⁴Jesus replied, "Friend, who has set me up as your judge or arbiter?" ¹⁵Then he told the crowd, "Avoid greed in all its forms. Your life isn't made more secure by what you own—even when you have more than you need."

¹⁶Jesus then told them a parable in these words: "There was a rich farmer who had a good harvest.

¹⁷" 'What will I do?' the farmer mused. 'I have no place to store my harvest. ¹⁸I know! I'll pull down my grain bins and build larger ones. All my grain and goods will go there. ¹⁹Then I'll say to myself: You have blessings in reserve for many years to come. Relax! Eat, drink and be merry!'

²⁰"But God said to the farmer, 'You fool! This very night your life will be required of you. To whom will all your accumulated wealth go?'

[21] "This is the way it works with people who accumulate riches for themselves, but are not rich in God."

[22] Then he said to the disciples, "That's why I tell you, don't worry about your life and what you are to eat. Don't worry about your body and what you are to wear. [23] For life is more than food, and the body is more than clothing. [24] Take a lesson from the ravens. They don't sow or reap. They have neither a food cellar nor a barn, yet God feeds them. And how much more valuable are you than birds? [25] Can any of you, for all your worrying, add a single hour to your life? [26] If even the smallest things are beyond your control, why worry about all the rest?

[27] "Notice how the flowers grow. They neither labor nor weave, yet I tell you, not even Solomon in all his splendor was robed like one of these! [28] If that is how God clothes the grass in the field—which is here today and thrown into the fire tomorrow—how much more will God look after you! You have so little faith!

[29] "As for you, don't set your hearts on what you'll eat or what you'll drink. Stop worrying! [30] All the nations of the world seek these things, yet your Abba God well knows what you need. [31] Set your sights on the kindom of God, and all these other things will be given to you as well.

[32] "Fear not, little flock, for it has pleased your Abba to give you the kindom.

[33] "Sell what you own and give the money to poorer people. Make purses for yourselves that don't wear out—treasures that won't fail you, in heaven that thieves can't steal and moths can't destroy. [34] For wherever your treasure is, that's where your heart will be.

[35] "Be dressed and ready, and keep your lamps lit. [36] Be like the household staff awaiting the owner's return from a wedding, so that when the owner arrives and knocks, you'll open the door without delay. [37] It will go well with those staff members whom the owner finds wide awake upon returning. I tell you the absolute truth, the owner will put on an apron, seat them at table and proceed to wait on them. [38] Should the owner happen to come at midnight, or before sunrise, and find them prepared, it will go well with them.

[39] "Understand this: no homeowner who knew when a thief was coming would have let the thief break in! [40] So be on guard—the Promised One will come when least expected."

[41] Peter said, "Do you intend this parable just for us, Teacher, or do you mean it for everyone?"

[42] Jesus said, "It's the faithful and farsighted steward that the owner leaves to supervise the staff and give them their rations at the proper time.

⁴³ Happy the steward whom the owner, upon returning, finds busy! ⁴⁴ The truth is, the owner will put the steward in charge of the entire estate. ⁴⁵ But let's say the steward thinks, 'The owner is slow in returning' and begins to abuse the other staff members, eating and drinking and getting drunk. ⁴⁶ When the owner returns unexpectedly, the steward will be punished severely and ranked among those undeserving of trust.

⁴⁷ "The staff members who knew the owner's wishes but didn't work to fulfill them will get a severe punishment, ⁴⁸ whereas the one who didn't know them—even though deserving of a severe punishment—will get off with a milder correction. From those who have been given much, much will be required; from those who have been entrusted much, much more will be asked.

⁴⁹ "I've come to light a fire on the earth. How I wish the blaze were ignited already! ⁵⁰ There is a baptism I must still receive, and how great is my distress until it is accomplished!

⁵¹ "Do you think I'm here to bring peace on earth? I tell you, the opposite is true: I've come to bring division. ⁵² From now on a household of five will be divided—three against two and two against three, ⁵³ father against son, son against father, mother against daughter, daughter against mother, mother-in-law against daughter-in-law, daughter-in-law against mother-in-law."

⁵⁴ Jesus said again to the crowds, "When you see a cloud rising in the west, you immediately say that rain is coming—and so it does. ⁵⁵ When the wind blows from the south, you say it's going to be hot—and so it is. ⁵⁶ You hypocrites! If you can interpret the portents of earth and sky, why can't you interpret the present time?

⁵⁷ "Tell me, why don't you judge for yourselves what is just? ⁵⁸ When you're going with your opponent to appear before a magistrate, try to settle with your antagonist on the way, lest you be turned over to the judge, and the judge deliver you to the bailiff, and the bailiff throw you into prison. ⁵⁹ I tell you, you won't be released until you've paid your opponent in full—to the last penny."

13:1 On the same occasion, there were people present who told Jesus about some Galileans whose blood Pilate had mixed with their own sacrifices.

² Jesus replied, "Do you think these Galileans were the greatest sinners in Galilee just because they suffered this? ³ Not at all! I tell you, you'll all come to the same end unless you change your ways. ⁴ Or take those eighteen who were killed by a falling tower in Siloam. Do you think they were

more guilty than anyone else who has lived in Jerusalem? [5]Certainly not! I tell you, you'll all come to the same end unless you change your ways."

[6]Jesus told this parable: "There was a fig tree growing in a vineyard. [7]The owner came out looking for fruit on it, but didn't find any. The owner said to the vine dresser, 'Look here! For three years now I've come out in search of fruit on this fig tree and have found none. Cut it down. Why should it clutter up the ground?'

[8]"In reply, the vine dresser said, 'Please leave it one more year while I hoe around it and fertilize it. [9]If it bears fruit next year, fine; if not, then let it be cut down.' "

ભ   ભ   ભ

[10]One Sabbath, Jesus was teaching in one of the synagogues. [11]There was a woman there who for eighteen years had a sickness caused by a spirit. She was bent double, quite incapable of standing up straight.

[12]When Jesus saw her, he called her over and said, "Woman, you are free of your infirmity." [13]He laid his hands on her, and immediately she stood up straight and began thanking God.

[14]The head of the synagogue, indignant that Jesus had healed on the Sabbath, said to the congregation, "There are six days for working. Come on those days to be healed, not on the Sabbath."

[15]Jesus said in reply, "You hypocrites! Which of you doesn't let your ox or your donkey out of the stall on the Sabbath to water it? [16]This daughter of Sarah and Abraham has been in the bondage of Satan for eighteen years. Shouldn't she have been released from her shackles on the Sabbath?" [17]At these words, Jesus' opponents were humiliated; meanwhile, everyone else rejoiced at the marvels Jesus was accomplishing.

[18]Jesus continued, "What does the kindom of God resemble? To what will I liken it? [19]It's like a mustard seed which a gardener took and planted in the garden. It grew and became a large shrub, and the birds of the air nested in its branches."

[20]Then he went on, "To what will I compare the kindom of God? [21]It's like the yeast which a baker added to three measures of flour and kneaded until the whole ball of dough began to rise."

ભ   ભ   ભ

[22]Jesus went through cities and towns teaching, all the while making his way to Jerusalem.

²³ Someone asked, "Will only a few people be saved?"

Jesus replied: ²⁴ "Try to come in through the narrow door. Many, I tell you, will try to enter and won't succeed. ²⁵ Once the head of the household gets up and locks the door, you may find yourselves standing outside, knocking and saying, 'Please open the door! It's us!' but the answer will come, 'I don't know you or where you come from.' ²⁶ Then you'll begin to say, 'But we ate and drank in your company. You taught in our streets.' ²⁷ But you'll hear, 'I tell you, I don't know where you come from. Get away from me, you evildoers!'

²⁸ "There will be wailing and the grinding of teeth when you see Sarah and Abraham, Rebecca and Isaac, Leah and Rachel and Jacob and all the prophets, safe in the kindom of God, and you yourselves rejected. ²⁹ People will come from the East and the West, from the North and the South, and will take their places at the feast in the kindom of God. ³⁰ Some who are last will be first, and some who are first will be last."

³¹ Just then, some Pharisees came to Jesus and said, "You need to get out of town, and fast. Herod is trying to kill you."

³² Jesus replied, "Go tell that fox, 'Today and tomorrow, I'll be casting out devils and healing people, and on the third day I'll reach my goal.' ³³ Even with all that, I'll need to continue on my journey today, tomorrow and the day after that, since no prophet can be allowed to die anywhere except in Jerusalem.

³⁴ "O Jerusalem, Jerusalem! You kill the prophets and stone those who are sent to you! How often have I wanted to gather your children together as a mother bird collects her babies under her wings—yet you refuse me! ³⁵ So take note: your house will be left to you desolate. I tell you, you will not see me again until you say, 'Blessed is the One who comes in the name of Our God!' "

ભ   ભ   ભ

14:1 One Sabbath, when Jesus came to eat a meal in the house of one of the leading Pharisees, the guests watched him closely. ² Directly in front of Jesus was a person who suffered from edema.

³ Jesus asked the experts on the Law and the Pharisees, "Is it lawful to heal on the Sabbath or not?" ⁴ But they kept silent. With that, Jesus laid hands on the individual and healed the swelling, then sent the person away.

⁵ Jesus said to the guests, "If one of you has a child—or even an ox—and

it falls into a pit, won't you rescue it immediately, even on the Sabbath day?" ⁶They had no answer to this.

⁷Jesus went on to address a parable to the guests, noticing how they were trying to get a place of honor at the table.

⁸"When you're invited to a wedding party, don't sit in the place of honor, in case someone more distinguished has been invited. ⁹Otherwise the hosts might come and say to you, 'Make room for this person,' and you would have to proceed shamefacedly to the lowest place. ¹⁰What you should do is go and sit in the lowest place, so that when your hosts approach you they'll say, 'My friend, come up higher.' This will win you the esteem of the other guests. ¹¹For all who exalt themselves will be humbled, and those who humble themselves will be exalted."

¹²Then Jesus said to the host, "Whenever you give a lunch or dinner, don't invite your friends or colleagues or relatives or wealthy neighbors. They might invite you in return and thus repay you. ¹³No, when you have a reception, invite those who are poor or have physical infirmities or are blind. ¹⁴You should be pleased that they can't repay you, for you'll be repaid at the resurrection of the just."

¹⁵One of the guests heard this and said to Jesus, "Happy are those who eat bread in the kindom of God!"

¹⁶Jesus responded, "A landowner was giving a large dinner and sent out many invitations. ¹⁷At dinnertime, the landowner instructed an aide to say to those invited, 'Come to the feast, everything is ready.' ¹⁸But they began to excuse themselves, each and every one. The first one said to the aide, 'I've just bought some land, and I need to go out and inspect it. Please send my regrets.' ¹⁹Another said, 'I've just bought five yoke of oxen, and I need to go out and test them. Please excuse me.' ²⁰A third said, 'I've just gotten married, so of course I can't come.'

²¹"The aide returned and reported all this to the landowner. The landowner became angry and said to the aide, 'Go into town, into the streets and alleys, and bring in those who are poor or crippled, and those who are blind or lame.' ²²After doing so, the aide reported, 'Your orders have been carried out, and there's still room.' ²³The landowner then said to the aide, 'Go out and scour the side roads and the back roads and make them come in. I want my house to be full! ²⁴But I tell you, not one of those I had initially invited will taste a bite of my dinner.' "

²⁵ Large crowds followed Jesus. He turned to them and said, ²⁶ "If any of you come to me without turning your back on your mother and your father, your loved ones, your sisters and brothers, indeed your very self, you can't be my follower. ²⁷ Anyone who doesn't take up the cross and follow me can't be my disciple.

²⁸ "If one of you were going to build a tower, wouldn't you first sit down and calculate the outlay to see if you have enough money to complete the project? ²⁹ You'd do that for fear of laying the foundation and then not being able to complete the work—because anyone who saw it would jeer at you ³⁰ and say, 'You started a building and couldn't finish it.' ³¹ Or if the leaders of one country were going to declare war on another country, wouldn't they first sit down and consider whether, with an army of ten thousand, they could win against an enemy coming against them with twenty thousand? ³² If they couldn't, they'd send a delegation while the enemy is still at a distance, asking for terms of peace.

³³ "So count the cost. You can't be my disciple if you don't say goodbye to all of your possessions.

³⁴ "Salt is useful, but if it loses its taste, how can it be resalted again? ³⁵ It's fit neither for the soil nor for the compost pile, so it's thrown away. Whoever has ears to hear, hear this."

☙ ☙ ☙

15·¹ Meanwhile, the tax collectors and the "sinners" were all gathering around Jesus to listen to his teaching, ² at which the Pharisees and the religious scholars murmured, "This person welcomes sinners and eats with them!"

³ Jesus then addressed this parable to them: ⁴ "Who among you, having a hundred sheep and losing one of them, doesn't leave the ninety-nine in the open pasture and search for the lost one until it's found? ⁵ And finding it, you put the sheep on your shoulders in jubilation. ⁶ Once home, you invite friends and neighbors in and say to them, 'Rejoice with me! I've found my lost sheep!' ⁷ I tell you, in the same way there will be more joy in heaven over one repentant sinner than over ninety-nine righteous people who have no need to repent.

⁸ "What householder, who has ten silver pieces and loses one, doesn't light a lamp and sweep the house in a diligent search until she finds what she had lost? ⁹ And when it is found, the householder calls in her friends and neighbors and says, 'Rejoice with me! I've found the silver piece I lost!'

¹⁰I tell you, there will be the same kind of joy before the angels of God over one repentant sinner."

¹¹ He added, "A man had two sons. ¹²The younger of them said to their father, 'Give me the share of the estate that is coming to me.' So the father divided up the property between them. ¹³Some days later, the younger son gathered up his belongings and went off to a distant land. Here he squandered all his money on loose living.

¹⁴"After everything was spent, a great famine broke out in the land, and the son was in great need. ¹⁵So he went to a landowner, who sent him to a farm to take care of the pigs. ¹⁶The son was so hungry that he could have eaten the husks that were fodder for the pigs, but no one made a move to give him anything. ¹⁷Coming to his senses at last, he said, 'How many hired hands at my father's house have more than enough to eat, while here I am starving! ¹⁸I'll quit and go back home and say, "I've sinned against God and against you; ¹⁹I no longer deserve to be called one of your children. Treat me like one of your hired hands."' ²⁰With that, the younger son set off for home.

"While still a long way off, the father caught sight of the returning child and was deeply moved. The father ran out to meet him, threw his arms around him and kissed him. ²¹The son said to him, 'I've sinned against God and against you; I no longer deserve to be called one of your children.' ²²But his father said to one of the workers, 'Quick! Bring out the finest robe and put it on him; put a ring on his finger and shoes on his feet. ²³Take the calf we've been fattening and butcher it. Let's eat and celebrate! ²⁴This son of mine was dead and has come back to life. He was lost and now he's found!' And the celebration began.

²⁵"Meanwhile the elder son had been out in the field. As he neared the house, he heard the sound of music and dancing. ²⁶He called one of the workers and asked what was happening. ²⁷The worker answered, 'Your brother is home, and the fatted calf has been killed because your father has him back safe and sound.'

²⁸"The son got angry at this and refused to go in to the party, but his father came out and pleaded with him. ²⁹The older son replied, 'Look! For years now I've done every single thing you asked me to do. I never disobeyed even one of your orders, yet you never gave me so much as a kid goat to celebrate with my friends. ³⁰But then this son of yours comes home after going through your money with prostitutes, and you kill the fatted calf for him!'

³¹" 'But my child!' the father said. 'You're with me always, and everything I have is yours. ³²But we have to celebrate and rejoice! This brother of

yours was dead and has come back to life. He was lost and now he's found.'"

16:1 Jesus said to the disciples, "There was a wealthy landowner who, having received reports of a steward mismanaging the property, 2 summoned the steward and said, 'What's this I hear about you? Give me an account of your service, for it's about to come to an end.' 3 The steward thought, 'What will I do next? My employer is going to fire me. I can't dig ditches. I'm ashamed to go begging. 4 I have it! Here's a way to make sure that people will take me into their homes when I'm let go.'

5 "So the steward called in each of the landowner's debtors. The steward said to the first, 'How much do you owe my employer?' 6 The debtor replied, 'A hundred jars of oil.' The steward said, 'Take your invoice, sit down quickly and make it fifty.' 7 To another the steward said, 'How much do you owe?' The answer came, 'A hundred measures of wheat,' and the steward said, 'Take your invoice and make it eighty.'

8 "Upon hearing this, the owner gave this devious worker credit for being enterprising! Why? Because the children of this world are more astute in dealing with their own kind than are the children of light. 9 So I tell you: make friends for yourselves through your use of this world's goods, so that when they fail you, you'll be welcomed into an eternal home. 10 If you can trust others in little things, you can also trust them in greater, and anyone unjust in a slight matter will also be unjust in a greater. 11 If you can't be trusted with filthy lucre, who will trust you with true riches? 12 And if you haven't been trustworthy with someone else's money, who will give you your own?

13 "Subordinates can't have two superiors. Either they'll hate the one and love the other, or be attentive to the one and despise the other. You can't worship both God and Money."

14 The Pharisees, who were greedy, heard all this and began to deride Jesus. 15 He said to them, "You justify yourselves in the eyes of mortals, but God reads your hearts. What people think is important, God holds in contempt.

16 "Up until the time of John, the Law and the prophets were proclaimed; but since then, the Good News of the kindom of God is taught, and everyone is trying to push their way into it. 17 Yet it's easier for heaven and earth to pass away than for the tiniest part of a letter to drop out of the Law.

¹⁸ "If you divorce your spouse and marry someone else, you're committing adultery. And if you marry someone who is divorced, you're committing adultery.

¹⁹ "Once there was a rich person who dressed in purple and linen and feasted splendidly every day. ²⁰ At the gate of this person's estate lay a beggar named Lazarus, who was covered with sores. ²¹ Lazarus longed to eat the scraps that fell from the rich person's table, and even the dogs came and licked Lazarus' sores. ²² One day poor Lazarus died and was carried by the angels to the arms of Sarah and Abraham. The rich person likewise died and was buried. ²³ In Hades, in torment, the rich person looked up and saw Sarah and Abraham in the distance, and Lazarus resting in their company.

²⁴ " 'Sarah and Abraham,' the rich person cried, 'have pity on me! Send Lazarus to dip the tip of his finger in water and cool off my tongue, for I am tortured by these flames!' ²⁵ But they said, 'My child, remember that you were well off in your lifetime, while Lazarus was in misery. Now Lazarus has found consolation here, and you have found torment. ²⁶ But that's not all. Between you and us there is a fixed chasm, so that those who might wish to come to you from here can't do so, nor can anyone cross from your side to us.'

²⁷ "The rich person said, 'I beg you, then, to send Lazarus to my own house ²⁸ where I have five siblings. Let Lazarus be a warning to them, so that they may not end in this place of torment.' ²⁹ But Sarah and Abraham replied, 'They have Moses and the prophets. Let your siblings hear them.' ³⁰ 'Please, I beg you,' the rich person said, 'if someone would only go to them from the dead, then they would repent.' ³¹ 'If they don't listen to Moses and the prophets,' Sarah and Abraham replied, 'they won't be convinced even if someone should rise from the dead!' "

17:1 Jesus said to the disciples, "Stumbling blocks will inevitably arise, but woe to those through whom stumbling blocks come! ² Those people would be better off thrown into the sea with millstones around their necks, than to make one of these little ones stumble.

³ "Be on your guard. If your sisters or brothers do wrong, correct them; if they repent, forgive them. ⁴ If they sin against you seven times a day, and seven times a day turn back to you saying, 'I'm sorry,' forgive them."

⁵ The apostles said to Jesus, "Increase our faith!"
⁶ Jesus answered, "If you had faith the size of a mustard seed, you could

say to this mulberry tree, 'Uproot yourself and plant yourself in the sea,' and it would obey you.

⁷"If one of you had hired help plowing a field or herding sheep, and they came in from the fields, would you say to them, 'Come and sit at my table?' ⁸Wouldn't you say instead, 'Prepare my supper. Put on your apron and wait on me while I eat and drink. You can eat and drink afterward'? ⁹Would you be grateful to the workers who were just doing their job? ¹⁰It's the same with you who hear me. When you have done all you have been commanded to do, say, 'We are simple workers. We have done no more than our duty.' "

⚜   ⚜   ⚜

¹¹On the journey to Jerusalem, Jesus passed along the borders of Samaria and Galilee. ¹²As Jesus was entering a village, ten people with leprosy met him. Keeping their distance, ¹³they raised their voices and said, "Jesus, Rabbi, have pity on us!"

¹⁴When Jesus saw them, he responded, "Go and show yourselves to the priests."

As they were going, they were healed. ¹⁵One of them, realizing what had happened, came back praising God in a loud voice, ¹⁶then fell down at the feet of Jesus and spoke his praises. The individual was a Samaritan.

¹⁷Jesus replied, "Weren't all ten made whole? Where are the other nine? ¹⁸Was there no one to return and give thanks except this foreigner?" ¹⁹Then Jesus said to the Samaritan, "Stand up and go your way; your faith has saved you."

²⁰The Pharisees asked Jesus when the reign of God would come.

Jesus replied, "The reign of God doesn't come in a visible way. ²¹You can't say, 'See, here it is!' or 'There it is!' No—look: the reign of God is already in your midst."

²²Jesus said to the disciples, "The time will come when you'll long to see one of the days of the Promised One, but you won't see it. ²³People will say, 'You can find the Promised One over here,' or 'Look over there!' But don't leave, and don't follow them. ²⁴No, it will be like the lightning that flashes from one end of the sky to the other, on the day of the Promised One. ²⁵First, however, the Promised One must suffer many things and be rejected by this generation.

²⁶"As it was in the days of Noah, so will it be in the days of the Promised

One. [27] They ate and drank, they took husbands and wives, right up to the day Noah entered the ark—and when the flood came, it destroyed them all. [28] It was the same in the days of Lot: they ate and drank, they bought and sold, built and planted. [29] But on the day Lot left Sodom, fire and brimstone rained down from heaven and destroyed them all.

[30] "It will be like that on the day the Promised One is revealed. [31] On that day, if people are on the rooftop and their belongings are in the house, they shouldn't go down to get them, nor should the farmer in the field turn back— [32] remember Lot's wife! [33] Those who try to save their lives will lose them, and those who lose their lives will save them. [34] I tell you, there will be two people in one bed; one will be taken and the other left. [35] Two millers will be grinding grain together; one will be taken and the other left. [36] Two farmers will be in the field; one will taken and the other left."

[37] The disciples interrupted him. "Where, Teacher?" they asked.

Jesus answered, "Wherever the carcass is, there will the vultures gather."

18[1] Jesus told the disciples a parable on the necessity of praying always and not losing heart: [2] "Once there was a judge in a certain city who feared no one—not even God. [3] A woman in that city who had been widowed kept coming to the judge and saying, 'Give me legal protection from my opponent.' [4] For a time the judge refused, but finally the judge thought, 'I care little for God or people, [5] but this woman won't leave me alone. I'd better give her the protection she seeks, or she'll keep coming and wear me out!' "

[6] Jesus said, "Listen to what this corrupt judge is saying. [7] Won't God then do justice to the chosen who call out day and night? Will God delay long over them? [8] I tell you, God will give them swift justice.

"But when the Promised One comes, will faith be found anywhere on earth?"

[9] Jesus spoke this parable addressed to those who believed in their own self-righteousness while holding everyone else in contempt: [10] "Two people went up to the Temple to pray; one was a Pharisee, the other a tax collector. [11] The Pharisee stood and prayed like this: 'I give you thanks, O God, that I'm not like others—greedy, crooked, adulterous—or even like this tax collector. [12] I fast twice a week. I pay tithes on everything I earn.'

[13] "The other one, however, kept a distance, not even daring to look up to heaven. In real humility, all the tax collector said was, 'O God, be merciful to me, a sinner.' [14] Believe me, the tax collector went home from the Temple right with God, while the Pharisee didn't. For those who exalt themselves will be humbled, while those who humble themselves will be exalted."

¹⁵ People even brought their infants forward for Jesus to touch. When the disciples saw this, they scolded the parents.

¹⁶ However, Jesus intervened by calling the children to himself. He said, "Let the children come to me. Don't stop them, for the kindom of heaven belongs to such as these. ¹⁷ The truth is, whoever doesn't welcome the kindom of God like a child will never enter it."

¹⁸ A young ruler asked him, "Good Teacher, what must I do to inherit eternal life?"

¹⁹ Jesus responded, "Why do you call me good? Only God is good! ²⁰ You know the commandments: 'No adultery. No killing. No stealing. No false testimony. Honor your mother and father.' "

²¹ The wealthy person replied, "I've observed all of these from my youth."

²² When Jesus heard this he said, "There is one thing left for you to do. Sell everything you own and give the money to those poorer than you— and you'll have treasure in heaven. Then come and follow me."

²³ This news was received with a heavy heart, because the ruler was extremely wealthy.

²⁴ Jesus looked at the ruler and said, "How hard it is for those who are wealthy to enter the kindom of God! ²⁵ It's easier for a camel to crawl through the Needle's Eye gate than for the wealthy to enter the kindom of God."

²⁶ Those who heard this said, "Then who can be saved?"

²⁷ Jesus replied, "What is impossible for mortals is possible for God."

²⁸ Then Peter said, "What about us? We have given up everything we own to follow you!"

²⁹ Jesus said, "The truth is, whoever gives up home or spouse or sisters or brothers or parents or children for the kindom of God ³⁰ will receive many times as much in this age, and eternal life in the age to come."

◌ॐ   ◌ॐ   ◌ॐ

³¹ Then Jesus took the Twelve aside and said to them, "Listen: we are going up to Jerusalem, and everything written by the prophets about the Chosen One will come to pass. ³² The Chosen One will be handed over to the Gentiles to be mocked, insulted, spat upon, ³³ beaten and finally killed— but on the third day, the Chosen One will rise again." ³⁴ But the Twelve couldn't make anything of this. The meaning of Jesus' words was hidden from them, and they didn't understand what he was telling them.

³⁵ As Jesus neared Jericho, a blind person sat at the side of the road, begging. ³⁶ Hearing a crowd go by, the beggar asked, "What's that?" ³⁷ They said that Jesus of Nazareth was passing by.

³⁸ The beggar shouted, "Jesus, Heir of David, have pity on me!" ³⁹ Those in the lead sternly ordered the blind beggar to be quiet, but the sufferer shouted all the more, "Heir of David, have pity on me!"

⁴⁰ Jesus stopped and had the blind beggar brought to him. ⁴¹ "What do you want me to do for you?" he asked.

"Rabbi, I want to see."

⁴² Jesus said to the beggar, "Receive your sight. Your faith has healed you."

⁴³ At that very moment, sight was restored to the beggar, who joined the crowd, giving praise to God. All the people witnessed it and they too gave praise to God.

19¹ Entering Jericho, Jesus passed through the city. ² There was a wealthy person there named Zacchaeus, the chief tax collector. ³ Zacchaeus was trying to see who Jesus was, but he couldn't do so because of the crowd, since he was short.

⁴ In order to see Jesus, Zacchaeus ran on ahead, then climbed a sycamore tree that was along the route. ⁵ When Jesus came to the spot, he looked up and said, "Zacchaeus, hurry up and come on down. I'm going to stay at your house today." ⁶ Zacchaeus quickly climbed down and welcomed Jesus with delight.

⁷ When everyone saw this, they began to grumble, "Jesus has gone to a sinner's house as a guest."

⁸ Zacchaeus stood his ground and said to Jesus, "Here and now I give half my belongings to poor people. If I've defrauded anyone in the least, I'll pay them back fourfold."

⁹ Jesus said to the tax collector, "Today salvation has come to this house, for this is what it means to be a descendant of Sarah and Abraham. ¹⁰ The Promised One has come to search out and save what was lost."

¹¹ While the crowd was listening, Jesus went on to tell a parable, because he was near Jerusalem where they thought the reign of God was about to appear. ¹² Jesus said:

"A member of the nobility went to a faraway country to become its ruler for a time. ¹³ Before leaving, the noble summoned ten overseers and gave them each ten minas—about three years' wages—and said to them, 'Invest this until I return.' ¹⁴ But the noble's new subjects rebelled and immediately sent a delegation with the message, 'We won't have you ruling over us!' ¹⁵ So the noble returned home, even though fully authorized to rule.

"The noble sent for the overseers to whom the money had been given, to learn what profit each had made. ¹⁶The first came and said, 'The sum you gave me was doubled for you.' ¹⁷'Well done,' the noble replied. 'You showed yourself capable in a small matter. For that you can govern ten cities.' ¹⁸The second came and said, 'Your investment has netted half again as much.' ¹⁹The noble said, 'Then you'll govern five cities.' ²⁰The third came in and said, 'Here's your money; I hid it for safekeeping. ²¹You see, I was afraid of you because you are notoriously exacting. You withdraw what you never deposited. You reap what you never sowed.'

²²"The noble replied, 'You worthless lout! I intend to judge you on your own evidence. So, you knew I was exacting, withdrawing what I never deposited, reaping what I never sowed? ²³Why, then, didn't you put the money on deposit with the moneylenders, so that upon my return I could get it back with interest?' ²⁴The noble said to those standing around, 'Take the money from this one and give it to the one who had the ten minas.' ²⁵'Yes, but that overseer already has ten,' they replied. ²⁶The noble responded, 'I tell you, whoever has will be given more, but those who don't have will lose the little they have. ²⁷Now, about those enemies of mine who didn't want me to be their ruler: bring them in, and kill them in my presence.' "

19:28–22:6

having said this, Jesus went ahead with the ascent to Jerusalem.

²⁹Approaching Bethphage and Bethany, near what is called the Mount of Olives, Jesus sent two of the disciples with these instructions: ³⁰"Go into the village ahead of you. Upon entering it, you'll find a tethered colt that no one has yet ridden. Untie it and lead it back. ³¹If anyone should ask you, 'Why are you untying it?' say, 'The Rabbi needs it.' "

³²They departed on their errand and found things just as Jesus had said. ³³As they untied the colt, its owners said to them, "Why are you doing that?"

³⁴They explained that the Rabbi needed it. ³⁵Then the disciples led the animal to Jesus and, laying their cloaks on it, helped him mount.

³⁶People spread their cloaks on the roadway as Jesus rode along. ³⁷As they reached the descent from the Mount of Olives, the entire crowd of disciples joined them and began to rejoice and praise God loudly for the display of power they had seen, saying,

³⁸"Blessed is the One who comes in the name of Our God!
Peace in heaven, and glory in the highest!"

[39]Some of the Pharisees in the crowd said to Jesus, "Teacher, rebuke your disciples!"

[40]Jesus replied, "I tell you, if they were to keep silent, the very stones would cry out!"

[41]Coming within sight of Jerusalem, Jesus wept over it [42]and said, "If only you had known the path to peace today! But now it has been hidden from your eyes. [43]Days will come upon you when your enemies will encircle you with a rampart, hem you in and press you hard from every side. [44]They'll wipe you out, you and your children within your walls, and won't leave one stone on top of another within you, because you failed to recognize the time of your visit from God."

[45]Then Jesus entered the Temple and began throwing out the vendors, [46]saying, "Scripture says, 'My Temple will be a house of prayer'—but you have made it a den of thieves!"

ॐ   ॐ   ॐ

[47]Jesus was teaching in the Temple area every day. Meanwhile, the chief priests and religious scholars were looking for a way to destroy him, as were the leaders of the people, [48]but they had no idea how to achieve it—the entire population was listening and hanging onto his every word.

20[1]One day as Jesus was teaching the people in the Temple and proclaiming the Good News, the chief priests and the religious scholars, together with the elders, approached him [2]and said, "Tell us by what authority you are doing these things. Who authorized you?"

[3]Jesus replied, "And I'll ask you a question. [4]John's baptism—did it come from heaven, or from mortals?"

[5]They discussed the question among themselves and concluded, "If we answer 'from heaven,' he'll ask, 'Then why didn't you believe him?' [6]But if we answer 'from mortals,' all the people will stone us, for they believe that John was a prophet." [7]So they said they didn't know where it came from.

[8]Jesus said, "Then I won't tell you by what authority I do these things."

[9]Then Jesus went on to tell the people this parable: "A landowner planted a vineyard, leased it to several farmers and left for a long journey. [10]When the time came, a worker was sent to the farmers to collect the landowner's share of the harvest. The farmers drove the worker off with a beating. [11]So

the landowner sent a second worker, who likewise was beaten and driven off emptyhanded. ¹²A third was beaten, and sent packing with none of the harvest.

¹³"The owner of the vineyard said, 'What will I do? I'll send my firstborn, whom I love; maybe that will get their respect.' ¹⁴But when the tenants learned of this, they conspired to kill the heir in order to gain control of the inheritance. ¹⁵So they murdered the firstborn outside the vineyard.

"What will the landowner do to them? ¹⁶The owner will come and execute those tenants and turn the vineyard over to others."

When the people heard this, they said, "God forbid!"

¹⁷But Jesus stared at them and said, "Then tell me what the scripture means when it says,

> 'The stone which the builders rejected
> became the cornerstone.'

¹⁸"All who fall on that stone will be dashed to pieces, and all those upon whom it falls will be scattered like powder."

¹⁹The religious scholars and the chief priests tried to lay hands on him that very hour, for they understood the parable to be about them. But they feared the people. ²⁰So they bided their time by sending spies, who pretended to be righteous in order to entrap Jesus by something he said. Then they would turn him over to the power and authority of the governor.

²¹So the spies asked him, "Rabbi, we know that what you say and teach is right. You show no partiality; you teach the way of God truthfully. ²²Is it proper for us to pay tribute to Caesar or not?"

²³Jesus saw through their deceitfulness and said, ²⁴"Show me a denarius. Whose picture and name are on it?"

They said, "Caesar's."

²⁵He said, "Then give to Caesar what belongs to Caesar. Give to God what is God's."

²⁶They were unable to find fault with his public statements. And they were so in awe of his answer that they fell silent.

²⁷Some Sadducees—the ones who claim there is no resurrection—came forward to pose this question: ²⁸"Teacher, Moses wrote that if a man's brother dies leaving a wife and no child, the brother should marry the woman now widowed, to raise up children with her. ²⁹Let's say that there were seven brothers. The first one married and died childless. ³⁰The second brother then married the woman, ³¹then the third, and so on. All seven died without leaving her any children. ³²Finally the woman herself died. ³³At the resurrection, who will be her husband? Remember, seven married her."

³⁴Jesus said to them, "The children of this age marry each other, ³⁵but those judged worthy of a place in the age to come and of the resurrection from the dead don't take husbands or wives. ³⁶They can no longer die, like the angels—they are children of God, since they are children of the resurrection. ³⁷That the dead rise again was even demonstrated by Moses when, in the passage about the bush, he called the Most High 'the God of Sarah and Abraham, and the God of Rebecca and Isaac, and the God of Leah and Rachel and Jacob.' ³⁸God is not the God of the dead, but of the living. All are alive to God."

³⁹Some of the religious scholars responded, "Well said, Teacher." ⁴⁰They didn't dare ask Jesus anything else.

⁴¹Then he said to them, "How can they say that the Messiah is the descendant of David? ⁴²For David himself says in the Book of Psalms,

'The Most High said to my Sovereign,
    "Sit at my right hand
⁴³until I place your enemies
        under your foot." '

⁴⁴"Now, if David calls the Messiah 'Sovereign,' how can the Messiah also be David's descendant?"

⁴⁵While all the people were listening, Jesus said to the disciples, ⁴⁶"Beware of the religious scholars, who love to go about in long robes and be greeted deferentially in the marketplace. They take the front seats in the synagogue and places of honor at banquets. ⁴⁷They swallow up the property of women who are widowed and make a show of offering lengthy prayers. People like them will be severely punished."

21¹Jesus looked up and saw rich people putting their offerings into the Temple treasury, ²and then he noticed an impoverished woman, a widow, putting in two copper coins. ³At that he said, "The truth is, this woman has put in more than all the rest. ⁴They made contributions out of their surplus, but she from her want has given what she couldn't afford—every penny she had to live on."

⁵Some disciples were speaking of how the Temple was adorned with precious stones and votive offerings. Jesus said, ⁶"You see all these things? The day will come when one stone won't be left on top of another—everything will be torn down."

⁷They asked, "When will this happen, Rabbi? And what will be the sign that it's about to happen?"

⁸Jesus said, "Take care not to be misled. Many will come in my name, saying, 'I am the One' and 'The time is at hand.' Don't follow them. ⁹And

don't be perturbed when you hear of wars and insurrections. These things must happen first, but the end doesn't follow immediately."

¹⁰ Then he said to them, "Nation will rise against nation, and empire against empire. ¹¹ There will be great earthquakes, plagues and famines in various places—and in the sky there will be frightening omens and great signs. ¹² But before any of this, they'll arrest you and persecute you, bringing you before synagogues and sending you to prison, bringing you to trial before rulers and governors. And it will all be because of my name— ¹³ this will be your opportunity to give your testimony. ¹⁴ So make up your minds not to worry about your defense beforehand, ¹⁵ for I'll give you the words, and a wisdom that none of your adversaries can take exception to or contradict. ¹⁶ You'll be betrayed even by your parents, brothers, sisters, relatives and friends, and some of you will be put to death. ¹⁷ Everyone will hate you because of me, ¹⁸ yet not a hair of your head will be harmed. ¹⁹ By patient endurance, you'll save your lives.

²⁰ "When you see Jerusalem encircled by soldiers, know that its devastation is near. ²¹ If you're in Judea at that time, flee to the mountains; if you're in the heart of the city, escape it; if you're in the country, don't go back to the city. ²² These indeed will be the days of retribution, when all that is written must be fulfilled.

²³ "Women who are pregnant or nursing will fare badly in those days! The distress in the land and the wrath against this people will be great. ²⁴ The people will fall to the sword; they'll be led captive into the lands of the Gentiles. Jerusalem will be trampled by the Gentiles, until the times of the Gentiles are fulfilled.

²⁵ "Signs will appear in the sun, the moon and the stars. On the earth, nations will be in anguish, distraught at the roaring of the sea and the waves. ²⁶ People will die of fright in anticipation of what is coming upon the earth. The powers in the heavens will be shaken. ²⁷ After that, people will see the Chosen One coming on a cloud with great power and glory. ²⁸ When these things begin to happen, stand up straight and raise your heads, because your ransom is near at hand."

²⁹ And he told them a parable: "Look at the fig tree, or any other tree. ³⁰ You see when they're budding and know that summer is near. ³¹ In the same way, when you see all these things happening, know that the reign of God is near. ³² The truth is, this generation will not pass away until all this takes place. ³³ The heavens and the earth will pass away, but my words will not pass away.

³⁴ "Be on your guard lest your spirits become bloated with indulgence, drunkenness and worldly cares. That day will suddenly close in on you like a trap. ³⁵ It will come upon all who dwell on the face of the earth, so be

on your watch. ³⁶Pray constantly for the strength to escape whatever comes, and to stand secure before the Chosen One."

³⁷Jesus taught in the Temple during the days, and he spent the nights on the hill called the Mount of Olives. ³⁸And all the people came to the Temple early each morning to hear him.

ℭℜ   ℭℜ   ℭℜ

22:1 Now the Feast of the Unleavened Bread, also known as Passover, drew near, ²and the chief priests and the religious scholars sought a way to kill Jesus, for they feared the people.

³Then Satan took possession of Judas, who was called Iscariot, one of the Twelve. ⁴He went to the chief priests and the Temple guards to discuss with them how he might betray Jesus. ⁵They were delighted and agreed to give him money. ⁶Judas accepted, then began to look for the opportune moment to hand Jesus over to them—when people were not present.

22:7–23:53

When the day of the Feast of the Unleavened Bread arrived, when the Passover lamb was to be sacrificed, ⁸Jesus sent Peter and John out with the instructions, "Go and make the preparations for us to eat the Passover."

⁹They asked, "Where do you want us to prepare the seder?"

¹⁰Jesus answered, "When you enter the city, a man will meet you carrying a jar of water. Follow him into the house he enters. ¹¹Say to the owner of the house, 'The Rabbi asks, "Where is the guest room where I can eat the Passover seder with my disciples?" ' ¹²The owner will show you a large furnished upper room. Make the preparations there."

¹³They went out and found everything as Jesus had told them. And they prepared the Passover.

¹⁴When the hour had come, Jesus took a place at the table with the apostles. ¹⁵Jesus said to them, "I've longed to eat this Passover with you before I suffer. ¹⁶I tell you, I will not eat it again until everything is fulfilled in the reign of God." ¹⁷Then taking a cup of wine, Jesus gave thanks and said, "Take this and share it among you. ¹⁸I tell you, I will not drink wine from now on, until the reign of God comes." ¹⁹Then Jesus took bread and gave thanks for it, broke it, and gave it to them, saying, "This is my body, which will be given for you. Do this in remembrance of me." ²⁰Jesus did

the same with the cup after supper and said, "This cup is the New Covenant in my blood, which will be poured out for you.

²¹ "Look! The hand of my betrayer is at this table with me. ²² The Chosen One is following the appointed course. But woe to the person by whom that One is betrayed!" ²³ Then they began to argue among themselves as to which of them would do such a deed.

²⁴ Another dispute arose among them about who would be regarded as the greatest. ²⁵ But Jesus said to them, "Earthly rulers domineer over their people. Those who exercise authority over them are called their 'benefactors.' ²⁶ This must not happen with you. Let the greatest among you be like the youngest. Let the leader among you become the follower. ²⁷ For who is the greater? The one who reclines at a meal, or the one who serves it? Isn't it the one reclining at table? Yet here I am among you as the one who serves you.

²⁸ "You are the ones who have stood by me faithfully in trials. ²⁹ Just as God has given me dominion, so I give it to you. ³⁰ In my reign, you will eat and drink at my table, and you'll sit on thrones judging the twelve tribes of Israel.

³¹ "Simon, Simon! Satan has demanded that you be sifted like wheat. ³² But I've prayed for you, that your faith may not fail. You, in turn, must give strength to your sisters and brothers."

³³ "Rabbi," Peter answered, "with you I'm prepared to face imprisonment and even death!"

³⁴ Jesus responded, "I tell you, Peter, before the rooster crows today you'll have denied three times that you know me."

³⁵ Jesus said to them, "When I sent you off without purse, traveling bag or sandals, were you in need of anything?"

"No, nothing!" they replied.

³⁶ He said, "Now, however, the one who has a purse had better carry it; the same with a travelling bag. And if they don't have a sword, they should sell their cloaks and buy one! ³⁷ For I tell you, what was written in scripture must be fulfilled in me: 'The suffering servant was counted among criminals'—for whatever refers to me must be fulfilled."

³⁸ And they said, "Look, Rabbi, here are two swords!"

Jesus answered, "That is enough."

ଔ   ଔ   ଔ

³⁹ Then Jesus went out and made his way as usual to the Mount of Olives; the disciples accompanied him. ⁴⁰ When they reached the place, Jesus said to them, "Pray that you not be put to the test."

⁴¹ Then Jesus withdrew about a stone's throw from them, knelt down and prayed, ⁴² "Abba, if it's your will, take this cup from me; yet not my will but yours be done."*

⁴⁵ When Jesus rose from prayer, he came to the disciples and found them sleeping, exhausted with grief. ⁴⁶ He said to them, "Why do you sleep? Wake up, and pray that you not be subjected to the trial."

⁴⁷ While Jesus was still speaking, a crowd suddenly appeared with Judas, one of the Twelve, at their head. Judas came over to Jesus to embrace him, ⁴⁸ but Jesus said, "Judas, are you betraying the Chosen One with a kiss?"

⁴⁹ Those who were around Jesus, realizing what was going to happen, said, "Rabbi, should we strike them with our swords?" ⁵⁰ One of them struck the attendant of the high priest, cutting off an ear.

⁵¹ But Jesus said, "Stop! No more of this!" Then Jesus touched the attendant's ear and healed it.

⁵² But to those who had come out against him—the chief priests, the chiefs of the Temple Guard and the elders—Jesus said, "Why do you come out with swords and clubs as if I were a robber? ⁵³ I was with you in the Temple every day, and you could have laid hands on me any time you wanted. But this is your hour—the triumph of darkness!"

℘   ℘   ℘

⁵⁴ They arrested Jesus and led him away, arriving at the house of the high priest. Peter followed at a distance ⁵⁵ and sat down in the midst of those who had kindled a fire in the courtyard and were sitting around it. ⁵⁶ One of the high priest's attendants saw him sitting there at the fire, and she stared at him and said, "This one was with Jesus, too."

⁵⁷ But Peter denied it. "I don't know him!" he said.

⁵⁸ A little later, someone else noticed Peter and remarked, "You're one of them too!"

But Peter said, "No, I'm not."

⁵⁹ About an hour later, someone else insisted, "Surely this fellow was with them, too. He even talks like a Galilean."

⁶⁰ "I don't even know what you are talking about!" Peter said.

Just then, as Peter was still speaking, a rooster crowed. ⁶¹ Jesus turned and looked at Peter. Then Peter remembered Jesus saying, "Before a rooster crows today, you'll deny me three times." ⁶² Peter went out and wept bitterly.

---

* Later manuscripts add: ⁴³ *An angel then appeared to Jesus from heaven to strengthen him.* ⁴⁴ *In anguish, Jesus prayed all the more fervently, and sweat, like drops of blood, fell to the ground.*

⁶³ Meanwhile, those who held Jesus in custody were amusing themselves at his expense. ⁶⁴ They blindfolded and slapped him, and then taunted him. "Play the prophet! Which one struck you?" they mocked. ⁶⁵ And they hurled many other insults at him.

⁶⁶ At daybreak the Sanhedrin—which was made up of the elders of the people, the chief priests and the religious scholars—assembled again. Once they had brought Jesus before the council, ⁶⁷ they said, "Tell us, are you the Messiah?"

Jesus replied, "If I tell you, you'll not believe me. ⁶⁸ And if I question you, you won't answer! ⁶⁹ But from now on, the Chosen One will have a seat at the right hand of the Power of God."

⁷⁰ Then all of them said, "So you are God's Own?"

Jesus answered, "Your own words have said it!"

⁷¹ "What need do we have of witnesses?" they said. "We have heard it from his own mouth!"

23:1 Then the whole assembly arose and led Jesus to Pilate. ² They began to accuse Jesus by saying, "We found this one subverting our nation, opposing the payment of taxes to Caesar and even claiming to be Messiah, a king."

³ Then Pilate questioned Jesus: "Are you the King of the Jews?"

"You have said it." Jesus answered.

⁴ Then Pilate reported to the chief priests and the crowds: "I find no guilt in him!"

⁵ But they insisted, "He stirs up the people wherever he teaches, through the whole of Judea, from Galilee to Jerusalem."

⁶ On hearing this, Pilate asked whether Jesus was a Galilean, ⁷ and learning that Jesus was from Herod's jurisdiction, sent Jesus off to Herod, who was also in Jerusalem at this time.

⁸ Now, at the sight of Jesus, Herod was very pleased. From the reports he had heard about Jesus, he had wanted for a long time to see him. Herod hoped to see Jesus perform some miracle.

⁹ Herod questioned him at great length, but Jesus wouldn't answer. ¹⁰ The chief priests and religious scholars stood there, accusing Jesus vehemently. ¹¹ So Herod and the soldiers treated Jesus with contempt and ridicule, put a magnificent robe upon him and sent him back to Pilate. ¹² Herod and Pilate, who had previously been set against each other, became friends that day.

¹³ Pilate then called together the chief priests, the ruling class and the

people, ¹⁴ and said to them, "You have brought this person before me as someone who incites people to rebellion. I have examined him in your presence and have found no basis for any charge against him arising from your allegations. ¹⁵ Neither has Herod, for Jesus has been sent back to us. Obviously, he has done nothing to deserve death. ¹⁶ Therefore, I will punish Jesus, but then I will release him."

¹⁷ Pilate was obligated to release one prisoner to the people at festival time. ¹⁸ The whole crowd cried out as one, "Take him away! We want Barabbas!" ¹⁹ Barabbas had been imprisoned for starting a riot in the city, and for murder.

²⁰ Pilate wanted to release Jesus, so he addressed them again. ²¹ But they shouted back, "Crucify him, crucify him!"

²² Yet a third time, Pilate spoke to the crowd, "What wrong has this Jesus done? I've found nothing that calls for death! Therefore, I'll have him flogged, and then I'll release him."

²³ But they demanded that Jesus be crucified, and their shouts increased in volume. ²⁴ Pilate decided that their demands should be met. ²⁵ So he released Barabbas, the one who had been imprisoned for rioting and murder, and Jesus was handed over to the crowd.

ଓ   ଓ   ଓ

²⁶ As they led Jesus away, they seized Simon—a Cyrenean who was just coming in from the fields—and forced him to carry the cross behind Jesus.

²⁷ A large crowd was following, many of them women who were beating their breasts and wailing for him. ²⁸ At one point, Jesus turned to these women and said, "Daughters of Jerusalem, don't weep for me! Weep rather for yourselves and for your children! ²⁹ The time is coming when it will be said, 'Blessed are the childless, the wombs that have never given birth and the breasts that have never nursed.' ³⁰ Then people will say to the mountains, 'Fall on us!' and to the hills, 'Cover us up!' ³¹ For if they do these things when the wood is green, what will happen when it is dry?"

³² Two others were also led off with Jesus, criminals who were to be put to death. ³³ When they had reached the place called The Skull, they crucified Jesus there—together with the criminals, one on his right and one on his left. ³⁴ And Jesus said, "Abba forgive them. They don't know what they are doing." Then they divided his garments, rolling dice for them.

³⁵ The people stood there watching. The rulers, however, jeered him and said, "He saved others, let him save himself—if he really is the Messiah of God, the Chosen One!" ³⁶ The soldiers also mocked him. They served Jesus sour wine ³⁷ and said, "If you are really the King of the Jews, save your-

self!" ³⁸ There was an inscription above Jesus that read, "This is the King of the Jews."

³⁹ One of the criminals who hung there beside him insulted Jesus, too, saying, "Are you really the Messiah? Then save yourself—and us!"

⁴⁰ But the other answered the first with a rebuke: "Don't you even fear God? ⁴¹ We are only paying the price for what we have done, but this one has done nothing wrong!"

⁴² Then he said, "Jesus, remember me when you come into your glory."

⁴³ Jesus replied, "The truth is, today you'll be with me in paradise!"

⁴⁴ It was about noon, and darkness fell on the whole land until three in the afternoon, ⁴⁵ because of an eclipse of the sun. Then the curtain in the sanctuary was torn in two, ⁴⁶ and Jesus uttered a loud cry and said, "Abba, into your hands I commit my spirit."

Saying this, Jesus breathed for the last time.

⁴⁷ The centurion who saw this glorified God, saying, "Surely this one was innocent." ⁴⁸ When the crowds that had gathered for the spectacle saw what had happened, they returned home beating their breasts and weeping. ⁴⁹ All the acquaintances of Jesus and the women who had come with him from Galilee stood at a distance, looking on.

ℭ   ℭ   ℭ

⁵⁰ There was a member of the Sanhedrin named Joseph, ⁵¹ who had not consented to their action. Joseph was from Arimathea and lived in anticipation of the reign of God. ⁵² He approached Pilate and asked for the body of Jesus. ⁵³ Joseph took the body down, wrapped it in fine linen and laid it in a tomb cut out of rock, where no one had yet been laid. ⁵⁴ It was Preparation Day, and the Sabbath was about to begin.

⁵⁵ The women who accompanied Jesus from Galilee followed Joseph, saw the tomb and watched as the body was placed in it. ⁵⁶ Then they went home to prepare the spices and ointments. But they rested on the Sabbath, according to the Law.

24:1-53

On the first day of the week, at the first sign of dawn, the women came to the tomb bringing the spices they had prepared. ² They found the stone rolled back from the tomb; ³ but when they entered the tomb, they didn't find the body of Jesus.

⁴ While they were still at a loss over what to think of this, two figures in dazzling garments stood beside them. ⁵ Terrified, the women bowed to the ground. The two said to them, "Why do you search for the Living One among the dead? ⁶ Jesus is not here; Christ has risen. Remember what Jesus said to you while still in Galilee—⁷ that the Chosen One must be delivered into the hands of sinners and be crucified, and on the third day would rise again." ⁸ With this reminder, the words of Jesus came back to them.

⁹ When they had returned from the tomb, they told all these things to the Eleven and the others. ¹⁰ The women were Mary of Magdala, Joanna, and Mary the mother of James. The other women with them also told the apostles, ¹¹ but the story seemed like nonsense and they refused to believe them. ¹² Peter, however, got up and ran to the tomb. He stooped down, but he could see nothing but the wrappings. So he went away, full of amazement at what had occurred.

¹³ That same day, two of the disciples were making their way to a village called Emmaus—which was about seven miles from Jerusalem—¹⁴ discussing all that had happened as they went.

¹⁵ While they were discussing these things, Jesus approached and began to walk along with them, ¹⁶ though they were kept from recognizing Jesus, ¹⁷ who asked them, "What are you two discussing as you go your way?"

They stopped and looked sad. ¹⁸ One of them, Cleopas by name, asked him, "Are you the only one visiting Jerusalem who doesn't know the things that have happened these past few days?"

¹⁹ Jesus said to them, "What things?"

They said, "About Jesus of Nazareth, a prophet powerful in word and deed in the eyes of God and all the people—²⁰ how our chief priests and leaders delivered him up to be condemned to death and crucified him. ²¹ We were hoping that he was the One who would set Israel free. Besides all this, today—the third day since these things happened—²² some women of our group have just brought us some astonishing news. They were at the tomb before dawn ²³ and didn't find the body; they returned and informed us that they had seen a vision of angels, who declared that Jesus was alive. ²⁴ Some of our number went to the tomb and found it to be just as the women said, but they didn't find Jesus."

²⁵ Then Jesus said to them, "What little sense you have! How slow you are to believe all that the prophets have announced! ²⁶ Didn't the Messiah have to undergo all this to enter into glory?" ²⁷ Then beginning with Moses and all the prophets, Jesus interpreted for them every passage of scripture which referred to the Messiah. ²⁸ By now they were near the village they

were going to, and Jesus appeared to be going further. ²⁹ But they said eagerly, "Stay with us. It's nearly evening—the day is practically over." So the savior went in and stayed with them.

³⁰ After sitting down with them to eat, Jesus took bread, said the blessing, then broke the bread and began to distribute it to them. ³¹ With that their eyes were opened and they recognized Jesus, who immediately vanished from their sight.

³² They said to one another, "Weren't our hearts burning inside us as this one talked to us on the road and explained the scriptures to us?" ³³ They got up immediately and returned to Jerusalem, where they found the Eleven and the rest of the company assembled. ³⁴ They were greeted with, "Christ has risen! It's true! Jesus has appeared to Simon!" ³⁵ Then the travelers recounted what had happened on the road, and how they had come to know Jesus in the breaking of the bread.

³⁶ While they were still talking about this, Jesus actually stood in their midst and said to them, "Peace be with you."

³⁷ In their panic and fright, they thought they were seeing a ghost. ³⁸ Jesus said to them, "Why are you disturbed? Why do such ideas cross your mind? ³⁹ Look at my hands and my feet; it is I, really. Touch me and see—a ghost doesn't have flesh and bones as I do." ⁴⁰ After saying this, Jesus showed them the wounds.

⁴¹ They were still incredulous for sheer joy and wonder, so Jesus said to them, "Do you have anything here to eat?" ⁴² After being given a piece of cooked fish, ⁴³ the savior ate in their presence.

⁴⁴ Then Jesus said to them, "Remember the words I spoke when I was still with you: everything written about me in the Law of Moses and the Prophets and the psalms had to be fulfilled."

⁴⁵ Then Jesus opened their minds to the understanding of the scriptures, ⁴⁶ saying, "That is why the scriptures say that the Messiah must suffer and rise from the dead on the third day. ⁴⁷ In the Messiah's name, repentance for the forgiveness of sins will be preached to all nations, beginning at Jerusalem. ⁴⁸ You are witnesses of all this.

⁴⁹ "Take note: I am sending forth what Abba God has promised to you. Remain here in the city until you are clothed with the power from on high."

⁵⁰ Then Jesus took them to the outskirts of Bethany, and with upraised hands blessed the disciples. ⁵¹ While blessing them, the savior left them and was carried up to heaven. ⁵² The disciples worshiped the risen Christ and returned to Jerusalem full of joy. ⁵³ They were found in the Temple constantly, speaking the praises of God.

the gospel according to
john

Ín the beginning
   there was the Word;
the Word was in God's presence,
   and the Word was God.
[2] The Word was present to God
   from the beginning.
[3] Through the Word
   all things came into being,
and apart from the Word
   nothing came into being
   that has come into being.
[4] In the Word was life,
   and that life was humanity's light—
[5] a Light that shines in the darkness,
   a Light that the darkness has never overtaken.

[6] Then came one named John, sent as an envoy from God, [7] who came as a witness to testify about the Light, so that through his testimony every-

one might believe.[8] He himself wasn't the Light; he only came to testify about the Light—the true Light that illumines all humankind.

[9] The Word was coming into the world—
[10] was in the world—
   and though the world was made through the Word,
   the world didn't recognize it.
[11] Though the Word came to its own realm,
   the Word's own people didn't accept it.
[12] Yet any who did accept the Word,
   who believed in that Name,
   were empowered to become children of God—
[13] children born not of natural descent,
   nor urge of flesh
   nor human will—
but born of God.
[14] And the Word became flesh
   and stayed for a little while among us;
we saw the Word's glory—
   the favor and position a parent gives an only child—
filled with grace,
   filled with truth.

[15] John testified by proclaiming, "This is the one I was talking about when I said, 'The one who comes after me ranks ahead of me, for this One existed before I did.' "

[16] Of this One's fullness
   we've all had a share—
   gift on top of gift.
[17] For while the Law was given through Moses,
   the Gift—and the Truth—came through Jesus Christ.
[18] No one has ever seen God;
   it is the Only Begotten,
ever at Abba's side,
   who has revealed God to us.

[19] Now the Temple authorities sent emissaries from Jerusalem—priests and Levites—to talk to John. "Who are you?" they asked.

This is John's testimony: [20] he didn't refuse to answer, but freely admitted, "I am not the Messiah."

[21] "Who are you, then?" they asked. "Elijah?"

"No, I am not," he answered.

"Are you the Prophet?"

"No," he replied.

²²Finally they said to him, "Who are you? Give us an answer to take back to those who sent us. What do you have to say for yourself?"

²³John said, "I am, as Isaiah prophesied, the voice of someone crying out in the wilderness, 'Make straight Our God's road!' "

²⁴The emissaries were members of the Pharisee sect. ²⁵They questioned him further: "If you're not the Messiah or Elijah or the Prophet, then why are you baptizing people?"

²⁶John said, "I baptize with water because among you stands someone whom you don't recognize—²⁷the One who is to come after me—the strap of whose sandal I am not worthy even to untie."

²⁸This occurred in Bethany, across the Jordan River, where John was baptizing.

²⁹The next day, catching sight of Jesus approaching, John exclaimed, "Look, there's God's sacrificial lamb, who takes away the world's sin! ³⁰This is the one I was talking about when I said, 'The one who comes after me ranks ahead of me, for this One existed before I did.' ³¹I didn't recognize him, but it was so that he would be revealed to Israel that I came baptizing with water."

³²John also gave this testimony: "I saw the Spirit descend from heaven like a dove, and she came to rest on him. ³³I didn't recognize him, but the One who sent me to baptize with water told me, 'When you see the Spirit descend and rest on someone, that is the One who will baptize with the Holy Spirit.' ³⁴Now I have seen for myself and have testified that this is the Only Begotten of God."

³⁵The next day, John was by the Jordan again with two of his disciples. ³⁶Seeing Jesus walk by, John said, "Look! There's the Lamb of God!" ³⁷The two disciples heard what John said and followed Jesus.

³⁸When Jesus turned around and noticed them following, he asked them, "What are you looking for?"

They replied, "Rabbi,"—which means "Teacher"—"where are you staying?"

³⁹"Come and see," Jesus answered.

So they went to see where he was staying, and they spent the rest of the day with him. It was about four in the afternoon.

⁴⁰One of the two who had followed Jesus after hearing John was Andrew, Simon Peter's brother. ⁴¹The first thing Andrew did was to find Simon Peter and say, "We've found the Messiah!"—which means "the Anointed One."

⁴²Andrew brought Simon to Jesus, who looked hard at him and said, "You are Simon, begot of Jonah; I will call you 'Rock' "—that is, "Peter."

⁴³The next day, after Jesus had decided to leave for Galilee, he met Philip and said, "Follow me." ⁴⁴Philip came from Bethsaida, the same town as Andrew and Peter.

⁴⁵Philip sought out Nathanael and said to him, "We've found the One that Moses spoke of in the Law, the One about whom the prophets wrote: Jesus of Nazareth, begot of Mary and Joseph."

⁴⁶"From Nazareth?" said Nathanael. "Can anything good come from Nazareth?"

"Come and see," replied Philip.

⁴⁷When Jesus saw Nathanael coming toward him, he remarked, "This one is a real Israelite. There is no guile in him."

⁴⁸"How do you know me?" Nathanael asked him.

Jesus answered, "Before Philip even went to call you, while you were sitting under the fig tree, I saw you."

⁴⁹"Rabbi," said Nathanael, "you're God's Own; you're the ruler of Israel!"

⁵⁰Jesus said, "Do you believe just because I told you I saw you under the fig tree? You'll see much greater things than that."

⁵¹Jesus went on to tell them, "The truth of the matter is, you will see heaven opened, and the angels of God ascending and descending upon the Chosen One."

CR   CR   CR

2⁻¹Three days later, there was a wedding at Cana in Galilee, and Mary, the mother of Jesus, was there. ²Jesus and his disciples had likewise been invited to the celebration.

³At a certain point, the wine ran out, and Jesus' mother told him, "They have no wine."

⁴Jesus replied, "Mother, what does that have to do with me? My hour has not yet come."

⁵She instructed those waiting on tables, "Do whatever he tells you."

⁶As prescribed for Jewish ceremonial washings, there were six stone water jars on hand, each one holding between fifteen and twenty-five gallons. ⁷"Fill those jars with water," Jesus said, and the servers filled them to the brim.

⁸"Now," said Jesus, "draw some out and take it to the caterer." They did as they were instructed.

⁹The caterer tasted the water—which had been turned into wine—without knowing where it had come from; the only ones who knew were those who were waiting on tables, since they had drawn the water. The caterer called the bride and groom over ¹⁰and remarked, "People usually serve the best wine first; then, when the guests have been drinking a while, a lesser vintage is served. What you've done is to keep the best wine until now!"

¹¹Jesus performed this first of his signs at Cana in Galilee; in this way he revealed his glory, and the disciples believed in him.

¹²After this Jesus went down to Capernaum with his mother, brothers and sisters, and disciples. They stayed there a few days.

2:13–3:21

Since it was almost the Jewish Passover, Jesus went up to Jerusalem.

¹⁴In the Temple, he found people selling cattle, sheep and pigeons, while moneychangers sat at their counters. ¹⁵Making a whip out of cords, Jesus drove them all out of the Temple—even the cattle and sheep—and overturned the tables of the moneychangers, scattering their coins. ¹⁶Then he faced the pigeon-sellers: "Take all this out of here! Stop turning God's house into a market!" ¹⁷The disciples remembered the words of scripture: "Zeal for your house consumes me."

¹⁸The Temple authorities intervened and said, "What sign can you show us to justify what you've done?"

¹⁹Jesus answered, "Destroy this temple, and in three days I will raise it up."

²⁰They retorted, "It has taken forty-six years to build this Temple, and you're going to raise it up in three days?" ²¹But the temple he was speaking of was his body. ²²It was only after Jesus had been raised from the dead that the disciples remembered this statement and believed the scripture—and the words that Jesus had spoken.

²³While Jesus was in Jerusalem for the Passover festival, many people believed in him, for they could see the signs he was performing. ²⁴But Jesus knew all people, and didn't entrust himself to them. ²⁵Jesus never needed evidence about people's motives; he was well aware of what was in everyone's heart.

3:1 A certain Pharisee named Nicodemus, a member of the Sanhedrin, **2** came to Jesus at night. "Rabbi," he said, "we know you're a teacher come from God, for no one can perform the signs and wonders you do, unless by the power of God."

3 Jesus gave Nicodemus this answer:

> "The truth of the matter is,
> unless one is born from above,
> > one cannot see the kindom of God."

4 Nicodemus said, "How can an adult be born a second time? I can't go back into my mother's womb to be born again!"

5 Jesus replied:

> "The truth of the matter is,
> no one can enter God's kindom
> > without being born of water and the Spirit.
> **6** What is born of the flesh is flesh;
> > what is born of the Spirit is Spirit.
> **7** So don't be surprised when I tell you that
> > you must be born from above.
> **8** The wind blows where it will.
> > You hear the sound it makes,
> but you don't know where it comes from
> > or where it goes.
> So it is with everyone
> > who is born of the Spirit."

9 "How can this be possible?" asked Nicodemus.

10 Jesus replied, "You're a teacher of Israel, and you still don't understand these matters?

> **11** "The truth of the matter is,
> we're talking about what we know;
> > we're testifying about what we've seen—
> > yet you don't accept our testimony.
> **12** If you don't believe
> > when I tell you about earthly things,
> how will you believe
> > when I tell you about heavenly things?
> **13** No one has gone up to heaven
> > except the One who came down from heaven—
> > the Chosen One.

¹⁴ As Moses lifted up the serpent in the desert,
    so the Chosen One must be lifted up,
¹⁵ so that everyone who believes in the Chosen One
    might have eternal life.
¹⁶ Yes, God so loved the world
    as to give the Only Begotten One,
that whoever believes may not die,
    but have eternal life.
¹⁷ God sent the Only Begotten into the world
    not to condemn the world,
but that through the Only Begotten
    the world might be saved.
¹⁸ Whoever believes in the Only Begotten avoids judgment,
    but whoever doesn't believe is judged already
for not believing in the name
    of the Only Begotten of God.
¹⁹ On these grounds is sentence pronounced:
    that though the light came into the world,
people showed they preferred darkness to the light
    because their deeds were evil.
²⁰ Indeed, people who do wrong hate the light and avoid it,
    for fear their actions will be exposed;
²¹ but people who live by the truth
    come out into the light,
so that it may be plainly seen
    that what they do is done in God."

After this, Jesus and the disciples went into Judea; Jesus spent some time with them there, and performed baptisms. ²³ John also was baptizing—in Aenon, near Salim, where water was plentiful—and people were constantly coming to be baptized. ²⁴ This was, of course, before John had been put in prison.

²⁵ A controversy about purification arose between some of John's disciples and a certain Temple authority. ²⁶ They came to John and said, "Rabbi, that person who was with you across the Jordan—the One about whom you've been testifying—is baptizing now, and everyone is going to him."

²⁷ John replied, "None can lay claim to anything unless it is given to them from heaven. ²⁸ You yourselves are witnesses to the fact that I said, 'I am

not the Messiah; I am the Messiah's forerunner.' ²⁹ The bride and the groom are for each other. The bridal party just waits there listening for them and is overjoyed to hear their voices. This is my joy, and it is complete. ³⁰ Now the Messiah must increase, and I must decrease.

> ³¹ The one who comes from above
>   is above all;
> the one who is of the earth
>   belongs to the earth
>   and speaks of earthly things.
> The one who comes from above
>   ³² testifies about things seen and heard above,
>   yet no one accepts this testimony.
> ³³ But those who do accept this testimony
>   attest to God's truthfulness.
> ³⁴ For the one whom God has sent
>   speaks the words of God,
>   for God gives the Spirit without reserve.
> ³⁵ Abba God loves the Only Begotten,
>   to whom all things have been entrusted.
> ³⁶ Everyone who believes in the Only Begotten
>   has eternal life.
> But everyone who rejects the Only Begotten
>   won't see life,
>   for God's wrath stays on them."

        CR   CR   CR

4:1 When Jesus learned that the Pharisees had heard he was attracting and baptizing more disciples than John ²—though it was really not Jesus baptizing, but his disciples—³ he left Judea and returned to Galilee. ⁴ This meant that he had to pass through Samaria.

⁵ He stopped at Sychar, a town in Samaria, near the tract of land Jacob had given to his son Joseph, ⁶ and Jacob's Well was there. Jesus, weary from the journey, came and sat by the well. It was around noon.

⁷ When a Samaritan woman came to draw water, Jesus said to her, "Give me a drink." ⁸ The disciples had gone off to the town to buy provisions.

⁹ The Samaritan woman replied, "You're a Jew. How can you ask me, a Samaritan, for a drink?"—since Jews had nothing to do with Samaritans.

¹⁰ Jesus answered, "If only you recognized God's gift, and who it is that is asking you for a drink, you would have asked him for a drink instead, and he would have given you living water."

¹¹ "If you please," she challenged Jesus, "you don't have a bucket and this well is deep. Where do you expect to get this 'living water'? ¹² Surely you don't pretend to be greater than our ancestors Leah and Rachel and Jacob, who gave us this well and drank from it with their descendants and flocks?"

¹³ Jesus replied, "Everyone who drinks this water will be thirsty again. ¹⁴ But those who drink the water I give them will never be thirsty; no, the water I give will become fountains within them, springing up to provide eternal life."

¹⁵ The woman said to Jesus, "Give me this water, so that I won't grow thirsty and have to keep coming all the way here to draw water."

¹⁶ Jesus said to her, "Go, call your husband and then come back here."

¹⁷ "I don't have a husband," replied the woman.

"You're right—you don't have a husband!" Jesus exclaimed. ¹⁸ "The fact is, you've had five, and the man you're living with now is not your husband. So what you've said is quite true."

¹⁹ "I can see you're a prophet," answered the woman. ²⁰ "Our ancestors worshiped on this mountain, but you people claim that Jerusalem is the place where God ought to be worshiped."

²¹ Jesus told her, "Believe me, the hour is coming when you'll worship Abba God neither on this mountain nor in Jerusalem. ²² You people worship what you don't understand; we worship what we do understand—after all, salvation is from the Jewish people. ²³ Yet the hour is coming—and is already here—when real worshipers will worship Abba God in Spirit and truth. Indeed, it is just such worshipers whom Abba God seeks. ²⁴ God is Spirit, and those who worship God must worship in spirit and truth."

²⁵ The woman said to Jesus, "I know that the Messiah—the Anointed One—is coming, and will tell us everything."

²⁶ Jesus replied, "I who speak to you am the Messiah."

²⁷ The disciples, returning at this point, were shocked to find Jesus having a private conversation with a woman. But no one dared to ask, "What do you want of him?" or "Why are you talking with her?"

²⁸ The woman then left her water jar and went off into the town. She said to the people, ²⁹ "Come and see someone who told me everything I have ever done! Could this be the Messiah?" ³⁰ At that, everyone set out from town to meet Jesus.

³¹ Meanwhile, the disciples were urging Jesus, "Rabbi, eat something."

³² But Jesus told them, "I have food to eat that you know nothing about."

³³ At this, the disciples said to one another, "Do you think someone has brought him something to eat?"

[34] Jesus explained to them,

> "Doing the will of the One who sent me
> > and bringing this work to completion
> > is my food.
> [35] Don't you have a saying,
> > 'Four months more
> > and it will be harvest time'?
> I tell you,
> open your eyes and look at the fields—
> > they're ripe and ready for harvest!
> [36] Reapers are already collecting their wages;
> > they're gathering fruit for eternal life,
> > and sower and reaper will rejoice together.
> [37] So the saying is true:
> > 'One person sows; another reaps.'
> [38] I have sent you to reap
> > what you haven't worked for.
> Others have done the work,
> > and you've come upon the fruits of their labor."

[39] Many Samaritans from that town believed in Jesus on the strength of the woman's testimony—that "he told me everything I ever did." [40] The result was that, when these Samaritans came to Jesus, they begged him to stay with them awhile. So Jesus stayed there two days, [41] and through his own spoken word many more came to faith. [42] They told the woman, "No longer does our faith depend on your story. We've heard for ourselves, and we know that this really is the savior of the world."

CR   CR   CR

[43] On the third day, Jesus left Samaria for Galilee. [44] Now Jesus had pointed out that a prophet is not esteemed in the prophet's own country. [45] So when he arrived in Galilee, it was the Galileans who welcomed him, because they themselves had been at the feast and had seen all that he had done in Jerusalem on that occasion. [46] That's why Jesus returned to Cana in Galilee, where he had turned the water into wine.

At Capernaum there lived a royal official whose child was ill. [47] Upon hearing that Jesus had returned to Galilee from Judea, the official went and begged Jesus to come down and restore health to the child, who was near death.

[48] Jesus replied, "Unless you people see signs and wonders, you won't believe!"

⁴⁹ "Rabbi," the official pleaded, "come down before my child dies."

⁵⁰ Jesus said, "Return home; your child lives."

The official believed what Jesus said and started for home. ⁵¹ On the way, the official was met by members of the household with the news that the child was going to live. ⁵² When the official asked at what time the fever broke, they said, "About one o'clock yesterday afternoon." ⁵³ The official realized that this was the very hour that Jesus had said, "Your child lives." The whole household then became believers.

⁵⁴ This was the second sign that Jesus performed, after he had left Judea for Galilee.

5:1-47

Some time after this, there was a Jewish festival and Jesus went up to Jerusalem. ² Now in Jerusalem, near the Sheep Gate, there is a pool with five porticoes; its Hebrew name is Bethesda. ³ The place was crowded with sick people—those who were blind, lame or paralyzed—lying there waiting for the water to move. ⁴ An angel of God would come down to the pool from time to time, to stir up the water; the first one to step into the water after it had been stirred up would be completely healed.*

⁵ One person there had been sick for thirty-eight years. ⁶ Jesus, who knew this person had been sick for a long time, said, "Do you want to be healed?"

⁷ "Rabbi," the sick one answered, "I don't have anyone to put me into the pool once the water has been stirred up. By the time I get there, someone else has gone in ahead of me."

⁸ Jesus replied, "Stand up! Pick up your mat and walk."

⁹ The individual was immediately healed, and picked up the mat and walked away.

This happened on a Sabbath. ¹⁰ Consequently, some of the Temple authorities said to the one who had been healed, "It's the Sabbath! You're not allowed to carry that mat around!"

¹¹ The healed one explained, "But the person who healed me told me, 'Pick up your mat and walk.' "

¹² They asked, "Who is this who told you to pick up your mat and walk?"

¹³ The healed person had no idea who it was, since Jesus had disappeared into the crowd that filled the place.

¹⁴ Later on, Jesus met the individual in the Temple and said, "Remember,

---

* Many of the manuscripts end verse 3 at ...or paralyzed, and delete verse 4 altogether.

now, you've been healed. Give up your sins so that something worse won't overtake you." ¹⁵The healed one went off and informed the Temple authorities that Jesus was the one who had performed the healing.

¹⁶It was because Jesus did things like this on the Sabbath that the Temple authorities began to persecute him. ¹⁷Jesus said to them, "Abba God is working right now, and I am at work as well." ¹⁸Because of this, the Temple authorities were even more determined to kill him. Not only was he breaking the Sabbath but, worse still, he was speaking of God as "Abba"—that is, "Papa"—thereby making their relationship one of intimacy and equality.

¹⁹This was Jesus' answer:

"The truth of the matter is,
the Only Begotten can do nothing alone,
   but can only follow Abba God's example.
For whatever Abba does,
   the Only Begotten does—
   and does in the same way.
²⁰For Abba God loves the Only Begotten,
   and teaches the Only Begotten by example.
And God will show the Only Begotten
   even greater works than you've seen—
   works that will astonish you.
²¹Indeed, just as Abba God raises the dead and gives them life,
   so the Only Begotten gives life to anyone at will.
²²For Abba God judges no one,
   having entrusted all judgment to the Only Begotten,
²³so that all may honor the Only Begotten
   as they honor Abba God.
Whoever doesn't honor the Only Begotten
   dishonors the One who sent the Only Begotten—
   Abba God.
²⁴The truth of the matter is,
whoever listens to my words
   and believes in the One who sent me
   has eternal life,
and isn't brought to judgment,
   having passed from death to life.
²⁵The truth of the matter is,
the hour will come—
   in fact is here already—
when the dead will hear the voice of God's Only Begotten,
   and all who hear it will live.

²⁶ For just as Abba God is the source of life,
    God has ordained that the Only Begotten
    also be the source of life—
²⁷ and be given authority to execute judgment
    as the Chosen One of God.
²⁸ Don't be surprised at this,
    because the hour is coming
when those in the grave
    will hear the Chosen One's voice
        ²⁹ and come forth:
those who did good will rise to life
    and those who did evil will rise to condemnation.
³⁰ I can do nothing by myself;
    I can only judge as I am told to judge.
And my judging is just,
    because my aim is to do not my own will,
    but the will of the One who sent me.
³¹ If I testify on my own behalf,
    my testimony is not valid;
³² but someone else is testifying on my behalf,
    and I know that this one's testimony is true.
³³ You've sent messengers to John,
    who has testified to the truth—
³⁴ not that I depend on human testimony;
    it's only for your salvation that I explain things this way.
³⁵ John was the lamp, set aflame and burning bright,
    and for a while you rejoiced willingly in his light.
³⁶ Yet I have testimony that is greater than John's:
    the works that Abba God has given me to do.
These very works that I do
    testify on my behalf that Abba God has sent me.
³⁷ Moreover the One who sent me
    has also testified on my behalf.
You've never heard God's voice;
    you've never seen God's form—
³⁸ nor have you ever had God's words abiding in your hearts,
    because you don't believe the one whom God has sent!
³⁹ Search the scriptures—
    the ones you think give you eternal life:
    those very scriptures testify about me.
⁴⁰ Yet you're unwilling to come to me
    to receive that life.

⁴¹ It's not that I accept human praise—
   ⁴² it is simply that I know you,
      and you don't have the love of God in your hearts.
⁴³ I have come in the name of Abba God,
      yet you don't accept me.
But let others come in their own name
      and you'll accept them!
⁴⁴ How can you believe,
      when you accept praise from one another,
yet don't seek the praise
      that comes from the One God?
⁴⁵ Don't imagine that I will be your accuser before Abba God;
      it is Moses who accuses you—
      the one in whom you've put your hope.
⁴⁶ For if you really believed Moses,
      you would believe me,
      for it was about me that Moses wrote.
⁴⁷ But if you don't believe what Moses wrote,
      how can you believe what I say?"

6:1-71

Some time later, Jesus crossed over to the other side of the Sea of Galilee—that is, Lake Tiberius— ² and a huge crowd followed him, impressed by the signs he gave by healing sick people. ³ Jesus climbed the hillside and sat down there with the disciples. ⁴ It was shortly before the Jewish feast of Passover.

⁵ Looking up, Jesus saw the crowd approaching and said to Philip, "Where can we buy some bread for these people to eat?" ⁶ Jesus knew very well what he was going to do, but asked this to test Philip's response.

⁷ Philip answered, "Not even with two hundred days' wages could we buy loaves enough to give each of them a mouthful!"

⁸ One of the disciples, Simon Peter's brother Andrew, said, ⁹ "There's a small boy here with five barley loaves and two dried fish. But what good is that for so many people?"

¹⁰ Jesus said to them, "Make the people sit down." There was plenty of grass there, and as many as five thousand families sat down. ¹¹ Then Jesus took the loaves, gave thanks, and gave them out to all who were sitting there; he did the same with the fish, giving out as much as they could eat.

¹² When the people had eaten their fill, Jesus said to the disciples, "Gather

up the leftover pieces so that nothing gets wasted." ¹³ So they picked them up and filled twelve baskets with the scraps left over from the five barley loaves.

¹⁴ The people, seeing this sign that Jesus had performed, said, "Surely this is the Prophet who was to come into the world." ¹⁵ Seeing that they were about to come and carry him off to crown him as ruler, Jesus escaped into the hills alone.

¹⁶ As evening approached, the disciples went down to the lake. ¹⁷ They got into their boat, intending to cross to Capernaum, which was on the other side of the lake. By this time it was dark, and Jesus had still not joined them; ¹⁸ moreover, a stiff wind was blowing and the sea was becoming rough.

¹⁹ When they had rowed three or four miles, they caught sight of Jesus approaching the boat, walking on the water. They were frightened, ²⁰ but he told them, "It's me. Don't be afraid." ²¹ They were about to take him into the boat, but suddenly the boat was ashore at their destination.

²² The next day, the crowd that had stayed on the other side of the lake saw that only one boat had been there; and they knew that Jesus had not gotten into the boat with the disciples—that the disciples had set off by themselves. ²³ Other boats, however, had put in from Tiberias, near the place where the bread had been eaten after the Rabbi had given thanks. ²⁴ When the people saw that neither Jesus nor the disciples were there, they got into those boats and crossed to Capernaum looking for Jesus.

²⁵ When they found Jesus on the other side of the lake, they said, "Rabbi, when did you get here?"

²⁶ Jesus answered them,

"The truth of the matter is,
you're not looking for me because you've seen signs,
but because you've eaten your fill of the bread.
²⁷ You shouldn't be working for perishable food,
but for life-giving food that lasts for all eternity;
this the Chosen One can give you,
for the Chosen One bears the seal of Abba God."

²⁸ At this they said, "What must we do to perform the works of God?"
²⁹ Jesus replied,

"This is the work of God:
to believe in the one whom God has sent."

³⁰ So they asked Jesus, "What sign are you going to give to show us that we should believe in you? What will you do? ³¹ Our ancestors had manna

to eat in the desert; as scripture says, 'God gave them bread from heaven to eat.' "

³²Jesus said to them,

> "The truth of the matter is,
> Moses hasn't given you bread from heaven;
>> yet my Abba gives you the true bread from heaven.
> ³³For the bread of God
>> is the one who comes down from heaven
>> and gives life to the world."

³⁴"Teacher," they said, "give us this bread from now on."

³⁵Jesus explained to them,

> "I am the bread of life.
> No one who comes to me will ever be hungry;
>> no one who believes in me will be thirsty.
> ³⁶But as I told you,
>> you see me and still don't believe.
> ³⁷Everyone Abba God gives me will come to me,
>> and whoever comes to me I won't turn away.
> ³⁸For I have come from heaven, not to do my own will,
>> but the will of the One who sent me.
> ³⁹It is the will of the One who sent me
>> that I lose none of those given to me,
>> but rather raise them up on the last day.
> ⁴⁰Indeed, this is the will of my Abba:
>> that everyone who sees and believes in
>> the Only Begotten will have eternal life.
> These are the ones I will raise up on the last day."

⁴¹The Temple authorities started to grumble in protest because Jesus claimed, "I am the bread that came down from heaven." ⁴²They kept saying, "Isn't this Jesus, begot of Mary and Joseph? Don't we know his mother and father? How can he claim to have come down from heaven?"

⁴³"Stop your grumbling," Jesus told them.

> ⁴⁴"No one can come to me
>> unless drawn by Abba God, who sent me—
>> and those I will raise up on the last day.
> ⁴⁵It is written in the prophets:
>> 'They will all be taught by God.'
> Everyone who has heard God's word
>> and has learned from it
>> comes to me.

⁴⁶ Not that anyone has seen Abba God—
　　 only the one who is from God has seen Abba God.
⁴⁷ The truth of the matter is,
　　 those who believe have eternal life.
⁴⁸ I am the bread of life.
⁴⁹ Your ancestors ate manna in the desert,
　　 but they died.
⁵⁰ This is the bread that comes down from heaven,
　　 and if you eat it you'll never die.
⁵¹ I myself am the living bread
　　 come down from heaven.
If any eat this bread,
　　 they will live forever;
the bread I will give
　　 for the life of the world
　　 is my flesh."

⁵² The Temple authorities then began to argue with one another. "How can he give us his flesh to eat?"

⁵³ Jesus replied,
　　 "The truth of the matter is,
　　 if you don't eat the flesh
　　　　 and drink the blood of the Chosen One,
　　　　 you won't have life in you.
⁵⁴ Those who do eat my flesh and drink my blood
　　　　 have eternal life,
　　　　 and I will raise them up on the last day.
⁵⁵ For my flesh is real food
　　　　 and my blood is real drink.
⁵⁶ Everyone who eats my flesh and drinks my blood
　　　　 lives in me, and I live in them.
⁵⁷ Just as the living Abba God sent me
　　　　 and I have life because of Abba God,
　　 so those who feed on me
　　　　 will have life because of me.
⁵⁸ This is the bread that came down from heaven.
　　　　 It's not the kind of bread your ancestors ate,
　　　　 for they died;
　　 whoever eats this kind of bread
　　　　 will live forever."

⁵⁹ Jesus spoke these words while teaching in the synagogue in Capernaum.

[60]Many of his disciples remarked, "We can't put up with this kind of talk! How can anyone take it seriously?"

[61]Jesus was fully aware that the disciples were murmuring in protest at what he had said. "Is this a stumbling block for you?" he asked them.

[62]"What, then, if you were to see the Chosen One
ascend to where the Chosen One came from?
[63]It is the spirit that gives life;
the flesh in itself is useless.
The words I have spoken to you
are spirit and life.
[64]Yet among you there are some
who don't believe."

Jesus knew from the start, of course, those who would refuse to believe and the one who would betray him. [65]He went on to say:

"This is why I have told you
that no one can come to me
unless it is granted by Abba God."

[66]From this time on, many of the disciples broke away and wouldn't remain in the company of Jesus. [67]Jesus then said to the Twelve, "Are you going to leave me, too?"

[68]Simon Peter answered, "Rabbi, where would we go? You have the words of eternal life. [69]We have come to believe; we're convinced that you are the Holy One of God."

[70]Then Jesus replied, "Haven't I chosen you Twelve? Yet one of you is a devil." [71]Jesus meant that one of the Twelve, Judas begot of Simon Iscariot, was going to betray him.

7:1–10:39

After this, Jesus walked through Galilee. He had decided not to travel to Judea, because the Temple authorities were trying to kill him.

[2]As the Jewish Feast of Tabernacles approached, [3]Jesus' sisters and brothers said to him, "Why not leave here and go to Judea so that your disciples there can also see the works you do. [4]Those destined for public life don't do things in secret. Since you're working these miracles, let the whole world know!" [5]For even his own siblings didn't believe in him.

[6]Jesus answered, "Now is not the right time for me. But for you, any time is right. [7]The world can't hate you. But it hates me because I testify that its

ways are evil. ⁸Go up to the feast yourselves. I am not going to this feast because my time is yet to come." ⁹Having said this, he stayed in Galilee.

☙   ☙   ☙

¹⁰Once Jesus' sisters and brothers had gone up to the festival, he too went up—not publicly, but in secret, as it were.

¹¹At the festival the Temple authorities were looking for Jesus and asking, "Where is he?" ¹²The crowd stood around whispering about him. Some said, "He's a good teacher." Others, however, said, "No, he is leading us astray." ¹³Yet no one spoke about Jesus openly for fear of the Temple authorities.

¹⁴When the Feast was half over, Jesus went to the Temple and began to teach. ¹⁵The crowd was amazed and said, "He certainly knows his letters! But how is that possible when he's never had any formal education?"

¹⁶Jesus answered,

"My teaching is not my own.
    It comes from the One who sent me.
¹⁷All who are prepared to do the will of God
    will know whether my teaching comes from God
    or whether I speak on my own.
¹⁸Those who speak on their own
    seek their own glory.
Those who seek the glory of the One who sends them
    are truthful, and do nothing unjust.
¹⁹Didn't Moses give you the Law?
    Yet not one of you keeps the Law!

"Why are you trying to kill me?"

²⁰The crowd answered, "You're possessed! Who is trying to kill you?"

²¹Jesus replied, "I worked one miracle, and you're all amazed by it. ²²Moses gave you circumcision as a sign of the Covenant—actually, it came from our ancestors and not from Moses—and you perform it on the Sabbath. ²³If a baby can receive the sign of the Covenant on the Sabbath in order to keep the Law of Moses, why are you angry with me for making a person whole on the Sabbath? ²⁴Stop judging for the sake of appearances! Start judging justly!"

²⁵Meanwhile some of the people of Jerusalem were saying, "Isn't this the one they want to kill? ²⁶And here he is, speaking freely, and they have nothing to say to him! Can it be true that the authorities have made up their minds that this is the Messiah? ²⁷Yet we all know where this fellow comes from, but when the Messiah comes, no one will know that one's origins."

²⁸ At this, Jesus, still teaching in the Temple area, cried out,

"So, you think you know me and my origins!
　Yet I haven't come of my own accord—
I was sent by One who is true,
　whom you don't even know.
²⁹ But I do know this One,
　because those are my origins,
　and by this One I was sent."

³⁰ They would have arrested Jesus then, but no one laid a hand on him because his time had not yet come.

³¹ There were many in the crowd, however, who believed in Jesus. They said, "Will the coming Messiah perform more miracles than this person?" ³² The Pharisees heard the crowd murmuring to this effect; so the Pharisees and the chief priests sent the Temple guards to arrest him.

³³ Jesus said, "I will be with you only a little longer, then I will go to the One who sent me. ³⁴ You'll look for me and won't find me. For where I am, you cannot come."

³⁵ Those gathered there said to one another, "Where is he going that we won't find him? Will he go abroad to our people scattered among the Greek Diaspora, and will he teach the Greeks? ³⁶ What is the meaning of the statement, 'You'll look for me and won't find me. For where I am, you cannot come'?"

ଔ　　　ଔ　　　ଔ

³⁷ On the last and greatest day of the festival, Jesus stood up and shouted,

"Any who are thirsty,
　let them come to me and drink!
³⁸ Those who believe in me, as the scripture says,
'From their innermost being
　will flow rivers of living water.' "

³⁹ Here Jesus was referring to the Spirit, which those who came to believe were to receive—though she had not yet been given, since Jesus had not been glorified.

⁴⁰ Several people in the crowd who had heard the words of Jesus began to say, "This must be the Prophet." ⁴¹ But others were saying, "He's the Messiah." Still others said, "Surely the Messiah is not to come from Galilee? ⁴² Doesn't scripture say that the Messiah, being of David's lineage, is to come from Bethlehem, the village where David lived?" ⁴³ So the people were sharply divided over this. ⁴⁴ Some of them even wanted to arrest Jesus. However, no one laid hands on him.

⁴⁵ The Temple guards went back to the chief priests and Pharisees, who said to them, "Why haven't you brought him in?"

⁴⁶ "No one ever spoke like that before," the guards responded.

⁴⁷ "So, you too have been taken in!" the Pharisees replied. ⁴⁸ "Do any of the Sanhedrin believe in him? Any of the Pharisees? ⁴⁹ This rabble knows nothing about the Law—and they are damned anyway!"

⁵⁰ One of their own, Nicodemus—the same person who had come to Jesus earlier—said to them, ⁵¹ "Since when does our Law condemn anyone without first hearing the accused and knowing all the facts?"

⁵² "Don't tell us you're a Galilean, too!" they taunted him. "Look it up. You'll see that no prophet comes from Galilee."

℞   ℞   ℞

* ⁵³ After that, everyone went home, ⁸:¹ and Jesus went out to the Mount of Olives.

² At daybreak, he reappeared in the Temple area, and when the people started coming to him, Jesus sat down and began to teach them.

³ A couple had been caught in the act of adultery, though the scribes and Pharisees brought only the woman, and they made her stand there in front of everyone. ⁴ "Teacher," they said, "this woman has been caught in the act of adultery. ⁵ In the Law of Moses, the punishment for this act is stoning. What do you say about it?" ⁶ They were posing this question to trap Jesus so that they could charge him with something.

Jesus simply bent down and started tracing on the ground with his finger. ⁷ When they persisted in their questioning, Jesus straightened up and said to them, "Let the person among you who is without sin throw the first stone at her." ⁸ Then he bent down again and wrote on the ground.

⁹ The audience drifted away one by one, beginning with the elders. This left Jesus alone with the woman, who continued to stand there. ¹⁰ Jesus finally straightened up again and said, "Where did they go? Has no one condemned you?"

¹¹ "No one, Teacher," came the reply.

"I don't condemn you either. Go on your way—but from now on, don't sin any more."

---

* John 7:53—8:11 is not found in most of the manuscripts.

¹² The next time Jesus spoke to them, he said,

> "I am the light of the world.
> Whoever follows me won't walk in darkness,
>> but will have the light of life."

¹³ The Pharisees said to him, "You're testifying about yourself, so your testimony isn't valid."

¹⁴ Jesus replied,

> "Even if I do testify about myself,
>> my testimony is valid,
> because I know where I came from
>> and where I am going.
> But you know neither where I come from
>> nor where I am going.
> ¹⁵ You people judge by external things;
>> I don't judge anyone at all.
> ¹⁶ But even if I were to judge,
>> my judgment would be true
> because I am not alone in it—
>> the One who sent me
>> joins me in that judgment.
> ¹⁷ Even in the Law it is written
>> that it takes two witnesses for testimony to be admissible.
> ¹⁸ Well, I bear witness about myself,
>> and my Abba, who sent me,
>> bears witness about me as well."

¹⁹ They asked Jesus, "Where is this 'Abba' of yours?"

Jesus replied,

> "You don't know me,
>> nor do you know my Abba;
> if you knew me,
>> you would know my Abba as well."

²⁰ Jesus spoke these words in front of the Temple treasury, while he was teaching. No one seized him, because his hour had not yet come.

²¹ Again he said to them:

> "I am going away.
> You'll look for me,
>> but you'll die in your sins.
> Where I am going
>> you cannot come."

²²At this, some of the Temple authorities said to one another, "Is he going to kill himself? Is this what he means by saying, 'Where I am going, you cannot come'?"

²³Jesus went on,

> "You belong to what is below;
>> I am from above.
> You're of this world;
>> I am not of this world.
> ²⁴I have told you already,
>> you'll die in your sins.
> Yes, you will surely die in your sins
>> unless you believe that I AM."

²⁵So they said to Jesus, "Who are you?"

Jesus answered,

> "What have I told you from the beginning?
> ²⁶About you I have much to say
>> and much to condemn;
> But the One who sent me is truthful
>> and what I have learned
>> I now declare to the world."

²⁷They didn't grasp that Jesus was speaking about Abba God. ²⁸Jesus continued,

> "When you have lifted up the Chosen One,
>> then you'll know that I AM
> and that I do nothing of myself;
>> I say only what Abba God has taught me.
> ²⁹The One who sent me is with me
>> and has not deserted me,
>> because I always do God's will."

³⁰While he spoke, many became believers. ³¹Jesus said to those who believed in him,

> "If you live according to my teaching,
>> you really are my disciples;
> ³²then you'll know the truth,
>> and the truth will set you free."

³³"We're descendants of Sarah and Abraham," they replied. "Never have we been the slaves of anyone. What do you mean by saying, 'You'll be free'?"

³⁴Jesus answered them,

> "The truth of the matter is,

everyone who lives in sin
  is the slave of sin.
³⁵ Now a slave doesn't always remain part of a household;
  an heir, however, is a member of that house forever.
³⁶ So if the heir—the Only Begotten—makes you free,
  you will be free indeed.
³⁷ I know that you're descended from Sarah and Abraham;
  but in spite of that you want to kill me
  because my message has found no room in you.
³⁸ I speak of what I have seen with Abba God,
  and you do what you learned from your parents."

³⁹ They repeated, "Our parents are Sarah and Abraham."
Jesus said to them,
  "If you were the children of Sarah and Abraham,
    you would do as they did.
⁴⁰ As it is, you want to kill me
    when I tell you the truth, which I heard from God.
  That is not what Sarah and Abraham did;
    ⁴¹ you're doing what your parents did."
They cried, "We're no illegitimate breed! We're born of God alone."
⁴² Jesus answered,
  "If you were born of God
    you would love me;
  for I came forth from God,
    and I was sent from God.
  I didn't come of my own will:
    it was God who sent me.
⁴³ Why don't you understand what I am saying to you?
    It's because you cannot bear to hear what I say.
⁴⁴ You're children of the Devil,
    and children want to do their parents' will.
  The Devil was a murderer from the beginning
    and is not grounded in truth,
    because there is no truth in it.
  When the Devil lies,
    it speaks its native tongue.
  The Devil is a liar—
    the source of all lies.
⁴⁵ But I speak the truth,
    yet you don't believe me.
⁴⁶ Can any of you convict me of sin?

If I do speak the truth,
  why don't you believe me?
⁴⁷ Whoever belongs to God
  hears the words of God.
And that's precisely why you don't hear them—
  because you're not of God."

⁴⁸ The Temple authorities replied, "Aren't we right to say that you're a Samaritan—a heretic—and that you're possessed by a devil?"

⁴⁹ Jesus answered, "I am not possessed. I honor God, my Abba, and you dishonor me. ⁵⁰ I don't seek my own glory. There is One who seeks it and judges it.

⁵¹ "The truth of the matter is,
anyone who keeps my word
  will never see death."

⁵² They retorted, "Now we're sure you're possessed! Sarah and Abraham are dead; the prophets are dead; yet you claim, 'Anyone who keeps my word will never know death.' ⁵³ Surely you don't pretend to be greater than our ancestors, Sarah and Abraham, who died! Or the prophets, who died! Who do you make yourself out to be?"

⁵⁴ Jesus answered,

"If I glorify myself,
  that glory comes to nothing.
But the One who glorifies me is Abba God,
  of whom you say, 'This is Our God.'
⁵⁵ You haven't come to know God,
  but I do,
and if I were to say, 'I don't know God,'
  I would be a liar, like you!
But I do know God,
  and I faithfully keep God's word.
⁵⁶ Your ancestors Sarah and Abraham rejoiced
  to think that they would see my day—
  and they did see it, and were glad."

⁵⁷ Then the authorities objected, "You're not yet fifty years old, and you say you've seen Sarah and Abraham?"

⁵⁸ Jesus answered them,

"The truth of the matter is,
before Sarah and Abraham ever were,
  I AM."

⁵⁹ At this, they picked up rocks to throw at Jesus. But he hid himself and slipped out of the Temple.

⁹¹ As Jesus walked along, he saw someone who had been blind from birth. ²The disciples asked Jesus, "Rabbi, was it this individual's sin that caused the blindness, or that of the parents?"

³ "Neither," answered Jesus,

> "It wasn't because of anyone's sin—
>   not this person's, nor the parents'.
> Rather, it was to let God's works shine forth
>   in this person.
> ⁴We must do the deeds of the One who sent me
>   while it is still day—
> for night is coming,
>   when no one can work.
> ⁵While I am in the world,
>   I am the light of the world."

⁶ With that, Jesus spat on the ground, made mud with his saliva and smeared the blind one's eyes with the mud. ⁷Then Jesus said, "Go, wash in the pool of Siloam"—"Siloam" means "sent." So the person went off to wash, and came back able to see.

⁸ Neighbors and those who had been accustomed to seeing the blind beggar began to ask, "Isn't this the one who used to sit and beg?" ⁹Some said yes; others said no—the one who had been healed simply looked like the beggar.

But the individual in question said, "No—it was me."

¹⁰ The people then asked, "Then how were your eyes opened?"

¹¹ The answer came, "The one they call Jesus made mud and smeared it on my eyes, and told me to go to Siloam and wash. When I went and washed, I was able to see."

¹² "Where is Jesus?" they asked.

The person replied, "I have no idea."

¹³ They took the one who had been born blind to the Pharisees. ¹⁴It had been on a Sabbath that Jesus had made the mud paste and opened this one's eyes. ¹⁵The Pharisees asked how the individual could see. They were told, "Jesus put mud on my eyes. I washed it off, and now I can see."

¹⁶ This prompted some Pharisees to say, "This Jesus cannot be from God, because he doesn't keep the Sabbath." Others argued, "But how could a sinner perform signs like these?" They were sharply divided.

¹⁷ Then they addressed the blind person again: "Since it was your eyes he opened, what do you have to say about this Jesus?"

"He's a prophet," came the reply.

¹⁸ The Temple authorities refused to believe that this one had been blind and had begun to see, until they summoned the parents. ¹⁹ "Is this your child?" they asked, "and if so, do you attest that your child was blind at birth? How do you account for the fact that now your child can see?"

²⁰ The parents answered, "We know this is our child, blind from birth. ²¹ But how our child can see now, or who opened those blind eyes, we have no idea. But don't ask us—our child is old enough to speak without us!" ²² The parents answered this way because they were afraid of the Temple authorities, who had already agreed among themselves that anyone who acknowledged Jesus as the Messiah would be put out of the synagogue. ²³ That was why they said, "Our child is of age and should be asked directly."

²⁴ A second time they summoned the one who had been born blind and said, "Give God the glory instead; we know that this Jesus is a sinner."

²⁵ "I don't know whether he is a sinner or not," the individual answered. "All I know is that I used to be blind, and now I can see."

²⁶ They persisted, "Just what did he do to you? How did he open your eyes?"

²⁷ "I already told you, but you won't listen to me," came the answer. "Why do you want to hear it all over again? Don't tell me you want to become disciples of Jesus too!"

²⁸ They retorted scornfully, "You're the one who is Jesus' disciple. We're disciples of Moses. ²⁹ We know that God spoke to Moses, but we have no idea where this Jesus comes from."

³⁰ The other retorted: "Well, this is news! You don't know where he comes from, yet he opened my eyes! ³¹ We know that God doesn't hear sinners, but that if people are devout and obey God's will, God listens to them. ³² It is unheard of that anyone ever gave sight to a person blind from birth. ³³ If this one were not from God, he could never have done such a thing!"

³⁴ "What!" they exclaimed. "You're steeped in sin from birth, and you're giving us lectures?" With that they threw the person out.

³⁵ When Jesus heard of the expulsion, he sought out the healed one and asked, "Do you believe in the Chosen One?"

³⁶ The other answered, "Who is this One, that I may believe?"

³⁷ "You're looking at him," Jesus replied. "The Chosen One is speaking to you now."

³⁸ The healed one said, "Yes, I believe," and worshiped Jesus.

³⁹ And Jesus said, "I came into this world to execute justice—to make the sightless see and the seeing blind."

⁴⁰ Some of the Pharisees who were nearby heard this and said, "You're not calling us blind, are you?"

⁴¹ To which Jesus replied, "If you were blind, there would be no sin in that. But since you say, 'We see,' your sin remains.

10:1 "The truth of the matter is,
whoever doesn't enter the sheepfold through the gate
but climbs in some other way
is a thief and a robber.
² The one who enters through the gate
is the shepherd of the sheep,
³ the one for whom the keeper opens the gate.
The sheep know the shepherd's voice;
the shepherd calls them by name
and leads them out.
⁴ Having led them all out of the fold,
the shepherd walks in front of them
and they follow
because they recognize the shepherd's voice.
⁵ They simply won't follow strangers—
they'll flee from them
because they don't recognize the voice of strangers."

⁶ Even though Jesus used this metaphor with them, they didn't grasp what he was trying to tell them. ⁷ He therefore said to them again:

"The truth of the matter is,
I am the sheep gate.
⁸ All who came before me
were thieves and marauders
whom the sheep didn't heed.
⁹ I am the gate.
Whoever enters through me will be safe—
you'll go in and out and find pasture.
¹⁰ The thief comes only to steal and slaughter and destroy.
I came that you might have life, and have it to the full.
¹¹ I am the good shepherd.
A good shepherd would die for the sheep.
¹² The hired hand, who is neither shepherd
nor owner of the sheep,
catches sight of the wolf coming
and runs away, leaving the sheep
to be scattered
or snatched by the wolf.

¹³ That's because the hired hand works only for pay
    and has no concern for the sheep.
¹⁴ I am the good shepherd.
I know my sheep
    and my sheep know me,
¹⁵ in the same way Abba God knows me
    and I know God—
and for these sheep
    I will lay down my life.
¹⁶ I have other sheep
    that don't belong to this fold—
I must lead them too,
    and they will hear my voice.
And then there will be one flock,
    one shepherd.
¹⁷ This is why Abba God loves me—
because I lay down my life,
    only to take it up again.
¹⁸ No one takes my life from me;
    I lay it down freely.
I have the power to lay it down,
    and I have the power to take it up again.
This command I received from my Abba."

¹⁹ These words once more divided the Temple authorities. ²⁰ Many said, "He is possessed, he's raving mad! Why do you listen to him?"

²¹ Others said, "These are not the words of a person possessed by a demon. Could a demon open the eyes of a blind person?"

ભ   ભ   ભ

²² The time came for Hanukkah, the Feast of the Dedication, in Jerusalem. ²³ It was winter, and Jesus was walking in the Temple area, in Solomon's Porch, ²⁴ when the Temple authorities surrounded him and said, "How long are you going to keep us in suspense? If you really are the Messiah, tell us plainly."

²⁵ Jesus replied,
    "I did tell you,
        but you don't believe.
    The work I do in my Abba's name
        gives witness in my favor,

²⁶ but you don't believe
    because you're not my sheep.
²⁷ My sheep hear my voice.
    I know them, and they follow me.
²⁸ I give them eternal life,
    and they will never be lost.
No one will ever
    snatch them from my hand.
²⁹ Abba God, who gave them to me, is greater than anyone,
    and no one can steal them from Abba God.
³⁰ For Abba and I are One."

³¹ With that, the Temple authorities reached again for rocks to stone him.

³² Jesus protested and said, "I have shown you many good works from Abba God. For which of these do you stone me?"

³³ "It's not for any 'good works' that we're stoning you," they replied, "but for blaspheming. You're human, yet you make yourself out to be God."

³⁴ Jesus answered,

"Isn't it written in your Law,
    'I said, You are gods?'
³⁵ So the Law uses the word 'gods'
    of those to whom the word of God was addressed—
    and scripture can't be broken.
³⁶ Yet you say—to someone whom Abba God has consecrated
    and sent into the world—
'You're blaspheming,'
    because I say, 'I am God's Only Begotten.'
³⁷ If I am not doing Abba God's work,
    there is no need to believe me;
³⁸ but if I am doing God's work—
    even if you don't believe me—
    at least believe in the work I do.
Then you'll know for certain
    that Abba God is in me
    and I am in Abba God."

³⁹ At these words, they again attempted to arrest Jesus, but he eluded their grasp.

Jesus went back again across the Jordan River to the place where John had been baptizing earlier, and while he stayed there, ⁴¹many people came to him. "John may never have performed a sign," they said, "but everything John said about this person was true." ⁴²And many of them believed in Jesus.

CR   CR   CR

11:1 There was a certain man named Lazarus, who was sick. He and his sisters, Mary and Martha, were from the village of Bethany. ²Mary was the one who had anointed the feet of Jesus with perfume and dried his feet with her hair, and it was her brother Lazarus who was sick. ³The sisters sent this message to Jesus: "Rabbi, the one you love is sick."

⁴When Jesus heard this, he said, "This sickness will not end in death; it is happening for God's glory, so that God's Only Begotten may be glorified because of it."

⁵Jesus loved these three very much. ⁶Yet even after hearing that Lazarus was sick, he remained where he was staying for two more days. ⁷Finally he said to the disciples, "Let's go back to Judea."

⁸They protested, "Rabbi, it was only recently that they tried to stone you—and you want to go back there again?"

⁹Jesus replied,

> "Aren't there twelve hours of daylight?
> Those who walk by day don't stumble,
>   because they see the world bathed in light;
>   ¹⁰those who go walking by night will stumble
>   because there is no light in them."

¹¹After Jesus said this, he said to the disciples, "Our beloved Lazarus has fallen asleep. I am going to Judea to wake him."

¹²The disciples objected, "But Rabbi, if he's only asleep, he'll be fine."

¹³Jesus had been speaking about Lazarus' death, but they thought he was talking about actual sleep. ¹⁴So he said very plainly, "Lazarus is dead! ¹⁵For your sakes I am glad that I wasn't there, that you might come to believe. In any event, let us go to him."

¹⁶Then Thomas, "the Twin," said to the rest, "Let's go with Jesus, so that we can die with him."

¹⁷When Jesus arrived in Bethany, he found that Lazarus had already been in the tomb for four days. ¹⁸Since Bethany was only about two miles from

Jerusalem, ¹⁹many people had come out to console Martha and Mary about their brother. ²⁰When Martha heard that Jesus was coming, she went to meet him, while Mary stayed at home with the mourners.

²¹When she got to Jesus, Martha said, "If you had been here, my brother would never have died! ²²Yet even now, I am sure that God will give you whatever you ask."

²³"Your brother will rise again!" Jesus assured her. ²⁴Martha replied, "I know he will rise again in the resurrection on the last day."

²⁵Jesus told her,

> "I am the Resurrection,
>   and I am Life:
> those who believe in me
>   will live, even if they die;
> ²⁶and those who are alive and believe in me
>   will never die.

"Do you believe this?"

²⁷"Yes!" Martha replied. "I have come to believe that you are the Messiah, God's Only Begotten, the One who is coming into the world."

²⁸When she had said this, Martha went back and called her sister Mary. "The Teacher is here, asking for you," she whispered.

²⁹As soon as Mary heard this, she got up and went to him. ³⁰Jesus hadn't gotten to the village yet. He was at the place where Martha had met him. ³¹Those who were there consoling her saw her get up quickly and followed Mary, thinking she was going to the tomb to mourn. ³²When Mary got to Jesus, she fell at his feet and said, "If you had been here, Lazarus never would have died."

³³When Jesus saw her weeping, and the other mourners as well, he was troubled in spirit, moved by the deepest emotions.

³⁴"Where have you laid him?" Jesus asked.

"Come and see," they said. ³⁵And Jesus wept.

³⁶The people in the crowd began to remark, "See how much he loved him!" ³⁷Others said, "He made the blind person see; why couldn't he have done something to prevent Lazarus' death?"

³⁸Jesus was again deeply moved. They approached the tomb, which was a cave with a stone in front of it. ³⁹"Take away the stone," Jesus directed.

Martha said, "Rabbi, it has been four days now. By this time there will be a stench."

⁴⁰Jesus replied, "Didn't I assure you that if you believed you would see the glory of God?" ⁴¹So they took the stone away.

Jesus raised his eyes to heaven and said, "Abba, thank you for having heard me. ⁴²I know that you always hear me, but I have said this for the sake of the crowd, that they might believe that you sent me!"

⁴³Then Jesus called out in a loud voice, "Lazarus, come out!"

⁴⁴And Lazarus came out of the tomb, still bound hand and foot with linen strips, his face wrapped in a cloth. Jesus told the crowd, "Untie him and let him go free."

⁴⁵Many of those who had come to console Martha and Mary, and saw what Jesus did, put their faith in him.

⁴⁶Some others, however, went to the Pharisees and reported what Jesus had done. ⁴⁷As a result, the chief priests and the Pharisees called a meeting of the Sanhedrin. "What are we to do," they said, "with this one who is performing all these miracles? ⁴⁸If we let him go on like this, everybody will believe in him, and then the Romans will come and destroy both our Temple and our nation."

⁴⁹One of them, Caiaphas, who was high priest that year, said, "You don't seem to have grasped the situation at all; ⁵⁰you fail to see that it is better for one person to die for the people, than for the whole nation to be destroyed." ⁵¹He didn't say this of his own accord; as high priest that year, he was prophesying that Jesus was to die for the nation—⁵²and not for the nation only, but to gather together into one body the scattered children of God.

⁵³From that day they were determined to kill him. ⁵⁴So Jesus no longer went about openly in Judea, but left the area for a town called Ephraim, in the region bordering on a desert, and stayed there with the disciples.

11:55–12:50

The Jewish Passover was near, and many of the country folk who had gone up to Jerusalem to purify themselves ⁵⁶were looking for Jesus, saying to one another as they stood in the Temple, "What do you think? Will he come to the festival or not?"

⁵⁷By now, the chief priests and the Pharisees had given their orders that anyone who knew where Jesus was should report it, so that they could arrest him.

12:¹Six days before Passover, Jesus went to Bethany, the village of Lazarus, whom Jesus had raised from the dead. ²There they gave a banquet in Jesus' honor, at which Martha served. Lazarus was one of those at the table. ³Mary brought a pound of costly ointment, pure nard, and anointed the feet of Jesus, wiping them with her hair. The house was full of the scent of the ointment.

⁴Judas Iscariot, one of the disciples—the one who was to betray Jesus—protested, ⁵"Why wasn't this ointment sold? It could have brought nearly a year's wages, and the money been given to poor people!" ⁶Judas didn't say this because he was concerned for poor people, but because he was a thief. He was in charge of the common fund and would help himself to it.

⁷So Jesus replied, "Leave her alone. She did this in preparation for my burial. ⁸You have poor people with you always. But you won't always have me."

⁹Meanwhile a large crowd heard that Jesus was there and came to see not only Jesus, but also Lazarus, whom he raised from the dead. ¹⁰So the chief priests planned to kill Lazarus as well, ¹¹since it was because of him that many of the people were leaving them and believing in Jesus.

☙   ☙   ☙

¹²The next day, the great crowd that had come for the Passover feast heard that Jesus was coming to Jerusalem, ¹³so they got palm branches and went out to meet him. They shouted joyfully,

> "Hosanna!
> Blessed is the One who comes
>   in the name of Our God—
>   the ruler of Israel!"

¹⁴Jesus rode in sitting upon a donkey, in accord with scripture:

> ¹⁵"Fear not, O people of Zion!
>   Your ruler comes to you
>   sitting on a donkey's colt."

¹⁶At the time, the disciples didn't understand all this, but after Jesus was glorified they recalled that the people had done to him precisely what had been written about him.

¹⁷Those who had been present when Jesus called Lazarus from the tomb and raised him from the dead continued to spread the word. ¹⁸A crowd gathered, and they went out to meet Jesus because they had heard he had performed this miraculous sign.

¹⁹Then the Pharisees said to one another, "See, this is getting us nowhere. Look—the whole world is running after him."

²⁰Among those who had come up to worship at the Passover festival were some Greeks. ²¹They approached Philip, who was from Bethsaida in Galilee, and put forth this request: "Please, we would like to see Jesus." ²²Philip went to tell Andrew, and together the two went to tell Jesus.

²³ Jesus replied,

> "Now the hour has come
>> for the Chosen One to be glorified.
> ²⁴ The truth of the matter is,
> unless a grain of wheat
>> falls on the ground and dies,
>> it remains only a single grain;
> but if it dies,
>> it yields a rich harvest.
> ²⁵ If you love your life
>> you'll lose it;
> if you hate your life in this world
>> you'll keep it for eternal life.
> ²⁶ Anyone who wants to work for me
>> must follow in my footsteps,
> and wherever I am,
>> my worker will be there too.
> Anyone who works for me
>> will be honored by Abba God.
> ²⁷ Now my soul is troubled.
> What will I say:
>> 'Abba, save me from this hour?'
> But it was for this very reason
>> that I have come to this hour.
> ²⁸ Abba, glorify your name!"

A voice came from heaven: "I have glorified it, and I will glorify it again."

²⁹ The crowds that stood nearby heard this and said it was a clap of thunder; others said, "It was an angel speaking."

³⁰ Jesus answered, "It was not for my sake that this voice came, but for yours.

> ³¹ "Sentence is now being passed on this world;
>> now the ruler of this world will be overthrown.
> ³² And when I am lifted up from this earth,
>> I will draw all people to myself."

³³ By these words Jesus indicated the kind of death he would die.

³⁴ The crowd answered, "We've heard from the Law that the Messiah will remain forever. So how can you say, 'The Chosen One must be lifted up.' Who is this Chosen One?"

³⁵ Jesus said to them,

> "The light will be with you
>> only a little while longer.

Walk while you have the light,
 before darkness overtakes you.
Those who walk in the dark
 don't know what they're doing.
³⁶ Believe in the light
 while you still have the light.
Only then will you become
 children of light."

After he said this, Jesus left and went into seclusion.

℞   ℞   ℞

³⁷ Even after Jesus worked so many miracles in their presence, they still didn't believe in him. ³⁸ This fact fulfilled the words of the prophet Isaiah:
 "O God, who has believed what we've heard?
  To whom has the authority of Our God been revealed?"
³⁹ This is why they could not believe—as Isaiah said again,
 ⁴⁰ "God has blinded their eyes
  and hardened their hearts,
 lest they see with their eyes
  and understand with their hearts
 and be converted,
  and I would have to heal them."
⁴¹ Isaiah said this because he saw Jesus glorified and spoke about him.

⁴² And yet many, even among the leaders, believed in Jesus. They refused to state their belief openly because they were afraid of the Pharisees and of being expelled from the synagogue. ⁴³ For they cared more about what people thought of them than about the glory of God.

⁴⁴ Jesus proclaimed publicly:
 "Whoever believes in me
  believes not so much in me
  as in the One who sent me;
 ⁴⁵ and whoever sees me
  sees the One who sent me.
 ⁴⁶ I have come as light into the world,
  so that whoever believes in me
  need not remain in the dark anymore.
 ⁴⁷ Anyone who hears my words
  and doesn't keep them faithfully

won't be condemned by me,
>> since I've come not to condemn the world
>> but to save it.
⁴⁸ Those who reject me and don't accept my words
>> already have their judge:
the message I have spoken
>> will be their judge on the last day.
⁴⁹ For I haven't spoken on my own;
>> no, what I was to say—how I was to speak—
>> was commanded by Abba God who sent me.
⁵⁰ Since I know that God's commandment is eternal life,
>> I say whatever Abba God has told me to say."

It was before the Feast of Passover, and Jesus realized that the hour had come for him to pass from this world to Abba God. He had always loved his own in this world, but now he showed how perfect this love was.

² The Devil had already convinced Judas Iscariot, begot of Simon, to betray Jesus. So during supper, ³ Jesus—knowing that God had put all things into his own hands, and that he had come from God and was returning to God—⁴ rose from the table, took off his clothes and wrapped a towel around his waist. ⁵ He then poured water into a basin, and began to wash the disciples' feet, and dry them with the towel that was around his waist.

⁶ When Jesus came to Simon Peter, Peter said, "Rabbi, you're not going to wash my feet, are you?"

⁷ Jesus answered, "You don't realize what I am doing right now, but later you'll understand."

⁸ Peter replied, "You'll never wash my feet!"

Jesus answered, "If I don't wash you, you have no part with me."

⁹ Simon Peter said to Jesus, "Then, Rabbi, not only my feet, but my hands and my head as well!"

¹⁰ Jesus said, "Any who have taken a bath are clean all over and only need to wash their feet—and you're clean, though not every one of you." ¹¹ For Jesus knew who was to betray him. That is why he said, "Not all of you are clean."

¹² After washing their feet, Jesus put his clothes back on and returned to the table. He said to them, "Do you understand what I have done for you? ¹³ You call me "Teacher," and "Sovereign"—and rightly, for so I am. ¹⁴ If I,

then—your Teacher and Sovereign—have washed your feet, you should wash each other's feet. ¹⁵ I have given you an example, that you should do as I have done to you.

>¹⁶ "The truth of the matter is,
>no subordinate is greater than the superior;
>>no messenger outranks the sender.
>¹⁷ Once you know all these things,
>>you'll be blessed if you put them into practice.
>¹⁸ What I say is not said about you all—
>>for I know the ones I chose—
>but so that scripture can be fulfilled:
>>'One who partook of bread with me
>>has raised a heel against me.'
>¹⁹ I tell you this now, before it takes place,
>>so that when it takes place you may believe that I AM.
>²⁰ The truth of the matter is,
>whoever accepts the one I send
>>accepts me,
>and whoever welcomes me
>>welcomes the One who sent me."

²¹ Having said this, Jesus became troubled in spirit and said, "The truth of the matter is, one of you will betray me."

²² The disciples looked at each other, puzzled as to whom he could mean. ²³ One of them, the disciple whom Jesus loved, was next to Jesus. ²⁴ Simon Peter signaled him to ask Jesus whom he meant. ²⁵ He leaned back against Jesus' chest and asked, "Rabbi, who is it?"

²⁶ Jesus answered, "The one to whom I give the piece of bread I dip in the dish." He dipped the piece of bread and gave it to Judas, begot of Simon Iscariot.

²⁷ After Judas took the bread, Satan entered his heart. Jesus said to him, "Be quick about what you're going to do." ²⁸ None of the others at the table understood the reason Jesus said this. ²⁹ Since Judas had charge of the common fund, some of them thought Jesus was telling him to buy what was needed for the festival, or to give something to the poor. ³⁰ As soon as Judas took the piece of bread, he went out into the night.

>³¹ Once Judas left, Jesus said,
>>"Now is the Chosen One glorified
>>>and God is glorified as well.
>>³² If God has been glorified,
>>>God will in turn glorify the Chosen One
>>>and will do so very soon.

³³ My little children,
   I won't be with you much longer.
You'll look for me,
   but what I said to the Temple authorities, I say to you:
where I am going,
   you cannot come.
³⁴ I give you a new commandment:
   Love one another.
And you're to love one another
   the way I have loved you.
³⁵ This is how all will know that you're my disciples:
   that you truly love one another."

³⁶ Simon Peter said, "Rabbi, where are you going?"
Jesus replied,

   "Where I am going,
      you cannot follow me now,
      though you'll follow me later."

³⁷ "Rabbi," Peter said, "Why can't I follow you now? I will lay down my life for you!"

³⁸ "Lay down your life for me?" exclaimed Jesus. "The truth of the matter is, before the cock crows you'll have disowned me three times!

14¹ "Don't let your hearts be troubled.
You have faith in God;
   have faith in me as well.
² In God's house there are many dwelling places;
   otherwise, how could I have told you
   that I was going to prepare a place for you?
³ I am indeed going to prepare a place for you,
   and then I will come back to take you with me,
that where I am
   there you may be as well.
⁴ You know the way that leads to where I am going."

⁵ Thomas replied, "But we don't know where you're going. How can we know the way?"

⁶ Jesus told him,

   "I myself am the Way—
      I am Truth,
      and I am Life.
No one comes to Abba God
   but through me.

⁷If you really knew me,
    you would know Abba God also.
From this point on,
    you know Abba God
    and you have seen God."

⁸"Rabbi," Philip said, "show us Abba God, and that will be enough for us."

⁹Jesus replied, "Have I been with you all this time, Philip, and still you don't know me?

    Whoever has seen me has seen Abba God.
        How can you say, 'Show us your Abba'?
¹⁰Don't you believe that I am in Abba God
    and God is in me?
The words I speak are not spoken of myself;
    it is Abba God, living in me,
    who is accomplishing the works of God.
¹¹Believe me that I am in God and God is in me,
    or else believe because of the works I do.
¹²The truth of the matter is,
anyone who has faith in me
    will do the works I do—
    and greater works besides.
Why? Because I go to Abba God,
¹³and whatever you ask in my name I will do,
    so that God may be glorified in me.
¹⁴Anything you ask in my name
    I will do.
¹⁵If you love me
    and obey the command I give you,
¹⁶I will ask the One who sent me
    to give you another Paraclete, another Helper
    to be with you always—
¹⁷the Spirit of truth,
    whom the world cannot accept
    since the world neither sees her nor recognizes her;
but you can recognize the Spirit
    because she remains with you
    and will be within you.
¹⁸I won't leave you orphaned;
    I will come back to you.
¹⁹A little while now and the world will see me no more;
    but you'll see me;

because I live,
    and you will live as well.
²⁰ On that day you'll know
    that I am in God,
and you are in me,
    and I am in you.
²¹ Those who obey the commandments
    are the ones who love me,
and those who love me
    will be loved by Abba God.
I, too, will love them
    and will reveal myself to them."

²² Judas—not Judas Iscariot—said, "Rabbi, why is it that you'll reveal yourself to us, and not to the whole world?"

²³ Jesus answered,

"Those who love me will be true to my word,
    and Abba God will love them;
and we will come to them
    and make our dwelling place with them.
²⁴ Those who don't love me
    don't keep my words.
Yet the message you hear is not mine;
    it comes from Abba God who sent me.
²⁵ This much have I said to you while still with you;
    ²⁶ but the Paraclete, the Holy Spirit
    whom Abba God will send in my name,
will instruct you in everything
    and she will remind you of all that I told you.
²⁷ Peace I leave with you,
    my peace I give to you;
but the kind of peace I give you
    is not like the world's peace.
Don't let your hearts be distressed;
    don't be fearful.
²⁸ You've heard me say,
    'I am going away but I will return.'
If you really loved me,
    you would rejoice because I am going to Abba God,
    for Abba is greater than I.
²⁹ I tell you this now, before it happens,
    so that when it happens you will believe.
³⁰ I won't speak much more with you,

because the ruler of this world,
who has no hold on me,
is at hand;
³¹ but I do this so that the world may know
that I love Abba God
and do as my Abba has commanded.
"Let's get up now, and be on our way.

15:1 "I am the true vine,
and my Abba is the vinegrower
² who cuts off every branch in me that doesn't bear fruit,
but prunes the fruitful ones
to increase their yield.
³ You've been pruned already,
thanks to the word that I have spoken to you.
⁴ Live on in me,
as I do in you.
Just as a branch cannot bear fruit of itself
apart from the vine,
neither can you bear fruit
apart from me.
⁵ I am the vine;
you are the branches.
Those who live in me and I in them
will bear abundant fruit,
for apart from me you can do nothing.
⁶ Those who don't live in me
are like withered, rejected branches,
to be picked up and thrown on the fire and burned.
⁷ If you live on in me,
and my words live on in you,
ask whatever you want
and it will be done for you.
⁸ My Abba will be glorified
if you bear much fruit
and thus prove to be my disciples.
⁹ As my Abba has loved me,
so have I loved you.
Live on in my love.
¹⁰ And you will live on in my love
if you keep my commandments,

just as I live on in Abba God's love
  and have kept God's commandments.
¹¹ I tell you all this that my joy may be yours,
  and your joy may be complete.
¹² This is my commandment:
  love one another as I have loved you.
¹³ There is no greater love
  than to lay down one's life for one's friends.
¹⁴ And you are my friends,
  if you do what I command you.
¹⁵ I no longer speak of you as subordinates,
  because a subordinate doesn't know a superior's business.
Instead I call you friends,
  because I have made known to you
  everything I have learned from Abba God.
¹⁶ It was not you who chose me;
  it was I who chose you
  to go forth and bear fruit.
Your fruit must endure,
  so that whatever you ask of Abba God in my name
  God will give you.
¹⁷ This command I give you:
  that you love one another.
¹⁸ If you find that the world hates you,
  remember that it hated me before you.
¹⁹ If you belonged to the world,
  the world would love you as its own;
but the reason it hates you
  is that you don't belong to the world—
  because I chose you out of the world.
²⁰ Remember what I told you:
  a subordinate is never greater than a superior—
so know that they will persecute you
  as they persecuted me,
they will respect your words
  as much as they respected mine.
²¹ They'll do all this to you because of my Name,
  for they know nothing of Abba God who sent me.
²² If I hadn't come and spoken to them,
  they would have been blameless.
But as it is,
  they have no excuse for their sin.

²³ All those who hate me
   also hate my Abba.
²⁴ If I had not done among them
   the works that no one else has ever done,
   they would be blameless.
But as it is, they have seen and hated
   both me and my Abba.
²⁵ Yet all this was only to fulfill
   what is written in the Law:
   'They hated me without cause.'
²⁶ When the Paraclete comes—
   the Spirit of Truth who comes from Abba God,
whom I myself will send from my Abba—
   she will bear witness on my behalf.
²⁷ You too must bear witness,
   for you've been with me from the beginning.
16:1 I have told you all this
   to keep your faith from being shaken.
² They will expel you from synagogues—
   and indeed, the hour is coming when anyone
   who kills you will claim to be serving God.
³ They will do these things
   because they know neither Abba God nor me.
⁴ But I have told you these things
   so that when the time comes,
   you'll remember that I told you ahead of time.
I didn't tell you this at first
   because I was with you.
⁵ Now I am going to the One who sent me—
   yet not one of you has asked, 'Where are you going?'
⁶ You're sad of heart
   because I tell you this.
⁷ Still, I must tell you the truth:
   it is much better for you that I go.
If I fail to go,
   the Paraclete will never come to you,
whereas if I go,
   I will send her to you.
⁸ When she comes,
   she will prove the world wrong
about sin, about justice
   and about judgment.

⁹ About sin—
    in that they refuse to believe in me;
¹⁰ about justice—
    because I go to Abba God
    and you will see me no more;
¹¹ about judgment—
    for the ruler of this world has been condemned.
¹² I have much more to tell you,
    but you can't bear to hear it now.
¹³ When the Spirit of truth comes,
    she will guide you into all truth.
She won't speak on her own initiative;
    rather, she'll speak only what she hears,
and she'll announce to you
    things that are yet to come.
¹⁴ In doing this, the Spirit will give glory to me,
    for she will take what is mine
    and reveal it to you.
¹⁵ Everything that Abba God has
    belongs to me.
This is why I said that
    the Spirit will take what is mine
    and reveal it to you.
¹⁶ Within a short time you won't see me,
    but soon after that you'll see me again."

¹⁷ At that, some of the disciples asked one another, "What can he mean, 'Within a short time you won't see me, but soon after that you'll see me'? And didn't he say he is going back to Abba God?"

¹⁸ They kept asking, "What is the 'short time'? We don't know what he means."

¹⁹ Since Jesus was aware that they wanted to question him, he said, "You're asking one another about my saying, 'In a short time you'll lose sight of me, but soon after that you'll see me again.'

²⁰ "The truth of the matter is,
you'll weep and mourn
    while the world rejoices;
you'll grieve for a time,
    but your grief will turn to joy.
²¹ When a woman is in labor
    she cries out, because her time has come.
When she has borne her baby
    she no longer remembers her pain,

because of her joy that a child
    has been born into the world.
²² In the same way,
    you are now grieving;
but I will see you again
    and then you'll rejoice,
    and no one will take away your joy.
²³ On that day you'll no longer
    question me about anything.
The truth of the matter is,
    if you ask Abba God for anything in my name,
    it will be given to you.
²⁴ Until now you haven't asked
    for anything in my name.
Ask, and you will receive
    so that your joy will be complete.
²⁵ I have spoken these things to you
    in veiled language.
A time is coming when I will no longer do so—
    I will tell you about Abba God in plain speech.
²⁶ On that day you will ask
    in my name.
Now, I am not saying that I'll petition Abba God for you—
    ²⁷ God already loves you,
because you have loved me
    and have believed that I came from God.
²⁸ I came from Abba God
    and have come into the world,
and now I leave the world
    to go to Abba God."

²⁹ His disciples said, "At last you're speaking plainly and not using metaphors! ³⁰ We're convinced that you know everything. There is no need for anyone to ask you questions. We do indeed believe you came from God."

³¹ Jesus answered them,
"Do you really believe?
³² An hour is coming—in fact, it has already come—
    when you will all be scattered
and go your own ways,
    leaving me alone;
yet I can never be alone,
    for Abba God is with me.

³³ I have told you all this
    that in me you may find peace.
You will suffer in the world.
    But take courage!
    I have overcome the world."

17:1 After Jesus said this, he looked up to heaven and said,
    "Abba, the hour has come!
Glorify your Only Begotten
    that I may glorify you,
² through the authority you've given me over all humankind,
    by bestowing eternal life on all those you gave me.
³ And this is eternal life:
    to know you, the only true God,
and the one you have sent,
    Jesus, the Messiah.
⁴ I have given you glory on earth
    by finishing the work you gave me to do.
⁵ Now, Abba, glorify me with your own glory,
    the glory I had with you before the world began.
⁶ I have manifested your Name
    to those you gave me from the world.
They were yours, and you gave them to me;
    and now they have kept your word.
⁷ Now they know that everything you've entrusted to me
    does indeed come from you.
⁸ I entrusted to them
    the message you entrusted to me,
    and they received it.
They know that I really came from you;
    they believe it was you who sent me.
⁹ And it's for them that I pray—
    not for the world,
but for these you've given me—
    for they are really yours,
¹⁰ just as all that belongs to me is yours,
    and all that belongs to you is mine.
It is in them
    that I have been glorified.
¹¹ I am in the world no more,
    but while I am coming to you,
    they are still in the world.

Abba, holy God,
  protect those whom you have given me
with your Name—
  the Name that you gave me—
that they may be one,
  even as we are one.
¹² As long as I was with them,
  I guarded them with your Name
  which you gave me.
I kept careful watch,
  and not one of them was lost,
except for the one who was destined to be lost
  in fulfillment of scripture.
¹³ Now I am coming to you;
  I say all this while I am still in the world
that they may have my joy
  fulfilled in themselves.
¹⁴ I gave them your word,
  and the world has hated them for it
because they don't belong to the world
  any more than I belong to the world.
¹⁵ I don't ask you to take them out of the world,
  but to guard them from the Evil One.
¹⁶ They are not of the world,
  any more than I am of the world.
¹⁷ Consecrate them—
  make them holy through the truth—
  for your word is truth.
¹⁸ As you have sent me into the world,
  so I have sent them into the world;
¹⁹ I consecrate myself now for their sakes,
  that they may be made holy in truth.
²⁰ I don't pray for them alone.
  I pray also for those
  who will believe in me through their message,
²¹ that all may be one,
  as you, Abba, are in me and I in you;
I pray that they may be one in us,
  so that the world may believe that you sent me.
²² I have given them the glory you gave me
  that they may be one, as we are one—

²³ I in them, you in me—
  that they may be made perfect in unity.
Then the world will know that you sent me,
  and that you loved them as you loved me.
²⁴ Abba, I ask that those you gave me
  may be here with me,
so they can see this glory of mine
  which is your gift to me,
because of the love you had for me
  before the foundation of the world.
²⁵ Righteous One, the world hasn't known you,
  but I have;
and these people know
  that you sent me.
²⁶ To them I have revealed your Name,
  and I will continue to reveal it
so that the love you have for me
  may live in them,
  just as I may live in them."

18:1–19:42

After Jesus had said all this, he left with the disciples and crossed the Kidron Valley. There was a garden there, and Jesus and the disciples entered it.

² Judas, the traitor, knew the place well, because Jesus often met there with his disciples. ³ Judas led the Roman cohort to the place, along with some Temple guards sent by the chief priests and Pharisees. All were armed and carried lanterns and torches.

⁴ Then Jesus, aware of everything that was going to take place, stepped forward and said to them, "Who are you looking for?"

⁵ "Are you Jesus of Nazareth?" they asked.

Jesus said, "I am." Now Judas, the traitor, was with them. ⁶ When Jesus said, "I am," they all drew back and fell to the ground.

⁷ Again, Jesus asked them, "Who are you looking for?"

They replied, "Jesus of Nazareth."

⁸ Jesus said, "I have already told you that I am the one you want. If I am the one you're looking for, let the others go." ⁹ This was to fulfill what he had spoken: "Of those you gave me, I have not lost a single one."

¹⁰Simon Peter, who had a sword, drew it and struck the high priest's attendant, cutting off his right ear. The name of the attendant was Malchus.

¹¹Jesus said to Peter, "Put your sword back in its sheath. Am I not to drink the cup Abba God has given me?"

¹²Then the cohort and its captain and the Temple guards seized and bound Jesus. ¹³They took him first to Annas. Annas was the father-in-law of Caiaphas, who was high priest that year. ¹⁴It was Caiaphas who had advised the Temple authorities that it was better to have one person die on behalf of the people.

¹⁵Simon Peter and another disciple followed Jesus. This disciple, who was known to the high priest, entered his courtyard with Jesus, ¹⁶while Peter hung back at the gate. So the disciple known to the high priest went back and spoke to the doorkeeper, and brought Peter inside.

¹⁷The doorkeeper said, "Aren't you one of this guy's followers?"

But Peter answered, "No, I'm not."

¹⁸Now the night was cold, so the attendants and guards had lit a charcoal fire and were warming themselves. Peter was with them as well, keeping warm.

¹⁹The high priest questioned Jesus about his disciples and his teachings. ²⁰Jesus answered, "I have spoken publicly to everyone; I have always taught in synagogues and in the Temple area where the whole Jewish people congregates. I have said nothing in secret. ²¹So why do you question me? Ask those who have heard me. Ask them what I said to them— they know what I said."

²²When Jesus said this, one of the guards standing by slapped him and said, "Is this how you answer the high priest?"

²³"If I've said anything wrong," Jesus replied, "point it out; but if I'm right in what I said, why do you strike me?"

²⁴Then Annas sent him, still shackled, to Caiaphas the high priest.

²⁵Meanwhile, Simon Peter was still standing there warming himself. Others asked him, "Aren't you one of his disciples?"

But Peter denied it, saying, "I am not!"

²⁶One of the attendants of the high priest, a relative of the attendant whose ear Peter had severed, spoke up: "Didn't I see you in the garden with him?"

²⁷Again Peter denied it. At that moment a rooster crowed.

CR   CR   CR

²⁸ At daybreak, they led Jesus from the house of Caiaphas to the Praetorium. The Temple authorities didn't enter the Praetorium, for they would have become ritually unclean and unable to eat the Passover seder. ²⁹ So Pilate went out to them and asked, "What charges do you bring against this person?"

³⁰ They responded, "We wouldn't have brought him to you if he weren't a criminal."

³¹ Pilate told them, "Take him yourselves, and judge him by your own Law."

The Temple authorities replied, "We don't have the power to put anyone to death." ³² This was to fulfill what Jesus had said about the way he was going to die.

³³ So Pilate reentered the Praetorium and summoned Jesus. "Are you the King of the Jews?" asked Pilate.

³⁴ Jesus answered, "Do you say this of your own accord, or have others told you about me?"

³⁵ Pilate replied, "Am I Jewish? It is your own people and the chief priests who hand you over to me. What have you done?"

³⁶ Jesus answered, "My realm is not of this world; if it belonged to this world, my people would have fought to keep me out of the hands of the Temple authorities. No, my realm is not of this world."

³⁷ Pilate said, "So you're a King?"

Jesus replied, "You say I'm a King. I was born and came into the world for one purpose—to bear witness to the truth. Everyone who seeks the truth hears my voice."

³⁸ "Truth? What is truth?" asked Pilate.

With that, Pilate went outside and spoke to the people. "I find no guilt in him," he said. ³⁹ "But according to your custom, I always release a prisoner at the Passover. Do you want me to release 'the King of the Jews'?"

⁴⁰ They shouted, "Not him! We want Barabbas!" Barabbas was a robber.

19:1 So Pilate ordered that Jesus be flogged. ² Then the soldiers wove a crown out of thorns and put it on his head, and dressed him in a purple robe. ³ They went up to him repeatedly and said, "All hail the King of the Jews!" And they struck him in the face.

⁴ Pilate came outside once more and said to the crowd, "Look, I'll bring him out here to make you understand that I find no guilt in him." ⁵ So Jesus came out wearing the purple robe and the crown of thorns, and Pilate said, "Look upon the one you accuse!"

⁶ When the chief priests and the Temple guards saw Jesus, they shouted, "Crucify him! Crucify him!"

Pilate told them, "Do it yourself. I find no reason to condemn him."

⁷ "We have a law," the Temple authorities replied, "that says he ought to die because he claimed to be the Only Begotten of God."

⁸ When Pilate heard this, he was even more afraid. ⁹ He went back into the Praetorium and asked Jesus, "Where do you come from?"

Jesus didn't answer.

¹⁰ Then Pilate said to Jesus, "You refuse to speak? Bear in mind that I have the power to release you—and the power to crucify you."

¹¹ "You would have no authority over me," Jesus replied, "unless it had been given to you by God. Therefore the person who handed me over to you has the greater sin."

¹² Upon hearing this, Pilate attempted to set Jesus free. But the crowd shouted, "If you set him free, you're no 'friend of Caesar.' Anyone who claims to be a king defies Caesar!"

¹³ Hearing these words, Pilate took Jesus outside and seated himself on the judge's seat at the place called the Pavement—"Gabbatha," in Hebrew.

¹⁴ Now it was almost noon on Preparation Day for the Passover. Pilate said to the people, "Here is your king!"

¹⁵ "Take him away!" they shouted. "Take him away! Crucify him!"

Pilate asked, "Do you want me to crucify your king?"

The chief priests said, "We have no king but Caesar!"

¹⁶ Then Pilate handed Jesus over to them to be crucified.

℞   ℞   ℞

So they took Jesus, ¹⁷ carrying his own cross, to what is called the Place of the Skull—in Hebrew, "Golgotha." ¹⁸ There they crucified him, along with two others, one on either side of Jesus.

¹⁹ Pilate wrote a notice and had it put on the cross. It read, "Jesus of Nazareth, King of the Jews." ²⁰ The notice, in Hebrew, Greek and Latin, was read by many people, because the place where Jesus was crucified was near the city. ²¹ The chief priests said to Pilate, "Don't write 'King of the Jews,' but, 'This one said, I am King of the Jews.' "

²² Pilate replied, "I have written what I have written."

²³ After the soldiers had crucified Jesus, they took his clothing and divided it into four pieces, one piece for each soldier. They also took the seamless robe. ²⁴ The soldiers said to one another, "Let's not tear it. We can throw dice to see who will get it."

This happened in order to fulfill the scripture, "They divided my garments among them and, for my clothing, they cast lots." And this is what they did.

²⁵ Standing close to Jesus' cross were his mother; his mother's sister, Mary, the wife of Clopas; and Mary of Magdala. ²⁶ When Jesus saw his mother and the disciple whom he loved standing there, he said to his mother, "Here is your son." ²⁷ Then he said to his disciple, "Here is your mother." From that moment, the disciple took her into his household.

²⁸ After this, Jesus knew that now all was completed, and to fulfill scripture perfectly, he said, "I am thirsty." ²⁹ There was a jar of cheap wine nearby, so they put a sponge soaked in the wine on a hyssop stick and raised it to his lips.

³⁰ Jesus took the wine and said, "It is finished." Then he bowed his head and gave up his spirit.

³¹ Since it was Preparation Day, the Temple authorities asked Pilate to let them break the legs of those crucified, and take their bodies from the crosses. They requested this to prevent the bodies remaining on the cross during the Sabbath, since that particular Sabbath was a solemn feast day.

³² So the soldiers came and broke the legs of first one and then the other who had been crucified with Jesus. ³³ But when they came to Jesus, they found that he was already dead, so they didn't break his legs. ³⁴ One of the soldiers, however, pierced Jesus' side with a lance, and immediately blood and water poured out. ³⁵ This testimony has been given by an eyewitness whose word is reliable; the witness knows that this testimony is the truth, so that you will believe. ³⁶ These things were done to fulfill the scripture, "Not one of his bones will be broken." ³⁷ And again, another scripture says, "They will look on the one whom they have pierced."

³⁸ After this, Joseph of Arimathea, a disciple of Jesus—but a secret one, for fear of the Temple authorities—asked Pilate for permission to remove the body of Jesus, and Pilate granted it. So Joseph came and took it away. ³⁹ Nicodemus came as well—the same one who had first come to Jesus by night—and he brought about one hundred pounds of spices, a mixture of myrrh and aloes. ⁴⁰ They took the body of Jesus and wrapped it with the spices in linen cloths, according to the Jewish burial custom.

⁴¹ There was a garden in the place where Jesus had been crucified, and in the garden was a new tomb where no one had ever been buried. ⁴² Since it was the day before the Sabbath and the tomb was nearby, they buried Jesus there.

early in the morning on the first day of the week, while it was still dark, Mary of Magdala came to the tomb. She saw that the stone had been rolled away from the entrance, ²so she ran off to Simon Peter and the other disciple—the one Jesus loved—and told them, "The Rabbi has been taken from the tomb! We don't know where they have put Jesus!"

³ At that, Peter and the other disciple started out toward the tomb. ⁴They were running side by side, but then the other disciple outran Peter and reached the tomb first. ⁵He didn't enter, but bent down to peer in and saw the linen wrappings lying on the ground. ⁶Then Simon Peter arrived and entered the tomb. He observed the linen wrappings on the ground, ⁷and saw the piece of cloth that had covered Jesus' head lying not with the wrappings, but rolled up in a place by itself. ⁸Then the disciple who had arrived first at the tomb went in. He saw and believed. ⁹As yet, they didn't understand the scripture that Jesus was to rise from the dead. ¹⁰Then the disciples went back to their homes.

¹¹ Meanwhile, Mary stood weeping beside the tomb. Even as she wept, she stooped to peer inside, ¹²and there she saw two angels in dazzling robes. One was seated at the head and the other at the foot of the place where Jesus' body had lain.

¹³They asked her, "Why are you weeping?"

She answered them, "Because they have taken away my Rabbi, and I don't know where they have put the body."

¹⁴No sooner had she said this than she turned around and caught sight of Jesus standing there, but she didn't know it was Jesus. ¹⁵He asked her, "Why are you weeping? For whom are you looking?"

She supposed it was the gardener, so she said, "Please, if you're the one who carried Jesus away, tell me where you've laid the body and I will take it away."

¹⁶Jesus said to her, "Mary!"

She turned to him and said, "Rabboni!"—which means "Teacher."

¹⁷Jesus then said, "Don't hold on to me, for I have not yet ascended to Abba God. Rather, go to the sisters and brothers and tell them, 'I'm ascending to my Abba and to your Abba, my God and your God!' "

¹⁸Mary of Magdala went to the disciples. "I have seen the Teacher!" she announced. Then she reported what the savior had said to her.

¹⁹ In the evening of that same day, the first day of the week, the doors were locked in the room where the disciples were, for fear of the Temple authorities.

Jesus came and stood among them and said, "Peace be with you." [20] Having said this, the savior showed them the marks of crucifixion.

The disciples were filled with joy when they saw Jesus, [21] who said to them again, "Peace be with you. As Abba God sent me, so I'm sending you."

[22] After saying this, Jesus breathed on them and said,

"Receive the Holy Spirit.
[23] If you forgive anyone's sins, they are forgiven.
If you retain anyone's sins, they are retained."

[24] It happened that one of the Twelve, Thomas—nicknamed Didymus, or "Twin"—was absent when Jesus came. [25] The other disciples kept telling him, "We've seen Jesus!"

Thomas' answer was, "I'll never believe it without putting my finger in the nail marks and my hand into the spear wound."

[26] On the eighth day, the disciples were once more in the room, and this time Thomas was with them. Despite the locked doors, Jesus came and stood before them, saying, "Peace be with you."

[27] Then, to Thomas, Jesus said, "Take your finger and examine my hands. Put your hand into my side. Don't persist in your unbelief, but believe!"

[28] Thomas said in response, "My Savior and my God!"

[29] Jesus then said,

"You've become a believer
because you saw me.
Blessed are those who have not seen
and yet have believed."

[30] Jesus performed many other signs as well—signs not recorded here— in the presence of the disciples. [31] But these have been recorded to help you believe that Jesus is the Messiah, the Only Begotten, so that by believing you may have life in Jesus' Name.

Ↄ   Ↄ   Ↄ

21[1] Later Jesus again was manifested to the disciples at Lake Tiberias. This is how the appearance took place.

[2] Assembled were Simon Peter, Thomas "the Twin," Nathanael of Cana in Galilee, Zebedee's children, and two other disciples. [3] Simon Peter said to them, "I'm going out to fish."

"We'll join you," they replied, and went off to get into their boat.

All through the night they caught nothing. [4] Just after daybreak, Jesus was standing on the shore, though none of the disciples knew it was Jesus. [5] He said to them, "Have you caught anything, friends?"

"Not a thing," they answered.

[6] "Cast your net off to the starboard side," Jesus suggested, "and you'll find something."

So they made a cast and caught so many fish that they couldn't haul the net in. [7] Then the disciple whom Jesus loved cried out to Peter, "It's the Teacher!"

Upon hearing this, Simon Peter threw on his cloak—he was naked—and jumped into the water.

[8] Meanwhile the other disciples brought the boat to shore, towing the net full of fish. They were not far from land—no more than a hundred yards. [9] When they landed, they saw that a charcoal fire had been prepared, with fish and some bread already being grilled. [10] "Bring some of the fish you just caught," Jesus told them. [11] Simon Peter went aboard and hauled ashore the net, which was loaded with huge fish—one hundred fifty-three of them. In spite of the great number, the net was not torn.

[12] "Come and eat your meal," Jesus told them.

None of the disciples dared to ask, "Who are you?" —they knew it was the savior.

[13] Jesus came over, took the bread and gave it to them, and did the same with the fish. [14] This marked the third time that Jesus had appeared to the disciples after being raised from the dead.

[15] When they had eaten their meal, Jesus said to Simon Peter, "Simon, begot of John, do you love me more than these?"

Peter said, "Yes, Rabbi, you know that I'm your friend."

Jesus said, "Feed my lambs."

[16] A second time Jesus put the question, "Simon, begot of John, do you love me?"

Peter said, "Yes, Rabbi, you know that I'm your friend."

Jesus replied, "Tend my sheep."

[17] A third time Jesus asked him, "Simon, begot of John, do you love me as a friend would?"

Peter was hurt because Jesus asked, "Do you love me?" a third time. So he said, "You know everything, Rabbi. You know that I am your friend."

Jesus said, "Feed my sheep.

    [18] The truth of the matter is,
      when you were young,

you put on your own belt
 and walked where you liked;
but when you get old,
 you will stretch out your hands
and someone else will put a belt around you
 and take you where you don't want to go."

[19] With these words, Jesus indicated the kind of death by which Peter would glorify God.

Then the savior said, "Follow me."

[20] Peter turned around and noticed that the disciple whom Jesus loved was following them—the one who had leaned over during the supper and asked, "Rabbi, which one will hand you over?" [21] Seeing him, Peter was prompted to ask, "But what about him, Rabbi?"

[22] Jesus replied, "If I want him to stay behind until I come, what does it matter to you? You're to follow me." [23] This is how the rumor spread among the sisters and brothers that this disciple would not die. Yet Jesus had not said to Peter, "He won't die," but rather, "If I want him to stay behind until I come, what does it matter to you?"

[24] This disciple is the one who was an eyewitness to these things and wrote them down, and we know that his testimony is true.

         ☙   ☙   ☙

[25] There are many other things that Jesus did—yet if they were written down in detail, the world itself, I suppose, couldn't hold all the books that would have to be written.

the
acts
of the apostles

1:1 – 2:47

I

n my earlier account, theophilus, i dealt
with everything that Jesus had done and taught, [2] from the beginning until
the day he was taken up, after he had given instructions through the Holy
Spirit to the apostles he had chosen. [3] After the Passion, Jesus appeared alive
to the apostles—confirmed through many convincing proofs—over the
course of forty days, and spoke to them about the reign of God.

[4] On one occasion, Jesus told them not to leave Jerusalem. "Wait, rather,
for what God has promised, of which you have heard me speak," Jesus
said. [5] "John baptized with water, but within a few days you will be baptized with the Holy Spirit."

[6] While meeting together they asked, "Has the time come, Rabbi? Are you
going to restore sovereignty to Israel?"

[7] Jesus replied, "It's not for you to know times or dates that Abba God
has decided. [8] You will receive power when the Holy Spirit comes upon
you; then you will be my witnesses in Jerusalem, throughout Judea and
Samaria, and even to the ends of the earth."

⁹Having said this, Jesus was lifted up in a cloud before their eyes and taken from their sight. ¹⁰They were still gazing up into the heavens when two messengers dressed in white stood beside them. ¹¹"You Galileans— why are you standing here looking up at the skies?" they asked. "Jesus, who has been taken from you—this same Jesus will return, in the same way you watched him go into heaven."

☙   ☙   ☙

¹²The apostles returned to Jerusalem from the Mount of Olives, a mere Sabbath's walk away. ¹³Entering the city, they went to the upstairs room where they were staying—Peter, John, James and Andrew; Philip, Thomas, Bartholomew and Matthew; James, begot of Alphaeus; Simon, a member of the Zealot sect; and Judah, begot of Jacob. ¹⁴Also in their company were some of the women who followed Jesus, his mother Mary, and some of Jesus' sisters and brothers. With one mind, they devoted themselves to constant prayer.

¹⁵One day Peter stood up in the midst of the believers, a gathering of perhaps a hundred and twenty. ¹⁶"Sisters and brothers," he said, "the saying in scripture, uttered long ago by the Holy Spirit through the mouth of David, was destined to be fulfilled in Judas, the one who guided those who arrested Jesus. ¹⁷He was one of our number and had been given a share in this ministry. ¹⁸He bought a field with the money he received for his injustice. He collapsed there, his body burst open, and his guts poured out. ¹⁹Everyone in Jerusalem heard about it, and the field became known as 'Akeldama,' the Field of Blood.

²⁰"But David wrote in the Book of Psalms,

> 'Let his encampment be desolate;
> may no one dwell on it.'

And,

> 'Let another take his office.'

²¹"It is necessary, therefore, that one of those who accompanied us all the time that Jesus moved among us, ²²from the baptism of John until the day Jesus was taken up from us, should be named as witness with us to the Resurrection."

²³At that, they nominated two—Joseph, called Barsabbas or Justus, and Matthias. ²⁴Then they prayed, "O God, you can read the hearts of people. Show us which of these two you have chosen ²⁵to occupy this apostolic ministry, replacing Judas, who turned away and went his own way." ²⁶They then drew lots between the two. The choice fell to Matthias, who was added to the eleven apostles.

CR   CR   CR

2:1 When the day of Pentecost arrived, they all met in one room. ²Suddenly they heard what sounded like a violent, rushing wind from heaven; the noise filled the entire house in which they were sitting. ³Something appeared to them that seemed like tongues of fire; these separated and came to rest on the head of each one. ⁴They were all filled with the Holy Spirit, and began to speak in other languages as she enabled them.

⁵Now there were devout people living in Jerusalem from every nation under heaven, ⁶and at this sound they all assembled. But they were bewildered to hear their native languages being spoken. ⁷They were amazed and astonished: "Surely all of these people speaking are Galileans! ⁸How does it happen that each of us hears these words in our native tongue? ⁹We are Parthians, Medes and Elamites, people from Mesopotamia, Judea and Cappadocia, Pontus and Asia, ¹⁰Phrygia and Pamphylia, Egypt and the parts of Libya around Cyrene, as well as visitors from Rome— ¹¹all Jews, or converts to Judaism—Cretans and Arabs, too; we hear them preaching, each in our own language, about the marvels of God!"

¹²All were amazed and disturbed. They asked each other, "What does this mean?" ¹³But others said mockingly, "They've drunk too much new wine."

¹⁴Then Peter stood up with the Eleven and addressed the crowd: "Women and men of Judea, and all you who live in Jerusalem! Listen to what I have to say! ¹⁵These people are not drunk as you think—it's only nine o'clock in the morning! ¹⁶No, it's what Joel the prophet spoke of:

¹⁷'In the days to come—
    it is Our God who speaks—
I will pour out my Spirit
    on all humankind.
Your daughters and sons will prophesy,
    your young people will see visions,
    and your elders will dream dreams.
¹⁸Even on the most insignificant of my people,
    both women and men,
 I will pour out my Spirit in those days,
    and they will prophesy.
¹⁹And I will display wonders
    in the heavens above
and signs on the earth below:
    blood, fire and billowing smoke.
²⁰The sun will be turned into darkness
    and the moon will become blood

before the coming of the
  great and sublime day of Our God.
  [21] And all who call upon the name
  of Our God will be saved.'

[22] "People of Israel, hear this: Jesus of Nazareth was sent to you with miracles, portents and signs as his credentials—which God performed through him in your midst, as you well know. [23] Jesus was delivered up by the set purpose and plan of God; you even made use of godless people to crucify and kill him. [24] God freed him from death's bitter pangs, however, and raised him up again, for it was impossible that death could keep its hold on him. [25] David says,

  'I have set Our God ever before me;
    God is at my right hand, and I will not be disturbed.
  [26] My heart has been glad, my tongue has rejoiced,
    my body will live on in hope,
  [27] for you will not abandon my soul to Hades,
    nor will you let your faithful one undergo decay.
  [28] You have shown me the paths of Life;
    you will fill me with joy in your presence.'

[29] "Sisters and brothers, I can speak confidently to you about our ancestor David. He died and was buried, and his grave is with us to this day. [30] But he was a prophet, and he knew that God had promised him with an oath that one of his descendants would sit upon his throne. [31] So what he was foreseeing and talking about was the resurrection of the Messiah: the one not abandoned to the underworld, whose body didn't decay. [32] God raised Jesus to life, and we are all witnesses to that.

[33] "Exalted to the right hand of God, Jesus received the promise of the Holy Spirit from Abba God, and what you now hear and see is the outpouring of that promise. [34] For David, who didn't ascend into the heavens, said,

  'God said to my Sovereign:
    "Sit at my right hand
    [35] until I place your enemies under your foot." '

[36] "Therefore, let the whole House of Israel know beyond any doubt that God made this Jesus—whom you crucified—both Messiah and Sovereign."

[37] When they heard this, they were deeply shaken. They asked Peter and the other disciples, "What are we to do?"

[38] Peter replied, "You must repent and be baptized, each one of you, in the name of Jesus the Messiah, that your sins may be forgiven; then you will receive the gift of the Holy Spirit. [39] It was to you and your children

that the promise was made, and to all those still far off whom Our God calls."

⁴⁰ In support of his testimony, Peter used many other arguments and kept saying, "Save yourselves from this corrupt generation!" ⁴¹ They were convinced by his arguments, and they accepted what he said and were baptized. That very day about three thousand were added to the number of those converted.

⁴² They devoted themselves to the apostles' instructions and the communal life, to the breaking of bread and the prayers. ⁴³ A reverent fear overtook them all, for many wonders and signs were being performed by the apostles. ⁴⁴ Those who believed lived together, shared all things in common; ⁴⁵ they would sell their property and goods, sharing the proceeds with one another as each had need. ⁴⁶ They met in the Temple and they broke bread together in their homes every day. With joyful and sincere hearts they took their meals in common, ⁴⁷ praising God and winning the approval of all the people. Day by day, God added to their number those who were being saved.

3:1–5:42

One day, when Peter and John were going up to the Temple for prayer at about three in the afternoon, ² a person who from birth was unable to walk was being carried in. Every day the individual was brought to the Temple gate called "the Beautiful," to beg from people as they came in.

³ Seeing Peter and John on their way in, the person being carried begged them for alms. ⁴ Peter fixed his gaze on the individual, as did John. "Look at us!" Peter said. ⁵ The person looked at them intently, hoping to get something.

⁶ Then Peter said, "I have neither silver nor gold, but what I have I give you! In the name of Jesus Christ of Nazareth, walk!"

⁷ Peter pulled the person up by the right hand. Immediately the beggar's ankles and feet became strong; ⁸ the individual jumped up, stood for a moment, began to walk around, then went into the Temple with them— walking, jumping about and praising God. ⁹ When the people saw the beggar walking and giving praise to God, ¹⁰ they recognized the one who used to sit and beg at the Beautiful Gate of the Temple. They were struck with astonishment—utterly stupefied at what had happened.

¹¹ As the person who had been healed stood clinging to Peter and John, the whole crowd rushed over to them excitedly in Solomon's Porch. ¹² When Peter saw this, he addressed the people as follows:

"Why does this surprise you? Why do you stare at us as if we had made this person walk by our own power or holiness? You are Israelites, ¹³and it is the God of Sarah and Abraham, Rebecca and Isaac, Leah and Rachel and Jacob, the God of our ancestors, who has glorified Jesus—the same Jesus you handed over and then disowned in the presence of Pilate, after Pilate had decided to release him. ¹⁴You disowned the Holy and Just One and asked instead for the release of a murderer. ¹⁵You put to death the Author of life, whom God raised from the dead—a fact to which we are witnesses. ¹⁶It is the name of Jesus, and faith in it, that has strengthened the limbs of this one whom you see and know well. Such faith has given this beggar perfect health, as all of you can see.

¹⁷"Yet I know, my sisters and brothers, that you acted out of ignorance, just as your leaders did. ¹⁸God has brought to fulfillment by this means what was announced long ago by the prophets: that the Messiah would suffer. ¹⁹Therefore, reform your lives! Turn to God, that your sins may be wiped away, ²⁰and that God may send a season of refreshment. Then Our God will send you Jesus, the preordained Messiah, ²¹whom heaven must keep until the restoration of all things comes, which God promised through the holy prophets in ancient times. ²²Moses, for example, said, 'Our God will raise up a prophet like me for you, from among your own kinfolk. You must listen to everything this prophet tells you. ²³Anyone who doesn't listen is to be cut off ruthlessly from the people.' ²⁴In fact, all the prophets who have ever spoken, from Samuel onward, have predicted these days.

²⁵"You are the heirs of the prophets, the heirs of the Covenant the Most High made with our ancestors when God told Sarah and Abraham, 'In your offspring all the families of the earth will be blessed.' ²⁶It was for you that God raised up and sent this Jesus, to bless you by turning every one of you from your wicked ways."

^{4:1}While the apostles were still addressing the crowd, the priests, the captain of the Temple guard and the Sadducees came up to them, ²angry because they were teaching the people and proclaiming the resurrection of the dead in the person of Jesus. ³It was evening by now, so the authorities arrested the apostles and put them in jail for the night. ⁴Despite this, many of those who had heard the speech believed—the total number had now risen to something like five thousand.

℞   ℞   ℞

⁵When the leaders, the elders and the scribes met the next day in Jerusalem, ⁶Annas the high priest, Caiaphas, Jochanan, Alexander and all who

were of the high priestly class were there. ⁷They brought Peter and John before them and began to interrogate them: "By what power and in whose name have you done this?"

⁸Then Peter, filled with the Holy Spirit, spoke up: "Leaders of the people! Elders! ⁹If we must answer today for a good deed done to a person who was unable to walk, and explain how this person has been made whole, ¹⁰then you and all the people of Israel must realize that it was done in the name of Jesus Christ of Nazareth, whom you crucified and whom God raised from the dead. In the power of that Name, this person stands before you perfectly sound. ¹¹This Jesus is 'the stone rejected by the builders which has become the cornerstone.' ¹²There is no salvation in anyone else, for there is no other name under heaven given to the human race by which we must be saved."

¹³They were amazed as they observed the self-assurance of Peter and John, and they realized that the speakers were uneducated and of no standing. Then they recognized them as having been with Jesus.

¹⁴When they saw the person who had been healed standing there with them, they could think of nothing to say, ¹⁵so they ordered them out of the court while they consulted. ¹⁶"What will we do with these two? Everyone who lives in Jerusalem knows what a remarkable show of power took place through them. We can't deny it. ¹⁷To stop this from spreading further among the people, we must give them a stern warning never to mention the Galilean's name to anyone again." ¹⁸So the priests and elders called the apostles back and made it clear that under no circumstances were they to speak the name of Jesus or teach anything about Jesus.

¹⁹Peter and John answered, "Judge for yourselves whether it's right in God's sight for us to obey you rather than God. ²⁰Surely we cannot help speaking of what we have heard and seen."

²¹At that point, they were dismissed with further warnings. The court could find no way to punish them, because all the people were praising God for what they had seen and heard. ²²The person who had been miraculously healed was over forty years old.

²³After being released, they went back to their own people and told them what the priests and elders had said. ²⁴On hearing the story, they all raised their voices in prayer to the Most High and said, "O Sovereign God, 'who made heaven and earth, the seas and all that is in them,' ²⁵you have said by the Holy Spirit through the lips of David, your servant,

'Why this arrogance among the nations,
    these futile plots among the peoples?
²⁶Rulers of the earth are setting out to war,
    and leaders are making alliances

> against the Most High
> and against God's Anointed One.'

²⁷ "This is what has come true: in this very city, Herod and Pontius Pilate made an alliance with the Gentiles and the peoples of Israel, against your holy child Jesus whom you anointed, ²⁸ but only to bring about the very thing that you in your strength and wisdom had predetermined should happen.

²⁹ "And now, O God, take note of their threats and help your faithful ones to proclaim your message with all boldness: ³⁰ stretch out your hand to heal and to work miracles and marvels through the name of your holy child Jesus." ³¹ As they prayed, the house where they were assembled was shaken; they were all filled with the Holy Spirit and began to proclaim the word of God boldly.

℘   ℘   ℘

³² The community of believers was of one mind and one heart. None of them claimed anything as their own; rather, everything was held in common. ³³ The apostles continued to testify with great power to the resurrection of Jesus Christ, and they were all given great respect; ³⁴ nor was anyone needy among them, for those who owned property or houses would sell them ³⁵ and give the money to the apostles. It was then distributed to any members who might be in need.

³⁶ There was a certain Levite from Cyprus named Joseph—to whom the apostles gave the name Barnabas, which means "encourager." ³⁷ He sold a farm that he owned and made a donation of the money, presenting it to the apostles.

⁵:¹ Now a couple, Ananias and Sapphira, sold a piece of their property too, ² but they conspired to keep part of the proceeds for themselves. Ananias brought the remainder and presented it to the apostles.

³ Peter said, "Ananias, has Satan so possessed you that you lie to the Holy Spirit by secretly withholding part of the proceeds of the property? ⁴ It belonged to you and Sapphira before you sold it, didn't it? And when you sold it, didn't you still have control of the money? How could you have conceived such a thing in your heart? You have not lied to people. You have lied to God!"

⁵ When Ananias heard this, he dropped dead on the spot. Great fear came upon all those present. ⁶ Young people in the crowd came up, wrapped up the body and took it away for burial.

⁷ About three hours later, Sapphira entered. She was unaware of what

had happened. ⁸Peter said to her, "Did you sell the property for such-and-such a price?"

"Yes," she replied, "that was the price."

⁹Peter said to her, "Why did you conspire to test the Spirit of Our God? Listen! The feet of those who buried your husband are at the door, and they will carry you out as well!"

¹⁰She immediately dropped dead at his feet. The young people entered and found her dead, so they carried her out and buried her next to her husband.

¹¹Great fear overcame the whole church and all who heard about this incident.

ॐ   ॐ   ॐ

¹²Through the hands of the apostles, many signs and wonders occurred among the people. By mutual agreement, they used to meet in Solomon's Porch. ¹³But none of the others dared to join them, despite the fact that the people held the apostles in great esteem.

¹⁴Even so, more and more believers, women and men in great numbers, were continually added to their community—¹⁵to the extent that people even carried their sick relatives and friends into the street and laid them on cots and mattresses, in the hope that when Peter passed by, his shadow might fall on one or another of them. ¹⁶Crowds from the towns around Jerusalem would gather, too, bringing their sick people and those who were troubled by unclean spirits, and they were all being healed.

¹⁷Then the high priest and all his supporters, who were members of the Sadducee party, were filled with jealousy; ¹⁸they arrested the apostles and threw them into jail.

¹⁹During the night, however, an angel of God opened the gates of the jail, led them out and said, ²⁰"Go and stand in the Temple and tell the people all about this Life." ²¹When they heard this, they went into the Temple at dawn and resumed their preaching.

When the high priest and his supporters arrived, they convened the Sanhedrin—the full senate of Israel—and sent word to the jail that the prisoners were to be brought in. ²²But when the Temple guard got to the jail, they couldn't find them, and they hurried back to report, ²³"We found the jail securely locked and the guards at their posts outside, but when we opened the cell, we found no one inside."

²⁴On hearing this report, the captain of the Temple guard and the high priests didn't know what to make of it. ²⁵Then a courier arrived with fresh news: "At this very moment those you put in jail are in the Temple. They're

standing there in the Temple, teaching the people." ²⁶ At that, the captain went off with the guard and arrested them once again, but without a show of force, for fear of being stoned by the crowd.

²⁷ The apostles were taken before the Sanhedrin, and the high priest began to interrogate them: ²⁸ "We gave you strict orders not to teach about that name, yet you have filled Jerusalem with your teaching—and you're determined to make us responsible for this Jesus' blood."

²⁹ To this, Peter and the apostles replied, "Better for us to obey God than people! ³⁰ The God of our ancestors has raised Jesus, whom you put to death by hanging him on a tree. ³¹ This One, who has been exalted to God's right hand as Ruler and Savior, is to bring repentance and the forgiveness of sins to Israel. ³² We are eyewitnesses to this. And so is the Holy Spirit, who has been given to those who obey God."

³³ When the Sanhedrin heard this, they were furious and intended to kill the apostles. ³⁴ However, a member of the Sanhedrin—a Pharisee named Gamaliel, an authority on the Law and respected by the people—stood up and asked that the apostles be removed from the room. ³⁵ Then he addressed the Sanhedrin:

"Israelites, think twice about what you are going to do with these people. ³⁶ Not long ago, a certain Theudas came around and tried to pass himself off as someone important. About four hundred joined him. But when he was killed, all his followers scattered, and that was the end of it. ³⁷ Then there was Judah the Galilean, at the time of the census. He attracted supporters too, but when he was killed, his support dissipated. ³⁸ The present case is similar. My advice is that you leave these people alone and let them be. If this movement, this activity, is of human origin, it will destroy itself. ³⁹ If, on the other hand, it comes from God, not only will you be unable to destroy them, but you might find yourselves fighting against God."

⁴⁰ They took Gamaliel's advice, and called in the apostles and flogged them. After ordering them not to speak again in the name of Jesus, they dismissed them. ⁴¹ The apostles left the Sanhedrin full of joy that they had been judged worthy to suffer shame for the sake of the Name. ⁴² Every day they preached in the Temple and in people's homes, continually proclaiming Jesus as the Messiah.

Ín those days, as the number of disciples grew, a dispute arose between the Hellenistic Jews and those who spoke Hebrew, that the Greek-speaking widows were being neglected in the daily distribution of food. ² The

Twelve assembled the community of disciples and said, "It's not right for us to neglect the word of God in order to wait on tables. ³ Look around among your numbers for seven people who are acknowledged to be deeply spiritual and prudent, and we will appoint them to this task. ⁴ This will permit us to concentrate on prayer and the ministry of the word."

⁵ The proposal was unanimously accepted by the community. They selected Stephen, full of faith and the Holy Spirit; Philip; Prochorus; Nicanor; Timon; Parmenas; and Nicolaus of Antioch, who had been a convert to Judaism. ⁶ They were presented to the apostles, who prayed over them and laid hands on them.

⁷ The word of God continued to spread, while at the same time the number of disciples in Jerusalem increased enormously, and a large group of priests became obedient to the faith.

ℛ   ℛ   ℛ

⁸ Stephen was filled with grace and power to work miracles and great signs among the people. ⁹ But then certain individuals came forward who were members of what was called the Synagogue of Freedom, and argued with Stephen; some were from Cyrene and Alexandria, others from Cilicia and Asia Minor. ¹⁰ They found they were no match for Stephen's wisdom, because Stephen was speaking through the Spirit.

¹¹ So they procured some false witnesses to say, "We heard him using blasphemous language against Moses and against God." ¹² They incited the people, the elders and the scribes, and together they seized Stephen and dragged him away, bringing him before the Sanhedrin.

¹³ Again they put up the false witnesses, who said, "This person is always making speeches against the Holy Place and the Law. ¹⁴ We've heard him say that Jesus of Nazareth is going to destroy the sanctuary and alter the traditions Moses handed down to us." ¹⁵ The members of the Sanhedrin looked intently at Stephen, whose face appeared to them like the face of an angel.

7:1 The high priest asked, "Is this true?"

² Stephen replied, "Sisters and brothers, mothers and fathers, members of the Sanhedrin, hear what I have to say! The God of Glory appeared to Sarah and Abraham, our ancestors, before they left Mesopotamia and before they settled in Haran. ³ God said to them, 'Leave this place—your land and your relatives—for the place I will show you.' ⁴ So they left Chaldaea and settled in Haran. After their parents died, they migrated to the place where you now live—⁵ without an inheritance and without a single square foot of land.

"But God promised this place to them and their descendants, even though they were childless. ⁶God said, 'Your descendants will be aliens in a foreign land, where they will be enslaved and oppressed for four hundred years. ⁷But I will pass judgment on the people who enslaved them. After that they will come out of bondage and worship me here.' ⁸Then God gave them the sign of the Covenant—they became the parents of Isaac, circumcising him on the eighth day. Isaac passed the Covenant on to Jacob and Rachel and Leah, and they passed it on to their twelve children.

⁹"These twelve grew jealous of Joseph, and sold him into slavery in Egypt. But God, who was with Joseph, ¹⁰rescued him from his troubles and gave him such wisdom that he caught the eye of Pharaoh, the ruler of Egypt, who made him governor of the country and ruler of the entire household.

¹¹"Then a famine struck Egypt and Canaan. It wrought such suffering that our ancestors couldn't find food to eat. ¹²But when Jacob heard that there was grain in Egypt, he sent our forebears there on a first visit. ¹³On their second visit, Joseph told his brothers who he was. He explained the same to Pharaoh about his family. ¹⁴Then he sent for Jacob, Rachel and Leah, along with all their relatives—about seventy-five families in all—¹⁵and they all went down into Egypt. When Jacob and our ancestors died, they were buried in Egypt, ¹⁶to be brought back eventually to Shechem and placed in the tomb that Sarah and Abraham purchased from the children of Hamor in Shechem.

¹⁷"When the time grew near for the fulfillment of the promise God made to Sarah and Abraham, the number of our people had grown very large. ¹⁸Then another ruler, who knew nothing about Joseph, came to power. ¹⁹He exploited our people and tyrannized them, forcing them to abandon their babies and let them die from exposure.

²⁰"It was at this time that Moses was born. Lovely in God's sight, Moses was nursed in his parents' house for three months. ²¹Then Moses too was abandoned to the elements, but was discovered by Pharaoh's daughter, who adopted and raised him as her own child. ²²He was educated in all the wisdom of the Egyptians, and grew powerful in speech and deeds.

²³"When Moses was forty years old he decided to visit his kinfolk, the Israelites. ²⁴When he saw one of them being abused by an Egyptian, he rescued the Israelite by killing the Egyptian. ²⁵Moses assumed that his kin would realize that God was offering them liberation through himself, but they didn't understand. ²⁶The next day, Moses came across two Israelites fighting; he tried to reconcile them by saying, 'Friends, you're related by blood—why are you hurting each other?' ²⁷One of them pushed Moses aside, saying, 'Who appointed you our ruler and judge? ²⁸Are you plan-

ning to kill me as you did the Egyptian yesterday?' ²⁹ Moses fled when he heard this, and settled in the land of Midian. While there he had two children with his wife Zipporah.

³⁰ "Forty years later, in the wilderness near Mount Sinai, an angel appeared to Moses in the fire of a burning thorn bush. ³¹ Moses was amazed when he saw it. As he approached the bush, the voice of Our God came out of it: ³²'I am the God of your ancestors—the God of Sarah and Abraham, of Rachel and Leah and Jacob, of Rebecca and Isaac.' Moses, shaking with fear, dared not look at it anymore. ³³ But Our God said to him, 'Take off your shoes, for the place where you stand is holy ground. ³⁴ I have witnessed the oppression of my people in Egypt. I have heard their groaning, and I have come down to set them free. Come now, and I will send you back to Egypt.'

³⁵ "This is the same Moses they rejected by saying, 'Who made you our ruler and judge?' Now, it was Moses who was being sent by God as both liberator and ruler, with the help of the angel who appeared to him in the burning bush. ³⁶ It was Moses who led them out of Egypt, and worked wonders and signs in Egypt, at the Red Sea and in the desert for forty years. ³⁷ It was Moses who said to the Israelites, 'God will send you a prophet like me from your own people.' ³⁸ It was Moses who, in the assembly in the desert, spoke with the angel on Mount Sinai and with our ancestors. It was Moses who was entrusted with the words of life to hand on to us.

³⁹ "But our ancestors refused to listen to him. Instead, they pushed him aside and turned their hearts back to Egypt. ⁴⁰ They said to Aaron, 'Make gods for us so they can lead us. We don't know what has happened to this Moses, who led us out of Egypt.' ⁴¹ So they made an idol shaped like a calf and offered sacrifices to it, rejoicing in what they had made with their hands. ⁴² But God turned away from them and abandoned them to the worship of the heavenly bodies. For it is written in the book of the prophets,

> 'Did you bring me sacrifices and offerings
> for forty years in the desert, O house of Israel?
> ⁴³ No, you carried the shrine of Moloch
> and the star of your god Rephan—
> those idols you made to adore—
> So now I will exile you even further than Babylon.'

⁴⁴ "Our ancestors had the Tabernacle of Testimony with them in the desert. It had been constructed by Moses as God had directed, according to the pattern Moses was shown. ⁴⁵ It was handed down to the next generation, who brought it along with Joshua when they dispossessed the nations that God drove out as they advanced. It stayed here until the time of David,

⁴⁶who so enjoyed God's favor that he asked God if he could build a dwelling place for the God of Jacob—⁴⁷though it was Solomon who actually built the Temple.

⁴⁸"Yet the Most High doesn't dwell in houses made by human hands, as it says in scripture:

⁴⁹'Heaven is my judgment seat,
 and the earth is my footstool.
What kind of house can you build for me?' says Your God;
 'or what is to be my resting place?
⁵⁰Didn't my hand make all these things?'

⁵¹"You stubborn people! Your hearts and ears are completely covered! You're always resisting the Holy Spirit, just as your ancestors did before you. ⁵²Was there ever any prophet whom your ancestors didn't persecute? In their day, they put to death those who foretold the coming of the Just One. And now it has been your turn as the Just One's betrayers and murderers. ⁵³You who received the Law by the hands of angels are the very ones who haven't kept it!"

⁵⁴They were infuriated when they heard this, and ground their teeth at him. ⁵⁵Stephen, meanwhile, filled with the Holy Spirit, looked to the sky and saw the glory of God, and Jesus standing at the right side of God. ⁵⁶"Look!" he exclaimed. "I see the heavens opened, and the Chosen One standing at God's right hand!"

⁵⁷The onlookers were standing there, shouting and holding their hands over their ears as they did so. They rushed at him as one, ⁵⁸and dragged him out of the city. The witnesses then stoned him, having laid their robes at the feet of a young man named Saul.

⁵⁹As they were stoning him, Stephen prayed, "O Jesus, receive my spirit." ⁶⁰He fell to his knees and cried out in a loud voice, "Please, don't hold this sin against them!" And with that, he died.

8:1Saul completely approved of the killing. On that day a great persecution broke out against the church at Jerusalem, and all except the apostles were scattered throughout Judea and Samaria. ²Godly women and men buried Stephen and mourned deeply for him. ³During this time, Saul worked for the total collapse of the church. Going from house to house, he dragged off women and men and put them in prison.

8:4–12:25

*t*hose who had been scattered began to proclaim the Good News wherever they went. ⁵Philip went down to the town of Samaria and there proclaimed the Messiah to them. ⁶Without exception, the crowds paid close attention to Philip, listening to his message and taking note of the miracles he performed. ⁷Many people were freed from unclean spirits, which came out of them shrieking loudly. Many people who couldn't move or couldn't walk were healed. ⁸The rejoicing in the town rose to a fever pitch.

⁹A man named Simon had been practicing magic in the city, astonishing the people of Samaria. He claimed to be someone great, ¹⁰and everyone, from prominent citizens to the lowly born, were paying attention to him and saying, "He is what is known as the Great Power of God." ¹¹They paid attention to him because he had astonished them with magic for so long. ¹²But they came to believe Philip as he preached the Good News of the kindom of God and the name of Jesus Christ, and both women and men were baptized. ¹³Even Simon became a believer. He followed Philip everywhere, constantly amazed when he saw the miracles and great signs that took place.

¹⁴When the apostles in Jerusalem heard that Samaria had accepted the word of God, they sent Peter and John to them. ¹⁵The two went down to these people and prayed that they would receive the Holy Spirit. ¹⁶She had not yet come down upon any of them, since they had only been baptized in the name of Jesus. ¹⁷Upon arriving, the pair laid hands on the Samaritans and they received the Holy Spirit.

¹⁸When Simon saw that the Spirit was given through the laying on of hands by the apostles, he offered them money, ¹⁹saying, "Give me this power, too, so that anyone I lay hands on will receive the Holy Spirit."

²⁰Peter replied, "May your money perish with you, for thinking that you can buy what God has given for nothing! ²¹You have no part or share in this ministry, for your heart isn't right before God. ²²Repent of your wickedness and pray to Our God, that you may still be forgiven for thinking as you did. ²³I can see that you are caught in the gall of bitterness and the bondage of iniquity."

²⁴Simon replied, "Pray to Our God for me yourselves, so that what you said may not happen to me."

²⁵After they gave their testimony and proclaimed the word of Christ, they returned to Jerusalem and preached the Good News to many Samaritan villages.

ଔ   ଔ   ଔ

²⁶An angel of God spoke to Philip and said, "Be ready to set out at noon along the road that goes to Gaza, the desert road." ²⁷So Philip began his journey.

It happened that an Ethiopian eunuch, a court official in charge of the entire treasury of Candace, the ruler of Ethiopia, had come to Jerusalem on a pilgrimage ²⁸ and was returning home. He was sitting in his carriage and reading the prophet Isaiah.

²⁹ The Spirit said to Philip, "Go up and meet that carriage."

³⁰ When Philip ran up, he heard the eunuch reading Isaiah the prophet and asked, "Do you understand what you are reading?"

³¹ "How can I," the eunuch replied, "unless someone explains it to me?" With that, he invited Philip to get in the carriage with him. ³² This was the passage of scripture being read:

> "You are like a sheep being led to slaughter,
> you are like a lamb that is mute in front of its shearers:
> like them, you never open your mouth.
> ³³ You have been humiliated
> and have no one to defend you.
> Who will ever talk about your descendants,
> since your life on earth has been cut short?"

³⁴ The eunuch said to Philip, "Tell me, if you will, about whom the prophet is talking—himself or someone else?"

³⁵ So Philip proceeded to explain the Good News about Jesus to him.

³⁶ Further along the road they came to some water, and the eunuch said, "Look, there is some water right there. Is there anything to keep me from being baptized?"*

³⁸ He ordered the carriage to stop; then Philip and the eunuch both went down into the water, and Philip baptized him. ³⁹ When they came out of the water, the Spirit of God snatched Philip away; the eunuch didn't see him anymore, and went on his way rejoicing.

⁴⁰ Philip found himself at Ashdod next, and he went about proclaiming the Good News in all the towns, until he came to Caesarea.

ও   ও   ও

9:1 Meanwhile Saul continued to breathe murderous threats against the disciples of Jesus. He had gone up to the high priest ² and asked for letters, addressed to the synagogues in Damascus, that would authorize him to arrest and take to Jerusalem any followers of the Way that he could find, both women and men.

---

* Later manuscripts add verse 37: *And Philip said, "If you believe with all your heart, you may." And the eunuch said, "I believe that Jesus Christ is the Only Begotten of God."*

³ As he traveled along and was approaching Damascus, a light from the sky suddenly flashed about him. ⁴He fell to the ground and heard a voice saying, "Saul, Saul, why are you persecuting me?"

⁵ "Who are you?" Saul asked.

The voice answered, "I am Jesus, and you are persecuting me. ⁶Get up now and go into the city, where you will be told what to do." ⁷Those traveling with him were speechless. They heard the voice, but could see no one.

⁸Saul got up from the ground unable to see, even though his eyes were open. They had to take him by the hand and lead him into Damascus. ⁹For three days he continued to be blind, during which time he ate and drank nothing.

¹⁰There was a disciple in Damascus named Ananias. Christ appeared to him in a vision, saying, "Ananias."

Ananias said, "Here I am."

¹¹Then Christ said to him, "Go at once to Straight Street, and at the house of Judah ask for a certain Saul of Tarsus. He is there praying. ¹²Saul had a vision that a man named Ananias will come and lay hands on him so that he would recover his sight."

¹³ But Ananias protested, "I have heard from many sources about Saul and all the harm he has done to your holy people in Jerusalem. ¹⁴He is here now with authorization from the chief priests to arrest everybody who calls on your name."

¹⁵Christ said to Ananias, "Go anyway. Saul is the instrument I have chosen to bring my Name to Gentiles, to rulers, and to the people of Israel. ¹⁶I myself will show him how much he will have to suffer for my name."

¹⁷With that Ananias left. When he entered the house, he laid his hands on Saul, saying, "Saul, my brother, I have been sent by Jesus Christ, who appeared to you on the way here, to help you recover your sight and be filled with the Holy Spirit."

¹⁸ Immediately, something like scales fell from Saul's eyes, and he regained his sight. He got up and was baptized, ¹⁹and his strength returned after he had eaten some food.

Saul stayed with the believers in Damascus for a few days, ²⁰and soon began proclaiming in the synagogues that Jesus was the Only Begotten of God.

²¹ Everyone who heard Saul was amazed. They said, "Isn't this the one who wiped out those in Jerusalem who called on the name of Jesus? Didn't Saul come here just so he could bring them in chains before the chief priests?"

²² But Saul kept growing in strength and confounding the Jewish authorities in Damascus by proving that Jesus is the Messiah.

²³ After many days had gone by, the Jewish authorities plotted together to do away with him, ²⁴ but Saul learned of their plot. They were watching the city gates day and night trying to put him to death, ²⁵ but one night his students came and got him, and had him escape through an opening in the wall, lowering him to the ground in a basket.

²⁶ When Saul arrived back in Jerusalem, he tried to join the disciples there, but they were all afraid of him, not believing that he was a disciple. ²⁷ Then Barnabas took charge of him and introduced him to the apostles. He explained to them how, on his journey, Saul had seen and conversed with Jesus, and how ever since that encounter, Saul had been speaking out fearlessly in the name of Jesus at Damascus.

²⁸ Saul stayed on with them, moving freely about Jerusalem and expressing himself quite openly in the name of Christ. ²⁹ He even addressed the Greek-speaking Jews and debated with them. They responded, however, by trying to kill him. ³⁰ When the sisters and brothers learned of this, some of them took Saul down to Caesarea and sent him off to Tarsus.

ʒʒʒ   ʒʒʒ   ʒʒʒ

³¹ Throughout all Judea, Galilee and Samaria, the church was at peace, building itself up, living in reverence of God and growing in numbers with the consolation of the Holy Spirit.

³² While Peter was traveling throughout the region, he also went to the saints living in Lydda. ³³ There he found a person named Aeneas, who was paralyzed and had been bedridden for eight years.

³⁴ Peter said to him, "Aeneas, Jesus Christ heals you. Get up and make your bed." Aenaeus got up at once. ³⁵ All the inhabitants of Lydda and Sharon, upon seeing him, were converted to Jesus.

³⁶ Now in Joppa there was a disciple, a woman named Tabitha—"Dorcas," in Greek—who never tired of doing kind things or giving to charity. ³⁷ About this time she grew ill and died. They washed her body and laid her out in an upstairs room.

³⁸ Since Lydda was near Joppa, the disciples sent two couriers to Peter with the urgent request, "Please come over to us without delay." ³⁹ Peter set out with them as they asked.

Upon his arrival, they took him upstairs to the room. All the townswomen who had been widowed stood beside him weeping, and showed him the various garments Dorcas had made when she was still with them.

⁴⁰ Peter first made everyone go outside, then knelt down and prayed. Turning to the body, he said, "Tabitha, stand up." She opened her eyes, then looked at Peter and sat up. ⁴¹ He gave her his hand and helped her to her feet. The next thing he did was to call in those who were believers—including the widows—to show them that she was alive.

⁴² This became known all over Joppa and, because of it, many came to believe in Jesus Christ. ⁴³ Peter remained awhile in Joppa, staying with Simon, a leather tanner.

ଔ   ଔ   ଔ

10:1 There was a centurion named Cornelius in the Italian cohort stationed in Caesarea. ² The household of Cornelius was full of God-fearing people; they prayed to God constantly and gave many charitable gifts to needy Jewish people.

³ One day at about three in the afternoon Cornelius had a vision. He distinctly saw an angel of God enter the house and call out, "Cornelius!"

⁴ Cornelius stared at the angel, completely terrified, and replied, "I'm at your service."

The angel said, "Your prayers and offerings to the poor are pleasing to God. ⁵ Send a deputation to Joppa and ask for a person named Simon who is called Peter. ⁶ He is staying with a tanner also named Simon, whose house is by the sea."

⁷ After the angel had departed, Cornelius called together three members of the household, ⁸ explained everything to them and sent them off to Joppa.

⁹ About noon the next day, shortly before they were to arrive in Joppa, Peter went up to the roof terrace to pray. ¹⁰ He was hungry and asked for something to eat. While the meal was being prepared he fell into a trance. ¹¹ Peter saw heaven standing open, and something like a large sheet being lowered to earth by its four corners. ¹² It contained all kinds of animals, birds and reptiles.

¹³ A voice said, "Stand up, Peter. Make your sacrifice, and eat."

¹⁴ But Peter said, "I can't, my God. I have never eaten anything profane or unclean."

¹⁵ The voice spoke a second time and said, "Don't call anything profane that God has made clean."

¹⁶ This happened three times, then the sheet disappeared into the heavens.

¹⁷ Peter was still pondering the vision when Cornelius' deputation ar-

rived. They had asked directions to Simon's house and were now standing at the door. ¹⁸ They called out to ask if Simon, known as Peter, was there. ¹⁹ While Peter reflected on the vision, the Spirit said, "A deputation is here to see you. ²⁰ Hurry down, and don't hesitate to go with them. I sent them here."

²¹ He went down and said to the deputation, "I'm the one you are looking for. What do you want?"

²² They answered, "Cornelius, a centurion—an upright and God-fearing person, respected by the Jewish people—was directed by a holy angel to send for you. We are to bring you to the household of Cornelius to hear what you have to say." ²³ Peter invited them in and gave them hospitality.

Peter left the next day, accompanied by some of the co-workers from Joppa. ²⁴ They reached Caesarea the day after. Cornelius was waiting for them, along with his household and many close friends.

²⁵ As Peter entered the house, Cornelius met him, dropped to his knees and bowed low. ²⁶ As he helped Cornelius to his feet, Peter said, "Get up! I'm a human being, just like you!"

²⁷ While talking with Cornelius, Peter went in and found many people gathered there. ²⁸ He said to them, "You know it's unlawful for a Jew to associate with Gentiles or visit them. But God made it clear to me not to call anyone unclean or impure. ²⁹ That's why I made no objection when I was summoned. Why have you sent for me?"

³⁰ Cornelius answered, "Four days ago, I was here praying at this hour—three in the afternoon. Suddenly a figure in shining robes stood before me ³¹ and said, 'Cornelius, your prayers have been heard and your charity has been accepted as a sacrifice before God. ³² Send to Joppa and invite Simon, known as Peter, who is staying in the house of Simon the tanner, who lives by the sea.' ³³ I sent for you immediately, and you were kind enough to come. Now we are all gathered here before you to hear the message God has given you for us."

³⁴ So Peter said to them, "I begin to see how true it is that God shows no partiality—³⁵ rather, that any person of any nationality who fears God and does what is right is acceptable to God. ³⁶ This is the message God has sent to the people of Israel, the Good News of peace proclaimed through Jesus Christ, who is Savior of all.

³⁷ "You yourselves know what took place throughout Judea, beginning in Galilee with the baptism John proclaimed. ³⁸ You know how God anointed Jesus of Nazareth with the Holy Spirit and with power, and how Jesus went about doing good works and healing all who were in the grip of the Devil, because God was with him. ³⁹ We are eyewitnesses to all that Jesus did in the countryside and in Jerusalem. Finally, Jesus was killed and hung

on a tree, ⁴⁰only to be raised by God on the third day. God allowed him to be seen, ⁴¹not by everyone, but only by the witnesses who had been chosen beforehand by God—that is, by us, who ate and drank with Christ after the resurrection from the dead. ⁴²And Christ commissioned us to preach to the people and to bear witness that this is the one set apart by God as judge of the living and the dead. ⁴³To Christ Jesus all the prophets testify, that everyone who believes has forgiveness of sins through this Name."

⁴⁴Peter had not finished speaking these words when the Holy Spirit descended upon all who were listening to the message. ⁴⁵The Jewish believers who had accompanied Peter were surprised that the gift of the Holy Spirit had been poured out on the Gentiles also, ⁴⁶whom they could hear speaking in tongues and glorifying God.

Then Peter asked, ⁴⁷"What can stop these people who have received the Holy Spirit, even as we have, from being baptized with water?" ⁴⁸So he gave orders that they be baptized in the name of Jesus Christ. After this was done, they asked him to stay on with them for a few days.

℞   ℞   ℞

11:¹The apostles and the community in Judea heard that Gentiles, too, had accepted the word of God. ²As a result, when Peter went up to Jerusalem, some of the Jewish believers took issue with him. ³"So you have been visiting the Gentiles and eating with them, have you?" they said.

⁴Peter then explained the whole affair to them step by step from the beginning: ⁵"One day when I was in the town of Joppa, I fell into a trance while at prayer and had a vision of something like a big sheet being let down from heaven by its four corners. This sheet came quite close to me. ⁶I watched it intently and saw in it all sorts of animals and wild beasts—everything possible that could walk, crawl or fly. ⁷Then I heard a voice that said to me, 'Now, Peter, make your sacrifice and eat.' ⁸I replied, 'I can't, my God. Nothing profane or unclean has ever entered my mouth!' ⁹And a second time the voice spoke from heaven, 'Don't call profane what God has made clean.' ¹⁰This happened three times, then the sheet and what was in it was drawn up to heaven again.

¹¹"Just at that moment, three couriers stopped outside the house where we were staying; they had been sent from Caesarea to fetch me, ¹²and the Spirit told me to have no hesitation about returning with them. These six believers came with me as well, and we entered Cornelius' house. ¹³He told us he had seen an angel standing in the house who had said, 'Send messengers to Joppa and bring back Simon, known as Peter; ¹⁴he has a message for you that will save you and your entire household.'

¹⁵"I had hardly begun to speak when the Holy Spirit came down on them in the same way she came on us in the beginning, ¹⁶and I remembered what Christ had said: 'John baptized with water, but you will be baptized with the Holy Spirit.' ¹⁷I realized then that God was giving them the same gift that had been given to us when we came to believe in our Savior Jesus Christ. And who am I to stand in God's way?"

¹⁸This account satisfied them, and they gave glory to God, saying, "God has granted the repentance that leads to life—even to Gentiles!"

ℛ   ℛ   ℛ

¹⁹Those scattered by the persecution that arose because of Stephen made their way as far as Phoenicia, Cyprus and Antioch, but they usually proclaimed the message only to Jews. ²⁰Some of them, however, who came from Cyprus and Cyrene, went to Antioch where they started preaching to the Greeks, proclaiming the Good News of Jesus Christ to them as well. ²¹Christ honored their efforts, and a large number of Greeks became believers.

²²The church in Jerusalem heard about this, so they sent Barnabas to Antioch. ²³Upon arriving, he rejoiced to see the evidence of God's favor. And he urged them to remain faithful to Christ with heartfelt devotion, ²⁴for he was good and faithful and filled with the Holy Spirit. And a large number of people was brought to Christ.

²⁵Barnabas then left for Tarsus to look for Saul, ²⁶and when he found him he brought him to Antioch. For a whole year they remained there, meeting with the church and instructing a large number of people. It was at Antioch that the disciples were first called Christians.

²⁷At this time, some prophets came down from Jerusalem to Antioch. ²⁸One of them, whose name was Agabus, stood up and—in the power of the Spirit—prophesied that a famine would spread throughout the entire Roman Empire. The same thing had happened before, during the reign of Claudius.

²⁹The disciples agreed that everyone, according to ability, should send relief to the sisters and brothers in Judea. ³⁰They did this and sent their contributions to the elders in care of Barnabas and Paul.

ℛ   ℛ   ℛ

12:1It was about this time that Herod, the ruler of Judea, began to persecute some members of the church. ²He put John's brother, James, to death with the sword. ³And when he noticed that this pleased the Jewish leaders, he decided to arrest Peter as well—which he did during the Feast of Unleavened Bread.

⁴Peter was taken into custody and put into prison. Herod assigned four squads of four soldiers each to guard him. He intended to put him up on public trial after the end of Passover week. ⁵So Peter was kept in prison, but the church prayed to God continually on his behalf.

⁶On the night before Herod was to open the trial, Peter slept, bound with double chains, between two guards—while more guards kept watch outside the door. ⁷Suddenly the angel of God stood before him and the cell was filled with light.

The angel nudged Peter in the side to awaken him. "Get up, and hurry," the angel said, and the chains fell from Peter's wrists. ⁸The angel continued, "And put on your belt and your sandals." Peter did so. Then the angel said, "Wrap your cloak around yourself and follow me." ⁹So he followed the angel out, unsure whether what he was experiencing was really happening, or whether he was having a vision.

¹⁰They passed by one guard post and then another, and came to the iron gate leading to the city, which opened for them by itself. They went through it and walked the length of one street, when suddenly the angel disappeared. ¹¹It was only then that Peter recovered his senses. "Now I know," he said, "that all of this is true—that Our God really did send an angel to rescue me from the hand of Herod and from all that the Jewish people were so certain would happen to me."

¹²When Peter realized this, he went to the house of Mary, the mother of John Mark. A number of people were gathered there praying. ¹³Peter knocked at the gateway door and an attendant named Rhoda came to answer. ¹⁴When she recognized Peter's voice, she was so overjoyed that she raced back without opening it and announced that Peter was at the gate.

¹⁵"You're out of your mind," they said.

But she kept insisting it was so.

"Then it must be his angel," they said.

¹⁶Meanwhile, Peter continued to knock. When they opened the door and saw that it was really him, they were amazed. ¹⁷Peter motioned with his hand for quiet and explained to them how God led him out of prison. He added, "Tell James and the sisters and brothers." Then he left for another place.

¹⁸At daybreak there was a huge commotion among the soldiers over what had become of Peter. ¹⁹Herod ordered a search, and when they didn't find Peter, Herod cross-examined the guards and then had them executed. Then he left Judea for a stay in Caesarea.

²⁰For some time, Herod had been on bad terms with the people of Tyre

and Sidon. Now they joined forces and sent a delegation to Blastus, Herod's chamberlain, and enlisted his support. With that in place, they negotiated a peace treaty, because they depended on Herod's territory for their food supply.

²¹On the appointed day, Herod—in royal robes and seated on the rostrum—addressed them. ²²The people proclaimed, "This is the voice of a god, not a man!" ²³Immediately, an angel of God struck Herod down because he didn't give God the glory. Herod was eaten away with worms and died.

²⁴The word of God continued to spread and increase. ²⁵Barnabas and Saul completed their mission and returned to Jerusalem, bringing John Mark with them.

13:1–15:35

*t*he church at Antioch had a number of prophets and teachers: Barnabas; Simeon, also known as Niger; Lucius of Cyrene; Manaen, who had been raised with Herod the tetrarch; and Saul.

²One day while they were worshiping God and fasting, the Holy Spirit said, "I want Barnabas and Saul set apart for the work to which I have called them." ³After the church members had fasted and prayed, they laid hands on the pair and sent them along.

⁴So the two of them, sent out by the Holy Spirit, went down to Seleucia and sailed from there to Cyprus. ⁵They arrived at Salamis and immediately went about proclaiming the word of God in the Jewish synagogues. John was with them as their assistant.

⁶They traveled the full length of the island. At Paphos they met a Jewish magician and false prophet named Bar-Jesus. ⁷He was one of the attendants of the proconsul Sergius Paulus, who was a person of great intelligence.

Sergius Paulus summoned Barnabas and Paul and asked to hear the word of God. ⁸But Elymas, as the magician's name is translated, opposed them to keep the proconsul from converting to the faith.

⁹At that moment, Saul, who had changed his name to Paul, was filled with the Holy Spirit. He looked Elymas full in the face and said, ¹⁰"You charlatan, you fraud, you child of the Devil, you enemy of all that is just! Stop distorting the right ways of the Most High! ¹¹Look now at how the hand of Our God is upon you. You will be blind and for a while unable to see the sun." Immediately, everything went dark and misty for him. He groped about asking for someone to take him by the hand. ¹²The procon-

sul—observing all that had happened, and astonished by the teaching about Christ—became a believer.

CR   CR   CR

¹³ Paul and his companions went by sea from Paphos to Perga in Pamphylia, where John left them and returned to Jerusalem. ¹⁴ They continued to travel on from Perga and came to Antioch in Pisidia.

On the Sabbath, they entered the synagogue and sat down. ¹⁵ After the readings from the Law and the Prophets, the leaders of the synagogue sent this message to them: "Friends, if you have any exhortation for the people, please speak up."

¹⁶ Paul stood up, raised his hand for silence and began to speak. "Fellow Israelites," he said, "and you others who revere Our God, listen to what I have to say! ¹⁷ The God of this nation Israel chose our ancestors, made our people great when they were living as foreigners in Egypt, then through divine power led them out, ¹⁸ and for about forty years took care of them in the desert. ¹⁹ After destroying seven nations in the land of Canaan, God gave them the inheritance of their land, ²⁰ after about four hundred and fifty years.

"After this God gave them judges, down to the prophet Samuel. ²¹ But then they demanded a ruler, and God gave them Saul, begot of Kish, a member of the tribe of Benjamin. ²² After forty years, God deposed him and made David their ruler, with these approving words: 'I have selected David, begot of Jesse, a person after my own heart, who will carry out my whole purpose.' ²³ To keep this promise, God has given to Israel a savior, one of David's descendants—Jesus, ²⁴ whose coming was heralded by John when he proclaimed a baptism of repentance for the whole people of Israel. ²⁵ Before John ended his ministry, he said, 'I am not the one you think I am; the one who is coming after me, I'm not fit to undo the sandals on his feet.'

²⁶ "Friends—children of the family of Sarah and Abraham, and you others who worship Our God—this message of salvation is meant for you. ²⁷ What the people of Jerusalem and their rulers did, though they didn't realize it, was in fact to fulfill the prophecies which are read on every Sabbath. ²⁸ Though they found no grounds for putting Jesus to death, they begged Pilate to carry out the execution. ²⁹ When they carried out everything that had been foretold, they crucified and then buried him in a tomb. ³⁰ But God raised Jesus from the dead, ³¹ and for many days he appeared to those who had accompanied him from Galilee to Jerusalem. And it's these same companions of Jesus who are now his witnesses before our people.

³² "We ourselves announce to you the Good News. It was to our ances-

tors that God made the promise. ³³ But it's to us, their children, that God fulfilled the promise, by raising Jesus from the dead. As scripture says in the second psalm, 'You are my Own; today I have begotten you.'

³⁴ "The fact that God raised Jesus from the dead, never to return to corruption, is affirmed in these words: 'I will give you the sure and holy blessings promised to David.' ³⁵ This is explained in another text: 'You will not allow your Holy One to suffer corruption.' ³⁶ Now, David died when he had served God's will in his lifetime. He was buried with his ancestors and underwent corruption. ³⁷ But the One whom God raised from the dead did not undergo corruption.

³⁸ "Sisters and brothers, let it be known that through Jesus the forgiveness of sins is proclaimed to you—and freedom from everything that kept you from being right with God, which the Law of Moses could not do. ³⁹ It is through Jesus that all who believe are made right with God. ⁴⁰ Take care that what the prophets said doesn't happen to you:

⁴¹ 'Observe, you scoffer, and marvel—
  and perish!
For I am accomplishing a work in your days,
  a work that you will never believe
  even if someone would describe it to you.' "

⁴² As Paul and Barnabas were leaving, they were invited to speak on this same theme the following Sabbath.

⁴³ When the synagogue service had broken up, many Jewish worshipers and God-fearing converts to Judaism joined Paul and Barnabas. In their talks, Paul and Barnabas urged them to continue in the grace of God.

ℛ   ℛ   ℛ

⁴⁴ On the next Sabbath, almost the whole city gathered to hear the word of God. ⁴⁵ When the leaders of the synagogue saw the crowds, they were filled with jealousy, and began to contradict everything Paul said and to revile him.

⁴⁶ Paul and Barnabas spoke out fearlessly nonetheless: "We had to proclaim the word of God to you first, but since you have rejected it—since you don't think yourselves worthy of eternal life—we now turn to the Gentiles. ⁴⁷ For this is what Christ instructed us to do:

'I have made you a light for the nations,
  so that my salvation may reach the ends of the earth.' "

⁴⁸ It made the Gentiles very happy to hear this, and they thanked God for the message. All who were destined for eternal life became believers. ⁴⁹ Thus the word of God was carried throughout that area.

⁵⁰ But the leaders of the synagogue worked on some of the notable, God-fearing members of the community and convinced them to turn against Paul and Barnabas. They finally expelled them from the territory.

⁵¹ So Paul and Barnabas shook the dust from their feet in protest and went on to Iconium. ⁵² But the disciples were filled with joy and with the Holy Spirit.

14·1 At Iconium Paul and Barnabas went to the Jewish synagogue. They spoke so effectively that a great number of Jews and Greeks came to believe. ² Some of the disbelieving Jews, however, stirred up and poisoned the minds of the Gentiles against the sisters and brothers. ³ So they stayed on for some time, speaking fearlessly about Christ, who then confirmed what they said about divine grace by granting that signs and wonders occur through them. ⁴ The people of the city, however, were divided—some supported the disbelievers, some supported the apostles.

⁵ Eventually a move was made by a group of Gentiles, Jews, and synagogue leaders to abuse Paul and Barnabas and have them stoned. ⁶ When they learned of this, the apostles fled to the safety of Lycaonia where, in the towns of Lystra and Derbe and in the surrounding countryside, ⁷ they preached the Good News.

⁸ At Lystra there was an individual who had never walked a step, afflicted from birth with no strength in the feet. ⁹ On one occasion this person was listening to Paul preaching, and they looked directly into each other's eyes. When Paul saw that the person had enough faith to be made whole, ¹⁰ he called out in a loud voice, "Stand up! On your feet!" And the person jumped up and began to walk around.

¹¹ When the crowds saw what Paul had done, they cried out in the Lycaonian language, "These two are gods who have come to us in the form of humans!" ¹² They addressed Barnabas as Zeus; Paul they called Hermes, since he was doing most of the talking. ¹³ Even the priest of the temple of Zeus, which stood outside the town, brought oxen and garlands to the gates, to offer sacrifice with the crowds.

¹⁴ When the apostles Barnabas and Paul heard this, they tore their garments and rushed out into the crowd. ¹⁵ "Friends, why are you doing this?" they shouted. "We are mortals like you. We have come with Good News to make you turn from these empty idols to the living God, who made heaven and earth and the sea and all that these hold. ¹⁶ In the past, God allowed each nation to go its own way. ¹⁷ But even then, God didn't leave you without personal evidence of the good things being done for you. God sends you rain from heaven, makes the crops grow when they should, and fills your hearts with food and gladness."

[18] Yet even with a speech such as this, they could hardly stop the crowds from offering sacrifice to them.

[19] Some members of the Jewish party from Antioch and Iconium arrived and won the people over. They stoned Paul and dragged him out of the town, leaving him there for dead. [20] His students quickly formed a circle about him, and before long he got up and went back into the town.

The next day, he left with Barnabas for Derbe. [21] After they had proclaimed the Good News in that town and made numerous disciples, they retraced their steps to Lystra and Iconium first, then to Antioch.

[22] They put fresh heart in the disciples there, encouraging them to persevere in their faith. "We all have to experience many hardships," they said, "before we enter the kindom of God." [23] In each church they appointed elders and, with prayer and fasting, commended them to God, in whom they had put their faith.

[24] Then they passed through Pisidia and came to Pamphylia. [25] After proclaiming the word in Perga, they went down to Attalia. [26] From there they sailed back to Antioch, where they had first been commended to the grace of God for the work they had now completed. [27] On their arrival, they assembled the church and gave an account of all that God had done with them, and of how they had opened the door of faith to the Gentiles. [28] Then they spent some time there with the disciples.

ᴄℛ   ᴄℛ   ᴄℛ

15[1] Then some Jewish Christians came down to Antioch and began to teach the believers, "Unless you follow exactly the traditions of Moses, you cannot be saved." [2] Paul and Barnabas strongly disagreed with them and hotly debated their position. Finally, it was decided that Paul, Barnabas and some others should go up to see the apostles and elders in Jerusalem about this question.

[3] All the members of the church saw them off, and as they made their way through Phoenicia and Samaria, Paul and Barnabas told how the Gentiles had been converted. Their story was received with great joy among the sisters and brothers. [4] When Paul's group arrived in Jerusalem, they were welcomed by that church, and by the apostles and the elders, to whom they gave an account of all that God had accomplished through them. [5] Some of the converted Pharisees got up and demanded that such Gentiles be forced to convert to Judaism first, before being baptized, and be told to follow the Law of Moses. [6] Accordingly, the apostles and the elders convened to look into the matter.

⁷ After much discussion, Peter said to them, "Friends, you know that God chose me from your midst a long time ago—so that the Gentiles would hear the message of the Gospel from my lips and believe. ⁸ God, who can read everyone's heart, bore witness to this by granting the Holy Spirit to them as the Spirit has been granted to us. ⁹ God made no distinction, but purified their hearts as well by means of faith.

¹⁰ "Why, then, do you put God to the test by trying to place on the shoulders of these converts a yoke which neither we nor our ancestors were able to bear? ¹¹ But just as we believe we are saved through the grace of Jesus Christ, so are they." ¹² At this, the whole assembly fell silent.

They listened to Barnabas and Paul as the two described all the signs and wonders God had worked among the Gentiles through them. ¹³ When they finished their presentation, James spoke up. "Sisters and brothers, listen to me," he said. ¹⁴ "Simon has told you how God initially became concerned about taking from among the Gentiles a people for God's name. ¹⁵ The words of the prophets agree with this, since the scriptures say,

¹⁶ ' "After that I will return
    and rebuild the fallen house of David;
I will rebuild it from its ruins
    and restore it.
¹⁷ Then the rest of humankind,
    all the Gentiles who are called by my Name,
    will look for God,"
¹⁸ says the Most High,
    who makes these things
    which were known so long ago.'

¹⁹ "It is my judgment, therefore, that we shouldn't make it more difficult for Gentiles who are turning to God. ²⁰ We should merely write to them to abstain from anything polluted by idols, from sexual immorality and from eating meat of unbled or strangled animals. ²¹ After all, for generations now Moses has been proclaimed in every town and has been read aloud in the synagogues on every Sabbath."

²² Then the apostles and elders decided, in agreement with the whole Jerusalem church, to choose delegates to send to Antioch with Paul and Barnabas. They chose Judas known as Barsabbas and Silas, both leading members of the community. ²³ They were to deliver this letter:

"From the apostles and elders,

"To our Gentile sisters and brothers in Antioch, Syria and Cilicia:

"Greetings! ²⁴ We hear that some of our number, without any instructions from us, have upset you with their discussions and disturbed your peace of mind. ²⁵ Therefore, we have unanimously resolved to choose representatives and send them to you, along with our beloved Barnabas and Paul, [26] who have risked their lives for the name of Jesus Christ. [27] So we are sending you Judas and Silas, who will convey this message by word of mouth: [28] it is the decision of the Holy Spirit, and ours as well, not to lay on you any burden beyond that which is strictly necessary— [29] namely, to abstain from meat sacrificed to idols, from meat of unbled or strangled animals and from fornication. You will be well advised to avoid these things. Farewell."

[30] The party left and went down to Antioch, where they called together the whole community and delivered the letter. [31] When it was read, there was great delight at the encouragement it gave them.

[32] Judas and Silas, themselves prophets, spoke for a long time, giving encouragement and strength to the sisters and brothers. [33] The two spent some time there, and then returned home bearing greetings of peace from the sisters and brothers to the apostles and elders who sent them. [34] But Silas decided to remain there. [35] Paul and Barnabas stayed in Antioch and, with many others, taught and proclaimed the Good News, the word of God.

After some time Paul said to Barnabas, "Let's return to all the cities where we preached the word of God and see how they're doing." [37] Barnabas suggested taking John Mark along with them as well. [38] But Paul said no, because he had deserted them in Pamphylia and had not continued to work with them. [39] The disagreement between Paul and Barnabas grew so sharp that they parted company. Barnabas took Mark and sailed to Cyprus. [40] Paul chose Silas and left—after being commended by the sisters and brothers to the grace of God. [41] Paul traveled through Syria and Cilicia, consolidating the churches along the way.

16:[1] Paul went to Derbe and from there to Lystra. There was a disciple there named Timothy, whose mother was Jewish and a believer, and whose father was Greek. [2] Since the sisters and brothers in Lystra and Iconium spoke highly of Timothy, [3] Paul was eager to have him come along on the journey. But because of the Jews who were in that region, Paul had Timothy circumcised, for everyone knew that his father was Greek. [4] As they made their way from town to town, they passed on the decisions reached by the apostles and elders in Jerusalem. [5] And the churches grew stronger in faith and daily increased in number.

[6] They next traveled through Phrygia and Galatian territory, because they had been prevented by the Holy Spirit from preaching the word in the

province of Asia. ⁷When they reached the frontier of Mysia, they thought to cross through it into Bithynia, but the Spirit of Jesus would not allow them to cross, ⁸so they went through Mysia and came down to Troas.

⁹Then one night Paul had a vision. A Macedonian stood before him and said, "Come over to Macedonia and help us." ¹⁰After this vision, we* immediately made efforts to get across to Macedonia, convinced that God had called us to bring them the Good News.

¹¹We put out to sea from Troas and set a course straight for Samothrace, and the next day on to Neapolis; ¹²from there we went to Philippi, which is one of the bigger cities in Macedonia and a Roman colony, and spent a few days there.

ᘓ   ᘓ   ᘓ

¹³On the Sabbath we went along the river outside the gates, thinking we might find a place of prayer. We sat down and preached to the women who had come to the gathering. ¹⁴One of them was named Lydia, a devout woman from the town of Thyatira who was in the purple-dye trade. As she listened to us, Christ opened her heart to accept what Paul was saying. ¹⁵After she and her household were baptized, she extended us an invitation: "If you are convinced that I am a believer in Christ, please come and stay with us." We accepted.

¹⁶Once when we were going to prayer, we met a household worker who was possessed by a spirit of divination, and who made a great deal of money for her employers through its fortune-telling. ¹⁷She began to follow Paul and the rest of us, shouting, "These are faithful followers of the Most High God, who proclaim to you the way of salvation!" ¹⁸She did this for many days.

Finally one day Paul lost his temper, and turned around and said to the spirit, "In the name of Jesus Christ I command you to leave this woman!" It left her that moment.

¹⁹When her employers saw that their profitable operation was now hopelessly dead, they seized Paul and Silas and dragged them before the authorities in the public square. ²⁰They brought them to the chief magistrates and said, "These people are Jews and are disturbing the peace ²¹by advocating practices which are unlawful for us Romans to accept or practice."

²²The crowd joined in the attack on them, and the magistrates stripped them and ordered them to be flogged. ²³They were whipped many times

---

* Luke, a physician and the author of *Acts*, apparently joins Paul's group at Troas.

and thrown into prison, and the jailer was told to keep a close watch on them. ²⁴ So, following these instructions, the warden threw them into the innermost cell of the prison and chained their feet to a stake.

²⁵ About midnight, Paul and Silas were praying and singing hymns to God as the other prisoners listened. ²⁶ Suddenly a severe earthquake shook the place, rocking the prison to its foundation. Immediately all the doors flew open, and everyone's chains were pulled loose. ²⁷ When the jailer woke up and found the doors wide open, he drew a sword and was about to commit suicide, presuming that the prisoners had escaped.

²⁸ But Paul shouted, "Don't harm yourself! We're all still here."

²⁹ The jailer called for a light, then rushed in and fell trembling at the feet of Paul and Silas, and, ³⁰ after a brief interval, led them out and asked them, "What must I do to be saved?"

³¹ They answered, "Believe in Jesus the Savior, and you will be saved—you and everyone in your household."

³² They proceeded to preach the word of God to the jailer and his whole household. ³³ At that late hour of the night he took them in and bathed their wounds; then he and the whole household were baptized. ³⁴ He led them up into his house, spread a table before them, and the whole family joyfully celebrated their newfound faith in God.

³⁵ In the morning the magistrates sent officers with the order, "Release them both."

³⁶ The jailer reported to Paul, "The magistrates have ordered your release. Go in peace."

³⁷ "What's this?" replied Paul. "They beat us publicly and throw us, Roman citizens, into prison without a trial. And now they want to release us quietly? No! They'll have to come and escort us out themselves!"

³⁸ The officers brought this news to the magistrates, who were horrified to learn that Paul and Silas were Roman citizens. ³⁹ So the magistrates came to assuage them, led them out of prison and begged them to leave the city.

⁴⁰ From prison Paul and Silas returned to Lydia's house, where they met with the sisters and brothers to give them encouragement. Then they left.

CR   CR   CR

17:1 When Paul and Silas had traveled through Amphipolis and Apollonia, they came to Thessalonica, where there was a Jewish synagogue. ² As was his custom, Paul visited the congregation; on three consecutive Sabbaths he debated with them from the scriptures—³ explaining and proving that the Messiah had to suffer and rise from the dead. "This Messiah," he said, "is the Jesus I am proclaiming to you." ⁴ Some of them were convinced, and joined Paul and Silas, along with a large number of God-fearing Greeks, and quite a few prominent women as well.

⁵ However, the Jews became jealous and, recruiting some reprobates from the marketplace, formed a mob and soon had the whole city in an uproar. They made for Jason's house, intending to find Paul and Silas there and bring them before the assembled people. ⁶ They weren't there, however, so they dragged Jason and some of the faithful off to the city council, shouting, "The people who have been turning the world upside down are now here. ⁷ Jason has been housing them. They all defy Caesar's edicts and claim that there is another ruler—Jesus." ⁸ The mob stirred up the crowd and city magistrates who, upon hearing the charges, ⁹ made Jason and the others post bond before releasing them.

¹⁰ When night fell, the sisters and brothers sent Paul and Silas to Berea. Once there, they went to the Jewish synagogue. ¹¹ These worshipers were more open-minded than those in Thessalonica. They heard the message willingly and studied the scriptures daily to determine whether it was true. ¹² Many of them became believers, as did many prominent Greek women and men.

¹³ But when the Jews of Thessalonica learned that the word of God was now being taught in Berea, they came there to make trouble and stir up the people. ¹⁴ The sisters and brothers immediately sent Paul to the seacoast, but Silas and Timothy stayed behind. ¹⁵ Paul was taken as far as Athens by an escort, who then returned with instructions for Silas and Timothy to join Paul as soon as possible.

℞   ℞   ℞

¹⁶ As Paul waited for them in Athens, his spirit was revolted at the sight of the city given over to idols. ¹⁷ So he debated in the Jewish synagogue with both the Jews and the God-fearing Greeks who worshiped there, and every day spoke in the marketplace to whomever came along. ¹⁸ Even some Epicurean and Stoic philosophers argued with him. Some said, "What is this chatter-box trying to say?" Others said, "He seems to be a promoter of foreign gods," because he was preaching about "Jesus" and "the Resurrection."

¹⁹ They invited Paul to accompany them to the Council of the Areopagus and said, "Let us learn of this new teaching you describe. ²⁰ You bring some strange notions to our ears, and we would like to know the meaning of all this." ²¹ The Athenians and the foreigners living there loved talking about and listening to the latest ideas whenever they could.

²² Then Paul stood up before the council of the Areopagus and delivered this address: "Citizens of Athens, I note that in every respect you are scru-

pulously religious. ²³ As I walked about looking at your shrines, I even discovered an altar inscribed, 'To an Unknown God.' Now, what you are worshiping in ignorance I intend to make known to you.

²⁴ "For the God who made the world and all that is in it, the Sovereign of heaven and earth, doesn't live in sanctuaries made by human hands, ²⁵ and isn't served by humans, as if in need of anything. No! God is the One who gives everyone life, breath—everything. ²⁶ From one person God created all of humankind to inhabit the entire earth, and set the time for each nation to exist and the exact place where each nation should dwell. ²⁷ God did this so that human beings would seek, reach out for and perhaps find the One who is not really far from any of us—²⁸ the One in whom we live and move and have our being. As one of your poets has put it, 'We too are God's children.'

²⁹ "If we are in fact children of God, then it's inexcusable to think that the Divine Nature is like an image of gold, silver or stone—an image formed by the art and thought of mortals. ³⁰ God, who overlooked such ignorance in the past, now commands all people everywhere to reform their lives. ³¹ For a day has been set when the whole world will be judged with justice. And this judge, who is a human being, has already been appointed. God has given proof of all of this by raising this judge from the dead."

³² When they heard about the resurrection of the dead, some sneered, while others said, "We must hear you on this topic some other time." ³³ At that, Paul left the council. ³⁴ A few women and men joined Paul and believed. Among them was Dionysius, a member of the Areopagus, a woman named Damaris and a few others.

ᴄ℞   ᴄ℞   ᴄ℞

18:1 After this, Paul left Athens and went to Corinth. ² There he met a Jew named Aquila, whose family came from Pontus. Aquila and his wife Priscilla had recently left Rome because an edict of Claudius had expelled all the Jews from Rome. Paul went to visit them, ³ and when he discovered that they were tent-makers—of the same trade as himself—he lodged with them, and they worked together. ⁴ Every Sabbath, in the synagogue, Paul led discussions in which he tried to persuade Greeks and Jews alike.

⁵ When Silas and Timothy came down from Macedonia, Paul was absorbed in preaching and giving evidence to the Jewish people that Jesus was the Messiah. ⁶ When they turned against him and started to insult him, he took his cloak and shook it out in front of them, saying, "Your blood is on your own heads; from now on I can go to the Gentiles with a clear conscience."

⁷Then he left the synagogue and moved to a house next door, which belonged to a worshiper of God named Justus. ⁸The president of the synagogue, Crispus, and his household became believers in Christ. Many Corinthians who heard Paul also believed and were baptized.

⁹One night God said to him in a vision, "Don't be afraid. Go on speaking and don't be silent, ¹⁰for I am with you. No one will attack you or harm you, because I have many people in this city." ¹¹So Paul stayed for a year and a half, teaching them the word of God.

ೞ   ೞ   ೞ

¹²While Gallio was proconsul of Achaia, the members of the local synagogue rose up in one accord against Paul, and brought him into court. ¹³"This one," they charged, "is persuading the people to worship God in ways that are against the Law."

¹⁴Paul was about to speak in self-defense when Gallio said to Paul's accusers, "If it were a serious crime or a serious fraud, I would give you a patient and reasonable hearing. ¹⁵But since this is a dispute about terminology and titles and your own law, you must see to it yourselves. I refuse to judge such matters." ¹⁶With that, he dismissed them from court.

¹⁷Then they all pounced on Sosthenes, a leader of the synagogue, and beat him in full view of the bench. But Gallio paid no attention to the incident.

¹⁸Paul stayed on in Corinth for some time. Eventually he left the sisters and brothers and sailed for Syria, in the company of Priscilla and Aquila. At the port of Cenchrea, he shaved his head because of a vow he had made.

¹⁹When they reached Ephesus, Paul left them and went alone to the Jewish synagogue to debate with the worshipers. ²⁰They asked him to stay longer, but he declined. ²¹Yet when he did leave, he said, "I will return if God wills it." After that he set sail from Ephesus. ²²When he landed at Caesarea, he went up to greet the church.

Then he came down to Antioch. ²³After spending some time there, Paul set out again, traveling systematically through Galatian territory and Phrygia to reassure all the disciples.

ೞ   ೞ   ೞ

²⁴A Jew named Apollos, a native of Alexandria with a reputation for eloquence, arrived by ship at Ephesus. He was both well-versed in scripture and instructed in the Way of Christ.

²⁵ Fervent in spirit, Apollos taught and spoke accurately about Jesus, although he knew firsthand only about John's baptism. ²⁶ He too began to express himself fearlessly in the synagogue. When Priscilla and Aquila heard Apollos, they took him home and explained the Way of Christ in greater detail. ²⁷ Apollos wanted to go to Achaia, and so the sisters and brothers encouraged him by writing the disciples there to meet him.

When Apollos arrived, he greatly strengthened those who through God's favor had become believers. ²⁸ He was vigorous in his public refutation of the Jewish party, as he went about establishing from the scriptures that Jesus was the Messiah.

19·¹ While Apollos was in Corinth, Paul passed through the interior of the country and came to Ephesus. There Paul found disciples, ² to whom he put the question, "Did you receive the Holy Spirit when you became believers?"

They replied, "No, we were never even told there was such a thing as a Holy Spirit."

³ "Then how were you baptized?" he asked.

"With John's baptism," they responded.

⁴ Paul then explained, "John's baptism was a baptism of repentance; he insisted that the people believe in the one who was to come after him—in other words, Jesus."

⁵ When they heard this, they were baptized in the name of Jesus Christ. ⁶ And the moment Paul laid his hands on them, the Holy Spirit came down on them, and they began to speak in tongues and prophesy. ⁷ There were about twelve of them.

ℭℜ   ℭℜ   ℭℜ

⁸ Paul entered the synagogue and, over a period of about three months, debated fearlessly, with persuasive arguments, about the reign of God.

⁹ But some among the congregation dissented, refused to believe and publicly disparaged the Way. Paul left them, along with his disciples, and held his daily debates in the lecture hall of Tyrannus. ¹⁰ This continued for two years, and all the Jews and Greeks throughout Asia heard the word of God.

¹¹ God worked such remarkable miracles through Paul ¹² that even handkerchiefs or aprons which touched him, when applied to sick people, healed them and drove evil spirits from them.

¹³ Then some roving Jewish exorcists tried invoking the name of Jesus Christ over those who had evil spirits, by saying, "I command you to come out—by Jesus, whom Paul preaches!"

¹⁴ Among the exorcists trying this were the seven children of Sceva, a Jewish high priest. ¹⁵ The evil spirit they were trying to exorcise came at them with, "Jesus I know, and Paul I know, but who are you?" ¹⁶ Then the person possessed by the demon sprang on them and overpowered them one by one. They were mauled so badly that they fled from the house naked and bleeding.

¹⁷ When the news of this incident reached the ears of Jews and Greeks living in Ephesus, they grew fearful, and the name of Jesus Christ became greatly esteemed. ¹⁸ Many believers came forward and confessed to practicing sorcery. ¹⁹ And a number of these brought their books of magic and made a public bonfire out of them. It was estimated that the value of the documents came to fifty thousand silver pieces—almost a hundred fifty years' wages. ²⁰ In this way the word of God spread widely and successfully.

19:21–28:31

When all this had come to pass, Paul decided to return to Jerusalem by way of Macedonia and Achaia. "And after that," he said, "I must visit Rome as well." ²² Then he sent Timothy and Erastus, two of his coworkers, ahead to Macedonia. He remained in the province of Asia a little longer.

²³ It was about this time that a controversy broke out concerning the Way. ²⁴ A silversmith named Demetrius, who employed a large number of workers crafting silver shrines to Diana, ²⁵ called together his workers and others in related crafts. "As you all know," he said, "we make a good living from this craft. ²⁶ Undoubtedly you have heard about this fellow Paul— who, not only in Ephesus but throughout most of Asia, has led astray a vast number of people by teaching that gods made by hand are not gods at all. ²⁷ This teaching threatens not only our very livelihood, but also the prestige of the temple of the Great Goddess—Diana. She who is worshiped throughout Asia and the whole world, may even be stripped of her divine majesty."

²⁸ When the workers heard this, they became enraged and started shouting, "Great is Diana of the Ephesians!" ²⁹ Their rage spread throughout the city, and the populace came together in the amphitheater, bringing with them two of Paul's Macedonian traveling companions, Gaius and Aristarchus. ³⁰ Paul intended to go in among the crowd, but was dissuaded by his disciples. ³¹ As a matter of fact, some friendly provincial officials sent word to Paul advising him not to venture into the theater.

³²By now mass confusion reigned in the gathering, and most of them didn't even know why they had assembled. Some shouted one thing, while others shouted another. ³³Members of the Jewish community there hustled Alexander to the front, who motioned with his hand for order. He intended to explain things to the gathering. ³⁴But when they realized he was Jewish, they shouted in unison, "Great is Diana of the Ephesians!"

They were at it for two hours ³⁵when the town clerk finally stilled the crowd and said, "Women and men of Ephesus, who among the living doesn't know that the city of the Ephesians is the guardian of the temple of the great Diana, and of her statue that fell from the heavens? ³⁶No one can contradict these facts! So there is no need for you to get so worked up and do something foolhardy. ³⁷The two you brought here have neither committed sacrileges against our Goddess nor blasphemed her. ³⁸If Demetrius and the silversmiths want to take action against anyone, the courts are in session and the proconsuls are available; let them press charges. ³⁹If you have anything more to bring up, let it be settled in the regular assembly. ⁴⁰As matters stand, we are already in danger of being accused of rioting for today's activities, since there's no real cause for it, and we don't have an explanation." ⁴¹With this, the town clerk dismissed the crowd.

20:1 Once the uproar was over, Paul sent for the disciples and encouraged them, said goodbye and left for Macedonia. ²As he passed through those places he gave the believers much encouragement, and eventually came to Greece, ³where he stayed for three months.

℞   ℞   ℞

As Paul prepared to set sail for Syria, he learned that the members of the local synagogue were plotting against him. So he changed his itinerary and returned by way of Macedonia. ⁴Traveling with him were Sopater, begot of Pyrrhus, from Beroea; Aristarchus and Secundus from Thessalonica; Gaius from Derbe; Timothy; and Tychicus and Trophimus from the province of Asia. ⁵They went on ahead and waited for us at Troas. ⁶We sailed from Phillipi after the Feast of Unleavened Bread and caught up with them in five days. We spent a week in Troas.

⁷On the first day of the week, we gathered to break bread. Paul spoke to them, and as he planned to leave the next day, he went on until midnight. ⁸There were a number of lamps in the upstairs room where they were gathered. ⁹And as Paul went on and on, a youth named Eutychus grew drowsy as he sat on a window sill; he fell asleep, tumbled out the window of the three-story building, and died. ¹⁰But Paul went down and flung himself on the youth and, cradling him in his arms, said, "Don't worry, he's still alive."

¹¹ Paul then returned to the upper room, broke bread and ate. He continued to talk until dawn; then he left. ¹² They took the youth away alive, to their great joy.

¹³ The plan was that we would now go ahead by sea. So we set sail for Assos, where we would meet up with Paul. He planned it this way, for he wanted to go by land. ¹⁴ When he met us at Assos, we took him aboard and went on to Mitylene. ¹⁵ The next day we left there and came to a point off Chios; the day after that we crossed over to Samos, and we made Miletas on the third day. ¹⁶ Paul had decided to sail past Ephesus and avoid Asia all together, since he was anxious to get to Jerusalem, if possible, in time for Pentecost.

¹⁷ Paul sent word from Miletus to Ephesus, summoning the elders of that church. ¹⁸ When they came he addressed these words to them: "You know how I lived among you from the first day I set foot in the province of Asia— ¹⁹ how I served Christ in humility through the sorrows and trials that came my way from the plotting of certain Jewish individuals and groups. ²⁰ I have not hesitated to do anything that might be helpful to you. I have taught you in public and in private, ²¹ urging both Jews and Greeks alike to turn to God and to believe in our Savior Jesus Christ.

²² "But now, as you see, I'm on my way to Jerusalem, compelled by the Spirit and not knowing what will happen to me there—²³ except that the Holy Spirit has been warning me from city to city that chains and hardships await me. ²⁴ However, I don't count my life of any value to myself. All I want is to finish my race and complete the task assigned to me by Jesus Christ—bearing witness to the Good News of God's grace. ²⁵ I know as I speak these words that none of you among whom I went about preaching the kindom will ever see my face again. ²⁶ Therefore, I solemnly declare today that I take the blame for no one's conscience, ²⁷ for I have never shrunk from announcing to you God's design in its entirety.

²⁸ "Keep watch over yourselves and over the whole flock the Holy Spirit has given you to guard. Shepherd the church of God, which was purchased with a high price—Christ's blood. ²⁹ I know quite well that when I am gone, savage wolves will invade you and will have no mercy on the flock. ³⁰ Even from your own ranks, there will be those coming forward with a travesty of the truth, to lead away any who will follow them.

³¹ "So be on your guard. Don't forget that for three years, night and day, I never ceased warning you individually, even to the point of tears. ³² I now commend you to God, and to the word of God's grace, which has the power to build you up and give you your inheritance among all the holy ones. ³³ Never did I set my heart on anyone's silver or gold or fine clothes. ³⁴ You yourselves know that these hands of mine have served both my needs and those of my companions. ³⁵ I have always pointed out to you that it's by

such hard work that you must help the weak. You need to recall the words of Jesus, who said, 'It is more blessed to give than to receive.'"

³⁶ After this discourse, Paul knelt down with them all and prayed. ³⁷ They began to weep without restraint, throwing their arms around him and kissing him, ³⁸ for they were deeply saddened to hear that they would never see his face again. Then they escorted him to the ship.

CR   CR   CR

21:1 Tearing ourselves away from them, we put to sea and sailed to Cos, and on the next day to Rhodes and from there to Patara. ² There we found a ship bound for Phoenicia, so we boarded and set sail. ³ When we came to Cyprus we passed it on the port side and headed for Syria, landing at Tyre. Here the ship unloaded its cargo. ⁴ Finding disciples there, we stayed with them for a week. Moved by the Spirit, they repeatedly counseled Paul not to go to Jerusalem. ⁵ But when our week was ended, we continued our journey. All the disciples and their families escorted us out of the city, and there on the beach we knelt to pray. ⁶ Then we made our goodbyes and boarded the ship, and they returned to their homes.

⁷ The voyage from Tyre ended when we came to Ptolemais, where we greeted our sisters and brothers and visited them for one day. ⁸ The next day we went to Caesarea. There we stayed with Philip the evangelist, one of the Seven. ⁹ He had four unmarried daughters who were prophets.

¹⁰ We had been there for several days when a prophet named Agabus came down from Judea. ¹¹ When he came to see us, he took Paul's belt, bound his own hands and feet with it and said, "The Holy Spirit says, 'The one who owns this belt will be bound this way in Jerusalem by the Temple authorities, and they will hand this person over to the Gentiles.' "

¹² When we heard this, all of us present begged Paul not to go up to Jerusalem. ¹³ Paul replied, "Are you trying to diminish my resolve by your crying? I am prepared not only to be bound but even to die for the name of Jesus Christ." ¹⁴ When it became obvious his mind was set, we fell silent, saying, "God's will be done."

¹⁵ After this, we made the necessary preparations for the journey and left for Jerusalem. ¹⁶ Some of the disciples from Caesarea accompanied us and led us to the house of our host, Mnason of Cyprus, who had been one of the earliest disciples.

¹⁷ When we arrived in Jerusalem, the sisters and brothers welcomed us warmly. ¹⁸ The next day Paul accompanied us to visit James; all the elders were present. ¹⁹ Paul greeted them and gave a detailed report of what God had accomplished among the Gentiles through Paul's ministry.

²⁰ They all gave praise to God when they heard the report. But they said to Paul, "You see, brother, how many thousands of our Jewish sisters and brothers are now believers—all of them resolute keepers of the Law! ²¹ They have heard that you teach people of the diaspora to abandon Moses, to stop circumcising their male children and to stop observing the various customs. ²² What are we to do? Certainly they will learn that you have arrived!

²³ "This is what we recommend: we have four believers here who have taken a Nazirite vow. ²⁴ Take them and purify yourself along with them; pay their expenses so that they may have their heads shaved. In this way, everyone will know that the reports they have heard about you are false, and that you still regularly live by the Law. ²⁵ Regarding our Gentile sisters and brothers, we sent them our decision that they are to abstain from food sacrificed to idols, from meat of unbled or strangled animals, and from sexual immorality."

²⁶ So the next day Paul took the four and was purified with them. Then he went to the Temple and gave notice when the day of purification would be completed and when the offering would be presented on their behalf.

CR   CR   CR

²⁷ When the seven days were almost over, some Jews from Asia Minor saw Paul in the Temple. They stirred up the crowd and seized him, ²⁸ shouting, "Children of Israel, help us! This is the person who preaches against our people, against our Law and against this place everywhere he goes, to anyone who will listen! Not only that, he has brought Greeks into the Temple and has defiled this holy place!" ²⁹ As it happened, they had previously seen Trophimus the Ephesian in the city with him, and presumed that Paul had brought him into the Temple.

³⁰ The whole city was in an uproar, with people scurrying about. They seized Paul and dragged him out of the Temple, and immediately the gates were closed behind them. ³¹ They were on the verge of killing him when news reached the commander of the cohort that all Jerusalem was breaking out in riot. ³² He immediately took soldiers and centurions and charged down to the crowd. When the crowd saw the commander and the troops, they stopped beating Paul.

³³ The commander approached, arrested Paul and had him bound with two chains. Then he attempted to find out who he was and what he had done. ³⁴ Different people in the crowd called out different charges. This resulted in such an uproar that it became impossible for the commander to gather the facts he needed. So he ordered Paul into the barracks. ³⁵ By the time Paul came to the steps, the soldiers had to carry him because of the violence of the crowd. ³⁶ The mob kept following from behind and shouting, "Away with him!"

³⁷ As Paul was about to be taken into the barracks, he asked the commander if he could have a word with him. The commander said, "So, you speak Greek! ³⁸ Aren't you the Egyptian who started the recent revolt and led the four thousand assassins into the desert?"

³⁹ Paul replied, "I am Jewish, a citizen of the well-known city of Tarsus in Cilicia. Give me your permission to speak to the people."

⁴⁰ The officer gave permission, and Paul, standing on the top step, motioned to the people to be quiet. When they grew silent he addressed them in Aramaic:

22 ¹ "Sisters and brothers, mothers and fathers, listen to my defense, which I now offer to you."

² When they realized he was speaking to them in Aramaic, they became utterly silent. He continued, ³ "I am Jewish, born at Tarsus in Cilicia. I was raised in this city and studied at the feet of Gamaliel. I was educated in the exact observance of the Law of our ancestors. I was as full of zeal for God as you are here. ⁴ I persecuted the followers of the Way to their death. I captured women and men and sent them to prison in chains. ⁵ The high priest and the elders will bear witness to this, for they sent me with letters of introduction to their peers in Damascus. I went there to deliver prisoners back here for punishment.

⁶ "As I neared Damascus, at about noon a bright light from heaven suddenly shone all around me. ⁷ I fell to the ground and heard a voice say to me, 'Saul, Saul, why are you persecuting me?' ⁸ 'Who are you?' I asked. The voice said to me, 'I am Jesus of Nazareth, and you are persecuting me.' ⁹ My traveling companions saw the light, but didn't hear the voice of the one speaking to me. ¹⁰ I asked, 'What must I do?' Jesus answered, 'Get up and go into Damascus. Once there, you will be told what to do.' ¹¹ Because I was blinded by the brightness of the light, my companions led me by hand into Damascus.

¹² "A person named Ananias, a devout observer of the Law and one highly regarded by the Jewish community in Damascus, came to see me. ¹³ He stood beside me and said, 'Saul, my brother, receive your sight.' My sight returned at that instant and I was able to see him. ¹⁴ He said to me,

'The God of our ancestors has chosen you to know the divine will, and to see the Just One and to hear the Messiah's voice. ¹⁵ You are to be the Messiah's witness to all humankind, bearing testimony about all you have seen and heard. ¹⁶ Now why do you delay? Go and get yourself baptized, wash away your sins and call on the name of Jesus.'

¹⁷ "When I returned to Jerusalem and was praying in the Temple, I fell into a trance ¹⁸ and saw Jesus. 'Hurry,' Jesus said, 'leave Jerusalem at once; for they refuse to accept your testimony about me.' ¹⁹ 'But my Sovereign,' I replied, 'it's because they know that I formerly moved from synagogue to synagogue, beating and imprisoning those who believe in you. ²⁰ They know that when the blood of your witness Stephen was shed, I stood by in full agreement, and even held the cloaks of the murderers while they stoned him.' ²¹ Then Jesus said to me, 'Go! I will send you far away to the Gentiles.' "

²² The crowd listened attentively up until he said this, then they began to shout, "Rid the earth of this one! He's not fit to live!" ²³ As they screamed, waved their cloaks over their heads and flung dust into the air, ²⁴ the commander had Paul taken into the barracks and interrogated with the whip, to figure out why the people were vilifying him like this.

²⁵ As they prepared him for the flogging, Paul said to the centurion on duty, "Is it lawful to scourge a person who is a Roman citizen and has not been brought to trial?"

²⁶ When he heard this, the centurion went to the commander and said, "Do you realize what you're about to do? This person is a Roman citizen!"

²⁷ The commander came to Paul and asked, "Are you a Roman citizen?"

"I am," he answered.

²⁸ The commander commented, "I bought my citizenship for a large sum of money."

Paul replied, "Actually, I was born a citizen."

²⁹ At this, those who were preparing to interrogate him withdrew, and the commander became frightened when he realized he had put a Roman citizen in chains.

ભ   ભ   ભ

³⁰ The next day, the commander released Paul from prison, intending to look carefully into the charge which the Temple authorities were bringing against him. He summoned the chief priests and the whole Sanhedrin to a meeting; then he brought Paul down and made him stand before them.

23:1 Paul looked intently at the Sanhedrin and said, "Friends, I have conducted myself before God in all good conscience to this day."

² At this the high priest Ananias commanded the attendants to strike Paul on the mouth. ³ Paul replied to this, "God is going to strike you, you white-washed wall! How dare you sit there to judge me according to the Law, and then break the Law by ordering me to be struck?"

⁴ Those nearby said, "You are insulting God's high priest!"

⁵ Paul answered, "I didn't realize he was the high priest, for scripture says, 'You will not curse a ruler of your people.'"

⁶ Now Paul was aware that some of them were Sadducees and some Pharisees. Consequently, he began his speech before the Sanhedrin this way: "I am a Pharisee, the descendant of Pharisees. I find myself on trial now because of my hope in the resurrection of the dead." ⁷ At these words, a dispute broke out between Pharisees and Sadducees, which divided the whole assembly. ⁸ The Sadducees, of course, maintain that there is no resurrection and deny the existence of angels and spirits, while the Pharisees believe in all these things.

⁹ A loud uproar ensued. Finally, some of the religious scholars who were Pharisees stood up and declared emphatically, "We don't find this man guilty of any crime. Perhaps a spirit or an angel has spoken to him." ¹⁰ At this, the commander feared they would tear Paul to pieces. He therefore ordered his troops to go down and rescue Paul from their midst and take him back to headquarters. ¹¹ That night God appeared at Paul's side and said, "Courage! Just as you have borne witness to me here in Jerusalem, so must you do the same in Rome as well."

¹² At daybreak, the Temple officials hatched a plot and bound themselves by oath that they would neither eat nor drink until they had killed Paul. ¹³ More than forty joined in the conspiracy. ¹⁴ They went to the chief priest and the elders and said, "We have made a solemn vow to eat nothing until we have killed Paul. ¹⁵ You and the Sanhedrin must now request the commander to bring him before you on the pretext that you need to examine his case more closely. For our part, we are prepared to kill him before he reaches you."

¹⁶ Now Paul's nephew heard of the plot and reported it to Paul in the barracks. ¹⁷ Paul called one of the centurions and said, "Take this youth to the commander. He has something to report."

¹⁸ The centurion took the youth to the commander and explained, "The prisoner Paul asked me to bring this youth to you, for he has something to report."

¹⁹ The tribune took him by the hand, pulled him aside and asked, "Now, what is it you want to tell me?"

²⁰ The youth said, "The Temple authorities have hatched a plot to ask you to bring Paul before the Sanhedrin tomorrow, as though they were going

to inquire more thoroughly into his case. ²¹Don't do it. For more than forty of them plan to ambush him. They have vowed not to eat or drink until they have killed him. They are ready and await your order."

²²The commander dismissed the youth with the counsel, "Don't tell anyone what you have told me."

²³Then he called for two of his centurions and said, "Call out two hundred soldiers, seventy cavalry and two hundred archers for a nine o'clock movement tonight. ²⁴Provide horses for Paul and deliver him to Felix the governor. Deliver him unharmed."

²⁵He also wrote the following letter:

²⁶"From Claudius Lysias,

"To His Excellency, Governor Felix:

"Greetings. ²⁷This person was seized by a Jewish mob with murder on its mind. But I, along with my troops, intervened and rescued him, for I learned that he was a Roman citizen. ²⁸With the intent to determine what charge to lay before him, I took him before their Sanhedrin. ²⁹I was able to ascertain that the accusations concerned questions about their Law, but that there was no charge worthy of imprisonment or the death penalty. ³⁰When I was informed that there was a conspiracy against him, I sent him to you immediately and ordered the accusers to state their case against him in your presence."

³¹So the soldiers, following orders, took Paul and escorted him to Antipatris after dark. ³²The next day, they returned to the barracks and left it up to the cavalry to complete the journey. ³³When the cavalry arrived in Caesarea, they delivered the letter and Paul to the governor. ³⁴The governor read the letter and asked Paul what province he was from. When he heard that Paul was Cilician, ³⁵the governor replied, "I will hear your case when your accusers arrive."

Then he ordered Paul to be held in Herod's Praetorium, the governor's official residence.

ଙ୍କ   ଙ୍କ   ଙ୍କ

^{24:1}Five days later, the high priest Ananias, accompanied by some elders and a lawyer named Tertullus, came down and filed formal charges against Paul before the governor.

²Paul was called, and Tertullus presented the case for the prosecution: "Your Excellency, Felix, we enjoy a longstanding peace and beneficial reforms because of your responsible stewardship. ³And we are grateful for

this. ⁴So, rather than take up too much of your time, in your kindness grant us a brief hearing.

⁵"This person is a troublemaker. He stirs up our Jewish sisters and brothers everywhere. He is a ringleader of the Nazarene sect, ⁶and he even attempted to desecrate the Temple. So we arrested him with the intent of judging him according to our Law, ⁷but the commander Lysias intervened and violently took him out of our jurisdiction. He then ordered us to appear before you. ⁸We invite you to learn for yourself the truth of our accusations against him." ⁹The high priest and the elders spoke up and agreed with the charge.

¹⁰Then the governor motioned Paul to speak. Paul said, "I know that you have administered justice over this nation for many years, so I will confidently make my defense. ¹¹As you can readily ascertain, it's no more than twelve days since I went up to Jerusalem on pilgrimage. ¹²But it's a lie that they found me arguing with anyone or stirring up a mob, either in the Temple or the synagogue or the city. ¹³Neither can they prove these charges they make against me. ¹⁴But I can admit that I worship the God of our ancestors in accordance with the Way, which they call a sect. I hold to my beliefs in accordance with the Law and with what the prophets have written. ¹⁵I trust in the same God that they do, that there will be a resurrection of the just and unjust alike. ¹⁶In view of this, I strive to keep a clear conscience before God and before all people.

¹⁷"After many years of absence, I came to Jerusalem to give alms for needy people and to make offerings. ¹⁸It was while I was doing this that they found me, after having been purified, in the Temple. There was no crowd and no disturbance. ¹⁹However, some Jewish authorities came down from Asia Minor—they should be here, if they have any reason to accuse me. ²⁰At least let those who are here say what crime I committed when I spoke before the Sanhedrin—²¹unless it's the one thing that I shouted out to them: 'It's over the issue of the resurrection of the dead that I am on trial before you today.' "

²²At this point Felix, who had accurate information about the Way, ordered a continuance of the case. "When Lysias the commander comes down," he said, "I will decide your case." ²³He then ordered the centurion to keep Paul in custody, but free from restrictions, and to allow his friends to care for his needs.

²⁴Several days later, Felix and his wife Drusilla—who was Jewish—came and sent for Paul, who told them about faith in Christ Jesus. ²⁵But when Paul touched on the subjects of justice, self-control and the coming judgment, Felix grew alarmed and said, "You are dismissed for now! I will send for you later at a more convenient time." ²⁶At the same time Felix had hopes

of being offered a bribe, so he sent for Paul quite often and had discussions with him.

CR　　　CR　　　CR

²⁷ After a period of two years, Felix was replaced by Porcius Festus. And since Felix was determined to win favor with the Jewish community, he left Paul in prison.

25:1 After Festus had been in the province for three days, he went up to Jerusalem from Caesarea. ² The chief priests and leaders of the Jewish community met with him and presented their charges against Paul. ³ They requested a concession: to have Paul be sent to Jerusalem. They were plotting to kill him along the way. ⁴ However, Festus replied that Paul would remain in custody in Caesarea, and that he himself would be going there before too long. ⁵ He added, "Let some of your authorities come down with me, and if he has done anything wrong they can file charges."

⁶ After spending eight or ten days there, Festus went down to Caesarea. The very next day, he took his seat on the tribunal and called for Paul to be brought before him. ⁷ Once Paul appeared, the Temple authorities who had come down from Jerusalem formed a circle around Paul and pelted him with unfounded accusations.

⁸ Paul said in his defense, "I have committed no crime against Jewish Law, against the Temple or against Caesar."

⁹ Festus, who wanted to be seen in a favorable light among Jewish people, said, "Are you willing to go up to Jerusalem and be tried before me there?"

¹⁰ Paul replied, "I am standing before the tribunal of Caesar, where I belong. I have not committed a crime against the Jewish people, as you very well know. ¹¹ If I am convicted of a capital crime, I don't refuse to die. But if their charges are specious, no one has the right to hand me over to them. I appeal to Caesar."

¹² Festus interrupted the proceedings to confer with his advisers. Then he said to Paul, "You have appealed to Caesar, you will go to Caesar."

CR　　　CR　　　CR

¹³ After a few days, Agrippa the ruler and Bernice, his sister, arrived in Caesarea and paid Festus a courtesy call. ¹⁴ Since they were to spend several days there, Festus referred Paul's case to the ruler. "There is a prisoner here," he said, "whom Felix left behind in custody. ¹⁵ While I was in Jerusalem, the chief priests and the elders presented their case against this man and demanded condemnation. ¹⁶ I replied that it was not a Roman

practice to hand accused persons over before they have been confronted by their accusers and given a chance to defend themselves against their charges. ¹⁷ When they came here, I didn't delay the matter. The very next day, I took my seat on the bench and ordered the accused brought in. ¹⁸ His accusers confronted him, but they didn't charge him with any of the crimes I suspected.

¹⁹ "Instead they differed with him over issues in their own religion, and about a certain Jesus who had died, but who Paul claimed is alive. ²⁰ Not knowing how to decide the case, I asked whether the prisoner was willing to go to Jerusalem and stand trial there on these charges. ²¹ Paul appealed to be kept here until there could be an imperial investigation of his case, so I issued orders that he be kept in custody until I could send him to Caesar."

²² Then Agrippa said to Festus, "I would like to hear this person, too."

"You will hear him tomorrow," Festus replied.

²³ The next day Bernice and Agrippa arrived with great pomp and ceremony, entering the auditorium attended by the commanders of the cohort and the notables of the city. Then Festus ordered Paul into the auditorium.

²⁴ Festus said, "Honored guests, Agrippa and Bernice, and notables of our city, look at this man! He is the one the whole Jewish community—both in Jerusalem and here—loudly declares doesn't deserve to live. ²⁵ But I have not found a capital offense. And as he has appealed to the emperor, I have decided to send him to Rome. ²⁶ But I find myself lacking something to write our sovereign about this case. So I have brought him here before all of you, and especially you, Agrippa, so that our hearing may result in material for my report. ²⁷ It seems absurd to send up the prisoner without indicating the charges against him!"

26:1 Agrippa then said to Paul, "You may speak on your own behalf."

² So Paul held up his hand and initiated his defense:

"I consider myself fortunate, your highness, that I am given the opportunity to state my case before you, and to address all the charges against me by the Jewish authorities. ³ This is especially so because you are an expert in issues pertaining to Jewish customs and controversies. Please, I beg you, be patient as you listen to me.

⁴ "The way in which I was raised as a child, beginning among my own people and later in Jerusalem, is well known among the Jewish community. ⁵ They have known from the beginning and could testify, if they were willing, that I have lived the life of a Pharisee—the strictest party of our religion.

⁶"And now I am on trial because of my hope in the promise of God to our ancestors. ⁷This is the promise our twelve tribes hope to attain as they zealously worship God night and day. Your highness, this hope is the reason I am put on trial by my Jewish sisters and brothers. ⁸Tell me why any of you consider it incredible that God should raise the dead?

⁹"Personally, I too once thought myself obligated to work fervently to oppose the name of the Nazarene known as Jesus. ¹⁰I did this in Jerusalem. I was authorized by the chief priests to imprison many of the believers. And I cast my vote against them when they were sentenced to death. ¹¹I moved from synagogue to synagogue punishing them and charging them with blasphemy. I even persecuted them in foreign cities.

¹²"I was on such a journey to Damascus, fortified with the authority and commission of the high priests. ¹³That day—around noon, your highness— I saw a light brighter than the sun come down from heaven. Its brilliance enveloped me and my travelers. ¹⁴We all fell to the ground, and I heard a voice saying to me in Aramaic, 'Saul, Saul, why are you persecuting me? It only hurts you to resist my prodding.' ¹⁵'Who are you?' I asked. And the reply came, 'I am Jesus, and you are persecuting me. ¹⁶Get up now on your two feet. I am appearing to you to appoint you as my servant, to bear testimony about what you have seen of me, and what you will be shown soon. ¹⁷I will deliver you from your own people, and from the Gentiles to whom I will send you. ¹⁸You will open their eyes, so that they will turn from darkness to light, from the control of Satan to God—that they may receive forgiveness of sins, and an inheritance among those who have been sanctified through faith in me.'

¹⁹"Consequently, your highness, I couldn't be disobedient to the heavenly vision. ²⁰So I proclaimed it originally to the citizens of Damascus, then to those in Jerusalem and all the inhabitants of Judea, and finally to the Gentiles. I preached repentance and turning to God, with good works as a sign of their repentance. ²¹It was because of this that the citizens of Jerusalem seized me in the Temple and tried to murder me. ²²But I have been blessed with God's help. That is why I stand to this very day, testifying to the great and lowly alike. I say nothing more than what the prophets and Moses predicted: ²³that the Messiah must suffer and, being the first to rise from the dead, would proclaim—both to our people and to the Gentiles as well—that the Light has come."

²⁴At this point in his defense, Festus loudly interrupted Paul: "Paul, you are deranged! Your immense learning is driving you to madness."

²⁵"Most excellent Festus," Paul replied, "I am not deranged. I speak nothing that isn't true and reasonable. ²⁶The ruler knows these issues, and I speak to him with assurance, since I'm confident that nothing spoken here

has escaped his notice—it was not done in a corner. ²⁷ Agrippa—do you believe the Prophets, your highness? I know that you do."

²⁸ Agrippa said to Paul, "In a short time you will have persuaded me to become a Christian!"

²⁹ "A short time or a long time!" Paul replied, "I pray to God that both you and all present who hear my words would come to be as I am—with the exception of these chains!"

³⁰ At this point the ruler arose, along with the governor, Bernice, and those sitting with them. ³¹ Once they had left the room, they compared notes and came to a consensus. "What this person is doing doesn't deserve the death penalty—or even imprisonment."

³² Then Agrippa said to Festus, "He might have been set free by now if he had not appealed to Caesar!"

ঙ   ঙ   ঙ

27:1 Once it was decided that we should sail for Italy, Paul and some other prisoners were put into the custody of a centurion named Julius, of the Augustan cohort. ² We embarked in a ship from Adramyttium, bound for ports along the province of Asia Minor. Accompanying us was Aristarchus, a Macedonian from Thessalonica. ³ The next day, we landed at Sidon, and Julius was considerate enough to allow Paul to go to his friends for provisions.

⁴ We embarked from there and sailed to the leeward side of Cyprus because of headwinds. ⁵ Then we sailed in open water along the coast of Cilicia and Pamphylia, and in two weeks arrived at Myra in Lycia. ⁶ There the centurion found a ship from Alexandria bound for Italy, and put us aboard. ⁷ For the next several days we made little headway and arrived off Cnidus only after much difficulty. The wind made it impossible to land there, so we sailed to the leeward side of Crete, off Cape Salmone. ⁸ We coasted along with difficulty until we reached a place called Fair Havens, near the town of Lasea.

⁹ All of this had consumed a huge amount of time, and sailing was now dangerous since it was so late in the year—even the Day of Atonement had come and gone. Paul warned everyone, ¹⁰ "Friends, I perceive that this voyage now faces dangerous weather; we run the risk of losing our cargo, our ship and even our lives." ¹¹ But the centurion gave more heed to the captain and the ship's owner than to Paul. ¹² Because the harbor was unsuitable for wintering, the majority agreed to set sail with the hope of reaching Phoenix, a harbor in Crete facing both southwest and northwest, to spend the winter there.

¹³ A mild breeze out of the south came up and, sensing this as a good omen, they weighed anchor and sailed close to the shore of Crete. ¹⁴ Before long, a hurricane force wind called a "northeaster" struck down on them from across the island. ¹⁵ The ship was enveloped by the storm and couldn't be turned into the wind, so we had to give way to the wind and allow ourselves to be driven along by its force.

¹⁶ As we ran along the leeward side of an island known as Clauda, we managed with difficulty to gain control of the ship's dinghy. ¹⁷ Next they passed cables under the ship itself. Then, for fear of running aground on the shallows of Syrtis, they lowered the sea anchor and let themselves be driven along. ¹⁸ We were being buffeted by the storm so violently that on the next day they tossed some of the cargo overboard. ¹⁹ On the third day, they tossed the ship's gear overboard with their own hands. ²⁰ For several days neither the sun nor the stars were visible, while the storm was assailing us. At last we gave up all hope of surviving.

²¹ Then, when they had been without food for a long time, Paul stood up among them. "Friends," he said, "had you heeded my advice and not set out from Crete, you would not have suffered all this loss, all this damage. ²² But now I ask you to hold on to your courage. For none of you will be lost, only the ship. ²³ Last night an angel of the God to whom I belong and whom I serve stood beside me ²⁴ and said, 'Don't be afraid, Paul. You are to stand trial before Caesar, so God has granted you the safety of all who sail with you.' ²⁵ So, take heart, friends, for I believe that events will take place just as I have been told. ²⁶ We are to run aground on an island."

²⁷ After another two weeks—we were still drifting and in the Adriatic Sea by now—the crew sensed that we were near land. ²⁸ They took soundings and measured twenty fathoms. A little later they measured fifteen fathoms. ²⁹ So, for fear of running aground on a reef, they let out four anchors from the stern and prayed for the sun to rise. ³⁰ The crew then tried to abandon ship. They lowered the dinghy into the water with the pretext that they were going to lay out anchors from the bow. ³¹ But Paul said to the centurion and his soldiers, "If the crew doesn't stay aboard, you won't be saved." ³² So the soldiers scuttled the dinghy by cutting its ropes.

³³ A little before daybreak Paul urged them all to eat something. "For the last two weeks," he said, "you have been under constant tension and have eaten nothing. ³⁴ I urge you to have something to eat; there is no doubt about your safety. Not a hair of your head will be lost." ³⁵ With this, he took some bread and gave thanks to God while standing before them all. Then he broke the bread and began to eat. ³⁶ They were all encouraged by this and began to eat as well. ³⁷ In all, there were two hundred seventy-six aboard. ³⁸ After they all had their fill, they lightened the load by tossing the wheat overboard.

³⁹ At daybreak, even though they didn't recognize the land, they spied a bay with a beach. Intending to run the ship aground at this point, ⁴⁰ they cut loose the anchors to abandon them to the sea, loosened the lines of the rudder, and hoisted the foresail to the wind and tried for the beach. ⁴¹ But the current carried the ship into a sandbar and grounded it. The bow was so wedged that it couldn't be moved, and the pounding surf began to break up the stern.

⁴² Initially, the soldiers intended to kill the prisoners to keep them from escaping by swimming away, ⁴³ but the centurion intervened and thwarted their plan, because he wanted to spare Paul's life. He ordered those who could swim to jump overboard and make for shore. ⁴⁴ He ordered the others to follow on planks or pieces of debris from the ship. All came ashore safe and sound.

28¹ Once safely ashore, we learned that the island was Malta. ² The inhabitants were especially friendly. They built a huge fire and bade us welcome, for it had started to rain and was cold. ³ Paul had collected an armful of firewood, and was putting it onto the fire when a snake, escaping from the heat, fastened itself onto his hand. ⁴ When the locals saw the snake hanging from his hand, they said to one another, "He must be a murderer. For divine justice would not let him live, even though he escaped the sea." ⁵ Paul, meanwhile, shook the snake into the fire with no ill effects. ⁶ They waited, expecting him to swell up and suddenly drop dead. After a long wait, and unable to detect anything unusual happening, they changed their minds and decided he was a god.

⁷ Nearby there were estates belonging to Publius, the chief official of the island. He welcomed us with open arms and entertained us cordially for three days. ⁸ It so happened that Publius' father was ill, suffering from dysentery and a fever. Paul went in to see him, and after praying, healed him by the laying on of hands. ⁹ Once this happened, others suffering from illnesses came and were healed. ¹⁰ They honored us with many gifts. When it came time to sail, they supplied the provisions.

℞   ℞   ℞

¹¹ After three months, we set sail on a ship which had wintered at the island. It was an Alexandrian ship with the figurehead of the twin gods Castor and Pollux. ¹² We put in at Syracuse and spent three days there, ¹³ and then moved along the coast to Rhegium. After a day there, a south wind sprang up, and two days later we made Puteoli. ¹⁴ Here we found some sisters and brothers, who invited us to spend a week with them.

At last we came to Rome. ¹⁵ When the sisters and brothers there learned of our arrival, they came from as far as the Forum of Appius and Three Taverns—thirty and forty miles away—to meet us. Paul took courage when he saw them, and gave thanks to God.

¹⁶ Upon arriving in Rome, Paul was allowed to take a lodging of his own, although a soldier was assigned as a guard.

¹⁷ Three days later, Paul invited the prominent members of the Jewish community for a visit. When they had gathered he said, "Friends, I have done nothing against our people or against our ancient customs. Yet in Jerusalem I was handed over to the Romans as a prisoner. ¹⁸ The Romans tried my case and wanted to release me because they found nothing against me deserving death. ¹⁹ When the Temple authorities objected, I was forced to appeal to Caesar, though I had no cause to make accusations against my own people. ²⁰ This is the reason, then, that I have asked to see you and to speak with you. I wear these chains solely because I share the hope of Israel."

²¹ They replied, "We received no correspondence from Judea about you, and none of the sisters and brothers arriving from there have reported any rumors or anything negative about you. ²² For our part, we want to hear what you think, for we understand that this sect is generally denounced everywhere."

²³ So they set a date to come to his lodgings. When the day arrived, people came in great numbers. From early morning until evening Paul set forth his position. He declared to them the kindom of God and tried to convince them about Jesus—arguing from the Law of Moses and from the prophets.

²⁴ Some were convinced by what he said, though most were skeptical; ²⁵ they argued among themselves and didn't come to any agreement. But before they left, Paul made one last effort. He said, "The Holy Spirit was right when she spoke to your ancestors through the prophet Isaiah:

²⁶ 'Go to this people and say,
     You will keep on listening but won't understand,
     you will keep on looking but won't perceive.
²⁷ For the heart of this people has become hardened;
     they hardly hear with their ears, and their eyes are shut.
Otherwise they might see with their eyes,
     hear with their ears,
understand with their heart
     and turn and be healed.'

²⁸ "Know, therefore, that this salvation of God has been sent to the Gentiles. They will listen to it."

²⁹ When Paul finished, his Jewish listeners left, arguing seriously over what had been said.

CR   CR   CR

[30] For two full years, Paul stayed on in his rented lodgings, welcoming all who came to visit. [31] With full assurance, and without any hindrance whatever, Paul preached the kindom of God and taught about our Savior Jesus Christ.

the letter of paul to the
ROMANS

Rom paul, servant of christ jesus, called to be an apostle and set apart to proclaim ²the Good News, which God promised long ago through the prophets, as the holy scriptures record—the Good News ³concerning God's Only Begotten, who was descended from David according to the flesh, ⁴but was made the Only Begotten of God in power, according to the spirit of holiness, by the resurrection from the dead: Jesus Christ our Savior. ⁵We have been favored with apostleship, that we may bring to obedient faith all the nations, ⁶among whom are you who have been called to belong to Jesus Christ;

⁷To all in Rome, beloved of God and called to be holy people:

Grace and peace from our Abba God and our Savior Jesus Christ.

⁸First, I thank my God through Jesus Christ for all of you and for the way your faith is proclaimed throughout the world. ⁹As God is my witness—the God I worship with my spirit by preaching the Good News of God's Only Begotten—I pray for you constantly. ¹⁰And I pray that, God willing, I will be able to find the way to visit you.

¹¹ I long to see you, either to share with you some spiritual gift ¹²or to find encouragement from you through our common faith. I want you to know, sisters and brothers, that I have often planned to visit you, but until now I have been prevented from doing so. ¹³ I want to work as fruitfully among you as I have done among the other Gentiles. ¹⁴ I owe a duty to both Greeks and non-Greeks, to the wise and the foolish alike. ¹⁵ That is why I am so eager to bring the Good News to you in Rome as well.

¹⁶ For I am not ashamed of the Good News: it is itself the very power of God, effecting the deliverance of everyone who believes the Good News—to the Jew first, but also to the Greek. ¹⁷ For in that Gospel, God's justice is revealed—a justice which arises from faith and has faith as its result. As it is written, "By being faithful, those who are upright will find life."

୯ ୯ ୯

¹⁸ At the same time, however, God's passionate and just anger is also being revealed; it rages from heaven against all of humankind's willful impiety and refusal to honor God, against the injustices committed by people who actively suppress the truth through their injustice.

¹⁹ For what is knowable about God is plain and obvious to everyone; indeed, it is God who has made it obvious to them. ²⁰ Though invisible to the eye, God's eternal power and divinity have been seen since the creation of the universe, understood and clearly visible in all of nature. Humankind is, therefore, without excuse.

²¹ For although they knew God, they didn't give God honor or praise and never even said, "Thank you"; instead, their reasoning became increasingly empty and inept, and their undiscerning hearts were darkened. ²² Professing to be wise, they became fools: ²³they exchanged the glory of the immortal and incorruptible God for mere images—images of mortal, corruptible humans, and birds, animals and reptiles. ²⁴ So God gave them over to their hearts' desire—to promiscuous immorality, to the devaluing of their bodies with each other. ²⁵ They exchanged the reality of God for a lie, and worshiped and served what was created rather than the Creator, who is forever praised. Amen.

²⁶ That is why God turned them over to their demeaning passions. Their women went from having sexual relations that were natural for them to relations that were contrary to their own natures. ²⁷ And their men who would have naturally had sexual relations with women abandoned those ways and became consumed with burning passions for one another. Thus both sexes acted against their nature, and received in their own personalities the consequences of their error.

²⁸Furthermore, since they didn't think it worthwhile to retain the knowledge of God, God abandoned them to their own depraved minds. They were driven to do things that shouldn't be done ²⁹and were filled with every kind of injustice, evil, greed and malice. They became full of envy, murder, bickering, treachery and deceit. They became gossips, ³⁰slanderers, God-haters; they were insolent, arrogant and boastful, inventors of evil, and rebellious to their parents. ³¹They were senseless, faithless, heartless and ruthless. ³²And even though they knew God's just mandate—that everyone who does such things deserves death—they not only continued to do these things, but encouraged others to do the same.

2:1 Yet every one of you who passes judgment has no excuse: by your judgment you convict yourself, since you do the very same things! ²We know that God's judgment rightly falls on people who do such things—³so how do you expect to escape God's judgment, since you who condemn these things in others do them yourselves? ⁴Or do you think lightly of God's rich kindness and forbearance? Don't you know that God's kindness is an invitation for you to repent?

⁵In spite of this, your hard and impenitent hearts are storing up retribution for that day of wrath when the just judgment of God will be revealed, ⁶when every person will be repaid for what they have done: ⁷eternal life to those who strive for glory, honor and immortality by patiently doing right; ⁸wrath and fury to those who selfishly disobey the truth and obey wickedness. ⁹Yes, affliction and anguish will come upon all who have done evil—the Jew first, then the Greek. ¹⁰But there will be glory, honor and peace for everyone who has done good—to the Jew first, then the Greek. ¹¹With God there is no favoritism.

2:12–3:26

$\mathcal{A}$ll who sin independently of the Law will also perish independently of the Law; and all who sin under the Law will be judged by the Law. ¹³It is not those who hear the Law who are just before God, but those who keep the Law who will be justified. ¹⁴For instance, when Gentiles do naturally things required by the Law, they are a Law unto themselves, even though they don't have the Law. ¹⁵They demonstrate that the demands of the Law are written on their hearts—they have a witness, their own conscience—and their conflicting thoughts accuse or even defend them. ¹⁶All this will occur—according to the Good News I preach—on the day when God judges the secrets of humankind through Jesus Christ.

¹⁷Now if you describe yourself as Jewish, if you rely on the Law, if you are proud of your relationship with the Most High, ¹⁸if you know God's will and can tell right from wrong since you've been instructed in the Law, ¹⁹if you are confident that you're a guide for the blind and a beacon for those in the dark, ²⁰if you teach the ignorant and instruct the immature—because you have in the Law the very embodiment of knowledge and truth—²¹then why don't you teach yourself as well as others? ²²You who preach against stealing, do you steal? You who condemn adultery, do you commit adultery? You who despise idols, do you rob temples? ²³You who boast of the Law, do you dishonor God by breaking the Law? ²⁴It says in scripture, "It is because of you that the name of God is reviled among the Gentiles."

²⁵The sign of the Covenant—circumcision—has value if you keep the Law. But if you break the Law, you might as well become a Gentile! ²⁶If those who are not members of the Covenant keep the spirit of the Law, won't they be judged as though they kept the Law? ²⁷Moreover, those who keep the Law but are not actual members of the Covenant will judge you as a lawbreaker, even though you have the written code and the sign of the Covenant.

²⁸Being Jewish is more than following the letter of the Law; the sign of the Covenant is more than a visible sign. ²⁹You are really Jewish if you are inwardly Jewish, and the real sign of the Covenant is on your heart. It is a matter of following the spirit, not the letter, of the Law. A person like this seeks praise not from humankind, but from God.

^{3:1}Then what benefit is there in being Jewish? What benefit is there in having the sign of the Covenant? ²Much, in every respect. First of all, the Jewish people were entrusted with the message of God. ³What if some of them were unfaithful? Will their unfaithfulness nullify God's faithfulness? ⁴Not at all! God will still be true, though all humankind lies—as scripture says, "That you may be right when you speak and prevail when you are judged."

⁵But if our lack of holiness provides proof of God's justice, what can we say? That God is unjust—I am using a human analogy—in being angry with us? ⁶Certainly not! That would imply that God could not judge the world. ⁷One might as well say, "If my lie makes God's truth all the more glorious by comparison, why am I being condemned as a sinner?" ⁸Why not say, "Do evil so that good may come of it!" Some slanderers have even accused us of teaching this; they are getting just what they deserve.

⁹What, then? Are Jews better than Gentiles? Not at all! We have already declared that Jews and Greeks alike are all subjects of sin. ¹⁰As it is written:
"There are no just, not even one;
¹¹there is not one who understands,

not one who seeks God.

¹² All have turned away,
  all alike have become worthless;
there is no one who does good,
  not a single one."

¹³ "Their throats are open graves;
  their tongues are full of deceit."

"Viper's venom is on their lips."

¹⁴ "Their mouths are full of bitter curses."

¹⁵ "Their feet are swift to shed blood;
  ¹⁶ they leave ruin and misery in their wake,
  and ¹⁷ they do not know the way of peace."

¹⁸ "There is no fear of God before their eyes."

¹⁹ Now we know that what the Law says is said to those under the Law. Therefore, let every mouth be silenced, and let all of humankind be open to God's judgment. ²⁰ This is because we are not justified in the sight of God by keeping the Law: law only makes us aware of sin.

²¹ But now the justice of God has been manifested apart from the Law, even though both Law and prophets bear witness to it; ²² the justice of God works through faith in Jesus Christ for all who believe. There are no exceptions: ²³ everyone has sinned; everyone falls short of the glory of God. ²⁴ Yet everyone has also been undeservedly justified by the gift of God, through the redemption wrought in Christ Jesus. ²⁵ God presented Christ as a propitiatory sacrifice, for the atonement of all who have faith in Christ's blood. And God did so to manifest divine justice—because God showed forbearance by remitting sins committed in the past, ²⁶ in order to demonstrate divine justice in the present—so that the Most High might be both a just judge and the One who justifies those who believe in Jesus.

3:27–4:25

*W*hat room is there then for boasting? It is ruled out. In what law do we boast—the law of works? No: only the law of faith. ²⁸ We maintain that one is justified by faith—apart from keeping the Law. ²⁹ Does God belong to the Jews alone? Isn't God also the God of the Gentiles? Yes, of the Gentiles too. ³⁰ And because there is only one God, it is the same God who will justify Jew and Gentile through the same faith. ³¹ Do we then render the Law null and void? Not at all—we give the Law its true value!

^{4:1} What will we say about Sarah and Abraham, our ancestors according

to the flesh? [2] Certainly if they were justified by their deeds they had grounds for boasting—but not in God's view. [3] For what does scripture say? "Sarah and Abraham believed God, and it was credited to them as righteousness."

[4] Now, when a person works, the wages are regarded not as a favor, but as what is due. [5] But when people do nothing except believe in the One who justifies the ungodly, their faith is credited as righteousness. [6] Thus David congratulates those to whom God credits righteousness without action on their part:

[7] "Blessed are they whose iniquities are forgiven,
    whose sins are covered over.
[8] Blessed is the person
    to whom God imputes no guilt."

[9] Is this blessedness only for Jewish people, or is it meant for others as well? Call Sarah and Abraham to mind: we have been saying that their faith justified them. [10] When did this justification occur? Was it before or after Abraham had received the sign of the Covenant? It was before, not after. [11] In fact, this sign of the Covenant—circumcision—was given after he believed, as a sign and a guarantee that his earlier faith had justified him. In this way Sarah and Abraham became the ancestors of all Gentile believers, who could then be considered justified as well. [12] These too are the ancestors of those under the Covenant—provided they follow the path of faith that Sarah and Abraham walked before they received the sign of the Covenant.

[13] The promise made to Sarah and Abraham and their descendants—that they would inherit the world—did not depend on the Law; it was made in view of the righteousness that comes from faith. [14] For if those who live by the Law are heirs, then faith is pointless and the promise is worthless. [15] The Law forever holds the potential for punishment. Only when there is no Law can there be no violation.

[16] Hence everything depends on faith; everything is grace. Thus the promise holds true for all of Sarah's and Abraham's descendants, not only for those who have the Law, but for all who have their faith. They are the mother and the father of us all, [17] which is why scripture says, "I will make you the parents of many nations"—all of which is done in the sight of the God in whom they believed, the God who restores the dead to life and calls into being things that don't exist.

[18] Hoping against hope, Sarah and Abraham believed, and so became the mother and father of many nations, just as it was once promised them: "Numerous as this will your descendants be." [19] Sarah and Abraham, without growing weak in faith, thought about their bodies, which were very

old—he was about one hundred, and she was well beyond child-bearing age. ²⁰Still they never questioned or doubted God's promise; rather, they grew strong in faith and gave glory to God, ²¹fully persuaded that God could do whatever was promised. ²²Thus, Sarah's and Abraham's faith "was credited to them as righteousness."

²³The words, "was credited to them," were not written with Sarah and Abraham alone in mind; ²⁴they were intended for us, too. For our faith will be credited to us if we believe in the One who raised Jesus our Savior from the dead, ²⁵the Jesus who was handed over to death for our sins and raised up for our justification.

5:1–6:23

𝓝*ow* since we have been made right in God's sight by our faith, we are at peace with God through our Savior Jesus Christ. ²Because of our faith, Christ has brought us to the grace in which we now stand, and we confidently and joyfully look forward to the day on which we will become all that God has intended. ³But not only that—we even rejoice in our afflictions! We know that affliction produces perseverance; ⁴and perseverance, proven character; and character, hope. ⁵And such a hope does not disappoint, because the love of God has been poured out in our hearts through the Holy Spirit, who has been given to us.

⁶At the appointed time, when we were still powerless, Christ died for us godless people. ⁷It is not easy to die even for a good person—though of course for someone really worthy, there might be someone prepared to die—⁸but the proof of God's love is that Christ died for us even while we were sinners.

⁹Now that we have been justified by Christ's blood, it is all the more certain that we will be saved by Christ from God's wrath. ¹⁰For if we were reconciled to God by Christ's death while we were God's enemies, how much more certain that we who have been reconciled will be saved by Christ's life! ¹¹Not only that, we go so far as to make God our boast through our Savior Jesus Christ, through whom we have now received reconciliation.

¹²Therefore, sin entered the world through the first humans, and through sin, death—and in this way death has spread through the whole human race, because all have sinned. ¹³Sin existed in the world long before the Law was given, even though it's not called "sin" when there is no law. ¹⁴Even so, death reigned over all who lived from our first parents until Moses, even

though their sin—unlike that of our first parents—was not a matter of breaking a law.

¹⁵ But the gift is not like the offense. For if by the offense of one couple all died, how much more did the grace of God—and the gracious gift of the One Jesus Christ—abound for all! ¹⁶ The gift that came to us is not at all like what came through the ones who sinned. In the one case, the sentence followed upon one offense and brought condemnation; in the other, the free gift came after many offenses and brought complete acquittal. ¹⁷ If death began its reign through one person because of an offense, so much more will those who receive the overflowing grace and the gift of justice live and reign through the One Jesus Christ.

¹⁸ To sum up, then: just as a single offense brought condemnation to all, a single righteous act brought all acquittal and life. ¹⁹ Just as through one person's disobedience, all became sinners, so through one person's obedience, all will become just.

CR   CR   CR

²⁰ When the Law came, the inability to obey the Law came all the more. But where sin increased, grace abounded all the more, ²¹ so that where sin had reigned in death, grace might reign through the justice that leads to eternal life, through Jesus Christ our Savior.

6:¹ What can we say, then? Should we go on sinning so that grace might abound? ² Of course not! We're dead to sin, so how can we continue to live in it?

³ Don't you know that when we were baptized into Christ Jesus, we were baptized into Christ's death? ⁴ We've been buried with Jesus through baptism, and we joined with Jesus in death, so that as Christ was raised from the dead by God's glory, we too might live a new life.

⁵ For if we have been united with Christ in the likeness of Christ's death, we will also be united with Christ in the likeness of Christ's resurrection. ⁶ We must realize that our former selves have been crucified with Christ to make the body of sin and failure completely powerless, to free us from slavery to sin: ⁷ for when people die, they have finished with sin.

⁸ But we believe that, having died with Christ, we will also live with Christ—⁹ knowing that Christ, having been raised from the dead, will never die again: death is now powerless over our Savior. ¹⁰ When Christ died, Christ died to sin, once for all, so that the life Christ lives is now life in God. ¹¹ In this way, you too must consider yourselves to be dead to sin—but alive to God in Christ Jesus.

¹² So don't let sin rule your mortal body and make you obey its lusts;

¹³ don't offer the members of your body to sin as weapons of injustice any more. Rather, offer yourselves to God as people alive from the dead, and your bodies to God as weapons for justice. ¹⁴Sin no longer has power over you, for you are now under grace, not under the Law.

¹⁵ Where does all this lead? Just because we are not under the Law but under grace, are we free to sin? By no means! ¹⁶You must realize that when you offer yourselves to someone else in obedience, you are bound to obey that person, whether you subject yourself to sin, which leads to death, or to obedience, which leads to justice. ¹⁷Thanks be to God, that though once you were slaves of sin, you became obedient from the heart to that rule of teaching imparted to you; ¹⁸freed from your sin, you became forever committed to justice.

¹⁹ I use the following example from human affairs because of your weak human nature. Just as you used to enslave your bodies to impurity and licentiousness for their degradation, now make them stewards of justice for their sanctification. ²⁰When you were slaves to sin, you felt no need to work for justice. ²¹What benefit did you enjoy from these things that you're now ashamed of, all of which lead to death? ²²But now that you are freed from sin and have offered yourselves to God in obedience, your benefit is that you are being made holy; your outcome is eternal life. ²³ The wages of sin is death, but the gift of God is eternal life in Christ Jesus our Savior.

7:1–8:13

Sisters and brothers, those of you who have studied law know that laws have power over us only during our lifetime. ²For example, married people are bound to each other only so long as they are alive, but all these obligations end when one of them dies. ³If one partner commits to someone else during the life of the marriage, that partner is legally an adulterer. But if one spouse dies, the other can marry again without becoming an adulterer.

⁴That is why you, my sisters and brothers, are now dead to the Law through the body of Christ. You are now able to belong to another—the One who rose from the dead—so that we might bear fruit for God. ⁵Before we were converted, our sinful passions were not controlled by the Law. Consequently, these passions, which were aroused by the Law, went to work in our bodies to bear fruit for death. ⁶But now we are freed from the Law, dead to what once bound us. Now we are free in the new way of the Spirit, not in the old way of a written Law.

⁷Does it follow that the Law is sin? Of course not! Yet I wouldn't have

known what sin was except for the Law. And I didn't know what "to covet" meant until I read, "No coveting." ⁸But sin, seizing the opportunity afforded by the commandment, produced in me every kind of covetousness. For apart from Law, sin is dead; ⁹and I once lived outside the Law. But when the commandment came, sin sprang to life, and I died. ¹⁰I found that the very commandment intended to bring life actually brought death. ¹¹For sin, seizing the opportunity afforded by the commandment, deceived me—and through the commandment put me to death.

¹²The Law is holy, and what it commands is holy, just and good. ¹³Does that mean that something good killed me? No. But sin, to show itself in its true colors, used that good thing to kill me. Thus sin, thanks to the commandments, exercised all its sinful power over me.

¹⁴We know that the Law is spiritual. But I am carnal. I've been sold to sin as a slave. ¹⁵I don't understand what I do—for I don't do the things I want to do, but rather the things I hate. ¹⁶ And if I do the very thing I don't want to do, I am agreeing that the Law is good. ¹⁷Consequently, what is happening in me is not really me, but sin living in me.

¹⁸I know that no good dwells in me, that is, in my human nature; the desire to do right is there, but not the power. ¹⁹What happens is that I don't do the good I intend to do, but the evil I do not intend. ²⁰But if I do what is against my will, it is not I who do it, but sin that dwells in me. ²¹This means that even though I want to do what is right, a law that leads to wrongdoing is always at hand. ²²My inner self joyfully agrees with the law of God, ²³but I see in my body's members another law, in opposition to the law of my mind; this makes me the prisoner of the law of sin in my members.

²⁴How wretched I am! Who can free me from this body under the power of death? ²⁵Thanks be to God—it is Jesus Christ our Savior! This, then, is the problem: I serve the law of God with my mind, but I serve the law of sin with my flesh.

8:1There is no longer any condemnation, however, for those who are in Christ Jesus. ²The law of the Spirit—the Spirit of life in Christ Jesus—has freed you from the law of sin and death. ³What the Law was powerless to do because human nature made it so weak, God did—by sending the Only Begotten in the likeness of sinful flesh as a sin offering, thereby condemning sin in the flesh.⁴In this way, the just demands of the Law could be fulfilled in us, who live not according to the flesh but according to the Spirit. ⁵Those who live according to the flesh have their mind set on the things of the flesh; those who live by the Spirit, on things of the Spirit.

⁶The mind of the flesh is death, but that of the Spirit is life and peace. ⁷The mind of the flesh stands in opposition to God; it is not subject to God's law—indeed, it cannot be, ⁸since those who are in the flesh cannot please

God. [9] But you are not in the flesh; you are in the Spirit, since the Spirit of God dwells in you. Those who do not have the Spirit of Christ do not belong to Christ. [10] But if Christ is in you, then though the body is dead because of sin, the spirit lives because of righteousness. [11] If the Spirit of the One who raised Jesus from the dead dwells in you, then the One who raised Christ from the dead will also bring your mortal bodies to life through the Spirit dwelling in you.

[12] Therefore, we are under an obligation, my sisters and brothers—but not to the flesh or to live according to the flesh. [13] If you live according to the flesh, you will die, but if you live by the Spirit, you will put to death the evil deeds of the body and you will live.

*t*hose who are led by the Spirit of God are the children of God. [15] For the Spirit that God has given you does not enslave you and trap you in fear; instead, through the Spirit God has adopted you as children, and by that Spirit we cry out, "Abba!" [16] God's Spirit joins with our spirit to declare that we are God's children. [17] And if we are children, we are heirs as well: heirs of God and co-heirs with Christ, sharing in Christ's suffering and sharing in Christ's glory.

[18] Indeed, I consider the sufferings of the present to be nothing compared with the glory that will be revealed in us. [19] All creation eagerly awaits the revelation of the children of God. [20] Creation was subjected to transience and futility, not of its own accord, but because of the One who subjected it—in the hope [21] that creation itself would be freed from its slavery to corruption, and would come to share in the glorious freedom of the children of God. [22] We know that from the beginning until now, all of creation has been groaning in one great act of giving birth. [23] And not only creation, but all of us who possess the firstfruits of the Spirit—we too groan inwardly as we wait for our bodies to be set free.

[24] In hope we were saved. But hope is not hope if its object is seen; why does one hope for what one sees? [25] And hoping for what we cannot see means awaiting it with patient endurance.

[26] The Spirit, too, comes to help us in our weakness. For we don't know how to pray as we should, but the Spirit expresses our plea with groanings too deep for words. [27] And God, who knows everything in our hearts, knows perfectly well what the Spirit is saying, because her intercessions for God's holy people are made according to the mind of God.

[28] We know that God makes everything work together for the good of

those who love God and have been called according to God's purpose. [29] They are the ones God chose long ago, predestined to share the image of the Only Begotten, in order that Christ might be the firstborn of many. [30] Those God predestined have likewise been called; those God called have also been justified; and those God justified have, in turn, been glorified.

[31] What should be our response? Simply this: "If God is for us, who can be against us?" [32] Since God did not spare the Only Begotten, but gave Christ up for the sake of us all, we may be certain, after such a gift, that God will freely give us everything. [33] Who will bring a charge against God's chosen ones? Since God is the One who justifies, [34] who has the power to condemn? Only Christ Jesus, who died—or rather, was raised—and sits at the right hand of God, and who now intercedes for us!

[35] What will separate us from the love of Christ? Trouble? Calamity? Persecution? Hunger? Nakedness? Danger? Violence? [36] As scripture says, "For your sake, we're being killed all day long; we're looked upon as sheep to be slaughtered." [37] Yet in all this we are more than conquerors because of God who has loved us. [38] For I'm certain that neither death nor life, neither angels nor demons, neither the present nor the future, [39] neither heights nor depths—nor anything else in all creation—will be able to separate us from the love of God that comes to us in Christ Jesus, our Savior.

9:1–11:12

I speak the truth in Christ; I'm not lying—my conscience bears me witness in the Holy Spirit [2] that there is great grief and constant pain in my heart. [3] Indeed, I would cut myself off from Christ if that would save my sisters and brothers, my kinfolk—[4] the Israelites. Theirs were the adoption as God's children, the glory, the covenants, the Law-giving, the worship and the promises; [5] theirs was the ancestry, and from them came the Messiah—at least, according to human ancestry. Blessed forever be God who is over all! Amen.

[6] It's not that the word of God has failed. It's just that not all who have descended from Israel are Israelites. [7] Nor are they all children of Sarah and Abraham simply because they're descended from them, because "it is through Isaac—not Esau—that your name will be carried on." [8] In other words, physical descent doesn't determine who are children of God, but rather belief in the promise. [9] For this is the wording of the promise: "This time next year I will return and Sarah will have a child."

[10] Even more relevant is what Rebecca was told while she was pregnant by our ancestor Isaac—[11] well before her twins were born, and long before

either child had done anything good or bad. In order to emphasize that God's choice is free—¹²for it depends on the One who calls, not on human deeds—Rebecca was told, "The older will serve the younger," ¹³or as scripture says elsewhere, "Jacob I loved, but Esau I hated."

¹⁴Does it follow that God is unjust? Certainly not. ¹⁵Consider what God says to Moses, "I will have mercy on whom I have mercy, and I will have compassion on whom I will have compassion." ¹⁶In other words, it doesn't depend on one's will or efforts, but on our merciful God. ¹⁷For the scripture says to Pharaoh, "I raised you up for this purpose, that I might show my power in you and that your name might be proclaimed in all the earth." ¹⁸Therefore, God has mercy and hardens hearts at will.

¹⁹You'll ask me, "If that's the case, how can God ever blame anyone, since no one can oppose the divine will?" ²⁰But what right have you, mere mortal, to question God? The pot has no right to say to the potter, "Why did you shape me this way?" ²¹Surely a potter can do what she wants with the clay! It is clearly for her to decide what lump of clay or what kind of pot, ordinary or special, is to be thrown.

²²Imagine that the Almighty is ready to show wrath and display divine power, yet patiently endures those people who test the divine mercy, however much those lumps of clay deserve to be destroyed. ²³The Most High puts up with them, all for the sake of those to whom God wants to mercifully reveal the wealth of divine glory—they are vessels prepared for this glory. ²⁴Well, we are those vessels. Whether we are Jews or Gentiles, we are the ones God has called. ²⁵As it says in Hosea:

> "Those who are not my people
>   I will call 'my people,'
> and those who are not my loved ones,
>   'my loved ones.' "

²⁶and,

> "In the very place where it was said to them,
>   'You are not my people,'
> they will be called
>   'daughters and sons of the living God.' "

²⁷Isaiah cried out concerning Israel:

> "Though the number of the Israelites
>   be like the sand of the sea,
>   only the remnant will be saved.
> ²⁸For Our God will execute sentence
>   on the earth decisively and quickly."

²⁹As Isaiah said earlier,

> "Unless the Most High
> had left us descendants,
> we would have become like Sodom;
> we would have been like Gomorrah."

[30] What then will we say? That the Gentiles, who were not looking for righteousness, found it all the same: a righteousness that comes from faith— [31] while Israel, looking for a righteousness that comes from the Law, failed to do what the Law required. [32] Why? Because Israel sought righteousness based not on faith, but on works. They stumbled over the "stumbling stone" [33] mentioned in scriptures:

> "Look: I lay in Zion a stone to make people stumble
> and a rock to trip them up,
> but whoever believes in God
> will not be disappointed."

10:[1] My sisters and brothers, my heart's desire and prayer to God for the Israelites is that they attain salvation. [2] For I can testify that they have zeal for God. But their zeal is not based on knowledge. [3] Not recognizing the righteousness that comes from God, they sought to establish their own instead of submitting to God.

[4] The Messiah, however, is the goal and fulfillment of the Law, and everyone who has faith will be made righteous.

ભ ભ ભ

[5] Moses writes about the righteousness that comes from the Law: "Those who do these things will live by them." [6] But the righteousness that comes from faith says, "Don't say in your heart, 'Who will ascend to heaven?' "— that is, to bring Christ down— [7] "or 'Who will descend into the underworld?' "—that is, to bring Christ up from the dead. [8] But what does it say? "The word is near you, on your lips and in your heart." This is the Word of faith. [9] For if you confess with your lips that Jesus is Sovereign and believe in your heart that God raised Jesus from the dead, you will be saved. [10] Faith in the heart leads to being put right with God, confession on the lips to our deliverance.

[11] Scripture says, "No one who believes in God will be put to shame." [12] Here there is no difference between Jew and Greek; all have the same Creator, rich in mercy toward those who call: [13] "Everyone who calls on the name of the Most High will be saved."

[14] How then can they call on the One in whom they have not believed? And how can they believe in the One about whom they have not heard? And how can they hear if no one preaches to them? [15] And how can they

preach unless they are sent? As scripture says, "How beautiful are the feet of those who bring the Good News!"

¹⁶ But not everyone has heeded the Good News. For Isaiah says, "O God, who has believed what we proclaimed?" ¹⁷ So you see that faith comes from hearing, and hearing from the word of Christ. ¹⁸ But I ask, didn't they hear? Of course they did: "Their voice has gone out into all the world, their words to the ends of the earth." ¹⁹ So I ask another question: Is it possible that Israel didn't understand? Moses answered this long ago:

> "I will make you envious of those
> who aren't even a nation;
> I will make you angry
> because of the Gentiles,
> who have no understanding."

²⁰ Isaiah said it even more clearly: "I was found by those who did not seek me; I revealed myself to those who did not ask for me." ²¹ But concerning Israel, Isaiah says, "All day long I stretched out my hand to a disobedient and obstinate people."

11:1 I ask, then, has God rejected the chosen people? Of course not! I myself am an Israelite, descended from Sarah and Abraham, of the tribe of Benjamin. ² No, God has not rejected the chosen people, who were foreknown long ago.

Don't you know what the scriptures say about Elijah—how he complained to God about Israel's behavior? ³ "O God, they've killed your prophets and torn down your altars. I'm the only one left, and they're trying to kill me." ⁴ What did God say to him? "I have reserved for myself seven thousand who have not bent the knee to Baal." ⁵ In the same way, today there's also a remnant—one chosen by grace. ⁶ And if it is by grace, then it is no longer by works—for if it were, grace would no longer be grace.

⁷ What follows? That what Israel sought so earnestly it did not achieve— but those who were chosen did. The rest were hardened, ⁸ as it says in scripture:

> "God gave them a sluggish spirit,
> eyes that could not see
> and ears that could not hear,
> down to this very day."

⁹ And David says:

> "May their own table become a trap and a snare,
> a stumbling block and a punishment.
> ¹⁰ Let their eyes grow dim so they cannot see,
> and bend their backs forever."

¹¹ I ask further, does their stumbling mean that they are forever fallen?

Not at all! Rather, by their transgressions salvation has come to the Gentiles, to stir Israel to envy. [12] But if their transgression and their diminishment have meant riches for the Gentile world, how much more will their fulfillment be!

I say this now to you Gentiles: inasmuch as I am the apostle of the Gentiles, I glory in my ministry, [14] trying to rouse my own people to jealousy and save some of them. [15] For if their rejection has meant reconciliation for the world, what will their acceptance mean? Nothing less than life from the dead!

[16] If the first part of the dough offered as firstfruits is holy, the whole batch is holy. If the root is holy, the branches are holy as well. [17] But if some of the branches have broken off, and you, a wild olive shoot, have been grafted in their place and share in the rich sap of the olive tree, [18] don't be arrogant toward those branches. If you find yourself feeling arrogant, remember that you don't support the root—the root supports you! [19] You might say, "Branches were broken off so that I could be grafted in." [20] That is so. But they were broken off for lack of faith. You stand there only through your faith. So don't become arrogant, but stand in awe. [21] For if God didn't spare the natural branches, neither will you be spared.

[22] Witness, then, both the kindness and severity of God: severity toward those who fell, and kindness to you—provided you remain in God's kindness, otherwise you too will be cut off. [23] And those who did not accept the Messiah—if they come to believe—will be regrafted: God is able to graft them in again. [24] After all, if you were cut from what is by nature a wild olive tree, and grafted, contrary to nature, into a cultivated tree, how much more readily will they, the natural branches, be grafted into their own olive tree!

[25] Sisters and brothers, I don't want you to be ignorant of this mystery, lest you be conceited: blindness has come upon part of Israel only until the full number of Gentiles enter in, [26] and then all Israel will be saved. As scripture says,

> "Out of Zion will come the Deliverer
>   who will remove all impiety from Jacob;
> [27] this is the Covenant I will make with them
>   when I take away their sins."

[28] With respect to the Good News, they are enemies of God because of

11:13-36

ROMANS 11

278

you; with respect to their call, however, they are beloved by the Most High because of their ancestors. ²⁹For God's gift and call are irrevocable.

³⁰Just as you were once disobedient to God and now have received mercy through Israel's disobedience, ³¹now they have become disobedient—since God wished to show you mercy—that they too may receive mercy. ³²God has imprisoned everyone in disobedience in order to have mercy on everyone.

³³Oh, how deep are the riches and the wisdom and the knowledge, how inscrutable the judgments, how unsearchable the ways of God! ³⁴For, "Who has known the mind of God or been God's counselor? ³⁵ Who has given God anything to deserve something in return?" ³⁶For all things are from God and through God and for God. To God be glory forever! Amen.

12:1–13:14

Sisters and brothers, I beg you through the mercy of God to offer your bodies as a living sacrifice, holy and acceptable to God—this is your spiritual act of worship. ²Don't conform yourselves to this age, but be transformed by the renewal of your minds, so that you can judge what God's will is—what is good, pleasing and perfect.

³In light of the grace I have from God, I urge each of you not to exaggerate your own importance. Each of you must judge yourself soberly by the standard of faith God has given you. ⁴Just as each of us has one body with many members—and these members don't have the same function—⁵so all of us, in union with Christ, form one body. And as members of that one body, we belong to each other.

⁶We have gifts that differ according to the grace given to each of us. If your gift is prophecy, use it in proportion to your faith. ⁷If your gift is ministry, use it for service. If you're a teacher, use your gift for teaching. ⁸If you're good at preaching, then preach boldly. If you give to charity, do so generously; if you're a leader, exercise your authority with care; if you help others, do so cheerfully.

⁹Your love must be sincere. Hate what is evil and cling to what is good.

¹⁰Love one another with the affection of sisters and brothers. Try to outdo one another in showing respect.

¹¹Don't grow slack, but be fervent in spirit: the One you serve is Christ.

¹²Rejoice in hope; be patient under trial; persevere in prayer.

¹³Look on the needs of God's holy people as your own; be generous in offering hospitality.

¹⁴ Bless your persecutors—bless and don't curse them.

¹⁵ Rejoice with those who rejoice, weep with those who weep. ¹⁶ Have the same attitude toward everyone.

Don't be condescending to those who aren't as well off as you; don't be conceited.

¹⁷ Don't repay evil with evil.

Be concerned with the highest ideal in the eyes of all people.

¹⁸ Do all you can to be at peace with everyone.

¹⁹ Don't take revenge; leave room, my friends, for God's wrath. To quote scripture, "'Vengeance is mine, I will pay them back,' says Our God." ²⁰ But there is more:

> "If your enemies are hungry, feed them;
> if they are thirsty, give them drink.
> For in doing so, you will heap burning coals
> upon their heads."

²¹ Don't be overcome by evil, but overcome evil by doing good.

13:1 Obey governing authorities. All government comes from God, so civil authorities are appointed by God. ² Therefore, those of you who rebel against authority are rebelling against God's decision. For this you are liable to be punished. ³ Good behavior is not afraid of authorities, only bad behavior. If you want to live without fear of authority, do what is right and authority will even honor you. ⁴ The state carries out God's will in order to serve you. However, if you do wrong, be afraid. For the state doesn't carry the sword for nothing: it does as God directs and is an agent of God's wrath, bringing punishment on wrongdoers. ⁵ That's why it's necessary to obey— not only out of fear of being punished, but for the sake of conscience as well. ⁶ That is also why you pay taxes, for the authorities carry out God's will, devoting themselves to this very cause. ⁷ Pay to all what is their due: taxes to tax collectors, tolls to toll collectors, respect to whom respect is due and honor to whom honor is due.

⁸ Owe no debt to anyone—except the debt that binds us to love one another. If you love your neighbor, you have fulfilled the Law. ⁹ The commandments—no committing adultery, no killing, no stealing, no coveting, and all the others—are all summed up in this one: "Love your neighbor as yourself." ¹⁰ Love never wrongs anyone—hence love is the fulfillment of the Law.

¹¹ Besides, you know the time in which we are living. It is now the hour for you to wake from sleep, for our salvation is closer than when we first accepted the faith. ¹² The night is far spent; the day draws near. So let us cast off deeds of darkness and put on the armor of light. ¹³ Let us live hon-

orably as in daylight, not in carousing and drunkenness, not in sexual excess and lust, not in quarreling and jealousy. ¹⁴ Rather, clothe yourselves with our Savior Jesus Christ, and make no provision for the desires of the night.

14:1–15:13

Ⱳelcome those whose faith is weak, and don't argue with them. ² The opinions of people range from those who believe they may eat any sort of meat, to those whose faith is so weak they eat only vegetables. ³ Those who eat everything must not despise those who abstain. The ones who abstain must not pass judgment on those who eat, for God has welcomed them. ⁴ Who are you to judge someone else's worker? It's for the employer to decide if the worker has succeeded or failed—and the worker will succeed, for Our God has the power to make it so. ⁵ One person considers one day more sacred than another, another considers all days equally sacred—and both are equally certain of their own opinions. ⁶ The person who observes special days does it for Our God. Whoever eats meat does it for Our God and gives thanks to God. Whoever abstains does it for Our God and gives thanks to God.

⁷ We don't live for ourselves, nor do we die for ourselves. ⁸ While we live, we live for Christ Jesus, and when we die, we die for Christ Jesus. Both in life and in death we belong to Christ. ⁹ That's why Christ died and came to life again—in order to reign supreme over both the living and the dead.

¹⁰ But you, how can you sit in judgment of your sisters or brothers? Or you, how can you look down on your sisters or brothers? We will all have to appear before the judgment seat of God. ¹¹ Scripture says, " 'As surely as I live'—it is Our God who speaks—'every knee will bend before me and every tongue will give praise to God.' " ¹² We will all have to give an account of ourselves before God.

¹³ So stop passing judgment on one another. Rather, we must resolve not to be stumbling blocks or obstructions to each other. ¹⁴ I know—and am convinced in our Savior Jesus—that no food is unclean in itself. But it is unclean for someone who is convinced it is unclean. ¹⁵ If your sister or brother is upset by what you eat, you are no longer acting in love. Don't cause their downfall, for whom Christ died, by your eating. ¹⁶ At the same time, don't let what is for you a good thing be spoken of as being evil. ¹⁷ For the kindom of God is a matter not of eating and drinking, but of justice, peace and joy in the Holy Spirit. ¹⁸ If we all serve Christ this way, we will be pleasing to God and respected by our sisters and brothers.

[19] Therefore, let us conduct ourselves in ways that lead to peace and mutual growth. [20] Don't destroy the work of God over a question of food. All food really is clean, but it's wrong for us to eat anything that is a stumbling block to another. [21] It's best not to eat meat or drink wine, or do anything else, if it will make somebody fall away. [22] On the other hand, be confident in your personal belief before God, and don't condemn yourself for doing something you really believe is all right to do. [23] If you have doubts about eating but you eat anyway, you are judged because your eating doesn't come from faith—[24] and whatever is not from faith is sin.

15[1] We who are strong have a duty to endure the failings of the weak, without trying to please ourselves. [2] We should be attentive to our neighbors and encourage them to become stronger. [3] For Christ was not self-serving, as it says in scripture: "The insults of those who insult you have fallen on me."

ʘʀ   ʘʀ   ʘʀ

[4] Everything written before our time was written for our instruction, that we might derive hope from the lessons of patience and the words of encouragement in the scriptures. [5] May God, the source of all strength and encouragement, enable you to live in perfect harmony with one another according to the Spirit of Christ Jesus, [6] so that with one heart and one voice, you may praise the God of our Savior Jesus Christ.

[7] Accept one another as Christ accepted us, for the glory of God. [8] Christ became a servant of the chosen people to live out the truth of God's promise to them, [9] and at the same time to give the Gentiles cause to glorify God for showing mercy. As scripture has it,

> "Therefore I will praise you among the nations
> and I will sing to Your Name."

[10] Again, it says,

> "Rejoice, all you nations, with God's people."

[11] And again:

> "Praise Our God, all you nations,
> and let all the peoples praise the Most High."

[12] And Isaiah too says,

> "The root of Jesse is coming
> and will arise to rule over the nations,
> and they will place their trust in the Coming One."

[13] May the God of hope fill you with such peace and joy in your faith, that you may be filled with hope by the power of the Holy Spirit.

I'm convinced, my sisters and brothers, that you are filled with goodness, that you have complete knowledge and that you are able to give good advice to one another. [15]Even so, I have written to you rather boldly in parts of this letter, by way of reminder. I take this liberty because God has given me the grace [16]to be a minister of Christ Jesus among the Gentiles, with the priestly duty of preaching the Good News of God, so that the Gentiles may be offered up as a pleasing sacrifice, consecrated by the Holy Spirit. [17]This means I can take glory in Christ Jesus for the work I have done for God.

[18]I will not dare to speak of anything except what Christ has done through me to win the Gentiles to obedience—by word and deed, [19]with mighty signs and marvels, by the power of God's Spirit. As a result, I have completed preaching the Good News of Christ, from Jerusalem all the way around to Illyria. [20]It has been a point of honor with me never to preach in places where Christ's name was already known, for I did not want to build on a foundation laid by another, [21]but rather to fulfill the words of scripture: "Those who received no word of God will see God, and those who have never heard of God will understand."

[22]That's why I've been kept from visiting you for so long. [23]But now, since I have no more work in these regions, [24]I hope to visit you on my way to Spain. I will spend some time with you and hope that you will help me on my journey. [25]For now, I must travel to Jerusalem to take a gift of money to the holy ones—[26]Macedonia and Achaia have made a generous contribution for those who are needy among them. [27]They were pleased to do so; actually, it pays a debt to Jerusalem. For if the Gentiles have come to share in their spiritual bounty, they owe it to our Jewish sisters and brothers to share with them their material bounty. [28]So when I have completed this task and officially handed over this contribution to them, I am off to Spain and will visit with you on the way. [29]I know that when I come to you I will bring rich blessings from Christ.

[30]I beg you, sisters and brothers, by our Savior Jesus Christ and by the love of the Holy Spirit, to join me in my struggle by praying to God for me. [31]Pray that I may be rescued from the unbelievers in Judea, and that my work in Jerusalem may be acceptable to the holy ones. [32]Then, God willing, I will come to you with joy, and together we will be refreshed.

The God of peace be with you all. Amen.

ℭ   ℭ   ℭ

16:[1]I commend to you our sister Phoebe, a deacon of the church at Cenchrea. [2]Welcome her, in the name of Our God, in a way worthy of the holy ones, and help her with her needs. She has looked after a great many people, including me.

³Give my greetings to Prisca and Aquila; they were my co-workers in the service of Christ Jesus, ⁴and even risked their lives for my sake. Not only I but all the churches of the Gentiles are grateful to them. ⁵Remember me also to the congregation that meets in their house.

Greetings to my beloved Epaenetus; he is the first convert to Christ from Asia.

⁶My greetings to Mary, who has worked hard for you, ⁷and to Andronicus and Junia, my kin and fellow prisoners; they are outstanding apostles, and they were in Christ even before I was. ⁸Greetings to Ampliatus, who is dear to me in Christ; ⁹to Urbanus, our co-worker in the service of Christ; and to my beloved Stachys. ¹⁰Greetings to Apelles, who has endured such trials for Christ. Greetings to those who belong to the household of Aristobulus; ¹¹greetings to my relative Herodian. Greetings to those in the household of Narcissus who are Christians. ¹²Greetings to the sisters Tryphaena and Tryphosa, who work hard for Our God; greetings to my friend Persis who has done so much for Our God. ¹³Greetings to Rufus, chosen in Our God, and to his mother, who has been a mother to me as well. ¹⁴Greetings to Asyncritus, Phlegon, Hermes, Patrobas, Hermas and all the others with them. Greetings to ¹⁵Philologus, Julia, Nereus and his sister, and Olympas, and all the holy ones with them.

¹⁶Greet one another with a holy kiss. All the churches of Christ send you greetings.

¹⁷I urge you, sisters and brothers, to be on your guard against those who foment trouble and put obstacles in your way, contrary to the teaching you learned. Steer clear of them. ¹⁸For such people don't serve Jesus Christ, but rather their own appetites. By smooth talk and flattering speech they deceive the hearts of the unsuspecting. ¹⁹While your obedience is famous everywhere—which fills me with joy over you—my counsel is that you are to be wise about what is good, and innocent of what is evil.

²⁰The God of peace will soon crush Satan under your feet. The grace of Our Savior Jesus Christ be with you.

²¹My co-worker, Timothy, sends greetings, as do my relatives, Lucius, Jason and Sosipater.

²²I, Tertius, who have written down this letter, send you my greetings in Christ. ²³Greetings also from Gaius, who is host to me and to the whole church. Erastus, the city treasurer, and our brother Quartus wish to be remembered to you.

²⁴ The grace of our Savior Jesus Christ be with you all. Amen.

²⁵ To God—who is able to strengthen you in the Good News that I pro-claim when I proclaim Jesus Christ, the Good News that reveals the mys-tery hidden for many ages, ²⁶ but has now been manifested through the writings of the prophets, and at the command of the eternal God made known to all the Gentiles, that they may believe and obey—to God ²⁷ who alone is wise, may glory be given through Jesus Christ to endless ages. Amen!

the first letter of paul to the
corinthians

f

rom paul, called by God's will to be an apostle of Jesus Christ, together with Sosthenes our brother,

² To the church of God in Corinth, you who have been consecrated in Christ Jesus and called to be a holy people, as well as to all who, wherever they may be, call on the name of Jesus Christ, their Redeemer and ours:

³ Grace and peace from our Loving God and our Savior Jesus Christ.

⁴ I continually thank my God for you because of the gift bestowed on you in Christ Jesus, ⁵ in whom you have been richly endowed with every gift of speech and knowledge. ⁶ In the same way, the testimony about Christ has been so confirmed among you ⁷ that you lack no spiritual gift, as you wait for the revelation of our Savior Jesus Christ. ⁸ God will strengthen you to the end, so that you will be blameless on the day of our Savior Jesus Christ. ⁹ God, through whom you have been called into intimacy with Jesus our Savior, is faithful.

I beg you, sisters and brothers, in the name of our Savior Jesus Christ, to agree in your message. Let there be no factions; rather, be united in mind and judgment. [11] I have been informed, my sisters and brothers, by certain members of Chloe's household, that you are quarreling among yourselves. [12] What I mean is, one of you is saying, "I belong to Paul," another, "I belong to Apollos," still another, "I belong to Cephas," still another, "I belong to Christ." [13] What—has Christ been divided into parts? Was it Paul who was crucified for you? Was it in Paul's name that you were baptized? [14] Frankly, I'm thankful I didn't baptize any of you, except Crispus and Gaius, [15] so that none of you can say you were baptized in my name! [16] Oh yes, I did baptize the household of Stephanas, but no one else as far as I can remember.

[17] The point is, Christ didn't send me to baptize but to preach the Gospel—not with human rhetoric, however, lest the cross of Christ be rendered void of its meaning! [18] For the message of the cross is complete absurdity to those who are headed for ruin, but to us who are experiencing salvation, it is the power of God. [19] Scripture says, "I will destroy the wisdom of the wise, and thwart the learning of the learned." [20] Where are the wise? Where are the scholars? Where are the philosophers of this age? Has not God turned the wisdom of this world into folly? [21] If it was God's wisdom that the world in its wisdom would not know God, it was because God wanted to save those who have faith through the foolishness of the message we preach.

[22] For while the Jews call for miracles and the Greeks look for wisdom, [23] here we are preaching a Messiah nailed to a cross. To the Jews this is an obstacle they cannot get over, and to the Greeks it is madness—[24] but to those who have been called, whether they are Jews or Greeks, Christ is the power and the wisdom of God. [25] For God's foolishness is wiser than human wisdom, and God's weakness is stronger than human strength.

[26] Consider your calling, sisters and brothers. Not many of you were wise by human standards, not many were influential, and surely not many were well-born. [27] God chose those whom the world considers foolish to shame the wise, and singled out the weak of this world to shame the strong. [28] The world's lowborn and despised, those who count for nothing, were chosen by God to reduce to nothing those who were something. [29] In this way no one should boast before God. [30] God has given you life in Christ Jesus and has made Jesus our wisdom, our justice, our sanctification and our redemption. [31] This is just as it is written, "Let the one who would boast, boast in Our God."

[2:1] As for myself, sisters and brothers, when I came to you I did not come proclaiming God's testimony with any particular eloquence or wisdom.

²No, I determined that while I was with you I would know nothing but Jesus Christ—Christ crucified. ³When I came among you, it was in weakness and fear, and with much trepidation. ⁴My message and my preaching did not rest on philosophical arguments, but on the convincing power of the Spirit. ⁵As a consequence, your faith rests not on human wisdom, but on the power of God.

⁶Still, there is a certain wisdom which we express among the spiritually mature. It is not a wisdom of this age, however, nor of the rulers of this age, who are headed for destruction. ⁷No, what we utter is God's wisdom: a mysterious, hidden wisdom. God planned it before all ages for our glory. ⁸None of the rulers of this age knew the mystery; if they had known it, they would never have crucified the Sovereign of Glory. ⁹Of this wisdom it is written,

> "Eye has not seen, ear has not heard,
>   nor has it so much as dawned on anyone
> what God has prepared
>   for those who love God."

¹⁰Yet God has revealed this wisdom to us through the Holy Spirit. She searches out all things, even the deep things of God. ¹¹After all, no one knows one's thoughts except one's own inner spirit; by the same token, no one knows God's thoughts except God's Spirit. ¹²We haven't received the spirit of the world but the Spirit of God, so that we can understand what God has freely given us. ¹³And this is precisely what we talk about, not using words taught us by human wisdom, but words taught by the Spirit, expressing spiritual thoughts in spiritual words.

¹⁴People without the Spirit do not accept what the Spirit of God teaches. Such teachings seem like foolishness to them because they can't understand them; such things must be spiritually discerned. ¹⁵Spiritual people, on the other hand, can discern all things, though they themselves can be discerned by no one—¹⁶for, "Who understands the mind of the Most High? Who would give instruction to God?" We, however, have the mind of Christ.

3:1 Unfortunately, sisters and brothers, I was unable to speak to you as spiritual people. I had to treat you as sensual people, still infants in Christ. ²I fed you with milk, not solid food, since you weren't ready for it. Indeed, you still aren't ready for it, ³since you're still far too carnal—a fact that should be obvious from all the jealousy and wrangling that there is among you, from the way that you go on behaving like ordinary people! ⁴What could be more nonspiritual than your slogans, "I belong to Paul," and "I belong to Apollos"?

⁵ After all, who is Apollos? And who is Paul? They are ministers through whom you came to believe. Even the different ways in which they brought the Gospel were assigned to them by God. ⁶ I did the planting, Apollos did the watering, but God caused the growth. ⁷ Neither the planter nor the waterer matters—only God, who makes things grow. ⁸ It is all one who does the planting and who does the watering; and all will be duly paid according to their share in the work. ⁹ We are co-workers with God; you are God's farm, God's building.

¹⁰ By the grace God gave me, I acted as a wise architect and laid the foundation. Someone else is doing the building. But each of you doing the building must do it carefully. ¹¹ For no one can lay a foundation other than the one already in place—Jesus Christ. ¹² You may build on this foundation using gold, silver, precious stones, wood, grass or straw. ¹³ Regardless of the material, the Day will come when your work will be revealed for what it is. It will be revealed in fire, and that fire will test the quality of your work. ¹⁴ If your building survives, you will receive your reward. ¹⁵ If it burns down, you will be the loser. You will survive, but only as one who goes through fire.

¹⁶ Aren't you aware that you are the temple of God, and that the Spirit of God dwells in you? ¹⁷ If you destroy God's temple, God will destroy you—for the temple of God is holy, and you are that temple.

¹⁸ Don't delude yourselves. Any who think themselves wise in a worldly way had better become fools. ¹⁹ In that way you will really be wise, for the wisdom of this world is absurdity with God—as scripture says, "God knows how empty are the thoughts of the wise," ²⁰ and again, "God is not convinced by the arguments of the wise." ²¹ So there is nothing to boast about in anything human, ²² whether it be Paul or Apollos or Cephas or the world or life or death or the present or the future—all these are yours, ²³ and you belong to Christ, and Christ belongs to God.

4:1-21

*t*herefore, we should be regarded as people in service to Christ, as people entrusted with the mysteries of God. ² The first requirement of those who have been given a trust is faithfulness. ³ It matters little to me whether you or any human court pass judgment on me. I do not even pass judgment on myself. ⁴ Mind you, I have nothing on my conscience. But that does not mean I am declaring myself innocent. Christ is the One to judge me—⁵ so stop passing judgment prematurely. Christ will bring to light what is hidden in darkness and manifest the intentions of hearts. At that time, all will receive from God the praise they deserve.

⁶Now, sisters and brothers, everything I have just said I have applied to Apollos and myself as examples to benefit you. Take a lesson from the saying, "Do not go beyond what is written." None of you should take pride in one person over another. ⁷What makes you superior to someone else? What do you have that was not given to you? And if it was a gift, how can you boast as if you had worked for it?

⁸You act as if you have all you need now—as if you were wealthy now, or had become rulers without us! Oh, how I wish you had become rulers— then we could share ruling with you!

⁹Rather, it seems to me God has put us apostles at the end of the parade, like those doomed to die in the arena. We have been made a spectacle to the whole universe, to angels and humans alike. ¹⁰Here we are fools for Christ's sake, but you are so wise in Christ! We are weak, but you are strong! You are honored, while they sneer at us! ¹¹At this very hour we go hungry and thirsty, we are in rags, we are roughly treated, we are homeless. ¹²We work hard at manual labor. When we are insulted, we give a blessing. When we are persecuted, we endure it. ¹³When we are slandered, we answer politely. We have become the scum of the earth, the dregs of humanity, to this very day.

¹⁴I am writing you this way not to shame you but to admonish you, my dear children. ¹⁵You may have ten thousand tutors in Christ, but you have only me as your parent. It was I who begot you in Christ Jesus through my preaching of the Gospel.

¹⁶Therefore, I beg you to imitate me. ¹⁷For this reason I send you Timothy, my beloved and faithful child in Our God. Timothy will remind you of the way I live in Christ, as I teach everywhere in all the churches.

¹⁸When it seemed that I was not coming to you, some of you assumed a role of self-importance. ¹⁹But I will be visiting you soon, God willing, and then I will see what you can really do—not what you boastfully say you can do. ²⁰For the kindom of God is not just words but power. ²¹What is your preference? Should I come to you with a paddle, or with a loving and gentle spirit?

5:1–6:20

I have been told that there is sexual immorality among you, and of a kind that does not occur even among the Gentiles—a man living with his father's wife. ²How can you be so proud of yourselves? You should be in mourning! Those who do such a thing ought to be expelled from the community. ³Though I am far away in body, I am with you in spirit, and have already passed judgment ⁴in the name of our Savior Jesus Christ on the ones who did this deed. United in spirit with you and empowered by our Savior Jesus Christ, ⁵I hereby hand them over to Satan for the destruction of their flesh, so that their spirits may be saved on the day of our Savior.

⁶This boasting of yours is an ugly thing. Don't you know that a little yeast has its effect all through the dough? ⁷Get rid of the old yeast to make for yourselves fresh dough, unleavened bread, as it were; Christ our Passover has been sacrificed. ⁸So let us celebrate the feast—not with the old yeast, the yeast of corruption and wickedness, but with the unleavened bread of sincerity and truth.

⁹Remember when I wrote to you to dissociate yourselves from immoral people? ¹⁰I did not mean to include all in the world who are sexually immoral, or all the greedy and the swindlers, or the idolators. To do this, you would have to leave the world! ¹¹What I wrote is that you must dissociate yourselves from any so-called Christians who are leading immoral lives, or are greedy or idolatrous, are slanderers or drunkards, or are dishonest. You shouldn't even eat with these people.

¹²It's not my business to judge outsiders. As for insiders, however, you be the judge. ¹³Let God judge the outsiders—you just get rid of the evildoers among you.

6¹But what do you do instead? You take your neighbor to court to be judged by the unjust instead of by God's holy people! How dare you! ²Don't you know that the holy ones will judge the world? And if you are to judge the world, why are you unfit to judge trifling matters? ³Since we are also to judge angels, it follows that we can judge matters of everyday life. ⁴But when you have had cases like that, you appoint as your judges people who are not respected members of the church! ⁵I say this to your shame: is there no one among you wise enough to judge a dispute among believers? ⁶Instead, sisters and brothers are taking each other to court—and having their cases heard by unbelievers!

⁷The very fact that you have lawsuits among you means that you're completely defeated already. Why not put up with injustice instead? Why not let yourselves be cheated? ⁸Instead, you yourselves injure and cheat your very own.

⁹Don't you realize that the unholy will not inherit the kindom of God? Do not deceive yourselves: no fornicators, idolaters, adulterers, hustlers,

pederasts, ¹⁰thieves, misers, drunkards, slanderers or extortionists will inherit God's kindom. ¹¹And such were some of you! But you have been washed, consecrated and justified in the name of our Savior Jesus Christ and in the Spirit of our God.

¹²"Everything is allowed"—but not everything is beneficial for me. "Everything is allowed"—but I will not be dominated by anything.

¹³"Food is for the stomach and the stomach for food, and God will do away with them both in the end"—but the body is not for immorality; it is for God, and God is for the body. ¹⁴God, who raised Jesus from the dead, will raise us also by the same power.

¹⁵Don't you see that your bodies are members of Christ? Would you have me take Christ's members and make them members of someone promiscuous? God forbid! ¹⁶Don't you know that when you sleep with someone, you're sleeping with all of their partners as well? For it is said, "The two will become one flesh." ¹⁷But whoever is joined to Christ becomes one spirit with Christ.

¹⁸Shun lewd conduct. Every other sin a person commits is outside that person's body, but sexual sins are sins against one's own body. ¹⁹You must know that your body is a temple of the Holy Spirit, who is within you—the Spirit you have received from God. You are not your own. ²⁰You have been bought with a price. So glorify God in your body.

7:1-40

𝕹ow for the matters about which you wrote.

Yes, it is a good thing for a woman or a man not to marry. ²But since there is so much immorality, each woman should have her own husband and each husband should have his own wife. ³The wife and husband should mutually fulfill their marital duties to each other. ⁴The husband's body belongs not to him alone, but also to the wife, and the wife's body belongs not to her alone, but also to the husband. ⁵Do not deprive each other except by mutual consent and within a time frame so that you can devote yourselves to prayer. But come together again lest you invite Satan to tempt you through your weakness. ⁶Let me make a suggestion—it is not a decree: ⁷I would hope that everyone could be like me. But we all have our own particular gifts from God. One has the gift for one thing and another has the gift for another thing.

⁸To the single, widows and widowers, I say: it is good for you to stay unmarried, as I am. ⁹But if you cannot control yourselves, then you should marry, for it is better to be married than to burn with passion.

¹⁰ I have this to say to you who are in relationships—and this is not from me but from God: you are not to leave your partners. ¹¹ But if you do separate, you must either remain single or be reconciled to each other; you are not to divorce each other.

¹² To the rest of you, I say—this is not from God but from me: ¹³ if one of you has a mate who is not a believer, and if the believer is willing to live with the unbeliever, then there must not be a divorce. ¹⁴ For the unbelieving member of the relationship is sanctified through the believing member. If this were not so, any children of the relationship would be unclean; as it is, they are holy.

¹⁵ Now if the unbeliever leaves, let it be. For the believing partner is not bound to the relationship in such circumstances. God has called us to live in peace. ¹⁶ For how do you know, wife, whether you will save your husband or not? And how do you know, husband, whether you will save your wife or not?

¹⁷ The point is, whatever lot God has assigned you, whatever God has called you to do, continue in it. This is the direction I give to all the churches. ¹⁸ Anyone who was Jewish at the time of the call need not disguise it. ¹⁹ Anyone who was a Gentile at the time of the call, need not convert to Judaism. Jew or Gentile, the only thing that matters is to keep the commandments of God. ²⁰ Let everyone remain in the condition they were in at the time of their call.

²¹ Were you a slave at the time of your call? Don't let it bother you. However, if you have a chance to gain your freedom, by all means do so. ²² For a slave, when called to be in Christ, is a free person. And a free person called to be in Christ becomes Christ's slave. ²³ You have all been bought and paid for, so do not become a slave to a human being. ²⁴ Sisters and brothers, continue in the state which you were in when God called you.

²⁵ I have not received any commandment from God with respect to remaining celibate, but I give my opinion as one who is trustworthy, thanks to the mercy of God. ²⁶ Because of the present crisis, it seems good to me for you to remain as you are. ²⁷ Are you married? Do not seek a divorce. Are you single? Do not go looking for a mate. ²⁸ But if you do marry—whether you are male or female, old or young—it is not a sin. However, those who do get married will face many problems in this life, and I want to spare you that.

²⁹ I tell you, sisters and brothers, the time is short. From now on, those with spouses should live as though they had none. ³⁰ Those who mourn should live as though they had nothing to mourn for, and those who rejoice should live as though they had nothing to laugh about. Buyers should conduct themselves as though they owned nothing, ³¹ and those who have

to deal with the world should live as if all their dealings meant nothing—for the world as we know it is passing away.

³²I would like you to be free of all worries. Unmarried people are busy with God's affairs, and are concerned with pleasing God, ³³but married people are busy with this world's demands and occupied with pleasing their spouses. ³⁴This means they are divided. Single women and men concern themselves with Our God's doings. Their aim is to be devoted to God in body and spirit. But married couples are troubled with the world's affairs, and they devote themselves to their spouses.

³⁵I tell you this for your own good. I have no desire to place restrictions on you, but I do want to promote what is good, what will help you to devote yourselves entirely to God.

³⁶If you feel that it is wrong to discourage your children from marrying as they grow older, and that you should do something about it, you are free to do as you like. You are not sinning if they marry. ³⁷But those who—while standing firm in their resolve, while not feeling forced, while in control of their own wills—have resolved not to discourage them from marrying are doing the right thing. ³⁸In other words, to marry is a good thing; not to marry is a better thing.

³⁹One mate is bound to the other throughout life. But if one dies, the other is free to enter into a new relationship—if the new intended belongs to Christ. ⁴⁰However, in my opinion, one is happier if one remains single, and I think I have the Spirit of God in this matter.

8:1-13

ⁿow, concerning food sacrificed to idols.

We all possess knowledge. But knowledge puffs up, whereas love builds up. ²You may think you know something, but you still won't know it the way you ought. ³But anyone who loves God is known—completely—by God.

⁴Well then, what about eating food sacrificed to idols? We know that idols have no real existence, that there is no God but the One. ⁵Even though there are so-called gods in the heavens—and on the earth as well, where there seem to be many gods and sovereigns—⁶for us there is only One God, Abba God, from whom all things come and for whom we live; there is one Sovereign, Jesus Christ, through whom everything was made and through whom we live.

⁷Some people, accustomed to idol worship until recently, are consumed with guilt every time they eat meat they buy in the market, because they

know that the meat had been sacrificed to idols—and their conscience, because it is weak, gets defiled every time they eat. ⁸But food cannot bring us closer to God. We lose nothing if we refuse to eat. We gain nothing if we choose to eat.

⁹Be on your guard, however, that this liberty of yours does not become a pitfall for the weak. ¹⁰Suppose someone who has this knowledge sees you eating in some idol's temple, won't this person be tempted to eat meat offered to idols? ¹¹Realize that your knowledge—that idols are nothing and thus it is all right to eat this meat freely—might be the ruination of a weak sister or brother, for whose sake Christ died. ¹²By sinning against your sisters and brothers in this way and injuring their weak consciences, you are sinning against Christ. ¹³Therefore, if meat causes my sister or brother to stumble, I will never eat it again—I don't want to be an occasion for sin to them.

9:1-27

am I not free? Am I not an apostle? Didn't I see our Savior Jesus, and aren't you yourselves my work in Christ? ²Even if I were not an apostle to others, I would still be an apostle to you, for you are the seal of my apostleship in Christ! ³So my answer to those who would sit in judgment of me is this: ⁴don't we have the right to eat and drink? ⁵Don't we have the right to have Christian spouses with us on our travels—as do all the other apostles, and Jesus' own family members, and Cephas? ⁶Or is it only Barnabas and I who must work for a living? ⁷Who has ever served in the army at one's own expense? Who plants a vineyard and refuses to eat its grapes? Who shepherds a flock and does not drink the milk from the flock?

⁸Sure, these are only human comparisons, but doesn't the Law say the same thing? ⁹It is written in the Law of Moses: "Do not muzzle the ox while it is treading out the corn." Is God concerned about oxen? ¹⁰Or is God really concerned about us? Yes, this was written for our sake to show that the plower plows and the thresher threshes in hope of receiving a share of the harvest. ¹¹If we have sown a spiritual harvest among you, can we not expect a material harvest from you? ¹²Others have the right of support from you. Surely our right to support is even greater.

In point of fact, we have never exercised any of these rights. On the contrary, we have put up with everything in order not to obstruct the Good News of Christ. ¹³Do you not know that those ministering in the Temple get their food from the Temple and those serving at the altar share in the sacrificial offerings? ¹⁴ In the same way, Christ directed that those who preach the Gospel should get their living from the Gospel. ¹⁵ Yet I have not claimed any of these rights. Nor do I write this to secure this treatment for myself. I would rather die than have anyone take away this boast.

¹⁶ Not that I do boast about preaching the Gospel; I am under compulsion and have no choice. I am ruined if I do not preach the Gospel! ¹⁷ If I do it willingly, I have my reward; if unwillingly, I am nonetheless entrusted with a charge. ¹⁸ What then is my reward? It is simply this: that when preaching, I offer the Gospel free of charge and do not assert the authority the Gospel gives me. ¹⁹ Although I am not bound to anyone, I put myself into the service of all so as to win over as many as possible.

²⁰ To the Jews I became even more Jewish, to win over the Jewish people; even though I am not subject to the Law, I made myself subject to the Law, to win those who are subject to the Law. ²¹ To those who have no law, I was free of the Law, too—though not free from God's Law, being subject to the Law of Christ—to win those who have no law. ²² To the weak I became weak to win the weak. I have become all things to all people, that I might save at least some of them. ²³ In fact, I do all that I do for the sake of the Gospel in the hope of having a share in its blessings.

²⁴ You know that in a race everyone runs, but only one wins the prize. So run in such a way as to win! ²⁵ Athletes deny themselves all sorts of things. They do this to win a laurel wreath, even though it withers. We, on the other hand, do so to win an imperishable crown.

²⁶ I don't run like one who loses sight of the finish line. I don't fight as if I were beating the air. ²⁷ What I do is discipline my body and keep it under control, for fear that, after having preached to others, I myself should be disqualified.

10:1-33

I want you to remember this: our ancestors were all under the cloud and all passed through the sea; ² by the cloud and the sea all of them were baptized into Moses. ³ All ate the same spiritual food. ⁴ All drank the same spiritual drink—they drank from the spiritual rock that was following them, and the rock was Christ, ⁵ yet we know that God was not pleased with most of them, for "they were struck down in the desert." ⁶ These things happened as an example to keep us from evil desires such as theirs.

⁷ Do not become idolators, as some of them were, for scripture says, "The people sat down to eat and drink and got up to indulge in revelry." ⁸ We must not take part in sexual immorality, as some of them did; twenty-three

thousand of them died in one day. ⁹We must not test Our God, as some of them did; they were killed by snakes.

¹⁰Nor are you to grumble as some of them did, for which they were killed by the destroying angel. ¹¹The things that happened to them serve as an example and have been written as a warning to us, upon whom the end of the ages has come. ¹²For all these reasons, let those who think they are standing upright watch out lest they fall!

¹³No test has overtaken you but what is common to all people. You can be confident that God is faithful and will not let you be tested beyond your means. And with any trial God will provide you with a way out of it, as well as the strength to bear the trial.

¹⁴I tell you, my dear friends, shun idolatry. ¹⁵I address you as sensible people; you may judge for yourselves what I am saying. ¹⁶The cup of blessing which we bless—is it not a sharing in the blood of Christ? The bread we break—is it not a sharing in the body of Christ? ¹⁷Because the loaf of bread is one, we who are many are one body, for we all partake of the one loaf. ¹⁸Or look at the people of Israel: those who eat the sacrifices are in communion with the altar.

¹⁹Now, I don't mean to imply that a sacrifice offered to an idol is anything, or that the idol itself is anything; ²⁰it's just that pagans make sacrifices to demons, not to God, and I do not want you to be in communion with demons. ²¹You cannot drink the cup of our Savior and the cup of demons too; you cannot partake of our Savior's table and the table of demons. ²²Do we want to provoke our Savior to jealous anger? Surely we are not that strong!

²³"Everything is allowed"—but not everything is good for you. "Everything is allowed"—but not everything is helpful. ²⁴So don't do things out of self-interest; always seek the good of others.

²⁵Feel free to eat anything that is sold in the meat market, without raising questions of conscience. ²⁶After all, "The earth is Our God's, and everything in it." ²⁷By the same token, if some nonbelievers invite you to a meal, feel free to go and eat whatever they put on the table with a clear conscience. ²⁸However, if someone says to you, "This food was offered in sacrifice to idols before it was sold," don't eat it, out of consideration for those who call it to your attention, and for conscience's sake—²⁹that is, for their conscience, not yours, since our freedom shouldn't be judged by someone else's conscience! ³⁰If I eat the meal with thankfulness, why should I be reviled over something for which I thank God?

³¹But whatever you eat or drink—whatever you do—do it all for the glory of God. ³²Give no offense, whether to Jew or to Greek or to the church of

God, [33] just as I try to please everyone in any way I can. I do this by seeking not my own advantage, but that of the many, that they may be saved.

Imitate me as I imitate Christ.

[2] You are to be praised for remembering me so constantly, and for maintaining the teachings just as I handed them down to you.

[3] You say in your letter, however, that since God is the head of Christ, then Christ is the head of man, and man is the head of woman. [4] And that if a man prays or prophesies with his head covered, it is a sign of disrespect for his "head," that is, Christ; [5] but that if a woman prays or prophesies with her head uncovered, it's a sign of disrespect for her "head," that is, man—and that this is just as disreputable as going around with her head shaved.

[6] If a woman won't cover her head, your argument goes, she really should have her hair cut off—but if she's too ashamed to do so, she should wear a head covering. [7] A man shouldn't cover his head, since he's the image and glory of God; woman, on the other hand, is the glory of man. [8] "Man did not come from woman," you say, "didn't the woman come from man? [9] And man was not created for the sake of woman—wasn't woman created for the sake of man?"

[10] The point I was trying to make was that women are to have an outward sign of prophetic *authority*—the covering of their "head"—because angels are always present when you worship. [11] You need to learn, however, that in Christ, woman is not different from man, and man is not different from woman. [12] Woman may come from man, but man is born of woman. And both come from God.

[13] So you be the judge. "Is it appropriate for a woman to pray to God with a bare head?" [14] Let nature herself be your teacher. Men generally feel it's not respectable to have long hair, [15] while women treat long hair as their glory—and besides, that way their head is always "covered"! [16] But if people still want to argue the matter, let's just say we have no other custom, nor do the churches of God.

What I now have to say is not said in praise.

Your meetings do more harm than good. [18] In the first place, I hear that when you gather for a meeting there are divisions among you, and I'm inclined to believe it. [19] No doubt there have to be factions among you, to distinguish those who are to be trusted from those who aren't. [20] The point is, when you hold your *agape* meals, it is not the Eucharist you've been commemorating, [21] for as you eat, each of you goes ahead without waiting for anyone else. One remains hungry, while another gets drunk. [22] Don't you have homes where you can eat and drink? Surely you have enough respect for the community of God not to embarrass poor people! What can I say to you? You'll get no praise from me in this matter!

[23] What I have passed on to you, I received from Christ—that on the night he was betrayed, our Savior Jesus took bread, [24] gave thanks and broke it, saying, "This is my body, which is broken for you. Do this in remembrance of me." [25] In the same way, after supper, he took the cup and said, "This cup is the New Covenant in my blood. Whenever you drink it, do it in remembrance of me." [26] For every time you eat this bread and drink this cup, you proclaim Jesus' death until Christ comes.

[27] Any unfit person who eats the bread or drinks from the cup sins against the body and blood of Christ. [28] Everyone, therefore, should examine themselves before they eat of the bread and drink of the cup, [29] because those who eat and drink without discerning the Body of Christ eat and drink condemnation on themselves. [30] This is why many of you are weak and ill, and some of you are dying.

[31] If only we judged ourselves rightly, we wouldn't be judged in this way. [32] But when God punishes us like this, we are being disciplined so that we will not be condemned along with the world. [33] Therefore, my sisters and brothers, when you assemble for a meal, wait for one another. [34] All who are hungry should eat at home, so that your meetings will not be the cause of your condemnation.

The other matters I will straighten out when I come.

12:1–14:40

Now dear sisters and brothers, I want to instruct you on the matter of spiritual gifts. [2] Remember how, when you were still nonbelievers, you were drawn to mute idols and led astray by them?

[3] It is for this reason that I want you to understand that no one can be speaking under the influence of the Holy Spirit and say, "Curse Jesus"; by the same token, no one can say, "Jesus Christ reigns supreme," unless under the influence of the Holy Spirit.

⁴There is a variety of gifts, but always the same Spirit. ⁵There is a variety of ministries, but we serve the same One. ⁶There is a variety of outcomes, but the same God is working in all of them. ⁷To each person is given the manifestation of the Spirit for the common good.

⁸To one, the Spirit gives wisdom in discourse, to another, the word of knowledge through the same Spirit. ⁹Through the Spirit, one person receives faith; through the same Spirit, another is given the gift of healing; ¹⁰and still another, miraculous powers. Prophecy is given to one; to another, power to distinguish one spirit from another. One receives the gift of tongues; another, that of interpreting tongues. ¹¹But it is one and the same Spirit who produces all these gifts and distributes them as she wills.

¹²The body is one, even though it has many parts; all the parts—many though they are—comprise a single body. And so it is with Christ. ¹³It was by one Spirit that all of us, whether we are Jews or Greeks, slaves or citizens, were baptized into one body. All of us have been given to drink of the one Spirit. ¹⁴And that Body is not one part; it is many.

¹⁵If the foot should say, "Because I am not a hand, I do not belong to the body," does that make it any less a part of the body? ¹⁶If the ear should say, "Because I am not an eye, I do not belong to the body," would that make it any less a part of the body? ¹⁷If the body were all eye, what would happen to our hearing? If it were all ear, what would happen to our sense of smell? ¹⁸Instead of that, God put all the different parts into one body on purpose. ¹⁹If all the parts were alike, where would the body be?

²⁰They are, indeed, many different members but one body. ²¹The eye cannot say to the hand, "I do not need you," any more than the head can say to the feet, "I do not need you." ²²And even those members of the body which seem less important are in fact indispensable. ²³We honor the members we consider less honorable by clothing them with greater care, thus bestowing on the less presentable a propriety ²⁴which the more presentable do not need. God has so constructed the body as to give greater honor to the lowly members, ²⁵that there may be no dissension in the body, but that all the members may be concerned for one another. ²⁶If one member suffers, all the members suffer with it; if one member is honored, all the members share its joy.

²⁷You, then, are the body of Christ, and each of you is a member of it. ²⁸Furthermore, God has set up in the church, first, apostles; second, prophets; third, teachers; then miracle workers, healers, assistants, administrators and those who speak in tongues. ²⁹Are all apostles? Are all prophets? Are all teachers? Do all work miracles ³⁰or have the gift of healing? Do all speak in tongues, or do all have the gift of interpretation of tongues?

³¹ Set your hearts on the greater gifts. But now I will show you the way which surpasses all the others.

13⁴¹ Even if I can speak in all the tongues of earth—and those of the angels too—but do not have love, I am just a noisy gong, a clanging cymbal. ² If I have the gift of prophecy such that I can comprehend all mysteries and all knowledge, or if I have faith great enough to move mountains, but do not have love, I am nothing. ³ If I give away everything I own to feed those poorer than I, then hand over my body to be burned, but do not have love, I gain nothing.

⁴ Love is patient; love is kind. Love is not jealous, it does not put on airs, and it is not snobbish; ⁵ it is never rude or self-seeking; it is not prone to anger, nor does it brood over injuries. ⁶ Love doesn't rejoice in what is wrong, but rejoices in the truth. ⁷ There is no limit to love's forbearance, to its trust, its hope, its power to endure.

⁸ Love never fails. Prophecies will cease, tongues will be silent, knowledge will pass away. ⁹ Our knowledge is imperfect and our prophesying is imperfect. ¹⁰ When the perfect comes, the imperfect will pass away. ¹¹ When I was a child, I used to speak like a child, think like a child, reason like a child. But when I became an adult, I put childish ways aside. ¹² Now we see indistinctly, as in a mirror; then we will see face to face. My knowledge is imperfect now; then I will know even as I am known.

¹³ There are, in the end, three things that last: faith, hope, and love. But the greatest of these is love.

14⁴¹ So pursue the way of love, but earnestly desire spiritual gifts as well, especially the gift of prophecy. ² Those who speak in tongues do not speak to us but to God—for no one understands them when they talk in the Spirit about mysterious things. ³ On the other hand, those who prophesy do talk to us—and they do so for our edification, encouragement and comfort. ⁴ Those who speak in tongues benefit only themselves, but those who prophesy benefit all the church. ⁵ While I would like all of you to speak in tongues, I would much rather that you prophesy. Because those who prophesy are more important than those who speak in tongues—unless they also interpret, in which case the church benefits, too.

⁶ Now, my sisters and brothers, if I were to come to you speaking in tongues, what good would it be if I didn't also give some revelation or knowledge or a prophecy or a teaching? ⁷ Think of a musical instument, a flute or a harp—how can you tell what tune is being played if all the notes sound alike? ⁸ Or if the trumpet gives an indistinct sound, who will be prepared for the attack? ⁹ So it is with you. If you don't produce intelligible speech, how will anyone know what you are saying? You will just be talk-

ing to the air. ¹⁰There are endless numbers of languages in the world, and all of them have meaning. ¹¹But if I don't know the meaning of a language, I am a foreigner to the person speaking, and the person speaking is a foreigner to me. ¹²So it is with you. As long as you eagerly desire spiritual gifts, desire those that benefit the entire community.

¹³It is for this reason that all of you who have the gift of tongues must pray for the gift to interpret them. ¹⁴For if I use the gift of tongues in my prayer, my spirit may be praying but my mind is not. ¹⁵What can we do about this? I will pray with my spirit, and I will pray with my mind also. And I will sing praises with my spirit, and with my mind as well. ¹⁶Otherwise, if you are praising God with the spirit only, how can the uninitiated say the "Amen" to your thanksgiving—they don't know what you are saying! ¹⁷You may be giving thanks well enough, but the other person is not edified.

¹⁸I thank God that I speak in tongues more than any of you. ¹⁹But when I am among the community, I would rather speak five intelligible words than ten thousand words in tongues.

²⁰Sisters and brothers, stop thinking like children. With respect to evil, be like children, but in your thinking, be like adults. ²¹It is written in the Law:

> " 'Through people speaking strange languages
>   and through the lips of foreigners
> I will speak to these people,
>   and still they will not listen to me,'
>   says Our God."

²²Tongues, therefore, are a sign for believers, but not for unbelievers. Prophecy, however, is for unbelievers, not believers.* ²³If inquirers or unbelievers were to come into the gathering of the whole church where everybody was speaking in tongues, wouldn't they decide that you were all mad? ²⁴But if you were all prophesying when inquirers or unbelievers entered—they'd find themselves convicted and called to repentance by everyone speaking. ²⁵When they find their secret thoughts laid bare, they'll fall on their faces, worship God and exclaim, "God is really with you!"

²⁶So, my dear sisters and brothers, what is to be done? When you gather, let everybody be ready with a hymn or a sermon or a revelation, or ready

---

* Our rendering, following the lead of famed translator J.B. Phillips, inverts the actual Greek text, which reads, *"Tongues, therefore, are a sign for unbelievers, but not for believers. Prophecy, however, is for believers, not unbelievers."* Phillips explained in his commentary that he "felt bound to conclude, from the sense of the next three verses, that we have here either a slip of the pen on the part of Paul, or, more probably, a copyist's error."

to use the gift of tongues or to give an interpretation. It must always be for the common good. ²⁷ If there are present those who speak in tongues, let two or three—no more—be allowed to do it. They should speak one at a time, and someone must be available to interpret. ²⁸ If no interpreter is present, the speakers should not speak in church and should speak only to themselves and to God. ²⁹ Let two or three of the prophets speak, with the others discerning if the message is true. ³⁰ If one of the discerners should receive a revelation, then the speaker should stop. ³¹ For you should all prophesy in turn, so that everybody will learn something and be encouraged. ³² Prophets can always control their spirit of prophecy. ³³ God is a God of peace, not disorder.

As in all the churches of the holy ones, ³⁴ only one spouse has permission to speak. The other is to remain silent, to keep in the background, as it says in the Law. ³⁵ If the silent one has questions to ask, ask them at home. It is disgraceful for a spouse to speak improperly in church.

³⁶ Did the word of God originate with you? Are you the only people it has reached? ³⁷ If any of you think you are a prophet or spiritually gifted, acknowledge that what I am writing to you is Christ's command. ³⁸ If you ignore this, you yourself will be ignored.

³⁹ Therefore, sisters and brothers, be eager to prophesy and do not forbid speaking in tongues. ⁴⁰ Let everything be done with propriety and order.

15:1-58

Sisters and brothers, I want to remind you of the Gospel I preached to you, which you received and in which you stand firm. ² You are being saved by it at this very moment, if you hold fast to it as I preached it to you. Otherwise you have believed in vain.

³ I handed on to you, first of all, what I myself received: that Christ died for our sins in accordance with the scriptures; ⁴ that he was buried and, in accordance with the scriptures, rose on the third day; ⁵ that he was seen by Peter, then by the Twelve. ⁶ After that, he was seen by more than five hundred sisters and brothers at once, most of whom are still alive, although some have fallen asleep. ⁷ Next he was seen by James, then by all the apostles. ⁸ Last of all he was seen by me, as one yanked from the womb.

⁹ I am the least of the apostles; in fact, because I persecuted the church of God, I do not even deserve the name. ¹⁰ But by God's favor I am what I am. This favor that God has given to me has not proven fruitless. Indeed, I have worked harder than all the others, not on my own but through the grace of

God. [11] In any case, whether it be I or they, this is what we preach and this is what you believed.

℞   ℞   ℞

[12] Tell me, if we proclaim that Christ was raised from the dead, how is it that some of you say there is no resurrection of the dead? [13] If there is no resurrection of the dead, then not even Christ has been raised. [14] And if Christ has not been raised, then all of our preaching has been meaningless—and everything you've believed has been just as meaningless. [15] Indeed, we are shown to be false witnesses of God, for we solemnly swore that God raised Christ from the dead—which did not happen if in fact the dead are not raised. [16] Because if the dead are not raised, then Christ is not raised, [17] and if Christ is not raised, your faith is worthless. You are still in your sins, [18] and those who have fallen asleep in Christ are the deadest of the dead. [19] If our hopes in Christ are limited to this life only, we are the most pitiable of the human race.

[20] But as it is, Christ has in fact been raised from the dead, the firstfruits of those who have fallen asleep.

[21] For since death came through one human being, in the same way the resurrection of the dead has come through one human being. [22] Just as in the first human all die, so in Christ all will come to life again, [23] but all of them in their proper order: Christ as the firstfruits, and then the faithful when Christ comes again. [24] After that will come the end, when Christ hands over the kindom to God the Creator, having done away with every sovereignty, authority and power. [25] Christ must reign until God has put all enemies under Christ's foot, [26] and the last enemy to be destroyed is death, [27] for everything is "put under" Christ's foot. But when it says that everything has been subjected, it is clear that this does not include God, who subjected everything to Christ. [28] When, finally, everything has been subjected to Christ, Christ will in turn be subjected to the God who had subjected everything to Christ—and so God will be all in all.

[29] Now, if there is no resurrection, what do people hope to gain by being baptized for the dead? If the dead are not raised at all, why be baptized on their behalf? [30] What about ourselves? Why do we constantly endanger ourselves? [31] I face death daily—I mean that, sisters and brothers—just as surely as I glory over you in Christ Jesus our Savior. [32] If at Ephesus I fought wild animals, so to speak, for personal gain, what have I gained? You are saying, "Let us eat and drink, for tomorrow we die." [33] Stop being led astray: "Bad company corrupts the noblest people." [34] Come to your senses. Be-

have properly and stop sinning! There are some of you who seem not to know God at all! Shame on you!

³⁵ Perhaps someone will ask, "How are the dead to be raised up? What kind of body will they have?" ³⁶ What a stupid question! The seed you sow does not germinate unless it dies. ³⁷ When you sow, you do not sow the full-blown plant but a kernel of wheat or some other grain. ³⁸ Then it is given the body God designed for it—with each kind of seed getting its own kind of body.

³⁹ Not all flesh is the same. Human beings have one kind, animals have another, birds another and fish another. ⁴⁰ Then there are heavenly bodies and earthly bodies. Heavenly bodies have a beauty of their own, and earthly bodies have a beauty of their own. ⁴¹ The sun has one kind of brightness, the moon another and the stars another. And star differs from star in brightness.

⁴² So it is with the resurrection of the dead. What is sown is a perishable body, what is raised is incorruptible. ⁴³ What is sown is ignoble, what is raised is glorious. Weakness is sown, strength is raised up. ⁴⁴ A natural body is sown, and a spiritual body is raised up. If there is a natural body, then there is also a spiritual body.

⁴⁵ The first Adam, as scripture says, "became a living soul," but the last Adam has become a life-giving spirit. ⁴⁶ That is, the natural comes first, not the spiritual; after that comes the spiritual. ⁴⁷ The first, being from the earth, is earthly by nature; the second is from heaven. ⁴⁸ As this earthly one was, so are we of the earth; and as the One from heaven is, so are we in heaven. ⁴⁹ And we, who have been modeled on the earthly, likewise will be modeled on the One from heaven.

⁵⁰ Put another way, sisters and brothers, I declare to you that flesh and blood cannot inherit the kindom of God. Neither can the perishable inherit what is imperishable. ⁵¹ I will share with you a mystery: we are not all going to die, but we will be changed. ⁵² It will be instantaneous, in the twinkling of an eye—when the last trumpet sounds. It will sound, and the dead will be raised, imperishable, and we will be changed, too. ⁵³ For our present perishable nature must put on imperishability, and our mortal nature must put on immortality.

⁵⁴ When this perishable nature has put on imperishability, and when this mortal body has put on immortality, then the words of scripture will come true: ⁵⁵ "Death is swallowed up in victory. Death, where is your victory? Death, where is your sting?" ⁵⁶ Now the sting of death is sin, and sin gets its power from the Law—⁵⁷ but thank God for giving us the victory through our Savior Jesus Christ!

⁵⁸ Be steadfast and persevering, my beloved sisters and brothers, fully

engaged in the work of Jesus. You know that your toil is not in vain when it is done in Christ.

16:1-24

now about the collection for the holy ones. Do what I told the Galatian churches to do: ²on the first day of the week, put aside what you can afford in order to avoid the collection being made after I come. ³Then, while I am there, I will send those whom you designate with letters of recommendation and your gifts to Jerusalem. ⁴If it is advisable for me to go, too, they may travel with me.

⁵I will come to you after I pass through Macedonia, for I intend to pass through Macedonia. ⁶And I may be staying with you for awhile, perhaps for the winter. That way you can help me on my journey, wherever that will be. ⁷I don't mean this to be just a passing visit. I hope to spend some time with you, if Our God allows.

⁸In any case, I will stay at Ephesus until Pentecost, ⁹for a huge door of opportunity has opened itself for me. Many people oppose me there.

¹⁰If Timothy comes, see that you don't scare him off, for he is doing God's work, as I am. ¹¹No one is to despise him simply because he is young. Send him on his way in peace that he may come to us. I am expecting him, as are the rest of us.

¹²Now about our brother Apollos: I begged him to come to you with the others. He was adamant not to go now, but he will come to you as soon as he can.

ଔ   ଔ   ଔ

¹³Be on your guard. Stand firm in the faith; be courageous; be strong. ¹⁴Let all that you do be done in love.

¹⁵There is one more thing. You know how the Stephanas family—the first converts in Achaia—have worked very hard in the service of the holy ones. ¹⁶Well, now you should put yourselves at the service of people like them, and of everyone who helps in that work. ¹⁷I am delighted that Stephanas, Fortunatus and Achaicus have arrived, because they make up for your absence. ¹⁸They refresh my spirit as well as yours. I hope you appreciate workers like these.

¹⁹The churches of Asia send you greetings. Aquila and Prisca, along with the community that meets in their house, send you their warmest greet-

ings in Christ. ²⁰ All the sisters and brothers greet you. Greet one another with a holy kiss.

²¹ I, Paul, write this greeting in my own hand.

²² Whoever does not love Our God is cursed. *"Marana tha!"*

²³ The grace of our Savior Jesus be with you. ²⁴ My love to all of you in Christ Jesus. Amen.

the second letter of paul to the

corinthians

1:1-7

from paul, an apostle of jesus christ by
the will of God, and Timothy our colleague,

To the church of God in Corinth, together with all the holy ones throughout Achaia:

²Grace and peace to you from God our Creator and our Savior Jesus Christ.

³Blessed be Abba God, the God of our Savior Jesus Christ, the Source of
all mercies and the God of all consoling, ⁴who comforts us in all our troubles
so that we can comfort those in any trouble with the same comforting God
has given us. ⁵For while the sufferings of Christ are abundantly ours, our
comforting is just as abundant through Christ.

⁶If we are troubled, it is for your comfort and salvation; if we are comforted, it too is for your comfort, which helps you patiently endure the same
sufferings we suffer. ⁷And our hope for you is firmly grounded, because
we know that though you share in our sufferings, you share in our consolation as well.

$\mathcal{W}$e want you to know, sisters and brothers, about the hardships we suffered in the province of Asia. We underwent severe stress, well beyond our ability to cope, to the point of despairing of life itself. ⁹In our hearts we felt we were doomed, which taught us not to rely on ourselves but on God, who raises the dead to life. ¹⁰God rescued us from so great a peril as death, and we will continue to be rescued by God, on whom we have set our hope. ¹¹ Please continue to help us through your prayers, though. The more you pray for us, the more others will give thanks for the blessings granted in answer to our prayers.

¹²Allow us to boast—and my conscience tells me this is true—that we have conducted ourselves in the world, and especially treated you, with a reverence and sincerity that comes only from God. We further attest, by God's grace, that it has been without ulterior motives. ¹³For we don't write anything you can't read and understand. And we hope that you will understand completely—¹⁴as you have come to understand partially—so that you can boast of us just as we will boast of you in the day of our Savior Jesus.

¹⁵Because I was so sure of this, I had meant to come to you first so that you might benefit twice—¹⁶I planned to visit you both on my way to Macedonia and on my return trip, then to have you send me on my way to Judea. ¹⁷And don't think I acted lightly, unsure of my intentions, when I planned this. Don't think I make my plans with ordinary human motives—so that I say "Yes, yes," then in the same breath, "No, no"! ¹⁸As sure as God is faithful, I declare that my word to you is not "yes" one minute and "no" the next.

¹⁹Jesus Christ, whom Sivanus, Timothy and I preached to you as the Only Begotten of God, was not alternately "yes" and "no"; Jesus is never anything but "yes." ²⁰No matter how many promises God has made, they are "yes" in Christ. Therefore it is through Jesus that we address our Amen to God when we worship together. ²¹God is the One who firmly establishes us along with you in Christ; it is God who anointed us ²²and sealed us, putting the Spirit in our hearts as our bond and guarantee.

²³As God is my witness, I swear that, in an attempt to spare your feelings, I did not return to Corinth. ²⁴I'm not a tyrant over your faith. Rather, I am a co-worker with you for your happiness. By faith you stand firm.

2:1So I made up my mind not to pay you a second painful visit. ²I may have hurt you, but if so I have hurt the only ones who could give me any comfort. ³I wrote what I did to make sure that when I came I would not be vexed by those same people who, under normal circumstances, would make me happy! Surely you know that my happiness relies on you all being happy. ⁴For I wrote to you with a heavy and anguished heart and many tears. I wrote not to grieve you, but that you might know how much I love you.

⁵One individual has been the cause of a great deal of pain, not just to me but, to a degree—not to exaggerate—to all of you. ⁶The punishment imposed by the majority on the person in question is sufficient. ⁷The appropriate next step is to forgive and encourage the offender, to avoid a breakdown because of so much misery. ⁸I urge you to reaffirm your love for this individual. ⁹For I really wrote to test your character, to see if you were obedient in everything. ¹⁰Whoever you forgive, I forgive. And what I have forgiven—if there has been anything to be forgiven—I have done so for your sake, in the presence of Christ. ¹¹And so we will not be outwitted by Satan, for we are aware of the Devil's intentions.

¹²Now, when I went to Troas to preach the Good News of Christ, I discovered a door open for me to minister. ¹³But I was particularly anxious over not meeting my brother Titus there, so I said goodbye to them and moved on to Macedonia.

¹⁴But thanks be to the Most High who makes us, in Christ, sharers in the divine triumph, and everywhere we go manifests through us the sweet aroma of the knowledge of God. ¹⁵For we are the incense of Christ that ascends to God on behalf of those being saved—and of those who are perishing. ¹⁶We are the stench of death to one, and the fragrance of life to the other.

Now I ask, who is qualified for work like this? ¹⁷At least we don't go around peddling the word of God for profit. Many others do, you know. We speak before God with sincerity—in Christ—as envoys of God.

3:1 Am I beginning to brag again? Or do I need letters of recommendation to you or from you, as others might? ²You are my letter, known and read by all, written on your hearts. ³Clearly you are a letter of Christ which I have delivered, a letter written not with ink, but with the Spirit of the living God; not on tablets of stone, but on tablets of flesh in the heart.

3:4–4:6

*T*he great confidence we have before God, we have because of Christ. ⁵It is not that we are entitled of ourselves to take credit for anything. Our sole credit is from God, ⁶who made us qualified ministers of a new Covenant, a covenant not of a written Law but of Spirit. The written Law kills, but the Spirit gives life.

⁷Now if the ministry that brought death, carved in writing on stone, was inaugurated with such glory that the Israelites could not look on Moses' face because of the radiance that shone on it, fading though it was—⁸how much greater will be the glory of the ministry of the Spirit? ⁹If the ministry of the Covenant that condemned had splendor, greater by far is the splendor of the ministry that justifies! ¹⁰Indeed, when you compare that limited glory with this surpassing glory, the former is no glory at all. ¹¹If what was destined to pass away was given in glory, greater by far is the glory that endures.

¹²With such hope we are very bold in what we say. ¹³And we are not like Moses, who covered his face with a veil to keep the Israelites from gazing at the radiance as it faded away. ¹⁴But their minds had been dulled, and to this day the same veil remains whenever the old Covenant is read—it has not been taken away, for only in Christ can it be removed. ¹⁵To this day, whenever Moses is read, a veil covers their understanding.

¹⁶But whenever anyone turns to Our God, the veil is removed. ¹⁷Now Our God is the Spirit, and where the Spirit of Our God is, there is freedom. ¹⁸And we, who with unveiled faces reflect Our God's glory, grow brighter and brighter as we are being transformed into the image we reflect. This is the work of Our God, who is Spirit.

4:1Therefore, because we have this ministry through God's mercy, we do not give in to discouragement. ²On the contrary, we renounce the shameful deeds that were kept hidden. We are not deceitful, nor do we adulterate the word of God. But by speaking the truth plainly, we commend ourselves to every person's conscience in the sight of God.

³If our Gospel can be called veiled in any sense, it is only for those who are headed toward destruction. ⁴Their unbelieving minds have been blinded by the god of the present age, so that they do not see the splendor of the Gospel showing forth the glory of Christ, the image of God. ⁵It is not ourselves we preach, but Christ Jesus as Sovereign, and ourselves as your workers for Jesus' sake. ⁶For God, who said, "Let light shine out of darkness," has shone in our hearts, so that we in turn might make known the glory of God shining on the face of Christ.

but this treasure we possess is in earthen vessels, to make it clear that its surpassing power comes from God and not from us. ⁸We are afflicted in every way possible, but we are not crushed; we are full of doubts, but we never despair. ⁹We are persecuted, but never abandoned; we are struck

4:7–6:2

down, but never destroyed. ¹⁰Continually we carry about in our bodies the death of Jesus, so that in our bodies the life of Jesus may also be revealed. ¹¹While we live, we are constantly being delivered to death for Jesus' sake, so that the life of Jesus may also be revealed in our bodies. ¹²So then, death is at work in us, but life is at work in you.

¹³But as we have the same spirit of faith that is mentioned in scripture— "I believed and therefore I spoke"—we too believe and therefore speak, ¹⁴ knowing that the One who raised Jesus to life will in turn raise us with Jesus, and place you with us in God's presence. ¹⁵You see, all of this is for your benefit, so that the grace that is reaching more and more people may cause thanksgiving to overflow, to the glory of God.

¹⁶That is why we don't lose heart. And though this physical self of ours may be falling into decay, the inner self is renewed day by day. ¹⁷These light and momentary troubles train us to carry the weight of an eternal glory which will make these troubles insignificant by comparison. ¹⁸And we have no eyes for things that are visible, but only for things that are invisible; visible things last only for a time, but the invisible are eternal.

5:1 For we know that when our earthly tent is folded up, there is waiting for us a house built by God, an everlasting home in the heavens, not made by human hands. ²And while in this tent, we lament—longing to be clothed with our heavenly home—³because when we are dressed we will not be found naked. ⁴While we are in this tent we groan and find it a burden, because we don't want to be naked, but to be clothed, so that what is mortal is swallowed up by life. ⁵God made us for this very purpose, and gave us the pledge of the Spirit to safeguard our future.

⁶And so we are always full of confidence, even though we realize that to live in the body means to be absent from Jesus Christ. ⁷We walk by faith, not by sight. ⁸We are full of confidence, I repeat, and would actually prefer to be absent from the body and make our home with Christ. ⁹Whether we are living in the body or absent from it, we are intent on pleasing Christ. ¹⁰For we must all appear before the judgment seat of Christ, and each of us will get what we deserve for the things we do while in the body, good or bad.

¹¹It is because we know "the fear of God" that we try to persuade others. What we really are is plain to God, and I hope it is also plain to your conscience. ¹²No, we are not attempting to commend ourselves to you once again. We are just giving you a reason to be proud of us. In that way you will have an answer for those who boast of what is seen, rather than what is in the heart. ¹³If we are beside ourselves, it is for the sake of God. If we are in our right minds, it is for you.

¹⁴The love of Christ overwhelms us whenever we reflect on this: that if

one person has died for all, then all have died. ¹⁵ The reason Christ died for all was so that the living should live no longer for themselves but for Christ, who died and was raised to life for them.

¹⁶ And so from now on, we don't look on anyone in terms of mere human judgment. Even if we did once regard Christ in these terms, that is not how we know Christ now. ¹⁷ And for anyone who is in Christ, there is a new creation. The old order has passed away; now everything is new!

¹⁸ All of this is from God, who ransomed us through Christ—and made us ministers of that reconciliation. ¹⁹ This means that through Christ, the world was fully reconciled again to God, who didn't hold our transgressions against us, but instead entrusted us with this message of reconciliation. ²⁰ This makes us Christ's ambassadors, as though God were making the appeal directly through us. Therefore we implore you in Christ's name: be reconciled to God. ²¹ For our sake, God made the One who was without sin to *be* sin, so that by this means we might become the very holiness of God.

6:1 As Christ's co-workers we beg you not to receive the grace of God in vain. ² For God says through Isaiah, "At the acceptable time I heard you, and on the day of salvation I helped you." Now is the acceptable time! Now is the day of salvation!

6:3–7:1

We take pains to avoid giving offense to anyone, for we don't want our ministry to be blamed. ⁴ Instead, in all that we do we try to present ourselves as ministers of God, acting with patient endurance amid trials, difficulties, distresses, ⁵ beatings, imprisonments and riots; in hard work, sleepless nights and hunger. ⁶ We conduct ourselves with innocence, knowledge, patience and kindness in the Holy Spirit, in sincere love, ⁷ with the message of truth and the power of God, wielding the weapons of justice with both right hand and left—⁸ regardless of whether we are honored or dishonored, spoken of favorably or unfavorably. We are called impostors, yet we are truthful; ⁹ we are called unknowns, yet we are famous; we are said to be dying, yet we are alive; punished, but not put to death; ¹⁰ sorrowful, though we are always rejoicing; poor, yet we enrich many. We seem to have nothing, yet we possess everything!

¹¹ We have spoken frankly to you, Corinthians; we've opened our hearts wide to you. ¹² We're not holding anything back; you, on the other hand, are holding back your affection from us. ¹³ It would be a fair exchange—I

speak as to my children—if you'd open your hearts as widely to us as we do to you.

¹⁴ Don't be harnessed in an uneven team with nonbelievers. Justice and inequity are not companions; light and darkness have nothing in common. ¹⁵ Christ is not allied with Belial, and a believer has nothing in common with a nonbeliever. ¹⁶ The Temple of God has nothing in common with idols, for we are the Temple of the living God. As God has said:

> "I will live with them
>   and move among them,
> and I will be their God,
>   and they will be my people."

¹⁷ " 'Therefore, come away from them,
>   and be separate,'
>   says Your God.
> 'Touch nothing that is unclean,
>   and I will welcome you.' "

¹⁸ " 'I will be a Parent to you,
>   and you will be daughters
>   and sons to me,'
>   says Your God Almighty."

7:1 Since we have these promises, dear sisters and brothers, let us wash off everything that contaminates body and spirit, working to make our holiness perfect out of reverence for God.

7:2-16

make room for us in your hearts. We have not wronged anyone or ruined anyone or exploited anyone. ³ I do not say this to put any blame on you. As I have already said, you are in our hearts—that we may live together or die together. ⁴ I have the greatest confidence in you. I take great pride in you. I am greatly encouraged and filled with joy all the more because of our troubles.

⁵ Even after we came to Macedonia, this body of ours found no rest. We were harrassed on all sides—quarrels on the outside, fear on the inside. ⁶ But God, who comforts the afflicted, comforted us with the arrival of Titus—⁷ and not only by his arrival, but also by the comfort you gave to him. He told us all about your yearning for me, how sorry you were and how concerned for me. I am happier now than I was before.

⁸ For even if I caused you sorrow by my letter, I don't regret it. I did re-

gret it before—I see that the letter saddened you, at least for a while—⁹but now I am happy. I rejoice not that you were made to suffer, but that your suffering led to your repentance. Your suffering is the kind of which God approves. And so you did not endure any kind of loss because of us. ¹⁰Godly sorrow means changing for the better and having no regrets. To suffer as the world suffers brings death. ¹¹See what salutary effects godly suffering has produced in you: what keenness, what earnestness, what indignation, what fear, what yearning, what concern, what zeal to see justice done! At every point you have shown yourselves blameless in this matter. ¹²So then, though I wrote the letter to you, it was not for the sake of the offender or the one offended. It was written so that you could see for yourselves how devoted to us you are in the sight of God. ¹³We are encouraged by this.

Besides this encouragement, we are especially delighted to see Titus so happy. Thanks to you, he has no more worries. ¹⁴I had boasted to him about you, and you have not embarrassed me. In fact, our boasting to Titus proved to be as true as anything we have said. ¹⁵His heart goes out to you all the more when he recalls how willing you all have been, and with what deep respect you welcomed him. ¹⁶I am very happy because I have complete confidence in you.

8:1–9:15

Now, sisters and brothers, we want to tell you how God's grace has been given to the churches in Macedonia. ²In the midst of severe trial, their overflowing joy and deep poverty have produced an abundant generosity. ³I can swear that they gave not only what they could afford but much more, spontaneously, ⁴begging and begging us for the favor of sharing in this service to God's holy ones and—⁵quite unexpectedly—they offered themselves first to God, and then to us, in keeping with God's will. ⁶This is why I have asked Titus, who has already begun this work of charity among you, to bring it to a successful completion: ⁷that just as you are rich in every respect, in faith and discourse, in knowledge, in total concern and in the love we inspired in you, you may also abound in this work of grace.

⁸It is not an order I am giving you, but the opportunity to test your generous love against the earnestness which others show. ⁹You are well acquainted with the favor shown by our Savior Jesus Christ, who, though rich, became poor for your sake, so that you might become rich by Christ's poverty.

¹⁰As I say, this is only a suggestion—it's my counsel about what is best

for you in this matter. A year ago, you were not only the first to act, but you did so willingly. ¹¹ Finish that work, so that your eagerness to begin can be matched by your eagerness to finish, according to your means. ¹² For so long as the heart is willing, it's what you have that is acceptable, not what you don't have.

¹³ This doesn't mean that by giving relief to others, you ought to make things difficult for yourselves! It's just a question of balancing ¹⁴ what happens to be your surplus now against their present need; one day they may have something to spare that will supply your own need. That is how we strike a balance, ¹⁵ as scripture says: "The one who gathered much had no excess, and the one who gathered little did not go short."

¹⁶ I thank God for putting into the heart of Titus the same concern for you that I have myself. ¹⁷ He did what he was asked, and because he is concerned, he is coming to you now on his own initiative. ¹⁸ And we are sending, along with Titus, someone who is praised in all the churches for being a brilliant preacher of the Gospel. ¹⁹ What's more, this individual has also been appointed as our traveling companion by the churches on this errand of mercy. We do it for the glory of God, and to show our eagerness to help. ²⁰ By doing so, we hope to avoid any criticism of the way we administer such a large fund. ²¹ For we are trying to do what is right in the sight of both God and people.

²² In addition, we're sending along another co-worker, who has proven diligent in earlier testings, but who is even more diligent now because of a tremendous faith in you. ²³ As for Titus, he is my colleague and co-worker among you. As for the other two co-workers, they are delegates of the churches and an honor to Christ. ²⁴ Therefore, before all the churches, give them a proof of your love, and prove to them that we are justified to be proud of you.

9¹ There's really no need for me to write to you about offering your services to the holy ones. ² For I know how anxious you are to help, and I've boasted about you to the Macedonians: "Achaia has been ready since last year." In fact, your zeal has stirred up most of them! ³ Even so, I'm sending the co-workers so that our boasting about you in this matter won't prove to have been empty—and to show that you are indeed ready, as I said you would be. ⁴ If any of the Macedonians should accompany me and find you unprepared, we—not to mention you!—would be humiliated after being so confident. ⁵ It's for this reason that I thought it necessary for the co-workers to precede us, and to arrange in advance for this generous gift you promised. In this way we will dispel all doubts that it comes as a bountiful and free gift, not an extorted one.

⁶ Keep this in mind: if you plant sparingly, you will reap sparingly, and

if you plant bountifully, you will reap bountifully. ⁷You must give according to what you have inwardly decided—not sadly, not reluctantly, for God loves a giver who gives cheerfully. ⁸There are no limits to the grace of God, who will make sure you will always have enough of everything and even a surplus for good works, ⁹as scripture says:

> "God scattered abroad
>   and gave to poor people;
> God's justice endures forever."

¹⁰The One who provides seed for the planter and bread for food will also supply and enlarge your store of seed and increase your harvest of justice. ¹¹You will be made rich in every way for your generosity, for which we give thanks to God.

¹²For the administration of this service not only supplies fully the needs of the holy ones, but also overflows in thanksgivings to God. ¹³By offering this service, you prove yourselves. And that makes them give glory to God for the way you obey and profess the Gospel of Christ, and for your generosity to them and to everyone. ¹⁴And their prayers also show how they are drawn to you because of the exceeding grace of God in you. ¹⁵Thanks be to God for such an indescribable gift!

10:1–11:15

I myself appeal to you by the gentleness and meekness of Christ—I who am so humble when face to face with you, but who bullies you when away! ²I only ask that I do not have to bully you when I come—for I'll be bold if I need to be—to confront some among you I could name, who think we live by worldly standards.

³Though we live in the world, we don't fight in a worldly way. ⁴Our weapons, however, have the power of God to destroy fortresses. ⁵We demolish every argument and pretension that resists the knowledge of God, and we take every thought captive and make it obedient to Christ. ⁶We're ready to punish every disobedience, once your obedience is complete.

⁷Look at what confronts you. Those who are convinced that they belong to Christ need to realize that we belong to Christ just as much as they do. ⁸And even if I should boast a little too much about our authority—which Christ gave for building up and not for tearing down—I will not be ashamed of it. ⁹I don't want you to think of me as someone who frightens you only by letter. ¹⁰Someone said, "His letters are weighty and forceful, but in person he is unremarkable and not even a preacher." ¹¹Such people

must understand that what we are in words when absent, we are in actions when present.

¹²We do not dare to classify or compare ourselves with some who recommend themselves. They are foolish because they measure and compare themselves only with themselves. ¹³We, on the other hand, won't boast without a measurable standard. Our standard is the measuring stick God gave us, which is long enough to reach you. ¹⁴We are not overreaching ourselves. Otherwise we would not have reached you—and we were the first to come all the way to you with the Gospel of Christ. ¹⁵Nor do we exceed our limits by boasting about the work of others. Yet our hope is that as your faith increases, our influence among you will increase accordingly—within proper limits—¹⁶so that we may carry the Gospel to places far beyond you. We won't boast of work completed in another person's territory. ¹⁷As scripture says, "Let those who boast, boast in Our God," ¹⁸for it is not those who commend themselves who are approved, but those who are commended by Our God.

11:1 Will you endure a little of my foolishness? Humor me, please. ²You see, the jealousy that I feel for you is God's own jealousy: I stood as witness to your marriage with Christ to testify about your purity before Christ. ³My fear is that you—just as our first parents were deceived by the cunning of the serpent—will let your ideas get corrupted and turned away from simple and pure devotion to Christ. ⁴I say this because when someone comes preaching a Jesus other than the one we preached, or telling you to receive a different spirit than the Spirit you received, or to accept a gospel other than the Gospel you accepted, you seem to endure it quite well.

⁵I consider myself not the least bit inferior to the "super apostles." ⁶I may be unskilled in speech, but I'm certainly not lacking in knowledge. We have made this evident to you in every conceivable way. ⁷I lowered myself to elevate you—I proclaimed the Gospel of God to you without cost. Was that a sin? ⁸I robbed other churches by receiving financial support from them while serving you. ⁹And while I was with you, I was careful not to be a burden to anyone—any time I needed something, my Macedonian coworkers supplied what I needed. I've kept myself from being a burden to you in any way, and I will continue to do so. ¹⁰As surely as the truth of Christ is in me, nobody in all of Achaia will prevent me from boasting. ¹¹And you think I don't love you? God knows I do!

¹²And what I am doing I intend to continue to do. I will leave no opportunity for those who want to boast that they are our equals. ¹³No—these people are false apostles and deceitful workers who pose as apostles of Christ. ¹⁴And no wonder: even Satan pretends to be an angel of light. ¹⁵One need not be surprised that the Devil's minions impersonate agents of righteousness. They will come to the end that their actions deserve.

i repeat, let no one take me for a fool. But if you must, treat me like a fool, and let me do a little boasting of my own. ¹⁷ What I am saying I say not as Christ would, but as a fool, in this overconfident boasting of mine.

¹⁸ Since many are boasting of their worldly accomplishments, I too will boast. ¹⁹ You gladly tolerate fools, since you yourselves are so wise. ²⁰ You've been patient with someone who enslaves you, devours you, takes advantage of you, puts on airs and hits you in the face. ²¹ I'm ashamed to say that we have a weakness for doing these very things!

But what anyone else dares to boast about—I speak with absolute foolishness now—I also dare to boast. ²² Are they Hebrews? So am I! Are they Israelites? So am I! Are they the seed of Sarah and Abraham? So am I! ²³ Are they ministers of Christ? Now I'm really talking like a fool—I am more of one! I have worked much harder, been in prison far more often, been flogged more severely and been exposed to death time and again. ²⁴ Five times I was given thirty-nine lashes by the Temple authorities. ²⁵ Three times I was beaten with sticks. They stoned me once. I was shipwrecked three times, once spending a night and a day in the open sea. ²⁶ And I have been constantly on the move—in danger from raging rivers, in danger from highway robbers, in danger from Jews, in danger from Gentiles, in danger in the city, in danger in the country, in danger at sea and in danger from false sisters and brothers. ²⁷ I have labored long and hard, often going without sleep; I've known hunger and thirst, often going without food; I've been cold and naked. ²⁸ And on top of everything, there is the daily stress of my anxiety for all the churches. ²⁹ Who is weak, that I don't feel that weakness? Who is led into sin, that I am not tortured by it? ³⁰ But if I must boast, I will boast of my shortcomings.

³¹ The God and Creator of our Savior Jesus, who is blessed forever, knows that I do not lie. ³² When I was at Damascus, the governor under the ruler Aretas stationed guards around the city to take me into custody. ³³ But I was lowered in a basket through a window in the wall and escaped.

12.¹ I must go on boasting, however useless it may be, and speak of visions and revelations from God. ² I know someone who fourteen years ago was caught up in the third heaven. Whether it was in the body or out of the body I do not know—only God knows. ³ And I know that this person— whether it was in the body or out of the body I do not know, only God knows—⁴ was caught up to paradise to hear words that cannot be uttered, words that no one may speak. ⁵ About this person I will boast, but I will do no boasting about myself, unless it be about my weaknesses. ⁶ And even if I were to boast, it wouldn't be foolish of me, because I am speaking the truth.

But I refrain, so that no one will think more of me than is justified by what I do or say. [7]Because of the surpassing greatness of the revelations, in order to keep me from becoming conceited, I was given a thorn in my flesh—a messenger of Satan to beat me—to keep me from exalting myself! [8]Three times I begged God that it might leave me. [9]And God said to me, "My grace is sufficient for you, for power is perfected in weakness." Most gladly, therefore, I would rather boast about my weaknesses, that the power of Christ may dwell in me. [10]So I am content with weakness, with mistreatment, with distress, with persecutions and difficulties for the sake of Christ; when I am powerless, it is then that I am strong.

12:11–13:14

I*'ve* been a fool, but you forced me to it. I ought to have been commended by you. Even though I am nothing, I am in no way inferior to these "super apostles." [12]The things that mark a true apostle—signs, wonders, miracles —were unfailingly produced among you. [13]How were you less privileged than the other churches—with the exception that I wasn't a burden to you? Forgive me this wrong!

[14]Now I'm ready to come to you a third time. I won't be a burden, for I want not what is yours, but you. After all, children are not expected to save money for their parents; rather, parents save for their children. [15]And I am perfectly willing to spend—and to be expended as well—for the sake of your souls. But if I love you more, am I to be loved less in return? [16]At least I wasn't a burden to you; but cunning as I am, I caught you by deceit. [17]Did I exploit you through any of those I sent to you? [18]I urged Titus to go and send our co-worker. Did Titus exploit you? It goes without saying that Titus and I have always been guided by the same Spirit and walk in the same path.

[19]Do you get the impression that we've been defending ourselves to you all along? We've been speaking in Christ, and in the sight of God. And it is all for your benefit, dearly beloved. [20]For I fear that when I come, I may find you not as I want you to be. And you may find me not as you want me to be. And there may be rivalry, jealousy, outbursts of anger, disputes, slander, gossip, deceit and disorder. [21]I am afraid that when I come again, my God may humiliate me before you. And I fear I will be grieving over many who have sinned earlier and have not repented of the impurity, immorality and debauchery they committed.

[13:1]This will be the third time I come to you: "Every charge must be established by the testimony of two or three witnesses." [2]I already gave you

321

2 corinthians 12

a warning when I was with you the second time. And I warn you now, before I come: I will have no mercy on those of you who sinned earlier, or on any of the others. ³ You want proof, you say, that Christ is speaking through me—me, whom you have known not as a weakling but as a power among you? ⁴ But our Savior was crucified through weakness and now lives through the power of God. Likewise, we are weak in Christ, yet we live in Christ by the power of God, to serve you.

⁵ Test yourselves to see if you're really walking in the faith. Examine yourselves! Don't you realize that Jesus Christ is in you? —That is, unless you fail the test! ⁶ I hope you come to see that we haven't failed it. ⁷ We pray to God that you won't commit any wrongdoing—not that we should appear to be in the right, but that you should do right, even if we appear to be in the wrong. ⁸ For we can't do anything against the truth—only for it. ⁹ And we rejoice when you are strong and we are weak. We pray that you will be made complete.

¹⁰ I write this while I am away from you, so that when I come, I need not be severe in my use of authority, which God gave me for building up, not for tearing down.

¹¹ And now, sisters and brothers, I must say goodbye. Mend your ways. Encourage one another. Live in harmony and peace, and the God of love and peace will be with you.

¹² Greet one another with a holy kiss. ¹³ All the holy ones send greetings to you.

¹⁴ The grace of our Savior Jesus Christ and the love of God and the friendship of the Holy Spirit be with you all!

the letter of paul to the

galatians

from paul, appointed to be an apostle, not through human agency but through Jesus Christ, and through Abba God, who raised Christ from the dead—²and from all the sisters and brothers who are here with us,

To the churches of Galatia:

³Grace and peace to you from God our Creator and our Savior Jesus Christ, ⁴whose self-sacrifice for our sins rescued us from this present wicked world, in accordance with the will of our God and Creator, ⁵to whom be the glory forever and ever!

⁶I'm astonished that you've so soon turned away from the One who called you by the grace of Christ, and have turned to a different gospel— ⁷one which is really not "good news" at all. Some who wish to alter the Good News of Christ must have confused you. ⁸For if we—or even angels from heaven—should preach to you a different gospel, one not in accord with the gospel we delivered to you, let us—or them—be cursed! ⁹We've

said it before and I'll say it again: if any preach a gospel to you that is contrary to the one you received, let them be cursed!

¹⁰Whom am I trying to please now—people or God? Is it human approval I'm seeking? If I still wanted that, I wouldn't be what I am—a servant of Christ! ¹¹I assure you, my sisters and brothers: the gospel I proclaim to you is no mere human invention. ¹²I didn't receive it from any person, nor was I schooled in it. It came by revelation from Jesus Christ.

1:13–2:21

*Y*ou've heard, I know, the story of my former way of life in Judaism. You know that I went to extremes in persecuting the church of God and tried to destroy it; ¹⁴I went far beyond most of my contemporaries regarding Jewish observances because of my great zeal to live out all the traditions of my ancestors.

¹⁵But the time came when God, who had set me apart before I was born, called me by divine grace, choosing ¹⁶to reveal God's Own through me, that I might spread Christ among the Gentiles. Immediately, without seeking human advisors ¹⁷or even going to Jerusalem to see those who were apostles before me, I went off to Arabia; later I returned to Damascus. ¹⁸Three years after that, I went up to Jerusalem to get to know Peter, with whom I stayed for fifteen days. ¹⁹I didn't meet any other apostle except James, the brother of Jesus. ²⁰I declare before God that what I have just written is true.

²¹After that I visited the regions of Syria and Cilicia. ²²The communities of Christ in Judea had no idea what I looked like; ²³they had only heard that "the one who was formerly persecuting us is now preaching the faith he tried to destroy," ²⁴and they gave glory to God because of me.

2¹After fourteen years, I went up to Jerusalem again with Barnabas, this time taking Titus with me; ²my going there was prompted by a revelation. Once there, I laid out for them the Gospel as I present it to the Gentiles. All of this took place in private conference with the leaders, to make sure that the course I was pursuing, or had pursued, was not useless.

³They even tried—unsuccessfully—to compel Titus, who had accompanied me, to be circumcised, since he was Greek. ⁴The question came up because some of the community infiltrated our ranks to spy on the freedom we have in Christ Jesus in order to enslave us. ⁵We didn't capitulate to them for one moment; we wanted to ensure that the truth of the Good News would remain intact for you. ⁶Consequently, the acknowledged

"leaders" there—importance is of no concern to me; we are all equal before God—had nothing to add to the Good News I preach.

⁷On the contrary, they recognized that I had been entrusted with the Good News for the Gentiles, just as Peter had for the Jewish people. ⁸The same One who appointed Peter as apostle to the Jewish people gave me a similar mission to the Gentiles. ⁹Recognizing the grace that had been given to me, James, Peter and John—these leaders, these pillars—shook hands with Barnabas and me as a sign of partnership: we were to go to the Gentiles and they to the Jews. ¹⁰The only thing they insisted on was that we should remember to help those poorer than we—the very thing I was eager to do.

¹¹When Peter came to Antioch, however, I opposed him to his face, since he was manifestly in the wrong. ¹²His custom had been to eat with the Gentiles but, after certain friends of James arrived, he stopped doing this and kept away from them altogether, for fear of the group that insists Gentiles must convert to Judaism first. ¹³The other Jews joined him in this hypocrisy, and even Barnabas felt obliged to copy this behavior.

¹⁴When I saw they weren't respecting the true meaning of the Good News, I said to Peter in front of everyone, "You're a Jew, yet you live like a Gentile and not a Jew. So why do you want to make the Gentiles adopt Jewish ways? ¹⁵Though we're Jewish by nature and not Gentile 'sinners,' ¹⁶we know that people aren't justified by following the Law, but by believing in Jesus Christ. That is why we too have believed in Christ—so that we can be justified by faith in Christ, not by obeying the Law. No one will be justified by keeping the Law!"

¹⁷But if it becomes evident that we ourselves are sinners while we seek justification in Christ, does this imply that Christ has induced us to sin? Absolutely not! ¹⁸If I rebuild what I had destroyed, then I prove that I am in fact a destroyer!

¹⁹It was through the Law that I died to the Law, to live for God. ²⁰I have been crucified with Christ, and it's no longer I who live, but Christ who lives in me. I still live my own life, but it's a life of faith in Jesus our Savior, who loves me and who gave himself for me. ²¹I will not nullify God's grace—for if justification is available only through the Law, then Christ died needlessly.

3:1-14

*Y*ou foolish Galatians! Who has cast a spell over you, in spite of the clear and public portrayal you've had of the crucifixion of Jesus Christ? ²Let me ask one question: was it because you practiced the Law that you received the Holy Spirit, or because you believed what was preached to you? [3] Are you so foolish that, having begun by the Spirit, you would now try to finish through human effort? [4] Was everything you suffered in vain? If this is how you're ending up, it has all been in vain indeed! [5] Does God give you the Spirit so freely and work miracles among you because you practice the Law, or because you believe what was preached to you?

[6] Recall that Sarah and Abraham "believed God, and it was credited to them as righteousness." [7] Realize, then, that those who believe are the children of Sarah and Abraham. [8] Because scripture saw in advance that God would justify the Gentiles through faith, it foretold this Good News to Sarah and Abraham: "All nations will be blessed in you." [9] So then all who believe are blessed along with Sarah and Abraham, who believed first.

[10] All who depend on observances of the Law, on the other hand, are under a curse. Scripture says, "Everyone who doesn't abide by everything written in the book of the Law and carry it out is cursed." [11] It should be obvious that no one is justified in God's sight by the Law, for "the just will live by faith." [12] But the Law doesn't depend on faith—its terms are that "those who keep the Law will live because of it."

[13] Christ, however, has redeemed us from the Law's curse by becoming a curse for us, as scripture says: "Anyone who is hanged on a tree is cursed." [14] This happened so that the blessing bestowed on Sarah and Abraham might come to the Gentiles in Christ Jesus, thereby making it possible for us to receive the promised Spirit through faith.

3:15–4:11

Sisters and brothers, take an example from daily life: no one can annul or amend a human contract once it is ratified. [16] Consider the promises that were addressed to Sarah and Abraham and their offspring. The scripture doesn't use "to your offspring" in the sense of many descendants, but "to your offspring" in the sense of a single individual—Christ. [17] What I mean is this: the Law, which came four hundred and thirty years later, doesn't annul the Covenant previously established by God, or it would cancel the promise. [18] For if you receive something through a legal inheritance, it doesn't come from a promise—yet it's precisely as a promise that God gave the gift to Sarah and Abraham.

[19] Why, then, was the Law added? It was added to teach people right from wrong until the "descendant" to whom the promise had been made would come. The Law was promulgated by angels through a mediator. [20] Now,

there can be a mediator only when there are two parties, whereas God is only one. ²¹ Does this mean that the Law is opposed to the promises of God? Certainly not! On the other hand, we could have been justified by the Law only if it had the power to give life.

²² Scripture has locked everything under the constraint of sin. Why? So that the promise might be fulfilled in those who believe because of their faith in Jesus Christ.

²³ Before faith came, we were under the constraint of the Law, locked in until the faith that was coming would be revealed. ²⁴ In other words, the Law was our monitor until Christ came to bring about our justification through faith. ²⁵ But now that faith is here, we are no longer in the monitor's charge.

²⁶ Each one of you is a child of God because of your faith in Christ Jesus. ²⁷ All of you who have been baptized into Christ have clothed yourselves with Christ. ²⁸ In Christ there is no Jew or Greek, slave or citizen, male or female. All are one in Christ Jesus.

²⁹ Furthermore, if you belong to Christ, you're the offspring of Sarah and Abraham, which means you inherit all that was promised. 4:1 What I'm saying is that as long as the heir remains a child, it's no different from being a slave—even if the child owns everything—² since the child is under the supervision of guardians and trustees until the time set by the parents. ³ In the same way, before we came of age, we were enslaved to the elemental principles of the world. ⁴ When the designated time had come, God sent forth the Only Begotten—born of a woman, born under the Law—to deliver from the Law those who were subjected to it, ⁵ so that we might receive our status as adopted heirs. ⁶ The proof that you're children of God is the fact that God has sent forth into our hearts the Spirit of the Child who calls out "Abba!" ⁷ You're no longer slaves, but daughters and sons! And if you're daughters and sons, you're also heirs, by God's design.

⁸ Once you were ignorant of God and enslaved to "gods" who are not really gods at all. ⁹ Now that you've come to know God—or rather, now that God knows you—how can you turn back to weak and worthless elemental powers? Do you want to be enslaved by them all over again? ¹⁰ You and your special days and months and seasons and years! ¹¹ You make me feel I've wasted all my time with you!

4:12–5:12

I beg you, sisters and brothers, become like me—for I have become like you. You've never treated me so coolly before. ¹³ Call to mind that an illness originally gave me the opportunity to preach the Good News to you. ¹⁴ You never gave the slightest indication of being revolted or disgusted because of my disease, which was such a trial to you. Rather, you treated me as if I were a messenger from God—or even as if I were Christ Jesus. ¹⁵ Where has all that joy of yours gone? I swear that, had it been possible, you would have plucked out your eyes and given them to me! ¹⁶ Has my telling you the truth made me your enemy?

¹⁷ The blame lies in those people who feign interest in you—their interest is self-serving. They intend to isolate you from us, so that you will be zealous for them instead. ¹⁸ To be zealous is admirable, if it's for a good purpose. But it must be this way always, and not just when I am with you. ¹⁹ My dear children, I must go through the pangs of giving birth to you once more, until Christ is formed in you. ²⁰ How I wish I were with you now! How I wish I could change my tone! How I wish I weren't so perplexed about you!

²¹ I ask you, you who strive to be subject to the Law—do you understand what the Law asks of you? ²² For scripture says that Abraham had two children—one by Hagar, who was a slave, and the other by Sarah, who was freeborn. ²³ The child of the slave had been begotten in the course of nature, but the child of the free woman was the fruit of the promise. ²⁴ All this is clearly an allegory: the two women stand for the two Covenants. One is from Mt. Sinai, and she gave birth to children in slavery: this is Hagar. ²⁵ Hagar represents Mt. Sinai in Arabia—which corresponds to the present Jerusalem, which is in slavery like Hagar's children.

²⁶ But the Jerusalem on high is freeborn, and it's she who is our mother. ²⁷ That is why scripture says,

> "Rejoice, you who are infertile,
> who has borne no children;
> break into song,
> you stranger to the pains of childbirth!
> For there are more born of the forsaken one
> than born of the wedded wife!"

²⁸ Now you, sisters and brothers, are children of the promise, like Rebecca and Isaac. ²⁹ At that time, the child born because of the urge of the flesh persecuted the child born through the urge of the Spirit. It's the same way now. ³⁰ For scripture says, "Drive away the slave woman and her child, for the child born of the slave woman will not share in the inheritance with the free woman's child." ³¹ Therefore, my sisters and brothers, we are children not of a slave, but of a mother who is free.

5:1 When Christ freed us, we were meant to remain free. Stand firm, therefore, and don't submit to the yoke of slavery a second time! ² Pay close attention to me—Paul—when I tell you that if you let yourself be subjected to the Law, Christ will be of no use to you! ³I point out once more to all who subject themselves to even one part of the Law that they are bound to keep the Law in its entirety. ⁴Any of you who seek your justification in the Law have severed yourselves from Christ and fallen from God's favor.

⁵It is in the Spirit that we eagerly await the justification we hope for, and only faith can yield it. ⁶In Christ Jesus, neither adherence to the Law nor disregard of it counts for anything—only faith, which expresses itself through love.

⁷You were running a good race. Who cut you off and made you cautious about obeying the truth? ⁸This persuasion doesn't come from the One who called you. ⁹The yeast seems to be spreading through the whole batch of you. ¹⁰I'm confident in Our God that you will agree with me. I'm equally confident that whoever is upsetting you in this matter will receive the appropriate judgment.

¹¹As for me, if I were still preaching the need to fulfill the Law's requirements, then I wouldn't continue to be persecuted the way I am—and my preaching about the cross would not be the stumbling block that it is. ¹²And as for those who keep harrassing Gentile Christians to submit to the Law and become circumcised: may their knives slip!

my sisters and brothers, you were called to freedom; but be careful, or this freedom will provide an opening for self-indulgence. Rather, serve one another in works of love, ¹⁴since the whole of the Law is summarized in a single command: "Love your neighbor as yourself." ¹⁵If you go on snapping at one another and tearing each other to pieces, be careful, or you may end up destroying the whole community.

¹⁶Let me put it this way: if you're guided by the Spirit, you will be in no danger of yielding to self-indulgence. ¹⁷Since our flesh is at odds with the Spirit—and the Spirit with our flesh—the two are so opposed that you cannot do whatever you feel like doing. ¹⁸If you're guided by the Spirit, you're not under the Law.

¹⁹It's obvious what proceeds from the flesh: lewd conduct, impurity, licentiousness, ²⁰idolatry, sorcery, hostility, arguments, jealousy, outbursts of anger, selfish rivalries, dissensions, factions, ²¹envy, drunkenness, orgies and so forth. I warn you as I've warned you before: those who do these sorts of things won't inherit the kindom of God!

²²By contrast, the fruit of the Spirit is love, joy, peace, patient endurance,

kindness, generosity, faithfulness, ²³ gentleness and self-control. Against these sorts of things there is no law! ²⁴ Those who belong to Christ Jesus have crucified their ego, with its passions and desires. ²⁵ So since we live by the Spirit, let us follow her lead. ²⁶ We must stop being conceited, contentious and envious.

⁶·¹ Sisters and brothers, if one of you is caught in any sin, the more spiritual among you should correct the offender in a spirit of gentleness—remembering that you may be tempted yourselves. ² Bear one another's burdens, and thus fulfill the law of Christ.

³ But if you think you're important when you're not, you're deceiving yourself. ⁴ Examine your own work, each of you. If you find something to boast about, at least it's something of your own and not just empty comparison with your neighbor. ⁵ Carry your own load!

⁶ Those under instruction in the word should always contribute to the support of the instructor.

⁷ Don't be deceived—God cannot be cheated: where you sow, there you will reap. ⁸ If you sow in the field of self-indulgence, you will reap corruption. If you sow in the field of the Spirit, you will reap the harvest of eternal life. ⁹ Never grow tired of doing good. We will reap a harvest at the proper time—if we don't grow weary. ¹⁰ So, while we still have time, do good to all and especially to those of the household of faith.

¹¹ Look how big these letters are when I write to you in my own hand!

¹² Those who are pressuring the men among you to be circumcised are only trying to win favor with others, so they won't be persecuted for the cross of Christ. ¹³ They themselves are circumcised but don't even keep the Law. They want you to accept circumcision just so they can boast about it.

¹⁴ May I never boast of anything but the cross of our Savior Jesus Christ! Through it the world has been crucified to me and I to the world. ¹⁵ It means nothing whether one bothers with the externals of religion or not. All that matters is that one is created anew.

¹⁶ Peace and mercy on all who follow this rule of life and on the Israel of God. ¹⁷ Henceforth, let no one trouble me, for my body bears the marks of Jesus.

¹⁸ Sisters and brothers, may the grace of our Savior Jesus Christ be with your spirit. Amen.

the letter of paul to the
ephesians

1:1-23

from paul, an apostle of christ jesus by the will of God,

To the holy ones in Ephesus who are faithful in Christ Jesus:

[2] Grace and peace to you from God our Creator and from our Savior Jesus Christ.

[3] Praised be the Maker of our Savior Jesus Christ, who has bestowed on us in Christ every spiritual blessing in the heavens! [4] Before the world began, God chose us in Christ to be holy and blameless and to be full of love; [5] God likewise predestined us through Christ Jesus to be adopted children— such was God's pleasure and will—[6] that everyone might praise the glory of God's grace which was freely bestowed on us in God's beloved, Jesus Christ.

[7] It is in Christ and through the blood of Christ that we have been redeemed and our sins forgiven, so immeasurably generous is God's favor [8] given to us with perfect wisdom and understanding. [9] God has taken plea-

sure in revealing the mystery of the plan through Christ, ¹⁰to be carried out in the fullness of time; namely, to bring all things—in heaven and on earth—together in Christ.

¹¹In Christ we were willed an inheritance; for in the decree of God—and everything is administered according to the divine will and counsel—we were predestined ¹²to praise the glory of the Most High by being the first to hope in Christ. ¹³In Christ you too were chosen. When you heard the Good News of salvation, the word of truth, and believed in it, you were sealed with the promised Holy Spirit, ¹⁴who is the pledge of our inheritance, the deposit paid against the full redemption of a people who are God's own—to the praise of God's glory.

¹⁵From the time I first heard of your faith in Christ Jesus and your love for all of the holy ones, ¹⁶I have never stopped thanking God for you and remembering you in my prayers. ¹⁷I pray that the God of our Savior Jesus Christ, the God of glory, will give you a spirit of wisdom and of revelation, to bring you to a rich knowledge of the Creator.

¹⁸I pray that God will enlighten the eyes of your mind so that you can see the hope this call holds for you—the promised glories that God's holy ones will inherit, ¹⁹and the infinitely great power that is exercised for us who believe. You can tell this from the strength of God's power at work in Jesus, ²⁰the power used to raise Christ from the dead and to seat Christ in heaven at God's right hand, ²¹far above every sovereignty, authority, power or dominion, and above any other name that can be named—not only in this age, but also in the age to come. ²²God has put all things under Christ's feet and made Christ, as the ruler of everything, the head of the church, ²³and the church is Christ's body; it's the fullness of the One who fills all of creation.

Y

2:1–3:21

ou were dead because of your sins and offenses, ²which you commited in your allegiance both to the present age and to the ruler of the power of the air—that spirit who is even now at work among "the children of rebellion." ³And all of us were among them; we lived at the level of the flesh, following every whim of the flesh, every fancy of this age, and so by nature deserved God's wrath like the rest.

⁴But God, rich in mercy and loving us so much, ⁵brought us to life in Christ, even when we were dead in our sins. It is through this grace that we have been saved. ⁶God raised us up and, in union with Christ Jesus,

gave us a place in the heavenly realm, ⁷to display in ages to come how immense are the resources of God's grace and kindness in Christ Jesus. ⁸And it is by grace that you have been saved, through faith—and even that is not of yourselves, but the gift of God. ⁹Nor is it a reward for anything that you have done, so nobody can claim the credit. ¹⁰We are God's work of art, created in Christ Jesus to do the good things God created us to do from the beginning.

¹¹Bear in mind that at one time the men among you who were Gentiles physically—called "the Uncircumcised" by those who call themselves "the Circumcised," all because of a minor operation—¹²had no part in Christ and were excluded from the community of Israel. You were strangers to the Covenant and its promise; you were without hope and without God in the world.

¹³But now in Christ Jesus, you who once were far off have been brought near by the blood of Christ. ¹⁴For Christ is our peace, who made both groups into one and broke down the barrier of hostility that kept us apart. ¹⁵In his own flesh, Christ abolished the Law, with its commands and ordinances, in order to make the two into one new person, thus establishing peace ¹⁶and reconciling us all to God in one body through the cross, which put to death the enmity between us. ¹⁷Christ came and "announced the Good News of peace to you who were far away, and to those who were near"; ¹⁸for through Christ, we all have access in one Spirit to our God.

¹⁹This means that you are strangers and aliens no longer. No, you are included in God's holy people, and are members of the household of God, ²⁰which is built on the foundation of the apostles and the prophets, with Christ Jesus as the capstone. ²¹In Christ the whole building is joined together and rises to become a holy temple in Our God; ²²in Christ you are being built into this temple, to become a dwelling-place of God in the Spirit.

3:1For I, Paul—a prisoner of Christ Jesus for the sake of you Gentiles—²am sure that you have heard of God's grace, of which I was made a steward on your behalf; ³this mystery, as I have briefly described it, was given to me by revelation. ⁴When you read this, you can understand my insight into the mystery of Christ, ⁵which was unknown to the people of former ages, but is now revealed by the Spirit to the holy apostles and prophets. ⁶That mystery is that the Gentiles are heirs, as are we; members of the Body, as are we; and partakers of the promise of Jesus the Messiah through the Good News, as are we.

⁷I became a minister of the Good News by the gift of divine grace given me through the working of God's power. ⁸To me, the least of all believers,

was given the grace to preach to the Gentiles the unfathomable riches of Christ⁹and to enlighten all people on the mysterious design which for ages was hidden in God, the Creator of all.

¹⁰ Now, therefore, through the church, God's manifold wisdom is made known to the rulers and powers of heaven, ¹¹in accord with the age-old design, carried out in Christ Jesus our Savior, ¹²in whom we have boldness and confident access to God through our faith in Christ. ¹³So, I beg you, never be discouraged because of my sufferings for you. They are your glory.

¹⁴ That is why I kneel before Abba God, ¹⁵from whom every family in heaven and on earth takes its name. ¹⁶And I pray that God, out of the riches of divine glory, will strengthen you inwardly with power through the working of the Spirit. ¹⁷May Christ dwell in your hearts through faith, so that you, being rooted and grounded in love, ¹⁸will be able to grasp fully the breadth, length, height and depth of Christ's love and, with all God's holy ones, ¹⁹experience this love that surpasses all understanding, so that you may be filled with all the fullness of God. ²⁰To God—whose power now at work in us can do immeasurably more than we ask or imagine—²¹to God be glory in the Church and in Christ Jesus through all generations, world without end! Amen.

4:1–5:20

I plead with you, then, in the name of our Redeemer, to lead a life worthy of your calling. ²Treat one another charitably, in complete selflessness, gentleness and patience. ³Do all you can to preserve the unity of the Spirit through the peace that binds you together. ⁴There is one body and one Spirit—just as you were called into one hope when you were called. ⁵There is one Savior, one faith, one baptism, ⁶one God and Creator of all, who is over all, who works through all and is within all.

⁷Each of us has received God's grace in the measure in which Christ has bestowed it. ⁸Thus you find scripture saying,

> "You ascended on high,
>> leading captives in your train,
>> and giving gifts to people."

⁹"You ascended"—what does this mean but that Christ first descended into the lower regions of the earth? ¹⁰The One who descended is the very One who ascended high above the heavens in order to fill the whole universe.

¹¹ And to some, the gift they were given is that they should be apostles; to some, prophets; to some, evangelists; to some, pastors and teachers. ¹² These gifts were given to equip fully the holy ones for the work of service, and to build up the body of Christ— ¹³ until we all attain unity in our faith and in our knowledge of the Only Begotten of God, until we become mature, attaining to the whole measure of the fullness of Christ.

¹⁴ Let us then be children no longer, tossed here and there, carried about by every wind of doctrine, or by human trickery or crafty, deceitful schemes. ¹⁵ Rather, let us speak the truth in love, and grow to the full maturity of Christ, the head. ¹⁶ Through Christ, the whole body grows. With the proper functioning of each member, firmly joined together by each supporting ligament, the body builds itself up in love.

¹⁷ So I declare and testify together with Christ that you must stop living the kind of life the world lives. Their minds are empty, ¹⁸ they have no understanding, they are alienated from the life of God—all because they have hardened their hearts. ¹⁹ They've dulled their sense of right and wrong, for they have abandoned themselves to sensuality in order to indulge in every form of licentiousness and greed.

²⁰ That is hardly the way you have learned from Christ, ²¹ unless you failed to hear properly, when you were taught what the truth is in Jesus. ²² You must give up your old way of life; you must put aside your old self, which is being corrupted by following illusory desires. ²³ Your mind must be renewed by a spiritual revolution, ²⁴ so that you can put on the new self that has been created in God's likeness, in the justice and holiness of the truth.

²⁵ Therefore, let's have no more lies. Speak truthfully to each other, for we are all members of one body.

²⁶ When you get angry, don't let it become a sin. Don't let the sun set on your anger, ²⁷ or you will give an opening to the Devil.

²⁸ You who have been stealing, stop stealing. Go to work. Do something useful with your hands, so you can have something to share with the needy.

²⁹ Be on your guard against foul talk. Say only what will build others up at that moment. Say only what will give grace to your listeners.

³⁰ Don't grieve the Holy Spirit of God, with whom you were sealed for the day of redemption. ³¹ Get rid of all bitterness, all rage and anger, all harsh words, slander and malice of every kind. ³² In place of these, be kind to one another, compassionate and mutually forgiving, just as God has forgiven you in Christ.

^{5:1} Try, then, to imitate God as beloved children. ² Walk in love as Christ

loved us, and offered himself in sacrifice to God for us, a gift of pleasing fragrance.

³ As for lewd conduct or promiscuousness or lust of any sort, let these things not even be mentioned among you, as befitting God's holy people. ⁴ Nor should there be any obscene, silly or suggestive talk; all that is out of place. Instead, give thanks. ⁵ Make no mistake about this: no promiscuous, unclean or lustful person—in effect an idolator—has any inheritance in the kindom of Christ and of God. ⁶ Let no one deceive you with worthless arguments: these are sins that bring God's wrath down on the disobedient; ⁷ therefore, have nothing to do with them. ⁸ There was a time when you were darkness, but now you are light in Christ. Live as children of the light.

⁹ Light produces every kind of goodness, justice and truth. ¹⁰ Be correct in your judgment of what pleases our Savior. ¹¹ Take no part in deeds done in darkness, which bear no fruit; rather, expose them. ¹² It's shameful even to mention the things these people do in secret; ¹³ but when such deeds are exposed and seen in the light of day, everything that becomes visible is light. ¹⁴ That's why we read,

> "Awake, O sleeper, arise from the dead,
>   and Christ will give you light."

¹⁵ Keep careful watch over your conduct. Don't act like fools, but like wise and thoughtful people. ¹⁶ Make the most of your time, for these are evil days. ¹⁷ Don't continue in ignorance, but try to discern the will of God. ¹⁸ Avoid getting drunk on wine—that is debauchery! Instead be filled with the Spirit, ¹⁹ meditating on psalms and hymns and spiritual songs, singing and making music to God in your hearts. ²⁰ Always give thanks to Abba God for everything, in the name of Jesus our Messiah.

5:21–6:9

Ⲇefer to one another out of reverence for Christ. ²² Those of you who are in committed relationships should yield to each other as if to Christ, ²³ because you are inseparable from each other, just as Christ is inseparable from the body—the church—as well as being its Savior. ²⁴ As the church yields to Christ, so you should yield to your partner in everything.

²⁵ Love one another as Christ loved the church. He gave himself up for it ²⁶ to make it holy, purifying it by washing it with the Gospel's message, ²⁷ so that Christ might have a glorious church, holy and immaculate, without mark or blemish or anything of that sort. ²⁸ Love one another as you love your own bodies. Those who love their partners love themselves.

²⁹ No one ever hates one's own flesh; one nourishes it and takes care of it as Christ cares for the church—³⁰ for we are members of Christ's body.

> ³¹ "This is why one person leaves home
> and clings to another,
> and the two become one flesh."

³² This is a great foreshadowing; I mean, it refers to Christ and the church. ³³ In any case, each of you should love your partner as yourself, with each showing respect for the other.

6:1 Children, obey your parents in Christ, for that is right. ² "Honor your mother and your father" is the first commandment to carry a promise with it: ³ "that it may go well with you, and that you may have long life on earth." ⁴ Mothers and fathers, don't anger your children. Bring them up with the training and instruction befitting Christ.

⁵ Workers, work diligently and support one another with the respect and sincere loyalty that you owe to Christ. ⁶ Don't render service just for appearance's sake, or only to please others, but do God's will with your whole heart as Christ's own workers. ⁷ Give your service willingly, doing it for Christ rather than for mortals. ⁸ You know that everyone, whether on the bottom rung or on the top, will be repaid by God for whatever they do. ⁹ When you are in a position of authority, act responsibly toward those in your charge. Stop threatening them. Remember that we all have a greater Authority over us in heaven who plays no favorites.

f

6:10-24

inally, draw your strength from Christ and from the strength of that mighty power. ¹¹ Put on the full armor of God so that you can stand firm against the tactics of the Devil. ¹² Our battle ultimately is not against human forces, but against the sovereignties and powers, the rulers of the world of darkness, and the evil spirits of the heavenly realms. ¹³ You must put on the armor of God if you are to resist on the evil day and, having done everything you can, to hold your ground. ¹⁴ Stand fast then, with truth as the belt around your waist, justice as your breastplate, ¹⁵ and zeal to spread the Good News of peace as your footgear. ¹⁶ In all circumstances, hold faith up before you as your shield; it will help you extinguish the fiery darts of the Evil One. ¹⁷ Put on the helmet of salvation, and carry the sword of the Spirit, which is the word of God.

¹⁸ Always pray in the Spirit, with all your prayers and petitions. Pray constantly and attentively for all God's holy people. ¹⁹ Pray also for me, that God will open my mouth and put words on my lips, that I may boldly make

known the mystery of the Good News—that mystery [20] for which I am an ambassador in chains. Pray that I may have courage to proclaim it as I ought.

[21] I would like you to have news of me and of what I am doing. My dear co-worker, Tychicus, a loyal minister in Christ, will tell you everything. [22] I am sending him to you precisely for this purpose—to reassure you and give you news of us.

[23] May God our Creator and our Savior Jesus Christ bring peace, love and faith to all our sisters and brothers. [24] May grace and eternal life be with all who love our Savior Jesus Christ.

the letter of paul to the

philippians

From paul and timothy, who serve christ
Jesus,

To all the holy ones in Christ Jesus at Philippi, together with their bishops
and deacons:

²Grace and peace be yours from our Abba God and from Jesus Christ, our
Savior.

³I thank my God every time I think of you. ⁴In every prayer I utter, as I
plead on your behalf, I rejoice ⁵at the way you have all continually helped
promote the Good News from the very first day. ⁶And I am sure of this
much: that God, who has begun the good work in you, will carry it through
to completion, right up to the day of Christ Jesus. ⁷It's only right that I
should entertain such expectations about you, since I hold all of you dear—
you who are all partakers of grace with me, even when I lie in prison or am
summoned to defend the solid ground on which the Good News rests.

⁸God knows how much I long for each of you with all the affection of

Christ Jesus! ⁹ My prayer is that your love may abound more and more, both in understanding and in wealth of experience, ¹⁰ so that with a clear conscience and blameless conduct you may learn to value the things that really matter, up to the very day of Christ. ¹¹ It's my wish that you be found rich in the harvest of justice which Jesus Christ has ripened in you, to the glory and praise of God.

1:12–2:18

I'm glad to announce to you, sisters and brothers, that what has happened to me has actually served to advance the Good News. ¹³ Consequently it has become clear throughout the Praetorium and everywhere else that I am in chains for Christ. ¹⁴ Because of my chains, most of our sisters and brothers in Christ have been encouraged to speak the word of God more fearlessly.

¹⁵ It's true that some preach Christ out of envy and rivalry, but others do so with the right intention. ¹⁶ These latter act out of love, aware that I am here in the defense of the Good News. ¹⁷ The others, who proclaim Christ for selfish or jealous motives, don't care if they make my chains heavier to bear.

¹⁸ All that matters is that in any and every way, whether from specious or genuine motives, Christ is being proclaimed! That is what brings me joy. ¹⁹ Indeed, I will continue to rejoice in the conviction that this will result in my salvation, thanks to your prayers and the support I receive from the Spirit of Jesus Christ. ²⁰ I firmly trust and anticipate that I will never be put to shame for my hopes; I have full confidence that, now as always, Christ will be exalted through me, whether I live or die.

²¹ For to me, "life" means Christ; hence, dying is only so much gain. ²² If, on the other hand, I am to continue living on earth, that means productive toil for me—and I honestly don't know which I prefer. ²³ I'm strongly attracted to both: I long to be freed from this life and to be with Christ, for that is the far better thing; ²⁴ yet it's more urgent that I remain alive for your sakes. ²⁵ This fills me with the confidence that I will stay with you and persevere with you all, for the sake of your joy and your progress in the faith. ²⁶ My being with you once again should make you even prouder of me in Christ.

²⁷ Conduct yourselves, then, in a way worthy of the Gospel of Christ. If you do, whether I come and see you myself or hear about your behavior from a distance, it will be clear that you're standing firm in unity of spirit,

and exerting yourselves with one accord for the faith of the Gospel, ²⁸ without being intimidated by your enemies. Standing together without fear is an indication that they will be destroyed and you will be saved. It's a divine signal that God— ²⁹ on behalf of our Savior—has given you the privilege of believing in and suffering for Christ. ³⁰ You're now experiencing the same struggle that you saw in me—and now hear that I still have.

2·¹ If our life in Christ means anything to you—if love, or the Spirit that we have in common, or any tenderness or sympathy can persuade you at all— ² then be united in your convictions and united in your love, with a common purpose and a common mind. That is the one thing that would make me completely happy. ³ There must be no competition among you, no conceit, but everybody is to be humble: value others over yourselves, ⁴ each of you thinking of the interests of others before your own. ⁵ Your attitude must be the same as that of Christ Jesus:

> ⁶ Christ, though in the image of God,
> > didn't deem equality with God
> > something to be clung to—
> ⁷ but instead became completely empty
> > and took on the image of oppressed humankind:
> born into the human condition,
> > found in the likeness of a human being.
> ⁸ Jesus was thus humbled—
> > obediently accepting death, even death on a cross!
> ⁹ Because of this, God highly exalted Christ
> > and gave to Jesus the name above every other name,
> ¹⁰ so that at the name of Jesus every knee must bend
> > in the heavens, on the earth and under the earth,
> ¹¹ and every tongue proclaim to the glory of God:
> > Jesus Christ reigns supreme!

¹² Therefore, my dear friends, you who are always obedient to my urging, work out your salvation with fear and trembling, not only when I happen to be with you, but all the more now that I'm absent. ¹³ It is God at work in you that creates the desire to do God's will.

¹⁴ In everything you do, act without grumbling or arguing; ¹⁵ prove yourselves innocent and straightforward, children of God beyond reproach, in the midst of a twisted and depraved generation—among which you shine like stars in the sky, ¹⁶ while holding fast to the word of life. As I look to the day of Christ, you give me cause to boast, proving that I didn't run the race in vain or work to no purpose. ¹⁷ Even if my life is to be poured out like a libation upon the sacrificial offering of your faith, I'm glad of it and rejoice

with all of you. ¹⁸ May you be glad for the same reason, and rejoice with me!

I hope in our Savior Jesus to send Timothy to you soon. And I will be cheered when I hear news of you. ²⁰ I have no one else here like him, and he's genuinely concerned about you. ²¹ All the others seem more interested in their own welfare than in Christ Jesus. ²² But you know how Timothy proved himself—as a child helping a parent—by working with me to further the Good News. ²³ So I intend to send him as soon as I see how things go with me. ²⁴ And I am confident in Christ that I, too, will be coming soon.

²⁵ I feel I need to send back to you Epaphroditus—brother, co-worker, spiritual warrior—who is also your messenger to me, the one you sent to be my companion in work and in battle. ²⁶ But he misses you all and was distressed when he learned that you had heard of his illness. ²⁷ Yes, he was sick; he almost died. But God had mercy on him—and on me as well, so that I wouldn't have one grief on top of another. ²⁸ I'll be sending him back as soon as I can. I know you'll be happy to see him again, and that will make me less worried about you. ²⁹ Welcome him heartily in Christ—people like him should be held in the highest regard. ³⁰ Know that he came so close to death in doing the work of Christ. He risked his life to give me the help that you were unable to provide.

3:1 Finally, my sisters and brothers, rejoice in Christ. To write the same things again is no burden for me, but I do it for your safety.

² Beware of the dogs! Beware of the trouble-makers! Beware of the mutilators, who insist that Gentile Christians must become circumcised! ³ We are the true circumcision—we are ourselves the sign of the Covenant—each and every one of us who worships in the Spirit of God and glories in Christ Jesus, rather than trusts in external signs.

⁴ Yet I can be confident even there! If they think they have the right to put their trust in external evidence, I have even more right! ⁵ I was circumcised on the eighth day, being of the stock of Israel and the tribe of Benjamin, a Hebrew of Hebrew origins; in legal observance I was a Pharisee, ⁶ and so zealous that I persecuted the church. I was above reproach when it came to justice based on the Law.

⁷ But those things I used to consider gain, I now count as loss for the sake of Christ. ⁸ What is more, I consider everything a loss in light of the surpassing knowledge of my Savior Jesus Christ, for whose sake I have for-

feited everything. I count everything else as garbage, so that Christ may be my wealth—⁹indeed, that I may be found in Christ, not having any justice of my own based on observance of the Law. The justice I possess is that which comes through faith in Christ. It has its origin in God and is based on faith. ¹⁰All I want is to know Christ, and the power of the resurrection, and how to share in Christ's sufferings by being formed into the pattern of Jesus' death—¹¹perhaps even to arrive at the resurrection from the dead.

¹²It's not that I have reached it yet, or have already finished my course; but I'm running the race in order to grab hold of the prize if possible, since Christ Jesus has grabbed hold of me. ¹³Sisters and brothers, I don't think of myself as having reached the finish line. I give no thought to what lies behind, but I push on to what is ahead. ¹⁴My entire attention is on the finish line as I run toward the prize—the high calling of God in Christ Jesus.

¹⁵We who are mature should adopt this attitude. And if you have a different opinion on any matter, God will make that clear to you as well. ¹⁶Just resolve to live up to what we have already attained.

3:17–4:23

Join in following my example, my sisters and brothers. Take as your guide those who follow the example that we set. ¹⁸Unfortunately, many go about in a way which shows them to be enemies of the cross of Christ. I have often said this to you before; this time I say it with tears: ¹⁹their end is destruction, their god is their belly, and their glory is in their shame. I'm talking about those whose minds are set on the things of this world.

²⁰But we have our citizenship in heaven; it's from there that we eagerly await the coming of our Savior Jesus Christ, ²¹who will give a new form to this lowly body of ours and remake it according to the pattern of the glorified body, by Christ's power to bring everything under subjection.

4:1 For these reasons, my sisters and brothers—you whom I so love and long for, you who are my joy and my crown—continue, my dear ones, to stand firm in Christ Jesus.

²I implore Euodia and Syntyche to come to an agreement with each other in Christ. ³And I ask you, Syzygus, to be a true comrade and help these co-workers. These two women struggled at my side in defending the Good News, along with Clement and the others who worked with me. Their names are written in the Book of Life.

⁴Rejoice in the Savior always! I say it again: Rejoice! ⁵Let everyone see your forbearing spirit. Our Savior is near. ⁶Dismiss all anxiety from your

minds; instead, present your needs to God through prayer and petition, giving thanks for all circumstances. [7] Then God's own peace, which is beyond all understanding, will stand guard over your hearts and minds in Christ Jesus.

[8] Finally, my sisters and brothers, your thoughts should be wholly directed to all that is true, all that deserves respect, all that is honest, pure, decent, admirable, virtuous or worthy of praise. [9] Live according to what you have learned and accepted, what you have heard me say and seen me do. Then will the God of peace be with you.

[10] It gave me great joy in Our God that your concern for me bore fruit once more. You had been concerned all along, of course, but lacked the opportunity to show it. [11] I don't say this because I am in need, for whatever the situation I find myself in, I have learned to be self-sufficient. [12] I know what it is to be brought low, and I know what it is to have plenty. I have learned the secret: whether on a full stomach or an empty one, in poverty or plenty, [13] I can do all things through the One who gives me strength.

[14] Still, it was kind of you to want to share in my hardships. [15] You yourselves know, my dear Philippians, that at the start of my evangelizing, when I left Macedonia, not a single congregation except yours shared with me by giving me something for what it had received. [16] Even when I was at Thessalonica, you sent something for my needs, not once but twice. [17] It's not that I am eager for the gift; rather, my concern is for the ever-growing balance in your account. [18] Here's my receipt—it says I've been fully paid, and more. I am well supplied because of what I received from you through Epaphroditus—a fragrant offering—a sacrifice acceptable and pleasing to God.

[19] In return, Our God will fulfill all your needs in Christ Jesus, as lavishly as only God can. [20] All glory to Our God and Creator for unending ages! Amen.

[21] Give my greetings to all the holy ones in Christ Jesus. The sisters and brothers who are with me send their greetings. [22] All the holy ones send their greetings, especially those who belong to Caesar's household.

[23] The grace of our Savior Jesus Christ be with your spirit.

the Letter of paul to the
colossians

1:1-20

from paul, an apostle of christ jesus by
the will of God, and our brother Timothy,

[2] To the holy and faithful sisters and brothers in Christ at Colossae:

Grace and peace to you from our Loving God.

[3] We always give thanks to the Abba God of our Savior Jesus Christ whenever we pray for you, [4] ever since we heard about your faith in Christ Jesus
and the love you show toward all the holy ones, [5] because of the hope stored
up for you in heaven. It is only recently that you heard of this, when it was
announced in the message of the truth. The Good News [6] which has reached
you is spreading all over the world; it is producing the same fruit there as
it did among you, ever since you heard about God's grace and understood
what it really is. [7] Epaphras, who taught you, is one of our closest co-workers and a faithful laborer of Christ on our behalf, [8] and it was he who told
us all about your love in the Spirit.

[9] Therefore, since the day we heard about you, we've been praying for

you unceasingly and asking that you attain the full knowledge of God's will, in perfect wisdom and spiritual understanding. [10] Then you'll lead a life worthy and pleasing to Our God in every way. You'll multiply good works of every sort and grow in the knowledge of God. [11] And by the might of God's glory you'll be endowed with the strength needed to stand fast and endure joyfully whatever may happen.

[12] Thanks be to God for having made you worthy to share in the inheritance of the holy ones in light! [13] God rescued us from the authority of darkness and brought us into the reign of Jesus, God's Only Begotten. [14] And it is through Jesus that we have redemption, the forgiveness of sins.

℺   ℺   ℺

[15] Christ is the image of the unseen God
　　and the firstborn of all creation,
[16] for in Christ were created
　　all things in heaven and on earth:
everything visible and invisible,
　　Thrones, Dominations, Sovereignties, Powers—
　　all things were created through Christ and for Christ.
[17] Before anything was created, Christ existed,
　　and all things hold together in Christ.
[18] The church is the body;
　　Christ is its head.
Christ is the Beginning,
　　the firstborn from the dead,
　　and so Christ is first in every way.
[19] God wanted all perfection to be found in Christ,
　　[20] and all things to be reconciled to God through Christ—
　　everything in heaven and everything on earth—
when Christ made peace
　　by dying on the cross.

1:21–2:8

At one time, you were alienated from God by the way you thought and the evil things you did. [22] But now you are reconciled in Christ's mortal body through death, so that you can now stand before God holy, pure and blameless—[23] provided you persevere and stand firm on the solid base of your faith. Never let yourselves drift away from the hope promised by the

Good News that you have heard, which even now is being preached to the whole human race, and for which I, Paul, was made a minister.

²⁴ Even now I find my joy in the suffering I endure for you. In my own body I fill up what is lacking in the sufferings of Jesus, for the sake of Christ's body, the church. ²⁵ I became a minister of this church through the commission God gave me, to preach among you the word in its fullness— ²⁶ that mystery hidden from ages and generations past, but now revealed to God's holy ones. ²⁷ God's will was to make known to them the priceless glory which this mystery brings to the nations—the mystery of Christ in you, the hope of glory. ²⁸ This is the Christ we proclaim while we admonish everyone and teach them in the full measure of wisdom, hoping to make everyone complete in our Savior. ²⁹ For this I work and struggle, impelled by Christ's own working, which is so powerful a force in me.

2:1 I want you to know how hard I am struggling for you and for the Laodiceans, and for the many others who have never seen me personally. ²I work so that their hearts will be strengthened, so that they will be knit together in love, enriched with full assurance by their knowledge of the mystery of God—namely Christ—³in whom every treasure of wisdom and knowledge is hidden.

⁴I say this so that no one deceives you with persuasive arguments. ⁵I may be absent in body, but I'm with you in spirit. I rejoice in seeing your good discipline and your firm faith in Christ.

⁶Since you have received Christ Jesus, live your whole life in our Savior. ⁷Send your roots deep and grow strong in Christ—firmly established in the faith you've been taught, and full of thanksgiving. ⁸Make sure that no one traps you and deprives you of your freedom by some secondhand, empty and deceptive philosophy that is based on the principles of the world instead of Christ.

2:9–3:17

In Christ the fullness of divinity lives in bodily form, ¹⁰and in Christ you find your own fulfillment—in the One who is the head of every Sovereignty and Power. ¹¹In Christ you have been given the Covenant through a transformation performed not by human hands, but by the complete stripping away of your body of flesh. This is what "circumcision" in Christ means. ¹²In baptism you were not only buried with Christ but also raised to life, because you believed in the power of God who raised Christ from the dead. ¹³And though you were dead in sin and did not have the Covenant, God gave you new life in company with Christ, pardoning all our sins. ¹⁴God has canceled the massive debt that stood against us with all its hostile claims, taking it out of the way and nailing it to the cross. ¹⁵ In this way God disarmed the Principalities and the Powers, and made a public display of them after having triumphed over them at the cross.

¹⁶ From now on, don't let anyone pass judgment on you because of what you eat or drink, or whether you observe festivals, new moons or Sabbaths. ¹⁷ These are mere shadows of the reality that is to come; the substance is Christ. ¹⁸ Don't let those who worship angels and enjoy self-abasement judge you. These people go into great detail about their visions, and their worldly minds keep puffing up their already inflated egos. ¹⁹ These people are cut off from the head that, with the ligaments and sinews, holds the whole body together, in order to attain its fullness of being in God.

²⁰ So if, in Christ, you've really died to the elemental principles of this world, why do you let regulations dictate to you, as though you were still living in the world? ²¹ "Don't handle this!" "Don't taste that!" "Don't touch those!" ²² These prohibitions concern things that perish with use. They are concerned with human values and regulations. ²³ These values and rules— through self-abasement, self-imposed religious practices and false humility—give the impression of true wisdom, but they have no value in restraining licentiousness.

ଔ   ଔ   ଔ

3:1 Since you've been resurrected with Christ, set your heart on what pertains to higher realms, where Christ is seated at God's right hand. ² Let your thoughts be on heavenly things, not on the things of earth. ³ After all, you died, and now your life is hidden with Christ in God. ⁴ But when Christ—who is your life—is revealed, you too will be revealed with Christ in glory.

⁵ So put to death everything in you that belongs to your old nature: promiscuity, impurity, guilty passion, evil desires and especially greed, which is the same thing as idolatry. ⁶ These are the sins which provoke God's wrath. ⁷ Your own conduct was once like this, when these things were your very life. ⁸ But now you must rid yourselves of them all: anger, rage, malice, slander and abusive language. ⁹ Stop lying to one another.

What you have done is put aside your old self with its past deeds ¹⁰ and put on a new self, one that grows in knowledge as it is formed anew in the image of its Creator. ¹¹ And in that image, there is no Greek or Hebrew; no Jew or Gentile; no barbarian or Scythian; no slave or citizen. There is only Christ, who is all in all.

¹² Because you are God's chosen ones, holy and beloved, clothe your-

selves with heartfelt compassion, with kindness, humility, gentleness and patience. ¹³ Bear with one another; forgive whatever grievances you have against one another—forgive in the same way God has forgiven you. ¹⁴ Above all else, put on love, which binds the rest together and makes them perfect.

¹⁵ Let Christ's peace reign in your hearts since, as members of one body, you have been called to that peace. Dedicate yourselves to thankfulness. ¹⁶ Let the Word of Christ, rich as it is, dwell in you. Instruct and admonish one another wisely. Sing gratefully to God from your hearts in psalms, hymns and songs of the Spirit. ¹⁷ And whatever you do, whether in speech or in action, do it in the name of Jesus our Savior, giving thanks to God through Christ.

3:18–4:6

*Y*ou who are in committed relationships, be submissive to each other. This is your duty in Christ Jesus. ¹⁹ Partners joined by God, love each other. Avoid any bitterness between you. ²⁰ Children, obey those responsible for you in everything, for this is what pleases God the most. ²¹ And if you are responsible for children, don't nag them, lest they lose heart.

²² Workers, work diligently in everything you do—not only to win favor, but wholeheartedly and reverently, out of respect for Christ. ²³ Do whatever you do from the heart. You are working for Christ, not for people. ²⁴ You know you'll be rewarded by God with an inheritance. You serve our Savior Jesus Christ. ²⁵ Anyone who does wrong will be paid in kind, without partiality. 4:1 When you are in a position of authority, treat your people with justice and fairness. We all have an Authority over us in heaven.

² Devote yourself to prayer and thanksgiving, but keep alert as well. ³ Pray for us, too, that God will open a door for proclaiming the mystery of Christ, for which I am in prison. ⁴ Pray that I may proclaim it as clearly as I should. ⁵ Be wise in your ways toward non-Christians. Make the most of every opportunity you have with them. ⁶ Talk to them tactfully, seasoned with salt as it were, and know how to respond to the needs of each one.

4:7-18

*t*ychicus will tell you all the news about me. He is a beloved brother, a loyal co-worker and companion in the service of Christ. ⁸ I send him to you for the express purpose of reassuring you with news about us—and to encourage your hearts. ⁹ Onesimus, who is one with you and a faithful and dear brother to me, will be accompanying Tychicus. They will tell you everything that is happening here.

¹⁰ Aristarchus, who is here in prison with me, sends greetings, as does Barnabas' cousin Mark, about whom you have received these instructions: if he comes to you, greet him warmly. ¹¹ Joshua, who is called Justus, sends greetings as well. Of those working with me for God's kindom, these three are the only Jewish believers. They are a great comfort to me. ¹² Epaphras, who is one of your number and who serves Jesus Christ, sends greetings. He never stops laboring in prayer for you, so that you'll stand firm and hold securely to the will of God. ¹³ I can speak for him that he works hard for you and for those at Laodicea and Hierapolis. ¹⁴ My dear friend Luke, the doctor, sends greetings, as does Demas.

¹⁵ Pass on my greetings to the sisters and brothers at Laodicea, to Nympha and to the church in her house. ¹⁶ After this letter has been read among you, send it to be read in the church of the Laodiceans, and get the letter I'm sending to Laodicea and read it to your church. ¹⁷ Tell Archippus, "See to it that you carry out the work that Our God wants you to do."

¹⁸ I, Paul, write this greeting in my own hand. Remember my chains. Grace be with you.

the first letter of paul to the

thessalonians

1:1-10

from paul, silas and timothy,

To the people of the church in Thessalonica, who belong to Abba God and our Savior Jesus Christ:

May grace and peace be yours.

[2] We always thank God for all of you and remember you in our prayers. [3] We call to mind before our God and Creator how you are proving your faith by your actions, laboring in love, and showing constancy of hope in our Savior Jesus Christ.

[4] We know, sisters and brothers beloved of God, that you have been chosen. [5] Our preaching of the Gospel was not a mere matter of words. It was done in the power of the Holy Spirit and with complete conviction. You know very well the sort of life we led when we were with you, which was for your sake.

[6] You, in turn, followed the example set by us and by Jesus—receiving

the word, despite great trials, with the joy that comes from the Holy Spirit. [7] In this way, you've become a model for all the believers in Macedonia and Achaia.

[8] The word of Christ has been resounding from you—and not only in Macedonia and Achaia: the news of your faith in God is celebrated everywhere, which makes it unnecessary for us to say anything more. [9] They themselves report to us what kind of reception we had among you, how you turned from idols to God, to be faithful witnesses of the living and true God, [10] and to await the appearance from heaven of Jesus, the Only Begotten, whom God raised from the dead and who will deliver us from the wrath to come.

2:1–3:8

And you yourselves know, sisters and brothers, that our coming among you was not without effect. [2] We had, as you know, been given rough treatment at Phillipi, and it was our God who gave us the courage to proclaim the Good News to you in the face of stiff opposition. [3] We don't preach because of impure motives or deceit or any sort of trickery; [4] rather, it was God who decided that we are fit to be entrusted with the Good News, and when we are speaking, we're trying to please not mortals, but God, who can read our inmost thoughts.

[5] You know very well—and we can swear it before God—that never at any time has our speech been simple flattery or a cover for trying to get money; [6] nor have we ever looked for any special honor from you or from anyone else—even though we could have imposed ourselves on you as apostles of Christ. [7] On the contrary, while we were with you we were as gentle as any nursing mother caring for her little ones. [8] So well disposed were we toward you, in fact, that we were willing to share with you not only the Good News, but our very lives as well—you had become that dear to us.

[9] Let us remind you, sisters and brothers, of our toil and hardship; we worked night and day in order not to be a burden to anyone while we preached the Good News of God to you. [10] You are witnesses, and so is God, that our treatment of you since you have become believers has been just, upright and impeccable. [11] You likewise know how we treated every one of you, as parents do their children—encouraging, comforting and urging you [12] to live lives worthy of God, who calls you into glory and the kindom. [13] And we constantly thank God for the way you received the words we

preached to you, not as our word but as the word of God, which it really was. And it changed your lives when you believed it.

[14] For you, sisters and brothers, have become imitators of the churches of God in Christ Jesus that are in Judea. You suffered the same things from your own compatriots as they, in turn, did from the Judeans—[15] who killed our Savior Jesus and the prophets, and drove us out of the country. They don't please God and are hostile to everyone else, [16] because they hinder us from preaching to the Gentiles—which fills the measuring cup of their sins to overflowing. But the wrath of God has finally started to overtake them.

[17] However, sisters and brothers, soon after we were separated from you—in body but never in heart—we were all the more desirous of seeing you face to face. [18] We wanted to come to you—I, Paul, tried more than once—but Satan prevented it. [19] For what is our hope, or joy, or the crown in which we glory in our Savior Jesus at the Coming? It's you: [20] you are our glory and joy.

3:[1] When we could bear it no longer, we decided to be left behind in Athens, [2] and instead sent Timothy, our companion and God's co-worker in spreading the Good News of Christ. His assignment was to encourage you and keep you strong in your faith, [3] so that none of you would become unsettled by the present troubles. You knew very well that we were destined to encounter them; [4] even when we were with you, we warned you to expect persecution. And that is exactly what you've found. [5] I couldn't stand it any more, so I sent someone to check on your faith; I was afraid the Tempter might have tried to test you, and our efforts might have been in vain.

[6] Now Timothy is back from visiting you, and he has told us good things about your faith and love, that you have fond memories of us and want to see us just as much as we want to see you. [7] We have been much consoled by your faith throughout our distress and persecution—[8] so much so that we will continue to flourish only if you stand firm in our Savior.

how can we thank God enough for you, for all the joy we feel before God on your account? [10] We earnestly pray night and day to be able to see you again and make up for any shortcomings in your faith. [11] May our loving Abba God and Jesus, our Savior, direct our steps back to you. [12] May Christ increase to overflowing your love for one another and for all people, even as our love does for you; [13] may Christ strengthen your hearts, making them blameless and holy before our Abba God at the coming of our Savior Jesus with all the holy ones.

4:1 Now, my sisters and brothers, we urge you and appeal to you in our Savior Jesus, to make more and more progress in the kind of life that you are meant to live—the life that God wants, as you learned from us, and as you are already living it. 2 You haven't forgotten the instructions we gave you by the authority of our Savior Jesus. 3 What God wants is for you all to be holy. God wants each of you to keep away from sexual immorality 4 and learn to control your own body in a manner that is holy and honorable, 5 and not be mired in passionate lust like the Gentiles who do not know God; 6 and in this matter no one should wrong their neighbors or take advantage of them. The Almighty will punish us for all such sins, as we have already told you and warned you. 7 God calls us not to immorality but to holiness. 8 Therefore, whoever rejects these instructions rejects not mortals but God, who gives you the Holy Spirit.

9 As regards love for other believers, there is no need for me to write you. God already has taught you to love one another, 10 and this you are doing toward all the sisters and brothers throughout Macedonia. Yet we exhort you to even greater progress. 11 Make it a point of honor to lead a quiet life and attend to your own affairs. Work with your hands as we directed you to do, 12 so that you'll be a good example to outsiders and not be dependent on anybody.

4:13–5:11

Sisters and brothers, we want you to be clear about those who sleep in death; otherwise you might yield to grief and lose all hope. 14 For if we believe that Jesus died and rose again, in the same way God will bring with Jesus all who have fallen asleep believing in Jesus. 15 We are speaking to you now just as if Jesus were speaking to you: we who live, who survive until Jesus returns, will have no advantage over those who have fallen asleep. 16 No, Jesus will personally come down from heaven with a shout, at the sound of the archangel's voice and the trumpet of God, and those who have died in Christ will rise first. 17 Then we the living, the survivors, will be caught up with them in the clouds to meet Jesus in the air— and thenceforth we will be with Jesus unceasingly. 18 Therefore console one another with these words.

5:1 But as to specific times and eras, sisters and brothers, you don't need me to tell you anything— 2 you know very well that the Day of God is coming like a thief in the night. 3 Just when people are saying, "At last we have peace and security," then destruction will fall on them with the suddenness of labor pains, and there will be no escape.

⁴But you, sisters and brothers, are not in the dark. The Day of God will not catch you like a thief. ⁵No, you are all children of light and children of the day. We don't belong to the darkness or the night. ⁶So let's not be asleep as others are—let's be awake and sober! ⁷Those who sleep do so at night, and those who get drunk do so at night. ⁸But we belong to the day, so let us be sober. Let us put on the breastplate of faith and love, and the helmet of the hope of salvation.

⁹God has destined us not to suffer wrath, but to receive salvation through our Savior Jesus Christ, ¹⁰who died for us so that, whether awake or asleep, we might live together with Christ. ¹¹So encourage each other and build each other up, just as you're already doing.

5:12-28

$\mathcal{W}$e ask you, sisters and brothers, to respect those who labor among you, who have charge over you in Christ as your teachers.¹³Esteem them highly, with a special love because of their work.

Live in peace with each other.

¹⁴We urge you, sisters and brothers, to warn the idlers, cheer up the fainthearted, support the weak and be patient with everyone. ¹⁵Make sure that no one repays one evil with another. Always seek what is good for each other—and for all people.

¹⁶Rejoice always, ¹⁷pray constantly, ¹⁸and give thanks for everything—for this is God's will for you in Christ Jesus.

¹⁹Don't stifle the Spirit; ²⁰don't despise the prophetic gift. ²¹But test everything and accept only what is good. ²²Avoid any semblance of evil.

²³May the God of peace make you perfect in holiness. May you be preserved whole and complete—spirit, soul, and body—irreproachable at the coming of our Savior Jesus Christ. ²⁴The One who calls us is trustworthy: God will make sure it comes to pass.

²⁵Sisters and brothers, pray for us.

²⁶Greet all the sisters and brothers with a holy kiss. ²⁷My orders, in the name of Christ, are that this letter is to be read to all the sisters and brothers.

²⁸The grace of our Savior Jesus Christ be with you.

the second letter of paul to the

thessalonians

from paul, silas and timothy,

To the church of the Thessalonians, who belong to our Abba God and our Savior Jesus Christ:

² Grace and peace be yours from our Abba God and our Savior Jesus Christ.

³ It's only right that we thank God unceasingly for you, sisters and brothers, because your faith grows more and more, and your love for each other increases—⁴ so much so that in God's churches we boast about your perseverance and faith in the midst of all the persecutions and trials you're enduring. ⁵ All this is evidence that God's judgment is right, and as a result you'll be counted worthy of the kindom of God, for which you are suffering.

⁶ Know that God is just, and will repay with affliction those who afflict you. ⁷ God will give relief to you who are suffering now, and to us as well, when our Savior Jesus will be revealed in blazing fire from heaven with the mighty angels. ⁸ Jesus will punish those who don't acknowledge God—

and those who don't obey the Good News of our Savior Jesus. [9] Their punishment will be eternal destruction—separation from the presence of Christ and the majesty of Christ's power—[10] on the day Christ comes to be glorified in the saints and to be marveled at by the faithful. You are included because you believed our testimony to you.

[11] Knowing all this, we pray continually that God will make you worthy of the call, fulfill all your desires for goodness, and empower all your works of faith. [12] In this way, the name of our Savior Jesus Christ will be glorified in you, and you in Christ, by the grace of our God and of our Savior Jesus Christ.

2:1-17

Concerning the coming of Jesus Christ and our being gathered to meet our Savior: we beg you, sisters and brothers, [2] don't become easily agitated or disturbed by some prophecy, report or letter falsely attributed to us, which says that the day of our Savior has come. [3] Let no one deceive you, in any way. It cannot happen until the Great Falling Away occurs, and the rebel, the Lost One, has appeared.

[4] This is the Enemy, the one who claims to be so much greater than all that people call "God," greater than every object of worship—so much so that it enthrones itself in God's sanctuary and claims to be God. [5] Surely you remember me telling you these things when I was with you?

[6] And now you also know what is holding the Lost One back now, only to appear at the proper time. [7] Rebellion is already at work, but secretly, and the one who holds it back must be removed first. [8] Then the Rebel will appear openly, whom Christ will destroy with nothing more than a breath, bringing that rebellion to an end with the revelation of Christ's presence.

[9] Christ's coming, however, will coincide with the activity of Satan. There will be all kinds of fake miracles, signs and wonders. [10] There will be every form of evil to deceive those already bound for destruction, because they would not grasp the love of the truth that could have saved them. [11] The reason God sends them such a delusive influence—and therefore makes them believe a lie—[12] is to condemn all who have not believed the truth, but chose evil instead.

[13] But we ought to thank God always for you, sisters and brothers loved by Christ, because God chose you from the beginning—to be saved by the sanctifying Spirit and by believing in the truth.

[14] God called you through our preaching of the Good News, so that you might gain the glory of our Savior Jesus Christ. [15] Therefore, sisters and

brothers, stand firm. Hold fast to the traditions you received from us, either by word of mouth or by letter. [16] May our Savior Jesus Christ and our Abba God—who loved us and in mercy gave us eternal consolation and hope—[17] console your hearts and strengthen them for every good work and word.

finally, sisters and brothers, pray for us that the message of Christ may spread rapidly and be honored, as it was with you. [2] Pray that we may be denied the interference of bigoted and wicked people. Faith is not given to everyone. [3] But Our God, who is faithful, will strengthen you and guard you from the Evil One. [4] We have confidence in Our God that what we taught you, you are now doing and will continue to do. [5] May Our God direct your hearts to the love of the Most High and the fortitude of Christ.

[6] In the name of our Savior Jesus Christ, we urge you, sisters and brothers, to keep away from anyone who refuses to work and live according to the teachings we passed on to you. [7] You know how you ought to imitate us. We didn't live undisciplined lives when we were among you, [8] nor did we depend on anyone for food. Rather, we worked night and day, laboring to the point of exhaustion so as not to impose on any of you—[9] not that we had no claim on you, but that we might present ourselves as an example for you to imitate. [10] Indeed, when we were with you we used to lay down the rule that anyone who didn't work didn't eat.

[11] We hear that some of you are undisciplined, doing no work at all, but acting like busybodies. [12] We command all such people and urge you strongly in our Savior Jesus Christ, to earn the food you eat by working hard and keeping quiet.

[13] My sisters and brothers, never tire of doing what is right. [14] Take special note of those who don't obey our teachings in this letter. Shame them by refusing to associate with them. [15] Even so, regard them not as enemies, but as sisters or brothers.

[16] Now may the God of peace give you peace at all times and in every circumstance. God be with you all!

[17] I, Paul, write this greeting in my own handwriting—the mark of authenticity in every letter—it is my own writing.

[18] May the grace of our Savior Jesus Christ be with you all.

the first letter of paul to
timothy

from paul, apostle of christ jesus by the command of God our Savior and Christ Jesus our hope,

[2] To Timothy, my true child in the faith:

May grace, mercy and peace be yours from Abba God and from Jesus Christ our Savior.

[3] I repeat the request I made when I was leaving for Macedonia: stay on at Ephesus, and insist that certain people stop teaching false doctrines [4] and cease devoting themselves to myths and endless genealogies. These things promote endless speculations rather than God's providential work—which is revealed by faith. [5] The purpose of this instruction is love from a pure heart, a clear conscience and a sincere faith. [6] Some people, however, have strayed from these and have turned to empty discussion. [7] They want to be teachers of the Law, but they don't know what they're asserting so confidently.

[8] We know that the Law is good, but only if it is treated like any law.

⁹Law is not meant for people who are just, but for the lawless and rebellious, for the irreligious and the wicked, for those who kill their parents, for murderers, ¹⁰for men and women who traffic in human flesh, for kidnappers, liars and perjurers. It is for everything else that is contrary to sound teaching— ¹¹that is, whatever conforms to the Good News of the blessed God, which was entrusted to me.

¹²I thank Christ Jesus our Savior, who has strengthened me, given me this work, and judged me faithful. ¹³I used to be a blasphemer, a persecutor, a violent man; but because in my unbelief I didn't know what I was doing, I have been treated mercifully, ¹⁴and the grace of our God has been granted to me in overflowing measure, as was the faith and love which are in Christ Jesus.

¹⁵Here's a saying that can be trusted and is worthy of your complete acceptance: "Christ Jesus came into the world to save sinners." Of these I myself am the worst. ¹⁶But I was dealt with mercifully for this reason: so that in me—the worst case of all—Jesus Christ might demonstrate perfect patience; and so that I might become an example to those who would later have faith in Christ and gain everlasting life. ¹⁷To the Ruler of ages, the immortal, the invisible, the only God, be honor and glory forever and ever! Amen.

1:18–3:16

I want to give you some instructions, Timothy, my child, in keeping with the prophecies that were made about you. Through them may you fight the good fight, ¹⁹with faith and a good conscience as your weapons. Others have put conscience aside and wrecked their faith—²⁰people like Hymenaeus and Alexander, whom I have handed over to Satan to be taught not to blaspheme.

2:1First of all, I urge that prayers be offered for everyone—petitions, intercessions and thanksgivings—²and especially for rulers and those in authority, so that we may be able to live godly and reverent lives in peace and quiet. ³To do this is right, and will please God our Savior, ⁴who wants everyone to be saved and to reach full knowledge of the truth. ⁵For there is only one God, and there is only one mediator between God and humankind—Christ Jesus, who was one of us, ⁶and who at the proper time sacrificed himself as a ransom and a testimony for all.

⁷Because of this I have been appointed to be a preacher, an apostle, and—this is the truth, now, I'm not lying—a faithful and honest teacher to the Gentiles.

⁸ Therefore, I want people everywhere to lift their hands up reverently in prayer, without anger or dissension.

⁹ I also want women to dress modestly and decently, not with braided hair or gold or pearls or expensive clothes. ¹⁰ Their adornment should be the good works that are proper for women who profess to be religious. ¹¹ Women are to be quiet and completely submissive during religious instruction. ¹² I don't permit a woman to teach or to have authority over a man. She must remain silent. ¹³ After all, Adam was formed first, then Eve. ¹⁴ And Adam was not the one deceived—it was the woman who was deceived and became a sinner. ¹⁵ But women will be saved through child-bearing—provided they continue in faith, love and holiness, with propriety.

      ℞   ℞   ℞

3⁻¹ You can depend on this: whoever wants to be a bishop aspires to a noble task. ² Bishops must be irreproachable, married only once, even-tempered, self-controlled, modest and hospitable. They should be good teachers. ³ They must not be addicted to drink. They shouldn't be contentious; instead, they should be gentle and peaceful. They must be free from the love of money. ⁴ They must be good managers of their own households, keeping their children under control without sacrificing their dignity. ⁵ For if bishops don't know how to manage their own households, how can they take care of the church of God? ⁶ They shouldn't be new converts, lest they become conceited and thus incur the punishment once meted out to the Devil. ⁷ They must also be well thought of by those outside the church, to ensure that they don't fall into disgrace, which is the Devil's trap.

⁸ In the same way, deacons must be dignified and straightforward. They may not overindulge in drink or give in to greed. ⁹ They must hold fast to the mystery of the faith with a clear conscience. ¹⁰ They should be put on probation first, and then—if there is nothing against them—they may serve as deacons. ¹¹ Their spouses, similarly, should be serious, mature, temperate and entirely trustworthy. ¹² Deacons must have been married only once and must be good managers of their children and their households. ¹³ Those who serve well as deacons gain a worthy place for themselves and acquire much assurance in their faith in Christ Jesus.

      ℞   ℞   ℞

¹⁴ Although I hope to visit you soon, I am writing you these instructions ¹⁵ so that if I should be delayed, you will know what kind of conduct befits a member of God's household—which is the church of the living God, the

pillar and foundation of the truth. ¹⁶ Wonderful indeed is the mystery of our faith, as we say in our profession of faith:

> "Christ appeared in the flesh,
>> was vindicated in the Spirit,
> was seen by angels,
>> was proclaimed among the nations,
> is believed in throughout the world
>> and was taken up into glory."

4:1–6:5

𝒏𝒐𝒘, the Spirit has explicitly said that during the last times some of us will desert the faith and listen to deceitful spirits and demonic teachings. ² These teachings come from hypocritical liars, whose consciences have been seared as with a red-hot iron. ³ They forbid people to marry. They also forbid certain foods, which God created to be accepted with thanksgiving by all who believe and know the truth. ⁴ For everything God created is good, and nothing is to be rejected provided thanksgiving is given for it; ⁵ it is made holy by the word of God and prayer.

⁶ If you will explain these instructions to the sisters and brothers, you will be a good minister of Christ Jesus, nourished on the truths of the faith and on the sound teachings you have followed. ⁷ Have nothing to do with godless myths and empty old fables.

Train yourself for godliness. ⁸ "Physical exercises have limited use, but spiritual exercises have unlimited value—they're a benefit both here and now and for all eternity." ⁹ —There's another saying that can be trusted and is worthy of your complete acceptance! ¹⁰ The focus of all our efforts is the trust we put in the living God, the Savior of the whole human race—particularly of those who believe.

¹¹ This is what you are to enforce in your teachings.

¹² Let no one look down on you because you are young, but be a consistent example for other believers in speech, in love, in life, in faith and in purity. ¹³ Until I arrive, give attention to the public reading of scripture, to preaching and to teaching. ¹⁴ Don't neglect the spiritual gift you received through the prophetic word when the presbyters laid their hands on you. ¹⁵ Attend to your duties with great devotion, so that everyone can see your progress. ¹⁶ Watch yourself and watch your teaching; persevere in both tasks. By doing so, you will bring salvation to yourself and to all who hear you.

5:1 Don't speak harshly to an older man, but appeal to him as a father.

Treat younger men as brothers. ²Treat older women as you would your mother, and younger women with propriety, as you would your sisters.

³Give proper recognition to women who have been widowed and are truly in need. ⁴For women who have been widowed while they still have children or grandchildren, their first duty is to practice godliness with their own families, and to try not to be a drain on their parents' finances. This is what pleases God. ⁵Those who are truly widowed, those who are really alone, should put their hope in God and continue in prayer and supplication night and day. ⁶But those who give themselves to willful pleasure are dead while they live. ⁷Remind the people of this, so that their lives may be irreproachable. ⁸People who don't provide for their relatives, especially those in the immediate household, have denied the faith and are worse than unbelievers.

⁹Let a widow be put on the list of widows to receive support if she is at least sixty years old and married only once. ¹⁰This woman must be known for her good deeds, such as the way she has raised her family, showed hospitality, washed the feet of the holy ones, helped those in need and involved herself in all kinds of good work.

¹¹Don't put young women who are widows on the list. Their sensual desires tend to get stronger than their dedication to Christ, and they want to remarry—¹²which invites others to judge them for being unfaithful to their original promise. ¹³Furthermore, they learn to become idlers, going from house to house. Not only that, they become gossips and busybodies, talking about things they ought not to. ¹⁴So I think it is better for young women who have been widowed to remarry, to have children, to manage a home, and not to give the enemy an opportunity for slander. ¹⁵There are already some who have turned away to follow Satan.

¹⁶If a Christian woman has relatives who are widowed, she must assist them and not let the church be burdened with them. Then the church can help those who are truly alone.

¹⁷Presbyters who do their work well are to be doubly honored, especially those who preach and teach. ¹⁸For scripture says, "Don't muzzle the ox while it is threshing the grain," and, "Workers deserve their wages." ¹⁹Don't accept an accusation against a presbyter if it doesn't have two or three witnesses. ²⁰If any are found to be at fault, reprimand them publicly, to warn the rest.

²¹Before God and before Jesus Christ and the chosen angels, enforce these rules without partiality. Show no favoritism. ²²Don't be too quick to ordain people—otherwise you'll share responsibility for the sins of others. Keep yourself pure.

²³ Stop drinking only water. Have a little wine because of your stomach and your frequent illnesses.

²⁴ The faults of some people are obvious long before anyone complains about them. Others have faults that are not discovered until afterwards. ²⁵ So it is with our work: good deeds are obvious. But even when they are not, they cannot be hidden forever.

⁶·¹ Those who are under the yoke of domination should consider their superiors as worthy of full respect, so that the Name of God and our teachings may not be brought into disrepute. ² If their overseers are believers, those who are in subjection should show their overseers even greater respect, for they are members of the same family. Indeed, they should be even more diligent in their work, because those who benefit from the work are believers, and they are beloved.

These are the things you are to teach and preach. ³ All those who advocate any other teaching, who don't hold to the sound doctrine of our Savior Jesus Christ and the teaching proper to true religion, ⁴ should be recognized as both conceited and ignorant. They have an unhealthy interest in controversies and debates. From these come envy, dissension, slander, evil suspicions—⁵ in other words, the bickering of those with twisted minds who have lost sense of the truth. Such people value religion only as a means of personal gain.

6:6-21

the**re** is, of course, great benefit in religion, but only for those who are content with what they have.

⁷ We brought nothing into the world, nor have we the power to take anything out. ⁸ If we have food and clothing, we have all that we need. ⁹ Those who want to be rich are falling into temptation and a trap. They are letting themselves be captured by foolish and harmful desires which draw us down to ruin and destruction. ¹⁰ The love of money is the root of all evil. Some people, in their passion for it, have strayed from the faith and have come to grief amid great pain.

¹¹ But you are to flee from these things. As one dedicated to God, strive to be a person of integrity and piety, filled with faith and love, patience and gentleness. ¹² Run the great race of faith. Take firm hold of the everlasting life to which you were called when, in the presence of many witnesses, you made your good profession of faith.

¹³ Before God, who gives life to all, and before Christ Jesus, who spoke

up as a witness for the truth in front of Pontius Pilate, I charge you [14] to keep God's command without fault or reproach until our Savior Jesus Christ appears. [15] This appearance God will bring to pass at a chosen time. God alone is the Sovereign over all, the blessed and only ruler above all earthly rulers, [16] who alone possesses immortality, and who dwells in un-approachable light, whom no human being has ever seen or can see. To God be the honor and the everlasting kindom! Amen.

[17] Warn those who are blessed with this world's goods not to look down on other people. They are not to put their hope in wealth, for it is uncertain. Instead, they are to put their hope in God, who richly provides us with all that we need for our enjoyment. [18] Tell them they are to do good and be wealthy in good works. They are to be generous and willing to share. [19] In this way, they'll create a treasure for the future, and guarantee the only life that is real.

[20] Dear Timothy, guard what has been entrusted to you. Avoid the blasphemous philosophical discussions and absurdities of what is falsely called knowledge. [21] Some have adopted it and have lost the faith.

Grace be with you.

the second letter of paul to
timothy

1:1–2:26

from paul, by the will of god an apostle
of Christ Jesus, sent to proclaim the promise of life in Christ Jesus,

² To Timothy, my dear child:

May grace, mercy and peace from God the Creator and from Christ Jesus our Savior be with you.

³ I thank God, the God of my ancestors—whom I worship with a clear conscience—whenever I remember you in my prayers, as indeed I do constantly, night and day.

⁴ When I recall your tears, I long to see you again, which would fill me with joy. ⁵ I'm reminded of your sincere faith, which first lived in your grandmother Lois, then in your mother Eunice, and now, I'm certain, in you as well.

⁶ That's why I want to remind you to fan into flame the gift of God, which is in you through the laying on of my hands. ⁷ For God didn't give us a spirit of timidity, but a spirit of power, of love, of self-discipline.

⁸So don't be ashamed to give your testimony about Christ, and don't be ashamed of me, Christ's prisoner. But join with me in suffering for the Gospel by the power of God, ⁹who has saved us and called us to a holy life—not because of anything we have done, but because of God's own purpose and grace. This grace was given to us in Christ Jesus before the beginning of time, ¹⁰but it has now been revealed through the appearing of our Savior Jesus Christ, who has destroyed death, and brought life and immortality to light through the Gospel.

¹¹And it was for this Gospel that I was appointed a herald and an apostle and a teacher. ¹²That's why I'm suffering as I am. Yet I'm not ashamed, because I know whom I have believed, and I'm convinced that Jesus Christ is able to guard what has been entrusted to me until that final Day.

¹³Take what you have heard me say as a model of sound teaching, in faith and love in Christ Jesus. ¹⁴Guard the rich deposit of faith with the help of the Holy Spirit, who dwells within us.

¹⁵As you know, Phygelus, Hermogenes and all the others from the province of Asia Minor have deserted me. ¹⁶But Our God will have mercy on the household of Onesiphorus. He was often a comfort to me and wasn't ashamed of my chains. ¹⁷On the contrary, when he came to Rome, he searched me out and found me. ¹⁸May God grant him divine mercy on that Day, for you know very well how much he helped me in Ephesus.

CR   CR   CR

2:1 Be strong, my child, in the grace that is in Christ Jesus. ²Everything that you've heard me teach in the presence of many witnesses—pass it on to trustworthy people, so that they, in turn, will teach others. ³Bear up under hardship, as I do: stay single-minded, in Christ Jesus. ⁴After all, those serving in national service don't get involved in business affairs—not if they want to keep their superiors happy. ⁵Or take athletes—they can't accept the winner's crown unless they play by the rules. ⁶And it is the hardworking farmer who has the first share of the crops. ⁷Reflect on what I'm saying and Our God will give you complete understanding in this matter.

⁸Remember that Jesus Christ, a descendent of David, was raised from the dead. This is the Gospel I preach; ⁹in preaching it I suffer as a criminal—even to the point of being thrown into chains—but there is no chaining the word of God! ¹⁰Therefore I bear with all of this for the sake of those whom God has chosen, in order that they may obtain salvation in Christ Jesus, and with it, eternal glory.

¹¹You can depend on this:

> If we have died with Christ,
>   we will also live with Christ;
> [12] if we hold out to the end,
>   we will also reign with Christ.
> If we deny Christ,
>   Christ will deny us.
> [13] If we are unfaithful,
>   Christ will remain faithful,
>   for Christ can never be unfaithful.

[14] Keep reminding people of these things. Warn them before God against quarrelling about words, which is of no value and only ruins those who listen. [15] Do your best to present yourself to God as one approved, a worker who doesn't need to be ashamed and who correctly handles the word of truth.

[16] Avoid profane, idle talk, for people who engage in it move further and further away from true religion. [17] This kind of talk spreads like gangrene. Among these talkers are Hymenaeus and Philetus, [18] who have deviated from the truth. They claim that the resurrection has already taken place—and they have destroyed the faith of some. [19] Nevertheless, God's foundation stands firmly, bearing this inscription: "Christ knows those who belong to God," and, "All who call on the Name of Our God must avoid wickedness."

[20] Not all the dishes in a large household are made of silver and gold. Some are made of wood, others are earthenware. Some are made for special occasions and some for everyday use. [21] Those who cleanse themselves from wickedness will become a vessel "for special occasions," useful to Christ and ready for any good work. [22] Run from youthful lusts; pursue justice, faith, love and peace, in union with all those who call on Our God with a pure heart. [23] Avoid futile and silly debates, for they breed quarrels. [24] And as a servant of Christ, you must not engage in quarrels; instead, be gentle with everyone—a good teacher, patient and tolerant. [25] Be gentle when you correct those who argue with you—perhaps God will grant them repentance, the grace to recognize the truth, [26] and they will come to their senses. Thus they may be freed of Satan's snare, where they have been captives to the Devil's will.

3:1–4:22

Realize that there are going to be terrible times in the last days. [2] People will be self-centered and money-grubbing, boastful, arrogant and abusive, disobedient of their parents, ungrateful, irreligious, ³callous and implacable. They will be slanderers, profligates, lovers of violence and haters of everything good. ⁴ They will be treacherous, reckless, and conceited; they'll be lovers of pleasure rather than lovers of God. ⁵ They will maintain the external form of religion, but will deny its power. Have nothing to do with these people.

⁶ They are the type who worm their way into families and gain control over the weak-willed—those oppressed by sin and driven by sinful desires. ⁷ These types are always learning, but are never able to come to the knowledge of the truth. ⁸ People like this defy the truth, just as Jannes and Jambres opposed Moses. Their minds are corrupt and their faith is a mockery. ⁹ But they won't continue much longer. Their foolishness, like that of those other two, will be obvious to all.

¹⁰ You have followed closely my teaching and my conduct. You have observed my purpose, faith, patience, love and endurance, ¹¹ and my persecutions and sufferings—like what happened to me in Antioch, Iconium and Lystra. What persecutions I endured—yet Our God rescued me from all of them! ¹² In fact, anyone who wants to live a godly life in Christ Jesus can expect to be persecuted. ¹³ But all the while, impostors and charlatans will go from bad to worse, deceiving others and deceiving themselves.

¹⁴ You, for your part, must remain faithful to what you have learned and believed, because you know who your teachers were. ¹⁵ Likewise, from your infancy you have known the sacred scriptures, the source of wisdom which through faith in Christ Jesus leads to salvation. ¹⁶ All scripture is inspired of God, and is useful for teaching—for reprimanding, correcting, and training in justice—¹⁷ so that the people of God may be fully competent and equipped for every good work.

4:1 In the presence of God and of Jesus Christ, who will judge the living and the dead, and in view of the appearance and reign of Christ, I charge you ² to preach the word; to be prepared in season and out of season; to correct, reprimand and encourage with great patience and careful instruction. ³ For the time is coming when people won't put up with sound doctrine. Instead, to suit their own desires, they will gather around them a great number of teachers who say what their fickle ears want to hear. ⁴ They will turn their ears away from truth and turn aside to myths. ⁵ But you, keep your head in all situations; endure hardship, perform your work as an evangelist and fulfill your ministry.

⁶ As for me, my life is already being poured out like a libation. The time of my dissolution is near. ⁷ I have fought the good fight; I have finished the race; I have kept the faith. ⁸ Now a laurel wreath awaits me; on that day

Our God, the just Judge, will award it to me—and not only to me, but to all who have longed for Christ's appearing.

ରେ   ରେ   ରେ

⁹Do your best to come to me as soon as you can. ¹⁰Demas, enamored of worldly things, left me and went to Thessalonica; Crescens has gone to Galatia, and Titus to Dalmatia. ¹¹Luke is the only one with me. Get Mark and bring him with you, for he is helpful to me in my work. ¹²I have sent Tychicus to Ephesus. ¹³When you come, bring the cloak I left with Carpus in Troas, and the scrolls—especially the parchment ones.

¹⁴Alexander the coppersmith caused me great harm. Our God will compensate him according to his actions. ¹⁵Be on your guard against him, for he has strongly opposed our preaching. ¹⁶I found myself alone and without a single witness at my first defense. Pray that they not be punished for it.

¹⁷Christ stood by my side and gave me strength, so that through me the proclamation might be completed and all the nations might hear the Gospel. That's how I was saved from the lion's jaws. ¹⁸Christ will continue to rescue me from all attempts to do me harm, and will bring me safe to the higher realm. To Jesus Christ be glory forever and ever! Amen.

¹⁹Greet Prisca, Aquila and the family of Onesiphorus. ²⁰Erastus remained in Corinth, and I left Trophimus behind at Miletus because he was ill. ²¹Do your best to get here before winter.

Greetings to you from Eubulus, Pudens, Linus, Claudia and all the sisters and brothers.

²²May Christ be with your spirit. Grace be with you.

titus

fROM PAUL, GOD'S SERVANT AND AN APOSTLE of Jesus Christ, sent to strengthen the faith of those whom God has chosen, and to promote their knowledge of the truth which godliness embodies, [2] all in the hope of that eternal life which God promised before the ages began—and God cannot lie. [3] This is the appointed time, manifested in the preaching entrusted to me by the command of God our Savior.

[4] To Titus, my own true child in our common faith:

May grace and peace be yours from Abba God and Christ Jesus our Savior.

[5] The reason I left you in Crete was so that you might accomplish what had been left undone, especially the appointment of presbyters in every town.

As I instructed you, [6] presbyters must be irreproachable, married only once, and the parents of children who are believers and are known not to be wild and insubordinate.

⁷Bishops, as God's stewards, must be blameless. They must not be self-willed or arrogant, addicted to drink, violent or greedy. ⁸On the contrary, they should be hospitable, and love goodness, and be steady, just, holy and self-controlled. ⁹In their teachings, they must hold fast to the authentic message, so that they'll be able both to encourage the faithful to follow sound doctrine, and to refute those who contradict it.

¹⁰This is necessary, frankly, because there are many rebellious types out there—idle talkers and deceivers, especially those who demand conversion to Judaism before becoming a Christian. ¹¹They must be silenced, for they're upsetting entire households by teaching things they shouldn't teach, and doing it for financial gain. ¹²One of their own prophets once said, "Cretans have always been liars, evil animals and lazy gluttons." ¹³This is a true statement.

Therefore, rebuke them sharply, so that they'll be sound in the faith. ¹⁴That should keep them from listening to empty myths and from heeding the commands of those who are no longer interested in the truth. ¹⁵To the pure all things are pure, but to those who are corrupted and lack faith, nothing can be pure. The corruption is both in their minds and in their consciences. ¹⁶They claim to know God, while denying it with their actions. They're vile, disobedient, and quite incapable of doing good.

2:1–3:9

As for yourself, let your speech be consistent with sound doctrine. ²Tell your older people that they must be temperate, reserved and moderate; ³they should be sound in faith, loving and steadfast; they must behave in ways that befit those who belong to God. They must not be slanderers or drunkards.

⁴By their good example, they must teach younger couples to love each other and their children, ⁵to be sensible, live pure lives, work hard, and be kind and submissive in their love relationships. In this way the message of God will not fall into disgrace. ⁶Tell young people to keep themselves completely under control—⁷and be sure that you yourself set them a good example. Your teaching must have the integrity of serious, ⁸sound words to which no one can take exception. That way no opponent will be able to find anything bad to say about us, and hostility will yield to shame.

⁹Tell workers that they're to obey their superiors and always do what they're told without arguing. ¹⁰And there must be no petty thieving. They must show complete honesty at all times. In this way they'll be a credit to the teaching of God our Savior.

¹¹The grace of God has appeared, offering salvation to all. ¹²It trains us to reject godless ways and worldly desires, and to live temperately, justly and devoutly in this age ¹³as we await our blessed hope—the appearing of the glory of our great God and our Savior Jesus Christ. ¹⁴It was Christ who was sacrificed for us, to redeem us from all unrighteousness and to cleanse a people to be Christ's own, eager to do what is right.

¹⁵Teach these things, whether you are giving instructions or correcting errors. Act with full authority, and let no one despise you.

CR   CR   CR

3:1Remind people to be loyally subject to the government and its officials, to obey the laws, and to be ready to do whatever is good. ²Tell them not to speak evil of anyone or to be quarrelsome. They must be forebearing and display perfect courtesy to all.

³We ourselves were once foolish, disobedient and far from the true faith; we were addicted to our passions and to pleasures of various kinds. We went our way in malice and envy, filled with self-hatred and hating one another. ⁴But when the kindness and love of God our Savior appeared, ⁵we were saved, not because of any righteous deeds we had done, but because of God's own mercy. We were saved through the baptism of new birth and renewal by the Holy Spirit. ⁶This Spirit God lavished on us through Jesus Christ, our Savior, ⁷that we might be justified through grace and become heirs to the hope of eternal life. ⁸This is doctrine you can rely on.

I want you to be quite uncompromising in teaching this. Then those who now believe in God will keep their minds occupied doing good works. These things are excellent and beneficial to everyone. ⁹But avoid pointless speculation, genealogies, rivalries and quarrels about the Law. They're useless and futile.

3:10-15

If people dispute what you teach, give them a first and even a second warning. After that, have no more to do with them. ¹¹Be assured that such people are twisted, sinful and self-condemned.

¹²As soon as I have sent Artemus or Tychicus to you, do your best to join me at Nicopolis. I have decided to spend the winter there. ¹³Send Zenas

the lawyer and Apollos on their journey, and see that they have everything they need.

¹⁴ All our people are to learn to do what is good for their practical lives as well. They'll then be able to provide for their daily needs and not be unproductive.

¹⁵ All who are with me send greetings. Grace be with you all.

the letter of paul to
philemon

from paul, a prisoner for christ jesus, and Timothy, our brother,

To Philemon, our dear friend and co-worker, ² to Apphia, our sister, to Archippus, our companion in the struggle, and to the church that meets in your house:

³ Grace and peace from Abba God and Our Savior Jesus Christ.

⁴ I always mention you in my prayers and thank God for you ⁵ because I hear of the love and faith you have for our Savior Jesus and for all the saints. ⁶ I pray that you'll be active in sharing your faith, so that you'll fully understand all the good things we're able to do for the sake of Christ.

⁷ I find great joy and comfort in your love, because through you the hearts of the holy ones have been refreshed. ⁸ Therefore, though I feel I have every right in Christ to command you to do what ought to be done, ⁹ I prefer to appeal in the name of love.

Yes, I, Paul, an ambassador and now a prisoner for Christ, ¹⁰ appeal to you for my child, of whom I have become the parent during my imprisonment. He has truly become Onesimus—"Useful"—[11] for he who was formerly useless to you is now useful indeed both to you and to me. [12] It is he that I am sending to you—and that means I'm sending my heart!

[13] I had wanted to keep him with me, that he might help me in your place while I'm in prison for the Good News; [14] but I didn't want to do anything without your consent, so that kindness might not be forced on you, but be freely bestowed. [15] Perhaps he was separated from you for a while for this reason—that you might have him back forever, [16] no longer as a subordinate, but as more—a beloved brother, especially dear to me. And how much dearer he'll be to you, since now you'll know him both in the flesh and in Christ!

[17] If you regard me as a partner, then, welcome Onesimus as you would me. [18] If he has done you any injury or owes you anything, charge it to me. [19] I, Paul, write this in my own hand: I agree to pay. And I won't even mention that you owe me your very self!

[20] You see, my friend, I want to make you "useful" to me in Christ. Refresh this heart of mine in Christ. [21] I write with complete confidence in your obedience, since I am sure you will do even more than I ask.

[22] There is one more thing. Prepare a guest room for me. I hope to be restored to you through your prayers.

[23] Epaphras, a prisoner with me in Christ Jesus, sends greetings. [24] And so do my colleagues Mark, Aristarchus, Demas and Luke.

[25] May the grace of our Savior Jesus Christ be with your spirit.

the letter to the
hebrews

1:1-14

Ín times past, god spoke in fragmentary
and varied ways to our ancestors through the prophets; ²in these final days,
God has spoken to us through the Only Begotten, who has been made heir
of all things and through whom the universe was first created. ³Christ is
the reflection of God's glory, the exact representation of God's being; all
things are sustained by God's powerful Word. Having cleansed us from
our sins, Jesus Christ sat down at the right hand of the Glory of heaven—
⁴as far superior to the angels as the name Christ has inherited is superior
to theirs.

⁵For to which of the angels did God ever say,

"You are my Own;
today I have begotten you,"

or,

"I will be your parent,
and you will be my child,"

⁶or, as when God said upon bringing the Firstborn into the world,

"Let all the angels of God worship you"?

⁷Of the angels God says,

"I make the angels winds,
my servants flames of fire."

⁸But to the Only Begotten, God says,

"Your throne, O God,
will last forever and ever,
and justice is the scepter
of your reign.
⁹You love justice as much
as you hate wickedness;
therefore, God, your God,
has set you above your companions
and anointed you
with the oil of gladness";

¹⁰and,

"In the beginning, O God,
you laid the foundations of the earth,
and the heavens
are the work of your hands.
¹¹They will perish,
but you will remain;
they will all wear out
like a garment.
¹²You will roll them up like a cloak,
and like a garment they will be changed.
But you are the same,
and your years never end."

¹³But to which of the angels did God ever say,

"Sit at my right hand
and I will place your enemies
under your foot"?

¹⁴The truth is, all angels are ministering spirits, sent out to serve those who will inherit salvation.

2:1–4:11

Chereﬁore, we must be more attentive to what we've been taught, so that we don't drift away. ²For if the promise made through angels was binding, and every infringement and disobedience received its just punishment, ³how will we escape if we ignore so great a salvation? This salvation, which was first announced by Christ, was confirmed for us by those who heard the message. ⁴God also confirmed their witness to it with signs, wonders, miracles of all kinds—and by freely distributing the gifts of the Holy Spirit.

⁵God didn't create the inhabited earth of which we speak to have it be ruled by angels. ⁶Somewhere this testimony is found:

> "Who are we that you should be mindful of us?
>> We are mere mortals, and yet you care for us!
> ⁷You have made us little less than the angels
>> and crowned us with glory and honor.
> ⁸You have put all things under our feet."

In subjecting all things to us, God left nothing unsubjected. At present, we don't see all things thus subject; ⁹but we do see Jesus, who was made "little less than the angels, crowned with glory and honor" by dying on the cross—so that, through the gracious will of God, Jesus might taste death for us all.

¹⁰Indeed, it was fitting that, when bringing many to glory, God, for whom and through whom all things exist, should make the author of their salvation perfect through suffering. ¹¹The one who makes holy and those who are made holy are all from the One God. And because of this, Jesus is not ashamed to call us sisters and brothers, ¹²as it is written:

> "I will proclaim your Name
>> to my sisters and brothers,
> I will sing your praise
>> in the midst of the assembly."

¹³And again,

> "I will put my trust in God."

And again, Jesus says,

> "Here I am,
>> with the children God has given me."

¹⁴Since the children of God are flesh and blood, Jesus likewise partook of that flesh and blood, that by dying he might render powerless the one who has the power of death—that is, the Devil—¹⁵and free those whose fear of death had enslaved them all their lives. ¹⁶Surely Jesus came to help not angels but rather the children of Sarah and Abraham! ¹⁷Therefore, Jesus had to become like his sisters and brothers in every way, in order to be a merciful and faithful high priest on our behalf, to make atonement for the sins of the people. ¹⁸And since Jesus suffered while being tempted, he is able to help others who are being tempted.

3:1 Therefore, holy sisters and brothers—and you all have the same heavenly call—fix your thoughts on Jesus, the apostle and high priest of our confession. 2 He was faithful to the One who appointed him, just as Moses stayed faithful, alone of all God's house. 3 But Jesus has been found worthy of greater honor than Moses, just as the builder of a house receives more honor than the house itself. 4 Of course, every house is built by someone, but the builder of all things is God. 5 Moses was faithful as a servant in all of God's house, serving as a witness to the things that were to be revealed later. 6 Christ, on the other hand, is faithful over God's house as the heir.

And we are God's house—if we persevere to the end, firmly holding on to our confidence and the hope of which we boast.

7 As the Holy Spirit says,

"Today,
      if you hear my voice,
8 don't harden your hearts
      as they did at the rebellion,
      in the day of testing in the desert,
9 when your ancestors tested and tried me
      and saw my works for forty years.
10 Because of this I was angry with that generation
      and I said, 'They have always been of erring heart
      and have never known my ways.'
11 So I swore in my anger,
      'They will never enter my place of rest.'"

12 Take care, my sisters and brothers, lest any of you have an evil and unfaithful spirit and fall away from the living God. 13 Encourage one another daily while it is still "today," so that no one grows hardened by the deceit of sin. 14 We have become partners in Christ, provided we maintain to the end that confidence with which we began.

15 For it is said,

"Today,
      if you hear my voice,
   don't harden your hearts
      as they did at the rebellion."

16 Who were those who heard and rebelled? Wasn't it all those who came out of Egypt with Moses? 17 And with whom was God angry for forty years? Wasn't it with those who sinned, whose bodies fell in the desert? 18 And to whom did God swear that they wouldn't enter into God's rest, if not those

who disobeyed? [19]Thus we see that they couldn't enter because they lacked faith.

4[1] Although the promise that all may enter God's rest still stands, you must be careful of falling short of it. [2]We've had the Good News proclaimed to us—and so did our ancestors. But the message they heard didn't profit them, for they didn't combine it with faith. [3]It is we who have believed who will enter into that rest, just as God said,

> "So I swore in my anger,
>   'They will never enter my rest.' "

Yet God's work was finished with the creation of the world, [4]for in reference to the seventh day one passage says, "And God rested from work on the seventh day," [5]and again in that passage, God says, "They will never enter my rest."

[6]Then we have established that some will reach it, and that those who formerly had the Good News proclaimed to them didn't enter because of their disobedience. [7]Therefore God has set a particular day—"Today"—when God spoke through David long ago, as we said earlier:

> "Today,
>   if you hear my voice,
>   don't harden your hearts."

[8]For if Joshua had led them into this rest, God wouldn't have spoken about another day to come. [9]Therefore, there must still be a rest reserved for God's people—the Sabbath rest. [10]For all those who enter God's rest also rest from their own work, just as God did.

[11]Therefore, let us strive to enter into that rest, so that no one may fall by imitating the example of our ancestors' disobedience.

4:12–8:6

𝓰oɒ's word is living and active, sharper than any double-edged sword. It pierces so deeply that it divides even soul and spirit, bone and marrow, and is able to judge the thoughts and intentions of the heart. [13]Nothing is concealed from God; all lies bare and exposed before the eyes of the One to whom we have to render an account.

[14]Since, then, we have a great high priest who has passed through the heavens—Jesus, the Firstborn of God—let us hold fast to our profession of faith. [15]For we don't have a high priest who is unable to sympathize with our weaknesses, but one who was tempted in every way that we are, yet

never sinned. ¹⁶ So let us confidently approach the throne of grace to receive mercy and favor, and find help in time of need.

5:¹ Every high priest taken from among the faithful is appointed on their behalf to deal with the things of God, to offer gifts and sacrifices for sins. ² The high priest is able to deal patiently with erring sinners, being likewise beset by weakness—³ and so must make personal sin offerings as well as those for the people. ⁴ One doesn't take on this honor by one's own initiative, but only when called by God, as Aaron was. ⁵ Even Christ didn't presume to take on the office of high priest. Christ was appointed high priest by the One who said,

> "You are my Own;
> today I have begotten you";

⁶ and in another place,

> "You are a priest forever,
> according to the order of Melchizedek."

⁷ In the days when he was in the flesh, Jesus offered prayers and supplications with loud cries and tears to God, who was able to save him from death, and Jesus was heard because of his reverence. ⁸ Firstborn though he was, Jesus learned to obey through suffering. ⁹ But having been made perfect, Jesus became, for all who obey, the source of eternal salvation, ¹⁰ and he was designated by God to be a high priest according to the order of Melchizedek.

ᘁ   ᘁ   ᘁ

¹¹ We have many things to say about this, but explaining is difficult because you have grown slow to understand. ¹² Really, even though you ought to be teachers by this time, you need someone to teach you anew the basic elements of God's word. You need milk, not solid food. ¹³ All those who are still living on milk cannot digest the doctrine of righteousness because they are still babies. ¹⁴ Solid food is for the mature, for those whose minds are trained to distinguish right from wrong.

6:¹ So let's leave behind the elementary teachings about Christ and move on to maturity, without laying the same foundation—repentance from dead works and faith in God, ² and teachings about baptism, the laying on of hands, the resurrection of the dead and eternal judgment. ³ And this, God willing, is what we will do.

⁴ As for those people who were once brought into enlightenment, who tasted the heavenly gift, who have shared in the Holy Spirit ⁵ and who have tasted the good word of God and the powers of the age to come—⁶ if they still fall away, it is impossible for them to come to repentance and renewal

a second time. They are crucifying—and publicly disgracing—the Only Begotten of God all over again. [7] A field that is well watered by frequent rain and yields a good crop useful to the farmer receives a blessing from God. [8] A field that grows thorns and thistles is abandoned as if it were cursed, and it will end up being burned.

[9] Even though we speak like this, beloved, we are confident of better results in your case, results related to salvation.

[10] God is not unjust, and will not forget your work and the love you have demonstrated by your past and present service to God's holy people. [11] Our one desire is that each of you show the same zeal to the end, to the perfect fulfillment of our hopes. [12] Don't grow careless, but imitate those who, through faith and perseverance, are inheriting the promises.

CR   CR   CR

[13] When God made the promise to Sarah and Abraham, it was made alone, for there was no one greater to swear by. [14] And God said to them, "I will indeed bless you and multiply you." [15] Because of that, Sarah and Abraham persevered and saw the promise fulfilled.

[16] People, of course, swear an oath by someone greater than themselves; an oath gives firmness to the promise and puts an end to all argument. [17] In the same way, God, wanting to make the heirs to the promise thoroughly realize that the divine promise was unalterable, guaranteed it by an oath. [18] Now, therefore, there are two unalterable things—the promise and the oath—in which it was impossible for God to be lying. We should now, having found safety, take a firm grip on the hope that is held out to us. [19] Like a sure and firm anchor of our lives, that hope extends beyond the veil [20] through which Jesus, our forerunner, has passed on our behalf, being made high priest forever according to the order of Melchizedek.

[7:1] Recall that Melchizedek, ruler of Salem, priest of the Most High God, went to meet Abraham, who was on his way back after the slaughter of the rulers, and blessed him; [2] and also that it was to Melchizedek that Abraham gave a tenth of all that he had. Melchizedek—which means "ruler of righteousness"—was also ruler of Salem—that is, "ruler of peace." [3] With no mother, no father, no genealogy, no beginning of days or end of life, Melchizedek is like God's Only Begotten and remains a priest forever.

[4] Try to fathom how great this person was. After all, the patriarch Abraham gave him a tenth of the treasure he had captured. [5] The descendants of Levi who receive the office of priesthood are, according to the Law, commanded to exact tithes from the people, their sisters and brothers, even though they also descended from Abraham. [6] But this person, not a descen-

dant of Levi, still exacted tithes from Abraham, and then blessed the partriarch—the one who had received the promises. ⁷Now, it's obvious that a lesser person is blessed by a greater person. ⁸Further, in the one case, the tithe is collected by mortals, who die; in the other case, by the one who, the testimony says, lives on. ⁹It could also be said that even Levi, who received tithes, actually paid them in the person of Abraham. ¹⁰For Levi was still in the loins of his ancestor Abraham when Melchizedek came to meet him.

¹¹Now if perfection came through the levitical priesthood—since because of this priesthood the Law was given to the people—why was a new priesthood necessary? And why one according to the order of Melchizedek, and not the order of Aaron? ¹²Because any change in the priesthood means a change in the Law as well.

¹³The one about whom these things were said came from a different tribe, and the members of that tribe never did service at the altar. ¹⁴Everyone knows that Christ came from Judah, a tribe that Moses didn't even mention when dealing with priests.

¹⁵The matter becomes even clearer when there appears a second Melchizedek, ¹⁶who is a priest not by virtue of a law about physical descent, but by the power of an indestructible life. ¹⁷Scripture testifies, "You are a priest forever, according to the order of Melchizedek."

¹⁸On the one hand, the former commandment is annulled because it is ineffective and useless: ¹⁹the Law wasn't able to make anything perfect. On the other hand, this commandment is replaced by a better hope—one that brings us nearer to God.

²⁰What's more, this didn't happen without the taking of an oath. ²¹The others became priests without an oath. But Jesus became a priest with an oath, when God said to him,

> "Our God has sworn,
> and will not renege on it:
> you are a priest forever."

²²Through this oath Jesus became the guarantee of a better covenant.

²³There's another difference: there were so many priests in the old Covenant because death prevented them from continuing their work. ²⁴But Christ lives on forever, and Christ's work as priest doesn't pass on to someone else. ²⁵And so Christ is able, now and always, to save those who come to God through Christ, because Christ lives forever to plead to God for them.

²⁶God ordained that we should have such a high priest—one who is holy, who has no fault or sin, who has been set apart from sinners and raised above the heavens. ²⁷Jesus is not like other high priests and doesn't need to

offer sacrifices every day, first for personal sins and then for the sins of the people. Christ's self-sacrifice was offered once and for all. ²⁸ For the Law appoints as high priests people who are weak; but God's sworn promise, which came later than the Law, appoints the Only Begotten, who has been made perfect forever.

8:1 The key to what we are saying is this: we have such a high priest, who sits at the right hand of the throne of Majesty in heaven, ² a minister of the sanctuary and of that true tabernacle set up by God and not by mortals. ³ Now every high priest is appointed to offer gifts and sacrifices—hence the necessity of this priest to have something to offer.

⁴ If this high priest were on earth, it would not be as a priest, for there are priests already offering the gifts which the Law prescribes. ⁵ They offer worship in a sanctuary which is only a copy and shadow of the heavenly one—for Moses, when about to erect the tabernacle, was warned, "See that you make everything according to the pattern shown you on the mountain."

⁶ But now Jesus, our high priest, has obtained a more excellent ministry as mediator of a better covenant, founded on better promises.

8:7–10:39

If that first Covenant had been faultless, there would have been no reason to have a second one. ⁸ But God, finding fault with them, says,

"Days are coming—it is Your God who speaks—
    when I will establish a new Covenant
    with the house of Israel and the house of Judah,
⁹ but not a covenant like the one I made with their ancestors
    on the day I took them out of the land of Egypt.
They abandoned that Covenant of mine,
    and so I deserted them—
        it is Your God who speaks.
¹⁰ No, this is the Covenant I will make
    with the house of Israel
    when those days arrive—
        it is Your God who speaks.
I will put my laws into their minds
    and write them on their hearts.
Then I will be their God
    and they will be my people.
¹¹ There will be no need

for neighbor to try to teach neighbor,
or sister and brother to say to each other,
'Learn to know Our God.'
No, they will all know me,
the least no less than the greatest,
¹²since I will forgive their iniquities
and never again remember their sins."

¹³In saying "a new covenant," God declares the first one obsolete. And what has grown old and become obsolete is ready to disappear.

CR   CR   CR

9:1 Now the first Covenant had regulations governing worship and a sanctuary, a sanctuary on this earth. ²Two tabernacles were constructed: the outer one, called the sanctuary, which held the lampstand, the table, and the showbread; ³and the inner tabernacle, behind the second veil, called the Holy of Holies, ⁴which held the gold altar of incense, and the gold-plated Ark of the Covenant. In it were the gold jar containing the manna, the staff of Aaron that had budded, and the stone tablets of the Covenant. ⁵Above the Ark was the throne of glory, with the glorious cherubim outspread over it. But we cannot go into further details now.

⁶Once these elements were in place, priests regularly entered the outer sanctuary to carry out their acts of worship. ⁷But only the high priest entered the inner sanctuary, once a year, and always with blood, which was both a self-offering and an offering for the sins of the people. ⁸In this way, the Holy Spirit is showing that the way into the inner sanctuary had not yet been revealed while the outer sanctuary was still standing. ⁹This is a symbol for the present time. Gifts and offerings made under these regulations cannot clear the conscience of the worshiper. ¹⁰They are rules about the outward life, relating to food and drink and ablutions at various times. They were intended to be in force only until the time of the new order.

¹¹But Christ, who came as high priest of the good things which came to be, entered once and for all into the greater and more perfect tabernacle, the one made not by human hands, that is, not belonging to this creation. ¹²It wasn't with the blood of goats and calves, but with our Savior's own blood that Christ entered the holy place, and once and for all obtained eternal redemption. ¹³For if the sprinkling of the blood of goats and bulls and a heifer's ashes can sanctify those who are defiled so that their flesh is cleansed, ¹⁴how much more will the blood of Christ, a perfect self-sacrifice to God through the eternal Spirit, cleanse our consciences from dead works, to worship the living God!

¹⁵Christ is the mediator of a new Covenant, so that the people who were

called by God may receive the eternal inheritance that was promised. This happens because a death has taken place which cancels the sins committed under the first Covenant.

¹⁶ In the case of a will, the death of the testator must be established, ¹⁷ for a will becomes valid only at death—it has no force while the testator is alive. ¹⁸ This is why even the first Covenant wasn't inaugurated without something being killed.

¹⁹ When Moses had given all the commandments of the Law to the people, he took the blood of calves and goats, together with some water, scarlet wool and branches of hyssop, and sprinkled both the book and the people. ²⁰ He said, "This is the blood of the Covenant that God has laid down for you." ²¹ In the same way, he sprinkled the tabernacle and the ceremonial vessels of worship. ²² In fact, according to the Law, almost everything has to be purified with blood. If there is no shedding of blood, there is no forgiveness.

²³ So if it was necessary for the copies of heavenly things to be purified this way, then the heavenly things have to be purified by a higher form of sacrifice than this. ²⁴ For Christ didn't go into a holy place made by human hands, a copy of the real one. Christ went into heaven itself and now appears on our behalf in the presence of God. ²⁵ High priests of old went into the Most Holy Place every year with the blood of an animal. But Christ didn't make a self-offering more than that one time; ²⁶ otherwise, Christ would have had to suffer many times ever since the creation of the world. But now that the Consummation is upon us, Christ has appeared once and for all, to remove sin through self-sacrifice. ²⁷ It is appointed that everyone must die once and then be judged by God. ²⁸ In the same way, Christ was offered once to bear the sins of many, and then will appear a second time— not to deal with sin, but to save those who are waiting for Christ's appearing.

10·1 Since the Law was only a reflection of the good things to come and not their true reality, it was quite incapable of perfecting the worshipers by the same sacrifices offered continually year after year. ² Otherwise, wouldn't the priests have stopped offering them because the worshipers, once cleansed, would no longer have had consciousness of sin? ³ But through these sacrifices there came only a yearly reminder of sins, ⁴ because it is impossible for the blood of bulls and goats to take away sins.

⁵ And this is what Jesus said, on coming into the world:
"You who wanted no sacrifice or oblation
    prepared a body for me.
⁶ In burnt offerings or sacrifices for sin
    you took no pleasure.
⁷ Then I said, just as it was written of me

> in the scroll of the book,
>> 'God, here I am!
>> I have come to do your will.' "

[8] In saying that God doesn't want burnt offerings and sacrifices—which are offered according to the Law—[9] and then saying, "I have come to do your will," Jesus abolishes the first Covenant in order to establish the second. [10] By God's will, we have been sanctified through the offering of the body of Jesus Christ once and for all.

[11] Every other priest performs services every day and offers the same sacrifices many times; but these sacrifices can never take away sins. [12] Christ, however, offered one sacrifice for sins, an offering that is effective forever. Then Christ sat down at the right hand of God, [13] and now waits there until God puts all enemies in their rightful place. [14] With one sacrifice then, Jesus has made perfect forever those who are being sanctified.

[15] The Holy Spirit also attests to this, first saying,

> [16] " 'This is the Covenant I will make with them
>> when those days arrive,' says Our God:
> 'I will put my laws into their hearts
>> and write them on their minds.' "

[17] Then she adds,

> "I will never again remember
>> their sins or offenses."

[18] So when sins and evil deeds have been forgiven, an offering to take away sins is no longer needed.

> ☙   ☙   ☙

[19] Therefore, sisters and brothers, since the blood of Jesus makes us confident to enter the holy place [20] by the new and living path opened for us through the veil—that is to say, the body of Jesus—[21] and since we have the supreme high priest presiding over the house of God, [22] let us enter it filled with faith and with sincerity in our hearts, our hearts sprinkled and cleared from any trace of bad conscience and our bodies washed with pure water. [23] Let us keep firm in the hope we profess, because the One who made the promise is faithful.

[24] Let us always think how we can stimulate each other to love and good works. [25] Don't stay away from the meetings of the community, as some do, but encourage one another; and do this all the more as you see the Day drawing near.

[26] For if we sin deliberately after we have received knowledge of the truth, there no longer remains any sacrifice for sins. [27] There only remains the fear-

ful prospect of judgment and of the raging fire that will consume the enemies of God. ²⁸ Anyone who rejects the Law of Moses is put to death without mercy on the testimony of two or three witnesses. ²⁹ So if you trample God's Only Begotten underfoot and treat the blood of the Covenant, which sanctified you, as if it were something unclean, insulting the Spirit of grace, how much more severely do you think you deserve to be punished? ³⁰ We know the One who said, "Vengeance is mine, I will repay!" and, "Our God will judge the people." ³¹ It is a terrifying thing to fall into the hands of the living God.

³² Call to mind those earlier days, after you had been enlightened, when you stood your ground in a great struggle of suffering. ³³ Sometimes you were exposed to insults and violence. Sometimes you stood by associates who received such treatment. ³⁴ You joined in the suffering of those in prison. You gladly accepted the confiscation of your property, for you knew that you possessed something better and lasting.

³⁵ So don't throw away your confidence. It will provide you with a great reward. ³⁶ You'll need endurance to carry out God's will and receive what has been promised.

> ³⁷ "In just a little while,
> the One who is coming will come
> and will not delay.
> ³⁸ The just will live by their faith,
> but if they hesitate,
> I will take no pleasure in them."

³⁹ You and I are not the sort to "hesitate" and be lost by it. We are the sort who have faith and are saved.

f

11:1–12:29

aith is the reality of all that is hoped for; faith is the proof of all that is unseen. ² Because of faith, our ancestors were approved by God.

³ By faith, we understand that the world was created by the word from God, and that what is visible came into being through the invisible.

⁴ By faith, Abel offered a better sacrifice to God than Cain, and for that was declared to be just; God spoke well of his offerings. And by faith Abel still speaks, even though he is dead.

⁵ By faith, Enoch was taken up and didn't have to experience death—"he was seen no more because God took him." Even before he was taken, he was commended as one who pleased God. ⁶ And without faith it is impos-

sible to please God, because anyone who comes to God must believe that God exists, rewarding those who earnestly seek the divine glory.

⁷ By faith, Noah—warned about things not yet seen—revered God and built an ark in order to save his household. By faith, Noah condemned the world and inherited the justice which comes through faith.

⁸ By faith, Sarah and Abraham obeyed when they were called, and went off to the place they were to receive as a heritage; they went forth, moreover, not knowing where they were going.

⁹ By faith, Sarah and Abraham lived in the promised land as resident aliens, dwelling in tents with their children and grandchildren, who were heirs of the same promise—¹⁰for they were looking forward to the city with foundations, whose designer and maker is God.

¹¹ By faith, Sarah received the ability to conceive, even though she was past child-bearing age, for she thought that the One who had made the promise was worthy of trust. ¹² As a result of this faith, there came forth from one woman and one man, themselves as good as dead, descendants as numerous as the stars in the sky and the sands of the seashore.

¹³ All of them died in faith. They didn't obtain what had been promised, but saw and welcomed it from afar. By acknowledging themselves to be strangers and exiles on the earth, ¹⁴they showed that they were looking for a country of their own. ¹⁵ If they had been thinking of the country from which they had come, they'd have been able to return to it. ¹⁶ But they were searching for a better country, a heavenly one. So God isn't ashamed of them, or ashamed to be called their God. That's why God has prepared a city for them.

¹⁷ By faith, Abraham, when put to the test, offered up Isaac. Abraham, who had received the promises, was ready to sacrifice his only son, ¹⁸ of whom it was said, "Through Isaac will your descendants be called." ¹⁹ He reasoned that God was able to raise Isaac from the dead, and so he received Isaac back as a symbol.

²⁰ By faith, Isaac blessed Jacob and Esau concerning their future.

²¹ By faith, Jacob, near death, blessed each of Joseph's sons, leaning on the top of his staff as though bowing in worship.

²² By faith, Joseph, near the end of his life, recalled the Exodus of the Israelites and made arrangements for his own burial.

²³ By faith, Moses was hidden by his parents for three months after his birth. They defied the royal edict because they saw he was such a fine child.

²⁴ By faith, Moses, now an adult, refused to be identified as the son of the Pharaoh's daughter. ²⁵ He chose to endure ill-treatment along with the people of God rather than enjoy the fleeting pleasures of sin. ²⁶ He consid-

ered disgrace for the sake of the Messiah something more precious than the treasures of Egypt. He was looking forward to his reward.

²⁷ By faith, he left Egypt, not fearing Pharaoh's rage. He persevered because he saw the Invisible One.

²⁸ By faith, he kept the Passover and the sprinkling of the blood, so that the Destroyer wouldn't touch the firstborn children of Israel.

²⁹ By faith, the people passed through the Sea of Reeds as though on dry land. When the Egyptians tried the same, they drowned.

³⁰ By faith, the walls of Jericho fell after being encircled for seven days.

³¹ By faith, Rahab the prostitute didn't perish with those who were disobedient, after she welcomed the spies in peace.

³² What more can I say? There is no time for me to give an account of Gideon, Barak, Samson, Jephthah, or David, Samuel and the prophets. ³³ These were those who through faith conquered nations, did what was just and earned the promises. They shut the jaws of lions, ³⁴ put out raging fires and emerged unscathed from battle. They were weak people who were given strength, became brave in battle and put foreign invaders to flight. ³⁵ Some came back from the dead to their spouses by resurrection. Others submitted to torture, refusing release so that they could rise again to a better life. ³⁶ Still others endured mockery, scourgings—even chains and imprisonment. ³⁷ They were stoned, sawed in half, even beheaded. They were homeless, dressed in the skins of sheep and goats; they were penniless and given nothing but ill treatment—³⁸ the world wasn't worthy of them!—and they wandered in deserts and slept on mountains and in caves and ravines. ³⁹ These are all heroes of our faith, but none of them received what was promised, ⁴⁰ since God had provided something better for us, so that they would not be made perfect apart from us.

∞   ∞   ∞

12:1 Therefore, since we are surrounded by such a great cloud of witnesses, let us lay aside everything that impedes us and the sin that so easily entangles us. Let us run with perseverance the race laid out for us. ² Let us not lose sight of Jesus, who leads us in our faith and brings it to perfection.

For the sake of the joy to come, Jesus endured the cross, heedless of its shame, and now sits at the right of God's throne. ³ Think of Jesus—who endured such opposition from sinners—so that you will not grow weary and lose heart. ⁴ In your struggles against sin, you still haven't resisted to the point of shedding your blood.

⁵ Moreover, you have forgotten the encouraging words addressed to you as daughters and sons,

"My children, when Our God corrects you,
  don't treat it lightly;
and don't get discouraged
  when you are reprimanded.
⁶ For God disciplines the ones God loves
  and punishes all whom God acknowledges
  as daughters and sons."

⁷ Endure your trials as the discipline of God, who deals with you as daughters and sons. Have there ever been any children whose parents didn't discipline them? ⁸ If you aren't disciplined—and everyone receives discipline—then you are illegitimate children and not heirs.

⁹ Moreover, we had our human parents to discipline us, and we respected them for it. Wouldn't we much rather submit ourselves to our spiritual Parent, and live? ¹⁰ Our parents applied discipline for the short term—doing what they thought best. But God does it for our own good—that we may share in the divine holiness.

¹¹ At the time it is administered, any discipline seems a cause for grief, not joy, but later it bears fruit in peace and justice for those formed by it. ¹² So hold up your drooping hands and steady your trembling knees. ¹³ Make straight the path you tread, that your halting limbs will not be dislocated, but healed.

¹⁴ Always strive for peace with everyone and for the holiness without which no one can see Our God. ¹⁵ See to it that no one falls short of God's grace, and that no bitter root starts growing, causing trouble and spreading defilement as it grows.

¹⁶ Take care that there be no immoral or godless person like Esau, who sold his own birthright for a single meal. ¹⁷ You know that later, when he wanted to inherit the blessing, he was rejected. Even though he sought it with tears, he couldn't bring about a change of heart.

ଔ   ଔ   ଔ

¹⁸ What you have come to is nothing known to the senses: not a blazing fire, or a gloom turning to total darkness, or a storm, ¹⁹ or trumpeting thunder, or the great voice speaking such that those hearing it begged that no more be said to them. ²⁰ They couldn't bear to hear the command, "If even an animal touches the mountain, it must be stoned." ²¹ Indeed, so fearful was the spectacle that even Moses said, "I am terrified and trembling."

²² What you have drawn near to is Mount Zion and the city of the living God, the heavenly Jerusalem, where myriad angels have gathered for the

festival with the whole church—[23] in which everyone is a "firstborn" and a citizen of heaven. You have come to God, the supreme Judge, and have been placed with the spirits of the holy ones who have been made perfect. [24] You have come to Jesus—the mediator who brings a new Covenant—and to the sprinkled blood which pleads even more insistently than that of Abel.

[25] Make sure that you never refuse to listen to the One who speaks. If the people who refused to listen to the warning while on earth didn't escape, how much less will we escape if we refuse to listen to the voice of warning that comes from heaven? [26] God's voice shook the earth then, but now God promises, "Once more I will shake not only the earth but also the heavens." [27] That promise means that the things being shaken are created things, so that only those things that cannot be shaken will remain. [28] Therefore, since we have inherited an unshakeable kindom, let us thankfully worship God in a way that is acceptable—in reverence and in awe. [29] For our God is a consuming fire.

13:1-25

Continue to love each other as sisters and brothers.

[2] Don't neglect to show hospitality to strangers, for by doing so some people have entertained angels without knowing it.

[3] Keep in mind those who are in prison, as though you were in prison with them. And be mindful of those who are being treated badly, since you know what they are enduring.

[4] Let marriage be honored by everyone, and let the marriage bed be kept undefiled, for God will judge covenant-breakers and adulterers.

[5] Put the love of money out of your lives and be content with what you have, for God has said, "I will never leave you or forsake you." [6] Thus we may say with confidence,

"God is my Helper,
and I will not be afraid;
what can mere humans do to me?"

[7] Remember your leaders, who preached the Word of God to you, and as you reflect on the outcome of their lives, imitate their faith. [8] Jesus is the same yesterday, today and forever.

[9] Don't be led astray by all kinds of strange teachings. It is better to rely on grace for inner strength than on dietary laws, which don't give spiritual benefits to those who live by them. [10] We have our own altar, from which even those who serve in the tabernacle have no right to eat. [11] The bodies of

animals whose blood the high priest brings into the sanctuary as a sin offering are burned outside the camp. [12] In the same way, Jesus suffered outside the city gate to sanctify the people with his own blood. [13] Let us, then, go to him outside the camp and share his degradation. [14] For there is no eternal city for us in this life—we seek the one which is to come.

[15] Through Jesus let us continually offer God a sacrifice of praise—that is, the fruit of lips that acknowledge God's Name.

[16] Keep doing good works and sharing your resources. These are the sacrifices that please God.

[17] Obey your leaders, acknowledge their authority, because they must give an account of how they look after your souls. Make this a joy for them to do, and not a burden, for that would be of no advantage to you.

[18] Pray for us. We are sure that we have a clear conscience, since we desire to live honorably in every way. [19] I ask you particularly to pray for my early return to you.

[20] May the God of peace, who brought back from the dead the great Shepherd of the sheep in the blood of the eternal Covenant, Jesus our Savior, [21] furnish you with all that is good, so you may do all that is pleasing to God. To Christ be glory forever! Amen.

[22] Sisters and brothers, I ask that you take these words of advice kindly, for I have written you only a brief letter.

[23] I want you to know that our brother Timothy has been released from prison. If he arrives in time, he will be with me when I see you. [24] Greetings to all your leaders and to all the saints. Those in Italy send you greetings.

[25] Grace be with you all. Amen.

the letter of
james

1:1-27

from james, a servant of god and our
Savior Jesus Christ,

To the twelve tribes of the diaspora:

Greetings.

² Think of it as pure joy, my sisters and brothers, whenever you face trials of any sort. ³ You understand that your faith is put to the test only to make you patient, ⁴ but patience too has its practical results—it's to make you fully mature and lacking in nothing.

⁵ If you lack wisdom, ask for it from God, who gives generously and ungrudgingly to all, and it will be given to you. ⁶ But you must ask in faith, never doubting, for the doubter is like the surf tossed and driven by the wind. ⁷ People like this must not expect to receive anything from God, ⁸ for they are devious and erratic in all they do.

⁹ Let sisters and brothers who are in humble circumstances take pride in their high position, ¹⁰ and let rich people take pride in their lowliness, for

they will disappear "like the flowers of the field." ¹¹ When the sun comes up with its scorching heat and parches the meadow, the flowers wither and the meadow's loveliness disappears. Just so will the rich people wither away amid their many concerns.

¹² Blessed are those who persevere under trial! Once their worth has been proven, they will receive the crown of life that God has promised to the faithful. ¹³ No one who is tempted is free to say, "I am being tempted by God." God, who is not touched by evil, tempts no one. ¹⁴ Those who are tempted are attracted and seduced by their own wrong desires. ¹⁵ Then the desires conceive and give birth to sin, and when that sin is fully grown, it too has a child—death.

¹⁶ Make no mistake about this, my dear sisters and brothers: ¹⁷ every worthwhile gift, every genuine benefit comes from above, descending from the Creator of the heavenly luminaries, who cannot change and is never in shadow. ¹⁸ God willingly gave birth to us with a word spoken in truth, so that we may be, as it were, the firstfruits of God's creatures.

¹⁹ Remember this, my dear sisters and brothers: be quick to listen, but slow to speak and slow to anger; ²⁰ for God's justice is never served by our anger. ²¹ So do away with all your filth and the last vestiges of wickedness in you. Humbly welcome the word which has been planted in you, because it has power to save you.

²² But act on this word—because if all you do is listen to it, you're deceiving yourselves. ²³ Those who listen to God's word but don't put it into practice are like those who look into mirrors at their own faces; ²⁴ they look at themselves, then go off and promptly forget what they looked like. ²⁵ But those who look steadily at the perfect law of freedom and make it their habit—not listening and then forgetting, but actively putting it into practice—will be blessed in all that they do.

²⁶ If those who don't control their tongues imagine that they are devout, they're deceiving themselves and their worship is pointless. ²⁷ Pure, unspoiled religion, in the eyes of our Abba God, is this: coming to the aid of widows and orphans when they are in need, and keeping oneself uncontaminated by this world.

2:1-26

My sisters and brothers, your faith in our glorious Savior Jesus Christ must not allow favoritism. ² Suppose there should come into your assembly a person wearing gold rings and fine clothes and, at the same time, a poor person dressed in shabby clothes. ³ Suppose further you were to take notice of the well-dressed one and say, "Sit right here, in the seat of honor"; and say to the poor one, "You can stand!" or "Sit over there by my footrest." ⁴Haven't you in such a case discriminated in your hearts? Haven't you set yourselves up like judges who hand down corrupt decisions?

⁵Listen, dear sisters and brothers: didn't God choose those who are poor in the eyes of the world to be rich in faith, and heirs of the kindom promised to those who love God? ⁶Yet you've treated poor people shamefully! Aren't rich people exploiting you? Aren't they the ones who haul you into the courts, ⁷and who blaspheme that noble Name by which you've been called?

⁸You're acting rightly, however, if you fulfill the venerable law of the scriptures: "Love your neighbor as yourself." ⁹But if you show favoritism, you commit sin, and that same law convicts you as transgressors. ¹⁰Those who keep the whole Law except for one small point are still guilty of breaking all of it. ¹¹The One who said, "No adultery," also said, "No killing." So even if you don't commit adultery, if you do commit murder, you still break the Law.

¹²Talk and behave as people who will be judged by the law of freedom, ¹³because judgment without mercy will be the lot of those who are not merciful. Mercy triumphs over judgment.

¹⁴My sisters and brothers, what good is it to profess faith without practicing it? Such faith has no power to save. ¹⁵If any are in need of clothes and have no food to live on, ¹⁶and one of you says to them, "Goodbye and good luck. Stay warm and well-fed," without giving them the bare necessities of life, then what good is this? ¹⁷So it is with faith. If good deeds don't go with it, faith is dead.

¹⁸Some of you will say that you have faith, while I have deeds. Fine: I'll prove to you that I have faith by showing you my good deeds. Now you prove to me that you have faith without any good deeds to show. ¹⁹You believe in the One God. Fine. But even the demons have the same belief, and they tremble with fear. ²⁰Don't you realize, you idiots, that faith without good deeds is useless?

²¹Wasn't our ancestor Abraham justified by his actions when he offered his child Isaac on the altar? ²²There you see proof that faith and deeds were working together and that faith was made complete by the deeds. ²³You also see that the scripture was fulfilled which says, "Abraham believed God, and it was credited to him as justice." This is why he is called "the friend of God." ²⁴So you see, people are justified by their works and not by faith alone.

²⁵And in the same way, wasn't even Rahab the prostitute justified by works when she welcomed the messengers and showed them a different way to leave?

²⁶ Be assured, then, that faith without works is as dead as a body without a spirit.

3:1–5:20

Only a few of you, my sisters and brothers, should be teachers. You should realize that those of us who are teachers will be called to a stricter account. ² After all, each of us falls from time to time.

However, those who never say anything wrong are truly close to perfection, because they can then control every part of themselves. ³ Once we put bits into the mouths of horses to make them obey us, we control the rest of their bodies. ⁴ The same with ships—no matter how large they are, and even if they are driven by fierce winds, they are directed by a very small rudder to wherever the captain wants to go.

⁵ The tongue is like that. It's a small part of the body, yet it makes great boasts. See how tiny the spark is that sets a huge forest ablaze! ⁶ The tongue is such a flame. Among all the parts of the body, the tongue is a whole wicked world in itself. It infects the entire body. Its flames encircle our course from birth, and its fire is kindled by hell. ⁷ All kinds of animals—birds, reptiles and creatures of the sea—can be tamed by us, ⁸ but no one can tame the tongue. It's a restless evil, full of deadly poison. ⁹ We use it to say, "Praised be our God and Creator"; then we use it to curse each other—we who are created in the image of God. ¹⁰ Blessing and curse come out of the same mouth. This shouldn't be, my sisters and brothers! ¹¹ Does a spring emit both pure water and brackish water? ¹² My sisters and brothers, can a fig tree produce olives, or can a grapevine produce figs? No—and neither can a fountain produce both salt water and fresh water.

¹³ If there are any wise and learned among you, let them show it by good living—with humility, and with wisdom in their actions. ¹⁴ But if you have the bitterness of jealousy or self-seeking ambition in your hearts, be careful or you'll find yourself becoming arrogant and covering up the truth with lies. ¹⁵ This kind of "wisdom" doesn't come from above. It's earthbound, animal-like and demonic. ¹⁶ Where there is jealousy and ambition, there is also disharmony and wickedness of every kind. ¹⁷ The wisdom from above, however, has purity as its essence. It works for peace; it's kind and considerate. It's full of compassion and shows itself by doing good. Nor is there any trace of partiality or hypocrisy in it. ¹⁸ Peacemakers, when they work for peace, sow the seeds which will bear fruit in holiness.

4:1 Where do these conflicts and battles among you first start? Isn't it that they come from the desires that battle within you? ² You want something but don't get it, so you're prepared to kill to get it. You have ambitions that you can't satisfy, so you fight to get your way by force. The reason you don't have what you want is that you don't ask for it in prayer. ³And when you do ask and don't get it, it's because you haven't prayed properly. You have prayed in order to indulge your own pleasures.

⁴You faithless people, don't you know that making the world your friend is making God your enemy? Those who want to befriend the world make themselves enemies of God. ⁵Do you think scripture says for no good reason that "the Spirit planted in us is passionate to the point of jealousy"? ⁶She bestows a greater gift, which is why scripture says, "God resists the proud and favors the humble."

⁷Submit yourselves, then, to God. Resist the Devil, and it will flee from you. ⁸Draw near to God, and God will draw near to you.

Clean your hands, you sinners; purify your hearts, you double-dealers! ⁹Look at your wretched condition and weep for it in misery. Be miserable rather than laughing, gloomy instead of happy. ¹⁰Humble yourselves before Our God, who will then raise you on high.

¹¹Sisters and brothers, don't slander one another. Whoever speaks evil of a sister or judges a brother, speaks against the Law and judges it. When you judge the Law, you cease keeping it and become a judge of it. ¹²But there is only one Lawgiver, one Judge—only one who is able to save or destroy. Who then are you to judge your neighbor?

¹³Come now, you who say, "Today or tomorrow we'll go to such-and-such a city, spend a year there, open a business and get rich." ¹⁴You can never tell what your life will be like or what will happen tomorrow. You're no more than a vapor that appears briefly and then disappears. ¹⁵Instead, you ought to say, "If it's Our God's will, we will live to do such-and-such." ¹⁶As it is, you boast and brag; all such boasting is evil. ¹⁷Anyone who knows the right thing to do and doesn't do so—to that person it is sin.

℘   ℘   ℘

5·¹Now an answer for the rich: weep and howl for the miseries that are coming to you. ²Your wealth is all rotting; your clothes are eaten up by moths. ³Your gold and silver are corroding, and the same corrosion will be your own sentence: it will consume your flesh like fire. This is what you've stored up for yourselves to receive on the last day. ⁴Laborers mowed your fields, and you cheated them! Listen to the wages that you kept back: they call out against you; realize that the cries of the reapers have reached the ears of Our God Most High. ⁵On earth you've had a life of comfort and luxury; you've been fattening yourselves for the day of slaughter. ⁶It was you who condemned the innocent and killed them; they offered you no resistance.

⁷ Be patient, my sisters and brothers, until the appearance of Christ. See how the farmer awaits the precious yield of the soil, looking forward to it patiently while the soil receives the winter and spring rains. ⁸ You, too, must be patient. Steady your hearts, because the coming of Christ is at hand.

⁹ Don't grumble against one another, my sisters and brothers, or you will be judged. The Judge is standing at the door! ¹⁰ To learn how to persevere patiently under hardship, sisters and brothers, take as your models the prophets who spoke in the name of the Most High. ¹¹ The ones we call "blessed" are the ones who persevered. You've heard of the patience of Job—do you remember what God, who is compassionate and merciful, did for him at the end of the story?

¹² Above all, my sisters and brothers, don't swear any oath by heaven or by earth or by anything else. Let your "yes" be yes and your "no" be no. In this way you're not liable to judgment.

¹³ Are any of you in trouble? Then pray. Are any of you in good spirits? Then sing a hymn of praise. ¹⁴ Are any of you sick? Then call for the elders of the church, and have them pray over those who are sick and anoint them with oil in the name of Christ. ¹⁵ And this prayer offered in faith will make them well, and Christ will raise them up. If they have sinned, they will be forgiven. ¹⁶ So confess your sins to one another, and pray for one another, that you may be healed.

The prayers of the just are powerful and effective. ¹⁷ Elijah was human just like us, yet he prayed that it wouldn't rain, and it didn't rain for three and a half years. ¹⁸ Then he prayed again, and the heavens gave rain and the earth produced its crop.

¹⁹ My sisters and brothers, if you should wander from the truth and another should bring you back, ²⁰ remember that whoever turns sinners from the error of their ways saves them from death and cancels a multitude of sins.

peter

from peter, an apostle of jesus christ,

To those who live as resident aliens dispersed throughout Pontus, Galatia, Cappadocia, Asia and Bithynia—²who have been chosen according to the foreknowledge of God the Creator, through the sanctifying work of the Spirit, that you may obey Jesus Christ and be sprinkled with Christ's blood:

May grace and peace be yours in abundance.

³Praised be the Abba God of our Savior Jesus Christ, who with great mercy gave us new birth: a birth into hope, which draws its life from the resurrection of Jesus Christ from the dead; ⁴a birth to an imperishable inheritance incapable of fading or defilement, which is kept in heaven for you ⁵who are guarded with God's power through faith; a birth to a salvation which stands ready to be revealed in the last days.

⁶There is cause for rejoicing here. You may, for a time, have to suffer the distress of many trials. ⁷But this is so that your faith, which is more pre-

cious than the passing splendor of fire-tried gold, may by its genuineness lead to praise, glory and honor when Jesus Christ appears. [8] Although you have never seen Christ, you love Christ; and without seeing, you still believe, and you rejoice with inexpressible joy touched with glory, [9] because you are achieving faith's goal—your salvation.

[10] This is the salvation the prophets were looking for and searching for so carefully; their prophecies were about the grace which has come to you. [11] The Spirit of Christ which was in them foretold the sufferings of Christ, and the glories that would come after those sufferings. They tried to find out at what time and in what circumstances all this was to happen. [12] However, it was revealed to them that the news they brought—regarding all the things that have now been announced to you by those who proclaimed the Good News, through the Holy Spirit who was sent from heaven—was for you and not for themselves. Even the angels long to catch a glimpse of such things.

1:13 – 2:10

So make your minds ready for action, and be sober. Put your hope in nothing but the grace that will be given you when Jesus Christ is revealed. [14] Be children of obedience. Don't behave the way you did when, in your ignorance, your desires were all you knew. [15] Be holy in everything you do, since it is the Holy One who has called you—[16] as scripture says, "You will be holy, for I am holy."

[17] When you pray, you call on Abba God, who judges everyone impartially on the basis of their actions. Since this is so, conduct yourselves reverently during your sojourn in a foreign land. [18] Realize that you were delivered from the futile way of life your ancestors handed on to you, not by any diminishable sum of gold or silver [19] but by Christ's blood, which is beyond all price: the blood of a spotless, unblemished lamb [20] foreknown before the world's foundation and revealed for your sake in these last days. [21] It is through Christ that you are believers in God, the God who raised Christ from the dead into glory. Your faith and hope, then, are centered in God.

[22] By obedience to the truth you have purified yourselves for a genuine love of your sisters and brothers. Therefore love one another constantly, from the heart. [23] Your rebirth has come not from a perishable seed but from an imperishable one—the living and enduring word of God. [24] For, as Isaiah says,

"All people are grass,
   and the glory of mortals is like the flower of the field.
The grass withers, the flower wilts,
   ²⁵but the word of Our God endures forever."
Now this "word" is the Good News which was proclaimed to you.

2:1 Therefore, never be spiteful, deceitful, hypocritical, envious or critical of each other.

²Like newborn babies, be hungry for nothing but milk—the pure milk of the word that will make you grow into salvation, ³now that you have "tasted that Our God is good."

⁴Come to Christ—a living stone, rejected by mortals but approved nonetheless, chosen and precious in God's eyes. ⁵And you are living stones as well: you are being built as an edifice of spirit, to become a holy priesthood, offering spiritual sacrifices to God through Jesus Christ. ⁶For scripture has it,

"See, I am laying a cornerstone in Zion;
   an approved stone, and precious.
Those who put their faith in it
   will not be shaken."

⁷The stone is precious for you who have faith. But for those without faith,

"The stone which the builders rejected
   has become the cornerstone,"

and, at the same time,

⁸"an obstacle and a stumbling block."

Those who stumble and fall are the disbelievers in God's word; it is their destiny to do so.

⁹You, however, are a "chosen people, a royal priesthood, a consecrated nation, a people set apart" to sing the praises of the One who called you out of the darkness into the wonderful, divine light. ¹⁰Once you were "not a people," but now you are the people of God; once there was "no mercy for you," but now you have found mercy.

Dear friends, I urge you, as strangers and aliens in this world, to abstain from sinful passions which attack the soul. ¹² Live such good lives among the Gentiles that, though they accuse you of doing wrong, they may see your good deeds and glorify God on the day of visitation.

¹³Accept the authority of every human institution for the sake of Christ,

whether it be the ruler as the supreme authority, ¹⁴ or the governors who are sent by the ruler to punish wrongdoers and to commend those who are good citizens. ¹⁵ For it is the will of God that by doing right you may silence those who are foolish in their ignorance. ¹⁶ Live as free women and men. Don't use your freedom to cloak evil, but to serve God.

¹⁷ Respect all people. Love the family of believers. Stand in awe before God. Honor the ruler.

¹⁸ You who are in bondage, show respect to your overseers—both to those who are good and considerate and to those who are cruel. ¹⁹ For grace is given if you endure unjust punishment for your conscience in the name of God.

²⁰ What credit is there if you patiently endure harsh punishment as a result of your sin? But if you put up with suffering for doing what is right, this is acceptable in God's eyes. ²¹ It was for this that you were called, since Christ suffered for you in just this way and left you an example. You must follow in the footsteps of Christ, ²² who did no wrong, who spoke no deceit, ²³ who did not return insults when insulted, who, when made to suffer, did not counter with threats. Instead, Christ trusted the One who judges justly. ²⁴ It was Christ's own body that brought our sins to the cross, so that all of us, dead to sin, could live in accord with God's will. By Christ's wounds you are healed. ²⁵ At one time you were straying like sheep, but now you have returned to the Shepherd, the Guardian of your souls.

☙   ☙   ☙

3:1 Those of you in relationships, be submissive to one another—so that spouses who have not yet submitted to the Word may be won over ² when they witness the example and respectful attitude of their partners. ³ Dress modestly, and not for show—without fancy hairstyles, gold jewelry or fine apparel. ⁴ Your attractiveness should reside inside, in the heart, with the imperishable quality of a gentle and calm disposition, which is precious in the sight of God. ⁵ We have the example of holy people of ages past who hoped in God and were attractive because of their humility. ⁶ Didn't Sarah confirm their destiny when she called Abraham "Sovereign One?" You are children of Sarah and Abraham when you fearlessly do what is good.

⁷ Husbands have a special obligation to be understanding and nurturing. Men, though physically stronger than women, must nonetheless acknowledge their equal status—that women are joint heirs of the gift of life. Doing so will ensure that your prayers are not hindered.

⁸ All of you must be of one mind. Be sympathetic, loving, compassion-

ate, humble. ⁹Never return evil for evil, or insult for insult, but give a bless-ing instead. You were called to do this, to inherit a blessing yourself. ¹⁰For,

"Whoever would love life
and see good days
must keep the tongue from evil
and the lips from deceitful talk.
¹¹They must turn from evil to good,
they must seek peace and pursue it.
¹²For the eyes of Our God
are on the just,
and the ears of Our God
attend to their prayers.
But the face of Our God
is turned against evildoers."

¹³Who is going to harm you if your goal is to do what is right? ¹⁴But even if you do suffer for what is right, count it a blessing. Don't fear what they fear. Don't be afraid, and don't worry.

¹⁵In your hearts, set Jesus apart as holy and sovereign. Should anyone ask you the reason for this hope of yours, be ever ready to reply, but speak gently and respectfully. ¹⁶Keep your conscience clear so that, whenever you are defamed, those who slander your way of life in Christ may be shamed. ¹⁷If it should be God's will that you suffer, it is better to do so for good deeds than for evil ones.

ଔ ଔ ଔ

¹⁸The reason Christ died for sins once for everyone—the just for the sake of the unjust—was in order to lead you to God. Jesus was put to death in the flesh but was given life in the Spirit. ¹⁹And in the Spirit, Jesus went and preached to the imprisoned spirits. ²⁰They had refused obedience long ago, while God waited patiently in the days of Noah and the building of the ark, in which a few persons, eight in all, were brought to safety through the water. ²¹That water prefigured the water of baptism through which you are now brought to safety. Baptism is not the washing away of physical dirt, but the appeal made to God by a good conscience: it brings salvation through the resurrection of Jesus Christ, ²²who entered heaven and is now at the right hand of God, having dominion over angelic authorities and powers.

4:1Accordingly, remind yourselves of what Christ suffered while among us, and equip yourselves with a similar attitude. For if you suffer in the body, you have broken with sin and, ²as a result, you won't spend the rest of your life on human desires, but on the will of God. ³ You dallied long enough in the past, living the kind of life some Gentiles choose: licentious living, lust, drunkenness, orgies, carousing and following false gods. ⁴ In all this, they consider it odd when you don't leap into the same flood of dissipation, and they slander you. ⁵ But they will eventually answer for it before the One who stands ready to judge the living and the dead. ⁶ This explains why the Gospel was preached also to the dead—that though judged in the flesh like the rest of humankind, they might live for God in the Spirit.

⁷ The end of all things is near. Therefore be clear-minded and self-controlled so that you can pray. ⁸ Above all, let your love for one another be constant, for love covers a multitude of sins. ⁹ Be mutually hospitable without complaining.

¹⁰ As generous distributors of God's manifold grace, put your gifts at the service of one another, each in the measure you have received. ¹¹ The one who speaks should deliver God's message. The one who serves should do so with the strength provided by God, so that in all things God may be glorified through Jesus Christ, who has been given all glory and dominion throughout the ages. Amen.

¹² Don't be surprised, my dear friends, that a trial by fire is occurring in your midst. It is a test for you, but it shouldn't catch you off guard. ¹³ Rejoice, instead, insofar as you share the Savior's sufferings, so that when the glory of Christ is revealed, you will rejoice exceedingly. ¹⁴ Happy are you when you are insulted for the sake of Christ, for then God's Spirit in her glory has come to rest on you.

¹⁵ See to it, however, that none of you suffers for being a murderer, a thief, an evildoer, or a destroyer of another's rights. ¹⁶ If anyone suffers for being a follower of Christ, however, that one ought not be ashamed, but rather should glorify God in virtue of that Name.

¹⁷ It is time for the judgment to begin with the family of God. And if we are only the beginning, what will happen by the time those who disobey the Good News of God are judged? ¹⁸ If it is hard for a good person to be saved, where will the wicked and the sinners be? ¹⁹ Therefore those who suffer according to God's will do the right thing, and commit themselves to their faithful Creator.

5:1-13

I send a word of advice to the elders among you. I, too, am an elder, as well as a witness to the sufferings of Christ and a partaker of the glory that will be revealed.

² Shepherd the flock entrusted to you. Shepherd it, not just out of duty, but eagerly, as God would have it. Don't do it for money, but do it freely.

³ Don't be pompous or domineering, but set an example for the whole community to follow. ⁴ Then when the chief Shepherd comes, you will receive a crown of unfading glory. ⁵ Let the young among you respect the leadership of the elders. Let all of you clothe yourselves in humility toward each other, for "God opposes the proud and gives grace to the humble." ⁶ Therefore, humble yourselves before God's mighty power, that you may be exalted by God on the appointed day.

⁷ Cast all your cares on God, who cares for you. ⁸ Be sober. Be watchful. For your adversary the Devil roams about like a roaring lion seeking someone to devour. ⁹ Stand up to the Devil as one strong in faith, fortified with the knowledge that your sisters and brothers throughout the world share the same afflictions.

¹⁰ But the God of all grace, who called you to eternal glory through Jesus Christ, will fulfill, restore, strengthen and establish you after you have suffered a little while. ¹¹ To God be glory and dominion forever and ever! Amen.

¹² This letter was dictated to Silas, a faithful co-worker I know and can trust. I have written this note to exhort you, and to testify that this is the true grace of God. Stand steadfast in it.

¹³ The church in "Babylon," chosen just as you are, sends greetings, as does my son Mark. ¹⁴ Greet one another with a holy kiss. Peace to all who are in Christ.

the second letter of
peter

from simon peter, servant and apostle

of Jesus Christ,

To those who received a faith equal to ours through the justice of our God and Savior Jesus Christ:

[2] May grace and peace be yours in abundance through your knowledge of Our God and of Jesus our Sovereign.

[3] Divine power has given us everything we need for life and godliness through our knowledge of God, who called us to share in the divine glory and goodness. [4] In bestowing these gifts, God has given us the guarantee of something very great and wonderful to come. Through them you'll be able to share the divine nature, and escape corruption from a world sunk in vice.

[5] For this very reason, make every effort to add to your faith, goodness; and to goodness, knowledge; [6] and to knowledge, self-control; and to self-

control, perseverance; and to perseverance, godliness; [7] and to godliness, familial love; and to familial love, truly unselfish love.

[8] For if these qualities are yours and they are growing in you, they will protect you from becoming ineffective and unfruitful; and they will bring you to a true knowledge of our Savior Jesus Christ. [9] But those who lack these qualities are blind and nearsighted, and have forgotten that they are cleansed of their past sins. [10] Sisters and brothers, you have been called and chosen. Strive that much harder to be up to your calling. In this way you will avoid stumbling, [11] and will ultimately receive a warm welcome into the eternal kindom of our Sovereign and Savior Jesus Christ.

1:12–2:22

My goal is to remind you constantly of these truths, even though you already know them and firmly possess them. [13] I consider it right, so long as I am in this tent that is my body, to motivate you with reminders. [14] For I know that I will soon be laying aside this earthly tent, as our Savior Jesus Christ has foretold to me. [15] I will be diligent in my teaching, so that even after I'm gone you will be able to recall these truths.

[16] We did not cleverly devise fables when we taught you of the power and coming of our Savior Jesus Christ; we ourselves saw the majesty of our Savior. [17] For Jesus was honored and glorified by our Creator God when the voice of the Majestic Glory spoke out, "This is my Own, whom I love, and with whom I am well pleased." [18] We heard this ourselves—this voice from heaven—when we were with Jesus on the holy mountain. [19] Moreover, we have the prophetic word, which is even more certain. Depend on it for your own good as a light shining in the dark, until first light breaks and the morning star rises in your hearts.

[20] At the same time, you need to know that no prophecy of scripture ever occurred by one's own interpretation. [21] Prophecy never comes through an act of human will, but comes as people have spoken for God under the power of the Holy Spirit.

[2:1] Even so, there were false prophets in the past among our people, and you will have your share of false prophets in the future. They will subtly introduce false heresies among you, to the point of denying the One who paid the price for their freedom. They will quickly fall to ruin, [2] but many will follow their licentious practices, and the Way of Truth will fall under a cloud of doubt because of them. [3] They will use lies to exploit you through greed.

But since the very beginning, their sentence has perpetually hung over them, and their damnation never sleeps. ⁴When the angels sinned, God did not spare them, but condemned them to the dungeons of the underworld to await the final judgment. ⁵Nor did the Most High spare the ancient world. God spared Noah, the paragon of justice, along with seven others, but flooded the ungodly world; ⁶God turned the cities of Sodom and Gomorrah into a pile of ashes as a warning to the ungodly about the future; ⁷God rescued the just Lot, who was oppressed by the filthy conduct of wicked people ⁸that he both witnessed and heard about as he lived among them; he suffered daily torment to his soul because of their lawlessness. ⁹But God knows how to rescue the godly from torment, and to incarcerate the unjust until the day of judgment.

¹⁰This pertains especially to those who succumb to the desires of the flesh, and to those who rebel against all authority. These bold and willful people are not afraid to revile the glorious angels— ¹¹even though the angels, with all their superior strength and power, don't speak a word of judgment against them in the presence of Our God. ¹²These people—who blaspheme anything they don't understand—are irrational animals, bred to be captured and killed, destroying themselves by their own destructive instincts. ¹³They will reap evil in reward for the evil they do. They revel in the daylight just for the fun of it. They are nothing but stains and blemishes. And they make amusement at your expense, even when you sit as a guest at their table. ¹⁴With their adulterous eyes they seduce the unstable because of their infinite capacity for sin. Their profession is greed—an accursed breed! ¹⁵They have abandoned the straight and narrow, straying onto the way of Balaam, begot of Beor, who lusted for the wages of injustice. ¹⁶But he was admonished by a mute animal, a donkey speaking with a human voice, which put an end to the prophet's madness. ¹⁷These people are waterless wells and storm-driven mists. Utter darkness is reserved for them. ¹⁸With their hollow, arrogant talk about the pleasures of the flesh, they seduce people who have only just escaped from those who live in error. ¹⁹They promise freedom, while they themselves are slaves to sin— for whatever dominates you makes you a slave.

²⁰If you've survived the enticements of the world through knowing our Sovereign and Savior Jesus Christ, you'll be ultimately worse off than at the start if you slip and are overcome a second time. ²¹Better not to have known the way of holiness, than to have known it and later reject the holy commandment. ²²What happens to that person shows the truth of the proverbs: "The dog turns back to its vomit," and, "The sow is bathed only to wallow again in the mud."

beloveɗ, this is the second letter I have written you. I wrote both of them to stir up your honest minds. ²Call to mind what the holy prophets of old taught us, and the commandments of our Savior Jesus Christ which you received from the apostles.

³Keep in mind that in the last days nay-sayers will show up to deride you, all the while following their own evil desires, ⁴and asking, "Where is this promised 'coming'? From the time our ancestors died, life goes on as it has from the creation!" ⁵They choose to ignore the fact that by God's word the heavens existed at the beginning, and that the earth was created out of water and through water. ⁶By this same word, waters flooded the world then in existence and destroyed it. ⁷The present heavens and earth are destined for fire by this same word, and are being preserved until the day of judgment when all the ungodly are destroyed.

⁸This point must not be overlooked, dear friends: in the eyes of the Most High, one day is like a thousand years, and a thousand years are like a day. ⁹God does not delay in keeping the promise, as some mean "delay." Rather, God shows you generous patience, desiring that no one perish but that all come to repentance.

¹⁰The day of Our God will come like a thief, and on that day the heavens will vanish with a roar; the elements will catch fire and fall apart, and the earth and all its works will be destroyed in the flames. ¹¹Since everything is to be destroyed in this way, what holy and devoted lives you should lead! ¹²Look for the coming of the Day of God, and try to hasten it along. Because of it, the heavens will be destroyed in flames and the elements will melt away in a blaze. ¹³But what we await are new heavens and a new earth where, according to the promise, God's justice will reside. ¹⁴So beloved, while waiting for this, make every effort to be found at peace and without stain or defilement in God's sight. ¹⁵Consider our God's patience as your opportunity for salvation.

Our dear brother Paul also wrote you about this, according to the wisdom he had been given. ¹⁶Paul writes this way and speaks of these issues in all of his letters—though he does, admittedly, write some things that are hard to understand, which ignorant and unbalanced people distort to their own undoing, as they do the other scriptures.

¹⁷But be forewarned, beloved sisters and brothers: do not be carried away by the errors of unprincipled people and thus forfeit the security you enjoy. ¹⁸Instead, grow in the grace and knowledge of our Sovereign and Savior Jesus Christ, who is glorified now and for all eternity. Amen.

1:1–2:17

*t*hat which was from the beginning,
which we have heard,
   and seen with our eyes,
and have looked at
   and touched with our hands:
the Word, who is Life—
   this is the subject of our letter.
² That life came to be;
   we saw it and bear witness to it.
We proclaim to you the eternal life
   which was with Abba God
   and was manifested to us.
³ What we have seen and heard
   we declare to you,
so that you may be one with us—
   as we are one with Abba God
   and with the Only Begotten, Jesus Christ.
⁴ We write this to fulfill our joy.

⁵ This, then, is the message we heard from Jesus
and declare to you:
God is light,
and in God there is no darkness at all.
⁶ If we say we have intimacy with God
while still living in darkness,
we are liars
and do not live in truth.
⁷ But if we live in the light,
as God is in the light,
we are one with each other,
and the blood of Jesus, the Only Begotten,
purifies us from all sin.
⁸ If we say we are without sin,
we lie, and the truth is not in us.
⁹ But if we admit our sins,
God, the faithful and just One,
will forgive our sins
and cleanse us from all injustice.
¹⁰ If we say we have not sinned,
we call God a liar
and show that God's Word is not in us.
2:1 My little ones,
I am writing this to keep you from sin.
But if anyone should sin,
we have an Advocate with God—
Jesus Christ, who is just.
² Jesus is the full payment for our sins,
and not for our sins only,
but for those of the whole world.
³ We can be sure that we know God
only by keeping the commandments.
⁴ Anyone who says, "I know God,"
and does not keep the commandments
is a liar and refuses to admit the truth.
⁵ But when anyone does obey God's word,
God's love comes to perfection in that person.

This is how you know that you are in God: ⁶ if you say you abide in
Christ, you ought to live the same kind of life as Christ. ⁷ Dear friends, this
is not a new commandment that I am writing to tell you, but an old

commandment—one that you were given from the beginning. The old commandment is the message you have heard. ⁸On the other hand, what I am writing to you is indeed a new commandment. Its truth is seen in Christ and in you, because the night is passing and the true light is already shining. ⁹Those who claim to be in the light but hate their neighbors are still in the dark. ¹⁰But those who love their neighbors are living in the light and need not be afraid of stumbling. ¹¹Those who hate their neighbors are in the darkness and do not know where they are going, because the darkness has blinded them.

> ¹²I am writing to you, my children,
>> because your sins have already been forgiven
>> through the name of Jesus.
> ¹³I am writing to you, mothers and fathers,
>> who have come to know the One
>> who has existed from the beginning.
> I am writing to you, young women and men,
>> who have already conquered the Evil One.
> I have written to you, children,
>> because you already know our Creator.
> ¹⁴I have written to you, mothers and fathers,
>> who have come to know the One
>> who has existed from the beginning.
> I have written to you, young women and men,
>> because you are strong,
> and the Word of God remains in you,
>> and you have overcome the Evil One.

¹⁵Do not love this passing world or anything that is in the world. The love of Abba God is not in anyone who loves this world, ¹⁶for anything that this world has to offer—the cravings of the flesh, the cravings of the eye, the boastful pride of life—could never come from Abba God, but only from this world. ¹⁷And this world, with its cravings, is passing away; but anyone who does the will of God will not pass away.

2:18–4:6

Children, it is the final hour; just as you heard that the Antichrist was coming, so now many such antichrists have appeared. This is how we know that these are the last days. ¹⁹These rivals of Christ came from our own numbers, but they never really belonged. If they had belonged, they would have stayed with us. But they left us, which proves that not one of them ever belonged to us.

²⁰ But you have been anointed by the Holy One, so that all knowledge is yours. ²¹ My reason for writing is not that you don't know the truth, but that you do, and that you already know that no lie can come from the truth.

²² Who is the liar? The person who denies that Jesus is the Christ. Such a person is an antichrist and is denying Abba God as well as the Only Begotten. ²³ No one who denies the Only Begotten has Abba God; whoever acknowledges the Only Begotten has Abba God as well.

²⁴ As for you, let what you heard from the beginning remain with you, then you in turn will remain in the Only Begotten and in Abba God. ²⁵ And this is the promise Christ gave us: eternal life. ²⁶ I write these things to you about those who are trying to lead you astray. ²⁷ As for you, the anointing you received from Christ remains in you, and you do not need anyone to teach you. The anointing that Christ gave you teaches you everything; you are anointed with truth, not with a lie. Remain in Christ, then, as the anointing taught you. ²⁸ Remain in Christ, then, my children, so that when Christ returns we need not hide in shame on the day of that coming.

²⁹ You know that God is righteous; you should know, then, that everyone whose life is righteous is born of God.

3:¹ See what love Abba God has lavished on us
   in letting us be called God's children!
Yet that in fact is what we are.
The reason the world does not recognize us
   is that it never recognized God.
² My dear friends,
   now we are God's children,
but it has not been revealed
   what we are to become in the future.
We know that when it comes to light
   we will be like God,
for we will see God
   as God really is.
³ All who keep this hope keep themselves pure, just as Christ is pure.

ℭ℞   ℭ℞   ℭ℞

⁴ Anyone who sins at all breaks the Law, because to sin is to break the Law. ⁵ Now, you know that Christ, who is sinless, appeared to abolish sin. ⁶ So everyone who lives in union with Christ does not continue to sin, but whoever continues to sin has never seen or known Christ.

⁷Dear children, do not let anyone lead you astray; to live a holy life is to be holy, just as Christ is holy. ⁸To lead a sinful life is to belong to the Devil, since the Devil was a sinner from the beginning. It was to undo everything the Devil has done that the Only Begotten of God appeared. ⁹Those who have been born of God do not sin. Because God's seed remains inside them, they cannot sin when they have been born of God. ¹⁰In this way, we distinguish the children of God from the children of the Devil. Any who do not live holy lives and love their sisters and brothers are not children of God.

¹¹This, remember, is the message you heard from the beginning: we should love one another. ¹²Do not be like Cain, who belonged to the Evil One and killed his brother. Why did Cain kill Abel? Because his own deeds were wicked and Abel's deeds were just.

¹³Do not be surprised, sisters and brothers, if the world hates you. ¹⁴We know that we have passed from death to life because we love our sisters and brothers; if we refuse to love we are still dead. ¹⁵Those who hate their sisters or brothers are murderers. And murderers, you know, do not have eternal life in them.

¹⁶This is how we know what love is: Jesus Christ died for us. And we, too, ought to lay down our lives for our sisters and brothers. ¹⁷If you have more than enough material possessions and see your neighbors in need yet close your hearts to them, how can the love of God be living in you? ¹⁸My children, our love must not be simply words or mere talk—it must be true love, which shows itself in action and truth. ¹⁹This, then, is how we'll know we belong to the truth; this is how we'll be confident in God's presence, ²⁰even if our consciences condemn us. We know that God is greater than our consciences and that God knows everything. ²¹And if our consciences do not condemn us, my friends, then we have confidence before God, ²²and we will receive whatever we ask from God's hand—because we keep the commandments and do what is pleasing in God's sight. ²³The commandments are these: that we believe in the name of God's Own, Jesus Christ, and that we love one another as we were told to do. ²⁴Those who keep these commandments live in God and God lives in them. We know that God lives in us by the Spirit given to us.

◌   ◌   ◌

4:1Dear friends, it is not every spirit that you can trust. Test them to see if they come from God. There are many false prophets in the world. ²This is how you can recognize the Spirit of God: every spirit that acknowledges that Jesus Christ came in the flesh is from God. ³And every spirit that does not acknowledge Jesus is not from God. This spirit is the Antichrist, which you have heard about and is already in the world.

⁴Dear friends, you have already overcome these false prophets, because you are from God and have in you the One who is greater than anyone in the world. ⁵As for them, they are of the world; they speak the language of the world, and the world listens to them. ⁶But we are from God, and those who know God listen to us. Those who are not of God refuse to listen to us. This is how we can tell the spirit of truth from the spirit of falsehood.

beloved,   4:7-21
let us love one another
 because love is of God;
everyone who loves is begotten of God
 and has knowledge of God.
⁸Those who do not love have known nothing of God,
 for God is love.
⁹God's love was revealed in our midst in this way:
 by sending the Only Begotten into the world,
 that we might have faith through the Anointed One.
¹⁰Love, then, consists in this:
 not that we have loved God,
but that God has loved us
 and has sent the Only Begotten
 to be an offering for our sins.
¹¹Beloved,
 if God has loved us so,
 we must have the same love for one another.
¹²No one has ever seen God.
Yet if we love one another,
 God dwells in us,
 and God's love is brought to perfection in us.
¹³The way we know that we remain in God and God in us
 is that we have been given the Spirit.
¹⁴We have seen for ourselves, and can testify,
 that God has sent the Only Begotten as Savior of the world.
¹⁵When any acknowledge that Jesus is the Only Begotten,
 God dwells in them
 and they in God.
¹⁶We have come to know and to believe
 in the love God has for us.

God is love,
    and those who abide in love
abide in God,
    and God in them.

[17] Love will come to perfection in us when we can face the day of judgment without fear—because our relation to this world is just like Christ's. [18] There is no fear in love, for perfect love drives out fear. To fear is to expect punishment, and anyone who is afraid is still imperfect in love.

[19] We love because God first loved us. [20] If you say you love God but hate your sister or brother, you are a liar. For you cannot love God, whom you have not seen, if you hate your neighbor, whom you have seen. [21] If we love God, we should love our sisters and brothers as well; we have this commandment from God.

5:1-21

*e*veryone who believes that Jesus is the Messiah
    has been born of God.
Everyone who loves God
    loves the One who has come from God.
[2] We can be sure that we love God's children
    when we love God and do what God has commanded.
[3] The love of God consists of this:
    that we keep God's commandments.
    And these commandments are not burdensome.
[4] Everyone born of God conquers the world,
    and the power that has conquered the world
    is our faith.
[5] Who then can overcome the world?
    The one who believes
    that Jesus is the Only Begotten of God.
[6] Jesus Christ came by water and blood—
    not by water alone,
    but with water and blood.
[7] It is the Spirit who testifies to this,
    and she is truth.

[8] So there are three witnesses: the Spirit, the water, and the blood, and all three of them are of one accord. [9] We accept the testimony of human witnesses, but God's testimony is much greater—and this is God's testimony, given as evidence of the Only Begotten of God. [10] Those who believe

in this One have this evidence within their hearts. Those who don't believe God have made God a liar by refusing to believe in the testimony given on behalf of the Only Begotten of God. ¹¹ The testimony is this: God has given us eternal life, and this life is in the Only Begotten. ¹² Whoever has the Only Begotten has life, and whoever does not have the Only Begotten does not have life.

¹³ I have written all this to you who believe in the Only Begotten of God, so that you may know that you have eternal life.

⊙   ⊙   ⊙

¹⁴ We are quite confident that if we ask anything of God, and if it is in accord with God's will, it will be heard. ¹⁵ And knowing that whatever we ask, we are heard, we understand that the request is already granted in the asking. ¹⁶ If any of you sees a sister or brother committing a sin that is not a deadly sin, you have only to pray and God will give life to the sinner. This is only for those whose sin is not deadly. There is a sin that leads to death, and I do not say that you must pray about that. ¹⁷ Every kind of wrongdoing is evil, but not all sin is deadly.

¹⁸ We know that everyone begotten of God does not sin, because the Only Begotten of God protects them, and the Evil One does not touch them. ¹⁹ We know that we belong to God, but the whole world lies in the power of the Evil One. ²⁰ We know, too, that the Only Begotten of God has come, and has given us knowledge about the One who is true. We are in the One who is true, and we are in our Savior Jesus Christ. This is the true God; this is eternal life.

²¹ Children, watch out for false gods.

1-13

from the elder,

To the chosen one and her children, whom I love in the truth—and not only I, but also all who have come to know the truth—²because of the truth that lives in us and is with us forever:

³May grace, mercy, and peace be with you in truth and love, from God our Creator and from Jesus Christ, God's Only Begotten.

⁴It has given me great joy to find some of your children walking in the path of truth, just as we were commanded by Abba God. ⁵Now I would make this request of you—but it is not as if I were writing you some new commandment; rather, it is a commandment we have had from the start: let us love one another. ⁶And this is love, that we walk according to the commandments; and as you have heard from the beginning, the commandment is the way in which you should walk.

⁷Many deceitful people have gone out into the world, people who do not acknowledge Jesus Christ as coming in the flesh. They are the spirit of the

Deceitful One! They are the Antichrist! [8] Look out that you yourselves do not lose what you have worked for; you must receive your reward in full. [9] Those who are so progressive that they do not remain rooted in the teaching of Christ do not possess God, while those who remain rooted in the teaching possess both Abba God and the Only Begotten.

[10] Any who come to your house without this doctrine are not to be welcomed. Don't even greet them, [11] for whoever greets them shares in their evil work.

[12] There are many things I have to tell you, but I choose not to use paper and ink. Rather, I choose to visit you and talk to you personally so that our joy may be complete.

[13] The children of your chosen sister send you their greetings.

from the elder,

To Gaius, my dear friend, whom I love in truth:

² My dear friend, I pray that all is well with you, and that you are as healthy physically as your soul is spiritually. ³ It was a source of great joy for me to receive from some of our co-workers word of your faithfulness to the truth, and your continued walk in the truth. ⁴ My greatest source of joy is to hear that my children live by the truth.

⁵ My friend, you demonstrate fidelity by all that you do for the travelling teachers and missionaries, even though they are strangers; ⁶ indeed, they have testified to your love before the church. And you will do a good thing if, in a way that pleases God, you help them to continue their journey. ⁷ It was for the sake of the Name that they set out, and they are accepting nothing from the Gentiles. ⁸ Therefore, we owe it to such people to support them and thus share in the work of truth.

⁹ I wrote a letter for the members of the church, but Diotrephes, who enjoys dominating, refuses to acknowledge us. ¹⁰ So if I do come, I will tell

everyone what he is doing, and how he spreads malicious gossip about us. As if that weren't enough, he not only refuses to welcome our co-workers, he also interferes with those who want to do so, and banishes them from the church.

¹¹ But as for you, my dear friend, don't imitate evil. Imitate what is good instead. Those who do what is right are children of God; those who do what is evil have never seen God.

¹² Everyone has good things to say about Demetrius—as does the truth itself. I too vouch for Demetrius, and you know that my word is true.

¹³ There are many other things I want to tell you, but I hesitate to put them to pen and ink. ¹⁴ However, I look forward to seeing you shortly, when we will talk face to face.

¹⁵ Peace be with you. Friends here send their greetings. Greet friends there by name.

the letteR of
juðe

ƒROM juðe, a seRʋant oƒ jesus chRist and a brother of James,

To those among the called who are dear to God the Creator and kept safe for Jesus Christ:

² May mercy, peace and love be yours in abundance.

³ My dear friends, I eagerly anticipated writing to you about the salvation we all share. But now I feel compelled to write and exhort you to contend for the faith which was once and for all time consigned to the holy people of God. ⁴ Certain individuals have infiltrated your ranks. These are the very ones we wrote you about long ago, when we condemned them for ungodliness. They turn the grace of our God into a license for immorality, and reject our Sovereign and Savior Jesus Christ.

⁵ Let me remind you what you already know—that Our God liberated a people from Egypt, but later destroyed those who did not believe. ⁶ Let me also remind you of the angels who held positions of supreme authority,

which they gave up, abandoning their assigned domain; God now keeps them chained in darkness awaiting the judgment of the great day. ⁷Likewise, Sodom and Gomorrah and their neighboring towns serve as a warning to us—they received the punishment of eternal fire because of their sexual promiscuity and their pursuit of fleshly vice.

⁸In the same way, these deluded people defile their bodies, reject authority and malign the glorious angels. ⁹Not even Michael the archangel, when arguing with the Devil about the body of Moses, dared to use such abusive language. All Michael said was, "May Our God rebuke you!" ¹⁰But these people speak abusively of anything they do not understand. And those things they do understand—instinctively, like mute animals—will eventually be their destruction. ¹¹Tragically, they will reap what they have sowed, for they have followed the path of Cain. They have rushed headlong into Balaam's mistake, and will receive the same reward. They rebelled—and will perish—as did Korah.

¹²These people are a dangerous element at your *agape* feasts. They come only for the food, and only for themselves. They are wind-blown, rainless clouds. They are twice-dead autumn trees, without roots or fruit. ¹³They are wild waves of the sea, foaming with shame. They are shooting stars destined for the darkness of the black hole. ¹⁴Enoch, in the seventh generation after Adam, had them in mind when he prophesied,

> "I tell you,
> Our God will come with tens of thousands of holy ones
> ¹⁵to execute judgment on all of humankind,
> to judge guilty the wicked for all their evil deeds
> and the ungodly for their defiant words
> against the Almighty."

¹⁶These people are mischief-makers and grumblers whose only goals are their selfish desires. Arrogance pours from their mouths, and they flatter people any time it will help them get their way.

¹⁷Remember, my friends, what the apostles of our Savior Jesus Christ told you to expect. ¹⁸"At the end-time," they told you, "there will be those who sneer at religion and follow only their own wicked desires." ¹⁹These are divisive people who, bereft of the Spirit, have only their natural instincts to rely on.

²⁰But you, dear friends, strengthen yourselves in your holy faith—pray in the Holy Spirit. ²¹Stay true to God's love and embrace the mercy of our Savior Jesus Christ, which leads to eternal life. ²²Reassure those who have doubts. ²³Rescue others by snatching them from the fire. With still others,

show them mercy tempered by fear—so much that you'd hate even to touch their clothing, so polluted are they by the flesh.

[24] But there is One who can prevent you from falling and make you stand pure and exultant in the presence of eternal glory. [25] To God, the only God, who saves us through Jesus Christ our Sovereign, be glory, majesty, authority and power—who was before all time, is now, and will be forever. Amen.

the
Revelation
of jesus christ

1:1-8

this is the Revelation of jesus christ,
given by God to show the faithful what must happen very soon. God made
it known by sending an angel to John, the faithful subject, ² who in writing
down everything he saw, bears witness to the word of God and the testimony of Jesus Christ. ³ Happy are those people who read this prophetic
message, and happy are those who hear it and heed what is written in it,
for the time is near!

⁴ From John,

To the seven churches in the province of Asia:

Grace and peace to you, from the One who is, who was and who is to
come, from the seven spirits before the throne ⁵ and from Jesus Christ, the
faithful witness, the Firstborn from the dead, sovereign of the rulers of the
earth.

To Christ—who loves us, and who has freed us from our sins by the shedding of blood, 6and who has made us to be a kindom of priests to serve Our God and Creator—to Jesus Christ be glory and power forever and ever! Amen.

> 7 Look! Christ is coming on the clouds
> for every eye to see,
> even those who pierced Jesus,
> and all the peoples of the earth
> will mourn over Christ.
> So be it! Amen.

8"I am the Alpha and the Omega," says Our God, "who is, who was and who is to come, the Almighty."

1:9–3:22

Í, John, your brother, who share with you the trial, the kindom and the perseverance we have in Jesus, was on the island of Patmos because I proclaimed God's word and bore witness to Jesus. 10 It was the first day of the week and I was in the Spirit, when suddenly I heard behind me a piercing voice like the sound of a trumpet, 11 which said, "Write on a scroll what you see, and send it to the seven churches: to Ephesus, Smyrna, Pergamum, Thyatira, Sardis, Philadelphia and Laodicea."

12 I turned around to see who spoke to me, and I saw seven lampstands of gold 13 and, among the lampstands, a figure of human appearance wearing an ankle-length robe with a golden sash across its chest. 14 The figure's head and hair were white as wool or snow, and its eyes were like a blazing flame. 15 Its feet were like burnished bronze refined in a furnace, and its voice was like the sound of crashing surf. 16 In its right hand the figure held seven stars, and out of its mouth came a sharp, double-edged sword. Its face shown like the sun at high noon.

17 When I saw it, I fell down as though dead. It touched me with its right hand and said, "Don't be afraid. I am the First and the Last, 18 the Living One. Once I was dead, but now I live forever and ever. I hold the keys of death and the underworld. 19 Write down, therefore, everything you see— things as they are now, and things that will take place in the future. 20 The seven stars you saw in my right hand, and the seven golden lampstands, are symbols: the seven stars are the angels of the seven churches, and the seven lampstands are the seven churches.

2:1 "To the angel of the church in Ephesus, write this:

The One who holds the seven stars in its right hand and walks among the seven golden lampstands says this: ²I know your deeds, your labors, your patient endurance. I know you cannot tolerate the wicked, that you have tested the impostors who claimed to be apostles and found them false. ³I know, too, that you have patiently endured hardship for my sake and have not become discouraged. ⁴I hold this against you, though: you have left your first love. ⁵Call to mind the heights from which you have fallen. Repent and do the good you did at first. If you don't repent, I will come to you and remove your lampstand from its place. ⁶But you have this in your favor: you loathe what the Nicolaitans are doing, which I also hate.

⁷Whoever has ears to hear, listen to what the Spirit says to the churches. To the one who overcomes, I will give the right to eat from the tree of life which stands in the paradise of God.

⁸"To the angel of the church in Smyrna, write this:

The First and the Last, who died and came to life, says this: ⁹I know your hardships and your poverty—yet you are rich. I know the slander of those who profess to be Jewish but are not; they are really members of the synagogue of Satan. ¹⁰Don't be afraid of the sufferings that come. I tell you, the Devil is about to send some of you to prison to test you, and you will undergo an ordeal for ten days. Be faithful until death, and I will give you the crown of life.

¹¹Whoever has ears to hear, listen to what the Spirit says to the churches. The one who overcomes will not be destroyed by the second death.

¹²"To the angel of the church in Pergamum, write this:

The One with the sharp, two-edged sword says this: ¹³I know that you live where Satan is enthroned. Yet you remain faithful to my name, and you did not renounce your faith in me—even in the days of Antipas, my faithful witness, who was martyred in your city, where Satan lives.

¹⁴Nevertheless, I have a few complaints against you. You have among you those who hold to the teachings of Balaam, who instructed Balak to put a stumbling block in front of the Israelites, tempting them to sin by eating food sacrificed to idols and by being sexually promiscuous. ¹⁵Likewise you also have among you those who hold to the teachings of the Nicolaitans. ¹⁶You must repent, or I will soon come to you and attack these people with the sword of my mouth.

¹⁷Whoever has ears to hear, listen to what the Spirit says to the churches. To the one who overcomes I will give the hidden manna and

a white stone—a stone with a new name written on it, known only to the person who receives it.

[18] "To the angel of the church in Thyatira, write this:

The Only Begotten of God, who has eyes like a blazing flame, and feet like burnished bronze, says this: [19] I know your works, your love and faith, your service and endurance, and that you're still making progress.

[20]Nevertheless, I have a complaint against you: you tolerate Jezebel, who claims to be a prophet, who leads my faithful astray so that they become promiscuous and eat food sacrificed to idols. [21] I have given her time to repent, but she refuses to give up her idolatry. [22]So I will cast her on a bed of suffering, and I will plunge those who join her into intense suffering, unless they repent of their ways. [23] I will kill her children with a plague. Then all the churches will realize that I search hearts and minds to give to each of you what your behavior deserves. [24]But I say to the rest of you in Thyatira, to you who have not held to her teachings and know nothing of Satan's so-called deep secrets: on you I will impose no other burden. [25] Just hold on to what you have until I come.

[26] To the one who overcomes and keep my ways until the end, I will give authority over the nations; [27] 'you will rule them with an iron scepter, you will shatter them like pottery,' just as I have received authority from Abba God. [28] And I will give you the morning star. Whoever has ears to hear, listen to what the Spirit says to the churches.

[3:1] "To the angel of the church in Sardis, write this:

The One who holds the seven spirits of God and the seven stars says this: I know your conduct; I know the reputation you have of being alive, when in fact you are dead! [2] Wake up and strengthen what remains before it dies. I find that the sum of your deeds is less than complete in the sight of my God. [3] Call to mind how you accepted what you heard; keep to it, and repent. If you don't rouse yourselves, I will come upon you like a thief, at a time you cannot know. [4] I realize you have in Sardis a few people who have not soiled their garments; these will walk with me in white because they are worthy.

[5] The one who overcomes will go clothed in white. I will never erase your name from the book of life, but will acknowledge you in the presence of Our God and the angels. [6] Whoever has ears to hear, listen to what the Spirit says to the churches.

[7] "To the angel of the church in Philadelphia, write this:

The One who is holy and true, who holds the key of David, who opens what no one can close, who closes what no one can open, says this: ⁸I know all about you. And now I have placed before you an open door, which no one can close. I know that though you have limited strength, you have kept my word and not denied my name. ⁹Now I will make the synagogue of Satan—those who claim to be Jewish and are not, for they are liars—I will make them come and fall at your feet and acknowledge that I have loved you. ¹⁰Because you have kept my command to endure all trials, I will also keep you safe in the time of trial that is going to come upon the whole world to test it. ¹¹I am coming soon. Hold fast to what you have, so that no one will take your crown.

¹²The one who overcomes I will make into a pillar in the Temple of my God, and you will stay there forever. I will inscribe on you the Name of my God and the name of the city of my God, the new Jerusalem which comes down from my God in heaven. On you I will also write my new name. ¹³Whoever has ears to hear, listen to what the Spirit says to the churches.

¹⁴"To the angel of the church in Laodicea, write this:

The Amen, the Witness faithful and true, the Source of God's creation, says this: ¹⁵I know your deeds, I know that you are neither cold nor hot. How I wish you were one or the other—hot or cold! ¹⁶But because you are lukewarm, neither hot nor cold, I will vomit you out of my mouth! ¹⁷You keep saying, "I am so rich and secure that I want for nothing." Little do you realize how wretched you are, how pitiable and poor, how blind and naked! ¹⁸Take my advice. Buy from me gold refined by fire, if you would be truly rich. Buy white garments to wear, if the shame of your nakedness is to be covered. Buy ointment to smear on your eyes, if you would see once more. ¹⁹Whoever is dear to me, I will correct and discipline. Be earnest about it, therefore. Repent! ²⁰Here I stand, knocking at the door. If any hear me calling and open the door, I will enter the house and have supper with them.

²¹To the one who overcomes I will give the right to sit with me on my throne, as I myself overcame and took my seat beside my Abba God on the heavenly throne. ²²Whoever has ears to hear, listen to what the Spirit says to the churches.

4:1–8:1

After this I saw a door standing open above me in heaven, and I heard the trumpetlike voice which had spoken to me before. It said, "Come up here, and I will show you what must take place in the time to come."

² Immediately I was caught up in the Spirit. A throne was standing there in heaven, and on the throne was seated ³ One who looked like jasper and carnelian. Around the throne was a halo the color of emerald.

⁴ Surrounding the throne were twenty-four other thrones, upon which were seated twenty-four elders; they were clothed in white garments and had gold crowns on their heads. ⁵ From the throne came flashes of lightning and peals of thunder; before it burned seven flaming torches, the seven spirits of God. ⁶ The floor around the throne was like a sea of glass that shone as crystal.

At the very center, around the throne itself, stood four living creatures; they were covered with eyes front and back. ⁷ The first creature resembled a lion, the second an ox, the third had a human face, while the fourth looked like an eagle in flight. ⁸ Each of the four living creatures had six wings and eyes all over, inside and out. Day and night, without pause, they sing,

"Holy, holy, holy, is Our God Almighty,
who was, who is, and who is to come!"

⁹ Whenever these creatures give glory and honor and praise to the One seated on the throne, who lives forever and ever, ¹⁰ the twenty-four elders fall down and worship the One seated on the throne, who lives forever and ever. They throw down their crowns before the throne and sing,

¹¹ "O God Most High, you are worthy
to receive glory and honor and power!
For you have created all things;
by your will they came to be and were made!"

5:1 In the right hand of the One who sat on the throne, I saw a scroll. It had writing on both sides and was sealed with seven seals.

² Then I saw a mighty angel proclaiming in a loud voice, "Who is worthy to open the scroll and break its seals?" ³ But no one in heaven, on earth or under the earth could be found to open the scroll or examine its contents. ⁴ I wept bitterly because no one could be found to open or examine the scroll.

⁵ One of the elders said to me, "Don't weep. The Lion of the tribe of Judah, the Root of David, has triumphed and will open the scroll with the seven seals."

⁶ Then, between the throne with the four living creatures and the elders, I saw a Lamb standing, a Lamb that had been slain. It had seven horns and seven eyes; these eyes are the seven spirits of God sent to all parts of the world. ⁷ The Lamb came and received the scroll from the right hand of the One who sat on the throne.

⁸ When it had taken the scroll, the four living creatures and the twenty-four elders fell down before the Lamb. Each of the elders held a harp, and golden bowls filled with incense, which are the prayers of God's holy people. ⁹ This is the new hymn they sang:

"Worthy are you to receive the scroll
and break the seven seals,
for you were slain.
With your blood you purchased for God
members of every race and tongue,
of every people and nation.
¹⁰ You made of them a kindom,
priests to serve Our God,
and they will reign on the earth."

¹¹ Then in my vision, I heard the voices of many angels who surrounded the throne together with the living creatures and the elders. They were numberless, thousands and tens of thousands, ¹² and they all cried out:

"Worthy is the Lamb that was slain
to receive power and wealth,
wisdom and strength,
honor and glory and praise!"

¹³ Then I heard the voice of every creature in heaven, on the earth, under the earth and in the sea. Everything in all creation cried aloud:

"To the One seated on the throne and to the Lamb,
be praise and honor,
glory and dominion,
forever and ever!"

¹⁴ The four living creatures said, "Amen!" and the elders fell on their faces and worshiped.

 CR   CR   CR

6:1 Then I watched as the Lamb broke the first of the seven seals, and I heard one of the four living creatures shout in a voice like thunder, "Come!"

² I looked, and there was a white horse with a rider holding a bow. The rider was given a victor's laurel and rode out as one bent on victory.

³ When the lamb broke the second seal, I heard the second living creature cry out, "Come!"

⁴ And out came another horse, a bright red one. Its rider was given a

sword, with the mandate to take away peace from the earth, so that people would slaughter one another.

⁵When the lamb broke the third seal, I heard the third living creature cry out, "Come!"

I looked, and there was a black horse, and its rider held a pair of scales. ⁶Then I heard what sounded like a voice from among the four living creatures say, "A ration of wheat for a day's wages, and three rations of barley for a day's wages, and take care not to harm the wine and the oil."

⁷When the lamb broke the fourth seal, I heard the voice of the fourth living creature cry out, "Come!"

⁸I looked, and there was a pale, ghastly green horse. Its rider was named Death, and the netherworld followed close behind. They were given authority over a quarter of the world to kill by the sword, by famine, by plague and by wild animals.

⁹When the lamb broke the fifth seal, underneath the altar I saw the souls of all the people who were killed because they had borne witness to the Word of God. ¹⁰They shouted in a loud voice, "How much longer, Holy Sovereign One, before you sit in judgment and avenge our blood on the inhabitants of the earth?"

¹¹Then each of them was given a white robe, and they were told to be patient a while longer, until the full number of the faithful—sisters and brothers who were to be killed just as they had been—was complete.

¹²I watched as the lamb broke the sixth seal. There was a great earthquake, and the sun turned black as coarse sackcloth. The moon turned blood red, ¹³and the stars of the sky fell to earth like figs falling from the tree in a strong wind. ¹⁴The sky tore and withdrew like two scrolls rolling up, and every mountain and island was removed from its place.

¹⁵Then all the rulers of the earth—the governors, the military leaders, rich and influential people—as well as every other person, enslaved or free, took to the mountains and hid in caves and among the rocks. ¹⁶They cried out to the rocks and the mountains, "Fall on us and hide us from the One who sits on the throne and from the wrath of the Lamb! ¹⁷The great day of their wrath has come! Who can survive it?"

ଔ　　ଔ　　ଔ

7:1 After this I saw the four angels that stood at the four corners of the earth, holding back the four winds of the world to prevent them from blowing on the land or on the sea or in the trees. ²Then I saw another angel rising from the east, carrying the seal of the living God. It called out in a powerful voice to the four angels who had been given the power to devastate the land and the sea: ³"Don't harm the land or the sea until we have put our God's seal on the foreheads of the faithful!"

⁴Then I heard the number of those who were marked with the seal: there were 144,000, out of all the tribes of Israel. ⁵From the tribe of Judah 12,000 were marked with the seal; from the tribe of Reuben, 12,000; from the tribe of Gad, 12,000;⁶from the tribe of Asher, 12,000; from the tribe of Naphtali, 12,000; from the tribe of Manasseh, 12,000;⁷from the tribe of Simeon, 12,000; from the tribe of Levi, 12,000; from the tribe of Issachar, 12,000; ⁸from the tribe of Zebulun, 12,000; from the tribe of Joseph, 12,000; and from the tribe of Benjamin, 12,000.

⁹After that, I saw before me an immense crowd without number, from every nation, tribe, people and language. They stood in front of the throne and the Lamb, dressed in long white robes and holding palm branches. ¹⁰And they cried out in a loud voice,

"Salvation is of our God,
who sits on the throne,
and of the Lamb!"

¹¹All the angels who were encircling the throne, as well as the elders and the four living creatures, prostrated themselves before the throne. They worshiped God ¹²with these words: "Amen! Praise and glory and wisdom and thanksgiving and honor and power and strength be to our God forever and ever! Amen!"

¹³Then one of the elders asked me, "These people in white robes—who are they, and where do they come from?"

¹⁴I answered, "You are the one who knows." Then the elder said to me, "These are the ones who survived the great period of testing; they have washed their robes in the blood of the Lamb and made them white. ¹⁵That's why they stand before God's throne and the One they serve day and night in the Temple; the One who sits on the throne will shelter them forever. ¹⁶Never again will they be hungry or thirsty; the sun and its scorching heat will never beat down on them, ¹⁷for the Lamb, who is at the center of the throne, will be their shepherd and will lead them to springs of living water. And God will wipe every last tear from their eyes."

⁸:¹ When the Lamb opened the seventh seal, there was silence in heaven for about half an hour.

8:2–11:18

t**hen** I saw the seven angels who stand before God being given seven trumpets.

³ Another angel, who had a golden censer, came and stood before the altar. It was given a large quantity of incense to offer with the prayers of all the holy ones, on the golden altar that stood before the throne. ⁴ The smoke of the incense, together with the prayers of the holy ones, went up before God from the angel's hand.

⁵ Then the angel took the censer, filled it with fire from the altar, and threw it down onto the earth. Immediately there came peals of thunder, loud noise, flashes of lightning and an earthquake.

⁶ The seven angels who had been given the seven trumpets prepared to blow them.

⁷ When the first angel blew its trumpet, there came hail and fire mixed with blood, which was hurled down on the earth. A third of the earth was burned up, as was a third of the trees, and all the green grass.

⁸ When the second angel blew its trumpet, something like a huge mountain blazing with fire was thrown into the sea. ⁹ A third of the sea was turned into blood, a third of all the creatures living in the sea died, and a third of the ships were destroyed.

¹⁰ When the third angel blew its trumpet, a great star burning like a torch fell from the sky. The star fell on a third of all the rivers and springs. ¹¹ The name of the star is Wormwood, and a third of the waters were poisoned as if by wormwood. Many people died from the waters which had become poisonous.

¹² When the fourth angel blew its trumpet, a third of the sun, a third of the moon and a third of the stars were struck, so that a third of them grew dark. A third of the day and a third of the night were without light.

¹³ As I watched, I heard an eagle flying overhead cry out in a loud voice,

"Sorrow! Sorrow! Sorrow to the inhabitants of the earth because of the trumpet blasts about to be sounded by the next three angels!"

9:1 Then the fifth angel blew its trumpet, and I saw a star that had fallen from the sky to the earth. The star was given the key to the shaft leading down to the Abyss. ²When it unlocked the shaft to the Abyss, smoke billowed out of the Abyss like smoke from a huge furnace. The smoke from the Abyss darkened the sun and the sky.

³Out of the smoke came locusts, and they rained down onto the earth. They were given power like the scorpions of the earth. ⁴They were instructed not to harm any of the grass, plants or trees of the earth—only those people who did not have the seal of God on their foreheads. ⁵They were instructed not to kill, but only to torment them for five months; their torment was a sting like the scorpion's. ⁶When this happens people will seek death, but will not find it; they will long to die, but death will shun them.

⁷The locusts looked like horses ready for battle. They had what looked like gold crowns on their heads, and their faces resembled those of humans. ⁸They had long hair on their heads, and their teeth were like those of a lion. ⁹They had scales like iron breastplates, and the noise of their wings sounded like many horses and chariots thundering into battle. ¹⁰They had tails like scorpions, complete with stingers, and their tails had the power to torment people for five months. ¹¹They had as their ruler the angel of the Abyss, whose name is Destroyer—in Hebrew, Abaddon; in Greek, Apollyon.

¹²The first sorrow has passed. Two more are yet to come.

¹³The sixth angel blew its trumpet, and I heard a voice coming from the four horns of the golden altar before God. ¹⁴It said to the sixth angel who had the trumpet, "Release the four angels who are bound at the great river Euphrates."

¹⁵So the four angels who had been kept ready for this very hour and day and month and year were released to slay a third of humankind. ¹⁶The number of the mounted troops was two hundred million—I heard their number.

¹⁷As the vision continued I saw horses and their riders: their breastplates were flame red, hyacinth blue and sulphur yellow; the horses had lion's heads, and fire, smoke and sulphur were coming out of their mouths. ¹⁸It was by these three plagues—the fire, the smoke, and the sulphur that came out of their mouths—that a third of humankind was slain. ¹⁹The power of

the horses was in their mouths and in their tails; their tails were like snakes, with heads that inflicted injury.

²⁰ The rest of humankind—those who were not slain by these plagues—refused to repent of the work of their hands. They didn't stop worshiping demons and idols made of gold, silver, bronze, stone and wood—idols that cannot see or hear or walk. ²¹ Nor did they turn from their murders, their sorcery, their debauchery or their stealing.

10¹ Then I saw another mighty angel coming down from heaven. It was robed in a cloud with a rainbow over its head. Its face was like the sun and its legs were like pillars of fire. ² In its hands it held a small scroll, unrolled. It put its right foot in the sea and its left foot on the land.

³ The angel shouted so loud that it was like a lion roaring. When it shouted, the seven thunders raised their voices, too. ⁴ And when the seven thunders had spoken, I was about to write it down when I heard a voice from heaven say to me, "Seal up what the seven thunders have spoken. Don't write it down."

⁵ Then the angel I saw standing on the sea and on the land raised its right hand to heaven. ⁶ And it swore, "By the One who lives forever and ever, who made heaven and all that is in it, and the earth and all that it bears, and the sea and all that it holds: the time of waiting is over! ⁷ When the seventh angel sounds its trumpet, the hidden plan of the Most High will be fulfilled, as was promised in the Good News to God's faithful, the prophets."

⁸ Then the voice that I had heard from heaven spoke to me again and said, "Go, take the scroll from the hand of the angel standing on the land and on the sea."

⁹ I went up to the angel and said, "Give me the little scroll."

The angel said to me, "Here, take it and eat it! It will be sour in your stomach, but in your mouth it will taste as sweet as honey."

¹⁰ I took the little scroll from the angel's hand and ate it. In my mouth it tasted as sweet as honey, but when I swallowed it my stomach turned sour. ¹¹ Then someone said to me, "You must once again prophesy about many peoples, nations, languages and rulers."

11¹ Then I was given a reed as a measuring rod, and I was told, "Go and measure the sanctuary of God, and the altar, and count the people worshiping there. ² Exclude the outer court of the sanctuary and don't measure it, for it has been handed over to the Gentiles who will trample the holy city for forty-two months. ³ And I will send my two witnesses, clothed in sackcloth, to prophesy for those 1,260 days."

⁴ These two witnesses are the two olive trees and the two lampstands which stand in the presence of the God of the earth. ⁵ If anyone tries to harm them, fire will come out of the mouths of these witnesses to devour their enemies. Anyone attempting to harm them must be killed in this way.

⁶ These witnesses have power to shut up the sky so that no rain will fall during the time of their mission. They also have power to turn water into blood and to afflict the earth at will with any kind of plague.

⁷ When they have finished giving their testimony, the beast that comes up from the abyss will wage war against them and will conquer and kill them. ⁸ Their corpses will lie in the streets of the great city—the one symbolically called "Sodom," and "Egypt"—where their Sovereign was crucified. ⁹ People from every race and civilization, language and nation, will stare at their corpses for three and a half days but refuse to bury them. ¹⁰ The earth's inhabitants will gloat over them, and in their merriment will exchange gifts, because these two prophets harassed everyone on earth.

¹¹ But after three and a half days, the breath of life returned to them from God. When they stood on their feet, sheer terror gripped those who saw them. ¹² The two prophets heard a loud voice from heaven say to them, "Come up here!" Then they went up to heaven in a cloud as their enemies looked on.

¹³ At that very hour there was a violent earthquake, and a tenth of the city collapsed. Seven thousand people were killed in the earthquake. The survivors were terrified and gave glory to the God of heaven.

¹⁴ The second sorrow has passed. The third is coming soon.

¹⁵ Then the seventh angel blew its trumpet. And loud voices in heaven began calling,

> "The kindom of the world
>   has become the kindom of our God
> and of God's Messiah,
>   who will reign forever and ever!"

¹⁶ And the twenty-four elders, who were seated on their thrones before God, prostrated themselves and worshiped God, ¹⁷ saying,

> "We give thanks to you, Sovereign God Almighty,
>   the One who is and who was,
> for using your great power
>   and establishing your reign.
> ¹⁸ The nations raged,
>   but now it is time for your own anger,

and time for judging the dead,
>and for rewarding your faithful and your prophets,
>and your holy ones and those who revere your Name—
>>both great and small—
>and for destroying those
>>who destroy the earth."

11:19–15:4

Then God's sanctuary in heaven was opened, and within it the Ark of the Covenant could be seen. There were flashes of lightning, loud noises, peals of thunder, an earthquake and a violent hailstorm.

12¹Then a great sign appeared in heaven: a woman clothed with the sun, with the moon under her feet, with twelve stars on her head for a crown. ²She was pregnant and in labor, crying out in pain as she was about to give birth.

³Then another sign appeared in heaven: a huge red dragon, with seven heads and ten horns, and each of the seven heads with a crown. ⁴Its tail swept a third of the stars from the sky and hurled them down to the earth.

The dragon stood before the woman about to deliver, to devour her child the moment she gave birth. ⁵The woman gave birth to a male child, a son, who is to rule the world with an iron rod. But the child was snatched straight up to God and God's throne. ⁶The woman fled into the desert, to a place prepared for her by God, where she will be kept safe for 1,260 days.

⁷Then war broke out in heaven. Michael and the angels fought against the dragon. The dragon and its angels fought back, ⁸but they were defeated and driven out of heaven. ⁹The great dragon, the primeval serpent who is called the Devil or Satan, who had deceived the whole world, was hurled down to the earth, and its angels were banished with it.

¹⁰Then I heard a loud voice in heaven shout:

>"Now have come salvation and power,
>>and the kindom of God,
>>and all authority for God's Anointed.
>For the accuser of our sisters and brothers,
>>who accused them before our God night and day,
>>has been brought down.
>¹¹They triumphed over the accuser
>>by the blood of the Lamb,
>>and by the word of their testimony;

their love of life
        did not dissuade them from death.
¹²Let the heavens rejoice
        and all who dwell in them;
but woe to you,
        earth and sea,
for the Devil has come down to you
        filled with fury,
for it knows
        that its days are numbered."

¹³When the dragon saw that it had been hurled to the earth, it pursued the woman who gave birth to the male child. ¹⁴The woman was given the two wings of the great eagle, so she could fly to the place prepared for her in the desert, where she was looked after for three and a half years, out of the serpent's reach. ¹⁵So the serpent vomited a river of water from its mouth to sweep the woman away in the current. ¹⁶But the earth came to the woman's rescue by opening its mouth and swallowing the river that the dragon had vomited up.

¹⁷Then the dragon was enraged with the woman, and went off to wage war with the rest of her offspring—those who keep God's commandments and hold to the testimony of Jesus.

Then I stood on the seashore, **13**·¹ and I watched a beast emerge from the sea. It had seven heads and ten horns, with a crown on each horn. Each head was marked with a blasphemous name. ²The beast looked like a leopard, with paws like a bear and a mouth like a lion. The dragon gave the beast its power and its throne and its world-wide authority.

³I noticed that one of its heads seemed to have been fatally wounded, but the wound had healed. The whole world marveled at that, and followed the beast. ⁴People worshiped the dragon because it had given authority to the beast; they also worshiped the beast and said, "Who can compare with the beast, and who can challenge it?"

⁵The beast was given a mouth to utter arrogant and blasphemous words, and to exercise authority for forty-two months. ⁶The beast opened its mouth to blaspheme God, and to slander the Name and the dwelling place of God and those who live in heaven. ⁷It was allowed to make war against the holy ones and to conquer them. And it was granted authority over every tribe, people, tongue and nation. ⁸All the inhabitants of the earth will worship the beast—all whose names have not been written in the book of life since the creation of the world, which belongs to the Lamb who was slain.

⁹Whoever has ears to hear, listen!
¹⁰Whoever is destined for captivity,
    into captivity will go.
Whoever is destined to die by the sword,
    by the sword will die.

This calls for patient endurance and faithfulness on the part of the holy ones.

¹¹Then I saw a second beast come out of the earth. It had two horns like a lamb, but it spoke like a dragon. ¹²It exercised all the authority of the first beast on its behalf, and made the earth and its inhabitants worship the first beast, whose fatal wound had healed. ¹³And it worked great miracles, even calling fire down from heaven onto the earth while people watched. ¹⁴It deceived the inhabitants of the earth with the miracles it was able to work.

And it ordered them to set up a statue in honor of the beast who had been wounded by the sword and revived. ¹⁵It was given permission to breathe life into the statue, so that the statue could speak and cause all who refused to worship the statue to be killed. ¹⁶It also forced everyone—small and great, rich and poor, free and oppressed—to be branded on the right hand or on the forehead. ¹⁷No one could buy or sell without the mark— that is, the name of the beast, or the number that stood for its name.

¹⁸Wisdom is required here. Let those who have insight figure out a number for this beast—a "human" number: 666.

14:1Then I saw the Lamb in my vision. It was standing on Mount Zion, and with it were the hundred forty-four thousand who had its name and the name of Abba God written on their foreheads.

²I heard a sound from heaven which resembled the roaring of the deep, or loud peals of thunder; the sound I heard was like the melody of harpists playing on their harps. ³They were singing a new hymn before the throne in the presence of the four living creatures and the elders. This hymn no one could learn except the hundred forty-four thousand who had been ransomed from the world. ⁴They are the ones who have never defiled themselves sexually: they are pure, and they follow the Lamb wherever it goes. They have been ransomed as the firstfruits of humankind for God and the Lamb. ⁵On their lips no deceit has been found; they are indeed without flaw.

⁶Then I saw another angel flying high overhead, sent to announce the Good News of eternity to all who live on the earth—every nation, race, language and tribe. ⁷It said in a loud voice, "Give reverence and glory to

God, for the hour of divine judgment has come. Worship the One who made the heavens, the earth, the sea and the springs of water."

⁸ A second angel followed and said, "Babylon has fallen! Babylon the Great has fallen, who made the whole world drink the wine of its corrupt passions."

⁹ A third angel followed them and shouted, "All who worship the beast and its image, or accept its mark on the forehead or the arm, ¹⁰ will drink the wine of God's fury, which has been poured, undiluted, into the cup of divine wrath. They will be tormented with burning sulphur in the presence of the holy angels and of the Lamb. ¹¹ The smoke of their torments will rise up forever and ever. There will be no rest, day or night, for those who worshiped the beast and its image, or accepted the mark of its name."

¹² This calls for the endurance of the holy ones, those who keep God's commandments and remain faithful to Jesus.

¹³ Then a voice from heaven said, "Write this down: Happy are they who die in Our God for all eternity."

"Yes," says the Spirit, "let them rest from their work, for their deeds accompany them."

¹⁴ In my vision a white cloud appeared, and on the cloud sat someone who looked like the Promised One, wearing a crown and holding a sharp sickle. ¹⁵ Then an angel came out of the Temple and in a loud voice cried out to the one sitting on the cloud, "Use your sickle and cut down the harvest, for now is the time to reap; the earth's harvest is fully ripe." ¹⁶ So the one sitting on the cloud wielded the sickle over all the earth and reaped the earth's harvest.

¹⁷ Then out of the Temple in heaven came another angel, who likewise held a sharp sickle. ¹⁸ A second angel, who was in charge of the fire at the altar of incense, cried out in a loud voice to the one who held the sharp sickle, "Use your sharp sickle and gather the grapes from the vines of the earth, for the clusters are ripe." ¹⁹ So the angel wielded the sickle over the earth and gathered the grapes of the earth. The angel threw them into the huge winepress of God's wrath. ²⁰ They were crushed in the winepress outside the city, and the blood poured out of the press to the height of a horse's bridle for sixteen hundred furlongs.

15:1 I saw another sign in heaven, great and awe-inspiring: seven angels holding the seven final plagues which would bring God's wrath to a climax.

² I then saw something like a sea of glass commingled with fire. On the

sea of glass were standing those who had won the victory over the beast and its image and the number that signified its name. They were playing the harps used in worshiping God, ³ and they sang the song of Moses, servant of God, and the song of the Lamb:

> "Mighty and wonderful are your works,
>> O God Almighty!
> Just and true are your ways,
>> O Ruler of the nations!
> ⁴ Who would dare refuse your honor,
>> or the glory due your Name, O God?
> Since you alone are holy,
>> all nations will come
>> and worship in your presence.
> Your mighty deeds are clearly seen."

15:5–16:21

After this I saw the Temple, the Tent of the Testimony in heaven, opened, ⁶ and out came seven angels with seven plagues. They were wearing pure white linen, each with a gold sash around its waist. ⁷ Then one of the four living creatures gave each of the seven angels a bowl filled with the fury of God, who lives forever and ever. ⁸ Then the Temple filled so completely with the smoke from the glory of God and from God's power, that no one could enter it until the seven plagues of the seven angels were completed.

16:1 Then I heard a loud voice speaking from the temple to the seven angels: "Go, and pour out the seven bowls of God's fury on the earth."

² The first angel went out and poured its bowl over the earth. Ugly and virulent sores broke out on the people who wore the mark of the beast and worshiped its image.

³ The second angel poured out its bowl onto the sea, which became like the blood of a corpse, and every living creature in the sea died.

⁴ The third angel poured its bowl onto the rivers and the springs of water. They also turned to blood. ⁵ Then I heard the angel in charge of the waters say,

> "You are just in these judgments,

Sovereign God Almighty,
    you who are and who were;
⁶for they have shed the blood
    of your holy ones and your prophets,
and you have given them blood
    to drink as they deserve."
⁷Then I heard the altar itself say,
    "Truly, Sovereign God Almighty,
      the punishments you give
      are true and just."

⁸The fourth angel poured its bowl on the sun. This angel had the power to burn people with fire. ⁹Even though people were scorched by the searing heat, they cursed the Name of God, who had the power to cause such plagues. And they refused to repent or give glory to God.

¹⁰The fifth angel poured its bowl onto the throne of the beast, and its empire was plunged into darkness. People bit their tongues in agony, ¹¹and cursed the God of heaven because of their pains and sores. But they did not repent of their deeds.

¹²The sixth angel emptied its bowl onto the great river Euphrates. Its water dried up so that an entrance was made for the rulers of the East. ¹³Then I saw, coming out of the mouths of the dragon, the beast and the false prophet, three foul spirits that looked like frogs—¹⁴demonic spirits who worked miracles. They went out to the rulers of the whole world, to call them together for battle on the great Day of Almighty God.

¹⁵"Behold, I will come like a thief. Blessed are those who stay awake and keep their clothes with them, so they need not go naked and be shamefully exposed."

¹⁶They then gathered the rulers together in the place that is called, in Hebrew, Armageddon.

¹⁷The seventh angel poured its bowl into the air, and out of the Temple came a loud voice that said, "It is finished." ¹⁸Then there were lightning flashes, peals of thunder and a great earthquake—such a violent earthquake that it was unmatched since humankind began on earth. ¹⁹The great city split into three parts, and the cities of the world collapsed. But God remembered Babylon the Great and made it drain the cup filled with the wine of God's fury. ²⁰Every island fled away and the mountains vanished. ²¹Huge, hundred-pound hailstones fell from the sky onto the people. Yet

the people still blasphemed God for the plague of hail, because it was the most terrible plague.

17:1–19:10

an angel who had been holding one of the seven bowls came to me and said, "Come here and I will show you the punishment of the famous Idolater who reigns near the place of many waters. ²The rulers of the earth joined in the Idolater's sin, and the inhabitants of the earth got drunk on the wine of their idolatry."

³Then the angel carried me away in the Spirit to a desert place, where I saw a figure on a scarlet beast that was covered with blasphemous names. The beast had seven heads and ten horns. ⁴The figure was dressed in purple and scarlet, and glittered with gold, precious stones and pearls. It held a gold wine cup filled with the abominable and sordid work of debauchery.

⁵This cryptic name was written on its forehead: "Babylon the Great, Source of All Idolatry and of the Abominations of the Earth." ⁶I saw that the figure was drunk on the blood of the holy ones and on the blood of the martyrs for Jesus.

When I saw this I was completely mystified. ⁷The angel said to me, "Why are you mystified? I will explain to you the mystery of the figure and of the beast it rides, which has the seven heads and the ten horns. ⁸The beast you saw once existed but is no more. It will arise from the Abyss, but only to go to its destruction. The inhabitants of the earth whose names have not been written in the book of life from the creation of the world will be amazed when they see the beast, because it once was, now is not, and yet is still to come.

⁹"Here is something for a shrewd mind: the seven heads represent seven hills, and the figure is sitting on them. ¹⁰They are also seven rulers. Five have fallen and one still lives. And the seventh has not yet come—but when it does, this ruler will remain only for a short time. ¹¹The beast that once was, and now is not, is the eighth ruler. It is the eighth, but it belongs to the seven—and it is going to its destruction.

¹²"The ten horns you saw are ten rulers; they have not yet received their realms, but for one hour they receive authority as rulers along with the beast. ¹³They are all of one mind, and they will put their powers at the beast's disposal. ¹⁴They will go to war against the Lamb, but the Lamb will defeat them. For the Lamb is the Sovereign of Sovereigns and the Ruler of

Rulers, and those who follow the Lamb are the called, the chosen and the faithful."

¹⁵ Then the angel said to me, "The waters you saw, beside which the famous Idolater sat, are peoples and multitudes and nations and languages. ¹⁶ But the time will come when the beast and the ten horns you saw will hate the Idolater. They will bring it to ruin and leave it naked; they will eat its flesh and burn the remains. ¹⁷ For God has influenced their minds to carry out the divine will: to delegate their rulership to the beast, until God's words are fulfilled. ¹⁸ The Idolater you saw is the great city that reigns over the rulers of the earth."

18¹ After this, I saw another angel coming down from heaven. Its authority was so great that the earth was lit up by its glory. ² The angel cried out in a strong voice,

"Fallen, fallen, is Babylon the great!
It has become the dwelling place for demons.
It is a haunt for every unclean spirit,
a cage for every filthy and disgusting bird.
³ For all the nations have drunk
the maddening wine of idolatry.
The rulers of the earth
joined in the Idolater's sin,
and the the earth's buyers and sellers
grew rich because of their idolatrous greed."

⁴ Then I heard another voice from heaven say,

"Come out of the Idolater, my people,
so that you will not share in its sins,
so that you will not receive any of its plagues,
⁵ for its sins are piled up to the heavens,
and God remembers such crimes.
⁶ Repay the Idolater as it has paid others!
Pay back double for what it has done!
Mix the Idolater a double portion
from its own cup!
⁷ Give back as much torture and grief
as the glory and luxury it wallowed in.
To itself the Idolater boasts,
'I reign above all!
I need no one,
nor will I ever mourn anyone.'

⁸So the Idolater's plagues will come in a single day:
disease, mourning and famine,
and then it will be consumed by fire.
For mighty is the God who judges the Idolater."

⁹The rulers of the earth who debauched and lived in luxury with the Idolater will mourn and weep. Seeing the smoke as it burns ¹⁰and terrified at its torment, they will keep their distance and cry out,

"Mourn, mourn for this great city,
Babylon, so powerful a city!
In one hour your doom has come!"

¹¹The merchants of the earth will weep and mourn for the great city, because nobody is left to buy their cargoes of goods—¹²cargoes of gold, silver, precious stones and pearls; fine linen, purple silk and scarlet cloth; all the fragrant woods, articles of ivory, bronze, iron and marble; ¹³cargoes of cinnamon and spices, incense, myrrh and frankincense; wine and olive oil, flour and wheat; cattle and sheep, horses and carriages; and the bodies and souls of women and men.

¹⁴"All the fruit you craved
is gone from you.
Gone forever, never to return,
is your life of riches and ease."

¹⁵The merchants who dealt in these things and gained their wealth from the great city will stand far off, terrified at its torment. Weeping and mourning, ¹⁶they will say,

"Mourn, mourn for this great city;
clothed in fine linen,
purple and scarlet,
for all your finery of gold,
jewels and pearls,
¹⁷in one hour this great wealth is destroyed."

All the sea captains and sailors, all who travel by sea, and all who earn their living off the sea will keep their distance. ¹⁸They will cry out, when they see the smoke from its burning, "What city was ever as great as this city?" ¹⁹And they will pour ashes on their heads, weep, mourn and cry out,

"Mourn, mourn for this great city,
where all who had ships at sea
grew wealthy through its riches.
In one hour it has been destroyed.
²⁰Rejoice over it, O heaven!
Rejoice, you holy ones, apostles and prophets.
God has judged it for all it did to you."

²¹ Then another angel picked up a stone like a huge millstone and hurled it into the sea, and said,

> "Babylon the great city
> will be cast down like this—
> with violence, and never more be found!
> ²² No tunes of harpists and minstrels,
> of flutists and trumpeters,
> will ever again be heard in you!
> Never again will you contain skilled workers;
> never again will the sound of the mill be heard in you!
> ²³ No light from a burning lamp
> will ever again shine out in you!
> No voice of bride and groom
> will ever again be heard in you!
> Because your merchants were the world's nobility,
> you led all nations astray by your sorcery.

²⁴ "In the Great Idolater you will find the blood of prophets and holy ones, and all the blood that was ever shed on earth."

19:1 After this I heard what sounded like the loud song of a great assembly in heaven. They were singing,

> "Alleluia!
> Salvation, glory, and power belong to Our God,
> ² whose judgment is true and just,
> who has condemned the Great Idolater
> that corrupted the earth with its idolatry,
> who has avenged the blood of its subjects
> which was shed by its hand."

³ And again they sang out,

> "Alleluia!
> The smoke from it
> rises forever and ever."

⁴ The twenty-four elders and the four living creatures prostrated themselves and worshiped God, who sat on the throne. And they cried, "Amen! Alleluia!"

⁵ Then a voice came from the throne, saying,

> "Praise our God,
> all you servants of God,
> you who fear the Most High,
> both small and great."

⁶Then I heard what sounded like a great multitude, like the sound of rushing water, like loud peals of thunder, shouting,

"Alleluia!
Our Sovereign God has begun to reign!
⁷Let us rejoice and be glad,
and give praise to God—
for the wedding day of the Lamb is at hand.
The betrothed is ready,
⁸and wearing a bright, clean linen garment."
The linen represents the righteous acts of the holy ones.

⁹The angel then said to me, "Write this down: 'Happy are they who have been invited to the wedding feast of the Lamb.' " And the angel added, "These are the true words of God."

¹⁰At this I fell at the angel's feet to offer worship. But it said, "Don't do that! I am a servant just like you and all your sisters and brothers who bear witness to Jesus. It is God you must worship! For the witness of Jesus is the spirit of prophecy."

19:11–21:8

*t*hen I saw heaven itself standing open, and a white horse appeared. Its rider was called Faithful and True—a warrior for justice, a judge with integrity. ¹²This warrior has eyes like a blazing flame, and is crowned with many crowns, inscribed with a name no one else has ever known. ¹³The warrior wears a cloak dipped in blood, and is known by the name "The Word of God."

¹⁴The armies of heaven were following the warrior, also riding on white horses. They were dressed in dazzling white linen. ¹⁵Out of the warrior's mouth comes a sharp sword to strike down the nations. They will be ruled with an iron rod, and the warrior will tread out the wine of Almighty God's fierce wrath. ¹⁶This is the name written on the warrior's robe and thigh: "Sovereign of Sovereigns and Ruler of Rulers."

¹⁷And I saw an angel standing in the sun. The angel cried out to all the birds flying overhead, "Come, gather together for God's great banquet! ¹⁸You will eat the flesh of rulers, military officers and those under their command, horse and rider alike—the flesh of all people, oppressor and oppressed, small and great."

¹⁹Then I saw the beast and the rulers of the earth and their armies, gath-

ered together to fight the army which the warrior led. ²⁰ But the beast was captured, as was the false prophet who had worked miracles on the beast's behalf. With these miracles, the false prophet had deceived all those who had been branded with the mark of the beast and who worshiped its statue. The two were thrown alive into the fiery lake of burning sulphur. ²¹ All the rest were killed by the sword that came out of the warrior's mouth. And all the birds gorged themselves on their flesh.

20:1 Then I saw an angel come down from heaven, holding in its hands the key to the Abyss and a huge chain. ² It seized the dragon, the ancient serpent—the one called "the Devil" and "Satan"—and chained it up for a thousand years. ³ The angel hurled it into the Abyss, which it closed and sealed over the dragon. It did this so that it might not lead nations astray until the thousand years are over. After this, the dragon is to be released for a short time.

⁴ Then I saw some thrones. Those who were sitting on them were empowered to pass judgment. I also saw the spirits of those who had been beheaded for their witness to Jesus and the word of God, those who had never worshiped the beast or its image or accepted its mark on their foreheads or their hands. They came to life again and reigned with Christ for a thousand years.

⁵ The rest of the dead did not come to life until the thousand years were over. This is the first resurrection. ⁶ Happy and holy are those who share in the first resurrection! The second death has no power over them. They will be priests of God and of Christ, and will reign with Christ for a thousand years.

⁷ When the thousand years are over, Satan will be released from prison, ⁸ and will go out to deceive the nations in the four quarters of the earth—Gog and Magog—to gather them for battle. In number they are like the sand on the seashore. ⁹ They will march the breadth of the earth and surround the camp of the holy ones, the beloved city. But fire will come down from heaven and consume them. ¹⁰ And Satan, who deceived them, will be thrown into the lake of fire and sulphur, where the beast and the false prophet are. They will be tormented day and night forever and ever.

¹¹ Next I saw a large white throne and the One who sat there. The earth and the sky fled from its presence until they could no longer be seen. ¹² I saw the dead, the great and the lowly, standing before the throne. Lastly, among the scrolls, the book of life was opened. The dead were judged according to their conduct as recorded in the scrolls. ¹³ The sea gave up its

dead; then Death and the netherworld gave up their dead. All given up were judged according to their conduct. [14] Then Death and the netherworld were hurled into the pool of fire, which is the second death; [15] anyone whose name was not found inscribed in the book of life was hurled into this pool of fire.

21 [1] Then I saw new heavens and a new earth. The former heavens and the former earth had passed away, and the sea existed no longer. [2] I also saw a new Jerusalem, the holy city, coming down out of heaven from God, beautiful as a bride and groom on their wedding day.

[3] And I heard a loud voice calling from the throne, "Look! God's Tabernacle is among humankind! God will live with them; they will be God's people, and God will be fully present among them. [4] The Most High will wipe away every tear from their eyes. And death, mourning, crying and pain will be no more, for the old order has fallen."

[5] The One who sat on the throne said, "Look! I'm making everything new!" and added, "Write this, for what I am saying is trustworthy and true."

[6] And that One continued, "It is finished. I am the Alpha and the Omega, the Beginning and the End. To those who are thirsty I will give drink freely from the spring of the water of life. [7] This is the rightful inheritance of the overcomers. I will be their God and they will be my daughters and sons. [8] But the legacy of cowards, the unfaithful, the depraved, the murderers, the fornicators, sorcerers, idolaters, and all liars is the burning lake of fiery sulphur, which is the second death."

21:9–22:22

*t*hen one of the seven angels that had held the seven bowls of the seven last plagues approached me and said, "Come and let me show you the betrothed of the Lamb."

[10] The angel then carried me away in the Spirit to the top of a very high mountain, and showed me the holy city Jerusalem coming down out of heaven from God. [11] It shone with God's glory and gleamed like a precious jewel, like a sparkling diamond. [12] Its wall was huge and very tall, and it had twelve gates with twelve angels as sentinels. On the twelve gates were written the names of the twelve tribes of Israel; [13] three of its gates faced east, three north, three south and three west. [14] The wall had twelve foun-

dation stones on which were written the names of the Lamb's twelve apostles.

¹⁵ The angel who talked with me carried a gold measuring rod to measure the city, its gates and its wall. ¹⁶ The city was laid out foursquare; it was as long as it was wide. The angel measured the city with the rod and found it to be 12,000 stadia—or 1,500 miles—in length, width and height. ¹⁷ The wall measured 144 cubits—or 2,160 feet—in thickness; the angel was using the standard measure.

¹⁸ The wall was made of jasper, and the city of pure gold, as pure as glass. ¹⁹ The foundation stones of the city wall were decorated with every kind of precious stone. The first one was jasper, the second was sapphire, the third was chalcedony, the fourth was emerald, ²⁰ the fifth was sardonyx, the sixth was carnelian, the seventh was chrysolite, the eighth was beryl, the ninth was topaz, the tenth was chrysoprase, the eleventh was jacinth, and the twelfth foundation was amethyst. ²¹ The twelve gates were twelve pearls, each gate made of a single pearl. The main street of the city was of pure gold, as pure as glass.

²² I saw no Temple in the city, for God Almighty and the Lamb were themselves the Temple. ²³ There was no sun or moon: God's glory was its light, and the Lamb was its lamp. ²⁴ The nations will walk by the city's light, and the rulers of the earth will bring their treasures. ²⁵ The city's gates will never be shut by day, and there will be no night there. ²⁶ The glory and honor of the nations will be brought into it. ²⁷ But nothing unclean will ever enter it, nor will anyone who does loathsome things or tells lies. Only those whose names are written in the book of life of the Lamb will enter.

22 ¹ The angel then showed me the river of life-giving water, clear as crystal, which issued from the throne of God and of the Lamb, ² and flowed down the middle of the streets. On either side of the river grew the trees of life which produce fruit twelve times a year, once each month; their leaves serve as medicine to heal the nations. ³ There will no longer be any curse.

The throne of the Almighty and of the Lamb will be there, and God's subjects will serve faithfully. ⁴ They will see the Most High face to face, and bear God's name on their foreheads. ⁵ Night will be no more. They will need no light from lamps or the sun, for Our God will give them light, and they will reign forever.

⁶ The angel said to me, "These words are trustworthy and true; the Most High, the God of the spirits of the prophets, has sent an angel to show the faithful what must happen very soon."

⁷ "Remember, I am coming very soon!
Happy are you who heed
the prophetic message of this book!"

⁸ I, John, am the one who heard and saw these things.

I prostrated myself in worship before the angel who had shown them to me. ⁹ But the angel said, "Don't do that! I am a servant, just like you and your sisters and brothers, the prophets, and those who treasure what you have written in this book. It is God you must worship."

¹⁰ Then the angel told me, "Don't keep the prophecies in this book a secret, for the appointed time is near. ¹¹ Let those who do wrong continue to do wrong. Let the vile continue to be vile. Let those who are just continue to do justice. Let those who are holy continue to be holy."

෴   ෴   ෴

¹² "Remember, I am coming soon!
I bring with me the reward
that will be given to all people
according to their conduct.
¹³ I am the Alpha and the Omega,
the First and the Last,
the Beginning and the End.
¹⁴ Happy are they who wash their robes
so as to have free access to the tree of life
and enter the city through its gates.
¹⁵ Outside are the dogs, the sorcerers,
debaucherers, murderers,
idolaters and the deceitful.

¹⁶ "It is I, Jesus, who has sent my angel to give you this testimony about the churches. I am the Root and Offspring of David, the Morning Star shining bright."

¹⁷ The Spirit and the Betrothed say, "Come!"

Let the one who hears it answer, "Come!"

Let the thirsty come forward. Let all who desire it accept the gift of life-giving water.

෴   ෴   ෴

¹⁸ I warn everyone who hears the prophetic words of this book: if anyone adds anything to them, God will add to that person the plagues described in this book; ¹⁹ if anyone excludes anything from this book of prophecy, God

will exclude that person from the tree of life and from the holy city, which are described here.

²⁰ The One who gives this testimony says, "Yes, I am coming soon!" Amen! Come, Jesus!

²¹ The grace of our Savior Jesus Christ be with you all. Amen.

Reproduction

appendix:

pronunciation guide

Abaddon	A-**BAD**-don	Antipatris	An-ti-**PA**-tris
Abiathar	A-bi-**ATH**-ar	Apelles	A-**PEL**-les
Abijah	A-bi-**JAH**	Apollos	A-**POL**-los
Abilene	Ab-i-le-**NAY**	Apollyon	A-**POL**-lyon
Abiud	A-bi-**OOD**	Apphia	**AP**-phi-a
Achaia	A-cha-**EE**-a	Appius	**AP**-pi-us
Achaicus	A-**CHA**-i-cus	Appolonia	Ap-ol-**LO**-ni-a
Achim	A-**CHIM**	Archelaus	Ar-che-**LA**-us
Adramyttium	Ad-ra-**MIT**-ti-um	Archippus	Ar-**CHIP**-pus
Adria	**A**-dri-a	Areopagite	Ar-e-**OP**-a-gite
Aeneas	Ae-**NE**-as	Areopagus	Ar-e-**OP**-a-gus
Aenon	**AE**-non	Aretus	A-**RAY**-tus
Agabus	**AG**-a-bus	Arimathea	Ar-i-ma-**THEE**-a
Ahaz	**A**-haz	Aristarchus	A-ris-**TAR**-chus
Akeldama	A-kel-**DA**-ma	Aristobulus	A-ris-**TO**-bu-lus
Amminidab	Am-**MIN**-a-dab	Armageddon	Ar-ma-**GED**-don
Amphipolis	Am-**PHIP**-o-lis	Arni	**AR**-ni
Ampliatus	Am-pli-**AH**-tus	Arphaxad	Ar-**PHA**-xad
Ananias	An-a-**NI**-as	Artemis	**AR**-te-mis
Andronicus	An-**DRON**-i-cus	Asiarchs	**A**-si-archs
Antipas	**AN**-ti-pas	Assos	**AS**-sos

Asyncritus .... A-**SYN**-cri-tus	Azor .... **A**-zor
Attalia .... At-**TA**-li-a	Azotus .... A-**ZO**-tus

b

Baal .... Ba-**AL**	Beroea .... Be-**ROE**-a
Balaam .... Ba-**LAAM**	Bernice .... Ber-**NEE**-kay
Barabbas .... Bar-**AB**-bas	Bethphage .... Beth-**PHA**-ge
Barachiah .... Bar-a-**CHI**-ah	Bethsaida .... Beth-sa-**EE**-da
Barsabbas .... Bar-**SAB**-bas	Bethzatha .... Beth-**ZA**-tha
Bartimaeus .... Bar-ti-**MAE**-us	Bithynia .... Bi-**THYN**-i-a
Beelzebul .... Be-**EL**-ze-bool	Boanerges .... Bo-a-**NER**-ges
Belial .... Be-**LEE**-al	Boaz .... **BO**-az
Beor .... **BE**-or	

c

Caesarea .... Caes-a-**RE**-a	Chloe .... **CHLO**-e
Caiaphas .... **CA**-ia-phas	Chorazin .... Ko-ra-**ZIN**
Cainan .... Ca-**EE**-nan	Chuza .... **CHU**-za
Candace .... Can-**DAH**-kay	Cilicia .... Si-**LEE**-kee-a
Capernaum .... Ca-**PER**-na-um	Cleopas .... Clay-**OH**-pas
Cappadocia .... Cap-pa-**DO**-ci-a	Clopas .... **CLO**-pas
Cauda .... **KOW**-da	Cnidus .... **KNEE**-dus
Cenchreae .... Ken-**CRAY**-eh	Colossae .... Col-**LOS**-sae
Cephas .... **CE**-phas	Cretans .... **CRE**-tans
Chaldeans .... Chal-**DE**-ans	Cyrene .... Cy-**RAY**-ne
Chios .... **CHI**-os	Cyrenians .... Cy-**RAY**-ni-ans

d

Dalmanutha .... Dal-ma-**NU**-tha	Derbe .... **DER**-bay
Damaris .... **DAM**-a-ris	Dionysius .... Di-o-**NYS**-i-us
Decapolis .... De-**CAP**-o-lis	Diotrephes .... Di-**OT**-re-phes
Demetrius .... De-**ME**-tri-us	Drusilla .... Dru-**SIL**-la

e

Elamites .... **EH**-lam-ites	Elymus .... **EL**-y-mus
Eleazar .... E-le-**AY**-zar	Emmanuel .... Em-**MAN**-u-el
Eliakim .... E-li-**AH**-kim	Emmaus .... Em-**MAY**-us
Eliezar .... E-li-**AY**-zar	Epaenetus .... Eh-pa-**EE**-ne-tus
Eliud .... E-li-**OOD**	Epaphras .... Eh-pa-**PHRAS**
Elmadam .... El-**MAH**-dam	Epaphroditus .... E-paph-ro-**DI**-tus
Eli, Eli, lama sabachthani	Ephphatha .... Eff-**FAH**-tha
.... **AY**-lee, **AY**-lee, **LA**-ma	Ephraim .... **EPH**-ra-im
.... sa-bach-**TA**-ni	Erastus .... E-**RAS**-tus
Eloi, Eloi .... E-lo-ee, E-lo-ee	Esli .... **ES**-li

Eubulus	Eu-**BU**-lus	Euphrates	Eu-**FRAY**-tees
Euodia	Eu-**O**-di-a	Eutychus	**EU**-ty-chus

f

Fortunatus	For-tu-**NAH**-tus

g

Gabbatha	**GAB**-ba-tha	Gerasenes	**GER**-a-senes
Gadarenes	**GAD**-a-reens	Gethsemane	Geth-**SEM**-a-ne
Gaius	**GUY**-as	Golgotha	**GOL**-go-tha
Gamaliel	Ga-**MA**-li-el	Gomorrah	Go-**MOR**-rah
Gennesaret	Gen-**NES**-a-ret		

h

Heli	**HE**-li	Herodion	He-**RO**-di-on
Hermas	**HER**-mas	Hezekiah	Hez-e-**KI**-ah
Hermes	**HER**-mes	Hezron	**HEZ**-ron
Hermogenes	Her-**MOG**-e-nes	Hierapolis	Hi-e-**RAP**-o-lis
Herodians	He-**RO**-di-ans	Hosea	Ho-**SE**-a
Herodias	He-**RO**-di-as	Hymenaeus	Hy-me-**NAE**-us

i

Iconium	I-**CO**-ni-um	Issachar	**IS**-sa-char
Idumea	Id-u-**MAY**-a	Ituraea	I-tu-**RAE**-a
Illyricum	Il-**LYR**-i-cum		

j

Jairus	**JA**-i-rus	Jezebel	**JEZ**-e-bel
Jambres	**JAM**-bres	Joanan	**JO**-a-nan
Jannai	Jan-**NAH**-i	Joanna	Jo-**ANN**-na
Jannes	**JAN**-nes	Joram	**JO**-ram
Jared	**JA**-red	Josech	**JO**-sech
Jechoniah	Jec-o-**NI**-ah	Josiah	Jo-**SI**-ah
Jehoshaphat	Je-**HOSH**-a-phat	Jotham	**JO**-tham
Jephthah	**JEPH**-thah	Junias	**JU**-ni-as

l

Lama sabachthani		Levitical	Le-**VIT**-i-cal
	LA-ma sa-bach-**TA**-ni	Linus	**LI**-nus
Laodicea	La-od-i-**CE**-a	Lois	**LO**-is
Laodiceans	La-od-i-**CE**-ans	Lycaonia	Ly-ca-**O**-ni-a
Lasea	La-**SE**-a	Lycaonian	Ly-ca-**O**-ni-an
Lazarus	**LAZ**-a-rus	Lycia	Ly-**SEE**-a

Lysanias	Ly-**SAH**-ni-us	Lysius	**LYS**-i-us

m

Maath	Ma-**ATH**	Matthias	Ma-**THI**-as
Macedonia	Ma-ce-**DO**-ni-a	Melchi	**MEL**-chi
Macedonians	Ma-ce-**DO**-ni-ans	Melchizadek	Mel-**CHIZ**-a-dek
Magadan	**MAG**-a-dan	Melea	Me-**LAY**-a
Magdala	**MAG**-da-la	Menna	**MEN**-na
Magog	**MA**-gog	Mesopotamia	Mes-o-po-**TAY**-mee-a
Mahalaleel	Ma-**HA**-lah-le-el	Miletus	Mi-**LE**-tus
Manaen	**MAN**-a-en	Mitylene	Mit-y-**LEH**-ne
Manasseh	Ma-**NAS**-seh	Mnason	**MNAH**-son
Mattatha	**MAT**-ta-tha	Mysia	**MY**-si-a
Mattathius	Mat-ta-**THI**-us		

n

Naaman	**NAH**-man	Nereus	Ne-**RAY**-us
Naggai	**NAG**-ga-i	Neri	**NEH**-ri
Nahor	Na-**HOR**	Nicanor	Ni-**CAH**-nor
Nahshon	Na-**SHONE**	Nicodemus	Nic-o-**DE**-mus
Nahum	**NAY**-um	Nicolaitans	Nic-o-**LA**-i-tans
Nain	**NAH**-in	Nicolaus	Ni-co-**LA**-us
Naphthali	Naf-**TAH**-li	Nicopolis	Ni-**COP**-o-lis
Narcissus	Nar-**CIS**-sus	Ninevah	**NIN**-e-vah
Nathanael	Na-**THAN**-a-el	Nympha	**NYM**-pha
Neapolis	Nay-**OP**-o-lis		

o

Obed	**O**-bed	Onesimus	O-**NES**-i-mus
Olympas	O-**LYM**-pas	Onesiphorus	O-ne-**SIPH**-o-rus

p

Pamphylia	Pam-**PHYL**-i-a	Philetus	Phi-**LE**-tus
Paphos	**PA**-phos	Philologus	Phi-**LO**-lo-gus
Parmenas	**PAR**-me-nas	Phlegon	**FLAY**-gon
Parthians	**PAR**-thi-ans	Phoenicia	Phoe-**NI**-ci-a
Patara	Pa-**TAH**-ra	Phrygia	**FRIDGE**-ee-a
Patrobus	Pa-**TRO**-bus	Phygelus	**FIG**-e-lus
Peleg	**PE**-leg	Pisidia	Pi-**SID**-i-a
Perez	**PER**-ez	Porcius	**POR**-cius
Pergamum	**PER**-ga-mum	Prisca	**PRIS**-ca
Phanuel	**PHAN**-u-el	Prochorus	**PROCH**-o-rus
Philemon	Phi-**LE**-mon	Ptolemais	Pto-le-**MA**-is

Pudens .... **PU**-dens	Pyrrhus .... **PYR**-rhus
Puteoli .... Pu-**TE**-o-li	

Quirinius .... Qui-**RIN**-i-us

Rabboni .... Rab-**BO**-ni	Rehoboam .... Re-**HO**-bo-am
Rahab .... **RA**-hab	Reu ....**RAY**-u
Ramah .... **RA**-mah	Rhegium .... **RAY**-gi-um

Sabachthani .... Sa-bach-**TA**-ni	Shealtiel .... She-**AL**-ti-el
Sadducees .... **SAD**-du-cees	Shechem .... **SHEH**-chem
Salamis .... **SAL**-a-mis	Shelah ....**SHAY**-lah
Salmon ....**SAL**-mon	Siloam ....Si-**LO**-am
Salmone .... Sal-**MO**-ne	Silvanus .... Sil-**VA**-nus
Salome .... Sa-**LO**-me	Sinai .... **SI**-nai
Samaria .... Sa-**MA**-ri-a	Sopater .... **SOP**-a-ter
Samos .... **SA**-mos	Sosipater .... So-**SIP**-a-ter
Samothrace .... **SAM**-o-thrace	Sosthenes .... **SOS**-the-nes
Sapphira ....Sap-**PHI**-ra	Stachys .... **STA**-chys
Sceva .... **SKAY**-va	Stephanus .... **STEPH**-a-nus
Scythian .... **SCYTH**-i-an	Sychar ....Si-**CAR**
Secundus .... Se-**CUN**-dus	Syntyche .... **SIN**-ti-key
Seleucia ....Se-**LEU**-ci-a	Syrophoenician
Semein .... **SEM**-e-in	.... **SY**-ro-phoe-**NEE**-cian
Serug .... Se-**ROOG**	Syrtis .... **SYR**-tis

Talitha koum .... **TAL**-i-tha **COOM**	Tiberias .... Ti-**BE**-ri-as
Tamar .... Ta-**MAR**	Tiberius .... Ti-**BE**-ri-us
Terah .... **TEH**-rah	Timaeus .... Ti-**MAE**-us
Tertius .... **TER**-tius	Trachonitus .... Trach-o-**NI**-tus
Tertullus .... Ter-**TUL**-lus	Troas .... **TRO**-as
Theophilus ....The-**OPH**-i-lus	Trophimus .... **TROPH**-i-mus
Thessalonians .... Thes-sa-**LO**-ni-ans	Tryphaena .... Try-**FAY**-na
Thessalonica .... Thes-sa-lo-**NI**-ca	Tryphosa .... Try-**PHO**-sa
Theudas .... **THEU**-das	Tychicus .... **TYCH**-i-cus
Thyatira .... Thy-a-**TI**-ra	Tyrannus .... Ty-**RAN**-nus

Urbanus .... Ur-**BA**-nus	Uriah .... Ur-**RI**-ah
	Uzziah .... Uz-**ZI**-ah

Zacchaeus	Zac-**CHAE**-us	Zebulun	**ZEB**-u-lun
Zadok	**ZA**-dok	Zechariah	Ze-cha-**RI**-ah
Zarephaph	**ZAR**-e-phaph	Zerah	**ZEH**-rah
Zebedee	**ZEB**-e-dee	Zerubbabel	Ze-**RUB**-ba-bel